The Supreme Court and
American Political Development

The Supreme Court and American Political Development

Edited by
Ronald Kahn and Ken I. Kersch

University Press of Kansas

Publication made possible, in part, by grants from The Witherspoon Institute, Princeton, New Jersey, and Oberlin College, Oberlin, Ohio.

Published by the University Press of Kansas (Lawrence, Kansas 66045), which was organized by the Kansas Board of Regents and is operated and funded by Emporia State University, Fort Hays State University, Kansas State University, Pittsburg State University, the University of Kansas, and Wichita State University

Library of Congress Cataloging-in-Publication Data

The Supreme Court and American political development / edited by
Ronald Kahn and Ken I. Kersch.
    p. cm.
  Includes bibliographical references and index.
  ISBN 0-7006-1438-9 (cloth : alk. paper) — ISBN 0-7006-1439-7 (pbk. :
alk. paper) 1. United States. Supreme Court—History. 2. Political
questions and judicial power—United States—History. 3. Constitutional
history—United States. 4. United States—Politics and government.
I. Kahn, Ronald. II. Kersch, Kenneth Ira, 1964-
  KF8742.S897 2006
  347.73'2609—dc22   2006000284

British Library Cataloguing-in-Publication Data is available.

For Theodore J. Lowi

Our Teacher and Friend

CONTENTS

ACKNOWLEDGMENTS

Our first, and deepest, debt is to the contributors to this volume for joining us in this prolonged—and ongoing—collaborative project. Over the past five years, they agreed to join us in a series of discussions aimed at thinking in fresh and interesting ways about the relationship between law, courts, and American political development. Many of these discussions took place in panels at annual meetings of the Western Political Science Association and the American Political Science Association and in stimulating and enjoyable colloquies in less formal settings at those meetings.

Karen Orren and Stephen Skowronek graciously provided us with drafts of their own works in progress, which helped us to think more clearly about many of the theoretical issues addressed in this book. Our outside readers, Karen Orren and Keith Whittington, provided constructive criticisms and helpful suggestions that significantly improved the collection. We are grateful to the University Press of Kansas, and particularly to our editor, Mike Briggs, for shepherding the book along with patience and sagacity. It is a privilege to work with one of the best in the business.

Ron Kahn would also like to thank his students in courses on American constitutional law, the Supreme Court in American political development, and seminars on contemporary constitutional theory, equal protection, and implied fundamental rights for providing a vibrant scholarly forum in which many of the ideas that inform this volume were discussed and revised. Two of his students, Sara Chatfield, Oberlin '06, and David A. Karpf, Oberlin '02, provided additional contributions as research assistants. Oberlin's Politics Department, the James Monroe Professorship Fund, the president of Oberlin College, and the dean of its College of Arts and Sciences provided essential financial support. Ron would also like to thank Diana Ceil Grossman Kahn for her friendship and love, essential ingredients in the quality of his life, and thus in the quality of this book.

Ken Kersch would also like to thank the students in his American constitutional development graduate seminar at Princeton in the spring of 2004, who helped him to think through many pertinent conceptual issues. Two of his doctoral students, Justin Crowe and Emily Zackin, read drafts of the chapters and provided helpful comments and suggestions. Creighton Page, Princeton '05, provided research assistance on the project. Princeton's Politics Department and its James Madison Program in American Ideals and Institutions provided indispensable financial and intellectual support. Ken especially thanks Ted Holsten for his friendship—although this contribution may have been less direct than that of others, it was every bit as crucial.

The editors would like to thank Oberlin College and the Witherspoon Institute for making this volume widely available to students.

No list of acknowledgments would be complete without our each pausing to recognize the contributions of the other. This book is the product of a collaboration in its fullest and richest sense. We barely knew each other at the time we began the project. But as we discussed and argued our way through it over the ensuing years, we became teachers to each other, and friends. The opportunity to develop such a friendship is one of the joys of a scholar's life.

Introduction

Ronald Kahn and Ken I. Kersch

The pedigree of Supreme Court decisions is often more complicated than is commonly supposed. In the landmark gay rights decision *Lawrence v. Texas* (2003), for instance, the Court, relying on the Fourteenth Amendment, struck down a Texas statute making same-sex sodomy a crime.[1] It is impossible, however, to imagine either those who ratified that amendment in the 1860s or the Supreme Court of that same era believing that it rendered such laws unconstitutional. What had changed? Certainly not the text of the Constitution itself, whose relevant provisions stood unaltered. It was, rather, the constitutional understandings of a majority of the Court's justices that had changed. How, in turn, can we explain these changes? We could say that in 2003 the justices favored policies that advanced gay rights, whereas justices in the 1860s (and 1880s, 1920s, and 1960s) did not (it is not clear they would have even understood the concept of "gay rights"). But this simply would move the question back a step. How did justices who—on the evidence of their votes—came to favor gay rights come to sit on the high court? We might think it is because they were appointed by a president (and, more broadly, a political party) who was committed to the cause and who sought to appoint "liberal" justices who are, today, most likely to harbor policy preferences committed to gay rights. But although this explanation would explain some of the votes in *Lawrence*—those of the Court's Democratic appointees (and possibly liberal Republicans like Justice John Paul Stevens, a Ford appointee)—it would not explain all of them. Key votes in the case were cast by the Republican appointees of conservatives Ronald Reagan (Justice Sandra Day O'Connor and Anthony Kennedy) and George H. W. Bush (Justice David Souter). Any true explanation for the result in *Lawrence* would thus need to be more capacious and complex.

In another landmark decision of the same term, the Court in *Grutter v. Bollinger* (2003) upheld both the constitutionality and the legality (in light of federal civil rights statutes) of the affirmative action admissions program at the University of Michigan Law School, which gave added weight to the

1

applications of certain racial minorities on account of their race. The university had justified these racial preferences with the claim that they contributed to the Law School's "diversity," an objective that they argued constituted a "compelling state interest." This interest, however, was virtually unknown a quarter-century earlier (its immediate origins in Court doctrine were to be found in the opinion of a single justice in a decision striking down a medical school affirmative action plan from the mid-1970s).[2] Moreover, those who sponsored and voted for the Civil Rights Act of 1964, one of the two most important civil rights laws of the twentieth century (along with the Voting Rights Act of 1965), repeatedly asserted and believed that the law forbade racial preferences.[3] Citing "diversity," however, the Court ignored both the law's text and its original intent. As in *Lawrence*, the politics of the decision was unusual. Justice O'Connor, a crucial vote for the university, was not only a Republican, but had routinely opposed the constitutionality of racial preference programs in other contexts (like the awarding of government contracts). How can we explain both the result and the emergence of important new constitutional doctrine in *Grutter*?

Questions like these, which are raised by both contemporary and historical Supreme Court decisions, are questions of what scholars call "constitutional development," or empirical questions about why and how the meaning of the Constitution changes over time. Sometimes the processes of constitutional change are formal and transparent, such as when new constitutional texts (or parts of texts) are proposed, debated, and adopted. Constitutional change, for instance, occurred when the Constitution (1789) replaced the Articles of Confederation (1781). Such change also occurs when amendments (like the Fourteenth Amendment, at issue in both the *Lawrence* and *Grutter* cases) are formally adopted through the explicitly specified procedures of Article V.[4] More often, however, the processes of constitutional change are informal and murky, such as when new meanings are arrived at. It is more common to undergo constitutional change through altered interpretations and understandings, whether by members of Congress, the president, activists, scholars, and the people at large, or by Supreme Court justices. Explanation becomes even more complicated when the constitutional understandings held by actors outside the Court come to influence the decisions and understanding of the justices within it.

This book's primary concern is with the development of constitutional doctrine (and meaning) as elaborated by the Supreme Court. In the chapters that follow, contributors canvass the breadth of American history to offer a series of case studies in constitutional change. These studies are designed both as efforts at illuminating important moments in constitutional history for their own sake and as contributions to a collaborative project aimed at constructing a broader theoretical model of the nature and processes of constitutional development. The understandings of constitutional development advanced in each of this book's chapters are often distinctive, with implied (and sometimes explicit) points of disagreement existing among our contributors. At the same time, however, each was selected as a contributor for this volume because he or she shared a common appreciation for the process of constitutional development as involving a complex interplay between factors internal to the Court itself as a legal institution called on to decide concrete cases according to preexisting law and institutional norms, and factors external to the Court, such as political, institutional, cultural, intellectual, and social forces. Thus, when considered together, the chapters that comprise this volume share a common outlook, broadly conceived, and, at the same time, provide enough room for fruitful disagreement and debate about the nature and processes of constitutional change in the Supreme Court.

The Benchmark: The Law Versus Politics Debate over the Nature of Supreme Court Decision Making

Since the behavioral revolution in political science in the 1950s, scholars have spent a considerable amount of time arguing over whether the choices made by judges in deciding cases like *Lawrence*, *Grutter*, and more mundane rulings, were, in the main, either legal or political in nature. For legalists, a judge's task was to take a law as written by others (such as the U.S. Congress) and to apply it to the facts of the case. In constitutional adjudication, as Supreme Court Justice Owen Roberts famously put it, the job of the judge was "to lay the Article of the Constitution which is invoked beside the statute which is challenged and to decide whether the latter squares with the former."[5] A judge's job, in other words, was legal and apolitical: it was to find the relevant law, and then in turn to follow and apply it. *Making* law was a political task: the law's content was determined by elected officials, acting on their own views (and the views of their constituents) on the best public policies. *Applying* law, however, was a legal task: a judge's views of the best public policy were irrelevant to his job as a judge.

Of course, even traditional legalists were not babes in the wood: they were hardly so naive as to believe that, in reaching all their decisions, judges hewed unwaveringly to settled legal doctrine. Nonetheless, they believed that when judges strayed from the doctrine—to pursue their policy preferences or to read that doctrine in light of their own (nonlegal) social theories (like social Darwinism), it was a corruption—a politicization—of the legal process. Legalists vigorously criticized these departures and expended a considerable amount of energy importuning the prodigal judges to return to their proper judicial role. For them, legal decision making for the most part was, and certainly should be, legal. As such, for legalists, understanding what courts and judges did involved, in significant part, understanding the commands of the law itself, whether in the form of constitutional or statutory text, or preexisting legal doctrine or precedent (that is, the declaration in previously decided cases of the meaning of a law).

In the 1950s, judicial behavioralists, casting a cold empirical eye to what judges actually did (in the form of their votes in particular cases)—as opposed to what they said they did—mounted a sustained challenge to the legalist model. Drawing on a long-standing "legal realist" criticism of law as indeterminate and a commitment to studying what it was that judges actually did as an empirical science, judicial behavioralists began collecting empirical observations about judicial decision making and working toward proving a causal relationship between a vote or decision (the dependent variable) and a series of causal factors (the independent variables—such as political ideology or public opinion). In time, scholars committed a political model of judicial decision making, which held that in most important respects, judges were indistinguishable from ordinary politicians (or legislators) gained ascendancy within contemporary political science, took its place within the discipline alongside traditional legalists and law-focused political scientists.

It was in this academic context that the "law versus politics" debate became central to the agenda of law and courts scholars. For behavioralists, the first task was to demonstrate that judges did not follow law (at least in any sense that that law was determinate), but rather made policy. Over time, leadership in this task was assumed by a group of scholars known as attitudinalists, who hypothesized that a political independent variable—judicial ideology or values—determined the dependent variable of primary interest, the voted outcome of a case.[6] Judicial attitudes, in other words, yielded judicial outcomes. This causal explanation, of course, might not be obvious from the opinions judges write in deciding cases, in which they cite statutes and the Constitution and prior rulings (or precedent), which, in classic legalist fashion, they claim simply to be following. But that, the attitudinalists claim, is window dressing. What matters to scientists of judicial behavior is not what the judges say, but what they do. And what they do is decide cases based not on law but on preexisting attitudes.[7] Early attitudinalist-inflected work (such as that of C. Herman Pritchett) was fairly ecumenical, holding that judicial decision making can be explained by a judge's attitudes along three dimensions: first, his attitude toward law itself, and his job to interpret law accurately; second, his attitude toward the institutional structure of government (or polity principles, including federalism and judicial power); and third, his policy preferences.[8] In later attitudinalist work, however, the first two considerations tended to drop out, and the last became predominant as the key explanatory variable. Beginning with Glendon Schubert of Michigan State University, attitudinalists began to devise techniques for measuring judicial ideology along a liberal-conservative axis. They then moved to tie attitudes toward particular fact patterns and model how judges with particular ideologies would "vote" on particular legal fact patterns. Attitudinalists ultimately concluded that "simply put, Rehnquist votes the way he does because he is extremely conservative; [Thurgood] Marshall voted the way he did because he was extremely liberal." Judges voted their policy preferences.[9]

The scientific study of judicial behavior has recently been supplemented by "rational choice" institutionalist approaches that take into account the possibility that to win the prize of having their policy preferences written into law in the form of a legal ruling, judges may have to depart from simply voting those preferences. Judges operated within the confines of institutions, not in a vacuum. As such, they were forced to act strategically to win over the allies on the Court necessary to assemble the majority vote necessary to win a case. Moreover, where statutes were being interpreted, judges also needed to act strategically to avoid having their ruling overturned by a vote of Congress. Judges, that is, operated within distinctive institutional settings both internal to the Court and externally, and they needed to take into account the limits imposed on them by those settings in working to achieve their policy objectives. Rational choice research agendas focused on "the collegial game" sought to model the justices' efforts to assemble majority coalitions. Separation of powers game-theoretical models, which focus on the strategic moves made by justices, sought to understand the ways in which the justices worked to avoid having their will (and policy preferences) thwarted by countervailing actions by Congress.[10]

As the behavioralist and rational choice models were being refined, other scholars deepened our understanding of the ways in which the policy preferences of non-Court actors and institutions were imported into the Supreme Court's inner sanctum. Important work looked at the influence political mobilization by legal advocacy groups has on the development of court doctrine.[11]

Political scientists have studied the processes of appointment and Senate confirmation, as well as the ways in which the Court acts to shape its own agenda in a way likely to advance the policy preferences of its justices.[12]

From Behavioralism to Development: The 1960s Spur a New Political Science

Judicial behavioralism, which was forged in the 1950s, sought to map the behavior of political actors with fixed preferences operating within mature, stable, preexisting institutions and relatively fixed constitutional and conceptual categories. In the mid- to late 1960s, scholars, students, and prominent segments of the general public launched a series of sustained challenges to many of the nation's key—and heretofore stable—institutions. At this time, many scholars began to evince less interest in how individuals with preexisting preferences operating within stable institutions made their choices and more interest in understanding the origins, character, and effects of the institutions themselves. In what ways did social and political institutions prevent individuals from acting on their "true" preferences? In what ways did they limit the options of individuals and political actors? Were people's expressed preferences independent of the web of institutions they inhabited? Or was the nature of their preferences themselves constructed by life within a given institutional environment? If a given institution either channeled or constructed individual preferences in a particular way, was that pure happenstance? Or was the institution designed to do so by a particular political, social, economic, or state interest or constellation of interests or movements? Did these groups or movements undertake this task to advance the broader public interest or rather to advance their personal interests and those of their allies?

A cascade of questions of this sort made behavioralism much less attractive as a vantage point from which to understand American politics. Leaving behavioralism behind, many scholars became increasingly interested in historical questions about how particular institutions came to assume their modern forms and about how prevalent public philosophies (or broad, widely shared understandings of the way the world works, including those that anchored the study of political science) came to pervade those institutions. These questions in turn spurred further questions about how institutions stabilized, how they altered, and how they decayed. Some of these questions lent themselves to the hard analysis of organizational theory. Others, however, lent themselves to questions of ideology: the more legitimate an organization or ordering seemed, the less vulnerable it would be to challenge. What were the ideologies that worked to sustain particular institutions? These were all empirical questions. But ultimately they raised normative ones. If political and social institutions are not timeless but instead constructed over the course of time, how do we explain how they are constructed? Do they advance the public interest? If they do not, what sort of institutions would? Would it be possible to create new institutions or alter existing ones to serve this purpose?[13]

In addressing these questions, institutionalists studying American politics drew extensively from a well of highly sophisticated studies of the development of political institutions around the world. After all, for comparative politics scholars, unlike scholars looking solely at American politics in the 1950s, the historical contingency of institutions, and their potential weaknesses, were apparent for all to see and hence could not be taken for granted. In the era of the cold war, scholars of comparative "political development"— or the construction of political order and institutions across time—lived in a world at a crossroads, poised between communism and capitalism, between democracy and dictatorship, between modern states that more or less provided for their people and newly independent, formerly colonial states that were perched on a razor's edge between stability and revolution. Scholars like Barrington Moore, Samuel P. Huntington, and Theda Skocpol formulated their animating research questions in the field of comparative politics where institutional structure and stability could not be and were not taken for granted. And in time, all, to greater or lesser degrees, moved on to ask these same questions about the institutional architecture of the United States.[14] All of these questions had potential implications for the study of American law, the U.S. Supreme Court, and the political, ideational, and institutional environment in which they operated.

The Emergence of American Political Development

Scholars who began to ask these same questions about the way in which institutions and the authority placed in them developed, stabilized, altered, and decayed over time within the United States itself gradually became known within political science as scholars of American political development, or "APD."* The work of these scholars is readily distinguishable from

---

*For clarity, when "American political development" is written out, it refers to the process of political change; when the acronym "APD" is used, it refers to the scholarly literature in those processes.

that of the behavioralists. Unlike behavioralist work, which looks at snap-
shots of individual decisions, APD scholars focus on the aspect of politics
that is like a moving picture. Its chief interest is not in the moment, but in
the passing of time. As such, although the questions APD work poses may
be motivated by contemporary politics, its focus is decidedly less presentist
and more historical. For similar reasons, it is less interested in decisions
made by individuals (at least as they are said to reflect the individual's
autonomous preferences) than on how the institutions structure their
choices. All these combine in shaping APD's preference for eschewing the
small-scale hypothesis testing of the behavioralists in favor of large-scale
historical studies asking big questions about the construction of political
authority across time.[15]

Seminal APD scholarship also has sparked ongoing debate about the
mechanisms that both sustain and erode the structures and practices of governance work, which would inevitably lead scholars to think about the
Court and constitutional law in new ways. Louis Hartz's *The Liberal Tradition in America* (1955), a landmark study of American political thought,
threw down the gauntlet for many who later came to identify themselves
as APD scholars by asserting that American political history was characterized by an aberrational uniformity and stability. Hartz traced the absence
of important political change in America to the peculiarly imprisoning
effect that a Lockean liberal ideology had on Americans. This ideology
stemmed from the fact that Americans, in contrast to Europeans, were (as
Tocqueville put it) born equal instead of having to become so. In contrast,
Europeans, noted Hartz (who started from Marxist premises), had experienced significant political change. They started from feudalism, and
through the mechanism of class struggle and social revolution, they had
fought hard to ascend to history's next stage, bourgeois capitalism. As
strong, centrally planned social welfare states were being established, Hartz
saw the Europeans advancing to the next developmental stage: socialism.
Americans, by contrast, had started from a clean slate in an abundant
wilderness. As such, they had never known feudalism. This meant that they
had never had to struggle to achieve their bourgeois capitalism; they inherited it. Having not had to fight for bourgeois capitalism, Americans, in turn,
lacked the drive to struggle against capitalism and for socialism. So far as
the stages of historical development were concerned, they were perma-
nently stuck in neutral. They were locked into a liberal capitalist ideology
that privileged private rights (including private property rights) and individualism over collective goals and social solidarity. For Hartz, America's

origins made the United States an exceptional country—a country that, in contrast to the nations of Europe, simply did not develop. How much, we might ask from a Hartzian perspective, was constitutional doctrine a pure reflection of this liberal capitalist ideology? If the answer is "to a considerable extent," did this mean that law was similarly stuck in neutral, without transformative potential? Questions of this sort about law and the Supreme Court are implicitly raised by the Hartzian paradigm.

Soon, an array of scholarship arose that challenged Louis Hartz's contention that, because the U.S. did not follow the familiar European developmental trajectory, its history was devoid of political change. Walter Dean Burnham, a student of Hartz's (and of the pioneering behavioral student of elections, V. O. Key) and a seminal APD scholar, accepted Hartz's liberal consensus thesis. But he went on to describe the ways in which important political change had taken place in the United States nonetheless—albeit within the boundaries set by the prevailing liberal consensus. Burnham stipulated that the Constitution played a highly significant part in institutionalizing liberal ideology: it enshrined individualism and private property rights and, through federalism and the separation of powers, fragmented state power. Nevertheless, over time, new needs and pressures inevitably bubbled up from the nation's political economy and civil society. These changes acted as disturbances to the ostensibly smoothly functioning governing order. They sparked contention over the nature and role of political actors and institutions that had been chosen and calibrated with a passing status quo in mind. In the context of new pressures and disturbances, prevailing and accepted institutions and arrangements came to be viewed by many as maladjusted and politicized. It was at times like these, Burnham argued, that critical realigning elections took place. In realigning periods, political parties fought over the fundamentals of state-society relations involving economic, sectional, and ethnocultural life which were suddenly up for grabs. The outcome of these battles upset the formerly stable party system. In the process, it reshaped the constituencies and the policy commitments of the parties themselves. The winners in these realignments—the Jeffersonians (1800), the Jacksonians (1828), the Civil War–era Republicans (1860), the progressives (1896), and the New Dealers (1932)—set the terms of the more stable governing orders ("party systems") that followed. Cyclical regime theory or punctuated equilibrium models of the sort advanced by Burnham have continued to anchor diverse developmental accounts of the shape and structure of American politics across time. If realigning elections were the "mainspring" of change in American politics, as Burnham argued, were they also the mainspring of change of Supreme Court decision making and constitutional doctrine? Burn-ham's revision of Hartz's consensus model implicitly raised such questions, presenting new challenges for law and courts scholars.[16]

In time, consensus models of American politics rooted in the Hartzian par-adigm were challenged on a number of fronts. While retaining Hartz's incli-nation to emphasize consensus and stability over development, some scholars either multiplied the number of ideologies they found to be influential in the United States or asserted that significant ideological conflict is possible within liberalism itself. Rogers M. Smith, for example, has argued that republicanism and ostensibly illiberal prescriptions of identity have been as pervasive and persistent within American political thought as liberalism itself.[17] Samuel P. Huntington has argued that although, broadly speaking, there has been a per-sistent consensus within American society converging on an American creed rooted in the values of liberty, equality, individualism, democracy, and the rule of law under a constitution, those commitments "constitute a complex and amorphous amalgam of goals and values, rather than a scheme for establish-ing priorities among values and for elaborating ways to realize values."[18] There are thus persistent tensions between these values. Moreover, in periods of "creedal passion," Huntington argued, gaps between ideals and institutions come to the political fore.[19] Both the conflicts between the basic creedal val-ues under ordinary conditions and the periodic outbreaks of passion over the gap between the promise of American ideals and the reality of American insti-tutions belie the notion that consensus implies an absence of conflict. Like Huntington, J. David Greenstone, in his study of Lincoln, both accepted the liberal consensus as a "boundary condition" and posited the persistence of conflict within that consensus.[20] Parting company from Huntington's more tragic vision, however, Greenstone viewed that conflict as potentially trans-formative, promising—and, in Lincoln, delivering—the possibility of revolu-tion even within consensus America. Greenstone's work (and that of his student, Ronald Kahn) suggested explicitly that the Supreme Court might play an important role in those societal transformations.[21]

Like Greenstone, other scholars have taken America's developmental potential seriously. Many of these scholars, however, have focused less on the role of ideas in this process and more on that of institutions.[22] Like Hartz, Stephen Skowronek built his developmental theory on a bedrock compari-son between the European and American case. Skowronek, however, empha-sized not ideas but an institutional comparison between European and American states. Rejecting the argument that the pre-twentieth-century United States was exceptional by virtue of an absence of a state—that is, an authoritative (and hence effective) system of governance and control—Skowronek argued rather that the American state was not absent but unusual: it was present not in the more familiar centralized bureaucratic form (on a French model, for instance), but instead in the form of a "state of courts and parties" that knit the nation together more or less successfully in the absence of a centralized American bureaucracy. Changes in the nation's political economy, however (particularly in the late nineteenth century) placed diverse and intense stresses on the state of courts and parties. Ultimately, reformers undertook a sustained project of building a "New American State" that was more centralized and bureaucratized along the lines of the more familiar baseline European central states. This project, however, like many projects of institutional construction, did not proceed on a cleared field. Rather, it was mediated by the persistence of preexisting institutions—of a decentralized constitutional order, of courts with common (or judge-made) law commitments, and of a cornucopia of preexisting political commitments embodied in prevailing institutions. Thus, at the same time the New American State was being constructed, it was simultaneously being thwarted in certain areas in diverse and uneven ways. In the end, the nation entered the twentieth century with a distinctive patchwork state that embodied a unique and incongruous admixture of developmental successes, failures, partial successes, and partial failures.[23] Law, courts, and constitutional doctrine, of course, were, in Skowronek's account, densely woven into the fabric of American politics and, in turn, of American political development.

In nuanced and ambitious large-scale historical studies that followed upon Skowronek's, other scholars modeled the processes of American state development, charting its causes and effects within and across extended historical periods. Some of these works retain ties to the literature on electoral realignments rooted in the work of Walter Dean Burnham. Many, however, chart long-term developmental processes that, if tied to electoral politics, are linked to them in more complex ways than the more familiar punctuated equilibrium models of development might suppose. These studies—by Martin Sklar, Richard Bensel, Elizabeth Sanders, Gretchen Ritter, Theda Skocpol, Scott James, Daniel Carpenter, and others—relate state construction to democratization, industrialization, sectionalism, professionalization, organized interests, social movements, and war, categories that have proved immensely useful to developmentally oriented students of comparative politics.[24]

These APD scholars, considered collectively, have constructed a remarkably rich account of the emergence and anatomy of the institutions that govern modern America. Whereas foundational work tended to focus on the nature of the processes by which we arrived at the New American State in the early twentieth century, second-generation APD scholars like Suzanne Mettler, David Plotke, Robert Lieberman, Jacob Hacker, and John David Skrentny, typically focusing on particular policy areas, have charted the processes of state development since the 1930s. Both literatures are now simultaneously vibrant. Although these works were not, strictly speaking, part of the public law literature within political science, many of them also made law and courts part of the accounts, or provided space where later scholars could make the contributions of legal doctrine to the processes of political change explicit.[25]

In the wake of these highly detailed and focused APD studies, certain scholars have turned toward reflecting more generally on theories of the processes of political development. For example, in recent years, comparativists like Paul Pierson and Kathleen Thelen and Americanists like Karen Orren and Stephen Skowronek have identified the dynamics of path dependency (the self-reinforcing aspects of certain decisions), sequencing (the effects of the chronological order of key decisions on institutional or political developments), layering (the superimposing of new institutional developments over older ones), conjunctures (the effects of collisions or crossings of developmental paths), unintended consequences (the implications of goal-directed decisions and institutions persisting through time and, in developing and moving through altering institutional environments, coming to have new, unintended effects), and of the life more generally of polities comprising multiple orders and patterns of intercurrence. Such theoretical work, which is informed inductively by a careful reading of the corpus of APD's more empirical work, has, needless to say, tended to call into question the neater and more schematic understandings of political order evident in the field's earlier work positing either long-term stability or consensus (such as Hartz) or punctuated equilibrium (such as Burnham). In their recent book, *The Search for American Political Development*, Orren and Skowronek, two of the field's pioneers, pause to review APD's history as a distinctive field of inquiry, set out its central insights, take stock of its failures and achievements, and spotlight what they see as its most importunate puzzles and challenges. Orren and Skowronek's critical overview of the field at the beginning of the century, *The Search for American Political Development*—and, we hope, this book—will provide a useful starting point for scholars aiming to move beyond the stock "law versus politics" and "institutionalist versus attitudinalist" debates of the 1990s and to arrive at new insights into the relation between the Supreme Court and American political development.[26]

The Law and American Political Development

Key APD works devoted considerable attention to law, with many placing law at the core of their analysis. In so doing, they advanced nuanced arguments about the role law—both private (contracts, property, and torts) and public (the Constitution; statutes like the Sherman Antitrust Act, the National Labor Relations Act, or the Civil Rights Act of 1964)—and the Supreme Court have played in catalyzing, constraining, and negotiating order and change over the course of American history.[27] These scholars made a major contribution to understanding the relationship between law and politics by refusing to isolate questions involving legal doctrines and judicial decisions and the special qualities of courts as decision-making units from the consideration of developments elsewhere in the political system— be they in ideologies, elite and popular political thought, social movements, or in formal institutions such as Congress, the presidency, state and federal bureaucracies, and state and federal court decisions. Nevertheless, we believe that the time has come for public law scholars who consider themselves part of the broader APD project to step up and provide a more subtle account of the way law works and of the role that the Supreme Court plays in American political development. This collection was conceived specifically with that aim.

This book represents what we hope will be a beginning in stimulating such a research agenda. Not all of the essays presented here, readers will note, make sustained reference to the classic works of APD and thought. But they were selected for inclusion in this collection because they evince pregnant conceptual affinities with the questions asked by APD scholars. We believe that the ties among scholars presented here, their students, and others with similar interests, and between them and APD scholars (and, we hope, comparativists) more generally will grow closer and thicker over time. We expect and hope that these ever-strengthening ties will stimulate new insights into and new questions about the role of the Supreme Court and American political development.

The Historical Institutionalist Challenge to
Judicial Behavioralism: Some Antecedents

An embryonic turn toward APD-like concerns, presaging the one we offer here, began in the public law literature in the late 1980s, when a group of historical institutionalist scholars mounted a sustained challenge to the attitudinalists and their conviction that the scientific study of judicial decision making on the Court had definitively demonstrated that, in nearly all cases of significance, judges simply voted their policy preferences. Although sharing with rational choice scholars the conviction that institutions mattered, historical institutionalists parted ways with many of them writing at that time in seeing institutions in temporal terms, as the product of history. Historical institutionalists concerned themselves not so much with the behavior of actors with fixed preferences operating within the constraints imposed by a fixed institutional environment, but with the behavior of actors who, although they certainly had policy preferences, some of which were fixed, also had strong, historically constituted beliefs involving institutional norms. As such, they had a strong belief about their duty as judges to follow law (such as by adhering to precedent) and to assume a particular relationship to other institutions of American government (such as Congress and the states). These competing considerations, the historical institutionalists studying public law asserted, broke the direct explanatory link between judicial policy preferences and case outcomes.[28]

This conceptual departure unleashed a cascade of new questions and interests. Some, for example, explored the way in which institutions outside of the Court, both formal and informal, shape decision making on the Court.[29] Others emphasized the degree to which understandings of judicial role and duty—of the appropriate place of the Court within the broader scheme of American government, of the relationship between structure and rights—have themselves—again, historically demonstratably—changed over time.[30] Historical institutionalists took as their primary task the illumination of long-term processes that lead to the construction of both judicial preferences and of the institutions that constrain the choices of judges as they pursue them.

The historical institutionalist challenge to the attitudinalist model was not of necessity a radical one, although it came to appear more radical as attitudinalism itself narrowed from the ecumenical work of C. Herman Pritchett toward the fundamentalism of Harold Spaeth.[31] Historical institutionalists never denied the long-standing attitudinalist assertion that judges often vote their policy preferences. Nor did they deny the rational choice insight that Supreme Court justices operate strategically within more or less stable institutional environments when they make decisions. What they did deny was the predominance of a single factor as applied to all significant cases at all times. Their point of departure is often one of emphasis: historical institutionalists frequently have longer time horizons and are often less interested in snapshot models of how judges behave at a given moment in time than in illuminating the way in which, over time, both preferences and institutions are constructed, stabilize, alter, and decay.[32]

Nonetheless, the historical institutionalist challenge was taken by many behavioralists as radical for two reasons, both of which led political science behavioralists to not only attack it, but to deride it. First, many behavioralists mistakenly understood it as a disinterment of the legalist understanding of judicial decision making, which, as they see it, they (or their teachers) had buried in the 1950s when the study of judicial decision making belatedly became a science. Although historical institutionalists take law seriously and treat courts as distinctive institutions and judges as a unique type of political actor, they never advanced the rather crude proposition that the law is both easily distinguishable from politics and (absent cases of unpardonable straying) determinative. On the contrary, historical institutionalist work involved sophisticated attempts to map the dynamic, mutually constitutive relationship between politics and law over time.

The second reason that historical institutionalism was attacked and derided by behavioralists is that, by choosing to focus on the processes by which preferences and institutions are constructed over time through the influence of many factors, the historical institutionalists have lost their ability to present their work in a way that contemporary behavioralists understand as scientific. Noninterpretive snapshot approaches to judicial decision making readily lend themselves to straightforward hypothesis testing in accordance with falsifiable models. Because they are often interested in the dynamics of the moving picture of judicial decision making over extended periods of time, as opposed to the snapshot model, and because these dynamics simultaneously reflect both recurrent patterns and unique historical departures, historical institutionalists rarely purport to arrive at timeless, strictly falsifiable conclusions.[33] As such, historical institutionalist public law scholarship tends to be simultaneously descriptive, interpretive, and empirical, and its conclusions about laws of behavior are either modest or abstract.

To make matters worse from a behavioralist perspective, the evidence adduced by historical institutionalist scholarship tends to be qualitative (although quantitative work can nestle within it), and thus lacking in science's contemporary raiment. As such, to the extent that it claims to be a social scientific study (as opposed to "mere" history), historical institutionalism has more in common with the traditional study of comparative politics than it does with the contemporary mainstream study of American politics. In some variants that emphasize the way in which broader currents of ideas influence legal thought, it also has more affinities with the study of the history of ideas, including the history of American political thought, than with the behavioral study of American politics.[34]

Historical institutionalists, in short, rejected a purely "political" model of judicial behavior, although they included in their model the impact of politics, among other factors. They have nonetheless been rejected by behavioralists as unscientific. A more thoughtful response on the part of attitudinalist and rational choice scholars would recognize that the historical institutionalist scholars are simply concerned with different problems, different dynamics, and different questions. Arguably, understanding how preferences are formed and how institutions change over time is crucial to a rich understanding of the nature of judicial politics—and politics more generally.

The Supreme Court and American Political Development

At the heart of this book's chapters are questions concerning the nature of the Supreme Court as a unique governmental institution. All the contributors to this volume understand the Court to be a political, and not simply a legal, institution. But at the same time, all appreciate that, as a court, it is distinctively political.[35] That courts are positioned at the juncture of law and politics had long been understood by serious historians and political theorists (if less so by modern behavioralist political scientists). The distinctiveness of courts is inherent in the nature of judicial power. As an historical matter, in the Anglo-American legal tradition, the judicial power was a component of the executive's power which involved the authority both to adjudicate disputes by the yardstick of "settled, known law, received and allowed by common consent to be the standard of right and wrong," and to enforce those rulings.[36] Given this history, it was understood that the threat to liberty in a political order premised on the rule of law came not from a merging of the judicial and executive powers but from the merging of either of these powers with the power to make laws—that is, the power to legislate. For this reason, the separation of legislative powers from the judicial (and executive) powers has been a foundational principle of liberal constitutionalism.[37]

Nonetheless, despite the long-standing caution that the power to make laws must be separated from the power to render judgments according to them and in turn to enforce those judgments, scholars have long since concluded that courts possess powers that can in some respects be described as involving lawmaking. Despite this foundational commitment, however, it has long been acknowledged that judicial lawmaking (perhaps inevitably) takes place, if only interstitially. But given its problematic nature, it is frequently disavowed.[38] In deciding cases, political scientists recognize that Supreme Court justices, like other judges, actually make law and set public policy, and vote on those laws and policies in a way that some have concluded is analogous to a nine-person legislature. Within this little legislature, justices pursue their policy goals and act strategically to do so; they engage in the sort of compromises and bargains that one sees in Congress and other legislatures.

This recognition, however, has often been too reductivist, and is an important but insufficient basis for arriving at a sophisticated understanding of the politics of Supreme Court decision making. Crucial to that understanding is the recognition that although the Court in some respects may be characterized as a little legislature, its claim to authority and the way it makes distinctions is distinguishable from those of either the executive or the legislature. The president and members of Congress are elected, which roots their authority in claims to democratic legitimacy. The Court's justices are appointed. The president and members of Congress (and executive branch administrative officials, including those of independent agencies) serve for limited terms. Federal judges, by contrast, serve for life.[39] As unelected, life-term appointees, the Court's authority derives chiefly from its claim to be exercising "neither force nor will, but merely judgment"—that is, to be acting as a neutral, apolitical applier of laws. Its chief claim to authority—its legitimacy—is premised, that is, on its status as a legal, as opposed to a political, institution.[40]

These distinctive wellsprings of legitimacy put a premium in courts on the notion that it is an institution governed by constraints. It is important for judges to both see themselves and publicly convey the impression that they are noninstrumental, exercising "neither force nor will," that they are not active, but passive. We call these constraints "internal" influences on judicial decision making. The law itself (whether in the form of the Constitution, statutes, or settled legal doctrine in the form of precedent) is one of the most important of these internal constraints on Supreme Court decision making. But there are other internal influences, including judicial norms and procedures, which are commonly the product of extensive professional training and socialization. Among these are the norm that judges be apolitical, a norm reinforced by the requirement that judges craft their legal rulings according to a "legal grammar" in which some forms of argument

(historical, textual, structural, prudential, and doctrinal) are considered legitimate and others (whim, personal policy preference) are not.[41] Although it
is important to recognize that these constraints are not unbreachable and
may not be determinate in any particular decision, they are crucial because,
in many respects, they are constitutive of who a judge thinks he is and what
he understands himself to be charged with doing. This, in turn, has a major
influence on what he does. These internal influences are unique features of
the kind of politics that courts do.[42]

Courts also are clearly tied to the "ordinary" politics that, in a democracy, has familiar influences on presidents, legislatures, and courts alike. We
call this set of influences on the Court "external" influences on judicial
decision making. These include election returns affecting both the powers
of particular political parties generally and the decisions of individual
officeholders on particular policy issues, changes in majority electoral coalitions, the politics of judicial appointments and confirmation, social and
intellectual movements, the opinions of (nonlegal) interpretive communities such as journalists and other opinion leaders, interest and advocacy
group activity, and threats by political actors to the Court's authority and
power (such as by impeachment or cabining the Court's jurisdiction in certain areas). One important potential influence on Supreme Court decision
making may straddle both categories. The opinion of members of the legal
interpretive community—law professors and social scientists—on key issues
is an internal influence in that it typically advances arguments for particular results in the legal grammar of the sort most likely to persuade legally
socialized justices that a particular result or conceptualization is a matter
of law rather than politics. At the same time, it is an external influence in
that the opinions of the legal interpretive community, although refracted
through a legal grammar, have, historically speaking, been closely tied to
the political visions of broader "external" intellectual and social movements, as well as of political interest groups.[43]

The law versus politics debate that has dominated much of the academic
debate over the nature of Supreme Court decision making in recent years is,
we believe, better conceptualized as a debate over the respective influences
of internal and external factors on Supreme Court decision making, with law
being an important potential internal influence, but a factor that does not
exhaust the category of internal influences, and electoral politics being a
significant potential influence that does not exhaust the category of external
influences. This interplay, we assert, is distinctive to courts as institutions,
and it is crucial to understanding them as such. It is because of this dynamic

perpetually playing itself out in courts that courts are not "little legislatures." The interplay of the internal and external taking place in courts gives them a certain autonomy from ordinary politics at certain times and in certain areas that leads them to ignore, resist, and even disregard robust political pressure. It thus gives them a special place in accounts of American political development. Accounts that simply seek to "link" the courts to events in the nation's "political" branches, although often helpful (indeed, they are key parts of the category we call "external"), flatten the unique properties and processes at work in courts in an effort to more easily assimilate them into models designed with other institutions in mind. Here, because we are looking at courts, we put courts first in our efforts to move toward the creation of new developmental models that involve them. What follow are developmentally oriented law and courts studies that are open to the idea that although they may share attributes with each others' political institutions, courts are not parties, not legislatures, not bureaucracies, and not the presidency.

We note that the payoff of the shift to a nomenclature of the interplay of the internal and the external would be minimal, and amount merely to rebottling old wine, if the essential character of the law versus politics debate were simply transposed into new arguments about whether internal or external factors predominate as explanations for Supreme Court decision making. The law versus politics debate was freighted by its normative implications for judicial power with a tendency toward asking dichotomous questions. A debate about internal and external influences can accommodate such questions. But it is more open to asking questions about the continuous interplay between those influences on the Court. It is because we believe this interplay to be at the heart of Supreme Court decision making that we adopt this nomenclature.[44]

American Constitutionalism as a Developmental Phenomenon

It is one of the central themes of this volume that sophisticated understandings of constitutional decision making in the Supreme Court must resist the tendency to posit the sorts of globalist theories that have long proved staples of the separate literatures on the subject by political scientists and legal academics (with the former giving pride of place to external and the latter to internal influences). We agree that questions involving the interplay between the internal and the external are central to constitutional analysis. But unlike those whose primary interest is in fixing the preeminence of either, we contend that that question cannot be properly considered without focusing simultaneously on the Court as an institution operating in the stream of time.

Internal and external influences, after all, are developmental phenomena. Both are constructed across time. Legalist scholars have emphasized that Court decisions are situated in streams of precedent; some scholars have also properly emphasized that they are also situated in a stream of future precedent, as the Court looks ahead to the probable legal implications of its constitutional holdings.[45] Political scientists have emphasized that Court decisions are situated in a stream of political developments that occur across time, particularly in the electoral sphere, including electoral realignments. But the influences on paths of development are much more complicated than these rigid formulations would have it. They include not simply precedent and electoral politics but also the continual process of the formation, transformation, interplay, and disintegration of a broad array of categories—legal, intellectual, political, social, cultural—that constitute constitutional analysis. We seek to trace decision making on the Court to the developmental life of these categories, many of which have yet to be mapped. This can only be done inductively, by a study of concrete trajectories in a theoretically open way. Our task is, first, to describe the life of these categories and their relationship to constitutional change, and second, to offer possible explanations for the dynamics of that change. In taking up this task in light of individual case studies of developmental trajectories, a number of common questions and themes will emerge.

One question that engages many of our authors is how to fix the precise way in which Supreme Court decisions situate themselves temporally within constitutional and political development in the United States, and how they come to alter (or fail to alter) that course. Another theme that emerges is that constitutional development and narratives about—or the memory of—constitutional development are not necessarily the same thing. Indeed, far from simply relating trajectories of decisions and events across time, many of our contributors either implicitly or explicitly conclude that after-constructed "constitutive stories" of constitutional development are an important form of constitutional construction, a construction which acts in an almost concrete way to shape the contours of constitutional development itself.[46] The question of where a particular constitutional decision fits into a story thus is highly significant. It is a question for which, our contributors find, answers are far from obvious.

Related is the question of how institutional channels or trajectories of development are carved, when (and if) Court decisions flow within those channels, and when they might leap over its banks. Other essays take up the questions of the relationship between the Court and constitutional development and the broader political and social order.

The Chapters That Follow

The chapters that follow spotlight in different ways the continuous and mutually constitutive dynamic relationship between the wide variety of patterns, habits, and norms internal to the Court itself, and the external social, political, economic, interpretive, and historical context within which the Court makes constitutional choices. With due recognition that divisions of this sort can be overly schematic, Part I asks us to rethink our standard approaches to the question of causation in judicial decision making. Part II focuses on the relationship between the Court and the ambient political order. Part III provides in-depth historical case studies in the development over time of authoritative constitutional meaning. And Part IV focuses on processes by which elites and marginalized communities negotiate the terms of constitutional inclusion. Thus, all the chapters in this book simultaneously engage the Supreme Court along two dimensions that are commonly treated separately: the judicial decision-making process *and* the long-term, big-picture processes of doctrinal change or development. The chapters speak to each other about each of these dimensions separately and about how they operate together. The book ends with a brief synopsis of what we see as the most important theoretical insights of this collection and suggestions for future research.

In the book's first part, Mark A. Graber and Ronald Kahn consider the relationship between the law, policy preferences, and strategic considerations in judicial decision making, and larger questions of explanation as to the role of the Supreme Court in American political development. Through an examination of two cases from the Civil War era and its aftermath, Graber deconstructs the distinctions political scientists ordinarily make between the legal, attitudinal, or strategic influences on judicial decision making. He demonstrates how each of those three ostensibly separate categories of influence is, in fact, significantly constituted by the others, and interacts with them in highly complex ways. In light of this, Graber concludes that pure social science—unless it is supplemented by interpretive claims about what makes good law and good strategy—can never fully explain judicial decision making. In the future, "the most fruitful investigations," he writes, "will explore the ways in which legal, strategic, and attitudinal factors interact when justices make decisions and not engage in fruitless contests to determine which single factor explains the most."

Ronald Kahn's chapter considers the relationship of long-term paths of constitutional change to judicial decision making by looking at decisions by the Supreme Court justices on whether to follow or overrule landmark precedents. Through an analysis of Rehnquist Court abortion and homo-sexual rights cases, Kahn demonstrates the presence of a "social construc-tion process" that is simultaneously inward (legal) and outward (society) looking and in which the normative and empirical elements of the case are mutually constitutive. Because this process cannot be segmented into wholly external or internal elements, Kahn contends, methodologies premised on externalist (attitudinalism, strategic, and historical) or inter-nalist (legal) assumptions of causation alone are wanting. The unique dynamics at work in this process, in individual decisions and across time, call into question the applicability of highly generalized APD theories like those involving path dependency for understanding the place of the Supreme Court in American political development.

The book's second part focuses on the relationship between the Court and the ambient political order. Mark Tushnet argues in his chapter that it would be helpful to understand the Court if we focused on the active col-laborative steps that the Court takes to "build a stable political order by helping some parts of the system destabilize other parts as a preliminary to the construction of a new system." He does so by examining the Court's affirmative order-building role in three episodes in constitutional history—the New Deal and its aftermath in the Roosevelt Court, the Warren Court and its relation to the Great Society, and the Rehnquist Court during the Reagan Revolution. Like Tushnet's chapter, Howard Gillman's emphasizes the usefulness of understanding the Court as a component part of a broader political regime. With an illustrative focus on the modern judicial liberal-ism of the Warren and post-Warren era, Gillman argues that constitutional change in the United States sometimes reflects an effort at "political entrenchment" by which a governing coalition attempts to protect a polit-ical agenda by placing supporters of the agenda on the bench, where they will stay long after the coalition that appointed them is out of power. Gill-man notes that efforts at entrenchment are mediated by a wide array of forces, including legal norms, the political possibilities at the time of the appointment, and independent-minded judges changing their views under altered conditions. In light of these and other considerations, he suggests when efforts at entrenchment are likely to take place and succeed, and when they are likely to be avoided or fail. In his study of the paths of development of constitutional doctrine concerning, first, the rights of organized labor, and then civil rights, Ken I. Kersch emphasizes the creative and highly ideological role the Court can play in attempting to accommodate a sequence of potentially antagonistic reform imperatives that are central to a political regime. He describes the way that, in its opinions, the Court's justices work to formulate a politically, emotionally, and intellectually plausible constitutional rapprochement between groups—blacks and labor— that, historically, have been political antagonists, but have come to be understood as core constituencies of an emerging governing coalition.

The chapters in the book's third part provide in-depth historical case studies in the development of authoritative constitutional meaning. Wayne D. Moore's chapter describes the complex process by which, after its ratification in 1868, particular interpretations of the Fourteenth Amendment gained and lost authority in the ensuing postbellum years. Moore demonstrates, in particular, the way in which debates reflecting a range of interpretive agendas, undertaken by a range of interpreters—almost all of which could be accommodated by the literal terms of the constitutional text—were gradually winnowed down into a small set of authoritative interpretations of the Fourteenth Amendment. From this, he distills six criteria by which authoritative constitutional interpretations are established as "rules of recognition." In her chapter, Pamela Brandwein traces the development of the emergence of a single—and highly significant—authoritative interpretation of the Fourteenth Amendment, the "state action doctrine," which holds the Fourteenth Amendment applicable to government action only, and not private conduct. She finds that the origins of this doctrine significantly postdate both the Amendment and the Supreme Court decision that, to this day, are commonly named as its source and that its emergence is explained, in significant part, by political developments and intellectual trends originating far outside the precincts of the High Court.

The book's fourth part focuses on the processes by which elites and marginalized communities negotiate the terms of constitutional inclusion. Julie Novkov's study of the development of state and federal constitutional law concerning interracial marriage in the postbellum era demonstrates the degree to which a complex constellation of open constitutional contingencies and possibilities existed in earlier years as part of a vibrant, state-level legal, political, and cultural battle over interracial marriage. She then details the processes by which most of these, in the ensuing years, were gradually foreclosed and constitutional settlements were reached which set out an authoritative and restrictive understanding of the constitutionality of state prohibitions of these marriages. Carol Nackenoff examines the way in which the necessity of dealing with the legal, political, and cultural claims of Native Americans in the late nineteenth and early twentieth centuries led state and federal judges, legislators, and an array of political actors to renegotiate the meaning of American citizenship. She shows how this negotiation, which was informed by a shifting cultural, constitutional, and political context, and by elite activism on behalf of Indians, ultimately came to inform authoritative Supreme Court interpretations of the Fourteenth Amendment's meaning, and the scope of permissible congressional authority over the governance of Indians and their tribes. Thomas M. Keck's account of the development of constitutional doctrine involving affirmative action demonstrates how the efforts of a single justice, Lewis Powell, to balance the Republican Party's competing ideological commitments to color-blindness and judicial restraint encouraged the development of conservative rights-based legal activists, who brought a series of test cases that spurred further doctrinal development. This campaign, in turn, spurred countervailing activism on the part of the affirmative action defenders. Ultimately, this led to the Court's decision to transmogrify Justice Powell's lone opinion into a five-vote ruling in the University of Michigan affirmative action case, and hence the law of the land.

Conclusion

In this introductory essay, we have provided students of law and courts with a brief overview of both the origins of the study of APD and the types of questions APD scholars are inclined toward asking about American politics, and suggested how those questions may be relevant to the study of the Supreme Court and American constitutionalism. For those law and courts scholars who have not been heretofore familiar with APD, we hope it has become clear that APD is not simply another method that, in a new departure for contemporary political science, uses history to answer the sorts of questions that have become standard lines of inquiry in the study of American politics. Students of APD have their own distinctive interests and will ask their own distinctive questions. Within political science, they are not agenda takers, but agenda setters. We believe that APD agendas are often more interesting, and more engaged with questions that truly matter, than much of the work that is done today within the mainstream of the contemporary study of American politics. Our enthusiasm for APD as a field stems from this belief.

But our purpose here has been more than to bring APD to law. It has also been to bring law to APD. As noted above, APD scholars have long evinced an interest in law as an instrumentality (perhaps the central instrumentality) of the state. We hope that the essays that follow will spur APD scholars to think about law and the Supreme Court in new and more sophisticated ways. We hope, moreover, that the insights provided here on the development of constitutional law and the Supreme Court will lead them to a more comprehensive understanding of the broader dynamic of the paths of American political development.

Notes

1. *Lawrence v. Texas*, 539 U.S. 558 (2003).

2. *Grutter v. Bollinger*, 539 U.S. 306 (2003); *Regents of the University of California v. Bakke*, 438 U.S. 265 (1978).

3. Hugh Davis Graham, *Collision Course: The Strange Convergence of Affirmative Action and Immigration Policy in America* (New York: Oxford University Press, 2002); John David Skrentny, *The Ironies of Affirmative Action: Politics, Culture, and Justice in America* (Chicago: University of Chicago Press, 1996); Thomas Sowell, *Civil Rights: Rhetoric or Reality* (New York: Quill, 1984).

4. See John R. Vile, *A Companion to the United States Constitution and Its Amendments* (Westport, Conn.: Praeger, 1997); David E. Kyvig, *Explicit and Authentic Acts: Amending the U.S. Constitution, 1776–1995* (Lawrence: University Press of Kansas, 1996).

5. *United States v. Butler*, 297 U.S. 1 (1936).

6. Jeffrey Segal and Harold Spaeth, *The Supreme Court and the Attitudinal Model* (New York: Cambridge University Press, 1993); Jeffrey Segal and Harold Spaeth, *The Supreme Court and the Attitudinal Model Revisited* (New York: Cambridge University Press, 2002).

7. See Harold J. Spaeth and Jeffrey A. Segal, *Majority Rule or Minority Will: Adherence to Precedent on the U.S. Supreme Court* (New York: Cambridge University Press, 1999).

8. Lawrence Baum, "C. Herman Pritchett: Innovator with an Ambiguous Legacy," in *Pioneers of Judicial Behavior*, ed. Nancy Maveety (Ann Arbor: University of Michigan Press, 2003); C. Herman Pritchett, *The Roosevelt Court: A Study in Judicial Politics and Values, 1937–1947* (New York: Macmillan, 1948).

9. Segal and Spaeth, *Supreme Court and the Attitudinal Model Revisited*, 86.

10. Walter F. Murphy, *The Elements of Judicial Strategy* (Chicago: University of Chicago Press, 1964); Lee Epstein and Jack Knight, *The Choices Justices Make* (Washington, D.C.: CQ Press, 1998); Forrest Maltzman, James F. Spriggs II, and Paul J. Wahlbeck, *Crafting Law on the Supreme Court: The Collegial Game* (Cambridge: Cambridge University Press, 2000); Rafael Gely and Pablo T. Spiller, "A Rational Choice Theory of Supreme Court Statutory Decisions with Applications to the 'State Farm'

and 'Grove City' Cases," *Journal of Law, Economics, and Organization* 6 (Autumn 1990): 263–300; Georg Vanberg, "Legislative-Judicial Relations: A Game-Theoretic Approach to Constitutional Review," *American Journal of Political Science* 45 (April 2001): 346–361. See Forrest Maltzman, James F. Spriggs II, and Paul J. Wahlbeck, "Strategy and Judicial Choice: New Institutionalist Approaches to Supreme Court Decision-making," in *Supreme Court Decisionmaking: New Institutionalist Approaches,* ed. Cornell Clayton and Howard Gillman (Chicago: University of Chicago Press, 1999); George I. Lovell, *Legislative Deferrals: Statutory Ambiguity, Judicial Power, and American Democracy* (New York: Cambridge University Press, 2003).

11. See J. W. Peltason, *58 Lonely Men: Southern Federal Judges and School Desegregation* (Urbana: University of Illinois Press, 1971); Lee Epstein, *Conservatives in Court* (Knoxville: University of Tennessee Press, 1985); Karen O'Connor, *Women's Organizations' Use of the Courts* (Lexington, Mass.: Lexington Books, 1980); Gregg Ivers, *To Build a Wall: American Jews and the Separation of Church and State* (Charlottesville: University of Virginia Press, 1995); Michael W. McCann, *Taking Reform Seriously: Perspectives on Public Interest Liberalism* (Ithaca, N.Y.: Cornell University Press, 1986); Charles R. Epp, *The Rights Revolution: Lawyers, Activists, and Supreme Courts in Comparative Perspective* (Chicago: University of Chicago Press, 1998).

12. See, e.g., Byron J. Moraski and Charles R. Shipan, "The Politics of Supreme Court Nominations: A Theory of Institutional Constraints and Choices," *American Journal of Political Science* 43 (1999): 1069–1095; Gregory A. Caldeira and John R. Wright, "Lobbying for Justice: Organized Interests, Supreme Court Nominations and the United States Senate," *American Journal of Political Science* 44 (1999): 499–523; Charles M. Cameron, Albert D. Cover, and Jeffrey A. Segal, "Senate Voting on Supreme Court Nominees: A Neoinstitutional Model," *American Political Science Review* 84 (1990): 525–534; Saul Brenner and John F. Krol, "Strategies in Certiorari Voting on the United States Supreme Court," *Journal of Politics* 51 (1989): 828–840; Gregory Caldeira, John R. Wright, and Christopher J. W. Zorn, "Strategic Voting and Gatekeeping in the Supreme Court," *Journal of Law, Economics, and Organization* 15 (1999): 549; H. W. Perry Jr., *Deciding to Decide: Agenda Setting in the United States Supreme Court* (Cambridge, Mass.: Harvard University Press, 1991).

13. See Edward A. Purcell Jr., *The Crisis of Democratic Theory: Scientific Naturalism and the Problem of Value* (Lexington: University of Kentucky, 1973), 267–272; Theodore J. Lowi, *The End of Liberalism: The Second Republic of the United States* (New York: W. W. Norton, 1969); Richard H. Pells, *The Liberal Mind in a Conservative Age: American Intellectuals in the 1940s and 1950s* (Middletown, Conn.: Wesleyan University Press, 1989).

14. Barrington Moore Jr., *Social Origins of Dictatorship and Democracy: Lord and Peasant in the Making of the Modern World* (Boston: Beacon Press, 1993); Samuel P. Huntington, *Political Order in Changing Societies* (New Haven: Yale University Press, 1968); Theda Skocpol, *States and Social Revolutions: A Comparative Analysis of France, Russia, and China* (Cambridge: Cambridge University Press, 1979). For a brief overview of this work, see Ira Katznelson, "Periodization and Preferences: Reflections on Purposive

Action in Comparative Historical Social Science," in *Comparative Historical Analysis in the Social Sciences*, ed. James Mahoney and Dietrich Rueschemeyer (Cambridge: Cambridge University Press, 2003). These questions were also at the heart of much of the work on American politics by midcentury pluralists like Robert Dahl and Seymour Martin Lipset. See Purcell, *Crisis of Democratic Theory*, 253–266.

15. See Paul Pierson, *Politics in Time: History, Institutions, and Social Analysis* (Princeton, N.J.: Princeton University Press, 2004); Karen Orren and Stephen Skowronek, *The Search for American Political Development* (New York: Cambridge University Press, 2004).

16. Orren and Skowronek, *Search for American Political Development*, chap. 2; William Nisbet Chambers and Walter Dean Burnham, eds., *The American Party Systems: Stages of Development* (New York: Oxford University Press, 1967); Walter Dean Burnham, *Critical Elections and the Mainsprings of American Politics* (New York: W. W. Norton, 1970). See also James Sundquist, *Dynamics of the Party System: Alignment and Realignment of Political Parties in the United States* (Washington, D.C.: Brookings Institution, 1973). For subsequent variations sharing a belief in punctuated equilibriums, see James A. Morone, *The Democratic Wish: Popular Participation and the Limits of American Government* (New York: Basic Books, 1990); Bruce Ackerman, *We the People 1: Foundations* (Cambridge, Mass.: Harvard University Press, 1991); Samuel P. Huntington, *American Politics: The Promise of Disharmony* (Cambridge, Mass.: Belknap Press of Harvard University Press, 1981).

17. Rogers M. Smith, "Beyond Tocqueville, Myrdal, and Hartz: Multiple Traditions in America," *American Political Science Review* 87 (September 1993): 549–566; Rogers M. Smith, *Civic Ideals: Conflicting Visions of Citizenship in U.S. History* (New Haven: Yale University Press, 1997).

18. Huntington, *American Politics*, 14–15.

19. Huntington names the Revolutionary, Jacksonian, and Progressive Eras, as well as "the years of protest, exposure, and reform of the 1960s and early 1970s," in Huntington, *American Politics*, 85.

20. He emphasized a humanist strand partial to negative, individualist conceptions of freedom and a reform liberal outlook that emphasizes commitments to positive, collectively defined social goals. J. David Greenstone, *The Lincoln Persuasion: Remaking American Liberalism* (Princeton, N.J.: Princeton University Press, 1993); J. David Greenstone, "Political Culture and American Political Development: Liberty, Union, and the Liberal Bipolarity," *Studies in American Political Development* 1 (1986): 1–49. See Karen Orren and Stephen Skowronek, "Study of Political Development," in *Political Science: The State of the Discipline*, ed. Ira Katznelson and Helen Milner (New York: W. W. Norton, 2002).

21. See J. David Greenstone, "Against Simplicity: The Cultural Dimensions of the Constitution," *University of Chicago Law Review* 55 (1988): 428–444; Ronald Kahn, "Liberalism, Political Culture, and the Rights of Subordinated Groups: Constitutional Theory and Practice at a Crossroads," in *The Liberal Tradition in American Politics*, ed. David F. Ericsson and Louise Birch Green (New York, Routledge, 1999), chap. 8.

22. Although the separation can be far from clear, many scholars take ideas to be a form of institution. See Rogers M. Smith, "Political Jurisprudence, the 'New Institu-

tionalism,' and the Future of Public Law," *American Political Science Review* 82 (1988): 89–108; Howard Gillman, *The Constitution Besieged: The Rise and Demise of Lochner Era Police Powers Jurisprudence* (Durham, N.C.: Duke University Press, 1993). See also Douglass North, *Institutions, Institutional Change, and Economic Performance* (Cambridge: Cambridge University Press, 1990).

23. Stephen Skowronek, *Building a New American State: The Expansion of National Administrative Capacities, 1877–1920* (Cambridge: Cambridge University Press, 1982).

24. Martin J. Sklar, *The Corporate Reconstruction of American Capitalism, 1890–1916: The Market, the Law, and American Politics* (Cambridge: Cambridge University Press, 1988); Richard F. Bensel, *The Political Economy of American Industrialization, 1877–1900* (Cambridge: Cambridge University Press, 2000); Elizabeth Sanders, *Roots of Reform: Farmers, Workers, and the American State, 1877–1917* (Chicago: University of Chicago Press, 1999); Gretchen Ritter, *Goldbugs and Greenbacks: The Antimonopoly Tradition and Politics of Finance, 1865–1896* (Cambridge: Cambridge University Press, 1997); Theda Skocpol, *Protecting Soldiers and Mothers: The Political Origins of Social Policy in the United States* (Cambridge, Mass.: Belknap Press of Harvard University Press, 1992); Scott C. James, *Presidents, Parties, and the State: A Party System Perspective on Democratic Regulatory Choice, 1884–1936* (Cambridge: Cambridge University Press, 2000); Daniel P. Carpenter, *The Forging of Bureaucratic Autonomy: Reputations, Networks, and Policy Innovation in Executive Agencies, 1862–1928* (Princeton, N.J.: Princeton University Press, 2001).

25. Suzanne Mettler, *Dividing Citizens: Gender and Federalism in New Deal Public Policy* (Ithaca, N.Y.: Cornell University Press, 1998); David Plotke, *Building a Democratic Political Order: Reshaping American Liberalism in the 1930s and 1940s* (Cambridge: Cambridge University Press, 1996); Robert C. Lieberman, *Shifting the Color Line: Race and the American Welfare State* (Cambridge, Mass.: Harvard University Press, 1998); Jacob Hacker, *The Divided Welfare State: The Battle over Public and Private Benefits in the United States* (Cambridge: Cambridge University Press, 2002); John David Skrentny, *The Minority Rights Revolution* (Cambridge, Mass.: Belknap Press of Harvard University Press, 2002).

26. Pierson, *Politics in Time*; Kathleen Thelen and Frank Longstreth, eds., *Structuring Politics: Historical Institutionalism in Comparative Analysis* (Cambridge: Cambridge University Press, 1992); Orren and Skowronek, *Search for American Political Development*.

27. Lowi, *End of Liberalism*; Sklar, *Corporate Reconstruction*; Skowronek, *Building a New American State*; Karen Orren, *Belated Feudalism: Labor, the Law, and Liberal Development in the United States* (Cambridge: Cambridge University Press, 1991); Victoria C. Hattam, *Labor Visions and State Power: The Origins of Business Unionism in the United States* (Princeton, N.J.: Princeton University Press, 1993).

28. See Cornell Clayton and Howard Gillman, "Beyond Judicial Attitudes: Institutional Approaches to Supreme Court Decision-making," and Cornell Clayton, "The Supreme Court and Political Jurisprudence: New and Old Institutionalisms," both in *Supreme Court Decision-making*, ed. Cornell Clayton and Howard Gillman (Chicago: University of Chicago Press, 1999).

29. Jeremy A. Rabkin, *Judicial Compulsions: How Public Law Distorts Public Policy*

(New York: Basic Books, 1989); R. Shep Melnick, *Regulation and the Courts: The Case of the Clean Air Act* (Washington, D.C.: Brookings Institution, 1983); Stanley I. Kutler, *Judicial Power and Reconstruction Politics* (Chicago: University of Chicago Press, 1968); Lovell, *Legislative Deferrals* (Cambridge: Cambridge University Press, 2003); Mark Graber, "Non-Majoritarian Difficulty: Legislative Deference to the Judiciary," *Studies in American Political Development* 7 (1993): 35–73.

30. Ronald Kahn, *The Supreme Court and Constitutional Theory, 1953–1993* (Lawrence: University Press of Kansas, 1994).

31. Keith Whittington, "Once More unto to the Breach: Post-Behavioralist Approaches to Judicial Politics," *Law and Social Inquiry* 25 (Spring 2000): 601–634, 608.

32. See Paul Pierson, "Not Just What, but When: Timing and Sequence in Political Processes," *Studies in American Political Development* 14 (April 2000): 72–92; Kathleen Thelen, "How Institutions Evolve: Insights from Comparative Historical Analysis," in *Comparative Historical Analysis in the Social Sciences*, ed. James Mahoney and Dietrich Rueschemeyer (Cambridge: Cambridge University Press, 2003).

33. See Katznelson, "Periodization and Preferences." See also Howard Gillman, "Robert G. McCloskey, Historical Institutionalism, and the Arts of Judicial Governance," in *Pioneers of Judicial Behavior*, ed. Nancy Maveety (Ann Arbor: University of Michigan Press, 2003), 337–338, 350.

34. See Purcell, *Crisis of Democratic Theory*; Kahn, *Supreme Court and Constitutional Theory*; Ken I. Kersch, *Constructing Civil Liberties: Discontinuities in the Development of American Constitutional Law* (Cambridge: Cambridge University Press, 2004); Robert G. McCloskey, *The American Supreme Court* (Chicago: University of Chicago Press, 1994).

35. McCloskey, *The American Supreme Court*, 11–13; Martin M. Shapiro, *Courts: A Comparative and Political Analysis* (Chicago: University of Chicago Press, 1981).

36. The melding of executive with judicial power is evident from the very word "court" itself: originally, English courts were a component part of the King's court.

37. John Locke, *Second Treatise of Government* (Indianapolis, Ind.: Hackett, 1980).

38. See Alexis de Tocqueville, *Democracy in America*, trans. Harvey C. Mansfield and Delba Winthrop (Chicago: University of Chicago Press, 2000); Friedrich von Hayek, *The Constitution of Liberty* (Chicago: University of Chicago Press, 1960); Benjamin N. Cardozo, *The Nature of the Judicial Process* (New Haven: Yale University Press, 1921). In the American constitutional system, although the legislative and executive powers are separated, some of the historically rooted ties between the executive and judicial power remain. It is the president who appoints the federal judges (subject to Senate confirmation). The Justice Department's position on pending cases is accorded special consideration in the Court's deliberations. Court rulings are enforced by the executive branch. And, functionally speaking, the Court, through its powers of judicial review, like the president, has the power to veto legislation that conflicts with the fundamental law of the Constitution. The president's powers in this regard are broader: he, unlike the Court, is permitted to veto a law on pure policy disagreement grounds. Because its judicial review powers are premised on the power of measuring ordinary laws

against the fundamental law of the Constitution, however, the Court is not supposed to do so.

39. Jack Balkin and Sanford Levinson argue that as a practical matter, justices—who, although appointed for life, serve an average term of eighteen years—are most analogous to similarly long-serving heads of independent agencies, like the head of the Federal Reserve Board. See Jack Balkin and Sanford Levinson, "Understanding the Constitutional Revolution," *Virginia Law Review* 87 (October 2001): 1045–1104.

40. Federalist 78, in James Madison, Alexander Hamilton, and John Jay, *The Federalist Papers*, ed. Clinton Rossiter (New York: Mentor Books, 1962).

41. Philip Bobbitt, *Constitutional Fate: Theory of the Constitution* (New York: Oxford University Press, 1982).

42. Kahn, *Supreme Court and Constitutional Theory.*

43. Purcell, *Crisis of Democratic Theory;* Kahn, *Supreme Court and Constitutional Theory;* Kersch, *Constructing Civil Liberties.*

44. See also Peter H. Russell and David M. O'Brien, eds., *Judicial Independence in the Age of Democracy: Critical Perspectives from around the World* (Charlottesville: University of Virginia Press, 2001); Kahn, *Supreme Court and Constitutional Theory.*

45. Shapiro, *Courts.*

46. Rogers M. Smith, *Stories of Peoplehood: The Politics and Morals of Political Membership* (Cambridge: Cambridge University Press, 2003); Kersch, *Constructing Civil Liberties.* See Keith E. Whittington, *Constitutional Construction: Divided Powers and Constitutional Meaning* (Cambridge, Mass.: Harvard University Press, 1999); William Novak, *The People's Welfare: Law and Regulation in Nineteenth-Century America* (Chapel Hill: University of North Carolina Press, 1996); Albert Alschuler, *Law without Values: The Life Work and Legacy of Justice Holmes* (Chicago: University of Chicago Press, 2000).

Part I

Rethinking the Law Versus Politics Dichotomy:
The Internal and External in
Supreme Court Decision Making

Chapter 1

Legal, Strategic or Legal Strategy: Deciding to Decide during the Civil War and Reconstruction

Mark A. Graber

Judicial decisions determining the constitutionality of wartime policies exhibit a disturbing pattern. The Supreme Court during a declared or undeclared war has refused to challenge any wartime policy clearly endorsed by both elected branches of the national government.[1] Nevertheless, official court doctrine rejects claims that *inter arma silent leges* is the law of the constitution. "No doctrine, involving more pernicious consequences," Justice David Davis declared in *Ex parte Milligan*, "was ever invented by the wit of man than that any of [the Constitution's] provisions can be suspended during any of the great exigencies of government."[2] Justice Frank Murphy's opinion in *Duncan v. Kahanamoku* proclaimed, "to retreat from [the] rule" of *Milligan* "is to open the door to rampant militarism and the glorification of war, which have destroyed so many nations in history."[3] These opinions were written after hostilities had ceased. The same judicial majorities that boldly asserted in peacetime that "the Constitution . . . is a law for rulers and people, equally in war and in peace"[4] consistently proved unwilling in wartime to protect fundamental civil liberties.[5] As Chief Justice Rehnquist succinctly observes, "courts are more prone to uphold wartime claims of civil liberties after the war is over."[6]

Supreme Court practice during the 1860s provides vivid examples of this judicial tendency to announce constitutional limits on military policy only after the need for military action is over. Many litigants during the Civil War urged federal justices to declare unconstitutional President Lincoln's decision to suspend habeas corpus, his decision to impose martial law in some northern communities, federal laws compelling creditors to take paper money in payment of existing debts, and other federal policies deemed necessary to support the Northern war effort. While Lee's army was in the field, the Supreme Court either sustained the federal policy under constitutional attack,[7] ruled that no jurisdiction existed to resolve cases presenting constitutional attacks on Civil War measures,[8] or postponed adjudication.[9] When the war ended, the justices struck down several wartime measures ducked during hostilities.[10] At the same time that the Chase Court declared unconstitutional several of the late President Lincoln's wartime policies, judicial majorities avoided interfering with the living Congress's Reconstruction policies. The very justices who in *Milligan* had boldly declared unconstitutional martial law in the North after that policy had been abandoned ruled in *Ex parte McCardle* that no jurisdiction existed to resolve the constitutionality of martial law in the South.[11]

The Supreme Court's behavior during and immediately after the Civil War inspired contemporary scholars to sharpen the strategic model of judicial decision making. Lee Epstein and Thomas Walker, when asserting that justices on the Supreme Court engage in sophisticated voting, highlight the difference between judicial activism on martial law in the North and judicial restraint on martial law in the South.[12] The best historical evidence, they point out, suggests that Chase Court majorities during the 1860s believed that imposition of martial law in the South was as unconstitutional as the imposition of martial law in the North. Nevertheless, the justices handed down opinions consistent with their political and legal convictions only when doing so did not challenge popular majorities in Congress. Military or military-related policies were declared unconstitutional only after they had been abandoned or were broadly recognized as no longer necessary to support a military effort.

Closer examination complicates the seemingly obvious strategic explanation for crucial judicial decisions during the 1860s. Legal precedents on federal appellate jurisdiction were abandoned in response to external pressures during the Civil War, but not during Reconstruction. The Supreme Court's decision in *Roosevelt v. Meyer* (1863) that the court had no jurisdiction to adjudicate an appeal from a state court decision sustaining the constitutionality of the Legal Tender Acts miscited previous holdings and was overruled immediately when felt needs for paper money passed. The judicial decision in *Ex Parte McCardle* (1868) that the court could not legally adjudicate an appeal challenging the constitutionality of martial law in the South after Congress withdrew jurisdiction, by comparison, was a straightforward application of nineteenth-century case law. The strategic decision *Roosevelt* had subtle legal foundations. The decision to ignore the plain meaning of the Judiciary Act of 1789 may have been a legitimate use of what Alexander

Bickel would later label "the passive virtues."[13] The legal decision in *McCardle* had subtle strategic and attitudinal foundations. The precedents that Chief Justice Chase correctly cited in his majority opinion embodied the strategic and sincere policy preferences of his judicial ancestors.

This chapter revisits *Roosevelt* and *Ex parte McCardle* with an eye to improving explanations of judicial decision making. Judicial decisions during the 1860s illustrate many interactions between legal, strategic, and attitudinal considerations too often separated in social science analysis. The justices in *McCardle* felt legally obligated to follow precedents decided partly on nonlegal grounds. *Roosevelt* was an instance where, arguably, law compelled the justices to make a strategic choice. Justices during the 1860s were concerned with public policy and judicial power, but they expressed these concerns as justices limited by legal logics. The forms of legal reasoning, although permitting and possibly even compelling some strategic behavior, also constrained the policies justices could advance and the strategic means by which judicial policy preferences could be achieved.

Judicial decision making, *Roosevelt* and *McCardle* reveal, is a practice that mixes legal, strategic, and attitudinal considerations in ways that cannot be fully isolated by scientific investigation. Behavioralists maintain that no judicial decision can be explained entirely as a legal exercise, but they fail to acknowledge that no judicial decision can be explained entirely as a sincere or sophisticated effort to secure policy preferences. Although persons use rules to further goals, the goals they pursue and the means they choose are largely constituted by the rules of the game. The progressive takes on *McCardle* and *Roosevelt* in this essay demonstrate how law both enables and constrains strategic and value choices, and how sincere and sophisticated policy preferences embodied in precedents mold the path of the law. Both justices and those who explain judicial decisions cannot avoid legal, strategic, and attitudinal analysis. Whether *Roosevelt* and *McCardle* are legal, strategic, or attitudinal decisions depends on contested interpretations of what constitutes competent legal, strategic or attitudinal practice.

The ways in which legal, strategic, and attitudinal considerations structured the *Roosevelt* and *McCardle* decisions help explain *inter arma leges silent* and the durability of judicial review in the United States. Judicial review thrives in the United States partly because at crucial moments, some legal norms facilitated strategic choices to avoid challenging administrative policy and other legal norms prevented less strategically minded justices from reaching constitutional decisions likely to provoke severe legislative retaliation. Justice Miller in *Roosevelt* believed the courts should not decide the constitutionality of wartime measures while hostilities were ongoing. Chief Justice Chase in *McCardle* hoped to have the opportunity to declare martial law in the South unconstitutional while Northern troops occupied the former slave states. Both justices refrained from acting. Legal norms permitted Justice Miller to interpret existing law as requiring a strategic denial of jurisdiction. Other legal norms explain why Chief Justice Chase interpreted existing law as forbidding an attitudinal decision on the merits of martial law. Both the precedents these justices followed and the precedents they created suggest the existence of a precedential spiral[14] or sequence in the United States evolving in ways that over time provides increased legal foundations for judicial decisions refraining from striking down military related policies and fewer legal grounds for judicial decisions declaring such policies unconstitutional.

Take One: The Legal *McCardle*

Ex Parte McCardle plays a central role in the strategic model of judicial decision making developed by Lee Epstein and her coauthors.[15] The Supreme Court in that case first delayed reaching a decision on the constitutionality of martial law in the South while legislation withdrawing jurisdiction was under legislative and executive consideration. The justices then denied jurisdiction immediately after Congress overrode a presidential veto and passed the Repealer Act of 1868. Epstein and Thomas Walker, in their seminal essay on judicial decision making, maintain that this exhibition of judicial restraint illustrates how judicial choices are "not merely the product of the individual policy preferences of the justices," but "also a function of the preferences of other political actors . . . and of the political context."[16] Epstein and Jack Knight, in their acclaimed book elaborating the strategic model of judicial decision making, similarly use *McCardle* when commenting on the judicial tendency to pursue personal policy preferences only in light of the political climate.[17] Both works assert that the attitudinal model associated with Harold Spaeth and Jeffrey Segal[18] does not explain why the Chase Court refused to use *McCardle* as a vehicle for declaring martial law unconstitutional. Spaeth and Segal regard Supreme Court decision making as unalloyed policy making.[19] Epstein and Walker declare, "*McCardle* did not reflect the sincere preferences of the Court." Epstein and Knight assert, "the justices acted in a sophisticated fashion; they acceded to the government's wishes and declined to hear the case."[20]

Proponents of the contemporary strategic model of judicial decision making assess whether the justices in McCardle engaged in sophisticated voting by examining judicial preferences on the underlying policy issue and determining probable legislative reactions to hostile judicial rulings. Their analysis begins by documenting that most Chase Court justices opposed martial law in the South. "The Court's sympathy," Epstein and Walker correctly observe, "lay with McCardle."[21] The justices had previously shown little sympathy toward military reconstruction. Political actors in the know thought the justices likely to free McCardle, and the private correspondence of the justices indicates that these suspicions were well founded.[22] Had the justices sincerely voted their policy preferences, they would have reached the merits in McCardle and struck down the offending government action. That decision declaring unconstitutional martial law might have provoked severe legislative retaliation. Epstein, Walker, and Knight point out that while McCardle was being litigated, Congress was debating the impeachment of President Johnson and proposals limiting judicial power. After oral argument, Congress passed the Repealer Act of 1868. This measure rescinded the Habeas Corpus Act of 1867, the statute under which McCardle claimed jurisdiction.[23] Given the evidence that the justices did not vote their policy preferences in McCardle, Epstein and others conclude that these legislative actions must have convinced the Chase Court that discretion was the better part of valor. The justices responded to changes in the external political environment by making the decision that best husbanded judicial power for the future, not the decision that best expressed immediate judicial policy preferences.

The justices were not completely obsequious in McCardle. The McCardle opinion, published the month after the ruling was announced, explicitly asserted that the legislation repealing the Habeas Corpus Act of 1867 did not affect the judicial power to hear habeas corpus appeals under the Judiciary Act of 1789. "The act of 1868 does not except from that jurisdiction any cases but appeals from Circuit Courts under the act of 1867," the chief justice stated. "It does not affect the jurisdiction which was previously exercised."[24] Ex parte Yerger,[25] decided six months later, made clear that the Supreme Court retained jurisdiction under the Judiciary Act of 1789 to consider constitutional challenges to Reconstruction. Epstein and Walker regard the quoted passage in the McCardle opinion and the Yerger decision as additional examples of strategic thinking by the justices. The Chase Court was more willing to express policy preferences in Yerger than in McCardle, they contend, because political enthusiasm for martial law had diminished considerably from the spring to the fall of 1868, "significantly reduc[ing] the probability of an adverse congressional response."[26]

Take Two: The Strategic *Roosevelt*

Roosevelt v. Meyer satisfies the criteria used to establish strategic decision making in *McCardle*. The justices did not vote their policy preferences when they rejected jurisdiction over an appeal from a New York decision sustaining the constitutionality of the Legal Tender Acts. Had the justices reached the merits, the eminent historian Charles Warren maintains, "it is probable that the Legal Tender Acts would have been held invalid by [a] large . . . majority of the Court."[27] The Jacksonian majority on the late Taney and early Chase Court abhorred paper money. Chief Justice Taney, who did not participate in the *Roosevelt* decision, wrote a draft opinion declaring the Legal Tender Acts unconstitutional. The principles stated in that draft became law shortly after Appomattox in *Hepburn v. Griswold* (1868).[28] A decision striking down legal tender laws during the Civil War, however, might not have been implemented and would have risked political retaliation. President Lincoln had previously refused to comply with a judicial order interfering with military concerns. "Are all the laws, but one, to go unexecuted, and the government itself go to pieces, lest that one be violated?"[29] Lincoln asked Congress when defending his decision to ignore the writ of habeas corpus issued in *Ex parte Merryman*.[30] Congress during the Civil War was no friendlier to an independent judiciary. The Republican majority had already added an extra justice to the bench, partly to secure favorable judicial decisions.[31] Antislavery advocates were looking for an opportunity to take revenge on the tribunal responsible for *Dred Scott*. These external threats seemingly explain why the justices in *Roosevelt* did not vote their sincere policy preferences. David Silver's analysis of the Supreme Court during the Civil War notes, "the Court did not desire to interfere with a measure devised by the administration to aid the war effort" when reaching the merits "might have led to a decision adverse to the administration."[32]

Law provides an additional reason for thinking *Roosevelt* an instance of strategic decision making. The decision to deny jurisdiction is plainly inconsistent with the clear commands set out in the Judiciary Act of 1789, precedent, and subsequent judicial decisions. The five justices in the *Roosevelt* majority still on the court when the jurisdictional issue was next litigated all confessed error. This unprecedented judicial reversal provides powerful evidence that legal logics neither permitted nor compelled the original decision to deny jurisdiction. Judicial decisions interpreting the Judiciary Act of 1789 responded to changes in the political environment, not the law of federal appellate jurisdiction.

The *Roosevelt* opinion is short, succinct, and superficially persuasive. Justice Wayne's two-sentence opus declared

> it to be the conclusion of their honors, upon an examination of the record, that as the validity of the act of February 25th, 1862, was drawn in question, and the judgment of the Court of Errors and Appeals of the State of New York was in favor of it, and of the right set up by the defendant, this court had no jurisdiction to reverse that judgment; that the dismissal of the case was accordingly to be directed. In support of the decision which he announced the learned Justice referred to various cases in this court which are mentioned in the note below.[33]

The four cases cited in that note all held that federal law did not permit the Supreme Court to exercise appellate jurisdiction whenever the final state court decision sustained an act of Congress.[34] These decisions relied on the clause in the Judiciary Act of 1789 that vests the Supreme Court with appellate jurisdiction over cases in which a state court declared a federal law unconstitutional. The New York court declared the Legal Tender Acts constitutional. Therefore, apparently, no basis for federal jurisdiction existed.

Justice Wayne's opinion is wrong and has been recognized as wrong by every prominent scholar who has commented on the case.[35] The Judiciary Act vests the Supreme Court with jurisdiction over state court decisions declaring federal laws unconstitutional and state court decisions rejecting claims of federal constitutional right. The relevant language in Section 25 declares, "any suit, . . . where is drawn in question the construction of any clause of the constitution . . . and the decision is against the . . . right . . . claimed by either party, . . . may be re-examined, and reversed or affirmed in the Supreme Court of the United States."[36] The plaintiff in *Roosevelt* asserted a constitutional right not to accept paper money as legal tender. The state court rejected that claim of constitutional right. Justices engaged in legal decision making would have taken jurisdiction under the Judiciary Act.

The justices recognized their mistake immediately after the Civil War. A unanimous Court in *Trebilcock v. Wilson* (1871) overruled *Roosevelt*. *Trebilcock* held that the Judiciary Act provided the Supreme Court with appellate jurisdiction to resolve a state court decision sustaining the Legal Tender Acts. Justice Field's opinion lamely asserted that the "court in [*Roosevelt*] confined its attention to the first clause of the 25th section of the Judiciary Act, and, in its decision, appears to have overlooked the third clause."[37] Belatedly interpreting federal law correctly, Field concluded that "the decision of the court below being against the right of the plaintiff in error claimed under the clauses of the Constitution, . . . he was entitled to have the decision brought before this court for re-examination."[38] The five justices (Miller, Field, Swayne, Davis, Clifford) in *Trebilcock* who overruled a decision in which they were previously in the majority set a record for judicial recantation that has never been broken and that has only once been approached.[39]

The "overlooking" in *Roosevelt* seems intentional. The justices in 1863 were presented with the correct legal grounds for a decision. Counsel for the plaintiffs asserted that jurisdiction was based on the third clause of Section 25, the clause vesting the Supreme Court with jurisdiction over appeals from state cases rejecting claims of federal constitutional right.[40] Justice Nelson dissented without opinion, but a reasonable inference can be made that he communicated this jurisdictional concern to his colleagues.[41] No great outcry took place between 1864 and 1871 that might have better informed the justices that they had misread the Judiciary Act of 1789. The justices got the law right in *Trebilcock* because the political climate in 1871 was more supportive of a legal decision than the political climate in 1864.

Take Three: The Legal *McCardle*

The legal reasons for thinking *Roosevelt* an instance of strategic decision making provide grounds for thinking that *McCardle* is an instance of legal decision making. Nineteenth-century case law and judicial practice supported the judicial choice to first delay the decision until Congress passed the Repealer Act and then deny jurisdiction. Precedent in 1868 permitted the Supreme Court to adjudicate appeals only when Congress passed and maintained statutes authorizing appellate jurisdiction. Recently decided cases held that the Supreme Court could not adjudicate appeals already pending before the justices after Congress withdrew jurisdiction. Jurisdiction had to exist at the time of final decision. Supreme Court justices, as a matter of long-standing practice, consistently delayed reaching decisions whenever Congress was actively considering changing the relevant law governing jurisdiction or the merits of an appeal. *McCardle* neither created new law nor inaugurated new judicial procedure. The case was a straightforward application of precedent and practice.

Federalist justices during the early republic ruled that Article III authorized judicial review only when federal statutes conferred appellate jurisdiction on federal courts. The justices in *Wiscart v. Dauchy* (1796) held that the Supreme Court could not adjudicate any appeal without statutory permission. Chief Justice Ellsworth declared, "if Congress has provided no rule to regulate our proceedings, we cannot exercise an appellate jurisdiction."[42] *Durousseau v. United States* (1810) agreed. The "affirmative description" of the jurisdiction laid out in the Judiciary Act of 1789, Chief Justice Marshall declared, "has been understood to imply a negative on the exercise of such appellate power as is not comprehended within it."[43] Some antebellum nationalists, most notably Justice Joseph Story, thought the Constitution requires Congress to vest the federal courts with original or appellate jurisdiction over cases raising certain constitutional issues.[44] *Wiscart* and *Durousseau* do not rule out this possibility. Nevertheless, both decisions clearly held that the Supreme Court could exercise appellate jurisdiction only in those cases where Congress chose to vest the justices with appellate jurisdiction. Legislative obligations under Article III, these precedents maintain, are not subject to judicial review.

Wiscart and *Durousseau* were established law throughout the nineteenth century. After Justice Story left the bench, suggestions that some amount of appellate jurisdiction was mandatory were abandoned. Robert N. Clinton thoroughly documents how "federal judicial authority" under Taney and Chase "was more a fragile creature of statutory grace, owing its life-blood to the largess of Congress."[45] Taney Court justices consistently maintained that federal appellate jurisdiction was given by the national legislature and could be taken away by the national legislature. "The disposal of judicial power (except in a few specified instances)," Justice Robert Grier declared in *Sheldon v. Sill* (1850), "belongs to Congress: and Congress is not bound to enlarge the jurisdiction of the Federal courts to every subject, in every form which the Constitution might warrant."[46] Justice Peter Daniel similarly ruled that "the judicial power of the United States . . . is . . . dependent for its distribution . . . entirely upon the action of Congress." "Congress," his majority opinion in *Cary v. Curtis* (1845) concluded, could "[withhold] jurisdiction from [federal courts] in the exact degree and character which . . . may seem proper for the public good."[47] These cases were not strategic retreats in the face of political pressure. Congress responded to *Cary* by passing a statute vesting the justices with the jurisdiction necessary to resolve the dispute in question.[48]

The Chase Court during the years before *McCardle* frequently reaffirmed the statutory foundations of federal appellate jurisdiction. A unanimous tribunal in *Daniels v. Railroad Company* held that "appellate jurisdiction . . . can be exercised only to the extent and in the manner prescribed by law." "It is wholly the creature of legislation," Justice Swayne's opinion asserted.[49] *Insurance Co. v. Ritchie* (1867) ruled that legislation withdrawing jurisdiction was valid even when the case was already pending before the Supreme Court. "When the jurisdiction of a cause depends upon a statute," every justice concluded, "the repeal of the statute takes away jurisdiction."[50]

Chief Justice Chase's unanimous opinion in *McCardle* relied heavily on these precedents. He began by citing *Wiscart* and *Durousseau* as establishing the rule that Congress determined the appellate jurisdiction of the Supreme Court.[51] He then cited *Ritchie* and *Norris v. Crocker*[52] as holding that courts could not decide a pending lawsuit after federal law removed the basis for jurisdiction.[53] Counsel for McCardle cited no contrary Supreme Court or federal precedent supporting jurisdiction.[54] Jeremiah Black, representing McCardle, demurred when the Chase Court offered him the opportunity to argue that the Repealer Act did not apply or could not constitutionally apply to cases after oral argument.

The precedential analysis in *McCardle* has largely escaped criticism for almost 150 years. The two justices who would have reached a decision before the Repealer Act became law, Justices Grier and Field, nevertheless acknowledged that no decision could be legally reached after the Repealer Act became law. Contemporary scholars agree. William Van Alstyne details "an unwavering line through five consecutive chief justices." He concludes, "the general position of the *McCardle* Court conforms entirely with virtually every other judicial construction previously and subsequently associated with the exceptions clause."[55] David Currie, who thinks "the issue was by no means so simple as Chase made it appear," regards *McCardle* as consistent with precedent.[56]

The judicial decision not to decide *McCardle* while the Repealer Act was before Congress was also consistent with past judicial practice. No statute or judicial opinion discussed what justices should do when Congress was considering legislation that might affect the outcome of a pending case. Still, this problem was not unprecedented. Supreme Court justices on several occasions had the opportunity to issue a decision while a change in the relevant law was being contemplated by the elected branches of the national government. On each occasion, the justices withheld judgment until proposed legal changes were adopted or abandoned.

Chief Justice Marshall in *United States v. Schooner Peggy*[57] refrained from making a final decision until the Senate had approved and President Jefferson promulgated a treaty that changed the legal rules in prize cases.[58] Marshall's opinion in *Schooner Peggy* did not discuss the reasons for this restraint. The Supreme Court did hold, however, that when Congress changed the relevant law while a case was being appealed, the appellate court must decide the case according to the new law unless doing so violated the ex post facto clause. In Marshall's view, "if . . . before the decision of the appellant court, a law intervenes and changes the rule which governs that law must be obeyed."[59] The Chase Court followed the precedent set by *Schooner Peggy* and subsequent decisions[60] by deciding *McCardle* consistently with federal law of appellate jurisdiction at the time of final decision rather than federal law at the time of the initial trial.

The Chase Court in a politically inconsequential matter withheld final judgment when Congress was considering changing the relevant jurisdictional rules. *Freeborn v. Smith*[61] was an appeal from a territorial court taken after the territory became a state. The Supreme Court had previously ruled that no jurisdiction existed to resolve such appeals in the absence of a federal statute.[67] Enabling legislation was proposed when *Freeborn* was pending, but Congress had not yet acted. The justices delayed their final decision until the bill vesting jurisdiction became law,[63] then adjudicated the merits. That no jurisdiction existed when the case first came before the Supreme Court was deemed irrelevant. Justice Grier's unanimous opinion held that "where there is no direct constitutional prohibition, a State may pass retrospective laws, such as, in their operation, may affect suits pending, and give to a party a remedy which he did not previously possess, or modify an existing remedy, or remove an impediment in the way of legal proceedings."[64] The justices in *McCardle* did exactly what they did in *Freeborn*. They withheld judgment while Congress was changing the relevant law of jurisdiction, then applied the new law when determining whether they could adjudicate the merits of the case.[65]

Supreme Court and congressional decisions associated with *McCardle* were influenced by the *Freeborn* precedent. During the last days of the legislative debate over the Repealer Act, Reverdy Johnson informed the House that "the Supreme Court have come to that determination—that as long as this bill is pending it is not their purpose to dispose of a case which has already been argued." "It has . . . been urged upon them," he continued, "that they should disregard the pendency of this and proceed to announce whatever decision they may have formed . . . upon the case which is before them; but they have determined, as they have upon former occasions, not to pursue such a course."[66] *Freeborn* was the "former occasion."

Johnson detailed that case history when asserting that the justices would delay a decision until Congress had finished debating changes in the relevant law.[67] Congress may already have been persuaded. Lyman Trumbull proposed the Repealer Act on February 17, 1868, two weeks before oral argument was scheduled. The bill was not passed until March 12, 1868, the week after oral argument had concluded. The Repealer Act did not become law over President Johnson's anticipated veto until March 27, 1868. Given the power of the Republican majority in Congress, Trumbull probably could have ensured passage of the Repealer Act before oral argument in *McCardle* was completed. Such dispatch would have removed any judicial temptation "to run a race" with elected officials in an attempt to strike down martial law before jurisdiction was legally withdrawn. Republicans may have taken that risk in theory only because they knew that in practice justices did not engage in such contests.

Justice David Davis in his private correspondence provides additional reasons for thinking *McCardle* an instance of legal decision making. Davis observed that the justices made several controversial rulings during the *McCardle* litigation. The first favored *McCardle*. The last favored Congress. He complained to his brother-in-law, Julius Rockwell, that all sides wanted "some decision that will help them, rather than the law pronounced." Republicans in January condemned the justices for advancing the case on the docket even though, Davis pointed out, that was the practice for "all criminal cases . . . under the rules." Democrats complained in late March when the justices "thought it unjudicial to run a race with Congress and especially as the Bill might be signed at any moment by the President." Efforts to make such a decision on the merits at the judicial conference held on March 21, David declared, would have been pointless, "for an opinion could not have been written until the Presdt & Congress had acted."[68] Justice Davis alluded to no change in the external environment that explains the judicial reversal. Pressures for favorable decisions seem to have been constant. Davis also appears not to have changed his views on the merits of Reconstruction while *McCardle* was under consideration. Instead, Davis pointed to preexisting legal practices as explaining why the court first expedited resolution of McCardle's appeal and then refused to consider that appeal. Davis changed his support for McCardle's appeal in response to changes in the law, not changes in the external political environment.

Reconstruction politics during the first months of 1868 do not explain the pattern of judicial decisions in *McCardle* and other cases challenging the constitutionality of martial law in the South. Republican legislators in January 1868 proposed a number of bills limiting judicial power and threatened to impeach justices perceived as hostile to Reconstruction. A bill requiring a supermajority to strike down federal laws passed the House on January 13, 1868.[69] Eight days later, House Republicans urged the court to rule that the Habeas Corpus Act of 1867 did not vest the justices with jurisdiction in *McCardle*. These expressions of legislative concern had no legal significance under preexisting law. None influenced the Court. The justices responded to legislative pressures only when the national legislature, by enacting a statute withdrawing jurisdiction, acted in ways that previous law regarded as having legal significance. That judicial response, however, was strictly limited by preexisting law. The same week the justices announced that *McCardle* would not be resolved during the 1868 judicial term, the justices declared they would resolve *Ex parte Martin and Gill*, another case challenging the constitutionality of the Reconstruction laws at issue in *McCardle*.[70] No event took place in late March or early April that explains why the justices thought the political climate too hostile to adjudicate a challenge to Reconstruction arising under the Habeas Corpus Act of 1867, but friendly enough to consider a similar challenge arising under the Judiciary Act of 1789. Lacking access to the mental states of Chase Court justices, strategic motivations cannot be ruled out. Nevertheless, the pattern of judicial decisions is far more closely tied to events regarded as having legal significance than events thought to have strategic significance.

Legal and strategic explanations both rely as much on interpretation as logic. Any finite series of decisions can be described without logical contradiction as good faith efforts to interpret the law or as sophisticated efforts to realize policy preferences. One cannot completely rule out the possibility that congressional passage of the Repealer Act finally convinced the Chase Court that threatening Reconstruction was politically too risky. Maybe the voting alignment in *Gore v. Bush* would have been identical to the voting alignment in *Bush v. Gore*. The extent to which any judicial decision was motivated by legal or strategic factors, at bottom, depends on contestable theories about what constitutes good legal and strategic practice. The claim that *McCardle* was a legal decision relies on the legal argument that case law in 1868 clearly required courts to dismiss pending cases whenever the statute granting jurisdiction was repealed. The argument that *McCardle* was a strategic decision relies on the strategic argument that sophisticated voters would ignore the political pressures to dismiss *McCardle* in February 1868, respond to those pressures in March 1868, then become less responsive to political pressure in April 1868. Legal practice, I have argued, explains why the justices responded to changes in the law of jurisdiction, but not to any other legislative threat leveled against the judiciary. Strategic practice provides no reason independent of law for thinking that justices would be responsive only to legislative decisions to change the relevant law. The crucial point, however, is less that the legal explanation of *McCardle* is better than the strategic explanation than that both at bottom depend on an interpretation of practices. Neither is more scientific than the other.

Take Four: The Legal, Strategic, and Attitudinal *McCardle*

From a different legal perspective, *McCardle* confounds any neat distinction between legal, strategic, and attitudinal decision making. The decision was a relatively straightforward application of precedents established in cases of no political consequence. Whether those previous precedents were instances of pure legal decision making is more doubtful. Prominent scholars using textual, historical, and structural legal logics conclude that federal appellate jurisdiction does not constitutionally exist wholly at the discretion of Congress. "If *Marbury* was right that the Framers provided for judicial review to keep legislatures in bounds," David Currie declares, "one may reasonably doubt that they meant to allow Congress to destroy that important check by the simple expedient of removing jurisdiction."[71] Even if the Chase Court in *McCardle* followed precedent, the decision to rely on precedent and the precedents relied on may not be entirely explainable within a legal framework.

Wiscart v. Dauchy, the case that provided the initial precedential foundations for congressional power over federal jurisdiction, may have been an instance of strategic judicial decision making. Anti-Federalists strongly objected to what they perceived to be the imperial federal court system laid out in Article III.[72] Partly to allay such concerns and increase support for the Constitution, members of the First Congress did not vest the Supreme Court with appellate jurisdiction over all federal questions. "The Judiciary Act," Maeva Marcus and Natalie Wexler detail, "was shaped by political forces rather than by the language of the Constitution."[73] Oliver Ellsworth, the person most responsible for the Judiciary Act, later penned the main judicial opinion in *Wiscart*. If Ellsworth acted strategically as a legislator in 1789 when he failed to provide the Supreme Court with jurisdiction over all cases and controversies mentioned in Article III, then he may have acted strategically as a judge in 1796 when he declared that the Supreme Court could exercise appellate jurisdiction only with statutory permission.

Durousseau may be a similar instance of strategic decision making. Most Federalists in 1801 believed that federal courts should have complete federal questions jurisdiction and the power to declare laws unconstitutional. Jeffersonians opposed the first. Many had qualms about the latter. *Durousseau* and *Marbury v. Madison* were part of a series of cases in which Chief Justice John Marshall "sought to preserve the judicial authority to declare laws unconstitutional . . . partly by permitting Congress to determine what cases the Justices would resolve."[74] Fears that a Federalist judiciary would strike down Republican programs were allayed by judicial decisions making clear that judicial review would be exercised only with legislative permission. "Jurisdiction," I have elsewhere detailed, "was partly sacrificed to help maintain authority."[75] If *Marbury* was an instance of sophisticated voting, *Durousseau* is probably another instance where the justices sacrificed immediate law and policy preferences to preserve as much judicial power as possible in a threatening political environment.

The attitudinal model of judicial decision making helps explain subsequent judicial rulings on legislative control over federal appellate jurisdiction. Taney Court justices had two reasons for following and extending the *Wiscart* line of precedents. First, the justices may have thought *Wiscart, Durousseau,* and other cases provided sufficient legal grounds for decisions upholding congressional power to determine what appeals the Supreme Court could adjudicate. Second, such congressional power was consistent with Jacksonian commitments to popular democracy. Judicial decisions on federal jurisdiction during the Jacksonian era, Clinton notes, "nicely matched the state-oriented, non-nationalist political orientation of the Taney Court."[76] Whereas Federalist justices may have announced the rule in *Wiscart* to avoid political troubles, Jacksonian justices may have maintained that rule to secure policy preferences.

The precedential evolution from *Wiscart* to *McCardle* illustrates how judicial rules once best explained by strategy (or values) may over time become best explained by law. The early Supreme Court frequently engaged in strategic decision making.[77] Chief Justice Marshall admitted as much in his private correspondence. He found a statutory excuse to avoid resolving the constitutional issues raised by state laws banning free blacks, Marshall informed Justice Story, because he was "not fond of butting against a wall in sport."[78] Salmon Chase expressed different sentiments when explaining his behavior in *McCardle*. He wrote John D. Van Buren that "it was especially desirable to me to have the case decided, for it is highly probable that I shall meet the question on the Circuit." Chase reluctantly concluded that because "Congress . . . had the undoubted right to except such cases as *McCardle* from its appellate jurisdiction," it was "an indecency to run a race in the exercise of that jurisdiction with the legislature."[79] This correspondence suggests that Chase did not think strategically or engage in sophisticated voting during Reconstruction. The chief justice was constrained by past legal practice, not present legislative threats. John Marshall's strategic decision in 1810 evolved into Salmon Chase's legal decision in 1868.

All judicial choices have legal, strategic, and attitudinal components. Even when the case law is clear at the time of a particular judicial decision, the relevant precedents may have foundations that cannot be entirely explained by law. The law of federal jurisdiction bequeathed to the Chase Court was rooted partly in the text of Article III and the original understanding of the framers, partly in Federalist efforts to forestall legislative attacks on judicial power, and partly in Jacksonian democratic commitments. The judicial decision to rely on precedent in *McCardle* was not based entirely on precedent. The Chase Court in *Trebilcock* and other cases proved willing to overrule past judicial rulings.[80] The justices probably adhered to precedent in *McCardle* because some justices thought past rulings a reasonable interpretation of the original text, some thought abandoning the *Wiscart/Durousseau* line of cases risked legislative retaliation, and some favored as a matter of public policy legislative control of the federal judicial docket. The justices may also have adhered to precedent in *McCardle* because they felt the policy and strategic stakes not sufficiently high to warrant abandoning clear law. Had the *McCardle* majority thought martial law in the South a gross violation of fundamental human rights, the Chase Court might have thrown law and strategy to the winds. Claims that justices vote consistently with their most cherished political commitments, however, differ significantly from claims that justices only vote their policy preferences. The line of cases from *Wiscart* to *Durousseau* indicate that precedent shapes and constrains normal judicial decision making, not that stare decisis never encompasses policy preferences and strategic considerations.

Take Five: The Legal, Strategic, and Attitudinal *Roosevelt*

Roosevelt v. Meyer also confounds neat distinctions between legal, strategic, and attitudinal decision making. Justice Miller's private conversation suggests he did not recognize a strict separation between rule by law and sophisticated voting. According to a friend, Miller

> said that during the war the most strenuous efforts were made to use the Court in such a way as to embarrass the Government in its conduct of operations by endeavoring to get decisions upon such questions as the right of Mr. Seward to confine obnoxious persons in the forts, the right of Mr. Stanton to confiscate the property of citizens in the rebellious states, etc. . . . The Justice did more to prevent interference by the court than perhaps any other member of it.[81]

This effort to "prevent interference by the court" might be interpreted as pure strategic action. Miller forestalled a judicial decision striking down policies he favored and husbanded scarce judicial resources for more favorable circumstances. The better reading may be that Justice Miller did not believe courts should interfere with wartime policies, even when he thought the policy wrong and the probability of political retaliation low. Justice Davis made a similarly ambiguous assertion in *Ex parte Milligan* when he declared,

> during the late wicked Rebellion, the temper of the times did not allow that calmness in deliberation and discussion so necessary to a correct conclusion of a purely judicial question. Then, considerations of safety were mingled with the exercise of power; and feelings and interests prevailed which are happily terminated. Now that the public safety is assured, this question, as well as all others, can be discussed and decided without passion or the admixture of any element not required to form a legal judgment.[82]

Perhaps Justices Miller and Davis thought law permitted or even required a strategic decision in the circumstances before the *Roosevelt* Court. *Inter arma leges silent* might be a legal rule, not simply a description of judicial practice.

Some prominent twentieth-century judicial opinions and constitutional commentators agree that strategic concerns ought to guide legal reasoning. Justice Robert Jackson, Alexander Bickel, and others maintain that justices must consider political circumstances when exercising judicial power. Law, their analyses claim, simultaneously permits and constrains strategic judicial choices. Prudential legal logics legitimate sophisticated voting while ruling out certain options that a differently located strategic actor might think the best means for securing desirable public policy. The crucial explanatory question in *Roosevelt* and related rulings is whether such decisions are instances when justices made a legal use of strategic (or attitudinal) considerations, not whether strategic (or attitudinal) considerations influenced the legal decision.

Justice Robert Jackson's dissent in *Korematsu v. United States* is the most famous instance of explicit prudential reasoning by a member of the Supreme Court. Jackson preferred not ruling on the constitutionality of a controversial war-related measure, in this instance, the internment of Japanese Americans during World War II. Unlike Miller, Jackson publicly justified judicial restraint on war-related measures. His *Korematsu* dissent asserted that the Supreme Court should be guided by *inter arma leges silent* when confronted with constitutional challenges to military policy. "It would be impractical and dangerous idealism," Jackson declared, "to expect or insist that each specific military command in an area of probable operations will conform to conventional tests of constitutionality. When an area is so beset that it must be put under military control at all, the paramount consideration is that its measures be successful rather than legal."[83] Judicial capacity provided additional reasons for a hands-off stance. "Military decisions," the Justice from upstate New York wrote, "are not susceptible of intelligent judicial appraisal."[84] Such reasoning supports both Jackson's decision not to determine the constitutionality of the Japanese internment and Miller's decision not to review the Legal Tender Acts. The *Roosevelt* opinion, written by Justice Jackson, would probably have contended that wartime financial policies are "not susceptible of intelligent judicial appraisal."

Alexander Bickel's famed "Passive Virtues" essay celebrates Justice Jackson's opinion in *Korematsu* and similar judicial writings that "decline the exercise of jurisdiction which is given."[85] Good legal reasons, Bickel claimed, justify judicial decisions not to make constitutional rulings. "The Passive Virtues" urges justices to refrain from constitutional adjudication when "the anxiety [is] not so much that judicial judgment will be ignored, as that perhaps it should be, but won't," when political circumstances highlight "the inner vulnerability of an institution which is electorally irresponsible," and when the justices conclude "on principle that there ought to be discretion free of principled rules."[86] These considerations specifically caution against judicial activism when the United States is at war. Bickel quoted with great enthusiasm Justice Jackson's rationale for thinking the federal judiciary should not have ruled on the constitutionality of the Japanese American internment.[87] *Roosevelt* decided by Bickel would have been simultaneously legal and strategic. A proper legal understanding of the judicial function, he would have concluded, required the justices to make a strategic decision declining jurisdiction.

Other scholars agree that justices may legally take political circumstances into account when resolving constitutional issues. Philip Bobbitt's analysis of legal logics insists that "prudential argument is constitutional argument." Of particular relevance to *Roosevelt*, Bobbitt notes, "prudentialists generally hold that in times of national emergency even the plainest of constitutional limitations can be ignored. Perhaps others share this belief; but the prudentialist makes it a legitimate, legal argument, fits it into opinions, and uses it as the purpose for doctrines."[88] Bobbitt regards strategy as more than a legitimate means for choosing between constitutional options justifiable by other legal logics. He thinks justices may examine the political climate, including the possibility of political backlash, when determining whether a possible judicial choice is constitutionally legitimate. Justice Jackson's assertion, "there is danger that, if the Court does not temper its doctrinaire logic with a little practical wisdom, it will convert the constitutional Bill of Rights into a suicide pact,"[89] Bobbitt believes, is a legal argument, a legal reason for discounting plain language in constitutional or statutory texts when simple textualism would trench too closely on vital government functions or entangle the justices too deeply in a political thicket.[90]

Legal strategies differ from nonlegal strategic behavior. Constitutionalists who urge justices to avoid making constitutional decisions on war-related policies and similar matters assert that justices must behave as justices when engaged in sophisticated voting or when using the passive virtues. "The antithesis of principle in an institution that represents decency and reason," Bickel declared, "is prudence,"[91] not arbitrary action. He maintained that prudent justices act consistently with their judicial obligations when manipulating jurisdictional rules, but violate their oaths of office when declaring a statute constitutional they believe unconstitutional.[92] Strategy was confined to the decision to decide, not decisions on the merits. Justice Jackson's *Korematsu* dissent anticipated Bickel's prudential guidelines. "If we cannot confine military expedience by the Constitution," the former wrote, "neither would I distort the Constitution to approve all that the military may deem expedient."[93] Jackson's opinion emphasized that when justices conclude that constitutional policy questions are not amenable to legal standards, the proper legal ruling is a refusal to adjudicate, not judicial approval of governmental actions. "A military order, however unconstitutional, is not apt to last longer than the military emergency," he declared, "but once a judicial opinion rationalizes such an order, . . . the Court for all time has validated the principle of racial discrimination in criminal procedure."[94] Jackson when condemning the majority opinion sustaining the internment policy did "not suggest that the courts should have attempted to interfere with the Army in carrying out its task." He simply rejected claims that justices "may be asked to execute a military expedient that has no place in law under the Constitution."[95]

The judicial decision in *Roosevelt* was consistent with the standards for prudential legal logics articulated by Jackson and Bickel. The opinion for the Court did not declare the Legal Tender Acts constitutional or give any judicial support to administration policy. Justices opposed to Lincoln's wartime policy did not make an effort to curry administration favor by sustaining some wartime policies they thought unconstitutional.[96] Justice Miller's private comments suggest he thought denying jurisdiction the appropriate legal strategy for not interfering with administration policy in war time. His understanding of the judicial function justified strategic action in the circumstances presented by *Roosevelt*, but limited the strategic choices open to the Court.

Strategic decision making (almost?) always takes place in the context of a practice whose norms sanction sophisticated choices under some circumstances while restricting the strategic options that may be chosen. In law, baseball, poker, and tag, some moves are permitted, others are questionable, and others are illegal. Assertions that persons engaged in any of these activities behaved strategically rarely suffice to explain their actions. Complete explanations explore the extent to which the actor felt permitted or perhaps even compelled to take strategic action, as well as what strategic actions that actor thought could legitimately by taken by a person engaged in that practice. Poker players bluff rather than peek. The former is strategic behavior within the rules. The latter is cheating. Although some bluffers refrain from peeking for fear of being caught, most limit sophisticated betting to bluffing because that is how poker is played. Norms similarly constrain legal practice. Legal considerations influence both judicial decisions to make a strategic choice and the particular strategic option selected. A justice who makes a strategic choice between two legitimate legal alternatives is behaving differently than a justice who for strategic reasons makes a decision that cannot be justified by prudential or any other legal logic.

Roosevelt occupies contested turf on the border between strategy and cheating. Bickel, Bobbitt, and others insist that justices are legally authorized to act prudentially. Prominent constitutionalists disagree. Gerald Gunther regarded the passive virtues as "100% insistence on principle, 20% of the time."[97] Nevertheless, even if the passive virtues are bad law, bad law differs from no law. Game theory recognizes a distinction between a contested interpretation of the rules, stretching the rules, or taking advantage of the rules, on the one hand, and outright cheating on the other. Unlike cheaters, interpreters are constrained by law, even as they advance contested understandings of what constitutes legitimate law. The strike zone in baseball is contested, but a pitch that bounces before reaching home plate is a ball.[98] Constitutional rules admit of similar degrees of certainty. Sanford Levinson observes that although many things are sayable in the language of American constitutional law, not every policy preference can be defended by legal logics.[99] One can argue in good faith that precedent sanctions presidential wars, but not that Article I mandates a parliamentary system of government.

Determining whether Justice Miller in *Roosevelt* used a contested legal strategy or cheated is difficult. Some indicia point to cheating. The *Roosevelt* opinion, unlike Jackson's *Korematsu* dissent, fails to make public the reasons that actually motivated the judicial decision to deny jurisdiction. Such subterfuge is more typical of cheating than interpreting. Other indicia point to law. Statutory misinterpretation was a common nineteenth-century practice.[100] The *Roosevelt* opinion may simply have respected a legal trope and not have been a self-conscious effort to deceive. Justice Miller claimed that he voted to sustain federal law in *Ex parte Garland*[101] even though he abhorred test oaths.[102] This is suggestive of a more general tendency to place law above policy concerns. Perhaps, however, Justice Miller felt compelled to rationalize his efforts to secure policy preferences.

Two reasons support claims that at least some justices in *Roosevelt* thought they were using a legal strategy to avoid resolving whether the Legal Tender Acts were constitutional. First, statutory misconstruction was sufficiently common to support the inference that justices regarded that practice as a legitimate means for not resolving constitutional questions. Second, justices engaged in pure strategic calculations would have considered sustaining such Civil War measures as the Legal Tender Acts in order to build up political capital that could be used to strike down Lincoln's suspension of habeas corpus, a constitutionally and politically more vulnerable Civil War measure. These claims involve evaluative as well as descriptive analysis. My argument that the justices thought statutory misconstruction to be legitimate rests on claims that the practice was sufficiently widespread as to be deemed legitimate legal behavior by competent lawyers. My argument about judicial trade-offs rests on claims that trading approval for the Legal Tender Acts in return for striking down habeas corpus was good strategy. Neither my legal nor my strategic analysis is written in stone. The crucial point is that any explanation of *Roosevelt* cannot take a purely external viewpoint. Claims about whether justices were influenced by a legal strategy inevitably encompass contestable claims about good law and efficacious strategy. Legal and strategic explanations require legal and strategic analysis.

Take Six: The Legal, Strategic, and Attitudinal
Roosevelt and *McCardle*

Combining legal, strategic, and attitudinal factors with an evolutionary perspective yields further insights into *Roosevelt* and *McCardle*. Path dependence theory highlights how particular actions are often explained largely by their place in a larger sequence. Random choices or decisions between available alternatives made at one moment in time typically limit or change the alternatives that may be selected at later moments in time.[103] *Wiscart* and *Durousseau* were decided early in Supreme Court history. Chief Justices Ellsworth and Marshall made their choices at a time when no clear law existed on whether the Supreme Court needed statutory authorization to exercise appellate jurisdiction under Article III. Both justices chose not to exercise judicial power. Salmon Chase probably would have chosen differently had he been the first decision maker. Chase's opinion in *Ex parte Yerger* intimated that had he been chief justice in 1803, the Supreme Court in *Marbury* would have exercised jurisdiction and awarded the writ of mandamus.[104] Chase, however, was not the first chief justice, or even the first great chief justice. His opportunity to choose came later in the precedential sequence. Legal options open to Marshall had been closed, partly because of the strategic choices Marshall made. The Supreme Court voted to deny jurisdiction in *McCardle*, a path dependence perspective suggests, because Chief Justice Chase decided after, not before, Chief Justices Ellsworth and Marshall.

A more complicated evolutionary perspective emphasizes how standard features of most judicial systems have strong tendencies to generate precedential sequences favoring restraint whenever policies favored by most elected officials are challenged in court. The processes by which courts are staffed in constitutional democracies normally yield justices who favor administration policies. Robert Dahl observes, "it would appear . . . somewhat unrealistic to suppose that a Court whose members are recruited in the fashion of Supreme Court Justices would long hold to norms of Right or Justice substantially at odds with the rest of the political elite."[105] Justices who oppose administration policies often elect for strategic reasons not to challenge elected officials. John Marshall spent his first decade on the bench finding ways not to antagonize the Jeffersonian majority.[106] Courts whose initial precedents favor government action are more likely to survive than courts whose initial precedents strike down popular measures. Ran Hirschl details numerous instances when elected officials responded to adverse judicial decisions by reconstituting the legal system.[107] This combination of attitudes, strategy, and backlash typically generates precedential sequences that yield strategic results and rules, even when few justices engage in sophisticated voting.

A simple hypothetical highlights how over time "survival of the passive" produces increased tendencies toward judicial restraint. Imagine a judicial system with three justices, Justice Law, Justice Strategy, and Justice Attitude, who are randomly selected to determine the constitutionality of martial law. Justice Law decides exclusively on precedent, flipping a coin when precedents are evenly balanced. Justice Strategy never strikes down martial law when troops are in the field. Justice Attitude is guided exclusively by policy preferences. On the less realistic version of this hypothetical, Justice Attitude is as likely to favor as oppose martial law. On a more realistic version, Justice Attitude, appointed by members of the dominant national coalition, favors martial law three-quarters of the time. A 50% probability exists that elected officials will respond to a decision striking down martial law by abolishing courts. The first judicial decision under these conditions is either twice (less realistic Justice Attitude) or three times (realistic Justice Attitude) more likely to refrain from declaring martial law unconstitutional. The next judicial decision is four or nine times more likely to refrain from declaring martial law unconstitutional. By the sixth and seventh decision, a strong precedent sequence favoring judicial restraint will almost always be in place in every surviving court system. The later the decision in the precedential sequence, the more likely Justice Law either denies jurisdiction (following precedents set by Justice Strategy) or sustains administration policy (following precedents set by Justice Attitude's votes favoring martial law). Justice Law exhibits the same deferential tendencies over time even when Justice Strategy's role is reduced or eliminated. Strategic rules are established, but not necessarily by strategic decisions.

"Survival of the passive" explains McCardle as the expected outcome of a mature judiciary. The later a judicial opportunity to strike down measures favored by powerful political actors occurs in the life of a court system, the more likely existing precedents will support either denying jurisdiction or sustaining regime policy. Chief Justices Ellsworth and Marshall were legally free to decide whether the Supreme Court needed statutory authorization to exercise appellate jurisdiction because they made the initial decisions in a precedential sequence. They were not equally free politically to establish either a precedential sequence favoring activism or a precedential sequence favoring restraint. Had Marshall in the wake of the election of 1800 boldly asserted a judicial right to decide cases without legislative permission, he probably would have been impeached and his activist precedents abandoned. Chief Justice Chase inherited a legal doctrine compelling restraint in McCardle partly because the Supreme Court probably would not have survived had previous chief justices attempted to hand down a different legacy.

Strategic Legislatures, Legal Courts

The interplay between legal, strategic, and attitudinal factors structured the way elected officials prevented the Supreme Court from declaring martial law and other military-related policies unconstitutional. Merryman aside, Republican presidents and Republican legislators acted within accepted legal frameworks when seeking to forestall adverse judicial decisions. On pure strategic grounds, assassination, abolition of judicial review, impeachment, and refusal to obey judicial decrees might have been superior means for ensuring that the justices did not strike down Civil War and Reconstruction measures. Nevertheless, elected officials consistently selected only means nineteenth-century constitutional norms clearly legitimated for influencing the course of judicial decision making. The strategies that executive and legislative actors chose for preventing judicial interference with martial law cannot be explained without reference to existing legal practices.

Republican presidents avoided judicial decisions declaring martial law unconstitutional by abandoning cases in which the Supreme Court had the necessary jurisdiction to strike down administration policies. Lincoln's attorney general, Edward Bates, ordered subordinates not to appeal adverse rulings in the lower federal courts.[108] Edward Yerger was freed after the Chase Court ruled that the justices would determine the constitutionality of his confinement.[109] These executive decisions were strategic. Republicans regarded releasing some persons less harmful than a Supreme Court decision declaring the entire confinement policy unconstitutional. Bates informed cabinet members that his failure to appeal adverse lower court decisions was based on his belief that "the Union could be furthered better without the Supreme Court decision than 'with decision *against* the power assumed by the President.'"[110] The strategy was also legal. Both the Constitution and long-standing legal practice recognized the right of the national executive to settle cases rather than risk an adverse Supreme Court decision.

The Repealer Act of 1868 was another legal strategy. The national legislature during Reconstruction considered various measures that might prevent the Supreme Court from striking down important Reconstruction policies. Means deemed illegitimate by existing practice were proposed, but did not become law. Imposing supermajoritarian voting requirements for decisions declaring laws unconstitutional was inconsistent with long-standing judicial precedent dating from 1791. Removing Supreme Court justices on political grounds was inconsistent with long-standing legislative precedent dating from the failed Chase impeachment.[111] Withdrawing appellate jurisdiction, by comparison, had been sanctioned by judicial rulings and federal law for more than seventy years. Previous Taney and Chase Court decisions established that Congress had the constitutional power to withdraw appellate jurisdiction, even when a case was pending before the Supreme Court. As did the national executive, the national legislature during the 1860s chose means that were simultaneously legal and strategic for preventing a Supreme Court decision on martial law.

The Repealer Act of 1868 was a legal strategy adopted by legislators interested in both limiting and expanding judicial power. Many political scientists and some law professors observe that elected officials often favor judicial review as a means for achieving cherished policies and for partly removing contentious issues from partisan politics.[112] Most, not all, Republicans during Reconstruction favored a strong judiciary for these reasons. Courts were considered good vehicles for carrying out Reconstruction policies and even better vehicles for rationalizing the emerging industrial order.[113] The challenge mainstream Republicans faced during the Johnson and early Grant administrations was how to prevent the Chase Court from making decisions on martial law that might obstruct desired congressional policies and weaken the political support necessary for more desirable judicial activism in the future. The Repealer Act secured both Republican ends. That measure ensured that the justices in 1868 would not rule on the constitutionality of martial law, but had no impact on federal jurisdiction in those areas of the law in which Republicans favored judicial intervention. Broader attacks on the federal judiciary were forestalled by laws preventing the Supreme Court from making decisions that probably would have increased the ranks of those committed to curtailing the judicial power to declare any law unconstitutional.

Elected officials were the strategic actors in *McCardle*. Given the legal opportunity, Chase would have declared martial law unconstitutional regardless of the consequences for the future exercise of judicial power. Republicans in the national legislature and national executive with long-term goals in mind exhibited more concern for husbanding judicial power than Republicans on the national bench. Lincoln, Trumbull, and other elected officials chose to prevent an adverse judicial ruling by making sophisticated decisions to release prisoners and withdraw jurisdiction. The Chase Court merely followed existing law.

Elected officials during the 1860s adopted legal strategies that assumed judicial officials would act legally. Releasing detainees seeking writs of habeas corpus prevented judicial decisions because the "case or controversy" requirement of Article III requires petitioners before the Court to demonstrate an actual injury. The Repealer Act of 1868 was based on a legislative expectation that the justices, guided by precedent, would refrain from deciding a pending case after appellate jurisdiction was withdrawn. These legal practices, in turn, served a vital strategic function for the Court. When judicial decisions to decide were based on clear legal rules, elected officials knew what had to be done politically to facilitate or prevent judicial decisions on constitutionally controversial policies. Elected officials could express their will clearly and narrowly. No need existed to impeach federal justices if everyone was confident that repealing a particular grant of jurisdiction would prevent adverse rulings on policies cherished by elected officials.

American constitutional politics by the Civil War had evolved in ways that gave a national majority substantial power to control the federal judicial docket. When most elected officials wanted the Supreme Court to resolve a contentious policy issue, as was the case with slavery in the territories, the national government possessed legal means for inviting judicial action.[114] When most elected officials preferred the Supreme Court not interfere with national policy, as was the case for martial law, legal means usually existed for securing judicial restraint. Exceptions existed, partly because the means by which elected officials could influence the Court were as much the result of evolution as a conscious choice by all branches of the national government at a specific point in time. *Roosevelt* was the product of one such loophole. The Judiciary Act of 1789 was primarily intended to allow federal courts to supervise state court decisions striking down federal law.[115] Until *Roosevelt*, both lawyers and elected officials seem to have forgotten the language in Section 25 permitting appeals when state courts sustained a federal law that a petitioner claimed violated federal constitutional rights. The decision, therefore, might be an instance where justices were guided by general constitutional principles manifested throughout the law rather than a statutory accident. Structuralist legal logics based on the constitutional relationships between governing institutions trumped legal reasoning based on long ignored language in a relatively ancient text.

More Takes?

Inter arma silent leges and judicial decision making are more complex than the simple strategic takes on *Roosevelt* and *McCardle* suggest. Law was not silent during the Civil War and Reconstruction. The Supreme Court gave legal reasons for not ruling on whether martial law in the South was constitutional. Legal reasons can be given for the judicial decision to refrain from determining whether the Legal Tender Acts were constitutional. The justices did not speak about the constitutional limits on federal legislative and executive power laid out in Articles I and II because they believed that conversation legally proscribed by the constitutional limits on federal judicial power laid out in Article III.

Law played different roles in *Roosevelt* and *McCardle*. Legal norms explain how Justice Miller avoided declaring the Legal Tender Acts unconstitutional. The *Roosevelt* Court ignored clear language in the Judiciary Act of 1789 when denying jurisdiction partly because statutory misconstruction in the nineteenth century was considered an appropriate legal strategy for avoiding delicate constitutional issues.[116] Legal norms help explain why Chief Justice Chase avoided declaring martial law unconstitutional. Unlike Justice Miller, Chase was eager to express his constitutional opinions officially on military related policies. The chief justice refrained from reaching the merits of *McCardle* because he believed law forbade justices from adjudicating appeals after Congress repealed the statutory basis for jurisdiction.

Had Justice Miller or Chief Justice Chase been in the executive or legislative branches of the national government, they probably would have behaved differently. Many legislators and cabinet members, most notably Treasury Secretary Salmon Chase, swallowed their constitutional scruples and supported the Legal Tender Acts.[117] No justice during the 1860s took that route. Justices voted to sustain only those laws they believed to be constitutional. The appropriate means by which justices avoided challenging wartime policies differed from appropriate means open to other political actors.

Simple legal explanations of *Roosevelt* and *McCardle* are no more accurate than simple strategic explanations. Jacksonian judicial appointees were far more eager than Lincoln's judicial appointees to adjudicate the constitutional merits of Civil War measures. The *McCardle* opinion relied heavily on precedents best explained by a combination of legal, strategic, and attitudinal factors. The legal roads to *Roosevelt* and *McCardle*, as well as the actual judicial decisions in those cases, were paved by a legal, strategic, and attitudinal mixture. No element of that compound can easily be isolated. The strategic aspects of *Roosevelt* are intertwined with legal norms concerned with when justices may behave strategically and what strategic considerations they may take into account when making legal decisions. The legal aspects of *McCardle* are intertwined with the strategic and attitudinal concerns that structured nineteenth-century case law on federal appellate jurisdiction.

Future research will develop new perspectives on legal strategies and strategic rules. An eighth take on *Roosevelt* and *McCardle* might explore the judicial practice during the 1860s of first deciding jurisdictional questions before entertaining oral argument on the merits. This procedure, which may not have had strategic origins, nevertheless facilitated strategic action on the part of elected officials. Republicans in 1868 could wait for the judicial decision on jurisdiction before settling *McCardle* or passing the Repealer Act. The various takes on *Roosevelt* and *McCardle* may help explain other judicial decisions or precedential sequences. The process by which judicial policy preferences and sophisticated votes harden into legal rules is likely to occur in many doctrinal areas. The evolution of the actual malice rule in libel cases from *New York Times Co. v. Sullivan*[118] to *Hustler Magazine v. Fallwell*[119] is a possible example. Justice Brennan's attitudinal decision may have become Chief Justice Rehnquist's legal decision.[120] Whatever areas of law scholars consider, the most fruitful investigations will explore the ways in which legal, strategic, and attitudinal factors interact when justices make decisions, and not engage in fruitless contests to determine which single factor explains the most.

Notes

1. In *Youngstown Sheet & Tube v. Sawyer*, 343 U.S. 579 (1952), the justices sided with the national legislature against the national executive. The judicial majority in *Ex parte Endo*, 323 U.S. 283 (1944), held that the executive orders issued during World War II authorizing the evacuation of Japanese American citizens from the West Coast did not authorize the military to hold citizens whose loyalty had been established in detention camps. *Endo*, 323 U.S., at 300–304. Justice Douglas's majority opinion began by declar-

ing that the justices would not resolve "the underlying constitutional issues which have been argued" (*Endo*, 323 U.S., 297). His opinion did adopt that interpretation of existing executive orders that had "the greater chance of surviving the test of constitutionality." *Endo*, 323 U.S., at 299. Justices Murphy and Roberts would have declared the detention practice unconstitutional, with Roberts explicitly stating that both branches of government had clearly authorized the detention policy. *Endo*, 323 U.S., at 307 (Murphy, J., concurring); *Endo*, 323 U.S., at 309–310 (Roberts, J., concurring).

2. *Ex parte Milligan*, 71 U.S. 2, 120–121 (1866).

3. *Duncan v. Kahanamoku*, 327 U.S. 304 (1946), 334–335 (Murphy, J., concurring).

4. *Ex parte Milligan*, at 120–121.

5. *Milligan* was handed down the year after the Civil War ended. The year before the Civil War ended, the justices in *Ex parte Vallandigham*, 68 U.S. 243 (1863), unanimously held that the Court did not have the jurisdiction necessary to determine whether the Lincoln administration had the power to suspend martial law in the North. *Duncan* was handed down the year after V-J Day. While hostilities were ongoing, the Supreme Court sustained executive orders banning Japanese Americans from living in the West Coast. See *Korematsu v. United States*, 323 U.S. 214 (1944); *Hirabayshi v. United States*, 320 U.S. 81 (1943).

6. William H. Rehnquist, *All the Laws but One: Civil Liberties in Wartime* (New York: Alfred A. Knopf, 1998), 222.

7. *The Prize Cases*, 67 U.S. 635 (1862).

8. *Ex parte Vallandigham*, 68 U.S. 243 (1863); *Roosevelt v. Meyer*, 68 U.S. 512 (1863).

9. See Charles Fairman, *Reconstruction and Reunion*, part 1 (New York: Macmillan, 1971), 55–58 (discussing *Ex parte Dugan*).

10. *Ex Parte Milligan*, 71 U.S. 2 (1866); *Hepburn v. Griswold*, 343 U.S. 579 (1869).

11. *Ex Parte McCardle*, 74 U.S. 506 (1869).

12. The seminal works in the strategic tradition are Lee Epstein and Jack Knight, *The Choices Justices Make* (Washington, D.C.: CQ Press, 1998); Jack Knight and Lee Epstein, "On the Struggle for Judicial Supremacy," *Law and Society Review* 30 (1996): 87; Lee Epstein and Jack Knight, "Mapping Out the Strategic Terrain: The Informational Role of *Amici Curiae*," in *Supreme Court Decision-making: New Institutional Approaches* (Chicago: University of Chicago Press, 1999); Lee Epstein and Thomas G. Walker, "The Role of the Supreme Court in American Society: Playing the Reconstruction Game," in *Contemplating Courts*, ed. Lee Epstein (Washington, D.C.: CQ Press 1995), 338–342. See also Frank B. Cross, "The Justices of Strategy," *Duke Law Journal* 48 (1900): 511, 513nn8–10 (citing numerous articles on judicial strategy published by positive political theorists).

13. Alexander M. Bickel, "Foreword: The Passive Virtues," *Harvard Law Review* 75 (1961): 40.

14. Gordon Silverstein and Dion Farganis, "Bridging the Gap: Precedent, Political Science and Law," paper presented at the 2001 American Political Science Association meeting.

15. Epstein and coauthors acknowledge the seminal work of Walter Murphy on justices as strategic decision makers. See Walter F. Murphy, *Elements of Judicial Strategy* (Chicago: University of Chicago Press, 1964).

16. Epstein and Walker, "Role of the Supreme Court," 317.

17. Epstein and Knight, *Choices Justices Make*, 154.

18. Jeffrey A. Segal and Harold J. Spaeth, *The Supreme Court and the Attitudinal Model Revisited* (New York: Cambridge University Press, 2002).

19. See Segal and Spaeth, Supreme Court and the Attitudinal Model Revisited, 2–3.

20. Epstein and Knight, *Choices Justices Make*, 153.

21. Ibid.

22. Epstein and Walker, "Role of the Supreme Court," 340. See Fairman, *Reconstruction*, 460–461, 465–467.

23. 15 Stat. 44 (1868).

24. *Ex parte McCardle*, 74 U.S. 506, 515 (1868); Epstein and Walker, "Role of the Supreme Court," 341–342.

25. 75 U.S. 85 (1868).

26. Epstein and Walker, "Role of the Supreme Court," 343.

27. Charles Warren, *The Supreme Court in United States History*, vol. 2, rev. ed. (Boston: Little, Brown, 1947), 387.

28. 75 U.S. 603 (1868).

29. Abraham Lincoln, *The Collected Works of Abraham Lincoln*, vol. 4, ed. Roy P. Basler (New Brunswick, N.J.: Rutgers University Press, 1953), 430.

30. 17 F. Cas. 144 (C.C.D. Mary. 1861).

31. See Henry J. Abraham, *Justices, Presidents, and Senators: A History of the U.S. Supreme Court Appointments from Washington to Clinton*, new and rev. ed. (Lanham, Md.: Rowman & Littlefield, 1999), 90.

32. David M. Silver, *Lincoln's Supreme Court* (Urbana: University of Illinois Press, 1956), 145.

33. *Roosevelt*, at 517.

34. *Roosevelt*, at 517n5. The cases were *Gordon v. Caldcleugh*, 7 U.S. 268, 269–270 (1806); *Fulton v. M'Affee*, 41 U.S. 149, 152 (1842); *Linton v. Stanton* 53 U.S. 423, 425–426 (1852); *Strader v. Baldwin*, 50 U.S. 261, 262 (1850).

35. See Warren, *Supreme Court*, 387; Daniel Meltzer, "The History and Structure of Article III," *University of Pennsylvania Law Review* 138 (1990): 1569, 1590n75.

36. 1 Stat 85, 86 (1789).

37. *Trebilcock v. Wilson*, 79 U.S. 687, 692 (1871).

38. *Trebilcock*, 79 U.S., at 693.

39. Three justices (Black, Douglas, Murphy) in *West Virginia State Board of Education v. Barnett*, 319 U.S. 624 (1943) voted to overrule a case, *Minersville School Dist. v. Gobitis*, 310 U.S. 586 (1940), in which they were in the majority.

40. See Silver, *Lincoln's Supreme Court*, 145.

41. See Meltzer, "The History of Structure and Article III," 1590n75.

42. *Wiscart v. Dauchy*, 3 U.S. 321, 327 (1796).

43. *Durousseau v. United States*, 10 U.S. 307, 314 (1810). See *United States v. Goodwin*, 11 U.S. 108 (1812) (Supreme Court has no appellate jurisdiction in the absence of legislation).

44. Justice Story insisted that the Constitution required that Congress vest at least one federal court with the power to decide federal questions, but he nevertheless believed that courts could not legally take this jurisdiction in the absence of a statute. *Martin v. Hunter's Lessee*, 14 U.S. 304, 328–335 (1816); *White v. Fenner*, 29 F. Cas. 1015 (C.C.D.R.I. 1818).

45. Robert N. Clinton, "A Mandatory View of Federal Court Jurisdiction: Early Implementation of and Departures from the Constitutional Plan," *Columbia Law Review* 86 (1986): 1515, 1608.

46. *Sheldon v. Sill*, 49 U.S. 441, 449 (1850).

47. *Cary v. Curtis*, 44 U.S. 236, 245 (1845). See Clinton, "Mandatory View," 1589–1592.

48. 5 Stat. 726 (1845).

49. *Daniels v. Railroad Company*, 70 U.S. 250, 254 (1865).

50. *Insurance Co. v. Ritchie*, 72 U.S. 541, 544 (1867).

51. *McCardle*, 74 U.S., at 513.

52. 54 U.S. 429 (1851).

53. *McCardle*, 74 U.S., at 514. See *Norris*, 54 U.S., at 440.

54. McCardle's attorney relied solely on several state cases which held that pending cases were not affected by subsequent changes in the substantive law. This was both a misstatement of federal law and irrelevant to the jurisdictional issue. Regardless of any change in the legal rights of parties as a result of new laws, courts had jurisdiction to decide cases only when they had jurisdiction at the time of decision.

55. William W. Van Alstyne, "A Critical Guide to Ex parte McCardle," *Arizona Law Review* 15 (1973): 229, 255, 233. See Van Alstyne, "Critical Guide," 255–258; Fairman, *Reconstruction*, 1395. David Currie questions only the constitutional soundness of the precedents underlying *McCardle*. See David P. Currie, *The Constitution in the Supreme Court: The First Hundred Years, 1789–1888* (Chicago: University of Chicago Press, 1985), 25–28.

56. Currie, *Constitution*, 305–306.

57. 5 U.S. 103, 110 (1801).

58. See Jean Edward Smith, *John Marshall: Definer of a Nation* (New York: Henry Holt, 1996), 298.

59. *Schooner Peggy*, 5 U.S. 103, at 110 (1801).

60. See especially, *Bell v. Maryland*, 378 U.S. 226, 231 n.2 (1964) ("the rule [of *Schooner Peggy*] has . . . been consistently followed and applied by this Court"); *Gulf, Colorado & Santa Fe Railroad Commission v. Dennis*, 224 U.S. 503, 505–506 (1912) (citing

numerous cases); *United States v. Tynen*, 78 U.S. 88, 94–95 (1871); *United States v. Preston*, 28 U.S. 57, 66–67 (1830); *Fairfax's Devisee v. Hunter's Lessee*, 11 U.S. 603, 632 (Johnson, J., dissenting) (agreeing with majority that "a treaty ratified subsequent to the decision of the Court appealed from, becomes a part of the law of the case and must control our decision").

61. *Freeborn v. Smith*, 69 U.S. 160 (1865).

62. See, i.e., *Benner v. Porter*, 50 U.S. 235 (1850); *Freeborn v. Smith*, 69 U.S. 160 (1865).

63. *Freeborn*, 69 U.S., at 174.

64. *Freeborn*, at 174–175. For a discussion of this case, see Fairman, *Reconstruction*, 468.

65. Chief Justice Chase withheld making an authoritative decision for similar reasons in very different circumstances the year before *McCardle* was decided. During the winter of 1867, Congress passed a bill requiring the chief justice to appoint registrars to assist bankruptcy justices. In part because of the Chief Justice's concerns about the constitutionality of the act, Congress during March of 1867 debated repealing the offending provision. Chase refused either to make appointments or publicly declare the bill unconstitutional while repeal was under serious legislative consideration. When Congress adjourned in late March without changing the law, Chase within a week determined that the law was constitutional and made the appointments. See Fairman, *Reconstruction*, 355–365.

66. Congressional Globe, 40th Cong., 2nd Sess., 2095.

67. Ibid.

68. Fairman, *Reconstruction*, 484 (quoting Davis to Rockwell).

69. See Epstein and Walker, "Role of the Supreme Court," 336–337.

70. Fairman, *Reconstruction*, 1394–1395.

71. Currie, *Constitution*, 27.

72. See especially Robert Yates, "Essays of Brutus," *The Complete Anti-Federalist*, vol. 2, ed. Herbert Storing (Chicago: University of Chicago Press, 1981), 422–442.

73. Maeva Marcus and Natalie Wexler, "The Judiciary Act of 1789: Political Compromise or Constitutional Interpretation?," in *Origins of the Federal Judiciary: Essays on the Judiciary Act of 1789*, ed. Maeva Marcus (New York: Oxford University Press, 1992), 29.

74. Mark A. Graber, "Establishing Judicial Review: *Marbury* and the Judiciary Act of 1789," *Tulsa Law Review* 38 (2003): 609, 641.

75. Ibid.

76. Clinton, "Mandatory View," 1592.

77. See Knight and Epstein, "Struggle"; Mark A. Graber, "Establishing Judicial Review?: *Schooner Peggy* and the Early Marshall Court," *Political Research Quarterly* 51 (1998): 221; Mark A. Graber, "The Passive-Aggressive Virtues: *Cohens v. Virginia* and the Problematic Establishment of Judicial Review," *Constitutional Commentary* 12 (1995): 67.

78. John Marshall, *The Papers of John Marshall: Correspondence, Papers, and Selected Judicial Opinions*, vol. 9, ed. Herbert Alan Johnson, Charles T. Cullen, and Charles F. Hobson (Chapel Hill: University of North Carolina Press, 1998), 338.

79. Fairman, *Reconstruction*, 486 (quoting Chase).

80. See *Mason v. Eldred*, 73 U.S. 231 (1868) (overruling *Sheehy v. Mandeville*, 10 U.S. 253 (1810)); *The Belfast*, 74 U.S. 624 (1869) (overruling *Allen v. Newberry*, 62 U.S. 244 (1858)); *Knox v. Lee*, 79 U.S. 457 (1871) (overruling *Hepburn v. Griswold*, 75 U.S. 603 (1870)).

81. Charles Fairman, Mr. *Justice Miller and the Supreme Court 1862–1890* (Cambridge, Mass.: Harvard University Press, 1939), 88–89.

82. *Ex parte Milligan*, 71 U.S. 2, 109 (1866).

83. *Korematsu*, 323 U.S., at 244 (Jackson, J., dissenting).

84. *Korematsu*, 323 U.S., at 245 (Jackson, J., dissenting).

85. Alexander M. Bickel, "Foreword: The Passive Virtues," 40; see also 43–46.

86. Bickel, "Foreword: Passive Virtues," 75.

87. Ibid., 49.

88. Philip Bobbitt, *Constitutional Fate: Theory of the Constitution* (New York: Oxford University Press, 1982), 61.

89. *Terminiello v. Chicago*, 337 U.S. 1, 37 (1949) (Jackson, J., dissenting).

90. Owen Fiss advances a similar understanding of constitutional prudentialism when he insists that judges remedying constitutional wrongs should emphasize what is feasible as much as what was required by other legal logics. "Instrumentalism," he writes, "may not only call for a departure from the interpretive paradigm, [but] may actually interfere with the interpretive process. It may make the judge settle for something less than he perceives to be the correct interpretation." Owen M. Fiss, "Objectivity and Interpretation," *Stanford Law Review* 34 (1982): 739.

91. Bickel, "Foreword: Passive Virtues," 51; see also 79.

92. Ibid., 48–49, 51, 74.

93. *Korematsu*, at 244 (Jackson, J., dissenting).

94. Ibid., at 246.

95. Ibid., at 248.

96. A judicial majority did, however, sustain the blockade. Justice Grier, the crucial fifth vote on the measure, fully supported the Civil War effort and does not appear to have voted strategically.

97. Gerald Gunther, "The Subtle Vices of the 'Passive Virtues'—A Comment on Principle and Expediency in Judicial Review," *Columbia Law Review* 64 (1964): 1, 3.

98. See Mark A. Graber, "Law and Sports Officiating: A Misunderstood and Justly Neglected Relationship," *Constitutional Commentary* 16 (1999): 293, 299–301.

99. Sanford Levinson and J. M. Balkin, "Law, Music and Other Performing Arts," *University of Pennsylvania Law Review* 139 (1991): 1597, 1603n25.

100. See Mark A. Graber, "Naked Land Transfers and American Constitutional Development," *Vanderbilt Law Review* 53 (2000): 73, 107.

101. 71 U.S. 333 (1867).

102. Charles Fairman, Mr. *Justice Miller*, 134.

103. Paul Pierson, "Not Just What, but *When*: Timing and Sequence in Political Processes," *Studies in American Political Development* 14 (2000): 72.

104. 75 U.S. 85, 97 (1868).

105. Robert A. Dahl, "Decision-making in a Democracy: The Supreme Court as a National Policy-Maker," *Emory Law Journal* 50 (2001): 563, 578.

106. See sources cited in footnote 77, above.

107. Ran Hirschl, "Beyond the American Experience: The Global Expansion of Judicial Review," in *Marbury v. Madison: Documents and Commentary*, ed. Mark A. Graber and Michael Perhac (Washington, D.C.: CQ Press 2002), 142–144.

108. Silver, *Lincoln's Supreme Court*, 123–125.

109. Fairman, *Reconstruction*, 584–585.

110. Silver, *Lincoln's Supreme Court*, 124 (quoting Edward Bates to Edwin M. Stanton, January 31, 1863).

111. See Keith E. Whittington, *Constitutional Construction: Divided Powers and Constitutional Meaning* (Princeton, N.J.: Princeton University Press, 1999), 20–71.

112. See Mark A. Graber, "The Non-Majoritarian Difficulty: Legislative Deference to the Judiciary," *Studies in American Political Development* 7 (1993): 35; Mark Silverstein and Benjamin Ginsberg, "The Supreme Court and the New Politics of Judicial Power," *Political Science Quarterly* 102 (1987): 371; Keith E. Whittington, "The Political Foundations of Judicial Supremacy," in *Constitutional Politics: Essays on Constitution Making, Maintenance and Change*, ed. Sotirios A. Barber and Robert P. George (Princeton, N.J.: Princeton University Press, 2001); Lucas A. Powe Jr., *The Warren Court and American Politics* (Cambridge, Mass.: Harvard University Press, 2000); Jack M. Balkin and Sanford Levinson, "Understanding the Constitutional Revolution," *Virginia Law Review* 87 (2001): 1045.

113. Howard Gillman, "How Political Parties Can Use the Courts to Advance Their Agendas: Federal Courts in the United States, 1875–1891," *American Political Science Review* 96 (2002): 511.

114. See Wallace Mendelson, "Dred Scott's Case—Reconsidered," *Minnesota Law Review* 38 (1953): 16; Graber, "Nonmajoritarian Difficulty," 35, 46–50.

115. See Jack N. Rakove, "The Origins of Judicial Review: A Plea for New Contexts," *Stanford Law Review* 49 (1997): 1031.

116. See note 100 above.

117. See Fairman, *Reconstruction*, 683–685.

118. 376 U.S. 254 (1964).

119. 485 U.S. 46 (1988).

120. Thomas Keck's study of the evolution of conservative activism in the United States similarly highlights path dependent influences of judicial decision making. Thomas M. Keck, *The Most Activist Supreme Court in History: The Road to Modern Judicial Conservatism* (Chicago: University of Chicago Press, 2004).

Chapter 2

Social Constructions, Supreme Court Reversals, and American Political Development: Lochner, Plessy, Bowers, *but Not* Roe

Ronald Kahn

Introduction

In this chapter, I explore the role of the social construction process (SCP) in the decision making of the mature Rehnquist Court from 1986 to 2003, with respect to the rights of privacy and personhood under the due process clause of the Fourteenth Amendment. This process—the continuous and mutually constitutive dynamic relationship between internal legalistic and external factors—has important implications for how we view the decision-making process of the Supreme Court and the Court's place in American political development. I will call this relationship a "mutual construction process," and emphasize that it is simultaneously normative and empirical, and internal and external.

In the first half of this chapter, I describe the SCP through an analysis of *Planned Parenthood of Southeastern Pennsylvania v. Casey* (1992)[1] and *Lawrence v. Texas* (2003).[2] I demonstrate the conditions under which the Supreme Court overturns landmark decisions, and I conclude that the mutual construction of internal-legal and external-social factors is central to defining those conditions that made *Plessy v. Ferguson* (1896),[3] *Adkins v. Children's Hospital of District of Columbia* (1923),[4] and *Bowers v. Hardwick* (1986)[5] ripe for overturning, but not *Roe v. Wade* (1973).[6] I show how in *Casey*, *Romer v. Evans* (1996),[7] and *Lawrence*, the Court engages in an informative debate on the merits of the SCP. My conclusion is that engaging in the SCP blends normative and empirical elements, including social facts, and therefore it is simultaneously inward (legal) and outward (society) looking. Because it is bidirectional, legal principles and the world outside the Court become symbiotic and mutually construct each other.

Through this lens, one recognizes that principles gain meaning through their application in the social, political, and economic world outside the Court. Moreover, the process results in a legal objectivity or secularism that, along with other factors, provides a (relative) autonomy for the Supreme Court from political pressures and institutions.

In the second half of the chapter, I explore the broader implications of Supreme Court decision-making process with its core SCP. The first implication is that originalists—those with fidelity to the original intent or meaning in interpreting the Constitution—accept many of the qualities of nonoriginalist decision making, but not a robust SCP. This suggests that a primary fissure on the mature Rehnquist Court, with regard to, among other things, the treatment of implied fundamental rights, was between originalists and nonoriginalists, rather than between conservatives, moderates, and liberals, and at the core of such differences was the legitimacy of a robust SCP.

The legal objectivity or secularism of the nonoriginalist SCP and the attendant Court autonomy are politically significant. For nonoriginalists, it is the basis for claims of Court legitimacy and uniqueness among governmental institutions; for originalists, it is the basis for undercutting the legitimacy of the Supreme Court. It also helps explain why a conservative Court in a conservative political era expands the jurisprudential basis for the right of abortion choice—moving from a concept of privacy to one of personhood—and also why personhood rights under the Constitution were extended to gay men and lesbians in the dramatic and unexpected expansionist decision in *Lawrence v. Texas* (2003).[8]

It also helps to explain why the role of the Supreme Court in American society is at the center of American politics today. The legal objectivity or secularism witnessed in the SCP in *Casey* and *Lawrence* is exactly what the religious right and social or cultural conservatives oppose—and what their secularist opposition admires. Thus, there is a feedback effect between differences on the Court over the legitimacy of a robust SCP, and the cases that result from such differences, and American politics, one that threatens to be with us for many years. These differences are not simply over controversial Court decisions, such as *Roe, Casey,* and *Lawrence;* they are over the nature of Court decision-making process and the place of the Court in American political development, as well as the politics of naming new Supreme Court justices.

One must assume that in deciding both *Casey* and *Lawrence,* the Court understood the possibility of heated political reactions to each of these decisions; however, in each case, the mutual construction of "the legal" and "the social" trumped such concerns. Moreover, although this conflict on the Court has had the feedback effect of controversy in American politics, this controversy has had a limited effect on the Supreme Court. This is because the SCP is engaged in, and thus supported by, nonoriginalists across the ideological board, and its legal objectivity fits with core elements of what they believe constitutes the rule of law and American political culture.

Because Supreme Court decision making cannot be segmented into internal or external elements, approaches to the study of the Supreme Court that rest on such segmentation—that is, on a vision of "law" versus "politics"—are wanting. These include attitudinalist, institutional-strategic, and historical approaches that seek to explain doctrinal change from the perspective only of external phenomenon, unmediated by the internal-legal through the Court's mutual construction process. These unique qualities of Supreme Court decision making also mean that the "legal time" of the Supreme Court is quite different from the "political time" of directly "political" institutions such as the presidency, as are the resulting path trajectories of the Supreme Court in American political development.[9] As explored in the last few sections of this chapter, scholars who wish to study the place of the Supreme Court in American political development should be wary of general theories of APD that are built on acceptance of increasing returns path dependence as an identifying element of American political institutions.[10]

Planned Parenthood of Southeastern Pennsylvania v. Casey (1992)

The central elements of the SCP are exemplified by the decision in *Planned Parenthood of Southeastern Pennsylvania v. Casey* (1992). In this rare joint opinion by Justices O'Connor, Kennedy, and Souter, the *Casey* Court does not simply explain why *Roe v. Wade* (1973) should not be overturned; it describes the internal legal and external social and political conditions that must be present before a landmark decision is overturned. More specifically, the joint opinion notes that the conditions that required the Supreme Court to overturn *Adkins v. Children's Hospital* (1923) (and *Lochner*-era principles) in *West Coast Hotel Co. v. Parrish* (1937)[11] and the *Plessy v. Ferguson* (1896) segregation decision in *Brown v. Board of Education* (1954) are absent in *Roe* and its progeny, and therefore *Roe* cannot legitimately be overturned.[12]

In outlining the factors that are necessary to make a landmark decision ripe for overturning, *Casey* provides a superb lens through which we can understand the basic elements of the SCP. In *Casey*, the Court suggests the following: (1) changing fact situations obligate the Court to rethink what constitutes individual rights; (2) workability and citizen reliance on rights are important in determining whether a right should be sustained; (3) the SCP increases the Court's legitimacy and institutional interests; and (4) engaging in the SCP requires the Court to apply rights principles to the lived lives of citizens under the law, rather than to respond to public opinion and political controversy.

Changed Factual Conditions, Social Constructions, and Overturning Landmark Decisions

In its discussion of whether it was proper for the Supreme Court to overturn *Adkins* in the *West Coast Hotel* case, the *Casey* Court specifically argues that false or changing factual conditions obligate the Court to rethink the nature of the rights involved and to evaluate the need for new or changed rights. The Court specifically identified the changed factual conditions in the fourteen years between *Adkins* and *West Coast Hotel*: "The facts upon which the earlier case had premised a constitutional resolution of social controversy had proven to be untrue, and history's demonstration of their untruth not only justified but required the new choice of constitutional principle."[13] In *Adkins*, the Court "held it to be an infringement of constitutionally protected liberty of contract to require the employers of adult women to satisfy minimum wage standards," whereas the Court in *West Coast Hotel* found that "the interpretation of contractual freedom protected in *Adkins* rested on fundamentally false factual assumptions about the capacity of a relatively unregulated market to satisfy minimal levels of human welfare."[14]

There is a similar repudiation of the factual basis of *Plessy* in *Brown v. Board of Education* (1954). The *Casey* joint opinion argues that the Supreme Court "repudiated" the "understanding of the facts and the rule" in *Plessy v. Ferguson* (1896).[15] The change in the role of public schools in the civil and political life of the African American community meant that the explanation provided and accepted in *Plessy*—that one could blame any feelings of inferiority on the African American children themselves—required repudiation by the Court in *Brown*. The Court in *Brown* addressed these changed facts by observing that whatever may have been the understanding in *Plessy*'s time regarding the power of segregation to stigmatize African Americans with a "badge of inferiority," it was clear by 1954 that legally sanctioned segregation had just that effect.[16]

Whether segregation in public schools is viewed as a badge of inferiority depends both on an interpretation of rights principles within the Fourteenth Amendment and on institutional shifts and changes in society. The Court is required to ask more than whether segregation was permitted at the time of the founding. The Court must continue to evaluate changes at the factual foundation in each case, and cumulatively in a line of cases, and ask whether it is required to impose new obligations on government with regard to individual rights. The joint opinion's comparison of *West Coast Hotel* and *Brown* illustrates this point:

> *West Coast Hotel* and *Brown* each rested on facts, or an understanding of facts, changed from those which furnished the claimed justifications for the earlier constitutional resolutions. Each case was comprehensible as the Court's response to facts that the country could understand, or had come to understand already, but which the Court of an earlier day, as its own declarations disclosed, had not been able to perceive . . . In constitutional adjudication as elsewhere in life, changed circumstances may impose new obligations, and the thoughtful part of the Nation could accept each decision to overrule a prior case as a response to the Court's constitutional duty.[17]

Therefore, use of the SCP is directly related to the conditions of citizens' lived lives, as they are shaped by the contours of the Constitution. Moreover, victories among scholars in the interpretive community or between legal advocacy groups are not to be the primary determinant of rights: "As the decisions were thus comprehensible, they were also defensible, not merely as the victories of one doctrinal school over another by dint of numbers (victories though they were), but as applications of constitutional principle to facts as they had not been seen by the Court before."[18] This does not mean that the scholarly community and its theories of justification are unimportant to the Court and the development of constitutional law; they are an important background condition for the justices, and they inform the amicus briefs sent to the Court. It means rather that regardless of what school of interpretation is dominant at a point in time, today or in the past, the Court's duty is to engage directly in the SCP. As the underlying factual conditions in society change, so must the application of the law to those facts and to the resulting principles.

In deciding whether *Roe* should be overturned, the *Casey* Court pinpoints the ways in which *Roe* differs from *Plessy* and *Lochner* with regard to its application of factors at the core of the SCP: "Because neither the factual underpinnings of *Roe*'s central holding nor our understanding of it has changed (and because no other indication of weakened precedent has been shown), the Court could not pretend to be reexamining the prior law with any justification beyond a present doctrinal disposition to come out differently from the Court of 1973."[19] The rights principles and the social constructions that link these principles to the lived lives of citizens not only made it difficult for the Court to overturn *Roe*; they also forced the Court to discuss the right of abortion choice in *Casey* as one of personhood, a far more filigreed social construction than that of privacy. Women and their families had grown to rely on the existence of rights of abortion choice, and that reliance provided the Court with additional reasons for its acceptance of the right of abortion choice as fundamental.[20] This expanded concept of personhood in *Casey* was a result of the mutual construction of legal precedents that increasingly recognized the active place of women in society and of rights principles that were extended as a reflection of that expanded role.

A willingness on the part of the Court to consider changes in the social, economic, and political landscape is the sine qua non of the SCP. The *Casey* Court analyzes the factual underpinnings of privacy rights in the years between 1973 and 1992 and recognizes that they were moving in the same direction as expanding interpretations of the right of privacy. For this reason, the *Casey* Court concluded that if it were to overturn *Roe*, nineteen years after it was decided, it would be seen as making the decision on raw policy grounds, or in response to politics, rather than on the basis of a determination by the Court whether the rights at issue in *Roe* were still valid in light of the lived experiences of our nation's citizens. Here, then, we see that justices are not restricted to a mathematical application of legal principle. Rather, they engage in a process that considers past principles and their application in the world outside the Court. These are core elements of the nonoriginalist vision of the rule of law. When changes in society are symbiotic with the Court's evaluation of the application of rights principles, landmark cases will not be overruled; when social constructions in past landmark cases are no longer tenable, landmark cases are ripe for serious modification, if not outright overturning.[21]

The Court Must Not Be Viewed as Political

The *Casey* Court demonstrates the importance of the SCP in Supreme Court decision making by linking that process to the justices' concerns about the Supreme Court as the legal arm of American governmental institutions. The Court emphasizes that its legitimacy is based on the quality of its decision making, which includes its ability to recognize when the social constructions prior rights were based on are no longer valid, and thus require the rejection or modification of the rights principles. For this reason, *Adkins* and *Plessy* were overturned, but not *Roe*.

> The examination of the conditions justifying the repudiation of *Adkins* by *West Coast Hotel* and *Plessy* by *Brown* is enough to suggest the terrible price that would have been paid if the Court had not overruled as it did. In [*Casey*], however . . . the terrible price would be paid for overruling. Our analysis would not be complete, however, without explaining why overruling *Roe's* central holding would not only reach an unjustifiable result under principles of stare decisis, but would seriously weaken the Court's capacity to exercise the judicial power and to function as the Supreme Court of a Nation dedicated to the rule of law. To understand why this would be so, it is necessary to understand the source of this Court's authority, the conditions necessary for its preservation, and its relationship to the country's understanding of itself as a constitutional Republic.[22]

The *Casey* Court reiterates that the mere application of the appropriate legal principle is not enough to protect Court legitimacy when deciding whether to overturn a landmark decision: "Even when justification is furnished by apposite legal principle, something more is required. Because not every conscientious claim of principled justification will be accepted as such, the justification claimed must be beyond dispute."[23] The "something more" that is required is the Court's engagement in the SCP.

The *Casey* Court stresses that the politically controversial nature of *Plessy* and *Lochner* is what links these cases with *Roe*. The Court describes these cases as being of "comparable dimension" because all three cases "responded to national controversies and take on the impress of the controversies addressed."[24] The justices discuss overruling under conditions of "intensely divisive controversy" and find that when such cases are decided, there is a "dimension present whenever the Court's interpretation of the Constitution calls the contending sides of a national controversy to end their national division by accepting a common mandate rooted in the Constitution."[25] In such situations, the Court emphasizes that it must ensure that its decisions are not perceived as giving in to political pressure if the Court wants to sustain its legitimacy.

Whatever the premises of opposition may be, only the most convincing justification under accepted standards of precedent could suffice to demonstrate that a later decision overruling the first was anything but a surrender to political pressure and an unjustified repudiation of the principle on which the Court staked its authority in the first instance. So to overrule under fire in the absence of the most compelling reason to reexamine a watershed decision would subvert the Court's legitimacy beyond any serious question.[26] The

Court recognizes that when cases are politically controversial, the institutional needs of the Court become even more prominent, thus signaling that the principles for overturning cases, and their application through the SCP, must be transparent, well grounded in principle, and "sufficiently plausible" to be accepted by the nation—even if all do not agree with their outcomes:

> The Court must take care to speak and act in ways that allow people to accept its decisions on the terms the Court claims for them, as grounded truly in principle, not as compromises with social and political pressures having, as such, no bearing on the principled choices that the Court is obliged to make. Thus, the Court's legitimacy depends on making legally principled decisions under circumstances in which their principled character is sufficiently plausible to be accepted by the Nation.[27]

Decisions that are viewed as "compromises with social and political pressures" lack plausibility because they are viewed as unprincipled, and they place the Court in the position of being viewed simply as a political body, and thus illegitimate. For nonoriginalists, the SCP adds to the plausibility of their decisions, and thus to the Court's legitimacy as an institution that is called upon to follow the rule of law, not politics. The Court highlights its institutional legitimacy concerns, specifically at issue if it were to overturn *Roe*.

> Whether or not a new social consensus is developing on [the abortion] issue, its divisiveness is no less today than in 1973, and pressure to overrule the decision, like pressure to retain it, has grown only more intense. A decision to overrule *Roe's* essential holding under the existing circumstances would address error, if error there was, at the cost of both profound and unnecessary damage to the Court's legitimacy, and to the Nation's commitment to the rule of law. It is therefore imperative to adhere to the essence of *Roe's* original decision, and we do so today.[28]

Moreover, engaging in a detailed, disciplined, and at times robust SCP adds to the legitimacy of the Court and the rule of law because it allows the Court to place its decision making among the competing claims within the nation's political culture. *Brown* gets its plausibility and moral force because its SCP recognizes that under the "reformed liberal" tradition of American political culture the state has a role in the development of persons, and a role in helping individuals become better citizens. This tradition recognizes that such development is only possible through nonsegregated public education.[29]

Likewise, the complex notion of the relationship between the level of individual agency of a woman with respect to personal choices about sex, birth control, and the right of abortion choice found in the *Casey* majority opinion means that the state has created a place and need for women in its social, economic, and political life. That place is partly sustained by the continued right of abortion choice. What Greenstone refers to as the "reformed liberal" dimension of American political culture also helps explain why the Court in *Casey* recognizes that it must respect the reliance of women on *Roe*'s right to abortion choice. This reliance, created by the state and allowed by the Court, placed a government institution in a position of supporting the manifestation of that right within the social, economic, and political system. No longer was sex, birth control, or the right of abortion choice simply a question of "address[ing] error, if error there was,"[30] in a formally legal sense of internal legal principles, uninformed by the lived lives under the *Roe* precedent. This view is at the core of what the *Casey* Court is thinking about when it writes, "the Court's legitimacy depends on making legally principled decisions in which their principle character is sufficiently plausible to be accepted by the nation."[31]

Finally, and ironically, for the Court to ignore these considerations of institutional role, legitimacy and, most importantly, the place of the SCP in achieving Court legitimacy would make the Court a less democratic institution as well. The consideration of rights in the context of the relationship of constitutional principles to the lived lives of citizens makes the Court democratic in terms of the special ways in which it makes decisions as it defines equality and liberty.[32]

Lawrence v. Texas (2003): Kennedy's Majority Opinion

One can see a confirmation of the importance of the SCP as outlined in *Casey* in *Lawrence v. Texas* (2003). *Lawrence* did not simply overturn *Bowers v. Hardwick* (1986), the case that permitted antisodomy laws, as applied only to gay men and lesbians—it eviscerated *Bowers*. The majority opinion in *Lawrence* was written by Justice Kennedy, joined by Justices Stevens, Souter, Ginsburg, and Breyer. Justice O'Connor wrote a concurring opinion. Justice Scalia, joined by Justices Rehnquist and Thomas, wrote a scathing criticism of the majority and concurring opinions, building on his dissents in *Romer* and *Casey* against a robust SCP.

The *Lawrence* decision starts with a condemnation of the *Bowers* Court for misapprehending primary liberty issues and for failing to properly engage in the process of stare decisis.[33] What did the Court mean when it emphasized that the *Bowers* Court failed to properly engage in the process of stare decisis?[34] The *Lawrence* Court suggests that *Bowers* was not a valid interpretation of the Constitution the day it was handed down, and since then, its validity has lessened. The *Bowers* Court erred by treating the issue as whether one had a constitutional right to engage in a particular sexual act, when in fact the issue was something much larger. At the heart of *Bowers* was a question about individual rights—the same rights that had formed the basis for the privacy protections established in such cases as *Griswold v. Connecticut* (1965),[35] *Eisenstadt v. Baird* (1972),[36] and *Roe v. Wade* (1973).[37]

> To say that the issue in *Bowers* was simply the right to engage in certain sexual conduct demeans the claim the individual put forward, just as it would demean a married couple were it to be said marriage is simply about the right to have sexual intercourse. The laws involved in *Bowers* and here . . . have more far-reaching consequences, touching upon the most private human conduct, sexual behavior, and in the most private of places, the home . . . When sexuality finds overt expression in intimate conduct with another person, the conduct can be but one element in a personal bond that is more enduring. The liberty protected by the Constitution allows homosexual persons the right to make that choice.[38]

The Court also considers the validity of *Bowers* in light of two antecedent cases, *Planned Parenthood of Southeastern Pa. v. Casey* (1992)[39] and *Romer v. Evans* (1996),[40] and finds them to "cast [*Bowers's*] holding into even more doubt"[41]: "The foundations of *Bowers* have sustained serious erosion from our recent decisions in *Casey* and *Romer*. When our precedent has been thus weakened, criticism from other sources is of greater significance."[42] Because the SCP is a continuing one, the *Casey* decision is especially significant. There is a shift in *Casey* toward recognition of abortion rights issues as involving the right of personhood, a far more forceful statement about liberty interests than the passive notion of privacy found in *Roe v. Wade* (1973). The *Lawrence* Court specifically refers to this critical social construction regarding the depth of women's right to abortion choice in *Casey*:

> These matters, involving the most intimate and personal choices a person may make in a lifetime, choices central to personal dignity and autonomy, are central to the liberty protected by the Fourteenth Amendment. At the heart of liberty is the right to define one's own concept of existence, of meaning, of the universe, and of the mystery of human life. Beliefs about these matters could not define the attributes of personhood were they formed under compulsion of the State.[43]

One also sees the SCP at work as the Court considers the continued validity of *Bowers* in light of *Romer v. Evans* (1996). The *Lawrence* Court wrote, "*Romer* invalidated an amendment to Colorado's Constitution, which named as a solitary class persons who were homosexuals, lesbians, or bisexual either by 'orientation, conduct, practices or relationships,'"[44] and noted that in *Romer* the Supreme Court had concluded that the amendment violated the equal protection clause because it was "'born of animosity toward the class of persons affected,'[45] and further that it had no rational relation to a legitimate governmental purpose."[46] The Court views the Colorado amendment as based on pure animus, even though it resulted from a vote of the people of Colorado.

Of equal importance for understanding the place of the SCP in determining why *Bowers* was overturned is the Court's specific reaffirmation in *Lawrence* of the conditions that must be present in order for the Court to overturn landmark decisions. These conditions required the *Lawrence* Court to consider (1) the substantive components (principles and social constructions) of what privacy meant before *Bowers*; (2) what personhood meant in *Casey*; and (3) what "pure animus" meant in *Romer*, while also realizing that Court decision making is also forward looking. The Court also had to consider what letting *Bowers* stand would do to key institutional norms that inform its legitimacy. More specifically, the importance of the SCP, in which rights principles are applied in light of the lived lives of persons, can be seen in *Lawrence* when the Court discusses why it does not simply follow public opinion, the will of the majority, as expressed by state legislatures, or the history of majority animus against gay men and lesbians. In so doing, the Supreme Court draws on its institutional norms that are quite distinct from those of political institutions. We see this when the Court explains why it cannot simply make decisions on a finding that there has been a moral condemnation of homosexual acts over the years by a majority of citizens, or the state legislature. Justice Kennedy, relying on *Casey*, notes that the Court's "obligation is to define the liberty of all, not to mandate our own moral code."[47]

> It must be acknowledged, of course, that the Court in *Bowers* was making the broader point that for centuries there have been powerful voices to condemn homosexual conduct as immoral . . . These considerations do not answer the question before us, however. The issue is whether the majority may use the power of the State to enforce these views on the whole society through operation of the criminal law.[48]

In such a setting, concepts such as emerging awareness, reliance, and workability take center stage. Supreme Court decision making does not start and stop at the founding: "History and tradition are the starting point but not in all cases the ending point of the substantive due process inquiry."[49] It is through the lens of the SCP, looking both backward and forward, that the Court articulates what liberty means. Through the SCP, application of concepts of emerging awareness, reliance, and workability, as used in *Casey*, becomes critical to understanding the *Lawrence* Court's decision to over-turn *Bowers*. Reliance is not the reliance of a majority in the state legislature, at the voting booth, or in opinion polls. The external world of the Court does not consist of a direct look by the Court at political choice or levels of contestation.

The Court directly confronts the important question of whether "the fact that the governing majority in a State has traditionally viewed a particular practice as immoral is sufficient reason for upholding a law prohibiting the practice."[50] In doing so, it affirms the importance of a continuous and continuing SCP when the Court interprets the Constitution.

> Had those who drew and ratified the due process clauses of the Fifth Amendment or the Fourteenth Amendment known the components of liberty in its manifold possibilities, they might have been more specific. They did not presume to have this insight. They knew times can blind us to certain truths and later generations can see that laws once thought necessary and proper in fact serve only to oppress. As the Constitution endures, persons in every generation can invoke its principles in their own search for greater freedom.[51]

The SCP involves recognition by the Court of the complexity of the social landscape and the lived lives of citizens. The Court's rejection of *Bowers* shows that flat, narrowly legalistic equations don't resolve key cases; rather, the Court relies on a process through which there is a mutual reconstruction of legal principles and the world outside the Court, while protecting the institutional interests of the Court and the rule of law.

O'Connor's Concurrence: Not Simply Strategic Decision Making

When legalists look at a case, they ask what "the law" is compared with dicta. Political scientists are not only concerned with what "the law" is in narrowly legalistic terms; they also study majority, concurring, and dissenting opinions to consider their implications for the development of individual rights in the future, in light of past decisions. Understanding social constructions in cases, and how they change, allows scholars to better understand the development of implied fundamental rights. When such an inquiry is undertaken, we begin to understand why Justice O'Connor, who voted with the majority in *Bowers*, now finds antisodomy laws aimed at gay men and lesbians to constitute a denial of equal protection of the law. O'Connor chooses not to directly overturn *Bowers*, or to accept an expansive due process liberty basis for deciding the case, in casting her vote against the constitutionality of the Texas antiabortion law.

However, in doing so, there is a great similarity between the social constructions in O'Connor's concurrence and Justice Kennedy's majority opinion, even though they differ on the constitutional basis for invalidating the Texas law. Justice Kennedy writes in *Lawrence* that Texas' homosexual sodomy law stimulates stigma against gay men and lesbians and encourages the imputation of inferiority by both government and private persons: "When homosexual conduct is made criminal by the law of the State, that declaration in and of itself is an invitation to subject homosexual persons to discrimination both in the public and in the private spheres . . . [*Bowers's*] continuance as precedent demeans the lives of homosexual persons."[52] Justice O'Connor agrees with the majority opinion that Texas' antihomosexual sodomy law constitutes an impermissible imputation of inferiority by the state against gay men and lesbians:

> The effect of Texas' sodomy law is not just limited to the threat of prosecution or consequence of conviction. Texas' sodomy law brands all homosexuals as criminals, thereby making it more difficult for homosexuals to be treated in the same manner as everyone else[53] . . . When a State makes homosexual conduct criminal, and not "deviate sexual intercourse" committed by persons of different sexes, "that declaration in and of itself is an invitation to subject homosexual persons to discrimination both in the public and in the private spheres."[54]

Moreover, O'Connor, like the majority, is willing to socially construct the problem with the Texas antisodomy law as a violation of equal protection principles because it is antagonistic to gay men and lesbians as a class:

> Texas argues, however, that the sodomy law does not discriminate against homosexual persons. Instead, the state maintains that the law discriminates only against homosexual conduct. While it is true that the law applies only to conduct, the conduct targeted by this law is conduct that is closely correlated with being homosexual. Under such circumstances, Texas' sodomy law is targeted at more than conduct. It is instead directed toward gay persons as a class.[55]

Most importantly, Justice O'Connor, unlike the majority, is willing to suggest a deeper social construction of the singling out of gay men and lesbians for special treatment, when she specifically draws on the maximalist *Plyler v. Doe* (1982)[56] decision to do so. In that case, Texas was not permitted to charge school tuition to parents of undocumented Mexican American children. Her more robust social construction is evident when she emphasizes that the sodomy statute subjects homosexuals to "a life-long penalty and stigma. A legislative classification that threatens the creation of an underclass . . . cannot be reconciled with the Equal Protection Clause."[57] This is a far more robust statement of the equal protection violation than one that rests simply on the view that the state cannot have sodomy laws that target homosexuals.

O'Connor, like the majority, sees the Texas law as violating the *Romer* mandate that government may not base a law on pure animus against a politically unpopular group. To do so is not permissible even under a rational basis (minimal scrutiny) test. The Texas law, like the invalidated state constitutional amendment in *Romer*, "singled out homosexuals 'for disfavored legal status,'"[58] and is therefore a violation of the equal protection clause.

One can see O'Connor's commitment to engaging in a robust SCP when she agrees with her nonoriginalist colleagues that the Court should not base its decision simply on accepting the moral disapproval of gay men and lesbians by the legislature or the public: "Moral disapproval of a group cannot be a legitimate governmental interest under the Equal Protection Clause because legal classifications must not be 'drawn for the purpose of disadvantaging the group burdened by the law.'"[59] Moreover, O'Connor specifically alludes to the importance of the liberty interests at stake in the case: "We have been most likely to apply rational basis review to hold a law unconstitutional under the Equal Protection Clause where, as here, the challenged legislation inhibits personal relationships."[60] The Kennedy majority differs with O'Connor and decides the case on due process privacy and personhood grounds, while also emphasizing many of O'Connor's equal protection concerns. However, Kennedy does not view the substantive issues raised by the Texas law as that different, whether it were to be decided on due process or equal protection grounds.[61]

O'Connor bases her decision on equal protection considerations in part because she, unlike the majority, places her trust in the political system. She believes that if the Court invalidated only antisodomy laws that targeted gay men and lesbians, states would not pass—and possibly would rescind—antisodomy laws that applied to both homosexuals and nonhomosexuals. For O'Connor, it is premature for the Court now to decide whether such a law is unconstitutional and to use the more broad-based due process clauses to do so, although she never makes a substantive argument against the legitimacy of due process arguments.[62]

Even though O'Connor wants a more toned-down response to *Bowers*, one based on the equal protection clause and the substantive elements in

Romer (and *Plyler*), an analysis of her SCP provides evidence that she agrees with many of the substantive conclusions at the core of the majority's opinion about the reasons to protect gay rights.[63] Considering the substantive components of O'Connor's analysis of the Texas law with regard to notions of permissibility of majoritarian views of sexuality, personhood, and morality, and her support of the SCP, there are far more similarities between O'Connor's views and those of the nonoriginalist justices in the majority, than there are between O'Connor and the originalists in dissent.[64] This is evident in Justice Scalia's stinging criticism of O'Connor's concurring opinion and conclusion that her equal protection argument will not necessarily lead to Court invalidation of laws banning same-sex marriages:

> This reasoning leaves on pretty shaky grounds state laws limiting marriage to opposite-sex couples. Justice O'Connor seeks to preserve them by the conclusionary statement that "preserving the traditional institution of marriage" is a legitimate state interest. But "preserving the traditional institution of marriage" is just a kinder way of describing the State's *moral disapproval* of same-sex couples. Texas's interest in [the antisodomy law] could be recast in similarly euphemistic terms: "preserving the traditional sexual mores of our society." In the jurisprudence Justice O'Connor has seemingly created, judges can validate laws by characterizing them as "preserving the traditions of society" (good); or invalidate them by characterizing them as "expressing moral disapproval (bad)."[65]

Scalia recognizes that O'Connor's SCP could be the basis for deciding future cases. Social constructions, even in concurrences, where the legal reasoning does not become part of "the law," can inform the development of doctrine. One cannot just look at the bottom-line conclusion that O'Connor bases her decision on equal protection grounds, whereas "the law" of the majority opinion rests on due process concerns. Scalia realizes that her definition of the substantive rights and social constructions and acceptance of the SCP do not augur well for future courts to simply defer to a state's moral disapprove of gays, and do so in a principled manner.

Scalia's Dissent: An Originalist Rejection of the Nonoriginalist SCP

I have argued that the nonoriginalist SCP in each new case involves a consideration of prior rights principles and social constructions, and asks whether past rights (or the lack of them) and the social constructions found in landmark cases continue to be valid. The most persuasive evidence for the importance of the nonoriginalist SCP in contemporary Supreme Court decision making is the vehement opposition to it by the Court's originalist justices, Scalia, Thomas, and Rehnquist. This opposition is most evident in Scalia's detailed, determined, and heartfelt dissent in *Romer*, where he was prescient in the view that *Romer* and *Bowers* could not stand together,[66] and in *Lawrence*, where he continued to attack both the conditions laid down in *Casey* under which the Supreme Court is to overturn landmark decisions,[67] and its robust SCP. Here, I concentrate on Scalia's dissent in *Lawrence*.

In contrast to nonoriginalists justices, Scalia believes that Supreme Court decision making is bounded by constitutional principles that existed at the establishment of the Constitution and its amendments, and not those formed by the Court's subsequent definition of implied fundamental rights. He believes that the Court should accept the policies of legislatures, as long as they do not violate the specific words of the Constitution, or cannot be directly inferred from those words. Scalia emphasizes that "fundamental rights" must be "so rooted in the traditions and conscience of our people as to be ranked as fundamental."[68] To see what Scalia means by this term, we need to consider the relationship between his view of the nonoriginalist SCP and tenants of his approach to constitutional interpretation. We need to look at his views on nonoriginalist positions on the importance of reliance, workability, and emerging awareness, and their relation to how he defines the place of history and tradition in Court decision making.

For nonoriginalist justices, evidence as to workability, reliance, and emerging awareness is a legitimate product of the Court's engagement in a robust SCP; the antisodomy law at issue in *Lawrence* is unconstitutional because its engagement in the SCP demonstrated that the rights principles and the social constructions of them were not significantly different from rights of privacy and personhood that the Court had defined for all citizens. Reliance, workability, and emerging awareness are based on engaging in the SCP in terms of the lived lives of its citizens and then making analogies from the findings for one group, and its actions, to that of a second group. For the nonoriginalists, the social facts—such as whether women have settled expectations as to liberty interests relating to contraception, right of abortion choice, and the place of women in the social, economic, and political world between 1973 and 1992—take form in terms of the principles about rights in *Roe* and the principles about liberty, privacy, and equal protection since *Roe*.

Scalia recognizes that the SCP is central to the *Lawrence* decision when he argues that one should not "believe" the majority opinion when it says the present case "does not involve whether the government must give formal recognition to any relationship that homosexual persons seek to enter."[69] This is because, for Scalia, the *Lawrence* decision builds on an illegitimate, decades-long SCP:

> More illuminating than this bald, unreasoned disclaimer is the progression of thought displayed by an earlier passage in the Court's opinion, which notes the constitutional protections afforded to "personal decisions relating to marriage, procreation, contraception, family relationships, child rearing, and education," and then declares that "[p]ersons in a homosexual relationship may seek autonomy for these purposes, just as heterosexual persons do . . ." If moral disapprobation of homosexual conduct is "no legitimate state interest" for purposes of proscribing that conduct; and if, as the Court coos (casting aside all pretense of neutrality) "[w]hen sexuality finds overt expression in intimate conduct with another person, the conduct can be but one element in a personal bond that is more enduring;" what justification could there possibly be for denying the benefits of marriage to homosexual couples exercising "[t]he liberty protected by the Constitution"?[70]

Moreover, as in *Romer*, where Scalia predicted that *Bowers* and *Romer* could not stand together, Scalia is predicting that if the SCP that began in *Griswold*, and was continued in *Roe, Casey, Romer,* and now *Lawrence,* is allowed to continue, establishing a right of same-sex marriage under the Constitution is just a matter of time.

Thus, we see the bases for Scalia's opposition to the Court's finding that there is "an emerging awareness that liberty gives substantial protection to adult persons in deciding how to conduct their private lives in matters pertaining to sex."[71] For him, an "emerging awareness" as defined by the nonoriginalists does not establish a "fundamental right." For Scalia, the continued presence of state laws and arrests for homosexual sodomy offer the only clear evidence that the protection of such acts is not "deeply rooted in the nation's history and traditions."[72] Scalia's rejection of a robust SCP, as well as his more general views of how to interpret the Constitution, also mean that his notion of what constitutes the mandate of history and tradition is dramatically different from the nonoriginalists.

In rejecting the emerging awareness and reliance arguments used in *Casey* and *Lawrence,*[73] Scalia opposes rights that evolve and are defined and redefined under the nonoriginalist SCP. One sees this when he seeks the narrowest reading of the *Lawrence* decision, and refuses to admit that *Casey* expanded the basis of abortion choice from a right of privacy to personhood. Scalia refuses to accept as controlling the language of what privacy and personhood means in *Casey,* as restated in the *Lawrence* majority, for that would be engaging in *substantive* due process, which he deplores. That would require the Court to engage in a robust SCP that considers concepts of reliance, workability, and emerging awareness as legitimate considerations when evaluating the substance of individual rights. He refuses to accept the view that a rule of law can include a changing definition by the Supreme Court of what constitutes liberty under the Constitution:

> As far as its holding is concerned, *Casey* provided a less expansive right to abortion than did *Roe, which was already on the books when Bowers was decided*. And if the Court is referring not to the holding of *Casey*, but to the dictum of its famed sweet mystery of life passage ("'At the heart of liberty is the right to define one's own concept of existence, of meaning, of the universe, and of the mystery of human life'"): That "casts some doubt" upon either the totality of our jurisprudence or else (presumably the right answer) nothing at all. I have never heard of a law that attempted to restrict one's "right to define" certain concepts; and if the passage calls into question the government's power to regulate *actions based* on one's self-defined "concept of existence, etc.," it is the passage that ate the rule of law.[74]

However, despite his claims to the contrary, Scalia does engage in a SCP, as do all originalists. Scalia engaged in a SCP when he approved the Court's invalidation of antimiscegenation laws in *Loving v. Virginia* (1965): "In *Loving*, however, we correctly applied heightened scrutiny, rather than the usual rational basis review, because the Virginia statute was 'designed to maintain White Supremacy.' A racially discriminatory purpose is always sufficient to subject a law to strict scrutiny, even a facially neutral law that makes no mention of race."[75] Thus, Scalia is willing to accept the social construction in *Loving* because, even though the Virginia law applied to people of all races, he was willing to view it as the subordination of African Americans to whites. In contrast to nonoriginalists on the *Lawrence* Court, Scalia argues that a SCP is not permissible with regard to laws against homosexual sodomy: "No purpose to discriminate against men or women as a class can be gleaned from the Texas law, so rational-basis review applies. That review is readily satisfied here by the same rational basis that satisfied it in *Bowers*—society's belief that certain forms of sexual behavior are 'immoral and unacceptable.'"[76]

Scalia's views on the difference between rejecting the constitutionality of antimiscegenation laws on the one hand, and accepting laws criminalizing acts when in engaged in by homosexuals, but not heterosexuals, suggest that, at some level, all cases pertaining to individual rights involve a SCP. It is the strict limitation that originalists place on the SCP that differentiates their jurisprudence from that of the nonoriginalists. Thus, the set of parameters as to the nature of the SCP, and its place in the Court's effort to define individual rights, is radically different for Scalia (and the originalists) as compared with nonoriginalists. This difference is the defining characteristic of the mature Rehnquist Court, and has become a defining fissure in contemporary American politics.

From this analysis of Scalia's rejection of the SCP, one can also gain a better understanding of why Scalia believes that nonoriginalist justices are simply responding to levels of political contestation, and why he believes they are inconsistent when doing so in *Casey* and *Lawrence*. In *Casey*, Scalia writes, "widespread criticism of *Roe* was strong reason to *reaffirm* it," but "today [in *Lawrence*], however, the widespread opposition to *Bowers* . . . is offered as a reason in favor of *overruling* it."[77] As explored above, majority and concurring justices in *Casey* and *Lawrence* do not rely on and strongly reject political contestation and majority public opinion as reasons on which to decide implied fundamental rights cases. When the *Casey* and *Lawrence* Courts engaged in the SCP, they considered whether the rights at issue in these cases, privacy and personhood, are still important and expanding and whether citizens have accepted these rights in their lives. Nonoriginalist justices accept the idea that because the Supreme Court is supposed to be a countermajoritarian institution, it should not make constitutional choices on the same bases as more directly political accountable institutions.

SCP and the Supreme Court in American Political Development

When the Supreme Court decides whether or not to overturn a landmark decision, as in *Casey* and *Lawrence*, a superb window into the SCP is provided. We saw that Supreme Court decision making involves the application of polity, or institutional, and rights principles. The SCP is the means through which the Court applies polity and rights principles, in light of the lived lives of citizens, as the complexity and the diversity of the nation's society, economy, and politics increase. Through a process of analogy, the Court considers whether a legal concept, such as liberty, should be extended to a group who heretofore had been denied such rights. We also witnessed robust debate between the originalists and nonoriginalists on the mature Rehnquist Court over the legitimacy of the SCP. We now shall explore the following core elements of the SCP: it is simultaneously empirical and normative, and inward and outward looking; the "interpretive turn" is the process through which the mutual construction process occurs; a special kind of legal objectivity, a "legal secularism," is inherent in the process; the process is cumulative; and the components of this process, including its objectivity, lead to the (relative) autonomy of the Supreme Court from political institutions, but not from the lived lives of citizens.

Empirical and Normative and Inward and Outward Looking

The SCP is both empirical and normative. It is empirical because justices engage in the application of legal concepts through a consideration of the lived lives of citizens and classes of citizens, both those who have and those who have not been granted constitutional protections in the past. Social constructs are informed by adduced social "facts," but they are not the social facts themselves.[78] Social facts gain meaning in constitutional law cases through the process of social construction; they gain resonance in light of definitions of polity and rights principles, social constructions in prior decisions, and the lived lives of citizens.[79]

The process is also normative. The empirical only gains meaning through application of core evaluative standards derived from what justice, liberty, and equality have meant in the past and present, with a concern for what rights and justice might mean in the future. This was demonstrated in *Casey* and *Lawrence*, when all justices engaged in a decision-making process that was simultaneously normative and empirical.

Supreme Court decision making has a second important quality: it is simultaneously internal ("inward looking") and external ("outward looking"). In the introduction to this volume, we noted that internal influences are such things as (1) the law itself (whether in the form of the Constitution, statutes, or settled legal doctrine in the form of precedent), and (2) judicial norms and procedures, including "the norm that judges be apolitical, a norm reinforced by the requirement that judges craft their legal rulings according to a 'legal grammar' in which some forms of argument (historical, textual, structural, prudential, and doctrinal) are considered legitimate and others (whim, personal policy preference) are not."[80]

Thus, the internal includes polity and rights principles, and the normative or evaluative standards in prior cases as to what constitutes privacy, personhood, liberty, or equal protection, as well as social constructions found in previous cases and institutional norms, such as what justices mean when they say that the Court is a legal institution that is guided by a rule of law. The "internal" might be thought of as the "law" (or the legal), when scholars mischaracterize Supreme Court decision making as "law" versus "politics," rather than conceptualizing it as a mutual construction process.

The process is also external or outward looking to social, political, institutional, cultural, historical, and intellectual forces. Here we focus in more direct terms on the lived lives of individuals and groups in the world outside the Court, as the Court engages in a mutual construction of the external with the internal. I note that the external also comes into the law as part of social constructions developed in prior cases, and the external is opened up again when the Court decides a case and engages in a new process of social construction.[81]

At the core of Supreme Court decision making is an "interpretive turn" in which the normative and empirical are mutually constructed through a consideration of the "internal" legal and "external" lived lives of citizens. The interpretive turn in the Supreme Court "locates the ground of (Court) objectivity as internal, rather than external to interpretation."[82] This means that the process produces an objectivity and separateness from the direct effect of either the internal legal or the external lived lives. This quality is distinctive of the Supreme Court, and is crucial to understanding its decision making and place in American political development. The mutual construction of the legal and empirical through the interpretive turn means that the process occurs through the simultaneous consideration of the normative and empirical, as applied within the contemporary social matrix.[83] The empirical is looked at through the prism of rights principles, notions of liberty and equality in the law. It centers on the Court's construction of the social, political, and economic world outside the Court, in light of rights and polity principles, precedent, and the social constructions that have been developed over the decades by prior Courts.

It is possible to identify social constructions in a case and line of cases and see which social constructions are accepted and rejected by the Court, as it engages in the SCP. Social constructions become clearer as case law develops within a doctrinal area. They become benchmarks in constitutional law, at times as important as polity and rights principles to the development of law. Because legal principles and social constructions gain clarity and depth as a line of cases develops, the first few cases in an emerging line of precedent may not yet have clear social constructions. For example, scholars wondered what the Supreme Court viewed as the rights violation when it invalidated an Idaho law that required state officials to select male family members over female to administer wills. The answer would only become clear in subsequent cases in which the Court considered possible levels of Court scrutiny of gender classifications through engaging in the SCP. With each new case, social constructions would further illuminate what gender discrimination means, and thus what constituted an equal protection violation.[84] As a line of cases develops, social constructions remain in place, are discussed and given more detailed filigree, and rights are given more clarity and depth; in rare times, as we saw above, the Court formally rejects social constructions developed over the decades. However, the development of rights usually is cumulative because there is a bridging process as rights are extended to classes of citizens who were previously excluded from Court protection as social constructions are refined. One sees this bridging process at work with regard to concepts of liberty, privacy, and personhood in the first half of the twentieth century, culminating in *Lawrence*.[85]

Legal Secularism (Objectivity) and Court Autonomy

There are two primary effects of the SCP that increase the chances for bridging precedents with future rights. The first effect is an objectivity, or universalism, in the way the Court thinks about legal questions. The second effect is a (relative) autonomy of the Supreme Court from the direct influence of politics and more directly politically accountable institutions, such as the presidency and Congress. These effects constitute important differences between the Supreme Court and political institutions.

The importance of the objectivity of the legal process cannot be overemphasized. Here objectivity does not refer to the objectivity of facts. Supreme Court decision making is objective because the Court engages in an analogical process in deciding whether a right defined in prior cases should apply in the case before the Court. In defining what equal protection or liberty means, objectivity is gained because the Court is asked to compare behaviors, rather than evaluate how society views those behaviors. If it looks like a duck, walks like a duck, then it must be a duck. To decide what constitutes equal protection or liberty, to remain objective and autonomous, the Court must focus on actions, not actors; comparison with contexts of actions that have been protected in the past plays a principal role in determining whether previously unprotected groups should come under the umbrella of constitutional protection.

In *Lawrence*, the Court felt it had an obligation, not honored in *Bowers*, to consider whether homosexual sodomy is covered by the right of privacy and personhood, in comparison to how those rights have been socially constructed in the past. When this consideration of principles and precedents is undertaken, and the Court determines that the rights of privacy and personhood in the past have protected similar actions when engaged in by other classes of citizens, the SCP points the Court to the conclusion that a constitutional injustice will be done if rights are not extended to the new group. It would deny a basic notion of fairness to decide otherwise; in such situations, the Court is prone to decide that government cannot criminalize citizens and groups for conduct that, when engaged in by others, is protected under the Constitution.

This process, which produces a legal secularism, is a defining characteristic of the Supreme Court, and most legal institutions, and of the rule of law itself. We see legal objectivity in *Roe* when the Court respects the differences among and between the religious and nonreligious as to their views about when life begins. We see it in *Lawrence* as well, when the Court considers whether it is appropriate for the Supreme Court to decide questions of rights on the basis of a society's Judeo-Christian values, and castigates former Chief Justice Warren Burger for his concurrence in *Bowers*, which justified the constitutionality of antihomosexual sodomy laws on the premise that sodomy violated Judeo-Christian values.[86] Deciding *Bowers* on such a consideration disregarded basic (nonoriginalist) institutional norms as to how individual rights are determined. As the *Lawrence* Court illustrates, it is not legitimate for the Supreme Court to decide questions of individual rights in general, and gay rights in particular, either on the premise that homosexual sodomy is a violation of Judeo-Christian values or on the basis that state legislatures, or the people themselves, think certain conduct is simply immoral; such decisions must be made after the Court *first* engages in the SCP.

The elements of Supreme Court decision making that result in legal objectivity help explain why justices do not see their role, and that of the Court, as one of responding to public opinion, the will of the majority, or levels of political contestation.[87] Through engaging in its process of mutual construction of the internal and external, the Court determines whether individual rights are to be protected. That is why in *Lawrence*, after discussing substantive rights questions and its rules for when to overturn landmark cases as outlined in *Casey*, it castigates the *Bowers* Court for allowing government to ban homosexual sodomy simply because the majority thinks such acts are immoral. This is not the way courts are supposed to decide whether a law violates the Constitution.

Many qualities of the Supreme Court make it a legal institution. I have emphasized the objectivity of its decision making, and its interpretive turn, with a mutual construction process that is simultaneously normative and empirical, and inward and outward looking. There are additional factors that make the Court (relatively) autonomous of politics, including its mandate to protect individuals from the tyranny of the state and the majority. This key institutional norm of autonomy is central to the Court's refusal to highly value and thus reflect in its decision making the direct effects of legal and political advocacy, other majoritarian pressures such as public opinion, high levels of political contestation, and pressures from more directly politically accountable institutions, such as Congress, the presidency, and the states.[88]

Originalists and Nonoriginalists

In the framework of a mutual construction process with a robust SCP, disagreements between originalists and nonoriginalists regarding how the Constitution should be interpreted become clearer. In this context, we can explain the response by Justice Scalia to the substance of *Casey* and its rules or conditions under which the Supreme Court may overturn landmark decisions. We also can better understand Justice Scalia's opposition to the acceptance of these conditions in both the *Lawrence* majority opinion and his even more heated response to Justice O'Connor's concurring decision. The doctrinal implications of her acceptance of a robust SCP with regard to future implied fundamental rights are what most concerned Justice Scalia. This also helps us understand why he viewed O'Connor as disingenuous when she argued that one should not fear that her invalidation of the Texas sodomy law on equal protection grounds might lead to a constitutional right to same-sex marriage. Scalia understands the implications of the Court's accepting a robust SCP, and he does not like them.

All justices, originalists and nonoriginalists alike, agree to follow precedent, consider polity and rights principles in making constitutional choices, and engage in analogical reasoning. All see themselves as dealing with the normative and empirical in ways that are special to courts. All see themselves as engaging in a process of interpretation. Both originalists and nonoriginalists acknowledge that Supreme Court decision making has normative and empirical elements, and that it is both inward and outward looking. Where they differ primarily pertains to what should be included in the process of social construction. The conflict between the originalists and nonoriginalists is over the relationship between the internal and external (and the normative and empirical). The outward-looking "empirical" of originalist justices may vary among them, but, for most, it is far more limited than for nonoriginalists. The "external" reference point for most originalists is the narrow time frame of founding periods. Originalists reject the permissibility of the external in Court decision making moving beyond the founding periods of the Constitution and its amendments. For Scalia, and most originalists, the manner in which privacy, personhood, and rights for gay men and lesbians have developed is not principled because the rights reflect the lived lives of citizens.

The use of concepts important to the nonoriginalists (and the SCP) such as reliance, workability, and emerging awareness to decide whether individual rights should be extended to new groups is viewed by Scalia as result-oriented jurisprudence, which is thus a violation of his vision of a rule of law. To consider the lived lives of citizens through a robust SCP is for justices to make decisions on the basis of policies they desire. The empirical for originalists is much more bounded. To make a decision that is based on implied fundamental rights is for the Court to be political and not legal. It is the Court engaging in cultural warfare over gay rights.[89] To consider the rights of gays in terms of looking at their lived lives, through the normative and empirical SCP, is also opposed by originalists because the normative bases of these rights come from implied fundamental rights that were established by an expansive notion of the empirical. The rights do not derive from the "original intent" of the Constitution—they are not tied directly to the words of the Constitution or its amendments. Therefore, Scalia refuses to accept the SCP and all rights based on that process, if that process moves beyond intentions derived from founding periods. Thus, *Roe*, *Casey*, *Romer*, and *Lawrence* are all illegitimate claims of "constitutional" law.

With each interpretive turn and SCP, the normative or evaluative support for the right increases, and on and on, as more filigreed notions of liberty, in the form of privacy, and then personhood develop in the law. As the normative and empirical elements of the SCPs build on each other, the rights, which they believe are built on improper theories of interpretation, are viewed as even more invalid by originalists. One can understand when Scalia says he has nothing against homosexuals in *Lawrence*, because he views his opposition to gay rights as not built on his attitudes, or his policy views about gays; it is built on a different vision of what constitutes proper Court decision making, and a robust SCP is viewed as an illegitimate form of decision making. In addition, the level of autonomy for the Court from political institutions, which results from the "objectivity" of the

SCP, is also viewed as illegitimate by originalists. These differences suggest that the central fissure on the mature Rehnquist Court, with regard to implied fundamental rights, was not between conservative, moderate, and liberal nonoriginalists, all of whom accept a robust SCP, but rather it was between originalist and nonoriginalist justices.

Many scholars argue that all justices, originalists as well as nonoriginalists, engage in the interpretive turn through a process of construction, and one is not more objective than the other in terms of the bases on which they make constitutional choices.[90] They are correct. However, the attack by the originalists on a core element of the nonoriginalist decision making, the SCP's application of principles to the lived lives of citizens, is tantamount to a rejection of the validity and legitimacy of the process itself, and thus of much of constitutional law.

Expanding Abortion and Gay Rights in a Conservative Political Age

Understanding the key components of nonoriginalist Supreme Court decision making helps explain why a conservative Court in a conservative age chooses to expand the rights to abortion choice and privacy and personhood for gay men and lesbians. It helps to explain why moderates and conservatives on the mature Rehnquist Court, such as Justices O'Connor, Kennedy, and Souter, and not simply liberal justices such as Stevens, Breyer, and Ginsburg, chose to solidify the right of abortion choice in *Casey*, and the rights of homosexuals in *Romer* and *Lawrence*. We also can get a better sense of why the Court overturned *Bowers*. *Bowers* rejected all the elements of the SCP. In so doing, it failed to have the legal objectivity that was present in *Roe*, continued in *Casey* and *Romer*, and was reaffirmed in *Lawrence*. Moreover, for the mature Rehnquist Court to overturn *Roe* and not overturn *Bowers*, it would have denied the important institutional value of Court autonomy from politics, a value that is fostered by the components of the SCP. Failing to overturn *Bowers* would prevent the Supreme Court from honoring rights principles and social constructions in cases decided prior to *Bowers*, and subsequent landmark cases such as *Casey* and *Romer*. It would force the Supreme Court to violate core elements of what the nonoriginalists believe to be the rule of law, the most important of which is the SCP, as outlined in *Casey*; it would also require the Court to disregard substantive visions of privacy, liberty, personhood, and equality, which also are informed by engaging in the SCP over the decades.

Thus, understanding the core elements of nonoriginalist Supreme Court decision making can help in understanding why a conservative court in a conservative political era can expand implied fundamental rights even as the political winds are going in exactly the opposite direction. It suggests there are important differences between legal and political decision making that conservatives, moderates, and liberals on the Court respect, and actively support. Originalists support these very same key differences between courts and political bodies—court autonomy and the interpretive turn. However, where they differ is in the defining of the components of the SCP.

SCP and American Politics

Social constructions become "pictures in precedents" of the rights principles of liberty, privacy, and personhood. As these pictures grow, new groups are viewed as possible candidates for protection under them. These core elements of objectivity and autonomy represent an invitation, a hope, to groups not currently afforded equal protection of law—that they also might partake in the protection of basic rights like liberty, privacy, and personhood. When these new groups step up to bat, they argue in court that they also deserve protection, and the mutual construction process, which links the normative and the empirical, makes it increasingly more difficult for courts to say no. The rights development process gains a persona of its own on the Supreme Court, in the legal-interpretive community of law professors and social scientists, and in the wider interpretive community of legal advocacy groups, journalists, bloggers, and the informed public. With such hopes, there continues to be an important role for legal advocacy groups and members of the wider interpretive community in American political development.[91]

However, the heated debate that abounds today over the place of the Supreme Court in our system of governance is caused in part by the effects of its objectivity and autonomy. Controversy is greatest as the Court engages in a SCP that applies principles, such as privacy and personhood, to groups in the society that do not have such rights. The objectivity of nonoriginalist decision making and the institutional norms of the SCP that lead to judicial autonomy from pressures of majoritarian politics infuriate the religious right and other cultural conservatives. The exercise of this legal secularism becomes politically charged and controversial especially when it brings new minority groups under the protection of law. This objectivism may not be understood, or appreciated, by the wider public and the politicians they elect. It is an anathema to citizens and groups who hold strong moral positions as to what constitutes proper behaviors and lifestyles, and seek government support of them. For these citizens, the Court's mandate to be legally objective appears as a legal secularism that does not respect *their* moral and ethical values, that is, their sectarianism.

One can ask: Why should views and votes of the people of Texas on questions of gay rights and the right to abortion choice be trumped by the Supreme Court?[92] One response is that its decision-making process, institutional norms, and place in American political development call on the Supreme Court to decide questions of individual rights, and do so in ways peculiar to it as a legal, not political, institution. The SCP, interpretive turn, consideration of internal-legal and external-social factors at the level of lived rights of citizens, and cumulative nature of the comparison of principles and past social constructions through a process of analogy led the Court to the *Casey* and *Lawrence* decisions—that is, to landmark decisions that are at loggerheads with the majority coalition.

Most importantly, the legitimacy of an expansive SCP and the nature of its components is not simply the defining fissure within the mature Rehnquist Court; it has become a core conflict within the interpretive community, and, more generally, within contemporary American politics. This was evident in 2005, as the Senate considered "nuclear options" to get rid of long-standing institutional rules that require sixty votes, rather than a simple majority, to close debate, and thus to stop a filibuster, on questions of appointment to federal courts. It was also evident in the Senate's consideration of President George W. Bush's nominee, Judge John Roberts, to replace Chief Justice Rehnquist on the Supreme Court, and the battle over Judge Samuel Alito to replace Justice O'Connor. In both instances, questions centered on whether they would honor precedents.

The key issue in this debate is whether a SCP is to occur in the future. The question debated today is not whether a conservative, moderate, or liberal will be appointed to the Court, but rather whether the nominee will be a nonoriginalist or originalist. Criticism from cultural conservatives now focuses on Justices Kennedy and O'Connor, not because they are liberal; they are not. Rather, they are criticized for the *Casey* and *Lawrence* decisions and their view of Court role. They are criticized because they accept the components of a Court decision making whose rules allow the continuation of implied fundamental rights of privacy and personhood, and their application to gay men and lesbians. The central question has become whether appointees will honor precedents that use the main components of that process and, most importantly, engage in the SCP in the future, with the possible result that implied fundamental rights will be expanded, as they were in the past, in *Casey*, *Romer*, and *Lawrence*.

In such a setting, the role of the SCP in Court decision making is closely linked to the place of the Supreme Court in American political development. There has been a feedback effect from conflicts over the SCP on the Court to more general American politics. This suggests that the bidirectionality between the internal Court and the world outside occurs at several levels, at the level of the lived lives of citizens, as the Court makes decisions about rights of privacy and personhood, and at the level of politics itself. However, institutional norms lead the Court to reject the politics from outside the Court to the Court, even as the opposition to the core elements of the SCP grows outside the Court.

Externalist Explanations Are Wanting

The unique qualities of this dual mutual construction process and the Supreme Court's autonomy from the direct effects of other political institutions have important ramifications for how we study the Supreme Court as an actor in American political development and the politics that surround the Court. In "system" terms, the unique qualities of the mutual construction process inform the boundary conditions of the Supreme Court. To view Supreme Court decision making as primarily internal or narrowly legalist is to proceed according to a faulty assumption—that the process is simply about rights as norms mechanically applied. However, few scholars today view Supreme Court decision making in such narrow legalist terms.

The greater problem in contemporary scholarship is not a belief in legalism, but the notion that Supreme Court decision making can be explained only by factors external to the Court. Externalist historical and "revolution" theorists have tried to make a link directly between specific historical events, such as a critical election or the "growth of the administrative state," and Court decision making—with no great success.[93] Externalists focusing on the agreement in policy terms between justices and the presidents who appointed them, election returns, and majority coalitions in power at a specific time, have fared little better. Studying the components of Supreme Court decision making, particularly the SCP, can help us understand the explanatory limitations of relying on externalist approaches to explain the place of the Supreme Court in American political development. This is because all externalist approaches are built on expectations of correlations of Court action with factors outside the Court, whether they are public opinion, international events such as the embarrassment during the cold war with the denial of equal rights to African Americans,[94] critical elections,[95] or the policy view of presidents and those they appoint to the Court.[96] Correlations do not explain Court actions. They are one dimensional; they only explore the external, and do not link them to the internal-legal. We have seen that external social, economic, and political facts do not come directly into judicial decision making. There is a process of mutual construction of the internal-legal and external that has a significant effect on doctrinal change and the place of the Court in American political development.

The problem with pure externalist scholarship is that it rejects the importance of the interpretive turn through which the internal-legal and external world are mutually constructed. Because of this, the explanation of Court decisions is not reducible to its normative or empirical elements. Because Supreme Court decision making is at the same time normative and empirical, and the two are intermingled through the interpretive turn, the study of Supreme Court decision making cannot successfully be isolated methodologically into an analysis of only the legal, or the empirical. Defining the nature of implied fundamental rights required the Court to apply the law and consider precedent based on lived lives of citizens—and this could not take place by the Court relying only on the law or on the lived lives alone.

Mark Graber demonstrates that the separation of the analysis of Supreme Court decision making into the legal, institutional-strategic, and attitudinal cannot adequately explain the reasons for doctrinal change. He finds that there is an intermingling of the legal, strategic, and attitudinal in Supreme Court decision making:

> Legal and strategic explanations both rely as much on interpretation as logic. Any finite series of decisions can be described without logical contradiction as good faith efforts to interpret the law or as sophisticated efforts to realize policy preferences . . . The extent to which any judicial decision was motivated by legal or strategic factors, at bottom, depends on contestable theories about what constitutes good legal and strategic practice.[97]

He concludes, "The most fruitful investigations will explore the ways in which legal, strategic, and attitudinal factors interact when justices make decisions, and not engage in fruitless contests to determine which single factor explains the most."[98]

The operation of the mutual construction process in implied fundamental rights cases provides additional evidence why the Supreme Court is not simply or primarily "strategic" in its decision making. In *Casey*, the Court provides a detailed explanation of the conditions under which landmark decisions are to be overturned, argues for a robust SCP, and specifically rejects political contestation and the votes of legislatures and the wider public as central to their determination of the implied fundamental rights. In *Romer*, the Court relies on the *Casey* conditions, and its support of a robust SCP, to find unconstitutional an Amendment to the Colorado Constitution that would deny gays the use of regular legislative, executive, and state court means to protect their rights. Finally, in *Lawrence*, the Court reaffirms *Casey*'s conditions for overturning landmark decisions, and engages in a SCP that results not simply in overturning *Bowers* on minimalist equal protection grounds, but makes a quite expansive decision extending rights of personhood and liberty to gays, one that does not preclude the Court from deciding that gays have a right to same-sex civil unions under the Constitution.

If the Supreme Court chose to be strategic with regard to its institutional needs, in *Casey* and *Lawrence*, it would be far more concerned about the political reactions by Congress, the states, and the people. Strategic factors, as explanations for Court action in *Casey* and *Lawrence*, are submerged because justices accept institutional norms that ask them to consider substantive constitutional questions as to what constitutes privacy, personhood, and liberty through the mutual construction process as described above. The Court does not focus on its strategic institutional interests; it engages in the process to decide whether rights have been violated by government, in comparison to what rights have been protected in the past.

This does not mean that justices never think strategically. Rather, they rarely think in solely strategic terms. There are indications of strategic considerations in *Casey* and *Lawrence*. This seems particularly so in O'Connor's concurrence in *Casey*, where she specifically decides to leave for another day the question of the constitutionality of laws that outlaw sodomy for both heterosexuals and homosexuals, trusting that state legislatures will not pursue such laws given the *Lawrence* decision. As much as one might want to argue that O'Connor is thinking strategically when she chooses not to overturn *Bowers* or invoke due process principles as the basis for her decision, it would be unwise to interpret her concurring opinion as primarily or simply strategic. If strategic institutional concerns of the Court with regard to political reaction to a decision on gay rights were central to her thinking, why did she engage in an expansive social construction of gay rights in her equal protection analysis?

Justice Scalia critiques O'Connor's position in *Lawrence* by arguing that O'Connor cannot have it both ways. She can't set up a social construction of rights that limits government from being able to say simply that a state's belief that homosexual sodomy is immoral is permissible (even under the rational basis, or minimal scrutiny test), and then argue that the very same SCP cannot lead to increased homosexual rights, even, perhaps, the right to marry. Scalia is arguing that the dynamics of the SCP as described in *Casey*, continued in *Romer*, and reaffirmed in *Lawrence*, are present in her non-originalist concurrence; that to accept her concurrence has left the fox in the chicken coop with regard to future increases in implied fundamental rights, including the rights of gay men and lesbians.

One could say that O'Connor chose to respect institutional concerns by not overturning *Bowers* and by using an equal protection basis to simply invalidate the Texas antisodomy law. However, even if one concludes this, and there is talk of trusting legislatures to do the right thing in O'Connor's concurrence, the nature of O'Connor's definition of the rights involved, and her respect for the SCP outlined in *Casey*, continue to be important to the future of implied fundamental rights. Rarely are cases only about strategic-institutional concerns, even, as Graber has demonstrated, in times when presidents are brought to the Court for abuses of power during times of war.

All political signals indicated that maximalist decisions in *Casey*, *Romer*, and *Lawrence* would trigger negative political reactions, and they did. If the Court simply had strategic concerns, it is difficult to understand why the Court in both *Casey* and *Lawrence* specifically rejected the importance of the presence of controversy and growing political contestation and controversy over abortion choice and gay rights, at a time when a center-piece of the governing majority, and the administration that it elected, was its opposition to the right of abortion choice and expanded gay rights.

Attitudinalism, an approach that seeks to explain Supreme Court decision making on the basis of the attitudes that justices have toward government policies, most clearly demonstrates the problem with simply externalist analyses of Supreme Court decision making.[99] Attitudinalism is far more questionable than legal and strategic explanations for Court action. This is because of the importance of institutional norms and processes on the Supreme Court, which severely restrict justices from making decisions on attitudinal grounds.[100] The presence of constituting institutional norms and practices means that Supreme Court rulings have objectivity and are independent of individual subjective policy opinions held by each participant in a majority opinion.[101] The collective nature of decision making acts as a constraint on individual preferences. Preexisting institutional norms and expectations of behavior limit the effect of a priori policy choices on judicial decision making. Because of this, Supreme Court decision making is not reducible to the sum total of individual private preferences of justices, in contrast to what the attitudinalists argue. Because of the dual mutual construction process (normative and empirical and internal and external), the act of decision making is also not reducible to historical and political events external to the Court.

Social Constructions, "Legal" Time, and Path Dependence

The presence of the SCP in Supreme Court decision making raises important questions about the place of the Supreme Court in American political development that cannot be addressed through a consideration of whether the Supreme Court is legal, strategic, or attitudinal in its decision making. Because the nonoriginalist SCP results in an objectivity in the definition of questions of individual rights and Court autonomy from politics, we need to consider their impact on the trajectory of the path of the law, and, most importantly, on the place of the Supreme Court in American political development. Moreover, basic constitutional principles, such as separation of powers, and the contemporary premise that the Court is the final arbiter of the Constitution, as evidenced by the lack of a sustained reaction against the Court as an institution after Bush v. Gore (2000), suggest that the Supreme Court may view its boundary conditions with other governmental institutions and the American people in quite different ways than nonlegal institutions.

When one looks at which landmark cases were overturned by the Supreme Court, and the reasons offered by the mature Rehnquist Court as to when it is proper to overturn them, we witness a general phenomenon. When the social construction(s) of the social, economic, and political world outside the Court that have been supporting an individual right or statement of government power in a landmark decision are so out of kilter with the world outside the Court, the landmark decision is likely to be overturned by the Supreme Court. This was true in the Court's overturning of Plessy, Adkins, and Bowers, and its decision not to overturn Roe.

What determines whether a landmark decision and an individual right, or the lack of one, is out of kilter? There is evidence that the legal-interpretive community of law professors and social scientists are important to influencing Supreme Court visions of the world outside the Court. The legal-interpretive community straddles both the internal and external of the Court, and additional evidence to this effect will be presented in subsequent chapters.

The analysis of why the Supreme Court overturned *Plessy v. Ferguson* (1896), *Lochner v. New York* (1905), and *Bowers v. Hardwick* (1986), but not *Roe v. Wade* (1973), and the centrality of the SCP in decisions by the Court whether to overturn a specific case, also raise important questions about the ability of increasing returns path dependence to explain doctrinal change and the place of the Supreme Court in American political development.[102] At the core of increasing returns path dependence is the notion that political institutions tend to stay on the same path and become dependent on that path because of the institutional costs and other difficulties of shifting to a new path. Those institutions that are first out of the gate have a strong incentive to focus on a single direction and to continue down a specific path once initial steps are taken in that direction. These dynamics are particularly important in politics because of the central role of collective action, the high density of institutions, the possibilities for using political authority to magnify power asymmetries, and the intrinsic complexity and opacity of political life.[103] However, some of the features found intrinsic to political institutions that result in increasing returns path dependence may not be intrinsic to the Supreme Court. These include the prominence of collective action problems, the prospects for the use of political authority to amplify asymmetries of power, short time frames of political actors, and the strong status quo bias associated with decision rules.

The Supreme Court may not be as change resistant as political institutions, and as change resistant as is assumed by Pierson's concept of path dependence, which is based on increasing returns. There may be fewer start-up costs for courts to develop new social understandings than in political institutions, in part because the SCP is continuous, and brings new understandings of the world outside the Court into Supreme Court decision making, as it decides cases.[104] Moreover, the Supreme Court has a mechanism to change the direction of the law when principles and social constructions of them become anachronistic: it can overturn landmark cases. The Court can distinguish prior decisions and reinterpret what the underlying social facts mean if the rights at issue are not so out of kilter with the world outside the Court. Thus, there are many reasons that there are far fewer costs for justices to reject a path-dependent strategy of increasing returns. This may sound ironic to those who view stare decisis as if it were a narrowly legalistic, mechanical process, but it is true.[105] The autonomy, universalism, and objectivity of the SCP results in the Supreme Court feeling less threatened by outside pressures than more directly accountable political institutions. The Supreme Court is the institution with the primary and final authority to arbitrate, circumscribe, and legitimate acts of state institutions through its power to establish "legally binding rules."

The basic constitutional theories of the "rule of law" over government, and constitutional law as a means to limit the abuse of government power, provide the Supreme Court with incentives to question the action of political institutions, rather than accept them. This gives the Supreme Court fewer incentives than political institutions to seek equilibrium with institutions at its boundaries. The Supreme Court, moreover, is subject to fewer "switching costs" for changing paths because it tends to hear cases and issues over which lower courts and society are in conflict; institutions outside the Court are not sure what the law is or what the Constitution requires, and in many cases are demanding an answer, in order to secure stability. Settled expectations may be needed by path dependent political institutions; however the Supreme Court engages in constitutive decision making and the mutual construction process to provide such answers. In other words, cases are not heard unless "reversals of course" or a change in the path of the law is a real possibility. The hypothetical alternatives, of changing paths, which political institutions are supposed to abhor under increasing returns path dependence, constitute the regular business of the Supreme Court. Although the "cost of exit" from paths for political institutions is high, the cost of exit and change for the Supreme Court is not as great.

For example, in the Court's considerations of the constitutionality of principles at the core of the *Plessy* and *Lochner* decisions, in order for the Court to avoid overturning those cases, it would have had it to continue constructions of the social, economic, and political world outside the Court that were no longer valid. As stated in the *Casey* joint opinion, if it had not overturned these landmark decisions, the Court would have had to accept social constructions that were locked in 1896 and 1905; these and the rights to which they were associated no longer had meaning and were hurting the legitimacy of the Court. Moreover, not to overturn *Plessy* and *Lochner* would have undermined the legitimacy of not only the Court, but of the rule of law. The rule of law gets its moral support, at least in part, from having the Constitution engage in what Lessig calls "translation with fidelity." The normal path of the law is incremental change although students of the law tend not to appreciate this because they study landmark cases, as they concentrate on doctrine.[106]

Ironically, externalist social scientists fail to emphasize the incremental yet constant nature of change in the law because they center their analysis only on landmark cases, asking whether they can be explained by specific historical events, rather than looking at the evolution of doctrine over the decades. Landmark cases, whether they overturn prior cases or not, tend to be a product of a long-term process during which rights principles and their supporting social, economic, and political constructions have been under attack.

The Difference between Legal Time and Political Time

The place of the SCP in Supreme Court decision making that results in the Supreme Court having more autonomy from governmental institutions, and the fact that the Supreme Court may be less subject to increasing returns path dependence, provides evidence for the position that the "legal" time of the Supreme Court may be quite different from the "political" time of more directly politically accountable institutions, such as the presidency, Congress, and states.

Stephen Skowronek argues that throughout the history of our nation, there has been "a waning of political time" in which each president can meet his commitments, in part as a result of the "thickening" of political institutions. Ever-increasing expectations of political change through presidential action are met with less time in which to meet such demands— even though resources of the office of the president have increased through the decades. This problem is most evident in presidents elected in periods of reconstructive politics. Presidents Lincoln, Roosevelt, and Reagan each had shorter time periods to carry out programs of reconstruction.[107]

The universalism and objectivity of the SCP, basic norms of what the rule of law means, and the place of the Supreme Court today as the final arbiter of the Constitution lead to a far greater autonomy of the Supreme Court from other governmental institutions than is found in the presidency, making the Supreme Court less subject to the sort of thickening that Skowronek describes in political institutions. The processes of increasing returns are weaker on the Court, and the Court's autonomy means that, to a large extent, the "reconstruction" of the law is in the hands of the Court. It is usually the end point of incremental moves in prior cases that pinpoint the anachronistic nature of the social constructions that supported prior individual rights, and thus the rights themselves. Thus, the Supreme Court is able to make constitutional choices in opposition to the primary commitments of the majority coalition, and the major political institutions that it may control, over a longer time frame than the president, who is more prone to the effects of the thickening of government with each passing decade.

Finally, I fear that the movement toward a general theory of American political development (as has been called for by the preeminent theorists of APD, Karen Orren and Stephen Skowronek) will be based on models of path dependence and institutional qualities found in political institutions. We cannot assume that the Supreme Court is subject to similar tendencies. When there is evidence of such assumptions, scholars of the Supreme Court have two choices: reject that theory, or make it more sensitive to the unique qualities of the Supreme Court, and courts in general. This chapter and the others in this volume are clearly dedicated to the second strategy.

Conclusion

The study of courts and law should be integrated into the study of American political development, but on terms that recognize the distinct relationship of the Supreme Court to its boundary conditions, as compared with the presidency, legislatures, and other political institutions that are more directly politically accountable. This will require scholars to rethink some general APD principles and concepts, such as increasing returns path dependence, as well as ideas and perspectives that may be dear to scholars of law and courts, such as the assumption that we can explain Supreme Court decision making as law versus politics.

In this chapter, I have concentrated on addressing implied fundamental rights with regard to the rights of privacy and personhood in matters of abortion choice and rights of gays and lesbians. If models of institutional expectations that are present in the theory of increasing returns path dependence are not found in these most controversial areas of public policy, then one would assume that these models of institutional expectation would be even less prevalent in less controversial and politically charged doctrinal areas. However, this hypothesis needs to be tested in other doctrinal areas and historical contexts.[108]

Notes

I thank Ken Kersch and Carol Nackenoff for their comments and criticisms. Research assistance was provided by Whitney Smith Pellegrino, Oberlin '99, and Sara Chatfield, Oberlin '06.

1. *Planned Parenthood of Southeastern Pennsylvania v. Casey*, 505 U.S. 833 (1992).

2. *Lawrence v. Texas*, 539 U.S. 558 (2003).

3. *Plessy v. Ferguson*, 156 U.S. 537 (1896).

4. *Adkins v. Children's Hospital of District of Columbia*, 261 U.S. 525 (1923).

5. *Bowers v. Hardwick*, 478 U.S. 186 (1986).

6. *Roe v. Wade*, 410 U.S. 113 (1973).

7. *Romer v. Evans*, 517 U.S. 620 (1996).

8. See Ronald Kahn, *The Supreme Court and Constitutional Theory, 1953–1993* (Lawrence: University Press of Kansas, 1994), 257–258; and Ronald Kahn, "Institutional Norms and Supreme Court Decision-making: The Rehnquist Court on Privacy and Religion," in *Supreme Court Decision-making: New Institutionalist Approaches*, ed. Cornell Clayton and Howard Gillman (Chicago: University of Chicago Press, 1999), 175–198, for details of the Court moving from a privacy to a personhood basis for the right of abortion choice. See Mark Graber, "The Clintonification of American Law: Abortion, Welfare, and Liberal Constitutional Theory," *Ohio State Law Journal* 58 (1997): 731–818, for the argument that abortion rights have such a staying power over rights of basic welfare because of the intellectual proclivities of liberal constitutional theorists and law professors.

9. See Stephen Skowronek, *The Politics Presidents Make: Leadership from John Adams to Bill Clinton* (Cambridge, Mass.: Harvard University Press, 1997), part 3, "The Waning of Political Time," 407–464, for discussion of the term *political time* and its application.

10. See Paul Pierson, "Increasing Returns, Path Dependence, and the Study of Politics," *American Political Science Review* 94 (June 2000): 251–267; and Paul Pierson, *Politics in Time: History, Institutions, and Social Analysis* (Princeton, N.J.: Princeton University Press, 2004), chap. 1.

11. *West Coast Hotel Co. v. Parrish*, 300 U.S. 379 (1937).

12. *Brown v. Board of Education*, 347 U.S. 483 (1954).

13. *Planned Parenthood of Southeastern Pennsylvania v. Casey*, 505 U.S. 833, 862 (1992).

14. Ibid., at 861–862. See Ken I. Kersch, *Constructing Civil Liberties: Discontinuities in the Development of American Constitutional Law* (New York: Cambridge University Press, 2004), for an analysis of the Supreme Court constructing rights in the *Lochner* era. See also Cass Sunstein, *The Partial Constitution* (Cambridge, Mass.: Harvard University Press, 1993), for the argument that the Court's treating of social facts in the outside world as neutral, rather than as created by government and questioning them, was a defining quality of the *Lochner*-era Court; moreover, Sunstein argues that the Supreme Court, in deciding cases, and constitutional scholars, in creating constitutional theory, should not see the outside world as "neutral." For a discussion of social constructions in what Lessig describes as the "process of translation" in Supreme Court decision making, see Lawrence Lessig, "The Regulation of Social Meaning," *University of Chicago Law Review* 62 (1995): 943–1045; and Lawrence Lessig, "Understanding Changed Readings: Fidelity and Theory," *Stanford Law Review* 47 (February 1995): 395–472.

15. *Planned Parenthood of Southeastern Pennsylvania v. Casey*, 505 U.S. 833, 862–863 (1992).

16. Ibid. at 863.

17. Ibid. at 863–864. See Lawrence Lessig, "Understanding Changed Readings," 424, for the reason why such constructions of the world outside the Court existed at the time of *Plessy*. He argues that changed readings in law relate to or are informed by changed discourses outside the law—in this case, science. He writes, "At the time *Plessy* was decided, science supported the racist status quo. Science, for example, told judges that interracial sex produces degenerate children—certainly one of the more extreme perversions of science from the period."

18. *Planned Parenthood of Southeastern Pennsylvania v. Casey*, 505 U.S. 833, 863–864 (1992). Was this due to a change in Court personnel, or to changes in society outside the Court? Although obviously it is both, the evidence presented here on abortion choice and gay rights suggests that even on Courts with very similar personnel, the SCP produces new definitions of rights. There was a breakdown of the right of contract well before the "Constitutional Revolution of 1937," and a change in Court personnel. There was a rejection of the Court's failure to engage in the SCP in *Bowers* by a 6–3 vote in *Lawrence*, even though there was not a dramatic change in Court makeup between 1986 and 2003.

19. Ibid. at 864.

20. See Ronald Kahn, *The Supreme Court and Constitutional Theory, 1953–1993* (Lawrence: University Press of Kansas, 1994), 257–258, and Kahn, "Institutional Norms," 175–198, for details of the Court moving from a privacy to a personhood basis for the right of abortion choice.

21. Many times there are Supreme Court decisions that signal the possibility of a landmark case being overturned, such as cases involving segregation in higher education before *Brown*. Also, in many *Lochner*-era cases, the right of contract and liberty under the due process clauses did not trump the police powers of government. See Kahn, "Institutional Norms," 50–59, for the place of the SCP in death penalty cases—one that has resulted in recent years in Supreme Court cases that reduce the instances in which the death penalty is permitted. Perhaps the Court will reconsider its failure to socially construct a relationship between government institutions, race, and the death penalty in *McCleskey v. Kemp* 481 U.S. 279 (1987). This is a case ripe for modification or even overturning.

22. *Planned Parenthood of Southeastern Pennsylvania v. Casey*, 505 U.S. 833, 864–865 (1992).

23. Ibid. at 865.

24. Ibid. at 861.

25. Ibid. at 866–867.

26. Ibid. at 867.

27. Ibid. at 865–866.

28. Ibid. at 869.

29. See J. David Greenstone, "Against Simplicity: The Cultural Dimensions of the Constitution," *University of Chicago Law Review* 55 (1988): 428–449, on the place of republican, reformed liberal, and humanist liberal strands of American political culture in theories of constitutional interpretation; see Ronald Kahn, "Liberalism, Political Culture, and the Rights of Subordinated Groups: Constitutional Theory and Practice at a Crossroads," in *The Liberal Tradition in American Politics: Reassessing the Legacy of American Liberalism*, eds. David F. Ericson and Louisa Bertch Green (New York: Routledge, 1999), 254–259, for how the conflicts among these strands of American political culture play themselves out through the Court's engaging in the SCP. The presence of conflicts among strands of American political culture is not only on the Court; they are also found in the interpretive community, among legal advocates, and in the wider polity, which supports the Court as a transformative venue in American political development.

30. *Planned Parenthood of Southeastern Pennsylvania v. Casey*, 505 U.S. 833, 869 (1992).

31. Ibid. at 866.

32. For two recent statements of how the Supreme Court helps make the nation more democratic, see Larry D. Kramer, *The People Themselves: Popular Constitutionalism and Judicial Review* (New York: Oxford University Press, 2004); and Christopher L. Eisgruber, *Constitutional Self-government* (Cambridge, Mass.: Harvard University Press, 2001). The SCP supports this role of the Supreme Court.

33. *Lawrence v. Texas*, 539 U.S. 558, 564–567 (2003).

34. See *Black's Law Dictionary*, 5th ed. (St. Paul, Minn.: West Publishing, 1979), 1261; here, *stare decisis* is defined as the "policy of courts to stand by precedent and not to disturb settled point." One can see the importance of the SCP as part of stare decisis, when the definition continues, "Doctrine that, when court has once laid down a principle of law as applicable to a certain state of facts, it will adhere to that principle, and apply it to all future cases, where facts are substantially the same; regardless of whether the parties and property are the same." The entry later notes, "there are occasions when departure [from stare decisis] is rendered necessary to vindicate plain obvious principles of law and remedy continued injustice." Exploration into the nature of the SCP with regard to implied fundamental rights of privacy and personhood suggests that we should not think of the term as based on a flat, legalistic notion of following the logic of the law.

35. *Griswold v. Connecticut*, 381 U.S. 479 (1965).

36. *Eisenstadt v. Baird*, 405 U.S. 438 (1972).

37. *Roe v. Wade*, 410 U.S. 113 (1973).

38. *Lawrence v. Texas*, 539 U.S. 558, 567 (2003).

39. *Planned Parenthood of Southeastern Pennsylvania v. Casey*, 505 U.S. 833 (1992).

40. *Romer v. Evans*, 517 U.S. 620 (1996).

41. *Lawrence v. Texas*, 539 U.S. 558, 573 (2003).

42. Ibid. at 576. The Court here refers to criticism in the interpretive community, drawing on work by Charles Fried and Richard Posner. Moreover, the courts of five

states have declined to follow *Bowers* in interpreting provisions in their own state con-stitutions parallel to the due process clause of the Fourteenth Amendment. In *Bowers*, one cannot see the level of settled expectations in the interpretive community and among jurists that the principles about privacy and personhood present before and after *Bowers* are sufficient to sustain its constitutional validity.

43. Ibid. at 574 (quoting *Casey*, 505 U.S. 833, 851).

44. Ibid. at 574 (quoting *Romer*, 517 U.S. 620, 624).

45. Ibid. (quoting *Romer*, 517 U.S. 620, 634).

46. Ibid.

47. Ibid. at 571 (quoting *Casey*, 505 U.S. 833, 850).

48. Ibid.

49. Ibid. at 572 (quoting *County of Sacramento v. Lewis*, 523 U.S. 833 at 857 (1998), Kennedy, J. [concurring]).

50. Ibid. at 577.

51. Ibid. at 578–579.

52. Ibid. at 575.

53. Ibid. at 581 (O'Connor concurring opinion).

54. Ibid. at 583 (O'Connor concurrence quoting Kennedy decision *Ante* at 575).

55. Ibid.

56. *Plyler v. Doe*, 457 U.S. 202 (1982).

57. *Lawrence v. Texas* 539 U.S. 558, 584 (2003).

58. Ibid.

59. Ibid. at 583 (quoting *Romer* 517 U.S. 620, 633).

60. Ibid. at 580. The phrase "the challenged legislation inhibits personal relation-ships" implies that Justice O'Connor, like the *Lawrence* majority, is concerned about the due process liberty interests of homosexuals.

61. Ibid. at 575. Scholars disagree on this point; for classic scholarly arguments about whether to rest rights of same-sex intimacy and marriage on equal protection or due process grounds, see Andrew Koppelman, *The Gay Rights Question in Contemporary American Law* (Chicago: University of Chicago Press, 2002); Evan Gerstmann, *The Constitutional Underclass: Gays, Lesbians, and the Failure of Class-based Equal Protection* (Chicago: University of Chicago Press, 1999); and Jean L. Cohen, *Regulating Intimacy: A New Legal Paradigm* (Princeton, N.J.: Princeton University Press, 2002).

62. *Lawrence v. Texas*, 539 U.S. 558, 584–585 (2003). This approach is very similar to that of the four members of the Court in *Frontiero v. Richardson* 411 U.S. 677, 692 (1973) (Powell, J. concurring), saying that they will wait to see whether the Equal Rights Amendment passes or not, to set the standard of scrutiny under the Equal Protection Clause for gender classifications. O'Connor will trust that the majoritarian pressures in the political system will do away with antisodomy laws aimed at both heterosexuals and homosexuals.

63. O'Connor is not minimalist in her analysis of the substantive rights at issue in *Lawrence*. She is a minimalist only in her conclusion to base this decision on the equal

protection rather than due process grounds. That is, O'Connor is engaged in a SCP that does not shy away from criticizing key substantive elements of the *Bowers* decision, including its key premise that moral disapproval of gays by government is a rational basis for denying rights.

64. The depth of O'Connor's social construction of rights at issue in the antisodomy law raises questions about the argument that we can view O'Connor simply as a centrist justice because of her views about judicial role, as lucidly explored by Thomas M. Keck, *The Most Activist Supreme Court in History* (Chicago: University of Chicago Press, 2004), 199–253. This view speaks only to minimalist outcomes, i.e., that O'Connor chose not to overturn *Bowers* and rested her argument on equal protection grounds. It does not speak to the effect and implications of her reasoning, including her social constructions, on future constitutional law.

65. *Lawrence v. Texas*, 539 U.S. 558, 601–602 (2003) (Scalia, J., dissenting).

66. *Romer v. Evans*, 517 U.S. 620, 620–644 (1996).

67. *Lawrence v. Texas*, 539 U.S. 558, 586–592 (2003) (Scalia, J., dissenting).

68. Ibid. at 593.

69. Ibid. at 604 (quoting Kennedy majority opinion at 578). For the argument that *Bowers* and *Romer* can't stand together, in *Romer*, as in *Lawrence*, Scalia sees the writing on the wall as to the implications for gay rights of the nonoriginalist justices' use of the SCP, see Scalia's dissent in *Romer v. Evans*, 517 U.S. 620, 640–644 (1996).

70. Ibid. at 604–605 (quoting Kennedy majority opinion at 574, 578, and 567).

71. Ibid. at 590.

72. Ibid. at 594.

73. Part of the opposition by Scalia and the other originalists on the Court to the *Casey* decision, and now to the *Lawrence* decision, is that the right to privacy itself is not found in the Constitution. For them, *Griswold*'s right of privacy was a misinterpretation of the Constitution, as was *Roe*. Therefore, the right of homosexual sodomy as part of the right of privacy is not a right protected in the Constitution. Any SCP that follows *Roe*, including the SCP outlined in *Casey*, is illegitimate. Originalists refuse to consider the effect on such rights of changes in the social, economic, and political world outside the Court since *Griswold* in 1965 and *Roe* in 1973. The attack by originalists on the nonoriginalist SCP takes quite direct forms. Scalia cannot rest his case against homosexual rights on the view that all rights not specifically stated in the Constitution cannot be fundamental rights. Thus, Scalia leaves the door ajar, conceptually, for the Court at times to define such implied fundamental rights when government is so abusive of its citizens.

74. *Lawrence v. Texas*, 539 U.S. 558, 588 (2003). In *Lawrence*, 539 U.S., at 595, Scalia admits *Roe v. Wade* (1973) recognized abortion of an unborn child as a "fundamental right" protected by the due process clause. However, he sees *Casey* as undermining this fundamental right because no longer "must regulations of abortion . . . be narrowly tailored to serve a compelling state interest." In so doing, Scalia rejects the nonoriginalists' expanded definition of personhood in *Casey*, the application of those

expanded rights in *Lawrence*, and any subsequent social constructions of rights that might follow these cases.

75. *Lawrence v. Texas*, 539 U.S. 558, 600 (2003).

76. Ibid. (quoting *Bowers*, 478 U.S. 186, 196 (1986)).

77. Ibid. at 587.

78. The analysis of the SCP is not centered simply or primarily on the question of whether the Supreme Court uses, misuses, or misinterprets social science data or social, economic, and political facts in a single case. Rosemary J. Erickson and Rita J. Simon, *The Use of Social Science Data in Supreme Court Decisions* (Urbana: University of Illinois Press, 1998), 149, finds that the Supreme Court gives far more weight to the decisions in prior cases or precedents, rather than the quality of the social science data used in precedents. Few citations are made to social science data when discussing precedents. This suggests that what are considered in later cases are not social facts or data, but rather the social constructions derived from the social facts. I would suspect that issues of the quality of data may be more central to other areas of law such as environmental law and torts, than to constitutional law.

79. See H. N. Hirsch, *A Theory of Liberty: The Constitution and Minorities* (New York: Routledge, 1992), chap. 4, "'The Most Willful Blindness': The Court and Social Facts," 115–193, for a lucid critique of the Supreme Court for disregarding social facts when defining liberty interests under the Constitution. Here I argue that it is through the SCP that the Court extends rights to groups previously unprotected.

80. See the Introduction to this book.

81. This is to be expected because Supreme Court decision making in the area of American constitutional law always has had significant common law roots, in which legal principles were applied in light of the economic, social, and political world outside the Court. See David A. Strauss, "Common Law Constitutional Interpretation," *University of Chicago Law Review* 63 (Summer 1996), 877–935. One can see it in *Marbury v. Madison* (1819); see Ronald Kahn, "*Marbury v. Madison* as a Model for Understanding Contemporary Judicial Review," in *Marbury versus Madison: Documents and Commentary*, ed. Mark Graber and Michael Perhac (Washington, D.C.: CQ Press, 2002), 155–180; and Edward H. Levi, *An Introduction to Legal Reasoning* (Chicago: University of Chicago Press, 1949).

82. See Dennis Goldford, *The American Constitution and the Debate over Originalism* (New York: Cambridge Press, 2005), 186.

83. See Ian Hacking, *The Social Construction of What?* (Cambridge, Mass.: Harvard University Press, 1999), 7–37, for the argument: "Ideas do not exist in a vacuum. They inhabit a social setting. Let us call that the *matrix* within which an idea, a concept or kind, is formed" (10). One can see this process at work when justices must determine whether a right has been violated.

84. For cases establishing the intermediate level of court scrutiny for gender classifications, in which a state must show the challenged gender classification serves "important governmental objectives and that the discriminatory means employed" are

"substantially related to the achievement of those objectives," see *Reed v. Reed*, 404 U.S. 71 (1971), *Frontiero v. Richardson*, 411 U.S. 677 (1973), culminating in *Craig v. Boren* 429 U.S. 190, 197 (1976). Also see *United States v. Virginia* 518 U.S. (1996), where the Court raised the *Craig* standard to a level at which government had to demonstrate an "exceedingly persuasive justification" when Virginia sought to retain gender-based military colleges. As in *Reed v. Reed* (1971), we don't yet know whether *Bush v. Gore* (2000) is a first case in a line of cases.

85. See *Meyer v. Nebraska* 262 U.S. 390 (1923), *Pierce v. Society of Sisters*, 268 U.S. 510 (1925), and *Skinner v. Oklahoma* 316 U.S. 535 (1942). In *Griswold v. Connecticut* 381 U.S. 479 (1965), the Court said there was a right to privacy that protected married people in the use of contraceptives. *Eisenstadt v. Baird* 405 U.S. 438 (1972) defined marriage as consisting of two individuals, each with separate privacy interests, and extended the right to use contraceptives to single individuals. In *Roe*, privacy is viewed as a key aspect of liberty that protects a woman's right of abortion choice; *Casey* premised the right of abortion choice on a right of personhood; and *Lawrence* applied rights of personhood to homosexuals.

86. *Lawrence v. Texas*, 539 U.S. 558, 571 (2003).

87. Thus, as an institutional norm, the Court is supposed to be autonomous from a *direct* concern with the plight of citizens, in ways that are different from political institutions. The outside is brought into a case through the principles that guide a specific area of doctrine. The best way to think of this is through comparing findings in the *Casey* and *Lawrence* decisions with the following quotation from Justice Sutherland's majority opinion in the *Lochner*-era case, *Carter v. Carter Coal Co.*, 298 U.S. 238. 308–309 (1936): "Much stress is put upon the evils which come from the struggle between employers and employees over the matter of wages, working conditions . . . and the resulting strikes, curtailment and irregularity of production . . . Such effect as they may have upon commerce, however extensive it may be, is secondary and indirect [under the majority opinion's interpretation of the commerce clause]. An increase in the greatness of the effect adds to its importance. It does not alter its character." Here we see the Court expressing its autonomy from the directness of external factors outside the Court, as it declared unconstitutional the Bituminous Coal Conservation Act of 1935. This act was intended to stabilize the coal industry during the crisis of the Depression. The Court's view of what "affecting commerce" meant under the commerce clause did not allow *national* regulation of external factors such as labor strikes, because they were at the state and local level, before goods entered the stream of commerce. Although one can question the substance of the *Lochner* Court's mutual construction of the internal and external, one can see the process at work in this case. To decide whether this law was constitutional required the Court to define a general principle of affecting commerce from prior cases through the construction of economic, social, and political factors in the outside, empirical world.

88. Given the nature of the SCP, one can also begin to see, in contrast to Cass Sunstein's view of *Lawrence*, why the Court did not base its decision to overrule *Bowers* sim-

ply on the fact that antisodomy laws are rarely enforced, or desuetude. One can also better understand why the Court is not simply minimalist and pragmatic in its decision making. The normative and empirical and inward- and outward-looking SCP is not primarily about the importance of strategic concerns for the Supreme Court as an institution—the central evaluative concern of Sunstein's argument for minimalism in Supreme Court decision making. See Cass Sunstein, "What Did *Lawrence* Hold?: Of Autonomy, Desuetude, Sexuality, and Marriage," *Supreme Court Review* (2003): 27–74; see also Ronald Kahn, "Why *Lawrence v. Texas* (2003) Was Not Expected: A Critique of Pragmatic Legalist and Behavioral Explanations of Supreme Court Decision Making," in *The Future of Gay Rights in America*, ed. H. N. Hirsch (New York: Routledge, 2005), 229–264.

89. See Justice Scalia's view that the Court has entered the culture wars in *Romer v. Evans*, 517 U.S. 620, 652 (1996). In *Lawrence v. Texas*, 539 U.S. 558, 577, and 602 (2003), he views the majority's view that criminalization of homosexual conduct is "an invitation to subject homosexual persons to discrimination both in the public and private spheres" as evidence "that the Court has taken sides in the culture war, departing from its role as assuring, as neutral observer, that the democratic rules of engagement are observed."

90. See Dennis Goldford, *American Constitution*, 186. Goldford writes, "Originalist intent itself . . . is not discovered, but rather constructed by interpretation, and thus cannot be the ground of objectivity in the sense in which originalism understands it." Thus, he finds originalism is not the obverse of nonoriginalism.

91. For evidence of the bidirectionality of influence between the Supreme Court and interpretive community, particularly with regard to the role of legal advocacy groups, see the contributions of Ken I. Kersch, Carol Nackenoff, Julie Novkov, and Thomas M. Keck in this volume.

92. For an anecdotal account of the conservative movement in Kansas' disdain for liberals, liberalism in general, and homosexuals in particular, see Thomas Frank, *What's the Matter with Kansas?: How Conservatives Won the Heart of America* (New York: Henry Holt, 2004). It seems that an important dimension of the disdain in Kansas is not simply against liberal social policies, but rather values found in the Court and the SCP: legal objectivity (secularism) and the autonomy from politics that goes along with it. The Terri Schiavo case, which involved a conflict over whether courts or Congress should make the decision whether Schiavo was to stay off life support systems, is an example of contemporary social conservative thinking that rejects legal objectivity for politics that will support their moral choices. Thanks to Jim Kennerly, Oberlin '05, for researching some of the implications of Court objectivity in the politics of same-sex marriage.

93. For the most comprehensive critique of arguments made by historians that external political events can explain *West Coast Hotel* and the judicial "revolution" of 1937, see Barry Cushman, *Rethinking the New Deal Court: The Structure of a Constitutional Revolution* (New York: Oxford University Press, 1998). Court decisions of 1937 can be explained by external political events. For an insightful discussion of the debate in the early twentieth century over whether the Constitution should be changed by evolution through interpretation or by amendment, see Howard Gillman, "The Collapse of

Constitutional Originalism and the Rise of the Notion of the 'Living Constitution' in the Course of American State-Building," *Studies in American Political Development* 11 (1997): 191–247. However, in this discussion, Gillman continues the traditional reification by externalist scholars of the importance of 1937 as the key dividing line between the Court following originalist thinking and one in which the Constitution is to be defined as a living document. See also Kahn, "*Marbury v. Madison* as a Model," 160–165.

94. See Mary L. Dudziak, *Cold War Civil Rights: Race and the Image of American Democracy* (Princeton, N.J.: Princeton University Press, 2000).

95. For a theory of doctrinal change that focuses on periods of "higher lawmaking" versus normal times and the effect of critical elections in the 1930s resulting in the formation of the post–*Lochner* era activist Supreme Court, see Bruce Ackerman, *We the People 1: Foundations* (Cambridge, Mass.: Harvard University Press, 1991), and *We the People 2: Transformations* (Cambridge, Mass.: Harvard University Press, 1998).

96. See Michael Comiskey, *Seeking Justices: The Judging of Supreme Court Nominees* (Lawrence: University Press of Kansas, 2004), chap. 7, "Court Packing and an Aberrant Court," for a fascinating review of the difficulties that presidents have had in attempting to pack the Supreme Court. See also Mark Silverstein and William Haltom, "You Can't Always Get What You Want: Reflections on the Ginsburg and Breyer Nominations," *Journal of Law and Politics* 12 (1996): 459–479.

97. See Mark Graber, "Legal, Strategic or Legal Strategy" (this volume).

98. Ibid.

99. See Jeffrey A. Segal and Harold J. Spaeth, *The Supreme Court and the Attitudinal Model* (New York: Cambridge University Press, 1993); and *The Supreme Court and the Attitudinal Model Revisited* (New York: Cambridge University Press, 2002), for classic statements of the attitudinal approach. See also Harold J. Spaeth and Jeffrey A. Segal, *Majority Rule or Minority Will: Adherence to Precedent on the U.S. Supreme Court* (New York: Cambridge University Press, 1999), for the view that, when justices disagree with the establishment of a precedent, they rarely shift from their previously stated positions in later cases. The analysis is in terms of end product policy, not in terms of a consideration of the principles and social constructions in prior cases as influential to how they engage in the interpretive turn in later cases.

100. See Goldford, *American Constitution*, 334.

101. Ibid., 348. Thus, the Constitution, in principle (and as constitutive practice) is distinct from whatever anyone says about it, including the founders. The Constitution can be invoked as a critical standard against current practices which are alleged to be unconstitutional.

102. See Pierson, "Increasing Returns"; and Pierson, *Politics in Time*, especially chap. 1, "Positive Feedback and Path Dependence," 17–53, for an analysis of the social qualities of political institutions that lead them to tend to stay with the status quo and to be reform-averse.

103. See Pierson, "Increasing Returns," 257. In contrast to economic institutions, political organizations are weak or absent in efficiency-enhancing mechanisms and gen-

erally have a stronger status quo bias built into them, and political actors have shorter time horizons than economic actors.

104. Ibid., 260–261.

105. This does not mean that the Court always engages in a (re)construction process and always seeks to interpret the Constitution in light of change outside the Court. Polity and rights principles and the social constructions on which they are built may become static. However, this is not the usual process of Supreme Court decision making and of doctrinal change.

106. See Lawrence Lessig, "Understanding Changed Readings," 424.

107. Stephen Skowronek, *The Politics Presidents Make: Leadership from John Adams to Bill Clinton*, especially part 3, "The Waning of Political Time," 407–464.

108. Social constructs may be less central to the development of First Amendment speech doctrine because of the importance of the concept of content neutrality in First Amendment theory and practice. This is evident in cases in which the Rehnquist Court has approved flag burning and banned content-based hate speech laws. See *Texas v. Johnson*, 491 U.S. 397 (1989) and R.A.V. *v. St. Paul*, 505 U.S. 377 (1992).

Part II

The Supreme Court and Governing
Political Orders and Regimes

Chapter 3

The Supreme Court and the National Political Order: Collaboration and Confrontation

Mark Tushnet

Introduction

As Martin Shapiro emphasized throughout his career, courts are part of the national political order. It would be surprising, then, to discover in a stable political system that courts were strongly at odds with the rest of that order for an extended period. Yet the institution of judicial review itself seems to *require* that constitutional courts sometimes set themselves against other parts of the political order. How can we understand judicial review as part of a stable political system?[1]

In this chapter I describe several ways in which the U.S. Supreme Court in the twentieth century contributed to the construction of the political order by means of judicial review.[2] The basic idea is simple. The Supreme Court can act against *parts* of the political system while at the same time collaborating with other parts.[3] A collaborative Court helps build a stable political order by helping some parts of the system destabilize other parts as a preliminary to the construction of a new system. A collaborative Court also can strengthen the normative case for judicial review, limiting the sting of the charge that judicial review is necessarily countermajoritarian.[4]

I develop my argument by examining several episodes in twentieth-century constitutional history: the New Deal and its aftermath in the Roosevelt Court, the Warren Court and its relation to the Great Society, and the Rehnquist Court during and after the Reagan Revolution. We can use the idea of a collaborative Court to illuminate some important features of each period, although much lies untouched by that idea.

Three Collaborative Courts

The history of the Court's response to the New Deal is so familiar that I simply sketch its outlines as a prelude to examining the Roosevelt Court as a collaborative Court. A majority of the Supreme Court's justices initially regarded many of the statutory innovations of the New Deal as constitutionally suspect. At best, the statutes took on existing due process and federalism doctrine extremely aggressively. The statutes assumed that, applied in the economic emergency of the Depression, federalism doctrine would justify substantially more national action than the national government had engaged in only a few years earlier, and that due process doctrine would justify substantially more regulatory action than governments at any level had engaged in. At worst, the statutes leaped over constitutional bounds separating the proper sphere of the national government from that of the states, and separating executive decision making from legislation.

The Court's first responses to the New Deal- and Depression-related legislation were lukewarm acceptances, but soon the Court's view changed. In 1937 the Court invalidated several statutes—not all of which were intrinsically important to the New Deal agenda as of that date—on grounds that the Roosevelt administration regarded as posing severe threats to statutes that *were* important, most notably the National Labor Relations Act and the federal Fair Labor Standards Act. Roosevelt responded with the famous Court-packing plan, and although the plan itself failed in Congress, Roosevelt ended up packing the Court anyway, as he appointed dedicated New Dealers to fill vacancies created by retirements from the Court.

The Roosevelt Court was a collaborative one. Of course, it upheld expansive exercises of national and state regulatory power against challenges that might have succeeded a decade or two earlier. Justice Felix Frankfurter, regarded by many as the Roosevelt Court's intellectual leader, articulated a jurisprudential theory of judicial deference to legislatures that was compatible with the New Deal program. New Dealers, and before them progressives, were primarily concerned about judicial interference with legislation in the interest of working people. Frankfurter's theory can be understood as premised on a vision of the legislative process as one of interest group pluralism. Labor's accomplishments during the New Deal (and earlier) showed that the courts could defer to legislatures seen as the locations for interest group bargaining because labor interests did well enough there.

But deference alone does not make a collaborative Court. In its generalized form, deference offers a normative rather than political account of judicial review. Collaboration, in contrast, can involve either deference to legislatures or confrontations with some of them, depending on the political requirements of the governing national coalition. Sometimes collaboration will mean that courts will have to invalidate legislative action—sometimes action by city councils or state legislatures, sometimes actions by a prior generation's Congress.

Deference—or, as it came to be called, judicial restraint—easily degenerates into an abandonment of judicial review itself, as it did in some of Frankfurter's more extreme formulations.[5] Linking Frankfurter's theory of deference to interest group pluralism exposes the major fault line in making deference a generalized approach. Perhaps labor interests did well enough in interest group bargaining, but not every interest group that liberals were concerned with did. Couple a more limited theory of deference predicated on interest group pluralism with an account of the defects of the pluralist system, and one could develop an account of judicial review as a collaboration with interest group pluralism.

The Roosevelt Court did just that. It became a collaborative Court as it developed the implications of the famous footnote 4 in *United States v. Carolene Products*.[6] The text the footnote was attached to offered a standard account of judicial deference to legislative judgment. The footnote said that deference sometimes might be abandoned. The occasions for more aggressive judicial review were when a statute was challenged as violating a specific rights-protecting provision of the Constitution, or as impairing the political processes that allow the repeal of unwise legislation, or as targeted at minorities because of prejudice against them. The "footnote 4" jurisprudence was the specific form the Roosevelt Court used to theorize its collaboration with the New Deal.

Treating judicial review as an institution that linked deference and protection of minorities within a broader framework of interest group pluralism solved another problem Shapiro identified. As he put it, the Roosevelt Court had captured the last bastion of opposition to the New Deal. Its members then had to decide whether to dismantle with weapons inside the citadel, or to turn those weapons against their enemies.[7] The justices might have thought, though, that there *were* no enemies to be fought any more, after the New Deal's successes. Yet anyone familiar with military campaigns knows that there is always work to be done after the major fighting ends. Pockets of resistance hold out, supporters of the defeated army may try to bide their time until conditions seem ripe for a new assault, and even those who supported the initial victory might be uncertain about efforts to extend the territory under control—or, to drop the military metaphor, to expand the scope of the New Deal's programs.

Deference where interest group pluralism worked well coupled with the footnote 4 jurisprudence was a combination that could be used to challenge the remaining resistance to the New Deal. The last criterion in footnote 4 was clearly adapted to address the condition of apartheid in the South, although as a theory it had a broader reach. From Roosevelt's point of view, the South was a problem for the New Deal, because Southern Democrats in Congress were a significant element in the anti–New Deal, conservative coalition that obstructed his legislative agenda. Roosevelt first took on the Southern Democrats directly, intervening in primary elections in an attempt to substitute Southern New Dealers for Southern obstructionists. His effort failed. But lawyers in the Department of Justice saw the possibilities— constitutional and political—opened up by the footnote 4 jurisprudence. Building on earlier precedents, they challenged the Southern white primary and became increasingly receptive to appeals from African Americans to intervene against white terrorism of the African American community.[8]

The Supreme Court's white primary decision in 1944 aligned the Court with this effort.[9] Notably, the decision was somewhat innovative doctrinally. In 1935 the Supreme Court upheld a white primary conducted, as the Court saw it, entirely without the participation of state government.[10] A 1941 decision arising out of an investigation of corruption in Huey Long's Louisiana gave the justices a chance to reconsider. The decision held that Congress had the power to regulate primary elections for national office, a holding that undermined the earlier holding that primary elections were outside the scope of "state action." By 1944 the Court was willing to overrule the 1935 decision, leading its author, who remained on the Court, to lament in a dissent that the earlier decision turned out to be like a limited railway ticket, "good for this day and train only."[11]

The Roosevelt Court collaborated with the political branches of the national government in other ways. The Roosevelt Court began to develop a First Amendment law protecting people's right to conduct demonstrations in public spaces in a case that pitted the Congress of Industrial Organizations, an important Roosevelt supporter, against Jersey City's antilabor mayor Frank "I am the Law" Hague.[12] The configuration of parties there was largely an accident, although in retrospect it certainly seems symbolic. More important, the Roosevelt Court extended the public forum doctrine in important cases upholding the rights of labor unions to engage in picketing, against claims, traditionally recognized by state courts, that picketing involved a tortious interference with the employers' business relations.[13] The Roosevelt Court contributed to the construction and deepening of the political coalition supporting New Deal programs in Congress and in the executive branch. It was a model of a collaborative Court.

The Warren Court was collaborative as well, this time with the Great Society's civil rights agenda and, more generally, with its challenge to a sort of traditionalism associated with the "Southern way of life" but dispersed more widely throughout the country. It is relatively easy—easier than in the case of the Roosevelt Court—to come up with specific examples of direct collaboration. For example, one provision in the Voting Rights Act of 1965 directed the Department of Justice to bring a lawsuit challenging the use of poll taxes as voter qualifications.[14] The Justice Department sued Texas, Alabama, and Mississippi, and the federal district courts in Texas and Alabama struck down the poll tax. At the Supreme Court the Attorney General had Solicitor General Thurgood Marshall present the government's anti–poll tax position by appearing as amicus curiae in a pending private lawsuit.[15] The Court agreed with the government and held the poll tax unconstitutional.

More dramatic were the maneuverings the Court went through to avoid interfering with the sit-in demonstrations that had become the hallmark of the civil rights movement. The Court faced a doctrinal difficulty. The sit-ins protested discrimination by owners of lunch counters and other private businesses. Generally, state law did not *require* the businesses to refuse to serve African Americans. But in the South, neither did state law prohibit such discrimination. The Constitution, though, had been interpreted since the *Civil Rights Cases* in 1883 to bar only discrimination by state actors or under color of state law. The doctrinal structure of the sit-in cases was that the sit-inners occupied places at lunch counters, were directed to leave the by owner, and then were arrested for violating general state trespass laws. Those trespass laws were not themselves discriminatory. The doctrinal problem then was to locate state action when private owners invoked general nondiscriminatory trespass laws as a basis for seeking police assistance to protect their rights as property owners.

There were some obvious, but far-reaching, theories under which enforcement of a private party's discriminatory wishes was state action. Justice William O. Douglas was attracted to a more limited version of such theories, seeing the sit-in cases as ones in which the private party was acting pursuant to a custom so widespread as to be "almost" lawlike.[16] Most of the Court, though, was unwilling to expand the state action doctrine a great deal. For several years the Court managed to come down on the sit-inners' side without confronting the doctrinal problem directly. In *Garner v. Louisiana*,[17] a majority found that there was no evidence to support the convictions of the peaceful sit-inners for disturbing the peace. It found in one case that the existence of a city ordinance requiring segregation was enough to overturn the convictions for trespass even though the store owner might have chosen to segregate on his own,[18] and in another case that public statements by city officials condemning sit-ins placed such pressure on store owners that the owners' decisions were, effectively, dictated by the city.[19]

By 1964 the Court could not evade the doctrinal issue any longer—or so it seemed. Having discussed the problem for three years, a majority seemed ready to use a Maryland case to find that trespass convictions were constitutionally permissible when store owners really did act on their own discriminatory preferences. The Court prepared to issue its decision in May 1964, at a time when Congress was engaged in a prolonged debate over adopting the Civil Rights Act of 1964, which included provisions that would have made unlawful discrimination in the places of public accommodation the sit-ins had focused on.

Justice William J. Brennan was alarmed at the prospect of a decision upholding the sit-inners' convictions, which he believed, probably correctly, would be taken in Congress to show that discriminatory store owners had the Constitution on their side. Brennan invented a new theory that avoided all the federal constitutional questions. He pointed out that Maryland had adopted an antidiscrimination statute after the state supreme court had upheld the sit-inners' convictions for trespass, and suggested that the state courts might conclude that the new statute somehow immunized the sit-inners from prosecution for actions taken *before* the statute was adopted. This was, at the least, an exceedingly creative reading of the Maryland and general common law precedents that Brennan invoked, but it was enough to get rid of the case and keep the Court from interfering with the progress of the Civil Rights Act through Congress.[20]

Lucas A. Powe sees the Warren Court's actions in a much wider range of cases as "an assault on the South as a unique legal and cultural region,"[21] pointing out that the Warren Court's most celebrated free speech decisions came in cases implicating civil rights. Similarly, Powe argues that the Warren Court decisions striking down organized prayer in public schools, despite coming from Northern states, were a challenge to the pervasive religiosity that characterized the South as a region. Powe recognizes, though, that the Warren Court expressed a vision of the Constitution that went beyond the South. Indeed, he describes the Warren Court as a collaborative one: "the Court was a functioning part of the Kennedy-Johnson liberalism of the mid and late 1960s. . . . The Warren Court seemed to combine Kennedy's rhetoric with Johnson's ability to do the deal."[22]

The Great Society was not simply the New Deal at age thirty, however. The Great Society continued to take interest group pluralism seriously. But it contained a strand deriving more substantially from the pre–New Deal progressives than the New Deal itself did. That strand was a commitment to policy making by an elite of professional specialists. The professionalization of reformism was reflected to some extent in an initially subtle, then grossly apparent, shift in interest groups themselves. During the 1960s interest groups began to transform themselves from organizations that derived their positions on public policy questions from the views of their members and then presented those positions to Washington policy makers into organizations whose professional leaders developed positions on public policy questions and then presented those positions to their members, who in turn placed pressure on Washington policy makers.

The Warren Court's criminal procedure revolution is probably the most important component of the Warren Court's collaboration with the professionalized reform movement in the Great Society. Powe and others have pointed out, correctly, that the criminal procedure revolution was intimately connected to the civil rights revolution. The Warren Court and its liberal supporters understood that African Americans were the primary victims of abusive police practices. Many major criminal procedure decisions involved minority defendants, a fact that the justices were of course aware of. The criminal procedure revolution was more than a civil rights revolution, though. It was a professionalist revolution too. Seen in the most general terms, the Warren Court's criminal procedure revolution gave criminal justice professionals—chiefs of large departments and prosecutors—the tools they needed to make sure that officers on the line adhered to the norms of policing understood as a profession.

Miranda v. Arizona is exemplary.[23] Generally taken as a challenge to standard police practices, Chief Justice Earl Warren's opinion in *Miranda* presented itself as articulating a "best practices" requirement. *Miranda* was actually a group of cases, one of which was a federal prosecution. At the oral argument Solicitor General Thurgood Marshall was asked what agents of the Federal Bureau of Investigation did when they arrested someone. Marshall described the warnings agents gave, and followed up with a more detailed letter to the Court after the argument. Warren's opinion emphasized that the warnings the Court required were only slightly different from the ones the FBI already gave. In Warren's eyes, then, the Miranda warnings would push local police forces to a point nearly reached already by the most professional police agencies.

The Warren Court's "stop and frisk" decision, *Terry v. Ohio*, had an identical managerial focus.[24] Warren's opinion was built around two propositions. First, what mattered was how to regulate the conduct of police officers on the street. Second, the only tool the courts had for regulating was the exclusion of evidence at subsequent trials. But, Warren observed, many police-citizen confrontations did not result in trials anyway. As a result, courts could do little to regulate those confrontations. Rather, police chiefs would have to train their offers to interact appropriately with citizens. And on a lower level of generality, Warren's opinion relied on the professional judgment of the experienced police officer in the case at hand to demonstrate why well-trained and experienced officers could be expected to balance well the public interests in law enforcement and privacy. The Warren Court's criminal procedure decisions were managerialist in their effort to use constitutional law as a tool for regulating the behavior of line officers—street-level police officers and ordinary prosecutors—to create or support a rationalized, rule-bound bureaucracy. In doing so, the decisions were part of a project of collaboration with the professional elites that were part of the Great Society coalition.

Collaboration may be a complex project, though, and is often incomplete and imperfect. The Warren Court's decisions on juvenile justice illustrate one form of complexity. The juvenile court system originated as a project of the new profession of social work, assisted by lawyers who conceptualized their job as a helping profession as well. The juvenile justice system was self-consciously antilegal, focusing on helping its clients through highly discretionary interventions. The Warren Court began to subject this system to the rule of law, in a way inconsistent with the social work norms that had animated the system. Justice Abe Fortas, the quintessential Great Society justice, wrote the Court's decision in *In re Gault*,[25] holding that the Constitution required juveniles to be given standard criminal procedure rights of notice, counsel, and confrontation. Yet by the time *Gault* was decided, even professional social workers had begun to question whether, as one recent history puts it, the "realities of juvenile incarceration" matched "the rehabilitative rhetoric of progressive juvenile jurisprudence."[26]

Justice Thurgood Marshall, reflecting a similar division within the Great Society coalition, wrote the prevailing opinion, and Fortas the dissent, in *Powell v. Texas*,[27] rejecting a constitutional challenge to the criminalization of public drunkenness. Fortas argued that punishing public drunkenness was unconstitutional because drunkenness was a condition that the victim had no control over—a standard theme in liberal criminal jurisprudence. In rejecting Fortas's argument, Marshall nonetheless invoked a progressive theme. For Marshall, what mattered was to ensure that criminal law focus on eliminating the "root causes" of crime. Noting that American society had dramatically failed to do so in the context of public drunkenness by refusing to develop facilities for treating alcoholics, Marshall regarded criminalization as a humane second-best response.

A final example of the complexity of the Warren Court's collaboration with the Great Society is the due process revolution in public assistance. As with criminal procedure, the Court's concern—like that of elite professionals—was that low-level bureaucrats exercised discretion, often in a discriminatory manner, in their ordinary interactions with recipients of public assistance. The Warren Court's solution, again like that of elite professionals, was to impose due process requirements and rules. As William Simon later pointed out, though, this strategy, however compatible with the views of elite professionals in the 1960s and early 1970s, made the welfare system particularly vulnerable to retrenchment.[28] The Warren Court's proceduralism was insensitive to the substance of the rules low-level bureaucrats were to apply, and when retrenchment came it meant that those bureaucrats could not exercise discretion in favor of recipients.

The Roosevelt and Warren Courts illustrate two elements of the idea of a collaborative Court. First, and more apparent on the surface, the collaboration is with a *national* political system that confronts resistance or indifference at the state and local level. The collaboration, one might say, is geographical: the Court collaborates with a national political system as that national system grapples with problems arising from the fact that the United States is a federal nation. Second, and less apparent, the Roosevelt and Warren Courts were in a position to be collaborative Courts because the national political system had an agenda with which the Courts could collaborate.

The geographical element of collaboration, as developed so far, means that the idea of collaborative Court will not work well when we consider the relation between the Supreme Court and the *national* political institutions—the president and Congress. By definition, judicial review of legislation means that the Court sets itself *against* what the legislature and executive have done. A Court can collaborate with the president and Congress against state and local governments, but with whom can the Court collaborate against a president and Congress that share a common political agenda? Pure deference would seem the only possibility, but, as I noted at the start, pure deference is incompatible with the idea of judicial review. One possibility is to switch from geographic to temporal collaboration. That is, a Court can collaborate with today's national political institutions against what is left over from a prior political system, most notably, laws enacted under the prior system that have the characteristic of being not merely unenactable today but actually contrary to the principles animating today's system.

We might see the Supreme Court of the early 2000s as engaged in this type of collaboration.[29] That Court collaborated with a political system characterized by either divided government or narrow majorities within a unified government, and polarized political parties. Procedural rules in Congress meant that, budget and tax matters aside, only legislation that had substantial bipartisan support could be adopted. This meant, in turn, that aside from tax reductions insulated from these procedural rules, Congress and the president found it impossible, for all practical purposes, to enact measures of the type characteristic of the New Deal and Great Society political systems. Collaborating with the system of the early 2000s entailed cleaning up the statute books by eliminating laws that could not be enacted under the prevailing conditions.

The Rehnquist Court's federalism decisions have been far more limited in their impact than some critics suggest. But in nearly every case, what the Court invalidated was a provision reflecting the policies preferred by a political coalition that could not be reassembled today. Consider the civil remedy provision of the Violence Against Women Act, held unconstitutional in *United States v. Morrison*.[30] The Violence Against Women Act reflected the deepening of the antidiscrimination agenda, exemplified as well by the Americans With Disabilities Act (ADA), in the 1980s and early 1990s. Although the question remains open, it seems to me defensible to assert that the deepening had ended by the late 1990s, leaving behind some degree of commitment to an antidiscrimination agenda that reached beyond the traditional areas of race, national origin, and religion. The congressional reaction to *Morrison* seems to me to support that assertion. Congress reauthorized the Violence Against Women Act, appropriating even more money to support programs assisting women who are victims of domestic violence. The invalidation of the civil remedy provision, in contrast, attracted a great deal of attention in the legal academy, but almost none in Congress.

The Rehnquist Court's decisions giving the ADA narrow interpretations provide probably the best example of temporal collaboration. The act was adopted in 1990 with bipartisan support. By the time the Rehnquist Court got around to interpreting the act, the national political system had changed. It seems quite unlikely that an act placing substantial regulatory burdens on businesses could be enacted today, and yet that is what the ADA does. The Rehnquist Court collaborated with the political system in place by reducing the costs of complying with the ADA, giving narrow interpretations to the act's coverage provisions, and casting aspersions on the act's requirement that employers accommodate their employees' disabilities.[31]

Some Descriptive Complexities

The idea that the Supreme Court should be a collaborative Court describes important episodes in constitutional history, but it requires an important qualification: Sometimes collaboration is impossible. I explore two variants of the impossibility of collaboration, one quite general and the other historically contingent. The general variant of impossibility has a specific institutional form. A Court cannot be a collaborative Court on questions of the separation of powers. Initially it might seem that that claim must be wrong. After all, in every separation of powers case, the Court takes the side of one or the other contending institutions. In holding that Congress has the power to create an independent counsel with power to investigate high officials without being subject to the president's control, for example, the Court sides with Congress against the president.[32] In holding that congressional creation of rights in ordinary citizens to sue to enforce environmental laws intrudes on the president's duty to take care to enforce the law, the Court sides with the president against Congress.[33]

The appearance of taking sides is misleading, however, for at least two reasons. First, it is often difficult to determine which side is favored by a decision invalidating or upholding a statute against a separation of powers challenge. Presidents sought the power to veto individual items in comprehensive budget bills, and members of Congress resisted. Whether a line-item veto would actually strengthen the president is quite unclear, with much depending on the way a line-item veto power would affect bargaining between the president and powerful members of Congress in repeated interactions. In striking down the Line Item Veto Act, did the Court side with Congress or with the president?[34]

Second, and probably more important, the Supreme Court has the opportunity to consider separation of powers challenges only after legislation has actually been enacted—which is to say, after *both* Congress and the president have agreed that the statute is desirable as a matter of public policy (and, of course, politics).[35] In such circumstances, judicial intervention is necessarily confrontational rather than collaborative. The statute embodies a deal struck between the president and Congress. To achieve the deal, each side might have had to compromise on questions of principle with respect to the statute itself. And, importantly, to achieve the deal each side might have had to compromise on some *other* item of legislation, having expended political capital on this one. Further, the deal struck with respect to the statute has implications for other deals that might be struck in the future. Judicial invalidation of the statute on separation of powers grounds undoes the bargain.

Of course, to the extent that deals between the president and Congress reflect the balance of political power between them, the two sides will have the incentive, and most likely the ability, to work around what the Court has said, achieving in substance what the invalidated statute achieved in a different form. But reaching the same point again, albeit in a new form, takes time and political energy away from other legislative and executive projects. Sometimes that will mean that the bargain will simply fall off the political agenda, displaced by other, apparently more important issues. In such situations, the Court will have displaced the policy compromises reached by the other components of the national political system. This sort of displacement might be collaborative in the temporal sense, if the balance of political power between Congress and the president has shifted between the time the statute was enacted and the time it is invalidated. Recent developments in statutory design reduce the time between enactment and the exercise of the power of judicial review. Over the past decade or so, Congress and the president have increasingly provided for fast track judicial review of statutes about which there are serious constitutional doubts. Such review makes it likely that the balance of political power will be unchanged by the time the Supreme Court considers the constitutional challenge. And if that balance is unchanged, the Court's displacement of policy compromise will be confrontational rather than collaborative.

It will be helpful to pause here to identify some themes about the relationships among institutions that my analysis suggests. First, and probably most obviously, the process of nominating and confirming justices is likely to produce justices who tend to side with the presidency in separation of powers controversies. A Senate jealous of Congress's prerogatives might block a president from nominating an extreme pro-executive justice, but the president's advantage in setting the agenda by nominating a particular person strongly suggests that any nominee—and appointee, after confirmation—will be closer to the president's position than to the Senate's.[36]

Second, it is important to emphasize that the interactions I have described between the Court and the other branches, and in particular the presidency, are systematic and not necessarily intentional. That is, I do not claim that the justices actually say to themselves that they are adopting a position *because* it is offered to them by the president. Rather, in the main they adopt the positions they do because those positions seem to them constitutionally correct. Each justice has or develops what some political scientists call a constitutional vision, a way of looking at constitutional law that gives them the sense that they are resolving constitutional controversies in accordance with the law, not their personal preferences. Some presidents, particularly forceful ones, have their own constitutional visions, and they try to nominate justices who, they believe, share those visions. This, too, induces the tendency of justices to side with the presidency.

Third, not everyone has a comprehensive constitutional vision, or holds whatever vision he or she has with the same degree of strength. This differential commitment to a constitutional vision generates some of the interactions between institutions. So, for example, the Roosevelt Department of Justice developed creative civil rights theories as part of the administration's assault on Southern conservatives, but the Roosevelt appointees accepted only some of the initiatives. Similarly, the Warren Court took the initiative in *Brown v. Board of Education*, and the Eisenhower Department of Justice only half-heartedly endorsed desegregation, acting forcefully only in the Little Rock school crisis when national authority, including that of the president, was directly challenged.

Collaboration is impossible in another way. There may be nothing for the Supreme Court to collaborate *with*. That is, a collaborative Court cooperates with the other elements of the national political system to advance the central political projects of those elements. But sometimes the other elements simply do not have a central project. Consider the standard periodization of the Warren Court, which identifies a first Warren Court lasting from Warren's appointment to the early 1960s, and a second Warren Court that began in 1962 and extended for some years after Warren's retirement.[37] The second Warren Court is the one to which scholars and the public refer in discussing the (unmodified) Warren Court. The reason is that history's Warren Court was a collaborative Court, working with the president and Congress in developing a constitutional law appropriate to the Great Society. In contrast, the first Warren Court faced a Republican president, Dwight

Eisenhower, who was somewhat reluctantly committed to a program of refusing to roll back the accomplishments of the New Deal, and a Congress controlled nominally by Democrats but actually by a coalition of Republicans and Southern Democrats. These institutions had no central ideological project around which a coherent constitutional agenda could develop. The president and Congress were committed to anticommunism and keeping the New Deal alive. The former commitment placed some limits on what the first Warren Court could do, but otherwise these commitments gave the Court little to work with.

The Rehnquist Court through most of its existence faced the same problem. The Reagan Revolution was incomplete, with Democrats retaining control of Congress. Reagan conservatives articulated a new constitutional vision, but interest group and substantive liberalism remained strong. As interest groups proliferated and transformed themselves in the Great Society, they produced a degenerate form of liberalism that was readily susceptible to attacks by conservatives. The Gun Free School Zones Act, which the Supreme Court invalidated in 1995,[38] was a ready poster child for Congress's critics, who called it a statute with little public policy justification that was simply the result of congressional grandstanding. The Supreme Court's reaction to the hypertrophy of interest group liberalism were cases that two scholars described as "Dissing Congress."[39] At the same time, the new conservative order failed to develop the kind of institutional substratum that interest groups had provided for the New Deal and the Great Society.

Congress itself drifted in a conservative direction, but when Newt Gingrich and his allies took over the House of Representatives and the Senate in 1994, they faced a Democratic president who was decidedly to their left and unenthusiastic about developing a constitutional vision compatible with the Republicans' conservatism. The Rehnquist Court's most ardent conservatives certainly would have liked to collaborate with the conservative Congress in developing such a vision, but they did not dominate the Supreme Court. As I have suggested, they were able to engage in temporal collaboration, but in general the Court, like Congress and the presidency, drifted to the right without articulating a new conservative constitutional vision.

Substantive liberalism did not disappear during the Rehnquist years, and indeed, in some ways it was cleansed of some of the interest-group-induced excesses of the Warren Court era. Commitments to equality continued to be important as nondiscrimination norms were extended to persons with disabilities and to gays and lesbians, albeit in less robust forms than such norms had taken at the height of the Warren Court. Even the somewhat chastened nondiscrimination norms applicable to these groups were consistent with the somewhat chastened nondiscrimination norms the Rehnquist Court applied to discrimination against African Americans and women.

We might see the drift in the Rehnquist Court as one effect of what Stephen Skowronek calls the "waning of political time."[40] According to Skowronek, the time cycle of changes in national political orders has accelerated, giving each president larger opportunities to exercise leadership than earlier presidents had, but posing increasingly difficult choices about *how* to lead. Without a president who addressed and solved the problems posed by the waning of political time, the Rehnquist Court could use only its own resources in developing a constitutional vision. But it lacked sufficient internal coherence to do more than drift to the right.

When collaboration is impossible, what can a Court do? In some ways, pretty much anything it wants. In the separation of powers context, for example, the Court will have allies in one of the political branches whatever it does. Those allies may be a minority, who objected to the compromise reached between Congress and the president and struck down by the Court. But congressional minorities are likely to be in a position to block any retaliation against the Court. When the Court rules in the president's favor, the president is likely to be its ally, again subject to the qualification that the Court will have undone a deal the president thought worth making.

The possibilities for a Court facing a national political system with no central project are probably more interesting. Here the Court can be a truly independent lawmaker, pursuing whatever projects its members can agree on. Of course, the justices may be unable to agree on central projects. This is particularly true because of the fact that justices arrive at and depart from the Court at unpredictable intervals. The nomination and confirmation processes in a political system without a central project may well generate almost random appointees. David Souter may be the most obvious example— a protégé of Warren Rudman, a moderately conservative Northeastern Republican senator, whose representations were sufficient to lead the conservative White House chief of staff John Sununu to reassure nervous conservatives that the appointment would turn out to be completely satisfying to them.

If the justices are able to locate a central project for themselves, they may be able to impose it as constitutional law. But the law they develop will be free-floating, disconnected from the remainder of the national political system. It will have shallow roots, liable to reversal once the national political system begins to generate a new central project. Here the threats—as yet unfulfilled—by conservatives to overturn the Court's decision upholding Congress's power to impose generally applicable regulations such as wage and hours laws on the states,[41] and the parallel threats by today's minority to overturn the Court's decisions on state immunity from suit,[42] illustrate the potential fluidity of the free-floating lawmaking characteristic of periods when the national political system has no central project. So too does the uncertain course of the first Warren Court's decisions on criminal procedure: the impulse toward liberalism pretty clearly predominated among the justices on that Court, but they were unable to give the first Warren Court a distinctive cast—because, in the terms I have been using, they were engaged in lawmaking in the absence of a central project of the political branches they might collaborate with.

So far I have examined the idea of a collaborative Court and the circumstances under which such a Court might exist. Before turning to normative questions about collaboration and constitutional law, I think it important to add another possibility to the mix. This is the possibility of what might be called an *anti*collaborative Court. Such a Court develops legal rules that come into play only when the Court finds one element in the national political system at odds with another. The model for such rules is the Court's recent law defining when Congress has the power under Section 5 of the Fourteenth Amendment to adopt legislation to enforce the prohibitions in Section 1 of that amendment.[43] According to the Court, exercises of the Section 5 power must have as their predicate the fact of reasonably widespread violations of Section 1 rights by state or local governments.[44] If Congress identifies such violations, it may adopt Section 5 legislation that is congruent with and proportional to the violations. What this means is that Congress must point its finger at, and criticize, state and local governments before it can invoke its Section 5 power. The Court identified the Voting Rights Act of 1965 as a valid exercise of Congress's enforcement power. Notably, though, that statute could be enacted precisely because of a large divergence between national political preferences and practices in a particular region, the segregated South.

It is not hard to understand why Congress might be reluctant to engage in finger-pointing with respect to some problem that is more dispersed throughout the country. One might design rules that would encourage Congress and state governments to work together to eliminate a practice that all agree is troublesome. The Court's Section 5 law, by requiring finger-pointing, pushes *against* that sort of collaboration. Indeed, the fact that state and local governments have begun to take action counts against the constitutionality of what Congress might do to supplement what has already been done.

Some Normative Issues

The possibility that the Court will be anticollaborative raises, in their most acute form, normative questions about the idea of collaboration. A collaborative Court is not merely a participant in a harmoniously operating political system, although it is that. Collaboration between the Court and the political system provides constitutional law with important normative support. The most general difficulty for constitutionalism in a democracy is to explain why the occurrent policy preferences of contemporary majorities should be displaced by contrary policy judgments made, in the first instance, by people long dead and enforced, most immediately, by judges. Sometimes, as with a Footnote 4 jurisprudence, the judges can demonstrate that the policies they are invalidating are in fact not the policies favored by true contemporary majorities. Collaboration provides an additional justification for democratic constitutionalism. This is clearest, of course, in geographical collaborations, where a local majority's preferences are displaced by a national one's.

Still, such collaborations—and collaboration more generally—might seem a strategy for democracy, but not for constitutionalism. For expository purposes, it is helpful to identify forms of collaboration in which the legislature takes some action and the courts go along with the legislature by expanding the coverage of the legislature's actions, as in geographical collaborations. The temporal collaboration I have described involves the reverse process of judicial contraction of legislative action to make it compatible with the preferences of today's political system. But in these forms, collaboration is simply the promotion of the occurrent preferences of today's political system. That is, it is democratic but not obviously constitutionalist.

The normatively more interesting forms of collaboration are those in which we can observe interactions between the courts and the rest of the political system. The national legislative response to the civil rights movement provided a normative justification for the Warren Court's actions, making it possible for that court to deepen commitments incompletely expressed in Congress. As Archibald Cox put it, "the principle of *Brown v. Board of Education* became more firmly law after its incorporation into . . . the Civil Rights Act of 1964."[45] And similarly, legislatures can pick up on constitutional decisions made by the courts, taking those decisions to express fundamental commitments reaching beyond the precise decisions the courts have made. Here the expansion of legal aid for the poor provides a good example. The Supreme Court held that the Constitution required the provision of legal assistance to criminal defendants unable to hire their own lawyers, and—much later—to people involved in a very narrow class of civil proceedings. Legislatures took these decisions as expressing something important about fundamental fairness, and they expanded programs of legal aid for the poor well beyond the minima demanded by the courts. Collaboration in this interactive way helps *construct* a normative constitutional order out of materials already at hand somewhere in the national political system, albeit not necessarily in the courts in the first instance.

Robert Post and Reva Siegel, in ongoing work, argue that a collaborative Court contributes to democratic constitutionalism in an even deeper way.[46] They begin by arguing that a court that treats constitutional law as completely autonomous from (contemporary) politics deprives constitutionalism of its democratic warrant. But, of course, a court that treats constitutional law as coextensive with occurrent majoritarian preferences deprives that law of its claim to constitutionalism. The interactions between courts and the national political system that take place with collaborative courts allow such courts to acknowledge the connection between constitutional law and politics, thereby making constitutionalism democratic, without forcing them to ratify everything that emerges from the national political system.

Judicial lawmaking when collaboration is impossible raises a normative question as well. It is desirable—although not, I think, strictly necessary—that constitutional law have some connection to the people for whom it is designed. That connection can be made in a number of ways, including through the development of consciousness among the people of their connection to some founding document. Another way is through collaboration between the courts and the political branches in developing constitutional law: the very fact of collaboration connects the courts' constitutional law to the people. Judicial lawmaking when collaboration is impossible eliminates this form of connection, weakening the overall connection between constitutional law and the people. Such lawmaking is not only peculiarly unstable; it also rests on a weaker normative foundation as well.

IN THIS CHAPTER, I developed, although only in a preliminary form, some descriptive and normative aspects of the idea of a collaborative court. Political scientists from Dahl to Shapiro have described in general terms how constitutional courts are parts of a national political system. The idea of a collaborative Court supplements their descriptions by indicating the roles constitutional courts can play in the dynamics of the political system. Their interactions with the other elements in political systems contribute to the construction and stabilization of different systems over time. In addition, the possibility that a constitutional court can be a collaborative one provides some modest normative support for democratic constitutionalism. Whether the idea of the Supreme Court as a collaborative Court contributes substantially to our understanding of the Court's role in constitutional and political history depends on further explorations, which I hope this chapter may provoke.

Notes

1. My terminology is intentionally imprecise in referring sometimes to a national political order, and more often to a national political system. The difficulty is that those terms, and others—such as *regime*—have connotations that I do not wish to invoke. My imprecision is designed to avoid the connotations.

2. I believe that my argument can be understood as an attempt to work out details of the argument underlying, but not explicitly made in, Robert Dahl's classic article, "Decision-making in a Democracy: The Supreme Court as a National Policy-Maker," *Journal of Public Law* 6 (1957): 279–295.

3. The term *parts* is only an approximation. It correctly suggests that the divisions may be geographical, but I later discuss divisions that are temporal—that is, between one political system and its predecessor.

4. The argument in this chapter was inspired by reflecting on Robert C. Post and Reva Beth Siegel, "Equal Protection by Law: Federal Antidiscrimination Legislation after *Morrison* and *Kimel*," *Yale Law Journal* 110 (2000): 441–526.

5. See *Dennis v. United States*, 341 U.S. 494, 517 (1951) (Frankfurter, J., concurring in the result). In this opinion, Frankfurter outlined the numerous considerations that had to be balanced in determining whether a sedition prosecution violated the First Amendment and concluded that the Court had to defer to Congress's determination of what the proper balance was.

6. *United States v. Carolene Products Co.*, 304 U.S. 144 (1938).

7. Martin Shapiro, "Fathers and Sons: The Court, the Commentators, and the Search for Values," in *The Burger Court: The Counter-Revolution that Wasn't*, ed. Vincent Blasi (New Haven, Conn.: Yale University Press, 1983), 220.

8. Kevin J. McMahon, "Constitutional Vision and Supreme Court Decisions: Reconsidering Roosevelt on Race," *Studies in American Political Development* 14 (2000): 20–50.

9. *Smith v. Allwright*, 321 U.S. 649 (1944).

10. *Grovey v. Townsend*, 295 U.S. 45 (1935).

11. 321 U.S., at 669.

12. *Hague v. CIO*, 307 U.S. 496 (1939).

13. The most important of these cases was *Thornhill v. Alabama*, 310 U.S. 88 (1940).

14. Voting Rights Act of 1965, §10, 79 Stat. 442.

15. *Harper v. Virginia State Board of Elections*, 383 U.S. 663 (1966). The decision cites the lower court decisions in the Alabama and Texas lawsuits.

16. *Garner v. Louisiana*, 368 U.S. 157, 177–181 (1961) (Douglas, J., concurring).

17. 368 U.S. 157 (1961).

18. *Peterson v. City of Greenville*, 373 U.S. 244 (1963).

19. *Lombard v. Louisiana*, 373 U.S. 267 (1963).

20. After the Civil Rights Act became law, the Court held that one of its provisions did indeed immunize sit-inners from prosecutions under state trespass laws. *Hamm v. City of Rock Hill*, 379 U.S. 306 (1964).

21. Lucas A. Powe Jr., *The Warren Court and American Politics* (Cambridge, Mass.: Harvard University Press, 2000), 490.

22. Ibid., 494.

23. 384 U.S. 436 (1966).

24. 392 U.S. 1 (1968).

25. 387 U.S. 1 (1967).

26. Barry C. Feld, "Race, Politics, and Juvenile Justice: The Warren Court and the Conservative 'Backlash,'" *Minnesota Law Review* 87 (2003): 1447–1577, at 1485.

27. 392 U.S. 514 (1968).

28. William H. Simon, "Rights and Redistribution in the Welfare System," *Stanford Law Review* 38 (1986): 1431–1516.

29. I have developed the argument in more detail in Mark Tushnet, *The New Constitutional Order* (Princeton, N.J.: Princeton University Press, 2003), on which the following paragraphs draw.

30. 529 U.S. 598 (2000).

31. *Sutton v. United Air Lines*, 527 U.S. 471 (1999); *Trustees of the University of Alabama v. Garrett*, 531 U.S. 356 (2001).

32. *Morrison v. Olson*, 487 U.S. 654 (1988).

33. *Lujan v. Defenders of Wildlife*, 504 U.S. 555, 577 (1992).

34. *Clinton v. City of New York*, 547 U.S. 417 (1998).

35. This point has to be qualified by the possibility that a statute was enacted over the president's veto, or that the president, while objecting in principle to the statue, recognized political reality and either let it go into effect without his signature or actually signed it to avoid a veto battle.

36. To some extent the Court's tendency to side with the executive is confirmed by the widely noted role the solicitor general plays in structuring the Court's agenda and offering the Court legal positions that the Court adopts more often than it does positions advocated by other lawyers.

37. For this periodization, see Powe, *Warren Court*.

38. *United States v. Lopez*, 514 U.S. 549 (1995).

39. Ruth Colker and James J. Brudney, "Dissing Congress," *Michigan Law Review* 100 (2001): 80–144.

40. Stephen Skowronek, *The Politics Presidents Make: Leadership from John Adams to George Bush* (Cambridge, Mass.: Harvard University Press, 1993), 442.

41. See *Garcia v. San Antonio Metropolitan Transit Auth.*, 469 U.S. 528, 580 (1985) (Rehnquist, J., dissenting) (referring to "a principle that will, I am confident, in time again command the support of a majority of this Court"), 589 (O'Connor, J., dissenting) (asserting that "this Court will in time again assume its constitutional responsibility").

42. *Alden v. Maine*, 527 U.S. 706, 814 (1999) (referring to the Court's doctrine as "probably fleeting").

43. I must note that this is the only example I have been able to think of to illustrate the possibility of an anticollaborative Court, and therefore acknowledge that I may be overgeneralizing in suggesting that there is some broader phenomenon of which Section 5 law is simply one illustration.

44. *City of Boerne v. Flores*, 521 U.S. 507 (1997). More precisely, Section Five clearly authorizes Congress to adopt a statute creating a federal cause of action for particular violations of Section One rights. The *Boerne* decision identifies the conditions under which Congress had addressed such violations by remedial schemes that go beyond simply invalidating or imposing liability for particular unconstitutional actions.

45. Archibald Cox, "The Supreme Court, 1966 Term—Foreword: Constitutional Adjudication and the Promotion of Human Rights," *Harvard Law Review* 80 (1966): 91–122, at 94.

46. See Post and Siegel, "Equal Protection by Law."

Chapter 4

Party Politics and Constitutional Change: The Political Origins of Liberal Judicial Activism

Howard Gillman

Introduction

It has been standard practice in public law scholarship to depict judges as self-interested policy makers competing against other policy makers. Judicial behavioralism fosters this one-against-the-other starting point by adopting a level of analysis that focuses on the preferences of individual judges and by treating the sources of judicial attitudes as exogenous to most models of decision making. Strategic approaches begin with this same starting point but then explore whether the dynamics of collegial or interinstitutional decision making complicate the ways in which judges pursue their individual preferences. These approaches shed light on important aspects of judicial politics, but—to use the lexicon of this volume—they do little to relate the "internal" points of view of judges with the "external" goals and preferences of those power holders who create courts and appoint judges.[1]

This chapter explores the advantages of explaining changes in judicial understandings of the Constitution—that is, nontextual "constitutional change"—with reference to the policy agendas of national governing coalitions. Following Terri Peretti, I assume that ideological voting by judges "is not merely the arbitrary expression of [their] idiosyncratic views [but rather] is the expression and vindication of those political views deliberately 'planted' on" courts by policy-conscious presidents and senators.[2] Rather than follow the standard practice in political science of analogizing judges to legislators, this approach recommends viewing federal courts as analogous to other institutions whose officeholders are appointed rather than elected, and who are responsible for a specialized subset of everyday policy making and/or particularized decision making—institutions such as bureaucratic agencies or independent regulatory commissions. For many such institutions, a desire to affect the decision-making bias of those institutions is foremost on the minds of those who are involved in staffing decisions; that is, power holders want the Federal Reserve to follow a certain approach to monetary policy, they want the Environmental Protection Agency (EPA) to strike a certain balance between industry and the environment, and so on. This concern about the overall decision-making bias of an institution is especially pointed when it comes to judicial appointments, because federal courts (ever since 1875) have decision-making authority over an extremely broad range of policy issues. This makes it even more important for parties in government to care about the political biases and allegiances of the nominee, which (along with patronage considerations) is why presidents and senators overwhelmingly select federal judges from among their own party activists or loyalists.[3]

Constitutional change, like changes in agency decision making, might result from a number of factors, including new information about the consequences of older decisions, the development of new constellations of interest group lobbying, or the need to address innovative issues. However, if there are times when it would seem natural to explain changes in agency decision making (at least in part) by referring to the goals and agendas of those who staff the agencies, then perhaps there are reasons to adopt the same approach when trying to explain changes in the way judges interpret the Constitution. On this view, to witness a shift on the Supreme Court from a more liberal to a more conservative understanding of the Constitution is to witness something that is no different in kind than a shift in the EPA from aggressive prosecution of industrial polluters to a more business-friendly approach to environmental protection. Both are changes in institutional behavior that, in all likelihood, can be traced to changing goals and agendas of other power holders in the regime.

There are a number of different political goals that might be pursued by dominant coalitions with an eye on courts, including simple support for a policy agenda (that is, elimination of a potential veto point or promotion of a "legitimation" function), front-line enforcement of special policies (for example, the return of fugitive slaves, the protection of black voting rights), the enhancement of "credible commitments" to favored constituencies, or the construction of a forum into which potentially divisive political issues might be channeled (such as slavery, antitrust policy, abortion, or even disputed presidential elections).[4] In this chapter I argue that constitutional change in the United States sometimes reflects an attempt at "political entrenchment"— that is, an effort of a governing coalition to transform or fortify the policy-making bias of the federal judiciary so that it is in a position to represent the goals of that coalition even if they lose control of the Congress or presidency.

Entrenchments become more conspicuous during periods of close party competition where the more ideological wing of one party is fortuitously in a position to gain representation of their views in federal courts before losing control over the appointment process.[5] Even if such a strategy is driven by short-term political considerations rather than anticipation of a possible loss of power, the effort might properly be considered "entrenchment" rather than mere "staffing" (as with the EPA) because a federal judge's tenure of office typically persists across a change in party governance.

Previously I developed and applied this perspective to the efforts of the post-Reconstruction Republican Party.[6] I argued that by the mid-1870s party leaders had begun to abandon a commitment to black civil rights in favor of a commitment to conservative economic nationalism, and that the institutionalization of this policy was largely accomplished through an expansion of federal judicial power. The party accomplished this goal by using two brief (lame duck) periods in which Republicans controlled the presidency and the entire Congress to pass legislation expanding the jurisdiction of federal courts (the Judiciary and Removal Act of 1875) and expanding the size and structure of federal courts (the Evarts Act of 1891). Even though Republicans lost the House of Representatives immediately after the passage of these acts they maintained control of the presidency and the Senate (sometimes with less than a majority of the popular vote for president, as in the case of Hayes in 1876 and Harrison in 1888), and with those institutions they were able to staff federal courts with conservative economic nationalists while at the same time fight off House Democratic efforts to roll back federal judicial power.

This time I want to explore whether the concept of political entrenchment provides a useful perspective for understanding the political origins of liberalism in the Warren- and post–Warren-era federal judiciary. Rather than view these developments as a by-product of unrestrained judicial activists intent of following personal political agendas, or even as a reflection of judges who act as if they are political blank slates who react to changes in public opinion, I want to see whether modern judicial liberalism can be traced to the self-conscious efforts of Democratic Party office holders in the 1960s. I hope to show that there are important similarities between the actions of Democrats in the 1960s and Republicans in the latter part of the nineteenth century, especially the use of legislation to reorganize and reconfigure access to federal courts, and the use of the appointment power to fundamentally alter the decision-making bias of the federal judiciary.

However, in order for this account to reflect the perspective of New

Institutionalist scholarship, it should be emphasized that "constitutional change as partisan entrenchment" never quite works out as a simple story of judges merely acting as faithful "agents" in service of their "principals." In part the problem has to do with the scope of the Court's decision making: it is comparatively more difficult to find decision makers who will be reliable on a wide range of issues than it is to find appointees who will act reliably over a narrowly defined set of policies—that is, getting someone who will do what you want over at the EPA is easier than getting a justice who will do what you want within the expansive universe of "constitutional law." Also, federal judges have more decision-making independence than many agency officials, and this means greater opportunities to strike out in surprising directions. Moreover, justices must reconcile their preferences with a web of "internal" institutional constraints, perspectives, and responsibilities, including (perhaps) legal norms.

Finally, it is an axiom of historical institutionalism that institutional politics rarely conforms to simple, linear models of causation or neatly schematized understandings of political "order"; instead, it is assumed that institutional politics is comprised of multiple orders and patterns of intercurrence that often create unintended consequences, paradoxes, and disjunctions. Institutional change—including constitutional change—inevitably triggers a dynamic whereby some mobilize in support of new developments and others begin work to block or roll back those developments. Thus, the political significance of 1960s Democratic entrenchment in the judiciary has as much to do with the way in which the political system reacted to the liberalization of the federal judiciary as with the resulting changes in constitutional policy making. Still, before pursuing the case of the 1960s, more should be said about the idea of political entrenchment as it relates to constitutional change.

Political Entrenchment and Judicial Politics

Jack Balkin and Sanford Levinson recently proposed a "theory of partisan entrenchment" as a way of understanding "how constitutional revolutions occur."[7] In their view, federal judges "resemble Senators who are appointed for 18-year terms [the average tenure of a Supreme Court justice] by their parties and never have to face election." They define partisan entrenchment as precisely this "temporal extension of partisan representation" that is so characteristic of the tenure of federal judges, and they argue that this extension of partisan representation through presidential appointment "is the best account of how the meaning of the constitution changes over time." More specifically, they argue that the balance of power between the president and the senate often shapes whether presidents are in a position to entrench strong party ideologues or party moderates. For example, even though Justices Blackmun and Scalia were both Republicans who were appointed by Republican presidents, they turned out different mostly because Nixon had to get his appointment through a Democratic Congress and Reagan did not. As a rule, "judges—and particularly Supreme Court justices—tend to reflect the vector sum of political forces at the time of their confirmation."[8] Presidents sometimes make notorious "mistakes," but a regrettable appointment "is a familiar feature of democratic politics," whether one is talking about the judiciary or the cabinet.[9]

One thing that prevents judges from being viewed as entrenched partisans is that they tend to represent the political agenda that was most salient at the time of their appointment. Unlike other elected partisans, they are under no pressure (as a condition of holding onto power) to update their views on the basis of new contexts, changing coalitions, and evolving electoral strategies. New Deal justices did their work by upholding the New Deal, and if later they diverged on issues relating to civil rights and liberties, that merely demonstrates that consensus on these issues was not a salient consideration for Roosevelt when he made his appointments. The fact that John Paul Stevens is now viewed as the Court's leading liberal is not inconsistent with the view that he was properly viewed as a lifelong moderate Republican at the time of his appointment.[10] In a nutshell:

> If you stock the federal judiciary with enough Reagan Republicans, you can expect that some fifteen to twenty years later they will be making a significant impact on the structure of constitutional doctrine. And so they are. . . . Indeed, given that the Democrats did not have a single Supreme Court nomination between 1967 and 1993, it is hard to expect otherwise. If one doesn't like the decisions of the Rehnquist Court, one should really have been putting more Democrats in the White House during the 1970s and 1980s. Put another way, if you don't like what the Court is doing now, you (or your parents) shouldn't have voted for Ronald Reagan.[11]

Once we pay attention to the relationship between conventional partisan politics and the shape of judicial decision making then (among other things) a more complicated relationship emerges between democratic theory and decision making by unelected federal judges. At a minimum, it should be acknowledged that the views represented by judges have some relationship to views considered acceptable by members of the dominant political coalition at some point in the (more or less) recent past, and it is very likely that they will continue to reflect the views of some portion of the party in government (for example, the ideological wing of a previously majoritarian party). This "temporal extension of partisan representation" also occurs when senators are given extended terms of office and (on a much more focused set of issues) when the board of governors of the Federal Reserve are given fourteen-year terms of office. Moreover, we should recall that parties "serve as sites for working out their adherents' views about constitutional politics. They collect, filter, co-opt and accumulate the constitutional beliefs and aspirations of the party faithful, of prospective voters, and, perhaps equally crucially, of social movements."[12] The successful entrenchment of these views by victorious parties might be considered one of the principal goals of majoritarian electoral politics.[13]

Balkin and Levinson are essentially right about how Supreme Court appointments determine constitutional change in the United States. My quibble is with their decision to label all judicial appointments as instances of a political phenomenon known as *entrenchment*. Instead, it may be useful to posit a variety of goals that governing coalitions might have when considering how the federal judiciary fits into their political agendas, only one of which might be the goal of using short-term control of key institutions to protect potentially vulnerable policies from electoral politics. One leading scholar of modern judicial appointments has suggested that there are at least three different kinds of agendas that presidents pursue in making judicial appointments: policy agendas, which refer to "the substantive policy goals of an administration, including its legislative and administrative objectives"; partisan agendas, which refer to efforts "to shore up political support for the president or for the party"; and personal agendas, which refer to an effort to "favor a personal friend or associate."[14] For example, after reviewing the record of federal court appointments under Eisenhower, Sheldon Goldman concluded that "Eisenhower did not consider the federal courts germane to his presidential agenda and his administration," and thus his appointments reflected "partisan" and "personal" considerations rather than "policy" considerations.[15] One might disagree with Goldman's assessment of Eisenhower's record and still acknowledge that, in the course of American constitutional history, there have been times when presidents have made appointments with more attention to simple patronage considerations than to the use of the judiciary to promote substantive political goals.

Also, if we are attentive to the condition of electoral vulnerability as a feature of political entrenchment, it may be possible to distinguish those circumstances where confident majority parties reconfigure the judiciary so that it is essentially in alignment with dominant coalitions in the rest of the national government.[16] Relatedly, we may want a separate category for those times when presidents and senators have focused more on removing judicial barriers to preferred agendas—a strategy of antientrenchment—rather than entrenching new agendas in courts.[17] One observable result of both of these alternatives would be that the decision-making bias of courts should be in the direction of upholding national legislation (and thus reducing the appearance of judicial activism). By contrast, one result of successful entrenchment would be a greater likelihood that national legislation would be struck down, because it is a condition of entrenchment that courts become (temporarily, anyway) out of sync with the prevailing constellation of power in the rest of the political system.[18]

Finally, during extended periods of divided government, when the political context is not conducive either to a strategy of entrenchment or alignment (especially when the presidency and the senate are controlled by different parties), it may be that partisans in government choose a second-best strategy of simple compromise, whereby they moderate their preferences and select what amounts to the median appointee. Although successful entrenchments may result in the Court being associated with a particular ideological wing of a party, the politics of compromise appointments may lead to a Court that seems to eschew sweeping declarations of constitutional principles in favor of a more prudential role in the political system.

It also should be emphasized that, even when decision makers intend a strategy of entrenchment, it is not always the case that the strategy is successful. Perhaps the most famous example of an attempted political entrenchment in American constitutional history is the decision of the outgoing Federalist Party to (in the words of Thomas Jefferson) "[retire] into the judiciary as a stronghold and from that battery all the works of republicanism are to be beaten down and erased." Balkin and Levinson cite this as an exemplar of their analysis, arguing that "Chief Justice John Marshall kept Federalist principles alive long after the Federalist Party itself had disbanded."[19] But it is not entirely clear that Marshall's tenure as chief justice is an example of effective entrenchment. The Judiciary Act of 1801 was quickly repealed, with the subsequent approval of the Supreme Court.[20] When Congress began targeting judges for impeachment, the remaining Federalists on the bench quickly learned that they had to give up on the hope of using their office as a partisan forum.[21] Over the years, John Marshall's Supreme Court did not challenge the dominant partisan coalitions in the national government; in fact, it was careful to tailor its decisions in a way that was conducive to the evolving preferences of the Virginia Dynasty.[22]

More obvious examples of political entrenchment in federal courts (as I define it) would be antebellum efforts by Southern politicians to construct five federal circuits that exclusively covered slave-owning states (thus ensuring a proslavery majority on the U.S. Supreme Court) and post-Reconstruction efforts by the Republican Party to transform the federal judiciary into a force for the promotion of conservative economic nationalism. In both of these cases, entrenchment involved not only favorable appointments, but also broader legislative efforts to reorganize and restructure federal courts. Do the efforts of the Democratic Party in the 1960s represent another example?

Partisan Entrenchment and the Creation of the New Frontier/Great Society Judiciary

No one would mistake the late 1950s Supreme Court, or the federal judiciary more generally, as a bastion of liberal decision making.[23] The Supreme Court's decision in *Brown v. Board of Education*, although controversial in the South and among many establishment lawyers in the American Bar Association (ABA) and elite law schools, was consistent with the urgings of the solicitor general and was seen by many in the Eisenhower State Department as vital for promoting the "image of American democracy" during the cold war.[24] By the end of the decade the Court attempted to extend some modest due process protections for witnesses called before the House Un-American Activities Committee, but Congress reacted strongly to these experiments and it was not long before the Court was in full retreat.[25] There were only four reliable liberals on the Court: Brennan, Warren, Douglas, and Black. Clark, Whittaker, Harlan, and Frankfurter had voting records that were reliably conservative on most issues. Stewart was a moderate Republican with a commitment to desegregation and free speech that was well known before his appointment by Eisenhower a few years after *Brown*.[26] In general, during the Eisenhower administration, the Supreme Court handed down "liberal" decisions in civil liberties cases about 58 percent of the time.[27] It was a very different Supreme Court, and a different federal judiciary, by the end of the Johnson administration.

In 1961 the Democratic Party took control of both the White House and the Congress for the first time in eight years. At the time Eisenhower left office there were 163 Democratic and 163 Republican federal judges.[28]

Over the next seven years, congressional Democrats increased the size of the federal judiciary three times. Immediately upon taking office, in July 1961, they added ten new appellate and sixty-three new district court judgeships (with Republican Senator Kenneth B. Keating suggesting that "the present urgency for action . . . smacks strongly of patronage politics").[29] In 1966 they added another ten appellate and thirty-five district court judgeships.[30] Another adjustment in 1968 created another thirteen circuit court positions.[31] In other words, between 1960 and 1968 the total number of permanent federal judges was increased by more than a hundred to 432, almost a 33 percent increase in the size of the federal judiciary.[32]

The Eisenhower administration had also pushed for an increase in federal judgeships, and modest expansion (amounting to a release of pressure resulting from extended congressional inaction) was authorized by a Republican Congress in February 1954.[33] However, after Democrats regained control of the Congress following the 1954 elections, legislators refused to give the Republican president the opportunity to fill more judicial positions, despite the Judicial Conference's pleas for as many as seventy new judgeships.[34] As a last-ditch effort, Eisenhower's Attorney General, William P. Rogers, conveyed to congressional Democrats that the president promised "to fill the posts on a 50–50 basis from the two parties."[35] But in the months before the 1960 presidential election, Democrats gambled that they might get an even better deal if they waited to see the result of the election. As explained by Representative Emanuel Celler, chairman of the House Judiciary Committee, "Very frankly I believe they [congressional leaders] contemplated a change in the Executive and the leadership gambled as it were—and won—that a new administration will make the appointments. That is nothing new in our political history."[36] And so instead of passing in the spring of 1960, the expansion was authorized in the spring of 1961.

As a result of this legislation, the Kennedy administration had the opportunity to appoint a huge number of new federal judges. When the new positions were combined with vacancies in preexisting positions, the administration was faced with filling 147 positions. The chairman of the ABA's Standing Committee on the Federal Judiciary, Bernard Segal, explained to the ABA House of Delegates on August 7, 1962, that "except for Presidents Truman and Eisenhower, this is more vacancies than any President of the United States has had to fill in two entire terms of office."[37] By October 1962 the White House, led by Attorney General Robert F. Kennedy and a Justice Department team made up of Byron White, Nicholas deB. Katzenbach, and Joseph F. Dolan, had received Senate confirmation of 128 of their nominees.[38]

The administration received two more confirmations before Kennedy's assassination, bringing the total number of judges appointed by Kennedy to 130.[39]

It would be implausible to assume that every one of these judges embodied the spirit of the New Frontier. Southern Democratic control of key Senate committees gave that wing of the party disproportionate influence over the fate of the president's political agenda, and the cultivation of that wing (combined with the practice of senatorial courtesy on lower court appointments) ensured that some federal judgeships would reflect the influence of Dixiecrat patronage. In March 1963 Governor Nelson A. Rockefeller of New York charged that the president had been appointing "segregationist judges" to the federal bench in the South, and the NAACP was critical of some of Kennedy's judges.[40] Senate politics also resulted in eleven Republican appointees (six of whom were nominated by Kennedy but confirmed during Johnson's administration).[41] Nevertheless, conscious efforts were made to ensure that these federal judges would have a different orientation toward the law than their Republican predecessors. Katzenbach declared that "judicial philosophy is important," in the sense that (whenever possible) the administration preferred "a judge who is a careful liberal, a good technician, liberal yet cautious."[42] More minority groups were represented than was the case with Eisenhower's appointments, including twenty Catholics, eleven Jews, five blacks, and three "foreign born" nominees;[43] by contrast, "unlike Roosevelt and Truman, Eisenhower did not name even one woman or black to a lifetime judgeship on a court of general jurisdiction."[44] More specifically, a special effort was made to check the civil rights attitudes of those who were nominated for judgeships in the South—especially important, given that the Justice Department would be bringing cases in those jurisdictions and wanted to ensure that they would receive a sympathetic hearing.[45] By contrast, Eisenhower's principal overseers on judicial nominations, Henry Brownell, William P. Rogers, and Lawrence E. Walsh, focused mostly on a candidate's feelings about law enforcement, and especially (after 1957) whether they exhibited a useful antagonism toward the U.S. Supreme Court with respect to decisions such as *Mallory v. U.S.* (a unanimous decision).[46]

Eisenhower's team also worked more closely with the (then conservative) American Bar Association, which was much less generous toward Kennedy's liberal nominees than his predecessor's conservative ones.[47] After the ABA rated James R. Browning "unqualified" for a position on the Ninth Circuit, despite experience in private practice, a stint in the Justice Department, and three years as a Supreme Court clerk, the administration

went ahead with the appointment largely on the strength of a memo prepared by a Justice Department official, James Rowe, who emphasized
Browning's liberalism and the fact that

> the Ninth Circuit [is] a weak[,] conservative bench quite out of step with the
> premises of the New Frontier. . . . In the great run of cases it does not much matter
> whether a judge is liberal or conservative if he is a good judge. There are a handful
> of cases, however . . . where the judicial mind can go either way, with probity, with
> honor, self-discipline and even with precedent. This is where the "liberal" cast of
> mind . . . can move this nation forward, just as the conservative mind can and does
> hold it back. This is intangible truth, but every lawyer knows it as reality![48]

Johnson (with the assistance of John W. Macy Jr., chairman of the Civil
Service Commission, Attorney General Nicholas Katzenbach, and deputy
attorney general Ramsey Clark) could also make controversial appointments, most notably his decision to nominate former Mississippi governor
(and segregationist) James P. Coleman for a position on the Court of Appeals of the Fifth Circuit: Coleman was opposed by Senate liberals as well
as professors such as Thomas Emerson and Louis Lusky before eventually
being confirmed 76 to 8.[49] At the behest of North Carolina's Democratic
senators, Sam Ervin and B. Everett Jordan, Johnson agreed to nominate
Woodrow Wilson Jones to a federal district court position, even though he
had been a signatory of the Southern Manifesto and was strongly opposed
by the North Carolina NAACP. Examples such as these reflected Johnson's
commitment to accommodate senatorial courtesy.[50] Still, overall his choices
reflected a concerted effort to reconstruct the ideological center of gravity
of the federal judiciary. Johnson, appointing judges in the wake of the Civil
Rights Act of 1964, was even more insistent than Kennedy on thoroughly
exploring his nominees' record on civil rights; "want this on every judge" was
his general written instruction, and presidential papers reveal consistent notes
on the civil rights views of potential candidates.[51] Johnson also made a serious
effort to recruit African Americans into the federal judiciary—an unprecedented 5 percent of all his judicial appointments.[52] Toward the end of his
presidency, when opposition to Johnson became more vocal, the president
became more insistent that judges be loyal to him personally and to the goals
of his administration.[53]

Even when Kennedy and Johnson were forced to accommodate senators in making certain lower court appointments, they nevertheless attempted to find judges who would not be obstructionist in the face of clear
Supreme Court directives. As Katzenbach explained it, they took steps to

ensure that even more conservative appointees would "follow the law of the land."[54] This made the appointment of Supreme Court justices a critical factor in reconstructing the overall decision-making bias of the federal judiciary. Presidents do not always have this opportunity, but with four acceptable liberals on the Court at the time of Kennedy's inauguration the White House was in a position either to fortify that wing or undermine it.

Despite the fact that Kennedy nominated a candidate who would eventually earn a reputation for judicial conservatism, the evidence is clear that these Democratic presidents were interested in appointing justices who would represent the more liberal wing of their party. When in March 1962 the conservative Eisenhower appointee Charles Whittaker informed the White House of his intention to retire from the Court, the initial assumption was that Kennedy would appoint Secretary of Labor Arthur J. Goldberg, who had been promised the seat on at least "a half dozen" occasions.[55] However, Kennedy concluded that he could not yet afford to part with his labor secretary, who was actively managing negotiations between U.S. Steel and the Steelworkers' Union. Attention then turned to Judge William Henry Hastie, the first black appointed to the federal circuit bench and one of only two black circuit court judges (the other being Thurgood Marshall, who was serving a recess appointment on the Second Circuit while awaiting a delayed Senate confirmation). Ironically, though, the nomination of this potentially historic candidate was sidetracked in part because the White House was explicitly trying to accommodate the liberal wing of the Court. Opposition came from Chief Justice Earl Warren and Justice William O. Douglas, who thought that Hastie was not liberal enough; this, combined with Dolan's assessment that the nomination would alienate Southern Democrats in the Senate and "blow everything we've got going on the Hill," was enough to shift the focus to a less controversial candidate, Kennedy loyalist Byron White, whose reputation and legal credentials would ensure no political problems for the administration.[56] Five months later, when Felix Frankfurter announced his retirement plans in August 1962 after suffering a stroke, Kennedy focused exclusively on Goldberg, who had completed his primary mission to prevent a nationwide steel strike.[57]

By all accounts, Johnson assumed as early as 1964 that his first Supreme Court appointee would be his close friend and advisor Abe Fortas. The president was so insistent on making the appointment that he famously schemed to convince the Court's newest justice, Goldberg, to step down and accept the position of UN ambassador. Although Johnson was single-minded about his choice of Fortas, he did ask Katzenbach to prepare a memo reviewing all possible options, and in that memo, Katzenbach emphasized the importance of appointing a Democrat (in order to avoid giving the Republicans a fourth seat on the Court), the advantages of considering a Jewish nominee, and the president's desire to appoint "an open-minded, judicious liberal." When Fortas proved resistant to the president's overtures, the White House arranged for the intervention of Justice Douglas, who was one of Fortas's original mentors at Yale. Fortas was eventually "ambushed" into accepting the nomination, and he quickly joined the Warren-Douglas-Brennan wing of the Court.[58]

Johnson was also single-minded about appointing Thurgood Marshall to the Supreme Court. After appointing him solicitor general to replace the retiring Archibald Cox, Johnson designed a political maneuver that he hoped would force conservative justice Tom Clark from the bench—a much better exchange than the Fortas-for-Goldberg deal, which maintained but did not increase the Court's newly constructed liberal majority. The plan was for LBJ to name Clark's son, Ramsey Clark, as attorney general, replacing Katzenbach, who left to become undersecretary of state, and thus create a perceived "conflict of interest." As Johnson told Ramsey Clark, "if my judgment is that you become attorney general, he [Tom Clark] would have to leave the Court. For no other reason than the public appearance of an old man sitting on his boy's case. Every taxi driver in the country, he'd tell me that the old man couldn't judge fairly what his old boy is sending up (laughter)."[59] Johnson was especially delighted that Marshall would be a completely reliable "liberal . . . chalk it up there 100 percent of the time." Ramsey Clark suggested that Marshall might be a liberal on civil rights but more moderate on criminal justice ("he reflects an older generation's attitude") but Johnson didn't think so. "I think we'd have to put Marshall on the Court. . . . And my judgment is with Hugo Black, Bill Douglas, the Chief, Abe Fortas . . . they'll just have a field day," not just on civil rights but on a range of constitutional issues, including the rights of criminal defendants. (Johnson quipped, "They wouldn't send a man to the penitentiary by God for raping a woman if you had a photograph of him."[60]) Just as planned, when Johnson announced the appointment of Ramsey Clark, the new attorney general's father immediately announced that he would resign from the Court at the end of the current term.

Johnson's final opportunity to fortify the liberal bloc on the Supreme Court came in June 1968 when Earl Warren conveyed his intention to retire. This sort of "strategic retirement" is a common way for justices to influence the Court's constitutional policy making; Warren knew that his constitutional agenda would be better protected if the selection emerged from a Democratic president (and Senate) than if it came from a Republican president, and by the spring of 1968 Democrats had every reason to be worried about whether they would be able to hold onto the White House.[61] (Warren sent word that he wanted to meet with the self-proclaimed lame-duck president on June 11, less than a week after Robert Kennedy was assassinated.) Once again Johnson considered his top adviser Fortas, who had continued to be a loyal servant of the president (by attending meetings and drafting speeches and executive orders) even after joining the Court. As David Yalof put it (citing the recollections of Joseph Califano), "Johnson viewed the Court as a means both of perpetuating his social reforms and of upholding various legislative compromises he had reached on controversial issues ranging from aid for parochial schools to consumer, health, and environmental legislation. Who better to protect the president's legacy than Fortas, who had played a key role in drafting much of that legislation in the first place?"[62]

To take over Fortas's spot as an associate justice, Johnson quickly focused on his old friend Judge William "Homer" Thornberry of the U.S. Court of Appeals for the Fifth Circuit and a "political clone of LBJ: a moderate-liberal Texan . . . who supported civil rights for minorities and liberal protections for free speech."[63] However, despite Johnson's intention to have his agenda retreat into the judiciary, the opportunities for political entrenchment were diminishing. Presidents historically have a more difficult time with Senate confirmation during the fourth year of their term. Compounding that conventional problem was Johnson's headstrong decision (against the advice of Secretary of Defense Clark Clifford and White House special counsel Larry Temple) to simultaneously nominate two old personal friends. Republicans from outside their own Senate leadership (led by Robert Griffin of Michigan and George Murphy of California) circulated a petition in the Senate cloakroom opposing any action on the nominations before the November elections. Proceedings went forward anyway, and opponents assaulted Fortas with criticisms of controversial Warren Court rulings, allegations of impropriety with respect to Fortas's ongoing relationship to the president, and revelations that Fortas had improperly accepted a huge lecture fee ($15,000) for participating in several college seminars arranged by his former law partner. When Democrats were unable to kill a filibuster (led by Republicans but also supported by Georgia's powerful Democratic Senator Richard B. Russell, who felt betrayed when Ramsey Clark temporarily held up a federal judgeship that Russell sponsored),

Fortas asked Johnson to withdraw his nomination.[64] In mid-October Johnson threw in the towel: he announced that Warren's replacement would be determined by the winner of the upcoming presidential election.[65]

As it turns out, even with the failure produced by this final overreaching, Democratic efforts to transform the federal judiciary in the 1960s were remarkably successful. Kennedy inherited a federal judiciary that was evenly split between Republicans and Democrats. By the end of Johnson's administration, over 70 percent of judges in this enlarged judiciary were appointed by Democratic presidents—more than 39 percent by Johnson himself.[66] In 1970 a Republican was in the White House and Democrats controlled the House and Senate by margins of 57 percent and 56 percent, respectively; that same year, Democrats made up 63 percent of circuit court judges and 66 percent of district court judges.

Moreover, even with the need to accommodate senatorial courtesy during the appointment process, these judges turned out to have remarkably liberal voting records. One study, examining the "percentage of liberal decisions rendered by district court appointees" of various twentieth-century presidents found Kennedy's appointees reaching more liberal outcomes than Eisenhower appointees; Johnson's judges were significantly more liberal.[67] A study of court of appeals decisions between 1961 and 1964 found that "the Democrats appear relatively more 'liberal' than Republicans in cases which involve what might be called 'economic liberalism'" but "equally 'liberal' on the criminal and civil liberties categories";[68] however, after the Kennedy and Johnson appointees had a chance to establish their record, the effects of liberal entrenchment on decisions across the board became more pronounced. In particular, Johnson's court of appeals judges had the highest liberalism score on issues relating to civil liberties and criminal procedure, compared with all other judges categorized by appointing president; Nixon's judges had the lowest liberalism scores on these issues.[69]

Similar changes were also apparent in the Supreme Court. Between 1958 and 1962 due process claims represented around 21 percent of the Supreme Court's docket; this rate grew to 31 percent during the 1968 through 1972 terms. Similarly, between 1958 and 1962 equality claims represented 5 percent of the Court's docket, compared with 12 percent between 1968 and 1972. As a percentage of the Supreme Court's overall docket, civil liberties claims skyrocketed in the latter part of the 1960s, while claims over federal regulation and economic matters declined dramatically.[70] A Supreme Court that, under Eisenhower, handed down "liberal" decisions in civil liberties cases 58 percent of the time now voted liberal in approximately 75 percent of cases during the Johnson administration. This is no surprise, given that Kennedy and Johnson justices were significantly more liberal than the justices they replaced.[71]

Partisan Entrenchment and the Politics of Constitutional Change

What Powe calls "History's Warren Court"—the Court that would usher in modern liberal constitutional jurisprudence—came into being in 1962 precisely because of Kennedy's commitment to Warren's constitutional vision, and it persisted throughout the decade because Johnson also aligned himself with the Court's liberal wing.[72] White and Goldberg together might have constituted the fifth and sixth votes for a solid liberal majority, but White was much less reliable on criminal procedure and civil liberties than he was on civil rights, and so it was the New Frontiersman Goldberg who (initially) became the pivot point for constitutional change. His 89 percent liberal voting record was second only to Douglas's. This fifth vote majority continued when Goldberg was replaced by Fortas (a protégé of Douglas), who voted with Warren 83–92 percent of the time, and was fortified in 1967 when Marshall replaced Clark.[73]

Powe is essentially correct that, during this period, the Court was (by design) "a functioning part of the Kennedy-Johnson liberalism of the mid and late 1960s."[74] Kennedy, who had to face questions about the separation of church and state during his presidential campaign, actively supported the Court's school prayer decisions. The justices declared the poll tax unconstitutional only after Congress encouraged the Justice Department to challenge those laws in federal court. The justices turned back legal challenges to the Vietnam War, and allowed (by a vote of 7–1) for the prosecution of protesters who burned their draft cards.[75] In *New York Times v. Sullivan*, the Court shielded the national press against harassing lawsuits from Southern officials and thus helped ensure a favorable media climate for passage of the Civil Rights Act of 1964. In reviewing civil rights legislation the Court provided forceful declarations of congressional power, thus "extending an offer to Congress to become a full partner" with the Court to promote the vision of the Great Society.[76]

This partnership was partially reciprocated in 1965, when the Johnson administration created the Legal Services Program (LSP) as part of the Office of Economic Opportunity, as an adjunct of the War on Poverty. The goal of the office was to give the poor greater access to courts—and, by so doing, give the justices greater opportunities to advance a more liberal agenda.[77] The

LSP's Supreme Court docket raised a wide variety of legal issues, including constitutional questions involving claims of equal protection, due process, the First Amendment, criminal procedure, and access to courts.[78] When the Court first decided a case in favor of welfare recipients it was in a lawsuit sponsored by the LSP; similarly, the landmark case *Shapiro v. Thompson* (1969), striking down residency requirements for welfare recipients, was also made possible by that program. More generally, during its nine-year tenure, the LSP sponsored 164 cases before the Supreme Court, 119 of which were accepted for review. The eighty cases that received plenary consideration represented 7 percent of all written opinions handed down by the Supreme Court during this era.[79] The LSP's success rate also inspired other liberal organizations dedicated to civil rights and liberties to beef up their litigation so as to "take full advantage of a favorable judicial climate."[80] Not to be outdone, the justices, on their own initiative, also made the Court more accessible to certain categories of litigants, not only by nationalizing bill of rights protections, but also through self-conscious adjustments in standing requirements.[81]

As a general matter, it should be easy to accept that much of the Court's constitutional decision making during this period cannot be understood without situating the Court in the larger context of 1960s Democratic Party politics. But it would also be misleading to leave the impression that the newly reconstructed federal judiciary was merely a harmonious partner with New Frontier and Great Society Democrats. To show a political relationship between the Court and the dominant political coalition is not to argue that the justices followed the instructions of party leaders. Even when the justices were upholding features of the Democratic agenda, they were also articulating specific doctrines of constitutional law, and nobody in the White House or the Senate was instructing the justices on the precise formulation of the constitutional tests associated with (for example) school prayer, seditious libel, or the scope of Congress' authority to pass civil rights legislation. In this respect, the justices often acted on their own initiative and not as a mere agent or partner.

In fact, one of the features of political entrenchment in an institution that has extremely broad policy-making jurisdiction is that the appointees' ideological disposition will inevitably manifest itself in ways that were not considered by the appointing parties. Sometimes this leads to decision making that presidents and senators did not anticipate but also did not oppose; other times it leads to unanticipated problems for the governing coalition. The liberals were central in establishing the specific legal rationale for

Reynolds v. Sims (1964) (with Harlan dissenting and Clark and Stewart concurring). Solicitor General Cox was pushed by the Kennedy White House to advocate a fairly egalitarian conception of reapportionment reform, but even he was surprised at the sweeping nature of the decision. (One of the victorious plaintiffs remarked, "We would have been satisfied with less than we got," and Anthony Lewis wrote in the *New York Times* that "even some liberal-minded persons, admirers of the modern Supreme Court, find themselves stunned.") In the wake of the decision the House (over the objections of the chairman of the Judiciary Committee) passed a jurisdiction-stripping bill, but liberal senators successfully filibustered similar efforts, and by 1968 all the fuss had passed.[82] Similarly, the new liberal majority allowed Brennan to turn his dissenting opinion in *Braunfeld v. Brown* (1961) into a majority opinion in *Sherbert v. Verner* (1963), thereby rewriting the constitutional standard governing protections for religious freedom.[83]

Maybe most notoriously (within the canonical history of American constitutional development), the new liberal majority took the lead in constitutionalizing the regulation of marital privacy and contraceptive use. The Court inherited by Kennedy ducked the issue in *Poe v. Ullman* (1961), but by 1965 there was plenty of support for jumping into the fray—even if there was no consensus among the justices over the proper constitutional justification for striking down Connecticut's antiquated ban on contraceptives. The significance of *Griswold v. Connecticut* lay not so much with the development of any coherent constitutional test, but with the signal that the Court was now in the business of resolving disputes over infringements on personal freedoms. This was not a move that either Black or Stewart considered appropriate, but there was a bipartisan consensus among the other justices that it was proper for the Court to provide protections against state intrusions into certain intimate decisions. Even the typically restrained Harlan agreed that the Court should use the due process clause to protect the unenumerated freedom of married couples to use contraceptives. For all the ink that would be spilled in subsequent decades about the appropriateness of such a role for the Court, the decision in *Griswold* itself was notably uncontroversial at the time, and the commitment to judicial protection for personal liberties remains bipartisan to this day.[84]

However, not all of the Court's initiatives proved as uncontroversial, or as benign for the Great Society coalition. After the well-regarded *Gideon v. Wainwright* in 1963, the Court's criminal procedure decisions proved extremely unpopular.[85] In *Escobedo v. Illinois* (1964), a bare liberal majority (over the dissents of Harlan, Stewart, White, and Clark) threw out an interrogation on the grounds that the suspect was questioned outside the presence of his lawyer, despite Escobedo's repeated requests to see his lawyer (who was in the station house trying to see his client). Goldberg's opinion was interpreted as a slap in the face of police efforts to get suspects to confess.[86] Complaints about liberal judges undermining law enforcement did not do Barry Goldwater much good, but the argument gained political traction after the urban rioting of 1965 and after public opinion began responding to rising crime rates. The decision in *Miranda v. Arizona* (1966) seemed to confirm the warnings of Court critics. This time, the five liberals imposed sweeping new police reforms on the nation. (In Powe's words: "*Gideon* required five backward states to change their laws and behavior. *Mapp* required half the states to change theirs. *Miranda* required *all* the states to change theirs."[87]) The decision worked against Democrats in the midterm 1966 elections, where the question of urban riots, "crime in the streets," and "law and order" framed many races. Undeterred, the Court hammered away at its agenda, ruling in 1967 that the government could not order a lineup for a suspect without the presence of defense counsel.[88] By 1968 many congressional Democrats were looking for cover and found some by passing the Omnibus Crime Control and Safe Streets Act, which (among other things) attempted to overturn a number of the Court's criminal procedure decisions.[89] Still, the Court's criminal procedure liberalism was successfully used against the Democrats by Richard Nixon as part of his "law-and-order" presidential bid in 1968. As candidate Nixon put it, certain judges had "gone too far in weakening the peace forces as against the criminal forces."

Because of the Fortas fiasco (which was made possible, in part, by Southern Democratic opposition to Warren Court liberalism), Nixon was able to mitigate the influence of the Kennedy and Johnson years on the U.S. Supreme Court. For his first appointment to the Court, replacing Chief Justice Warren, Nixon chose someone who was arguably the most prominent critic of the Warren Court in the federal judiciary, chief judge of the D.C. Circuit Warren Burger. Nixon's efforts to disentrench liberalism on the U.S. Supreme Court continued with the nominee chosen to replace the retiring Fortas, South Carolinian Clement Haynsworth Jr. of the U.S. Court of Appeals for the Fourth Circuit, but Senate Democrats defeated the nomination. There was a similar fate awaiting Georgian G. Harrold Carswell, when the Senate, for the first time in American history, turned down a second consecutive presidential nomination for the Supreme Court. The result of these battles was that Nixon was forced to turn to the more moderate Harry Blackmun, who ended up voting in a liberal direction on civil liberties issues more than half the time and who supported the liberal position on civil rights more than 61 percent of the time.[90] Within a few years Black and Harlan retired and were replaced by Lewis Powell (37 percent pro–civil liberties voting record) and William Rehnquist (21.8 percent pro–civil liberties voting record).[91] More generally, a Democratic Congress was extremely stingy about authorizing new judgeships for a Republican president, and unlike virtually every president since Grant, he left the White House with the judiciary still under the control of the opposition party.[92]

After Nixon, the Court no longer had the sort of reliable liberal majority that characterized the heyday of the Warren Court; only Douglas, Brennan, and Marshall remained from that group. But to a considerable extent, the constitutional innovations of the 1960s remained alive even after changes in the Court's personnel. Although the entrenchment of a majority of liberal judges did not survive for long, the entrenchment of liberal constitutional policies continued for some time, at least in many areas of the law. This was because Warren Court liberals were not merely deciding case outcomes; they were constructing a series of "jurisprudential regimes"—that is, constitutional doctrines, standards, and tests that framed the ways in which justices approached the issues in particular cases—and most of these jurisprudential regimes were acceptable to the Court's new majorities.[93] The liberal justices' innovations in free speech jurisprudence survived. Expanded protections for free exercise of religion were embraced by Burger in *Wisconsin v. Yoder* (1973), and Brennan's approach in *Sherbert* remained the prevailing framework for analyzing free exercise claims for a quarter century, until a more conservative Court rolled back special protections for religious liberty in *Employment Division v. Smith* (1988).[94] In the area of the establishment clause the unanimous decision in *Lemon v. Kurtzman* built upon (and even expanded) the more separationist approach advocated by the liberals in the 1960s.[95] Maybe most notably, the innovative right to privacy (or freedom of choice over certain intimate decisions) was expanded in *Eisenstadt v. Baird* (1972) and *Roe v. Wade* (1973)—with Burger dissenting in the former but not the latter.[96] The entrenchment of these 1960s precedents was successful enough that, by the mid-1980s, it could be said that the Burger Court was "the counter-revolution that wasn't."[97]

On the other hand, Nixon's reconstructed Court was able to roll back some of the Warren Court's revolution in criminal procedure. For example, in *Harris v. New York* (1971), the *Miranda* dissenters joined forces with Burger and Blackmun in holding that confessions excluded under *Miranda* could be used to impeach a defendant's trial testimony; other exceptions to

Miranda (and to the exclusionary rule) would follow.[98] The requirement that lineups be done in the presence of counsel was gutted when Nixon appointees (over dissents by Brennan, Douglas, and Marshall) ruled that this right did not attach prior to indictment.[99] Over the years similar steps were taken in other areas of criminal procedure to rein in the vision of due process advanced in the mid-1960s. However, even in this area of the law, some of the Warren Court's innovations were quite long-lasting, including the fundamental holding in *Miranda* itself, which was reiterated by the Rehnquist Court as late as 2000.[100]

Conclusion

Because of their embrace of the liberal wing of the Supreme Court, Kennedy and Johnson set in motion an important constitutional legacy. The decisions of that era fundamentally changed constitutional law in many areas, and a good number of those changes persisted well after the liberals no longer constituted a majority on the Court. It may not be over-stating it to say that those decisions framed constitutional politics—and constitutional theory—in the United States for a generation.

There were a number of factors that allowed 1960s constitutional deci-sion making to persist even after Republican appointees changed the Court's composition. The Congress remained under the control of the Democratic Party, and this prevented the appointment of justices who may have been more inclined to roll back Warren-era precedents. Precedents such as *Reynolds v. Sims*, *Sherbert v. Verner*, or *New York Times v. Sullivan*, although revolutionary at the time, were largely accepted by the late 1960s (or at least had become uncontroversial) and thus were easy enough for new justices to embrace (or at least tolerate). Largely, changes in the political system—such as the women's movement—provided a political context whereby the lib-eralization of certain constitutional norms was increasingly acceptable to moderates in both parties.

Still, it is unlikely that liberal constitutionalism would have emerged without the efforts of Kennedy and Johnson to create reliable liberal majori-ties on the Supreme Court. Their appointments turned over the authorship of pathbreaking opinions to the most liberal justices ever appointed; thus, rather than grudging or constrained accommodation of constitutional change, the Court took the lead and offered a full embrace. In the language of New Institutionalist scholarship, these developments highlight the role of sequencing and dynamics of path dependency on the specific shape of constitutional change. If Nixon had won the 1960 election, or if Kennedy and Johnson preferred to marginalize the judiciary by fortifying the Harlan-Frankfurter wing of the Court, then it is difficult to imagine a scenario whereby similar precedents have an opportunity to earn the respect or toleration of later Court majorities. Then again, all such imagined alternative histories are matters of speculation. In the actual history of American constitutional development in the 1960s the changes in our constitutional practices came about because of choices made by those who appointed the justices.

The political consequences of these efforts were less straightforward than Democrats would have preferred. Kennedy and Johnson certainly created a partner in promoting many features of Great Society liberalism. The Court also took the lead in other policy areas that were broadly acceptable to the party. At the same time, the justices articulated constitutional views that proved politically damaging to the Democrats, both in 1966 and 1968. It is, if you will, a "nonequilibrium" account of political change, as well as one that incorporates unintended consequences.

Nevertheless, there is reason to believe that parties consider the potential unanticipated consequences of partisan entrenchment in the judiciary to be outweighed by the advantages of having sympathetic decision makers in relatively insulated policy-making institutions. After all, one of the explicit goals of the Reagan Justice Department was to use judicial appointments, not simply to reverse some of the more unwelcome features of the modern judicial liberalism, but also to institutionalize key features of the political agenda of the New Right, including a rollback of the scope of federal power over commerce and civil rights and an expansion of the idea of state sovereignty. The Office of Legal Policy under Reagan prepared a 199-page guide to judicial appointments, entitled *The Constitution in the Year 2000: Choices Ahead in Constitutional Interpretation*, which was premised on the assumption that "there are few factors that are more critical to determining the course of the Nation, and yet more often overlooked, than the values and philosophies of the men and women who populate the third co-equal branch of the national government—the federal judiciary."[101] The Reagan and Bush I White Houses appointed four of the five justices who became known as the "federalism five" and elevated the fifth to the position of chief justice.[102] As is made clear by the recent appointments of Chief Justice John Roberts and Justice Samuel Alito, constitutional change has as much to do with the decisions made by power holders outside the judiciary as with the constitutional visions and institutional circumstances of the justices themselves.

Notes

I thank Mark Graber, Keith Whittington, the editors of this volume, the anonymous reviewer, and the organizers and participants at the Constitutional Law Workshop at the University of Chicago Law School, the Yale Legal Theory workshop, and the Legal History Workshop at the UCLA Law School. Lingering mistakes and weaknesses are there despite all their best efforts.

1. See the editors' Introduction to this volume.

2. Terri Jennings Peretti, *In Defense of a Political Court* (Princeton, N.J.: Princeton University Press, 1999), 133.

3. For example, Harding appointed 57 Republicans and 3 Democrats (95 percent from his own party); Coolidge appointed 92 Republicans and 8 Democrats (92 percent); Hoover appointed 67 Republicans and 14 Democrats (87.2 percent); FDR appointed 229 Democrats and 12 Republicans (95 percent); Truman appointed 143 Democrats and 14 Republicans (91 percent); and Eisenhower appointed 186 Republicans and 15 Democrats (92.5 percent). See Harold W. Chase, *Federal Judges: The Appointing Process* (Minneapolis: University of Minnesota, 1972), 72 (citing *Congressional Quarterly* 20 [1962]: 1175). Between 1869 and 1992, the "same party appointment rate" of district and circuit court judges was around 93 percent; see Deborah J. Barrow, Gary Zuk, and Gerard S. Gryski, *The Federal Judiciary and Institutional Change* (Ann Arbor: University of Michigan Press, 1996), 15. For an overview of the political background of selected court of appeals judges in the mid-1960s, see J. Woodward Howard Jr., *Courts of Appeals in the Federal Judicial System: A Study of the Second, Fifth, and District of Columbia Circuits* (Princeton, N.J.: Princeton University Press, 1981), 92. Recall Griffin B. Bell's famous remark: "For me, becoming a federal judge wasn't very difficult. I managed John F. Kennedy's presidential campaign in Georgia. Two of my oldest and closest friends were the two senators from Georgia. And I was campaign manager and special, unpaid counsel for the governor" (93). Obviously, a different political dynamic exists in systems where party leaders do not staff constitutional courts.

4. See Robert A. Dahl, "Decision-making in a Democracy: The Supreme Court as a National Policy-Maker," *Journal of Public Law* 6 (1957): 279; Mark A. Graber, "The Non-Majoritarian Difficulty: Legislative Deference to the Judiciary," *Studies in American Political Development* 7 (1993): 35; Howard Gillman, "Judicial Independence through the Lens of *Bush v. Gore*: Four Lessons from Political Science," *Ohio State Law Journal* 64 (2003): 249. On the various motivations that legislators might have when delegating authority to other institutions, see Stefan Voigt and Eli M. Salzberger, "Choosing Not to Choose: When Politicians Choose to Delegate Powers," *Kyklos* 55 (May 2002).

5. For a discussion of this issue from a more comparative perspective, see Ran Hirschl, "Israel's 'Constitutional Revolution': The Legal Interpretation of Entrenched

Civil Liberties in an Emerging Neo-Liberal Economic Order," *American Journal of Comparative Law* 46 (Summer 1995): 427–452; and Hirschl, "The Political Origins of Judicial Empowerment through Constitutionalization: Lessons from Four Constitutional Revolutions," *Law and Social Inquiry* 25 (Winter 2000): 91–148.

6. "How Political Parties Can Use the Courts to Advance Their Agendas: Federal Courts in the United States, 1875–1891," *American Political Science Review* 96 (2002): 511–524.

7. Jack M. Balkin and Sanford Levinson, "Understanding the Constitutional Revolution," *Virginia Law Review* 87 (October 2001): 1045; see especially 1066–1083.

8. Ibid., 1067–1069. For examples of the political science literature demonstrating the effect of Senate politics on presidential Supreme Court nominations, see Lilliard E. Richardson Jr. and John M. Scheb II, "Divided Government and the Supreme Court," *American Politics Quarterly* 21 (1993): 458–472; Byron J. Moraski and Charles R. Shipan, "The Politics of Supreme Court Nominations: A Theory of Institutional Constraints and Choices," *American Journal of Political Science* 43 (October 1999): 1069–1095. For a study of the factors influencing whether senators vote to confirm Supreme Court nominees (including the ideology of the senator and the preferences of interest groups), see Jeffrey A. Segal, Charles M. Cameron, and Albert Cover, "A Spatial Model of Roll Call Voting: Senators, Constituents, Presidents, and Interest Groups in Supreme Court Confirmations," *American Journal of Political Science* 36 (February 1992): 96–121.

9. Balkin and Levinson, "Understanding the Constitutional Revolution," 1071.

10. Similarly, the fact that conservatives control the leadership of the Republican Party in Congress and the White House does not mean that someone like David Souter is not still properly regarded as a Republican—a moderate to liberal northeastern Republican in the mold of Susan Collins or (maybe more appropriately) Jim Jeffords.

11. Balkin and Levinson, "Understanding the Constitutional Revolution," 1075–1076.

12. Ibid., 1077.

13. Balkin and Levinson appropriately distinguish their view from Bruce Ackerman's overly formulaic and ultimately unconvincing conception of constitutional change as a by-product of a certain kind of special electoral politics that qualifies as a "constitutional moment." Balkin and Levinson, "Understanding the Constitutional Revolution," 1079–1080.

14. Sheldon Goldman, *Picking Federal Judges: Lower Court Selection from Roosevelt through Reagan* (New Haven, Conn.: Yale University Press, 1997), 3.

15. Goldman, *Picking Federal Judges*, 153.

16. This is the main argument developed by Dahl, "Decision-making in a Democracy."

17. See, for example, Michael J. Klarman, "Majoritarian Judicial Review: The Entrenchment Problem," *Georgetown Law Review* 85 (1997): 491.

18. It seems to me that the New Deal reconfiguration of the federal judiciary is better understood either as an example of alignment or antientrenchment (likewise Grant's focus on removing constitutional barriers to paper money).

19. Balkin and Levinson, "Understanding the Constitutional Revolution," 1068.

20. *Stuart v. Laird*, 5 U.S. 299 (1803).

21. See Keith E. Whittington, *Constitutional Construction: Divided Powers and Constitutional Meaning* (Cambridge, Mass.: Harvard University Press, 1999).

22. See Mark A. Graber, "Federalist or Friends of Adams: The Marshall Court and Party Politics," *Studies in American Political Development* 12 (1998): 209; and Michael J. Klarman, "How Great Were the 'Great' Marshall Court Decisions?," *Virginia Law Review* 87 (October 1998): 1111.

23. See Goldman's *Picking Federal Judges*, especially chap. 5, entitled "The New Frontier/Great Society Judiciary."

24. Mary L. Dudziak, *Cold War Civil Rights: Race and the Image of American Democracy* (Princeton, N.J.: Princeton University Press, 2000).

25. See Walter F. Murphy, *Congress and the Court: A Case Study in the American Political Process* (Chicago: University of Chicago Press, 1962); and C. Herman Pritchett, *Congress Versus the Supreme Court, 1957–1960* (Minneapolis: University of Minnesota Press, 1961).

26. Potter Stewart's nomination was opposed by many Southern Democrats in the Senate. Senator Richard B. Russell of Georgia charged that his nomination was "part of a deliberate policy by the Department of Justice to perpetuate some recent decisions of the Court in segregation rulings, which decisions were partly based on amicus curiae briefs submitted by the Department of Justice." See Henry J. Abraham, *Justices, Presidents, and Senators: A History of the U.S. Supreme Court Appointments from Washington to Clinton*, new rev. ed. (Lanham, Md.: Rowman and Littlefield, 1999), 205, citing Congressional Record, 86th Cong., 1st sess., May 5, 1959, 6693. Voting no on the nomination were senators from Alabama, Arkansas, Georgia, Louisiana, Mississippi, North Carolina, South Carolina, and Virginia (plus one of Florida's senators, Spessard L. Holland). Democratic Senators George Smathers of Florida, Estes Kefauver and Albert Gore of Tennessee, and Lyndon B. Johnson and Ralph Yarborough of Texas joined all Senate Republicans in support of Stewart's appointment (205, 351).

27. Jeffrey A. Segal and Harold J. Spaeth, *The Supreme Court and the Attitudinal Model Revisited* (Cambridge: Cambridge University Press, 2002), 220.

28. Barrow et al., *Federal Judiciary*, 62.

29. PL 87-36; Barrow et al., *Federal Judiciary*, 54.

30. PL 89-372.

31. PL 90-347.

32. Barrow et al., *Federal Judiciary*, 45.

33. Ibid., 51–52; the bill was Public Law 83-294, creating three new circuit court positions and thirty-one district court positions. The fact that there was extended congressional inaction under a previously unified Democratic government shows that parties in power do not always pursue strategies of partisan entrenchment in the judiciary.

34. Actually, four positions were authorized during this period, three of which reflected the granting of statehood to Alaska and Hawaii. Barrow et al., *Federal Judiciary*, 52.

35. 15 *Congressional Quarterly Weekly Report* 1206 (1959), cited in Chase, *Federal Judges*, 74; see also *Federal Courts and Judges*, Hearings before Subcommittee No. 5 of the House Judiciary Committee, 86 Cong. 2 sess. (February 2, 3, and 29, 1960), 51, cited in ibid., 214 (Deputy Attorney General Walsh reassuring Representative Celler that the Democratic nominees would be acceptable to the Democratic Party and would not merely be "Eisenhower Democrats").

36. *Federal Courts and Judges*, Hearings before Subcommittee No. 5 of the House Judiciary Committee, 87 Cong. 1 sess. (March 1 and 2, 1961).

37. Cited in Chase, *Federal Judges*, 48. Of the 147 vacancies, 62 were for new district court judges and 10 were for new circuit court judges. The figure also includes the two Supreme Court vacancies filled by Kennedy through October 1962. See ibid., 49.

38. Ibid., 49.

39. Ibid., 77.

40. See Goldman, *Picking Federal Judges*, 167. For a strong critique of Kennedy's Southern appointments see Victor S. Navasky, *Kennedy Justice* (New York: Atheneum, 1971), 243–276.

41. Chase, *Federal Judges*, 78.

42. Goldman, *Picking Federal Judges*, 163. Goldman goes on to report that "Justice Department officials did not ordinarily look at the decisions of those who had a judicial record, and 'there was no saliva test for liberalism,' according to Joseph Dolan."

43. Chase, *Federal Judges*, 78.

44. Goldman, *Picking Federal Judges*, 152.

45. Justice Department officials were not starry-eyed about their ability to get progressives in these posts. As Katzenbach explained, "We do not expect to find and to be able to obtain confirmation for a militant civil rights advocate in the South. What Southern senator could afford not to oppose confirmation? What we seek is to assure ourselves that nominees will follow the law of the land. We are satisfied with that much." Chase, *Federal Judges*, 80–81. In the case of Southern circuit court appointments, Goldman reports that "in every instance the administration sought to discover the candidate's views on racial segregation, and in only one instance [Pat Mehaffy of Arkansas, personal counsel to Governor Faubus and supported by Arkansas Democratic senator John McClellan and Senator J. William Fulbright] did the administration knowingly appoint a segregationist." Goldman, *Picking Federal Judges*, 168.

46. *Mallory v. U.S.*, 354 U.S. 449 (1957); Chase, *Federal Judges*, 104–105; see also Sheldon Goldman, *Picking Federal Judges*, 126 (although "Rogers did not link changing the course of court decisions to the appointment process," Justice Department officials were "alert to the policy views of candidates on issues of criminal procedure"). It should be noted, however, that there is no evidence that Eisenhower's appointees had a worse record on civil rights issues than Democratic appointees, which is no surprise, given that Brownell, Rogers, and Walsh were more liberal than Eisenhower. Jack Peltason, in *Fifty-eight Lonely Men* (New York: Harcourt, 1961), 46–51, castigated Eisenhower for contributing to a climate in which local leaders believed they could get away with resisting

Brown and other unpopular Supreme Court decisions, and also argued that the president's "nonintervention policy has had its impact on the judges as well," who knew they could not count on the president's backing. However, when the *Yale Law Journal* reviewed the record of Fifth Circuit district court judges on civil rights, they focused their criticism on two Roosevelt appointees, three Truman appointees, and four Kennedy appointees. See the discussion in Chase, *Federal Judges*, 117, citing and reviewing (in addition to Peltason) "Judicial Performance in the Fifth Circuit," *Yale Law Journal* 73 (1963): 90; and Mary Hannah Curzan, *A Case Study in the Selection of Federal Judges in the Fifth Circuit, 1953–1963* (Ann Arbor: University Microfilms, 1968). In fact, Curzan noted that "if one takes the total number of civil rights cases decided by all the Eisenhower and Kennedy judges in each year and determines the percentage of those cases that favored the Negro plaintiff, the Eisenhower judges have a more liberal record than do the Kennedy judges" (60). See also Goldman, *Picking Federal Judges*, 128–130.

47. Goldman, *Picking Federal Judges*, 114–115. On the ABA's conservatism see Chase, *Federal Judges*, 160–161, citing John R. Schmidhauser, *The Supreme Court* (New York: Holt, Rinehart and Winston, 1960), 77–78 (reviewing the ABA's views on a variety of policies between 1937 and 1960). When Kennedy nominated labor lawyer David Rabinovitz, the ABA rated him "not qualified." Civil rights lawyer Constance B. Motley was rated only qualified (the second lowest rating), as were Anthony Celebrezze (Department of Health, Education, and Welfare secretary and former mayor of Cleveland), Congressman Oren Harris, and George C. Edwards (a Detroit police commissioner who previously served for six years on the Michigan Supreme Court) (see Chase, *Federal Judges*, 163). By contrast, when Kennedy appointed the racist William Harold Cox to the district bench in Mississippi (at the behest of the chairman of the Senate Judiciary Committee, James Eastland), the ABA gave him their highest rating, "exceptionally well qualified." Robert Kennedy later explained that Cox personally assured him that he would faithfully follow the law, including the Supreme Court's civil rights rulings. "I was convinced he was honest with me, and he wasn't" (see Goldman, *Picking Federal Judges*, 167).

48. Cited in Goldman, *Picking Federal Judges*, 164–165. As Goldman points out, Browning was confirmed without difficulty and became a leading liberal on the Ninth Circuit, earning the praise of Chief Justice Rehnquist for his innovative leadership as chief judge; see William H. Rehnquist, foreword to Arthur D. Hellman, ed., *Restructuring Justice* (Ithaca, N.Y.: Cornell University Press, 1990), xi.

49. Chase, *Federal Judges*, 170–172; Goldman, *Picking Federal Judges*, 171.

50. Goldman, *Picking Federal Judges*, 171. Goldman notes that Johnson might have felt more comfortable accommodating North Carolina's senators given that the Jones nomination came two weeks after he had named Thurgood Marshall to the Supreme Court.

51. Ibid., 170.

52. Ibid., 196.

53. Ibid., 172.

54. Chase, *Federal Judges*, 81.

55. David Alistair Yalof, *Pursuit of Justices: Presidential Politics and the Selection of Supreme Court Nominees* (Chicago: University of Chicago Press, 1999), 72.

56. Ibid., 76–80; Goldman, *Picking Federal Judges*, 166; Abraham, *Justices, Presidents, and Senators*, 209. (The source on Warren's and Douglas's views was Robert Kennedy.) Paul Freund was also seriously considered, but he was adamantly opposed by Robert Kennedy, possibly because Freund turned down an offer to become solicitor general in part because he did not want to serve under the president's brother. Goldman reports that Hastie's voting record became more liberal by the mid-1960s.

57. Yalof, *Pursuit of Justices*, 80–81. In his career, White ended up voting mostly with Stewart, which suggests where the moderate center of both parties was located in the early 1960s.

58. Ibid., 81–85; Abraham, *Justices, Presidents, and Senators*, 215. After Fortas reiterated his refusal to accept the nomination, Johnson caught him just before the president was scheduled to announce plans to escalate the war in Vietnam: "I'm going to send your name to the Supreme Court, and I'm sending fifty thousand boys to Vietnam, and I'm not going to hear any argument on either of them."

59. Phone conversation between Ramsey Clark and Lyndon Johnson, Tape No. K67.01, 1/25/67, 8:22 P.M., PNO: 6, LBJL, cited in Yalof, *Pursuit of Justices*, 88.

60. Yalof, *Pursuit of Justices*, 89, 239n100.

61. More generally, there is a partisan "generational" pattern to replacement appointments on district and circuit courts since the New Deal, in the sense that Roosevelt and Truman appointees typically left the bench under Kennedy and Johnson, and the appointees of Kennedy and Johnson tended to retire under Carter. See Barrow et al., *Federal Judiciary*, 20.

62. Yalof, *Pursuit of Justices*, 91.

63. Ibid., 92.

64. Goldman, *Picking Federal Judges*, 171–172; Bruce Allen Murphy, *Fortas* (New York: Morrow, 1988), 337–359; Abraham, *Justices, Presidents, and Senators*, 218; John Massaro, "LBJ and the Fortas Nomination for Chief Justice," *Political Science Quarterly* 97 (Winter 1982–1983): 4. The federal judge was Alexander Lawrence, and Clark's concern was that Lawrence had given an allegedly racist speech in the 1950s.

65. Yalof, *Pursuit of Justices*, 93–94. The episode demonstrates that the politics of entrenchment can be exceeding complicated, requiring difficult strategic decisions. For example, the entrenchment thesis might be criticized on the grounds that Kennedy and Johnson spent too much time accommodating senatorial courtesy and compromised on certain nominees. However, had Johnson heeded the advice of those recommending a less bold course of action (for example, by nominating a moderate Republican for the lower court position—someone like Albert Jenner, who was chairing the ABA's Standing Committee on the Federal Judiciary), his efforts at ensuring a lasting liberal entrenchment on the Supreme Court would have been even more successful.

66. Barrow et al., *Federal Judiciary*, 62.

67. Robert A. Carp and Ronald Stidham, *The Federal Courts*, 4th ed. (Washington, D.C.: CQ Press, 2001), 99. More generally, when comparing Democratic and Republican district court judges between 1932 and 1998, these authors found that Democratic judges reached significantly more liberal decisions when issues involved the right to privacy, affirmative action, local economic regulation, race discrimination, women's rights, freedom of religion, criminal convictions, and freedom of expression. On other issues (Indian rights, state habeas corpus pleas, union members versus unions, rent control or excess profits), the differences between these categories of judges was much less pronounced (134). For a thorough review of the literature on how party affiliation influences judicial voting behavior, see Daniel R. Pinello, "Linking Party to Judicial Ideology in American Courts: A Meta-Analysis," *Justice System Journal* 20 (1999): 219–254.

68. Sheldon Goldman, "Voting Behavior on the United States Courts of Appeals, 1961–1964," *American Political Science Review* 60 (June 1966): 374–383, 381.

69. Sheldon Goldman, "Voting Behavior on the United States Courts of Appeals Revisited," *American Political Science Review* 69 (June 1975): 491–506. For example, Goldman pointed out that Nixon's judges had the lowest liberal score in criminal procedure and civil liberties cases, whereas Johnson's judges had the highest liberal scores in both those categories (n24).

70. Susan E. Lawrence, *The Poor in Court: The Legal Services Program and Supreme Court Decision Making* (Princeton, N.J.: Princeton University Press, 1990), 113; Richard L. Pacelle Jr., "The Dynamics and Determinants of Agenda Change in the Rehnquist Court," in *Contemplating Courts*, ed. Lee Epstein (Washington, D.C.: CQ Press, 1995), 251–274, 257.

71. Segal and Spaeth, *The Supreme Court and the Attitudinal Model Revisited*, 220–221.

72. Lucas A. Powe Jr., *The Warren Court and American Politics* (Cambridge, Mass.: Harvard University Press, 2000), 207.

73. Ibid., 211–212. Of course, by the time of Marshall's arrival, Justice Black had entered the phase of his career when his liberalism was much less reliable (to say the least), and this meant that there was still a tenuous five-person liberal majority on the Court in 1967.

74. Powe, *Warren Court*, 490.

75. *U.S. v. O'Brien*, 391 U.S. 367 (1968).

76. Powe, *Warren Court*, 189–190, 265; Mark A. Graber, "Constitutional Politics and Constitutional Theory: A Misunderstood and Neglected Relationship," 27 *Law and Social Inquiry* 309 (2002): 311.

77. The office had its genesis in an influential *Yale Law Journal* article written by Edgar S. and Jean C. Cahn, "The War on Poverty: A Civilian Perspective," *Yale Law Journal* 73 (1964): 1317. Edgar Cahn received an appointment as a special assistant to Sargeant Shriver, who was heading the president's task force on poverty. The LPS lasted nine years. In July 1974 Congress passed the Legal Services Corporation Act, creating the entity that replaced the LSP. Lawrence, *Poor in Court*, 12n29, 24–25.

78. Lawrence, *Poor in Court*, 59–61, 93–94. This political commitment continued even after LSP started to establish a record. When in 1967 Republican George Murphy introduced an amendment that would have severely curtailed LSP's appellate work, it was defeated in the Senate by a vote of 52–36 (116).

79. Ibid., 9–10, 98. LSP lawyers received the most support (in descending order) from Justices Douglas, Marshall, Brennan, Fortas, Warren, and White, and relatively less support (still in descending order) from Justices Stewart, Blackmun, Powell, Harlan, Rehnquist, Burger, and Black. Ibid., 99–100, 106. For a review of the influence that LSP had on the development of law, including constitutional law, see ibid., 123–147.

80. Karen O'Connor and Lee Epstein, "Beyond Legislative Lobbying: Women's Rights Groups and the Supreme Court," *Judicature* 67 (1983): 134, 138. Conversely, as Republican presidents retooled the federal judiciary to make it more conservative, conservative public interest litigation increased. See Karen O'Connor and Lee Epstein, "The Rise of Conservative Interest Group Litigation," *Journal of Politics* 45 (May 1983): 432.

81. The obvious examples are *Flast v. Cohen*, 392 U.S. 83 (1968) (relaxing taxpayer standing to allow for greater Supreme Court review of establishment clause claims and other bill of rights protections) and *Sierra Club v. Morton*, 405 U.S. 727 (1972) (adjusting the concept of "injury in fact" to allow environmental groups to challenge government action that allegedly harmed the environment). On the politics associated with changes in standing requirements, see Karen Orren, "Standing to Sue: Interest Group Conflict in the Federal Courts," *American Political Science Review* 70 (1976): 723–741.

82. *Reynolds v. Sims*, 377 U.S. 533 (1964); Powe, *Warren Court*, 246–247, 252–254. Opponents eventually had to satisfy themselves by giving the justices a pay raise that was $3,000 less than that given to the rest of the federal judiciary. (Powe comments that "the justices' loss of part of a pay raise was more than compensated for by the losses suffered by their opponents as 'Goldwater Freshmen' poured into both the House of Representatives and state legislative chambers across the country" [254]).

83. *Sherbert v. Verner*, 374 U.S. 398 (1963).

84. *Poe v. Ullman*, 367 U.S. 497 (1961), *Griswold v. Connecticut*, 381 U.S. 479 (1965). As Michael J. Klarman points out, *Griswold* is another example of the Court imposing a national political consensus on "regional outliers." "Rethinking the Civil Rights and Civil Liberties Revolutions," *Virginia Law Review* 82 (1996): 1–67. See also Powe, *Warren Court*, 372 ("the South was an outlier on segregation; the Northeast on contraception; and the Court was tolerating no outliers").

85. *Gideon v. Wainwright*, 372 U.S. 335 (1963).

86. *Escobedo v. Illinois*, 378 U.S. 478 (1964).

87. Powe, *Warren Court*, 394; *Miranda v. Arizona*, 384 U.S. 436 (1966).

88. *U.S. v. Wade*, 388 U.S. 217 (1967) and *Gilbert v. California*, 388 U.S. 263 (1967).

89. The act included provisions that attempted to repeal *Miranda* and *Wade*. An effort to strip the Court's jurisdiction in state-based confession cases failed.

90. It was not long before Harlan and Black were replaced by Powell and Rehnquist. Overall Nixon's judicial appointees had "liberal" voting records hovering around 30 percent, compared to the almost 70 percent averages of the justices they replaced.

91. See Segal and Spaeth, *The Supreme Court and the Attitudinal Model Revisited*, 322.

92. Nixon got close, though; 49.5 percent of federal judges were appointed by Republican presidents at the time of his departure. (When Ford left the percentage of Republican federal judges was 54.2.) The only other president since Grant who left office with a judiciary that was under the control of the other party was Cleveland, whose terms came amidst periods of Republican domination. Congressional Democrats in 1969 did respond to caseload pressures and authorize a relatively small number of new judgeships (64, fewer than the number recommended by the Judicial Conference), but then kept the judiciary at that level until after Carter was elected, when 152 new judgeships were authorized (PL 95-486). Barrow et al., *Federal Judiciary*, 23, 68–71, 84.

93. On the idea of "jurisprudential regimes," see Mark J. Richards and Herbert M. Kritzer, "Jurisprudential Regimes in Supreme Court Decision Making," *American Political Science Review* 96 (2002): 305.

94. *Wisconsin v. Yoder*, 406 U.S. 205 (1972); *Employment Division v. Smith*, 485 U.S. 660 (1988).

95. *Lemon v. Kurtman*, 403 U.S. 602 (1971); see *Abington School District v. Schempp* 374 U.S. 203 (1963) (creating the "secular purpose and primary effect").

96. *Eisenstadt v. Baird*, 405 U.S. 438 (1972) and *Roe v. Wade*, 410 U.S. 113 (1973).

97. Vincent Blasi, ed., *The Burger Court: The Counter-Revolution that Wasn't* (New Haven, Conn.: Yale University Press, 1986).

98. *Harris v. New York*, 401 U.S. 422 (1971).

99. *U.S. v. Ash*, 413 U.S. 300 (1973).

100. *Dickerson v. U.S.*, 530 U.S. 428 (2000).

101. Office of Legal Policy, U.S. Department of Justice, *Report to the Attorney General, The Constitution in the Year 2000: Choices Ahead in Constitutional Interpretation* (1988), v, cited in Dawn E. Johnsen, "Ronald Reagan and the Rehnquist Court on Congressional Power: Presidential Influences on Constitutional Change," *Indiana Law Journal* 78 (Winter/Spring 2003): 363.

102. See Johnsen, "Ronald Reagan and the Rehnquist Court"; see also Dawn Johnsen, "Tipping the Scale," *Washington Monthly*, July/August 2002, 15.

Chapter 5

The New Deal Triumph as the End of History? The Judicial Negotiation of Labor Rights and Civil Rights

Ken I. Kersch

Introduction

To a degree not widely appreciated, popular and scholarly understandings of the trajectories of twentieth-century constitutional change have been shaped by the intense gravitational pull of a progressive narrative or "constitutive story" of American history. That story begins with the conviction that constitutional modernity was born in a dramatic fight against the barriers imposed by the old legal-constitutional order and a triumphant breakthrough to a new one. The story then holds that after the thoughtways defining the old order—chiefly a blinkered unwillingness, in applying legal rules, to take account of altering political, social, economic, and institutional conditions, often characterized as legal "formalism"—were challenged, seen through, and discarded, a new "living," postformalist constitutionalism was fashioned. This constitutionalism looked beyond forms to social facts and to substance, and evinced a new, more humane concern for personal rights and, in sequence over time, the rights of disempowered groups. The result was a transcendent constitutionalism for the modern world: a constitutionalism without illusions, and a constitutionalism that cared.[1]

This constitutive story, I argue in the illustrative case study that follows, is an origins myth. The evidence that forms the basis of this story—the Constitutional Revolution of 1937 and the subsequent growth of the Court's civil rights and civil liberties jurisprudence in subsequent years—are, of course, very real. But interpretations of it that posit a radical breakthrough in the nature of constitutional adjudication are to a significant extent highly ideological efforts designed to legitimate the prevailing post–New Deal regime. The barrier-and-breakthrough metaphor, I argue here, has for too long obscured key patterns in the trajectory of twentieth-century constitutional development. In its tutelary simplicities involving lessons about legal formalism, judicial power, and the need for progressives to fight the good fight, this story has rallied the troops and sustained the regime.[2] But ultimately, the barrier-and-breakthrough model of constitutional development—what Julie Novkov has dubbed "monumental history"—has done justice to the nature of neither of the old order nor of the new. Scholars have recently come to appreciate that the "conservative" justices of the old pre–New Deal U.S. Supreme Court were hardly so heedless of the changes taking place in the world around them as is commonly supposed. In sometimes subtle ways, they had always brought the outside world into the sinews of the decisions issuing from the internal world of the Court.[3] Only more recently, however, have scholars come to appreciate the extent to which, over the course of the twentieth century, the justices of the new order constructed new legal categories and templates that would screen out of their decisions changes that were taking place in the world that surrounded them. This suggests that—at least in their mature forms—the old constitutionalism and the new were less dissimilar than is commonly supposed.[4]

My emphasis here is on the nature of the new order. To limn its character as I see it, I focus not on obscure, ostensibly unappreciated byways, but on an area at the heart of the New Deal breakthrough: labor law. And I follow two key developmental dynamics separately and as they interact with each other in post–New Deal labor law: first, institutionalization (or consolidation), and second, sequential development (or assimilation). When considered together, these two axes supply the dimensions that allow us to see constitutional development as a perpetual affirmative and ideologically infused process of consolidation and assimilation, or, put otherwise, as a process of patterned (yet provisional) relationships between stability and change. In looking at institutionalization or consolidation in labor law, I identify the ways in which, in the aftermath of that breakthrough, the Supreme Court, far from leaving behind the ostensibly discredited thought-ways and commitments, negotiated new formalisms (and sometimes simply revived old ones) in an altered ideational and institutional context.[5]

The pre–New Deal Court, as part of its "formalist" liberty of contract doctrine under the Fourteenth Amendment and Fifth Amendment's due process clauses, repeatedly voided state and federal employment legislation on the grounds that it interfered with the freedom of the employer-employee bargaining relationship. In the process, the Court was excoriated for refusing to look behind its models of that relationship to its true nature, particularly as it was experienced by the manifestly weaker party: the employee whom the legislation was aimed at empowering and protecting. The New Deal breakthrough ostensibly ushered in an "antiformalist" approach to these contracts, which would be sensitive to the real dynamics of the outside world and would be committed to deciding cases based on real consequences and with a due regard for social facts. I find, however, that after the New Deal, in decisions involving labor picketing, the Court, as part of its initiative to place a constitutional imprimatur on legislation extending new privileges to organized labor as an identifiable class—in opinions written by its ostensibly most vehemently antiformalist justices— brutally dismissed as irrelevant the highly plausible assertions by aggrieved individuals that in light of newly prevailing power relations, those new privileges would bankrupt them or otherwise prove immensely harmful. In doing so, the Court self-consciously turned its focus away from the individual and to the broader requirements of the new governing system, in much the same way as the *Lochner* Court had done before it.

The pre–New Deal Court rejected the constitutional legitimacy of "class legislation" (or legislation identifiably aimed not at advancing the public interest generally, but rather the interest of an identifiable subset of the population at the expense of another) and publicly committed itself to the principle of legislative neutrality. The New Deal constitutional breakthrough ostensibly unmasked the pretenses of neutrality and frankly accepted as legitimate legislation aimed at buttressing the power of particular classes (the paradigm case being organized labor), as needed in light of altering (external) socioeconomic conditions.[6] As civil rights succeeded the labor problem in sequence as the key developmental imperative, however, in the process pitting a newly powerful constitutionally preferred class (labor) against a would-be class (African Americans), the Court recommitted itself to the proposition ostensibly discredited by the breakthrough that legislation, to be constitutionally legitimate, must be class neutral.

In addition, the pre–New Deal Court, to the consternation of many, seemed untroubled by the problems raised by aggressive assertions of judicial power. Such assertions became especially incendiary in cases involving labor injunctions and the voiding of social and economic regulations on the grounds that they trenched upon individual rights. The New Deal breakthrough ostensibly rang down the curtain on the "cult of the Constitution" and "government by judiciary." But I find that, in ways that are partially acknowledged but only along a single familiar (and obfuscating) dimension— the Court's new inclination to exercise its powers of judicial review in the service of "personal" as opposed to "economic" rights—the post–New Deal Court quickly (indeed, immediately, without a moment's pause) began reconstructing its powers to aggressively assert the precise sort of equitable remedies that had inspired the attack on "government by judiciary" in the first place.[7]

These three examples—the turning away from individual power relations to formal systems requirements, the revival of class neutrality as an ideal, and the rebuilding of judicial injunctive powers—illustrate the ways in which the Court after the breakthrough worked to institutionalize the achievements of the New Deal constitutional transformation. This process did not involve a broad openness to altering political, social, and economic conditions, as the prevailing origins myth would have it, but rather a process of negotiating new formalisms in new contexts—formalisms consistent with the ideology of and advancing the substantive ends of the new regime. As it turned out, and has not been sufficiently recognized, these new formalisms assumed forms that in many ways mirrored those of the days of old. This is the consolidationist side of constitutional development. That development, as noted earlier, also has an assimilationist side, which worked to accommodate change after the foundations of the new regime were well on their way to being set. In labor law (and in much of constitutional law besides), the assimilationist imperative was driven by a "layering" or sequencing of reformist political imperatives that followed unexpectedly, and almost immediately, on the triumphs of the Constitutional Revolution of 1937 and the successful resolution of "the labor problem": the emergent commitment to civil rights.[8]

The foundation setting the first layer in this sequence was a "constitutional construction," which involved a highly public commitment by the regime to group rights rubrics (understood in context chiefly as a commitment both to the strength and autonomy of organized labor or labor union voluntarism), and, relatedly, to the cabining of judicial power (which was understood to be clearing the way for legislatures to enact protective labor legislation and for unions to organize and act free of court-imposed labor injunctions).[9] As the progressives took the reins of power and became New Dealers with control of the Court, however, their institutional position shifted. They were no longer reformers on the outside looking in. Henceforth, any constitutional reforms would amount to an alteration not of an alien regime made by "the conservatives" or the "Nine Old Men," but of an order they themselves had designed and institutionalized with the primary objective of solving "the labor problem." The New Dealers were progressives who won. "Liberals," it soon became apparent, were New Dealers who, without jettisoning their founding commitments, successfully negotiated the assimilation of the next reformist imperative: civil rights.[10]

In working to consolidate the new order and assimilate the next reformist imperative, constitutional liberals were forced to operate within "layered text," or developmental sequence that constrained them both ideologically and, if the rapids were not run properly, politically. To maintain credibility and broader public legitimacy, and to sustain their political coalition as well as possible in light of both its initial base and an altering environment and commitments, liberals sought to retain commitments to labor union autonomy and judicial restraint at the same time that the new imperative, civil rights, seemed to call for a piercing of the labor union autonomy and a commitment to judicial activism. Race discrimination cases involving labor unions—cases in which the sequential imperatives of twentieth-century liberalism are pitted against one another at the very moment in which a new institutional order was being consolidated—provide a window on the way in which the Court worked in an assimilationist spirit to negotiate a new constitutional order beyond the breakthrough in the aftermath of the Constitutional Revolution of 1937. What follows is a woven account of the post-1937 developmental process of consolidation and assimilation in light of reformist achievements and emergent reformist imperatives. So far as this process was concerned, the Constitutional Revolution of 1937 was not so much the end of history as the beginning.

From *Lochner* to *Senn:* The Persistence of Formal Models of Social Organization after Modernity

The essence of the constitutionalism of the old, pre–New Deal Court can be distilled for many into a single word: *Lochnerism.* The reference is to the Supreme Court decision, *Lochner v. New York* (1905), in which the Court held unconstitutional a New York state law that limited the working hours of bakers to sixty hours per week. The Court's *Lochner* decision—which repeated the jurisprudential commitments and patterns of other decisions of about the same time—literally defined an era: Whereas other periods in the history of the Court are known by the name of the chief justice who presided over them, the late nineteenth and early twentieth centuries became, and remain, broadly known as the *Lochner* era. Lochnerism became a synonym for an aggressive approach to judging that insisted on rigidly applying old legal templates in a world of new socioeconomic conditions. In the process, it voided as unconstitutional a significant amount of very popular protective legislation for workers that had been passed to meet the new problems thrown up by these conditions. The story of the triumph over Lochnerism became a central thread in the constitutive story charting the nation's achievement of constitutional modernity.[11]

The Court in *Lochner* held that the baker's hours law violated the fundamental right (protected by Fourteenth Amendment's guarantee that no state shall "deprive any person of life, liberty, or property, without due process of law") of employers and employees to freely bargain and reach an agreement over the terms of employment, a "substantive due process" right that came to be known as the "liberty of contract." The baker's hours law at issue in the case was of no particular significance. The rule of the case, however, was: it called into question the constitutional legitimacy of a raft of broadly applicable labor laws that had recently been passed by state legislatures around the country concerning workplace health and safety, minimum wages, and maximum hours, and the legality of organizationally effective labor unions.[12]

The liberty of contract doctrine appealed to many of the Court's justices because it was consonant with a deeply rooted understanding of the employer-employee relationship that had long been anchored in self-evident social facts. For the preponderance of the nation's pre-*Lochner* history, individual workers (slaves and indentured servants excepted), as farmers and small tradesmen, worked chiefly not for others but for themselves. For Americans, a wage laborer was a late nineteenth-century novelty, and a disturbing one at that, given prevailing understandings of the conditions of individual freedom.[13] As wage labor became increasingly prevalent in the United States, it first won grudging acceptance as a temporary expedient, as a stage of dependence tolerable in a longer life of work that would, over the long term, be characterized chiefly by the independence born of self-employment. As the frontier closed and urbanization and industrialization proceeded apace, more and more workers made their way from farm to factory. For many, wage labor became a way of life. A form of dependence tolerated as regrettable but temporary now became the rule.

At the same time, the prevailing understanding of the worker as a free and independent contractor, with full liberty to hire himself out at terms he would negotiate and to move on if unsatisfied, lingered. Many continued to see workers not as they now were but as they had been: as free and autonomous actors with the full power to bargain for the conditions of their employment. Others, though, came to see them as newly helpless to control the conditions of their working lives. Particularly when as lone individuals they confronted powerful new corporations, many workers lacked the effective power to bargain for minimally safe and healthy working conditions and for fair pay and equal treatment. Progressives who believed that power relations in the workplace had been altered irredeemably came to believe that under emergent political economic conditions, it was appropriate to shore up the power of workers by acting collectively to alter the rules on their behalf. Proceeding through political parties and political movements (including populism, progressivism, and the labor movement), they won power in the legislatures and, in turn, succeeded in passing protective legislation governing the workplace, including laws affecting health and safety, minimum wage, and maximum hours. It was in setting itself against this tide that *Lochner* came as such an affront. It seemed to hew ritualistically, formalistically, and atavistically to discredited categories of thought born of defunct conditions. This called into question the future of these hardwon achievements.

In defending the constitutionality of the new protective legislation, reformers appealed to the traditional authority of state legislatures, pursuant to their "police powers" to advance the public health, safety, and morals. Justice Peckham, writing for the *Lochner* majority, however, parried the police powers argument with one appealing to fundamental rights. State police powers, Peckham acknowledged, of course existed. But appeals to their authority could all too easily be advanced as a "pretext" for the violation of basic constitutional rights such as the liberty of contract. To determine whether the appeal to the police powers was legitimate or simply being used as a subterfuge for subverting fundamental constitutional rights, the Court would have to take a hard look at the substance of the law at issue. Was there a reasonable case to be made that the law was aimed at advancing the public health, safety, and morals? The answer here, Peckham concluded, was clear: "There is no reasonable ground for interfering with the liberty of the person or the right of free contract, by determining the hours of labor, in the occupation of a baker."[14]

Peckham's conclusion in *Lochner* has been broadly understood both at the time and now as a paradigmatic case of legal formalism, and as an illustration of its perniciousness. In a dissenting opinion in *Lochner* itself, Justice John Marshall Harlan scored Peckham for his categorical assumption that in negotiating an employment contract, employers and employees were possessed of equal bargaining power. "It may be that the statute had its origin, in part, in the belief that employers and employees in such establishments were not upon an equal footing, and that the necessities of the latter often compelled them to submit to such exactions as unduly taxed their strength," he suggested. If this was so, the legislature's invocation of its police powers was hardly a pretext. Citing a social science treatise (Hirt's *Diseases of the Workers*), Harlan alluded to the lesser known physical hardships of bakery work. Under modern conditions, he found it quite plausible that individual wage laborers would be unable to protect themselves against these harms through individual bargains.[15]

Harlan's *Lochner* dissent was not simply an attack on Peckham's opinion in the case, viewed narrowly, but on a style of reasoning that became known as "legal formalism." A constitutional rule that presumed that individual workers would be able to effectively negotiate the terms of their employment was formalistic in the sense that it was "abstract, formal, conceptualistic, [and] categorical." Peckham's aim had not been "a fair equitable result in the particular case, but rather a uniform, undeviating, impartial application of supposedly neutral rules in all cases." Moreover, it involved the application of an internal rule that had fallen out of harmony with external conditions. The construction of the outside world that had lent it its sense— the presumption of an equality of bargaining power between employers and individual employees—no longer defined the typical case of employer-employee relations. As such, liberty of contract rested on an abstraction, and an outmoded one at that, and the Court's invalidation of the baker's hours law rested on a deduction from this abstraction. A modern constitutionalism, Harlan's dissent suggested, would rest not on such rigidities and aridities, but rather on an inductive historicism that accorded due attention to "life, experience, process, growth, context, [and] function."[16]

The New Deal Constitutional Revolution of 1937 was billed at that time, and has long been remembered, as a repudiation of Lochnerism with its attendant legal formalism, and, thus, as a vindication of Justice Harlan's (and Justice Holmes's) famous dissents. Facing a Fourteenth Amendment liberty of contract challenge, the Court, in *West Coast Hotel v. Parrish* (1937), in a stunning about-face, upheld the constitutionality of a Washington state minimum wage law for women. After noting that "the Constitution does not speak of freedom of contract," Chief Justice Hughes, writing for the Court, rejected abstract readings of the due process clause, asserting that "liberty in each of its phases has its history and connotation," and that "the liberty safe-guarded is liberty in a social organization." "Liberty under the Constitution," he asserted, "is . . . necessarily subject to the restraints of due process, and regulation which is reasonable in relation to its subject and is adopted in the interests of the community is due process."[17]

In *West Coast Hotel*, Hughes adopted the essence of the construction of the employer-employee relationship favored by Justice Harlan. But rather than simply vindicating Harlan's approach, he did so in a way that was distinctive and foreign to the spirit of Harlan's *Lochner* dissent, and was plainly influenced not simply by a reading of the employer-employee bargain under modern conditions (a reading he shared with Harlan), but also by an identifiably new and systemic constitutional vision. Harlan had reasoned that protective legislation was constitutional because the legislature must be possessed of the authority to empower the individual bakery worker who had been disempowered by modern conditions. Chief Justice Hughes, in contrast, perhaps influenced both by ambient social and political ideas and by the conditions of the Great Depression itself, focused less than Justice Harlan on the position of the individual worker than on "the exploitation of a class of workers who are in an unequal position with respect to bargaining power and are thus relatively defenseless against the denial of a living wage." Hughes, moreover, moved beyond considering the effects an old-school liberty of contract ruling would have on the individual worker (or even the working class) to a broader consideration of the effects such a ruling would have on the broader social welfare *system*, of which he considered the terms of private employment contracts to be a part. The unequal bargaining position of workers "is not only detrimental to their health and well being," Hughes wrote, "but casts a direct burden for their support upon the community. What these workers lose in wages the taxpayers are called upon to pay. . . . The community is not bound to provide what is in effect a subsidy for unconscionable employers." Rather than simply mimicking the Harlan dissent of 1905, that is, Hughes fashioned his opinion in *West Coast Hotel* in ways that were consonant with an emergent class and systems based constitutional vision.[18]

As such, the decision amounted to more than a negative constitutional achievement involving "the systematic removal of ancient institutions" and the task of "clear[ing] . . . ancient hedgerows, and of roots that repeatedly undermine finished work."[19] It was simultaneously an affirmative substantive achievement that mirrored and helped legitimate the underlying ideology, ethos, and institutional affinities of the new order. In this sense, *West Coast Hotel* was certainly evidence that a constitutional revolution was afoot. But it has been insufficiently emphasized that certain jurisprudential patterns declared to have been interred in the 1930s alongside the *Lochner* decision persisted, or were reinvented and revived after 1937, as part of the process of institutionalizing or consolidating the new order. The breaks and continuities were woven into complex developmental patterns.

The Supreme Court negotiated this tapestry of breaks and continuities, amongst other places, in its understudied New Deal–era Norris-LaGuardia decisions, *Senn v. Tile Layers Union* (1937) and *Lauf v. Shinner* (1938).[20] In those decisions, in interpreting the Fourteenth Amendment due process clause, the Court, in a broad, anti-*Lochner* spirit, publicly acknowledged the altered nature of the American political economy and its effects on employer-employee power relations. But in doing so, it rejected the individual-oriented antiformalism of Harlan's *Lochner* dissent (which had focused on the actual harm to the individual worker concealed by the formalist abstractions of the "liberty of contract" construct), and instead, in the spirit of Hughes's decision in *West Coast Hotel*, both cast the incidence of those abstractions as falling not on individuals, but rather on identifiable classes (in this case, the laboring class) and gave due weight to systemwide concerns. By recasting the problem this way, the Court was able to lay the constitutional foundations for holding constitutionally legitimate state efforts to regulate class relations and broader swathes of economic life regardless of the actual harm such efforts might have occasioned for individual workers. So long as the legislation in question was reasonably aimed at alleviating the harms to labor as a class and served a broader, systemic regulatory purpose that legislation would be presumed constitutional. A simple adoption of Justice Harlan's *Lochner* dissent on its own terms, which focused on the heretofore obscured harms that befell individuals, would not have achieved this result. As it turned out, this affirmative ideological vision, which accorded new constitutional cognizance to classes and systems, proved no less prone to abstractions, categorical applications, and formalisms than its newly discredited predecessor.[21]

At issue in *Senn* and *Lauf* was the constitutionality of the Norris-LaGuardia Act (1932), a pre–New Deal law sharply restricting the power of the courts to issue labor injunctions.[22] Norris-LaGuardia, an underdiscussed legislative landmark, represented what many reformers hoped would be the coup de grâce in a half-century of institutional struggle between "conservative" courts and progressive labor activists and legislators. In the immediate aftermath of its passage, most courts yielded to the initiative to cabin their prerogatives and construed the act liberally in line with Congress's apparent intent.[23] An outlier court, the Seventh Circuit Court of

Appeals, however, stubbornly resisted by construing the phrase "labor dispute" in the statute narrowly. In the *Senn* and *Lauf* decisions, the Supreme Court tamped down the Seventh Circuit's resistance.[24]

Senn was something of a trial run in this process, involving not the Norris-LaGuardia Act itself, but rather Wisconsin's "little Norris-LaGuardia" Act (which was the fruit of labor activism by many of the same people who had pushed for passage of the federal act—including Felix Frankfurter and Nathan Greene).[25] *Senn* interpreted the anti-injunction provisions of the act broadly. The case involved a sole proprietor who ran his business with the help of one or two assistants and who, despite a professed willingness to make his business into a union shop, faced sustained picketing by picketers with no connections to any of Senn's employees alleging that he was "unfair to labor" for, while retaining his position as an owner and manager, refusing to quit his job as a laborer. Given the state of the law at the time, the case raised questions about whether the situation involved a "labor dispute" under the terms of the statute. In *Senn*, the Court held that the facts of the case did involve such as dispute because the phrase "labor dispute" was properly defined not by the particular people involved in it (that is, whether there was a dispute between any given company and its employees)—an approach to the question known as the "proximate relations test"—but rather by the classes or categories to which the people involved in the dispute belonged. If the dispute involved an employer and either employees or potential employees—even if these workers had no connection to that particular business—the Court held that a "labor dispute" was taking place under the terms of the statute. The job of effectuating a separation of these categories for regulatory purposes—and not the unionization of Senn's shop per se—was at the heart of this case. After all, Senn had readily agreed to unionize his shop. What he had not agreed to do was personally lay down his tools in accordance with union rules that required a hermetic separation in all union shops between management and labor.[26]

Senn resisted with individualist rights claims that would have been both cognizable and persuasive under the *Lochner* regime of only a few years before. The Fourteenth Amendment's due process and equal protection clauses, he argued, forbade legislation passed under the pretext of the police power that conferred public power upon a special interest or class, thereby permitting it to advance its collective interests at the expense of an individual freely exercising his constitutional rights (here, the right to work and earn a living). Additionally, Senn argued that the Wisconsin Labor

Code, which prevented the Court from enjoining picketers attempting to deny him his right to work, had deprived him of his property rights without due process of law. In so doing, it forced Senn to give up his fundamental individual rights to further collective class interests, because had the unions not represented other workers in the same line of business as that in which Senn himself employed others, an injunction would certainly have been issued.

In an opinion written by Justice Brandeis that drew affirmatively on the new constitutional ethos of groups and systems, however, the Court categorically rejected Senn's individual rights arguments. Brandeis opened with a systems analysis that spotlighted economic interdependence as the foundational social fact of his times.[27] This social fact necessitated adherence to a broadly conceived, societywide, systems-regarding constitutional vision. Accordingly, Brandeis began not with a consideration of Senn's individual rights claims but rather with the observation that, at the time the union made its demands, the tile industry was in a "demoralized state." The Wisconsin law permitted the union to combine and to act collectively for a now thoroughly legitimate constitutional purpose, namely to "[enhance] their opportunity to acquire work for themselves and those whom they represent," to "[protect] . . . themselves as workers and craftsmen in the industry." Because they were advancing their collective interests as a class or a group, there was nothing either ethically or morally wrong with what they had done. "There is no basis for a suggestion that the unions' request that Senn refrain from working with his own hands . . . was malicious; or there was a desire to injure Senn." Moreover, "there was no effort to induce Senn to do an unlawful thing." "There was no violence, no force was applied, no molestation or interference, no coercion."[28] "Each member of the unions, as well as Senn, has the right to strive to earn his living," Brandeis explained. "Senn seeks to do so through the exercise of his individual skill and planning. The union members seek to do so through combination." So far as the Constitution is concerned, this was all a matter of state policy and "not our concern. The Fourteenth Amendment does not prohibit it." "A hoped-for job is not property guaranteed by the Constitution."[29]

In his discussion of the only section of the Tile Layers' Union contract that Senn refused to sign—the part that would have required him to give up his trade, in the interest of effectuating a hermetic separation of labor from management—Brandeis again recurred to a group-oriented, class-based approach to labor relations. He noted that however unfair this section of the contract might seem, given the "necessities of employment

within the industry and [the need] for the protection of themselves as workers and craftsmen in the industry," it was "a reasonable rule." "The unions
acted, and had the right to act as they did, to protect the interests of their
members against the harmful effect upon them of Senn's actions. . . .
Because his action was harmful, the fact that none of Senn's employees was
a union member, or sought the union's aid, is immaterial."[30]

Far from leaving Lochnerism behind, in one respect Justice Brandeis's
opinion in *Senn* shares much of the spirit of Justice Peckham's infamous
opinion in that case. Certainly, in its groups and systems orientation, it
marked a sharp departure from *Lochner* (including, as I have explained
above, from Justice Harlan's *Lochner* dissent). But in its approach to real-
world power relations, it was *Lochner*'s mirror image. In his famous dissent
in that case responding to Justice Peckham, Justice Harlan asked the Court
to look past the formalities of the doctrine of liberty of contract to the
actual unequal bargaining power between an employer and an employee.
Brandeis's opinion in *Senn* is actually closer in spirit to Justice Peckham's
majority opinion in its formalism: Senn had a choice to make, and, so far
as Brandeis was concerned, it was a choice made in total freedom—either
give up his trade, or go out of business. It seems that the chief difference
between Peckham and Brandeis is not one of formalism versus antiformalism, but rather in their respective commitments to individualist or collec-
tivizing goals.[31]

Whereas Brandeis applied a class and society-level systems analysis in the
Senn case, Pierce Butler, joined by McReynolds, Van Devanter, and Sutherland—the infamous Lochnerite "Four Horsemen of the Apocalypse"—
responded with an antiformalist analysis crafted in the spirit of Justice
Harlan's *Lochner* dissent. Butler appraised the situation from the perspective
of the actual power relations manifested in the case, looking at the effects
those power imbalances had on an aggrieved individual seeking to negotiate
the future terms of his employment. Eschewing Brandeis's abstract and distancing class and systems analysis, Butler focused instead on the seemingly
absurd predicament into which Paul Senn had been placed. What the case
amounted to, Butler pointed out, was a union refusal to allow Senn either to
unionize or to carry on his business solely because he personally worked with
his hands. This, Butler declared, was an unlawful purpose. Under the law, he
declared, strikes and picketing for unlawful purposes are plainly illegal. As
such, the *Senn* decision "violat[ed] a principle of fundamental law: That no
man may be compelled to hold his life or the means of living at the mere will
of others."[32]

Senn was followed by another Wisconsin case, *Lauf v. Shinner* (1938), this one calling on the Court to construe the Norris-LaGuardia Act itself. *Lauf* involved the efforts of an unincorporated AFL-affiliated union to organize about thirty-five workers at a small chain of privately owned Milwaukee meat markets. By all accounts these workers were content with their jobs and their relationship with their employers. They had organized their own employee association and were pleased with that as well. At some point, however, the union officials, who had no connection to either the meat markets or its employees, called up the owner of the markets and demanded that all his employees join the union. The owner told the union representative that the employees had their own association, and that he did not think they would be interested in an outside union. Nonetheless, he told the union that he would raise the issue with them, and did so, telling his employees that the union had expressed an interest in organizing them and that they were free to join up if they wanted to. The employees responded that they were not interested, and the owner in turn relayed the message back to the union. Outraged, the union instructed the owner that they intended "to declare war on you."

The union then demanded that the owner present his employees with an ultimatum: join the union and designate it as your exclusive agent and collective bargaining representative, or be fired. When the owner refused (as indeed he was obligated to do under the labor laws, which ostensibly prohibited him from using the threat of dismissal to coerce his employees regarding their decisions about whether to join a union), the union began its war to drive him out of business. It declared that the owner was "unfair to labor." It picketed, marched, threatened, and intimidated the owner and the meat market employees.

The lower court in *Lauf* had held that under these circumstances, no labor dispute had existed under the federal (or state) law because Shinner was bound to allow its employees a free choice concerning whether to join a labor union. It was thus entirely appropriate for a court to issue an injunction against the union prohibiting it from coercing the meat market owner into dismissing his employees for failing to make the "proper" choice. The Supreme Court granted certiorari on the basis of an apparent conflict with its ruling in *Senn*.[33]

In an opinion by Justice Owen Roberts, who had just recently broken the standoff between the Court and the president by joining his pro–New Deal colleagues in the 5–4 majorities in *West Coast Hotel* (1937) and *Jones and Laughlin Steel* (1937), the Court easily found that the district court's interpretation of the Wisconsin Labor law diverged from the state court's interpretation of its own statutes, and that that divergence was impermissible and in error. As for the federal act, the Court was obligated to follow its own lights. Adopting the ethos and ideology of the state court decision interpreting the little Norris-LaGuardia Act (if not, strictly speaking, following it as a matter of law), the Court quickly and peremptorily held that the lower courts had not made the legal findings necessary to justify an injunction. And for good measure, it held that there was no employee associational right that warranted such an injunction.

As he had done in *Senn*, Pierce Butler penned an impassioned dissent in *Lauf*, reminding the Court in emphatic italics drawing attention to facts over abstractions, that there had been "a demand by the union that [Shinner] compel its employees, on pain of dismissal from their employment, to join the union and constitute it their bargaining representative and agent." Because Shinner had refused to coerce its employees into making choices that were consonant with an emergent, group-oriented regulatory order concerning labor relations, the union, Butler concluded, had falsely declared in banners, picketing, and placards that the meat market was "unfair to labor."[34] In issuing an injunction, Butler insisted, the lower courts had simply enforced the provisions of the Norris-LaGuardia Act itself, which clearly stated that a worker must be "free to decline to associate with his fellow workers," that he should "have full freedom of association, self-organization, of representatives of his own choosing," and that he should "be free from the interference, restraint, or coercion of employers of labor, or their agents, in the designation of such representatives."[35] "If a demand by a labor union that an employer compel its employees to submit to the will of the union, and the employer's refusal, constitute a labor controversy," he concluded, "the highwayman's demand for the money of his victim, and the latter's refusal to stand and deliver, constitute a financial controversy."[36]

Unsurprisingly, in the aftermath of the Constitutional Revolution of 1937, the Court rejected Butler's approach. But what is more surprising is that this rejection has been broadly understood as a triumph over formalism or abstraction. The new approach, in a broad sense, certainly represented an engagement with new social facts. But it did not represent an unbounded openness to the lived harms suffered by individuals in labor cases. An "economic theory" infused *Senn*, *Lauf*, and *West Coast Hotel* every bit as much as Herbert Spencer's *Social Statics* had infused *Lochner*. And the social facts the Court considered relevant were mediated by that theory which posited the need for a new, global regulatory order anchored in collective bargaining concerning labor.[37] In the interest of labor as a class, as seen through the prism of that theory, the harms suffered by disempowered individuals obstructing the new order, whether sole proprietors who doubled as laborers (classified under the new system as "management") or employees, were no longer cognizable. The relative powerlessness of the individual when confronted with a powerful labor union was no longer cognizable. Looking at what it took to be the greater good, the Court freely adopted whatever abstractions and conceptual formalities were necessary to achieve this result.[38]

West Coast Hotel and the Court's Norris-LaGuardia decisions represented a departure from Lochnerism in notable respects. They evinced a new affinity for groups or class-based understandings of the political-economic order. And they seem to suggest a retreat from the aggressive exercise of judicial power. But they share with Justice Peckham's majority opinion in *Lochner* a willingness to abstract from the lived power relations in a particular employer-employee relationship before them in the interest of sustaining a broader political-economic system. In each case, the nature of that system is perceived through the lens of a substantive, affirmative working theory of social organization. In this regard the revolt against Lochnerism was far from global.

Constitutionalizing Industrial Democracy

As we have seen, a group-oriented ethos suffused the opinions of the Court's progressive and New Deal justices, including those in the Norris-LaGuardia cases. Indeed, the emergence of this new ethos motivated the Court's abandonment of its traditional defense of constitutional proscriptions against "class legislation," or laws aimed at advancing the interests of part of the polity rather than the whole. Under new conditions, the Court's new majority concluded, that proscription had ossified into a lifeless formalism. Taking judicial notice of the class-based nature of power in the modern world became a touchstone of modern "pluralist" constitutionalism.[39]

Lochner itself had most immediately frustrated efforts to render unambiguously constitutional protective legislation involving health and safety and minimum wage and maximum hours rules. But it also had plain implications for the constitutionality of legislative efforts to empower labor unions as collectivities, where they were understood to be representatives of the working class operating as a countervailing and balancing force to capitalists. As *West Coast Hotel* (1937) had cleared away the barriers to protective legislation imposed by Lochnerism, *NLRB v. Jones and Laughlin Steel* (1937) cleared away similar barriers to unionism.[40]

The call for giving collective power to labor unions, and supporting that power with the authority of the state, clearly dovetailed with—indeed, inspired—much of the new social scientific thinking on politics as the study of the functional system of group interaction.[41] But the call for according group power to labor also came to be identified by progressives with a normative commitment to democracy itself. The fusing of a social scientific model of the modern social order with a normative defense of that order anchored in claims of democracy within progressive thought proved powerful. By justifying an emergent regulatory order on both descriptive and proscriptive grounds, it ultimately helped undergird New Deal constitutionalism concerning labor.

In the early twentieth century, "industrial democracy," which came to be associated with labor union power culminating in collective bargaining arrangements, developed into a high-profile and defining progressive imperative.[42] In his landmark early work, *Drift and Mastery* (1914), Walter Lippmann declared that "without democracy in industry . . . there is no such thing as democracy in America."[43] And many spanning the Progressive Era through the New Deal, including John Dewey, Herbert Croly, Louis Brandeis, and Felix Frankfurter, agreed, spinning out variations and refinements on the theme.[44] As early as 1894 (the year of the Pullman strike), John Dewey had added "industrial democracy" to civil and political democracy as the third pillar of a truly democratic society. To conceptualize the workplace as a purely private space was to stand in the way of the realization of the full ethical potential of human beings and, in turn, the ethical potential of society. "All industrial relations," he wrote, "are to be regarded as subordinate to human relations, to the law of personality. . . . They are to become the material of an ethical realization; the form and substance of a community of good (though not necessarily of goods) wider than any now known." This approach was anchored in republicanism: just as citizens should actively govern their civil and political life, so too, thought Dewey, should they govern their lives as workers.[45]

Although the spirit of "industrial democracy" in Dewey's work was clear, its practical import remained hazy. Others, however, anchored and developed the concept. Walter Lippmann, for example, specifically identified "industrial democracy" and "industrial citizenship" with what labor unions were fighting for.[46] Traditional Jeffersonian, Jacksonian, and Free Labor strains of American political thought held that only the autonomous individual was fit for and capable of self-government. Picking up on Dewey's industrial republicanism, Lippmann denied this, claiming that only the man who participated collectively in industrial governance acquired the political education that prepared him to govern America. If labor unions, as currently constituted, did not seem up to that ambitious educative mission, it was because they had yet to be trusted with the kind of responsibility that would hone their democratic and republican instincts and skills. Change, however, was at hand. "Private industry has got to prepare itself for democratic control," Lippmann asserted.[47] "Men are fighting for the beginning of industrial self-government. . . . They have got to win civilization, they have got to take up the task of fastening a worker's control upon business."[48] What would that control look like? Lippmann expected that it would involve worker partnerships with management and the right of laborers to choose their own foremen, elect company directors, and share company profits. Joint employer-worker governance would eventually expand outward. In time, it would become a part of a nationwide system of economic governance in which the tasks of industrial planning would be coordinated with the governing plans of consumers and the state. This project—in which labor unions would play a central part—would involve "adjust[ing] . . . conflicts and to reach some working plan." Bringing labor unions into the heart of this grand endeavor, Lippmann declared, represented "the extension of civilization into the wilderness," "the first feeble effort to conquer the industrial jungle for democratic life."[49]

This was plainly a constitutional vision, as was apparent in Lippmann's choices of similes and metaphors. Employers, he observed:

> fight unions as monarchs fight constitutions, as aristocracies fight the vote. When an employer tells about his own virtues, he dilates upon his kindness, his fairness, and all the good things he has done for his men. That is just what benevolent autocrats do: they try to justify their autocracy by their benevolence. Indeed, the highest vision of those who oppose unions is that the employer will develop the virtues of a good aristocrat.[50]

To place political power in the hands of labor unions, indeed, raised anew all the thrilling problems of a constitutional founding:

> In this movement to eat into economic absolutism, very perplexing questions . . . arise. What is the proper structure for a union? Shall it be organized by crafts, or occupations, or industries? With amalgamation or by federation? How shall the unions be governed: by representative or by direct vote? In fact, there is hardly a problem of constitutional government which doesn't appear in acute form among

the workers. And in passing, one might suggest that scholars who wish to see sovereignty in the making cannot do better than to go among the unions.[51]

Herbert Croly also followed Dewey in making his own case for industrial democracy. Like Lippmann, Croly argued that the practice of industrial democracy would amount to a "genuinely formative popular political experience," conducive of "individual and social fulfillment." "As the result of such action," he contended, "a progressive democracy will gradually learn to be progressively democratic. . . . The creation of an industrial organization . . . will serve to make individual workers enlightened, competent and loyal citizens of an industrial commonwealth."[52]

Croly's vision was also constitutional: "The wage-earner," he wrote, "must have the same opportunity of being consulted about the nature and circumstances of his employment that the voter has about the organization and policy of the government. The work of getting this opportunity for the wage-earner is the most important task of modern democratic social organization."[53] Only by granting the worker legal security in and control of his work life on a par with the legal security and effective control enjoyed by the property owner would the worker cease "to separate himself from his fellows by becoming a property owner" and join in a socialized democracy.[54] Labor unions would play a crucial role in this process. Participation in a union would counteract the tendency of the individual in a capitalist society to separate himself from his fellows and to stake his claims to freedom as an autonomous individual. By "mak[ing] the economic emancipation of the individual depend on the emancipation of the whole class," unions, Croly concluded, counteracted the atomistic tendencies of modern capitalism.[55]

Croly was nonetheless critical of the objectives of the contemporaneous labor movement. By focusing on the extraction of collective bargaining agreements and concrete, but limited, concessions from employers, unions were insufficiently radical: they were not committed to midwifing the birth of a new republican politics. Croly interpreted their aims as reflecting a stubbornly persistent commitment to private property—class property, perhaps—but property all the same. He condemned craft unionism as "a parasite" and decried the labor movement's appropriation of a reactionary, property-holding ideology. While distancing himself somewhat from syndicalist methods, which called upon unions, in a series of revolutionary acts, to seize the means of production, he praised syndicalist ends, and called for the establishment of "industrial constitutionalism," of "constitutional government in industry," in which workers would control the structure of government in industry and, by extension, their own lives. The establishment of this new form of constitutional government in industry would involve the hiring of "a well equipped general staff" of "expert administrators" to run the new system.[56]

Louis Brandeis, the future Supreme Court justice and author of many of the Supreme Court's key labor opinions (including its Norris-LaGuardia opinions) swam in the same currents of thought as Dewey, Lippmann, and Croly. For Brandeis, part of the "curse of bigness" in business corporations was that it stifled the creativity and initiative of workers, in the process subtracting from the sum total of human happiness. Besides making businesses smaller, one of the chief antidotes to "industrial absolutism," in Brandeis's view, involved the empowerment of workers by inviting them to be active participants in "industrial government."[57] Such government, he argued, "will make the employee to a very much larger extent a thinker; it will make him realize that his work is his best field for development, and he will look to that as the employer looks to that—as a place for his greatest satisfaction in life."[58] Like Croly, Brandeis believed that labor unions would play an important part in this new democratic-republican industrial order. "America must breed only free men," he insisted. "It must develop citizens. It cannot develop citizens unless the workingmen possess industrial liberty; and industrial liberty is impossible if the right to organize be denied."[59] Like Croly, however, Brandeis, also speaking in constitutional terms, conceived of unionization itself as only a way station on the road to industrial democracy:

> We have already had industrial absolutism. With the recognition of the unions, this is changing into a constitutional monarchy, with well-defined limitations placed about the employer's formerly autocratic power. Next comes profit sharing. This, however, is only to be a transitional, halfway stage. Following upon it will come the sharing of responsibility, as well as of profits. The eventual outcome promised to be full-grown industrial democracy.[60]

Felix Frankfurter (friend and disciple of Brandeis, future Supreme Court justice, and major influence on the development of early twentieth-century labor law) echoed these by now familiar themes. Frankfurter scored "modern industry" for "its grinding pressure and spiritual starvation," "its failure to use the creative qualities of men, its deadening monotony and its excessive fatigue." "Nowhere," Frankfurter worried,

> save in directive and professional work, is there the opportunity for individual expression which was characteristic of the medieval handicraft. The result is to ensure a stunted citizenship, since only in a really adequate leisure and a training in the facility of its use can the qualities of democratic life be made manifest. For it is

very certain that without facilities for the cultivation of the amenities of civilized life the mass of the people will remain incapable of disciplined democracy.[61]

Frankfurter's vision of industrial democracy was more restrained and pragmatic than that of Dewey, Croly, Lippmann, and even Brandeis. Frankfurter, for instance, put in a good word for the social value of leisure, one of the labor movement's decidedly nonrevolutionary goals. And he took the rhetoric of industrial democracy down a notch by implying that in many ways corporatist collective bargaining and craft unionism represented not the fledgling beginnings of a move toward the *beau idéal* of industrial democracy proper but rather the achievement of the thing itself. Frankfurter's decision to accept collective bargaining and craft unionism went a long way toward domesticating the concept and reworking it into a socially and politically acceptable form.

Central for Frankfurter was stemming the tide of industrial unrest. Labor disturbances are "bound to continue," Frankfurter contended, "just so long as the present state of mind and feeling of workers is generated by growing disparity between their participation in politics and their exclusion from industrial direction." Collective bargaining, in his estimation, showed promise as a starting point for a solution. "This principle," he argued, "must, of course, receive ungrudging acceptance. It is nothing but belated recognition of economic facts—that the era of romantic individualism is no more." "The collectivity," he declared, "must be represented and must be allowed to choose its representatives."[62]

The National Labor Relations Act or "Wagner Act"—the keystone of New Deal labor policy—at long last gave collectivity its representation.[63] The act represented a radical assault on the prevailing Lochnerite constitutional conception of the workplace that envisaged the employment relation as one in which employers and employees freely bargained over the terms of the labor contract. In contrast, it envisaged that relation as structured by the power of antagonistic groups and as amounting, in its fundamentals, as a bargain between the collectivities of "business" and "labor." Under the institutional arrangements it created, the state supported union power. It prohibited company unions (where, ostensibly, workers were compelled to become outsiders to their class by working too closely with the capitalist-managerial class). It obligated employers to accept rather than fight unionization. And it institutionalized a variant of the workplace constitutionalism that Lippmann and Croly had dreamed of by providing labor unions with exclusive power within plants and workplaces to represent the interests of all workers as a class. The principle of industrial democracy was enshrined by allowing unions to govern themselves by majority vote in government-supervised elections, echoing the principled commitment to majoritarianism progressives had made in defending protective legislation against the countermajoritarian assaults of the courts.[64]

The Supreme Court put its imprimatur on this new constitutionalism of labor in *Jones and Laughlin Steel*.[65] The explicitly constitutional nature of this achievement was celebrated in 1947 when, in the early days of the Cold War, a Freedom Train toured America with originals of a handful of the nation's iconographic documents: the Declaration of Independence, the Mayflower Compact, and the Gettysburg Address. The Wagner Act was slated to join this elevated company of the nation's foundational texts. Only the intercession of the American Heritage Foundation, a business-backed sponsor, prevented the act from taking its proper place at their side.[66]

The passage of the Wagner Act, however, was not simply a culminating breakthrough that wiped away the old restraints. It reflected a substantial and affirmative constitutional vision, and it embodied that vision in new institutions. These, in turn, posed new barriers to the achievement of the next reformist imperative. With "the labor problem" solved, "the race problem" moved to the head of the queue as the chief progressive reformist imperative. Sympathy for blacks—for southern blacks in particular—began to replace a sympathy for the working man as the most salient commitment of political progressives (now becoming known, after FDR's appropriation of the term, as "liberals").[67] The liberal mind was soon confronted with a "layered text," created by this developmental sequence.[68] As an ideological matter, it was important for liberals to recognize and theorize these two commitments as part of a natural trajectory of principle, first labor rights, then civil rights. Within the context of American politics (if not necessarily in theory), however, the commitments were highly conflictual. The new collective powers, anchored in majoritarianism, accorded to one class, posed serious problems for a rising other. Labor rights and civil rights—at least as they were understood in advance of serious midcentury ideological negotiation and construction by liberal scholars—were highly antagonistic causes.

The Breakthrough as Barrier: From Class Representation to Fair Representation

From the late nineteenth century through the New Deal, African Americans were staunch opponents of the rights of labor: they opposed the right to strike, supported the constitutionality of yellow dog contracts (employment contracts that made a commitment not to join a union a condition of employment), and feared New Deal collective bargaining arrangements. Unlike progressives, New Dealers, and liberals, they did not romanticize the white working class. Because they were on intimate terms with them, many regarded the prospect of their constitutional empowerment with horror. "The first large-scale exclusion of Negroes by private organizations in the post-bellum period," they knew, was the handiwork "not of owners of railroad cars, hotels, and places of public amusement," but rather "of organized labor."[69] Before the mid-1960s, union power meant black exclusion. In this context, every victory for labor was a defeat for blacks.[70]

White workers resented the potential competition for their jobs from black workers. Moreover, they refused blacks admission to their "brotherhoods" on the grounds that this would force them to associate with blacks as social equals. They were less comfortable with the white working class than with white capitalists, whom they had been allied with since the founding of the Republican Party. Capitalism, in the mind and experience of many blacks, was color-blind: it looked only to the abstraction of profit. Collectivist unionism, on the other hand, promised an impenetrable exclusion. Astonished (and progressively inclined) Columbia University researchers heard much of this while interviewing black workers during the 1920s and early 1930s. "The excuse, 'I have no objection to hiring colored labor but my employees would quit if I did,' has been heard so often by Negro job seekers," the scholars noted incredulously, "that they have come to believe it and to assume that if only the opposition of white labor were removed the Negro could readily find employment."[71]

The very public—and heavily theorized—identification of labor union power and autonomy with the cause of majoritarian democracy, thus presented a distinct institutional and ideological problem for those committed to the next reformist imperative, civil rights. By loudly trumpeting industrial democracy and identifying it with labor union "sovereignty" or autonomy, progressives had constructed a new obstacle that threatened to scuttle the achievement of the next reformist imperative.[72] It was not clear how liberals would respond to this dilemma. One possibility was that liberal elites would acknowledge the error of the earlier commitment, and repudiate it in service of the achievement of the newer one. This, however, was not an attractive option. With their political ascendancy built on a half-century's crusade fought in the name of "democracy," understood in significant part in terms of securing broad powers of majoritarian self-government to organized labor, the loss of credibility would have been arresting. It would, moreover, have amounted to an open betrayal of the Democratic Party's newly consolidated political base.[73] The more attractive possibility was to fudge, or muddle through. Liberals could set themselves to reconciling commitments in a way that, if not logically plausible, was at least plausible emotionally and politically. A successful ideological negotiation of this sequence of reformist imperatives would involve maintaining a staunch rhetorical commitment to the first—labor union self-government and autonomy—while at the same time prudently trimming its prerogatives in service of the second—civil rights. Crucial to winning acceptance for a policy program that strained to reconcile these seemingly irreconcilable commitments would be the negotiation of an affirmative constitutional vision that posited not compromise or trimming but rather a linear progression. The second reformist imperative, the ideological negotiation of modern liberals would come to believe, was the logical next step in the fulfillment of the principles of the first.

This process of ideologically negotiating the relationship between sequential reformist imperatives took place broadly in liberal political and intellectual discourse. It is on display in perhaps its most concentrated form in the jurisprudence of the Supreme Court. During the 1940s and the 1950s, the Court acted as the political theorist for the emergent regime, negotiating a modus vivendi between these sequentially arrayed antagonistic imperatives.[74]

In the thick of repeated, publicized findings by the Fair Employment Practices Commission (1941–1946)—which had no enforcement powers—that labor unions were rife with race discrimination, the Roosevelt and Truman Courts, in an intriguing series of statutory interpretation cases, took up the project of negotiating the reconciliation of a layered reformist commitment to labor rights and civil rights.[75] The problem of defining the scope of labor union autonomy in the face of race discrimination charges was thrust before the Court in two cases heard during the same term, *Railway Mail Association v. Corsi* (1944) and *Steele v. Louisville and Nashville Railroad* (1944). In these cases, heard less than a decade after the celebrated constitutional breakthrough, the NAACP and the ACLU argued stridently on behalf of the black plaintiffs against a labor union's right to democratic self-government (understood in classically progressive, majoritarian terms) and associational freedom.[76]

At issue in *Corsi* was a New York State civil rights law that provided that no labor organization shall deny a person membership by reason of race, color, or creed, or deny to any of its members, by reason of race, color, or creed, equal treatment in the designation of its members for employment, promotion, or dismissal by an employer. In Article III of its constitution, the Railway Mail Association, an AFL affiliate group of 22,000 postal clerks of the Railway Mail Service, in a provision typical of the sort of racial exclusions practiced by American labor unions (either tacitly or explicitly), limited membership to those who were either white or American Indian. Strikingly enough, given that the case was heard a full seven years after the Constitutional Revolution of 1937, the labor union defendant in *Corsi*, in a precise echo of the ostensibly dead formalist arguments that employers had used in an attempt to deflect state regulation in the interests of organized labor, defended itself by asserting that the New York law trampled on its Fourteenth Amendment due process liberty rights to choose its own members and to have those members freely contract with each other, and its Fourteenth Amendment rights to manage its own property as it saw fit.

The Court began its opinion in *Corsi* by rebuffing the union's efforts to revive these pre–New Deal forms of argument in service of the ends of the substantive winners of the New Deal, organized labor. As the New Deal Court had ultimately rejected these constitutional claims when employers had made them in resistance to organized labor seeking to advance its interests as a group, the Court now, in turn, rejected the same claims made by organized labor in resistance to African American efforts to advance their own interests as a group. The Court rejected the union's claims of autonomy, claiming that it was an organization "functioning under the protection of the state," and as such was subject to state regulation in the service of state-declared policy interests. One such policy was that against racial discrimination. Because "the terms imposed by a dominant union apply to all employees, whether union members or not," the Court wrote, African Americans were deprived of all means of protection from unfair treatment by the racially discriminatory policies and practices of labor unions.[77]

Thus, the *Corsi* Court set out down the road that, mindful of the recent "revolt against formalism" and the dispelling of the illusion of the state's neutrality in the face of contending social powers, one might have expected it to take: it had declared that unions were now intertwined with the state and were, in important respects, instruments of state policy. But this vision was problematic. It clashed too sharply with notions of labor union autonomy and majoritarian industrial democracy that had been central to the earlier reformist struggle. The solution to achieving both labor rights and civil rights offered in *Corsi*—to simply declare unions to be instruments of the state—threw too much of its weight on one side of the equation. As such, it did not represent a satisfactory or stable ideological settlement.

In *Steele*, the Court rose to meet this problem by negotiating a new and affirmative constitutional vision. *Steele* raised a related question under the terms of the 1926 Railway Labor Act (a model for New Deal collective bargaining legislation). The Brotherhood of Locomotive Firemen had been granted the exclusive collective bargaining authority for train firemen under the terms of the act. This was industrial democracy in action, and the union operated democratically—by majority rule. The majority of union members were white, and by the act's terms, the black union members were governed by the white majority.[78] In the years preceding *Steele*, technological advances in the industry had made the job of a railway fireman cleaner (and hence more desirable). Given the high unemployment levels of the Great Depression, the fireman's job, formerly a "Negro position," became much more attractive to whites. It was in the context of these changes that the railway union, acting by majority vote, began to systematically drive black workers out of the fireman's slot and into less attractive positions. As part of this effort, the *Steele* plaintiff and his black peers were pushed out of their jobs as locomotive firemen and replaced by whites with less seniority and no more professional competence. The black firemen were reassigned to lower-paying and less attractive jobs.

In its decision invalidating these union initiatives, the *Steele* Court went beyond the simple assertion that the labor union whose case was before it was now, post–New Deal, a creature of the state and an instrument of state policy. At the same time, it rejected a simple adherence to the principle of majority rule. Instead, urged on by amicus briefs filed by the Justice Department and the NAACP, the Court made a juris-generative argument anchored in an analogy between a labor union and a legislature. And interestingly enough for a Court that had recently abandoned its requirement of legislative neutrality and impartiality in cases involving contention between capital and labor— on the antiformalist grounds that claims to neutrality in these matters belied the reality of underlying power relations[79]—the Court then went on to assert that it was a statutory requirement under the Railway Labor Act that all "legislatures" operate impartially. This the Court held despite the fact that the act had no nondiscrimination provision, and despite the fact that the act clearly had not intended to racially integrate the railway labor unions:

> If, as the state court has held, the Act confers this power on the bargaining representative of a craft or class of employees without any commensurate statutory duty

toward its members, constitutional questions arise. For the representative is clothed with power *not unlike that of a legislature* which is subject to constitutional limitations on its power to deny, restrict, destroy or discriminate against the rights of those for whom it legislates and which is also under an affirmative constitutional duty equally to protect those rights.[80]

This "union as legislature" had, in the Court's estimation, an affirmative fiduciary duty to act impartially with the best interests of all in mind—a duty that came to be known as the "duty of fair representation." "We think that the Railway Labor Act," Chief Justice Harlan Fiske Stone continued, "imposes upon the statutory representative of a craft at least as exacting a duty to protect equally the interests of the members of the craft as the Constitution imposes upon a legislature to give equal protection to the interests of those for whom it legislates."[81] In *Steele*, that is, Stone reads into the Railway Labor Act a proscription on class legislation favoring one race over another, thus signaling a major constitutional revival of the old pattern of formalist constitutionalism in a new context and for an altered purpose.[82]

The reasoning of Frank Murphy's concurrence, however, proceeded somewhat differently. Murphy frankly acknowledged that organized labor was accorded special, state-sanctioned group power by the terms of the 1926 act (and Murphy, the former pro-labor Governor of Michigan, was very much in sympathy with these developments). "While such a union is essentially a private organization," Murphy emphasized, "its power to represent and bind all members of a class or craft is derived solely from Congress." Unlike Stone, who interpreted the act in line with what he saw as newly emerging policy imperatives, Murphy correctly noted that the act, which evinced a broad trust in industrial democracy, "contains no language which directs the manner in which the bargaining representative shall perform its duties." For the Court to assert that unions like the Brotherhood were limited in the ways in which they could govern themselves and take positions in their dealings with management was to make a constitutional rather than a statutory decision. Murphy insisted that the Court should base its holding not on statutory grounds, but on the grounds that the statute (and presumably other collective bargaining arrangements such as the Wagner Act that were based on its model) was in contravention of the Constitution's Fifth Amendment.

Murphy, a judge known for his forthright, and, at times, nonlegalistic, opinions—was simply too direct about all this to present an ideologically serviceable line of analysis. There were two major drawbacks to his approach.

First, it was ahead of its time so far as the Court's understanding of the Fifth Amendment's due process clause was concerned. The Court came to apply the Fifth Amendment as a guarantee of equal protection of the laws in race discrimination cases only in *Bolling v. Sharpe* (1954) as part of its sweeping extension of the ruling of *Brown v. Board of Education* (1954).[83] And second, it simply refused to profess the ultimate constitutional commensurability between industrial democracy and the civil rights of African Americans.[84] The Court eventually arrived at the same substantive end as Murphy. But its ideological needs and commitments drove it to arrive there by a more tortured and roundabout statutory path.[85] In passing the Wagner Act, Congress did not, either deliberately or by default, "punt" the issue of the racial integration of labor unions to the courts.[86] Antidiscrimination provisions were proposed in Congress at the time the law was being considered. Those proposals were roundly rejected. Nor was there any intention in framing the language of the bill to invite an antidiscrimination jurisprudence. The focus of Congress was rather on the basic structure of majority rule. For the Court to read a racial nondiscrimination requirement into the collective bargaining provisions of the law was an aggressive act of judicial policy making, amounting to the rewriting of the act itself.[87]

As a matter of pure legal logic, the constitutional route clearly made more sense. It was, after all, federal legislation that called into being the entire system of collective bargaining at issue in the fair representation cases. It certified the unions as bargaining agents, supervised union elections, and oversaw both disputes concerning those elections and between employers and unions. As such, the connection between federal action and any racial discrimination that occurred was strong—at least as strong as it was in other areas of the law where the conduct of ostensibly private organizations was deemed to be public for constitutional purposes.[88] Strictly speaking, the Fourteenth Amendment's equal protection clause applied to the states, not the federal government (as Justice Murphy had noted). But the due process clause of the Fifth Amendment was an available, if audacious, means to the same end, as was (possibly) even the Fifteenth Amendment, which proscribed racial discrimination in voting by "the United States or by any State." In an era in which "formalism" was ostensibly a thing of the past, and the Court was ostensibly looking beyond the rigidities of the public/private distinction, there would seem to be no reason for the Court to hold back from resting its race discrimination cases involving labor unions on constitutional grounds.[89]

If we consider legal initiatives in this area as an ideologically infused developmental process, however, the statutory route had a signal advantage: in its refusal to find governmental action in the conduct of labor unions it maintained a public commitment to labor union voluntarism in a high-profile area of law. A rights-based constitutional ruling, by contrast, would achieve its result by penetrating the union, thus permitting the claims of the second developmental imperative (civil rights) to publicly trump those of the first (labor rights). At this relatively early stage, before the full consolidation of the New Deal regime—typically linked to (Republican) President Eisenhower's decision in the 1950s to accept rather than roll back its key commitments—such a rights-based ruling, besides being a bold substantive move, would amount to an ideological whipsawing. It was highly desirable, at least at this point in time, to avoid the confrontational and penetrating rights-based approach.[90]

The statutory approach, moreover, had the further advantage of downplaying the sharpness of the confrontation between labor unions and the federal courts—a sensitive subject for labor in light of a half-century's history that had culminated in the passage of the Norris-LaGuardia Anti-Injunction Act (1932) and of the Wagner Act (1935). Rather than conferring *rights* on African Americans, who could then assert them against labor unions, the statutory approach allowed courts to focus on *duties*, or on imposing norms of governance on the unions that were consistent with broader norms said to be ambient in the wider polity. In effect, of course, the hoped-for result would be the same by either rule. But the approach anchored in statutory interpretation took the decision out of the realm of judicial review. An equal protection ruling was essentially made norm based, rather than rights based, and the commitment to labor power and labor voluntarism was effectively preserved.[91]

Although standard barrier-and-breakthrough accounts of the emergence of constitutional modernity focus on the removal of formalist obstacles to labor union power and the gradual extension of civil rights protections to those within, and attempting to join, labor unions, the process I describe here emphasizes conflict between the rights of labor and the rights of blacks, and the revival of pre-1937 constitutional constructions to obscure that antagonism, which was ideologically problematic for modern liberalism. The state's conferral of broad powers of (majoritarian) self-government on labor unions had been the culmination of a half-century of highly public political and intellectual work advocating that power on pluralist (group), republican, and democratic grounds. Once the labor problem had been solved, and civil rights became the chief reformist imperative, it was thus extremely difficult for liberals to frankly repudiate these commitments. This made constitution-based antidiscrimination rulings in cases involving labor unions highly unpalatable. To assimilate the next reformist imperative while doing as little damage as possible to the consolidation of the first, the Court, in its statutory decisions, revived the idea that a legislature had a duty to act in a class-neutral way (now christened "the duty of fair representation")—an idea that had ostensibly been discarded as a species of "formalism" at the birth of constitutional modernity. The revival of the idea that legislation must be class neutral (in this high-profile context, at least), thus joined the renewed willingness of the Court to abstract from lived employer-employee power relationships in the service of the interests of the new system, as paradoxical pillars of the post-1937 Constitutional order. Far from having been discarded, the old forms—in service of new substantive ends—were very much alive.

Reconstructing Judicial Power: The Labor Injunction is Dead— Long Live the Labor Injunction

The next step in the ideological project of reconciling the first reform imperative of labor union autonomy with the subsequent imperative of civil rights involved reconstructing the legitimacy of aggressive assertions of judicial power. To a significant extent, the early twentieth-century struggle against Lochnerism amounted to a broad and concerted attack on aggressive assertions of judicial power. Indeed, it was in the fight against Lochnerism that the preoccupation of modern constitutional theorists with the countermajoritarian "problem" of judicial power began. "Government by injunction" and, more broadly, "government by judiciary"—calls to arms sounded chiefly in response to court decisions involving protective legislation and labor unions—were at the core of what constitutional progressives understood themselves to be fighting against. A normative commitment to majoritarianism in labor relations thus dovetailed ideologically with the progressive commitment to majoritarianism in politics more broadly. The emergent imperative of civil rights raised serious problems for this commitment and self-understanding.[92]

The problem was joined when emergent civil rights activists made the strategic decision to model their movement activity on the successful strategies of the labor movement, and to construct their constitutional vision in light of the opportunity structures organized labor had newly built into the sinews of the state.[93] New Deal labor decisions, like the Court's Norris-LaGuardia decisions of the late 1930s, along with other developments, had signaled to American blacks the altered nature of the regime's political and constitutional opportunity structure. One obvious change was that the courts had backed away from their formerly narrow interpretations of the term "labor dispute" in the Norris-LaGuardia Act (in, for example, formulating the "proximate relations doctrine"). *Senn* and *Lauf* signaled that courts would now categorize a more expansive array of social disturbances as "labor disputes," in the process sharply cabining their power to issue injunctions. The collective, coercive muscle of organized labor, it became apparent, could at long last be asserted (even to the point of trampling on plausible and seemingly sympathetic individual rights claims, as was the case in the *Senn* and *Lauf* decisions themselves), and these assertions would no longer meet with rights-protective judicial intervention from the state.[94]

Given this turn against judicial power in the Court's statutory jurisprudence, and the constitutional ethos of groups that undergirded it, the civil rights leadership came to appreciate, first, that it would be newly advantageous to press their case as a group or class, and, second, that their interests as a group would benefit from having courts categorize race discrimination disputes as a species of class-based "labor dispute." In the process, they would be free to flex their collective muscle as a group through movement activity without court interference.[95] The designation of blacks as a formal constitutional group akin to organized labor for purposes of injunctions was negotiated in a series of state and federal decisions arising out of the "Don't Buy Where You Can't Work" campaigns launched during the 1930s by urban blacks against white business owners operating in black neighborhoods. These campaigns, which had a special intensity given the dearth of jobs during the depths of the Depression, deployed an array of direct action tactics appropriated from the repertoires of contention of organized labor, including publicity, boycotts, and pickets. The demands of the "Don't Buy Where You Can't Work" campaigns were straightforward: targeted businesses were asked to either hire all-black staffs or to fulfill a specified proportion or quota of black workers. Failure to do so would bring down a hail of protest on the defiant business.[96]

Two of the earliest legal rulings arising out of these campaigns, *A. S. Beck v. Johnson* (1934) and *Green v. Samuelson* (1935), were issued by state courts.[97] In *A. S. Beck*, a white-owned Harlem shoe store was systematically picketed by a group of blacks having no connection with the store, its employees, or, indeed, with any labor organization (and thus with no "proximate relation" to the business). The picketers demanded that the store employ a fixed percentage of black workers and urged Harlem residents not to shop there if the store refused. A. S. Beck, resisting these threats, sought and won an injunction against the picketing. The New York Supreme Court (a trial court) based its decision on the *sic utere tuo* principle that Beck's business was being hurt by an organized protest campaign that lacked a lawful purpose, a ruling that seemed to fit more comfortably with the old order's constitutional ethos than the new one's. Picketing in New York State (as elsewhere) had recently been accorded statutory protection from judicial injunctions. But the pickets at issue in *A. S. Beck*, the court plausibly declared, were different: because they were aimed at having the store dismiss white employees so that black workers could be hired to replace them, they lacked a lawful purpose. The New York court also held, again quite plausibly, that the confrontation did not involve a labor dispute: rather, it was a racial dispute. As such, the state's new anti-injunction statute was inapplicable. Thus, although blacks were deploying labor movement tactics in *A. S. Beck*, the fact remained that they were not a recognized class like organized labor, and their use of those tactics to advance their interests as a group did not fall under the anti-injunction laws as applied to labor disputes. Under these circumstances, individual rights considerations of the sort that were at the heart of the old order concerning labor regulations would remain decisive.[98]

In *Green v. Samuelson*, another state case decided the following year, the Jewish owners of a number of stores in black neighborhoods in Baltimore were targeted by civil rights boycotts and pickets insisting they hire only black workers. At the time the boycotts and pickets began, some of these Jewish-owned stores had staffs that were a full 50 percent black, a percentage the protesters had deemed inadequate. In issuing a permanent injunction against black pickets and boycotts, the Maryland court, as in *A. S. Beck*, cited the *sic utere tuo* principle and maintained that it was inappropriate to invoke the rules applicable to labor disputes in a race case involving different issues. "In our opinion," the Maryland court concluded, "this is a racial or social question, and as such, the rules heretofore announced and applied to labor disputes have no application." In 1935, the effort "to promote the interests of the colored race generally" was still seen as constitutionally distinct from analogous efforts on behalf of organized labor.[99]

Soon, however, some of the nation's most elite law journals began the process of ideologically reconstructing the meaning of these decisions. This began in articles that were supportive of the rulings. Even there, however, transformative ambitions were apparent. In backing the *A. S. Beck* decision, for example, a comment in the *Harvard Law Review* was quick to call attention to the fact that "the picketing in the instant case, definitely for the purpose of aiding members of the Negro race, seems similar to the organized labor cases in that it involves the possibilities of riots and injury to the business of the employer as well as a demand for the betterment of the position of the picketing class." The crucial difference for this commentator, however, was "the lack of any policy favoring racial privileges comparable to that favoring labor demands." This difference, he concluded, "seems an adequate reason for a different result."[100]

A commentator writing in the *University of Pennsylvania Law Review*, however, took a different approach. The author first noted the court's holding that the case "involved no dispute over working conditions, and no attempt to unionize." This, the court had held, had essentially dictated that the protesters possessed no right to avail themselves of the "privilege" of picketing. The commentator objected to this line of reasoning, however: "The impossibility of fitting the situation into the category of a labor dispute should not necessitate such a result. There may well be considerations in favor of giving such privileges to the negro race quite as compelling as those which have brought about the liberalization of the judicial attitude toward labor."[101] Continuing the conceptual analogy between blacks and labor as cognizable groups or classes, the commentator continued:

> Some degree of violence seems to be an inevitable concomitant of any self-enforced improvement in the lot of previously subjected groups, as the turbulence of many labor disputes will bear witness. The alternative of abandoning all attempts at progress is scarcely preferable. . . . The essential purpose behind the liberal attitude toward labor would seem to be the advisability of raising living standards and ultimately reducing the sociological and economic burdens upon the community as a whole which accompany the subjugation of any large group therein. The economic progress of the negro race should, for this same reason, be a proper subject of community concern.[102]

The issues raised in these state court decisions soon reached the Supreme Court. And it was not long before that court, in turn, adopted as the law of the land the analogy urged by the University of Pennsylvania law student, an analogy, of course, that sat well, if not with the law, per se, then at least with the new, group-oriented constitutional ethos.

The High Court took the key step in the term immediately after its "switch-in-time" decisions in the *West Coast Hotel* and *Jones and Laughlin*

Steel and at about the same time as its Norris-LaGuardia decisions in *Senn* and *Lauf*. The opinion in which it conferred constitutionally cognizable status on blacks as a group was *New Negro Alliance v. Sanitary Grocery* (1938), a decision penned by the key switch-in-time justice, Owen Roberts (an alumnus, professor, and later dean of the University of Pennsylvania Law School—and thus a man who was likely to have perused the school's law review comment involving the state court picketing decisions).[103] In *New Negro Alliance*, the Court held, contrary to the thrust of the state-level *A. S. Beck* and *Green* decisions, that antirace discrimination picketing indeed constituted a "labor dispute" under the terms of the Norris-LaGuardia Act. And the Court further held that this was the case even if the picketers had no employment relationship (or proximate relation) with targeted business. In applying the terms of the act to these disputes, the Court—for picketing purposes at least—elevated blacks as a group to the same status of labor as a group within the parameters of the new constitutional order.

New Negro Alliance involved the legality of the picketing of a Washington, D.C. grocery store by a black civic and racial improvement association. That store operated in a black neighborhood and employed both white and black employees. None of the employees at the store was affiliated with the New Negro Alliance.[104] The Alliance insisted both that the store employ more blacks and that those blacks newly hired in response to their protests be appointed to sales and managerial positions. When Sanitary Grocery refused to accede to the Alliance's demands, its members threatened to boycott and ruin the business. As part of their protest campaign, they paraded before the store with signs reading, "Do Your Part! Buy Where You Can Work! No Negroes Employed Here!"

In his opinion in *New Negro Alliance*, Justice Roberts brought African Americans—considered not as individuals but as a group or class—under the wing of the new state-administered order set out in the Norris-LaGuardia Anti-Injunction Act. Roberts justified the Court's decision to do so with the argument that race discrimination in employment was "quite as important" as discrimination arising out of labor union affiliation or other grievances about the conditions of employment (the *Pennsylvania Law Review* article had called it "quite as compelling"). "The [Norris-LaGuardia] Act," Roberts wrote, "does not concern itself with the background and motives of the dispute."

> The desire for fair and equitable conditions of employment on the part of persons of any race, color, or persuasion, and the removal of discriminations against them

by reason of their race or religious beliefs is quite as important to those concerned as fairness and equity in terms and conditions of employment can be to trade or craft unions or any form of labor organization or association. Race discrimination by an employer may reasonably be deemed more unfair and less excusable than discrimination against workers on the ground of union affiliation.[105]

Accordingly, henceforth, injunctions in such cases—like those in pure labor cases—could not be issued. The barrier of judicial power was removed for blacks as well, placing the labor movement and the fledgling civil rights movement on par.

These decisions will seem readily assimilable by key legal and developmental models of constitutional change. Legalists can read them as extending principle of equality from one deserving group (labor) to another (blacks). Developmentalists committed to theories of path dependency can read them as amounting to a step by blacks along an institutionalized path that had been paved earlier by organized labor. Both readings run into problems, however, when, in the next developmental stage, the principles conflict and the paths cross. The illusion of linearity was sustained in these decisions only because the defendants in the "Don't Buy Where You Can't Work" cases were independent businesses and not labor unions. Under these circumstances, it was easy enough to take the status accorded to labor unions in similar cases, draw an analogy between labor and blacks (in the classic legal analogical style) and then extend the coverage of that status to what was taken to be a similarly disempowered group. The courts had declared, consistent with regard to the bedrock commitments of constitutional progressivism, that judges would not stand in the way of the assertion of coercive powers of either group. What would happen, though, when blacks then took this newly won constitutional status and sought to assert it against the very group that it had been fashioned to empower in the first place? Here, the Court would be called on to make a stark choice between the darling of the old progressive politics, and the emerging darling of the new one. These circumstances—an "abutment" or "abrasion"—forced the Court, in a key area, to fundamentally reassess what was assumed to be its bedrock progressive commitment to limited judicial power. The Court was forced to negotiate a new modus vivendi.[106]

Blacks forced the issue in injunction cases in the late 1940s and early 1950s. In the process they drove the Court to knit together the jurisprudence of its injunction cases (with its origins in the first reformist campaign concerning labor) and its fair representation cases (itself the product of the negotiated assimilation of labor rights and civil rights) into a single, functional and ideologically plausible constitutional vision that played a signal role in reconstructing the power of the federal courts. In *Graham v. Brotherhood of Locomotive Firemen and Enginemen* (1949), the Court extended its decision in *New Negro Alliance* by holding that civil rights disputes between excluded (that is, nonunion) black workers and an all-white railway union were "labor disputes," and accordingly were to be governed by the terms of Norris-LaGuardia Anti-Injunction Act.[107] But at the same time—remarkably enough, given that the purpose of that act was to constrain court power in labor disputes—the Court not only held that blacks had recourse to a court injunction against racial discrimination (because the statutory right to "fair representation" must have a remedy), but also boldly declared that the power of courts to issue injunctions was at the heart of the act.

Looked at from the perspective of traditional narratives of constitutional development hewing to a teleological view of the emergence of civil rights as the gradual realization of the principles of political equality underlying either the New Deal or "liberal justice," *Graham* would appear to be routine, one more step along the path of progress.[108] Looked at developmentally, however, it is extraordinary. Because the very purpose of the Norris-LaGuardia Act was to take injunctive power away from the courts in labor disputes in the service of labor union autonomy, its deployment here as a wellspring of judicial power represents nothing less than a major reconstruction of the meaning of one of the nation's seminal labor laws.[109]

One of the most remarkable aspects of Justice Robert Jackson's opinion for the Court in *Graham* is Jackson's decision, when forced into the uncomfortable position of choosing between the claims of one newly preferred group and another, to extricate himself by conferring the beneficent label of "labor" on the nonunion black men rather than on the labor union itself. Jackson asserted that the Court must be able to aggressively wield its injunctive powers to constrain the power of labor unions because, if it could not, this would constrain the power of "labor." Specifically, he wrote, "to depart from those views [that the Norris-LaGuardia Act did not deprive federal courts of jurisdiction to compel compliance with positive mandates of the Railway Labor Act] would be to strike from labor's hands the sole judicial weapon it may employ to enforce such minority rights as these petitioners assert and which we have held are now secured to them by federal statute." Injunctions against labor unions are entirely appropriate under the Norris-LaGuardia Act, considered in light of fair representation guarantees, Jackson had ingeniously concluded in inventively melding the sequential reform imperatives, because issuing them advances the cause of labor.[110]

In *Brotherhood of Railroad Trainmen v. Howard* (1952) the Court continued the process of negotiating a successful modus vivendi in this ongoing ideological project. *Howard* involved the evolving practice in the railroad industry of pushing black employees who performed the duties of brakemen out of the "white" category of "brakemen" and into the black category of "porters" (where they organized in all-black porters unions). The Court handed a victory in the case to outsider blacks challenging the discriminatory practices of the (white) brakemen's union. The Railway Labor Act, the Court held, "prohibits bargaining agents it authorizes from using their position and power to destroy colored workers' jobs in order to bestow them on white workers." Moreover, the *Howard* Court gave a ringing endorsement to the fashioning of a strong judicial remedy in the case. "Our conclusion is that the District Court has jurisdiction and power to issue necessary injunctive orders," Justice Black declared, writing for the Court, "notwithstanding the provisions of the Norris-LaGuardia Act."[111]

A dissent by Sherman Minton (joined by Chief Justice Fred Vinson and Stanley Reed), however, emphasized the private status of the labor union, and appealed to the old progressive imperative of labor union autonomy and self-government. "The [Court] majority reaches out to invalidate the contract," Minton wrote,

> not because the train porters are brakemen entitled to fair representation by the Brotherhood, but because they are Negroes who were discriminated against by the carrier at the behest of the Brotherhood. I do not understand that private parties such as the carrier and the Brotherhood may not discriminate on the ground of race. Neither a state government nor the Federal Government may do so, but I know of no applicable federal law which says that private parties may not.[112]

This, however, was about as far as the Court was willing to go. In *Oliphant v. Brotherhood of Locomotive Firemen and Engineers* (1958), a federal appellate court negotiated the outer limits of this jurisprudence—limits that the Supreme Court let stand. In *Oliphant* the court was confronted with a constitutional (as opposed to statutory) fair representation argument in what would now seem to be a much more hospitable post-1954 climate. Specifically, the court explained that petitioners'

> first argument is that, inasmuch as racial exclusion from public schools is inherently a denial of the equal protection of the laws guaranteed by the Fourteenth Amendment

[citing *Brown v. Board*] and of due process of law guaranteed by the Fifth Amendment [citing *Bolling v. Sharpe*] it follows that denial of membership in the duly elected statutory bargaining representative, based on race, is inherently incompatible with the rights afforded by the Fifth Amendment to the Constitution of the United States and by the equal protection and equal representation guaranteed to them by [the doctrine of the *Steele* case]. Plaintiffs then go on to draw a direct analogy to this situation and the cases in which the Court rejected "separate but equal" in schools [citing *Missouri ex rel. Gaines*; *Sweatt v. Painter*].[113]

Despite the new environment, however, the Court in *Oliphant* demurred. It emphasized that the chief purpose of the collective bargaining arrangements set up by the federal government was to create "industrial tranquility in the arteries of commerce" and "industrial peace and stabilized labor-management relations."[114] Blacks were put in the position they were not by the federal government, but by a private, autonomous labor union. "The accusing finger is pointed at the Congress," the court noted. But "only one analysis could tend to lay the responsibility for appellants' situation on our national legislative branch of government; that is, the violation of the Fifth Amendment by the Congress, in its enactment of the Railway Labor Act without including therein a provision requiring a labor union—when duly elected as collective bargaining representative of a craft—to extend membership privileges to all members of the craft, regardless of race." This line of argument, however, the court dismissed as a "fine-spun hypothesis," which it found easy to reject. *Brown* and *Bolling* both involved legislation that affirmatively discriminated against blacks. Here, the court concluded that "this record does not show an agency of the federal government to have been responsible for the appellants' plight." Here, the culprit was not the government, but a labor union. "The Brotherhood is a private association, whose membership policies are its own affair." And the Court underlined its holding by appealing to virtues of judicial restraint.[115]

The Settlement

From the time of the passage of the Wagner Act and the passing of the labor problem as the defining reformist imperative, and its sequential displacement by the cause of civil rights, courts, component institutions of the new regime, were placed in the difficult position, in cases involving race discrimination by labor unions, of negotiating the assimilation of the second imperative without undermining the consolidation of the first. They did so through a highly creative statutory jurisprudence that clung to the idea of labor union autonomy and self-government while taking important steps toward compelling those unions to be nondiscriminatory. Once this regime was fully consolidated, and the New Deal's collective bargaining arrangements (and other aspects) were fully accepted as part of the twentieth-century state's governing philosophy in the early 1960s, however, this ideological high-wire act was no longer necessary. The second imperative could now be followed without an overlying restricting obeisance to the ideology of the first.[116] Decisions of the Court in other areas of the law began to call into question the constitutional legitimacy of the public-private distinction when it was used as a shield for race discrimination.[117]

Labor unions, once at the center of the liberal program, came under increasing criticism for their corruption, and interest group politics, as notions of participatory democracy began to undercut the appeal of the more sanguine understandings of interest group pluralism.[118] The Civil Rights movement culminated in the passage of the 1964 Civil Rights Act, which, in Title VII, directly forbade race discrimination by labor unions.[119] At the very same time, the National Relations Labor Board had begun to (newly) declare that race discrimination in unions amounted to an "unfair labor practice" under Section 9(a) of the act and was hence remediable in the federal courts.[120] Moreover, since 1954, the Court had boldly committed itself to using whatever remedies it believed necessary to achieve its goals concerning civil rights. The aggressive wielding of equitable power—including injunctive powers—by the Court spread from civil rights proper to a variety of related areas that came to be associated with modern liberalism.[121] By the 1970s, the Court had no problem, notwithstanding Norris-LaGuardia, in granting injunctions against organized labor even in cases not involving racial issues.[122] Under the influence of sequential reform imperatives, both within labor law and outside it, by the 1970s, the relationship between labor unions and the courts had been radically transformed.

Conclusion

The traditional constitutive story of the emergence of constitutional modernity in the Constitutional Revolution of the 1930s does a certain amount of justice to events. That revolution was born in a highly political fight against the Lochnerite liberty of contract doctrine that served to invalidate the passage of protective legislation, against overly restrictive readings of the Constitution that worked to thwart labor unions' power, and against what more generally was taken to be a disposition on the part of judges to make too ready use of their powers against labor unions and legislatures that (unlike the judges) were elected by the people. After the revolution, when legislatures were free to pass minimum wage, maximum hours, and health and safety laws, the ability of courts to issue labor injunctions had been sharply curtailed, and constitutional challenges to collective bargaining arrangements were all but eliminated. Courts seemed suddenly quiescent. A rigid jurisprudence of economic rights had been swept away. And a new, more humane jurisprudence of personal rights was on the horizon. These events form the foundations of the barrier-and-breakthrough narrative of the nation's passage to constitutional modernity.

In this chapter, I have argued not so much that this narrative is false as that its elevated status as an origins myth marking the end of history—the end of rigid formalisms, an unwillingness on the part of the Court to bring the outside world as lived and experienced into its decision-making process, and of aggressive assertions of judicial power—has tended to obscure the nature of the processes of constitutional development that followed the breakthrough of the 1930s. In particular, the predisposition to viewing the New Deal triumph as a clean breakthrough to a new order has tended to thwart a clear-sighted appreciation for the ways in which the post-1937 Court recurred to ostensibly old-order habits as part of the process of consolidating the new regime. The breakthrough of the 1930s, I argue here, may have permitted the bold new public policy initiatives that came to characterize the twentieth-century American state. But in the wake of that breakthrough, the Court did not jettison a reliance on broad social theories, or evince a new openness to the lived experience of individuals facing power, or abandon the ideal of class neutrality, or forswear judicial power. What it did was simply turn all of these to new purposes consistent with the needs and public philosophy of the new regime.

This conclusion, in its broadest sense, is consistent with the understanding of political scientists holding that judges vote their "attitudes" or, in a variant, pursue the policy preferences of the political coalition that appointed them. But this understanding, although of course true in important respects, does not explain anything that is truly interesting about constitutional law or development. It fails to capture the dynamism of the process of constitutional change. Looking at the area I have focused on here, liberal legalists have charted a principled, linear progression adding the rights of blacks to the rights of labor, whereas attitudinalists and behavioralists (more dependent on liberal legal philosophers than they suppose) accept these categories and measure them in electoral or interest group terms.[123] But what if the rights of one group within a coalition conflict with the rights of another, in principle and in practice, as labor rights and civil rights did, after 1937? And what if according rights to a disempowered group worked to limit a key individual liberty? As the fight for the rights of labor and civil rights, and the movements pursuing them, formed the backbone of modern liberalism and played a critical role in the constitution of the modern state, these are hardly idle questions. What the Court did—as political parties do (in a different institutional context, a comparison well worth exploring)—is endeavor to negotiate a modus vivendi that holds the coalition together, consolidating its achievements while assimilating new sequential imperatives in a changing institutional and ideational context. Understanding how it does so while maintaining its legitimating appearance as a legal (as opposed to a "political") institution is an ideological process, and an interesting one at that, for besides helping us to understand the nature of courts and institutions, and the dynamics of legal and political change, it helps us to appreciate the way in which the very categories that attitudinalists trustingly tally as votes "for" civil rights and liberties came into being. They chart the genealogy of contemporary common sense.

In the mid-twentieth century, I find, the Supreme Court negotiated the sequential reform imperatives of labor rights and civil rights by recurring as much as possible to statutory (as opposed to constitutional) interpretation, an approach that served to downplay the tensions between them. The Court also subtly altered its construction of the meaning and symbol of "labor," ultimately coming to identify it rhetorically with blacks against labor unions themselves. At first, while the regime was new and unsettled, the Court was cautious in its steps, emphasizing consolidation of the achievements of labor. As its foundations grew firmer, the Court, although it never disregarded the task of consolidation, grew bolder in its assimilation of the next reform imperative. In both, as part of the process of striving to maintain its legal authority and legitimacy, it made use of formalisms, categories, and (when needed and safer) aggressive assertions of its power that had ostensibly been discredited in the 1930s. Neither the legalist nor the political models do justice to this distinctive developmental process.

Notes

I thank Paul Frymer, Ron Kahn, Karen Orren, and Keith Whittington for their comments, criticisms, and encouragement. Research assistance was provided by Creighton Page, Princeton '05, and Nancy Danch of the Bobst Center for Peace and Justice of Princeton's Department of Politics.

1. See, e.g., Howard Gillman, "The Collapse of Constitutional Originalism and the Rise of the Notion of the 'Living Constitution' in the Course of American State-building," *Studies in American Political Development* 11 (Fall 1997): 191–247; Howard Gillman, "Preferred Freedoms: The Progressive Expansion of State Power and the Rise of Modern Civil Liberties Jurisprudence," *Political Research Quarterly* 47 (September 1994): 623–653; Karen Orren, *Belated Feudalism: Labor, the Law, and Liberal Development in the United States* (Cambridge: Cambridge University Press, 1991); William M. Wiecek, *The Lost World of Classical Legal Thought: Law and Ideology in America, 1886–1937* (New York: Oxford University Press, 1998). For a critique of barrier and breakthrough models of institutional change, see Kathleen Thelen, "How Institutions Evolve: Insights from Comparative Historical Analysis," in *Comparative Historical Analysis in the Social Sciences*, ed. James Mahoney and Dietrich Rueschemeyer (Cambridge: Cambridge University Press, 2003), 211. On constitutive stories (which, I argue, are supportive of such models), see Rogers M. Smith, *Stories of Peoplehood: The Politics and Morals of Political Membership* (New York: Cambridge University Press, 2003). See also Benedict R. O'G. Anderson, *Imagined Communities: Reflections on the Origin and Spread of Nationalism* (London: Verso, 1983); William Novak, "The Legal Origins of the Modern American State," in *Looking Back on Law's Century*, ed. Bryant Garth, Robert Kagan, and Austin Sarat (Ithaca, N.Y.: Cornell University Press, 2003).

2. Julie Novkov, *Constituting Workers, Protecting Women: Gender, Law, and Labor in the Progressive Era and New Deal Years* (Ann Arbor: University of Michigan Press, 2001), 254. Constitutive stories recalling the "lessons" learned from the New Deal breakthrough are at the core of the ideology of contemporary constitutional liberalism. See *Planned Parenthood of Southeastern Pennsylvania v. Casey*, 505 U.S. 833 (1992); *United States v. Lopez*, 514 U.S. 549 (1995) (dissent).

3. Ronald Kahn, "*Marbury v. Madison* as a Model for Understanding Contemporary Judicial Review," in *Marbury v. Madison: Documents and Commentary*, ed. Mark A. Graber and Michael Perhac (Washington, D.C.: CQ Press, 2003); G. Edward White, *The Constitution and the New Deal* (Cambridge, Mass.: Harvard University Press, 2000); Barry Cushman, *Rethinking the New Deal Court: The Structure of a Constitutional Revolution* (New York: Oxford University Press, 1998); See Melvin Urofsky, "Myth and Reality: The Supreme Court and Protective Legislation in the Progressive Era," *Yearbook of the Supreme Court Historical Society* (1983): 53–72.

4. See, e.g., Keith E. Whittington, "Dismantling the Modern State? The Changing Structural Foundations of Federalism," *Hastings Constitutional Law Quarterly* 25 (Summer 1998): 483–527; Howard Gillman, "Political Development and the Rise of the 'Preferred Freedoms' Rubric in Constitutional Law," paper presented at the University of Maryland Georgetown Constitutional Discussion Group, College Park, Md., April 2002; Howard Gillman, "How Political Parties Can Use the Courts to Advance Their Agendas: Federal Courts in the United States, 1875–1891," *American Political Science Review* 96 (2002): 511–524.

5. See Thelen, "How Institutions Evolve," 221, advocating that scholars "distinguish more clearly at both an empirical and an analytic level between the *mechanisms of reproduction* and the *logic of change* at work in particular instances" and "suggest modes of change going beyond the familiar but perhaps ultimately empirically quite rare cases of institutional 'breakdown' or wholesale replacement as implied in a punctuated equilibrium model." On the dynamic of negotiation as central to much of constitutional development, see Stephen Skowronek, *Building a New American State: The Expansion of National Administrative Capacities, 1877–1920* (Cambridge: Cambridge University Press, 1982); Ken I. Kersch, "The Reconstruction of Constitutional Privacy Rights and the New American State," *Studies in American Political Development* 16 (Spring 2002): 61–87. Ken I. Kersch, *Constructing Civil Liberties: Discontinuities in the Development of American Constitutional Law* (Cambridge: Cambridge University Press, 2004); Ronald Kahn, *The Supreme Court and Constitutional Theory, 1953–1993* (Lawrence: University Press of Kansas, 1994); Keith Whittington, *Constitutional Construction* (Cambridge, Mass.: Harvard University Press, 1999); Novkov, *Constituting Workers, Protecting Women*, 14–22.

6. Howard Gillman, *The Constitution Besieged: The Rise and Demise of Lochner Era Police Powers Jurisprudence* (Durham, N.C.: Duke University Press, 1993).

7. Louis B. Bodin, *Government by Judiciary* (New York: William Godwin, 1932); William G. Ross, *A Muted Fury: Populists, Progressives, and Labor Unions Confront the Courts, 1890–1937* (Princeton, N.J.: Princeton University Press, 1994); Abram Chayes, "The Role of the Judge in Public Law Litigation," *Harvard Law Review* 89 (May 1976): 1281–1316; Malcolm Feeley and Edward S. Rubin, *Judicial Policymaking and the Modern State: How the Courts Reformed America's Prisons* (New York: Cambridge University Press, 1998); Lino A. Graglia, *Disaster by Decree: The Supreme Court Decisions on Race and the Schools* (Ithaca, N.Y.: Cornell University Press, 1970).

8. Thelen, "How Institutions Evolve," 231–214, 222, 225, 226–228; Jeffrey Tulis, *The Rhetorical Presidency* (Princeton, N.J.: Princeton University Press, 1987); Eric Schickler, *Disjointed Pluralism: Institutional Innovation and the Development of the U.S. Congress* (Princeton, N.J.: Princeton University Press, 2001); Novkov, *Constituting Workers, Protecting Women*, 243–255; Paul Pierson, "Not Just What, but When: Timing and Sequence in Political Processes," *Studies in American Political Development* 14 (Spring 2000): 72–92; Kathleen Thelen, "Timing and Temporality in the Analysis of Institutional Evolution and Change," *Studies in American Political Development* 14 (Spring 2000): 101–108.

9. Theodore J. Lowi, *The End of Liberalism: The Second Republic of the United States* (New York: W. W. Norton, 1979); Grant McConnell, *Private Power and American Democracy* (New York: Knopf, 1966). On constructions, see generally Whittington, *Constitutional Construction*; Pamela Brandwein, *Reconstructing Reconstruction: The Supreme Court and the Production of Historical Truth* (Durham, N.C.: Duke University Press, 1999).

10. David Green, *The Language of Politics in America: Shaping Political Consciousness from McKinley to Reagan* (Ithaca, N.Y.: Cornell University Press, 1987). See David

Plotke, *Building a Democratic Political Order: Reshaping American Liberalism in the 1930s and 1940s* (New York: Cambridge University Press, 1996).

11. *Lochner v. New York*, 198 U.S. 45 (1905). See William Leuchtenburg, *The Supreme Court Reborn: The Constitutional Revolution in the Age of Roosevelt* (New York: Oxford University Press, 1999); Novkov, *Constituting Workers, Protecting Women*, 4–7. The *Lochner* era loosely comprises the chief justiceships of Melville Weston Fuller (1888–1910) and Edward Douglass White (1910–1921).

12. Gillman, *Constitution Besieged*; Novkov, *Constituting Workers, Protecting Women*.

13. See Eric Foner, *Free Soil, Free Labor, Free Men: The Ideology of the Republican Party before the Civil War* (New York: Oxford University Press, 1970); John Patrick Diggins, *The Lost Soul of American Politics: Virtue, Self-Interest, and the Foundations of Liberalism* (New York: Basic Books, 1984); James Henry Hammond, speech in U.S. Senate, 4 March 1858 ("Mud-Sill Speech"). Slaves and indentured servants, although denied this status, nonetheless aspired to it.

14. *Lochner*, 198 U.S., at 57.

15. Ibid. at 69.

16. Wiecek, *Lost World*, 4–5; Morton White, *Social Thought in America: The Revolt against Formalism* (New York: Oxford University Press, 1976), 132; Edward A. Purcell Jr., *The Crisis of Democratic Theory: Scientific Naturalism and the Problem of Value* (Lexington: University of Kentucky Press, 1973). See also Judith Shklar, *Legalism: Law, Morals, and Political Trials* (Cambridge, Mass.: Harvard University Press, 1986), 1–28.

17. *West Coast Hotel v. Parrish*, 300 U.S. 379, 391 (1937).

18. Ibid. at 399. The emphasis on systems analysis in the labor cases as a constitutional construction meshed effectively with the Court's commerce clause analysis, which was central to the Constitutional Revolution of 1937, including in cases involving labor, and analysis of the federal power to tax to advance the general welfare. *National Labor Relations Board v. Jones and Laughlin Steel Co.*, 301 U.S. 1 (1937); *United States v. Darby Lumber*, 312 U.S. 100 (1941); *Wickard v. Filburn*, 317 U.S. 111 (1942); *Steward Machine v. Davis*, 301 U.S. 548, 588 (1937); *Helvering v. Davis*, 301 U.S. 619, 641–645 (1937). See also *Home Building and Loan Association v. Blaisdell*, 290 U.S. 398, 442.

19. Karen Orren and Stephen Skowronek, "Institutions and Intercurrence: Theory Building in the Fullness of Time," in *Nomos: Political Order*, ed. Ian Shapiro and Russell Hardin (New York: New York University Press, 1996).

20. *Senn v. Tile Layers Union*, 301 U.S. 468 (1937); *Lauf v. Shinner*, 303 U.S. 323 (1938).

21. See *Lochner*, 198 U.S., at 75 (1905) (J. Holmes, dissenting, on Herbert Spencer's *Social Statics*). My analysis here, which focuses on developmental patterns, is agnostic as to the moral defensibility of the old formalisms and the new ones (although I would say that, given the often mutable and unforeseen consequences of any formalism in the long term, the moral implications of the new formalisms are never so clear as it might initially appear). It is also possible (as Ron Kahn has suggested to me) that the new categories, abstractions, and formalisms were less all-encompassing and rigid than those the Court

relied on in cases like *Lochner* and *Carter Coal*. It is also possible that the formalisms, abstractions, and categories match more closely in intensity those of the Courts before the *Lochner* era. But I leave these judgments and determinations to others. My interest here is in countering the constitutive story positing a sweeping "revolt against formalism" and the rise of a freewheeling and open "living constitution."

22. 47 Stat. 70 (1932).

23. The contrast was with the language of the Clayton Act, whose (minimal) ambiguities had been seized by the Court. See generally George I. Lovell, *Legislative Deferrals: Statutory Ambiguity, Judicial Power, and American Democracy* (Cambridge: Cambridge University Press, 2003).

24. For rare discussions of the act in the political development literature, see Lovell, *Legislative Deferrals*; Ruth O'Brien, *Worker's Paradox: The Republican Origins of New Deal Labor Policy, 1886–1935* (Chapel Hill: University of North Carolina Press, 1998); Kersch, *Constructing Civil Liberties*. See *Lauf v. Shinner*, 82 F.2d 68 (7th Cir. 1935); *United Electric Coal Co. v. Rice*, 80 F.2d 1 (7th Cir. 1935), cert. denied, 297 U.S. 714 (1936); *Newton v. Laclede Steel Co.*, 80 F.2d 636 (7th Cir. 1935); *Scavenger Service Corp. v. Courtney*, 85 F.2d 825 (7th Cir. 1936). See also Erwin B. Ellman, "Comment: When a 'Labor Dispute' Exists Within the Meaning of the Norris-LaGuardia Act," *Michigan Law Review* 36 (1938): 1146–1176, esp. 1152, 1154.

25. *Senn v. Tile Layers Union*, 301 U.S. 468 (1937).

26. See Nelson Lichtenstein, *State of the Union: A Century of American Labor* (Princeton, N.J.: Princeton University Press, 2002), 38. For a fuller discussion of the origins of the proximate relations test, and its roots in the Court's Clayton Act jurisprudence, see Kersch, *Constructing Civil Liberties*, 167–169. On the proximate relations test, see *Duplex Printing v. Deering*, 254 U.S. 443, citing *Traux v. Corrigan*, 257 U.S. 312; *Butcher's Union v. Crescent City Live Stock Co.*, 111 U.S. 746; *Hitchman Coal & Coke Co. v. Mitchell*, 245 U.S. 229; *Coppage v. Kansas*, 236 U.S. 1; *Traux v. Raich*, 239 U.S. 33; *Adair v. U.S.*, 208 U.S. 161. For a progressive argument from the state-building era supporting the view that to establish a new regulatory order concerning labor, worthy individual rights claims must be sacrificed, see Herbert Croly, *The Promise of American Life* (New Brunswick, N.J.: Transaction, 1980), 387–388: "In the majority of discussions of the labor question the non-union laborer is figured as the independent working man who is asserting his right to labor when and how he prefers against the tyranny of the labor union. . . . [He is conceptualized as] fighting the battle of individual independence against the army of class oppression. Neither is this estimate of the non-union laborer wholly without foundation. The organization and policy of the contemporary labor union being what they are, cases will occasionally and even frequently occur in which the non-union laborer will represent the protest of an individual against injurious restrictions imposed by the union upon his opportunities and his work. But such cases are rare compared to the much larger number of instances in which the non-union laborer is to be considered as essentially the industrial derelict. . . . Under existing conditions, [independence] must be bought by association. Worthy individuals will sometimes be sacrificed by this process of associa-

tion; but every process of industrial organization or change . . . necessarily involves individual cases of injustice." The fact that to this day individuals are held to have a fundamental right to pursue a lawful trade did not alter the result in *Senn*. See *Hicklin v. Orbeck*, 437 U.S. 518 (1978).

27. This assumption was at the core of the posttraditional constitutional order. See *NLRB v. Jones and Laughlin Steel*, 301 U.S. 1 (1937); Thomas L. Haskell, *The Emergence of Professional Social Science: The American Social Science Association and the Nineteenth Century Crisis of Authority* (Urbana: University of Illinois Press, 1977); Theodore J. Lowi, "The Welfare State: Ethical Foundations and Constitutional Remedies," *Political Science Quarterly* 101 (1986): 197–220; *Wickard v. Filburn*, 317 U.S. 111 (1942); *West Coast Hotel v. Parrish*, 300 U.S. 379 (1937). The critique of the notion that the nation's economy could be managed by a decentralized federalism that imagined "a widespread similarity of local conditions," and that the states could manage the complexities of the regulation of interstate commerce in the state-building era had long been critiqued by progressives outside the Court before it finally made its way into Court doctrine. David W. Levy, *Herbert Croly of the New Republic: The Life and Thought of an American Progressive* (Princeton, N.J.: Princeton University Press, 1985), 110–113.

28. *Senn*, 301 U.S., at 480–481. See Oliver Wendell Holmes Jr., "Privilege, Malice and Intent," *Harvard Law Review* 8 (April 1893): 3, 7; Daniel W. Ernst, *Lawyers against Labor: From Individual Rights to Corporate Liberalism* (Urbana: University of Illinois Press, 1995), 81–85; Lovell, *Legislative Deferrals*, chap. 2.

29. *Senn*, 301 U.S., at 481–482. Needless to say, this assertion would in time be rejected as antiprogressive when the next reformist movement—that of civil rights— took hold. The position advanced by Brandeis in *Senn*, incidentally, was supported by the ACLU in an amicus brief filed in the case.

30. *Senn*, 301 U.S. 480. In making this ruling in *Senn*, the Court simply deferred to the state supreme court's interpretation of a state statute in light of the requirements of the state constitution as binding in the U.S. Supreme Court. *Senn*, 301 U.S., at 477.

31. See also *Duplex Printing* (J. Brandeis, dissenting).

32. *Senn*, 301 U.S., at 491.

33. *Lauf v. Shinner*, 82 F.2d 68 (7th Cir. 1936); *Lauf v. Shinner*, 90 F.2d 250 (1937).

34. *Lauf*, 303 U.S., at 332.

35. *Lauf*, 303 U.S., at 333, citing 29 U.S.C. Section 102 (Section 2 of the Norris-LaGuardia Act, 23 March 1932, 47 Stat. 70).

36. *Lauf*, 303 U.S., at 336. It should be noted that the rhetoric of "choice" concerning a worker's decision whether or not to join a labor union had hardly been at the core of progressive thought. Herbert Croly, for instance, frankly argued in 1908 that because, in a new, modern order, the power of "labor" as a collectivity was needed to counterbalance the power of capital as a collectivity, workers who refused to join a union had to be stripped of their right to work. Croly asserted that "the labor unions deserved to be favored [by the state], because they are the most effective machinery which has yet been forged for the economic and social amelioration of the laboring class. . . . As

a type the non-union laborer is a species of industrial derelict. He is the laborer who has gone astray and who either from apathy, unintelligence, incompetence, or some immediately pressing need prefers his own individual interest to the joint interests of himself and his fellow laborers. From the point of view of a constructive national policy he does not deserve any special protection. In fact, I am willing to go farther and assert that the non-union industrial laborer should, in the interest of a genuinely democratic organization of labor, be rejected; and he should be rejected as emphatically . . . as the garderner rejects weeds in his garden for benefit of fruit-and flower-bearing plants." Croly, *Promise of American Life*, 387. Along the same lines, Croly condemns "the politician who solemnly declares that he believes in the right of the laboring man to organize, and that labor unions are deserving of approval, but . . . also believes in the right of the individual laborer to eschew unionism whenever it suits his individual purpose or lack or purpose" (388). See also Levy, *Herbert Croly*, 114.

37. *Lochner v. New York*, 198 U.S. 45 (1905) (J. Holmes, dissenting).

38. The Norris-LaGuardia decisions I present here are only illustrative of a broader point. Reuel Schiller has demonstrated at length that, in an effort to sustain the power of labor unions considered as groups in the context of a post–New Deal governing philosophy based on interest group pluralism, the Court routinely worked to circumscribe individual rights claims in a wide variety of areas, including those involving exclusive representation, fair representation, and free speech. Reuel F. Schiller, "From Group Rights to Individual Liberties: Post-War Labor Law, Liberalism, and the Waning of Union Strength," *Berkeley Journal of Employment and Labor Law* 20 (1999): 1–73. I should also note here that *Senn* and *Lauf* were not decided on free speech grounds. Picketing had long been considered "conduct" and not "speech." The decision to reclassify it as speech, however, was imminent—the product of labor movement cases. See *Hague v. Congress of Industrial Organizations*, 307 U.S. 496 (1939); *Thornhill v. Alabama*, 310 U.S. 88 (1940). The decision to make this move was a pillar of the ideological institutionalization of the new regime: it enabled the Court to meet the trampling upon individual rights in favor of group-oriented regulatory systems with the counterassertion that they were actually championing a key individual right. In reality, the Court championed the "individual" right of free speech when it served labor unions as groups, but circumscribed it in service of the group when appeals were made to it by individual labor union members. Schiller, "From Group Rights to Individual Liberties," 29–41. For an explication of this point at greater length, see Kersch, *Constructing Civil Liberties*, 226–233. See also Ken I. Kersch, "How Conduct Became Speech and Speech Became Conduct: A Political Development Case Study in Labor Law and the Freedom of Speech," *University of Pennsylvania Journal of Constitutional Law* (forthcoming, 2006).

39. See generally, Kahn, *Supreme Court and Constitutional Theory*; Howard Gillman, *Constitution Besieged*; Haskell, *Emergence of Professional Social Science*; Arthur F. Bentley, *The Process of Government: A Study of Social Pressures* (Chicago: University of Chicago Press, 1908).

40. *National Labor Relations Board v. Jones and Laughlin Steel Co.*, 301 U.S. 1 (1937).

Labor union power was inhibited not simply by *Lochner*-ism proper, but by long-standing common law doctrine concerning conspiracy. See Victoria C. Hattam, *Labor Visions and State Power: The Origins of Business Unionism in the United States* (Princeton, N.J.: Princeton University Press, 1993); Daniel Ernst, *Lawyers against Labor*; Kersch, *Constructing Civil Liberties*.

41. See Bentley, *Process of Government*, 17–18, 245; Kahn, *Supreme Court and Constitutional Theory*. See also Katherine Van Wezel Stone, "The Post-War Paradigm in American Labor Law," *Yale Law Journal* 90 (1981): 1509–1580; Schiller, "From Group Rights to Individual Liberties."

42. Lichtenstein, *State of the Union*, 9, 13, 32–35.

43. Walter Lippmann, *Drift and Mastery: An Attempt to Diagnose the Current Unrest* (1914; reprint, Madison: University of Wisconsin Press, 1985), 59.

44. On the carry-over of the rhetoric of "industrial democracy" into New Deal–era labor struggles, see David Plotke, *Building a Democratic Political Order*, 98–99; Ruth Horowitz, *Political Ideologies of Organized Labor: The New Deal Era* (New Brunswick, N.J.: Transaction Books, 1978), 175–177.

45. John Dewey, *Ethics and Politics* (1894), quoted in Robert B. Westbrook, *John Dewey and American Democracy* (Ithaca, N.Y.: Cornell University Press, 1991), 49. Across the ocean, the Fabian socialists in England were also calling for "industrial democracy." The phrase, and the push for it, were thus transnational. See Sidney and Beatrice Webb, *Industrial Democracy* (London: Longmans, Green, 1897). Lichtenstein, *State of the Union*, 10. Karl Marx, of course, had attributed a similar centrality to work in constituting human meaning under capitalism. Marx, "Economic and Philosophical Manuscripts," in *The Marx-Engels Reader*, ed. Robert C. Tucker (New York: W. W. Norton, 1978). On the republican strain within progressive thought, see Michael Sandel, *Democracy's Discontent: America in Search of a Public Philosophy* (Cambridge, Mass.: Belknap Press of Harvard University Press, 1996); Ruth O'Brien, *Worker's Paradox*.

46. See Lippmann, *Drift and Mastery*, chap 5.

47. Ibid., 59.

48. Ibid., 60.

49. Ibid., 65.

50. Ibid., 57. See also William Leiserson, "Constitutional Government in American Industries," *American Economic Review* 12 (1922, suppl.), 56, 60–61; Lichtenstein, *State of the Union*, 7, 36; Stone, "Post-War Paradigm," 1514–1516; Schiller, "From Group Rights to Individual Liberties," 5–6.

51. Lippmann, *Drift and Mastery*, 65.

52. Herbert Croly, *Progressive Democracy* (1914; reprint, New Brunswick, N.J.: Transaction Publishers, 1998), 378, 379, 390. Both Lippmann's *Drift and Mastery* and Croly's *Progressive Democracy*, which appeared at about the same time, were effusively praised by Theodore Roosevelt, who declared that "no man who wishes seriously to study thought and action so as to work for national betterment in the future can afford not to read these books through and through and to ponder and digest them." Theodore

Roosevelt, "Two Noteworthy Books on Democracy," *Outlook* 108 (18 November 1914): 648–651. The imagination of industrial democracy as an explicitly *constitutional* order was one of its defining features in the American context. In this imagining, Lippmann's characterization is illustrative rather than distinctive. See Steve Fraser, "The Labor Question," in *The Rise and Fall of the New Deal Order, 1930–1980*, ed. Gary Gerstle and Steve Fraser (Princeton, N.J.: Princeton University Press, 1989), 59–60.

53. Croly, *Progressive Democracy*, 384–385.

54. Ibid.

55. Ibid., 386.

56. Ibid., 386–402.

57. Louis Brandeis, quoted by Treadwell Cleveland Jr. in *LaFollette's Weekly Magazine*, 24 May 1913, cited in Louis Brandeis, *The Brandeis Guide to the Modern World*, ed. Alfred Lief (Boston: Little, Brown, 1941), 93.

58. Brandeis, *Boston Sunday Post*, 14 February 1915, cited in Brandeis, *Brandeis Guide*, 96.

59. Brandeis, "Trusts, Efficiency, and the New Party," *Collier's Weekly*, 14 September 1912, 15.

60. Brandeis, quoted in Cleveland, *LaFollette's Weekly Magazine*, 24 May 1913, cited in Brandeis, *Brandeis Guide*, 93–94.

61. Felix Frankfurter, "The Eight Hour Day," *Boston Herald*, 9 October 1916, reprinted in Frankfurter, *Law and Politics: Occasional Papers of Felix Frankfurter, 1913–1938*, ed. Archibald MacLeish and E. F. Pritchard Jr. (New York: Harcourt Brace, 1939), 203–204.

62. Frankfurter, "Law and Order," *Yale Review* (Winter 1920), reprinted in Felix Frankfurter, *Law and Politics: Occasional Papers of Felix Frankfurter, 1913–1938* (New York: Capricorn Books, 1962), 213–215. This concern was paramount for many New Dealers. See Karl E. Klare, "The Quest for Industrial Democracy and the Struggle Against Racism: Perspectives from Labor Law and Civil Rights Law," *Oregon Law Review* 61 (1982): 157–200, 170–172; Karl E. Klare, "Labor Law as Ideology: Toward a New Historiography of Collective Bargaining Law," *Industrial Relations Law Journal* 4 (1981): 450–482, 452, 456.

63. See *J. I. Case Co. v. National Labor Relations Board*, 321 U.S. 332, 338–339 (1944); *American Communications Ass'n v. Douds*, 339 U.S. 382, 401 (1950); Schiller, "From Group Rights to Individual Liberties," 21–23.

64. See Schiller, "From Group Rights to Individual Liberties," 9–23; Stone, "Post-War Paradigm," 1521–1525; Klare, "Quest for Industrial Democracy," 165; William Leuchtenburg, *Franklin D. Roosevelt and the New Deal, 1932–1940* (New York: Harper & Row, 1963), 150–152. Christopher Tomlins and others have characterized the act as amounting to a failure of a more radical labor vision. See Christopher L. Tomlins, *The State and the Unions: Labor Relations, Law, and the Organized Labor Movement in America, 1880–1960* (Cambridge: Cambridge University Press, 1985); Lichtenstein, *State of the Union*, 148–162; Klare, "Quest for Industrial Democracy," 166. For a critique of the

"deradicalization theorists" for failing to situate the post–New Deal system of labor governance within the context of broader, dominant interest group pluralist understandings of the nature of political life, see Schiller, "From Group Rights to Individual Liberties."

65. *National Labor Relations Board v. Jones and Laughlin Steel Corp.*, 301 U.S. 1 (1937). See also Statement of Robert F. Wagner, 79 *Congressional Record* 2372 (1935): "Without [the majority rule provisions of the NLRA] the phrase 'collective bargaining' is devoid of meaning." *J. I. Case Co. v. National Labor Relations Board*, 321 U.S. 332, 338–339 (1994); *Ford Motor Co. v. Huffman*, 345 U.S. 330, 338 (1953); *Emporium Capwell Co. v. Western Addition Community Organization*, 420 U.S. 50, 62 (1975).

66. Eric Foner, *The Story of American Freedom* (New York: W. W. Norton, 1998), 249–250. Also slated to go but eliminated was an original of FDR's order establishing the Fair Employment Practices Commission.

67. Plotke, *Building a Democratic Political Order;* Fraser, "Labor Question," 55–84. Green, *Language of Politics in America;* Lichtenstein, *State of the Union*, 12–13, 20. This is not to deny that important elements of the labor movement were nondiscriminatory: the Congress of Industrial Organizations (CIO) was integrated from its inception in 1937. Nor is it to deny the existence of important vanguard elements of black unionism, such as A. Philip Randolph's Brotherhood of Sleeping Car Porters. At the time of the initial building of the modern American State, both groups were outsiders. My interest here is in charting the progression of the nondiscriminatory union norm and the black-labor alliance at the core of mid- to late-century liberalism, from hope to assumption. It is in limning the ideological negotiation over time of these norms and political coalitions, rather than simply making the teleological assumption that their seeds were somehow rooted in the nature of the modern liberal state. I discuss the emergence of black unionism, with a focus on Randolph, at greater length in my book, Kersch, *Constructing Civil Liberties*, 188–210. This transformation was reflected in an array of spheres.

68. See Thelen, "How Institutions Evolve," 232: "It may be that the [institutional] conversion processes are more associated with the incorporation of new or previously excluded groups (pursuing different, perhaps though not necessarily entirely contradictory goals) into a pre-existing institutional framework." See also Tulis, *Rhetorical Presidency*, 17. I note that it is possible for efforts at negotiation of change to fail, amounting to what Mark Brandon and Mark Graber have called "constitutional failures." Mark E. Brandon, *Free in the World: American Slavery and Constitutional Failure* (Princeton, N.J.: Princeton University Press, 1998); Mark A. Graber, "*Dred Scott* and the Problem of Constitutional Evil," paper presented at the Public Law Colloquium, Politics Department, Princeton University, Spring 2003. The more or less successful judicial negotiation of a layered developmental sequence is a less catastrophic alternative that seems to be plausible in certain circumstances under certain conditions.

69. Rayford W. Logan, *The Negro in American Life and Thought: The Nadir, 1877–1901* (New York: Dial Press, 1954), 142. See generally Herbert Hill, *Black Labor and the American Legal System: Race, Work, and the Law in the American Legal System* (Madison: University of Wisconsin Press, 1985); David E. Bernstein, *Only One Place of*

Redress: African Americans, Labor Regulations, and the Courts from Reconstruction to the New Deal (Durham: Duke University Press, 2001); Eric Arnesen, *Brotherhoods of Color: Black Railroad Workers and the Struggle for Equality* (Cambridge, Mass.: Harvard University Press, 2001); Lichtenstein, *State of the Union*, 40–42, 73.

70. Kersch, *Constructing Civil Liberties*, 188–195. One foreign observer who did appreciate this—writing as late as the 1940s—was Gunnar Myrdal, who worried that "there are grave risks . . . in the increased union power. A greatly strengthened union movement holding power over employment might, if dominated by monopolistic and prejudiced white workers, finally define the Negro's 'place' as outside industrial employment." Gunner Myrdal, *An American Dilemma* (New York: Harper & Row, 1944), 401; see also 643, 787.

71. Sterling D. Spero and Abram L. Harris, *The Black Worker: The Negro and the Labor Movement* (New York: Columbia University Press, 1931), 133–134. Only recently has this confluence between economic theory and historical fact been seriously explored. See David E. Bernstein, *Only One Place of Redress*; Lichtenstein, *State of the Union*, 72–74, 76; David Roediger, *Toward the Abolition of Whiteness* (London: Verso, 1994), 37–45. Some of the best recent work on civil rights now takes the procapitalist, anti-labor views of blacks of this era seriously. See Michael J. Klarman, *From Jim Crow to Civil Rights: The Supreme Court and the Struggle for Racial Equality* (New York: Oxford University Press, 2004) (discussing distinct black preference for paternalism over labor union power).

72. This sequence of events is probably the rule rather than the exception in constitutional development because what is considered "conservative" is often simply the institutionalized spirit of progress of an earlier day. Liberal individualism itself was advanced as a progressive ideology. See Kramnick, *Republicanism and Bourgeois Radicalism: Political Ideology in Late Eighteenth Century England and America* (Ithaca, N.Y.: Cornell University Press, 1990). Howard Gillman's *Constitution Besieged* makes a similar argument about the progressive-spirited Jacksonian origins of the anticlass legislation doctrines of what was later taken to be the Supreme Court's late-nineteenth-century doctrinaire conservatism. The progressive triumphs on behalf of the rights of labor in the 1930s should be understood to have inaugurated a similar dynamic. What is unusual in that case, however, is the rapidity with which the next reformist imperative followed upon the heels of the former one. See Lichtenstein, *State of the Union*, 172–174.

73. John Gerring, *Party Ideologies in America, 1828–1926* (New York: Cambridge University Press, 1998), 202–203.

74. This reflects my broader theory that the Court, at least from about the time in the late nineteenth and early twentieth centuries that the Court was forced by developmental imperatives to put its imprimatur on the New American State, has taken it upon itself to regularly reconcile agonistic creedal commitments into what serves as a reasonably coherent ideology, in the process erasing those agonisms and re-presenting them as a commitment to principles each of which coheres with the other. See Kersch, *Constructing Civil Liberties*. Theoretically speaking, this need not have been done by the courts. The conflicts between the perceived imperative of labor union autonomy and

civil rights might have been resolved in Congress through the passage of antidiscrimination laws targeted at labor unions. Although some state legislatures did pass such laws, Congress, under control of an uneasy Democratic Party amalgam of Southern whites, white unionists, and (relatively newly) black workers before 1964, was unwilling to touch the issue. See Paul Frymer, "Acting When Elected Officials Won't: Federal Courts and Civil Rights Enforcement in U.S. Labor Unions, 1935–1985," *American Political Science Review* 97 (2003); Ira Katznelson, Kim Geiger, and Daniel Kryder, "Limiting Liberalism: The Southern Veto of Congress: 1930–1950," *Political Science Quarterly* 108 (Summer 1993): 283–306; John David Skrentny, *The Ironies of Affirmative Action: Politics, Culture and Justice in America* (Chicago: University of Chicago Press, 1996), chap. 8. On congressional delegations to the courts in cases of political controversy, including (prominently) controversy concerning labor issues, see generally Lovell, *Legislative Deferrals*. See also Mark A. Graber, "The Nonmajoritarian Difficulty: Legislative Deference to the Judiciary," *Studies in American Political Development* 7 (Spring 1993): 35–73.

75. Kevin J. McMahon, *Reconsidering Roosevelt on Race: How the Presidency Paved the Road to* Brown (Chicago: University of Chicago Press, 2004), on President Franklin Roosevelt's role in encouraging Court involvement in civil rights issues. For an exception, see Frymer, "Acting When Elected Officials Won't"; Kryder, *Divided Arsenal: Race and the American State during World War II* (New York: Cambridge University Press, 2000); Hill, *Black Labor*, 106–107.

76. *Railway Mail Association v. Corsi*, 326 U.S. 88 (1944); *Steele v. Louisville and Nashville Railroad Co.*, 323 U.S. 192 (1944). See also *Tunstall v. Brotherhood of Locomotive Firemen and Enginemen*, 323 U.S. 210 (1944).

77. *Corsi*, 326 U.S., at 94. See also *J. I. Case Co. v. National Labor Relations Board*, 321 U.S. 332 (1944) (reaffirming majority rule principle of the Railway Labor Act).

78. See *Virginian R. Co. v. System Federation*, 300 U.S. 515, 545 (1937) (holding that the majority of any craft has the right to determine who shall be the representative of the class for purposes of collective bargaining with the employer); Arnesen, *Brotherhoods of Color*, 126–127. It is worth noting that the ethos—rather than the law being interpreted—is crucial. Here, the case involves not the National Labor Relations Act, but rather the Railway Labor Act. And it involves statutes rather than the Constitution itself. But the ethos or construction underlies all three situations and bleeds across them. Being overly legalistic in one's approach can lead one to miss these dynamics.

79. See Gillman, *Constitution Besieged*. This appeal to democracy and its rhetoric was serviceable in this context in significant part because, as most people conversant in the politics of the era knew, the labor movement itself had relied on arguments concerning the "right of representation" as part of their fight to secure the passage of the Wagner Act in 1935 (as in many instances before). See Plotke, *Building a Democratic Political Order*, 97–98. I borrow the concept of jurisgenerative ideas from Robert Cover, "Nomos and Narrative," *Harvard Law Review* 97 (1983): 4–68.

80. *Steele*, 323 U.S., at 198 [emphasis added]. See also, e.g., Archibald Cox, "The Duty of Fair Representation," *Villanova Law Review* 2 (1957): 151–177, 152. On the

recourse made by labor lawyers (and the Court) to broader theories of governance—an understanding that I have shown repeats patterns pioneered by earlier twentieth-century progressive political thought more generally—see Karl Klare, "Labor Law as Ideology: Toward a New Historiography of Collective Bargaining Law," *Industrial Relations Law Journal* 4 (1981): 450, 458–480; Klare, "Quest for Industrial Democracy," 196–197; Stone, "Post-War Paradigm," 1514–1516; Lichtenstein, *State of the Union*, 7, 36.

81. *Steele*, 323 U.S., at 202. Bernstein characterizes Stone's intellectual moves in the *Steele* decision as "legal gymnastics" that were "perhaps" disingenuous. Bernstein, *Only One Place of Redress*, 63. Without denying some truth in this characterization, it is important to note the way in which, admittedly animated by a reformist policy goal, Stone is rethinking the nature of representative democracy within American constitutionalism. His patterns of thought, as revealed in the *Steele* decision, are notable (and will prove influential) in ways that extend beyond his decision to vote "for" civil rights, in line with his policy preferences.

82. This neutrality and impartiality was later abandoned by "progressives" on the Court in its later affirmative action cases. See, e.g., *Adarand Construtors, Inc. v. Pena*, 515 U.S. 200 (1995) (J. Stevens, dissenting; J. Ginsburg, dissenting).

83. *Bolling v. Sharpe*, 347 U.S. 497 (1954); *Brown v. Board of Education*, 347 U.S. 483 (1954); *Mayor and City Council of Baltimore v. Dawson*, 350 U.S. 877 (1955); *Holmes v. Atlanta*, 350 U.S. 879 (1955); *Gayle v. Browder*, 352 U.S. 903 (1956); *New Orleans v. Detiege*, 358 U.S. 54 (1958); *Burton v. Wilmington Parking Authority*, 365 U.S. 715 (1961); *Johnson v. Virginia*, 373 U.S. 61 (1963); *Watson v. City of Memphis*, 373 U.S. 526 (1963). See also *Hurd v. Hodge*, 344 U.S. 24 (1948).

84. Murphy's view, which has never been adopted by the Supreme Court, mounts a direct challenge to the core ideology of twentieth century liberalism, which posits that labor and blacks do not have interests that are opposed but rather are each analogous, oppressed, socially disadvantaged groups that are properly situated within the same political coalition.

85. *Bolling v. Sharpe*, 347 U.S. 497 (1954). The *Steele* opinion, of course, applied only to unions that already had black members. It did not require unions to admit blacks as members. Nor did it alter other antiblack rules operating within labor unions. In any case, as Bernstein notes, the *Steele* opinion was not energetically enforced. Bernstein, *Only One Place of Redress*, 64.

86. See Hill, *Black Labor*, 93–106; Karl Klare, "The Public/Private Distinction in Labor Law," *University of Pennsylvania Law Review* 130 (1982): 1358–1422, 1382.

87. See Frymer, "Acting When Elected Officials Won't." See Hill, *Black Labor*, 94, 101: "Because the Act itself deals inadequately with the entire problem of racial discrimination in employment, and because the NLRB has been loath to bring its administrative power to bear on the problem. . . . Creative interpretation by the courts has been necessary, but it has emerged very slowly." See also *Williams v. Yellow Cab Co.*, 200 F.2d 302 (3rd Cir. 1952): the National Labor Relations Act "was directed primarily to the prevention of unfair labor practices in order to open the way for free collective bargaining rather than

to the regulation of the course of such bargaining and the settlement of disputes." See *Syres v. Oil Worker International Union*, 223 F.2d 739 (5th Cir. 1955) (distinguishing *Steele* and *Howard*, which involved disputes concerning the designation of the official bargaining representative from the instant case involving a race discrimination case internal to the certified representative). Contra, *Conley v. Gibson*, 355 U.S. 41, 44 (1957).

88. See *Nixon v. Herndon*, 273 U.S. 536 (1927); *Nixon v. Condon*, 286 U.S. 536 (1927); *Smith v. Allwright*, 321 U.S. 649 (1944); *Terry v. Adams*, 345 U.S. 461 (1953) (white primary cases).

89. U.S. Constitution, Fifteenth Amendment. See *Bolling v. Sharpe*, 347 U.S. 497 (1954); *Smith v. Allwright* (1944); *Terry v. Adams* (1953); *Railway Employee's Department v. Hanson*, 351 U.S. 225 (1956). And indeed (as Reuel Schiller notes), "the cases the Court cited for the proposition that racial discrimination was impermissible under the [Railway Labor Act] (*Yick Wo v. Hopkins*, 118 U.S. 356 (1886); *Yu Cong Eng v. Trinidad*, 271 U.S. 500 (1926); *Missouri ex rel Gaines v. Canada*, 305 U.S. 337 (1938); *Hill v. Texas*, 316 U.S. 400 (1942)) were all equal protection cases." Schiller, "From Group Rights to Individual Liberties," 24. See also Klare, "Public/Private Distinction," 1373, 1390: "It is remarkable that at a time when the viability of the public/private distinction was under attack in most political and legal contexts [including by the reform-oriented Legal Realists], the philosophy of labor law reform embodied such resolute faith in the distinction. . . . The NLRA was grounded upon and justified by reference to a . . . version of public/private rhetoric." See also Klare, "Quest for Industrial Democracy," 183.

90. See Stone, "Post-War Paradigm"; Lichtenstein, *State of the Union*, 172; Schiller, "From Group Rights to Individual Liberties," 28; Grant McConnell, *Private Power and American Democracy*. See Arneson, *Brotherhoods of Color*, 225–226. Hill, *Black Labor*, 109—in fact, "the DFR [Duty of Fair Representation] concept established in *Steele* has become a prolific source of litigation in cases having nothing to do with race discrimination. . . . DFR law has become today one of the primary vehicles of government intervention in the internal affairs of labor unions." Klare, "Quest for Industrial Democracy," 187–188, 195–196. See Schiller, "From Group Rights to Individual Liberties," 62–64. Note that these same concerns were *not* present in the white primary cases. Seen in developmental context, in the first half of the twentieth century, the cause of labor union autonomy was unique. See generally Karen Orren, "The Primacy of Labor in American Constitutional Development," *American Political Science Review* 89 (June 1995): 377–388. By the time of the passage of the Civil Rights Act of 1964, which (in Title VII) did penetrate labor unions and control their membership practices, the New Deal regulatory regime had been consolidated, and hence the developmental context had shifted. 42 U.S.C. Sec. 2000e(2)(c). See *Alexander v. Gardner-Denver*, 415 U.S. 36 (1974). On the consolidation of the regime by this point, see Lowi, *End of Liberalism*.

91. For professional praise of this approach, see Harry Wellington, *Labor and the Legal Process* (New Haven, Conn.: Yale University Press, 1968), 145, cited in Hill, *Black Labor*, 109.

92. See Keith E. Whittington, "Constitutional Theories and the Faces of Power," in *The Judiciary and American Democracy: Alexander Bickel, the Countermajoritarian Difficulty, and Contemporary Constitutional Theory*, ed. Kenneth D. Ward and Cecilia R. Castillo (Albany: State University of New York Press, 2005); Keith E. Whittington, " 'To Support this Constitution': Judicial Supremacy in the Twentieth Century," in *Marbury v. Madison: Documents and Commentary*, ed. Mark A. Graber and Michael Perhac (Washington, D.C.: CQ Press, 2003); Barry Friedman, "The Birth of an Academic Obsession: The History of the Countermajoritarian Difficulty," *Yale Law Journal* 112 (2002): 153; Karl Klare, "Labor Law and the Liberal Political Imagination," *Socialist Review* 62 (1982): 45; Ross, *Muted Fury*.

93. Sidney Tarrow, *Power in Movement: Social Movements, Collective Action, and Politics* (New York: Cambridge University Press, 1994).

94. Karl Klare describes this turn as an apparent " 'deregulation' of labor conflict." Klare, "Public/Private Distinction," 1392.

95. In their consideration of the relationship between labor unions and emergent civil rights, Lichtenstein and Schiller conceptualize civil rights as a species of individual rights claims asserted against the group rights claims of organized labor. This, I believe, underestimates the group rights underpinning of much of modern civil rights law, an underpinning appropriated from labor. As I see it, the developmental dynamic operating in this area involves the claims of one group against another, and not simply one of individual versus group rights. See Lichtenstein, *State of the Union*, 171–177; Schiller, "From Group Rights to Individual Rights."

96. In the discussion of the political campaigns and cases that follow, I have profited from Paul D. Moreno, *From Direct Action to Affirmative Action: Fair Employment Law and Policy in America, 1933–1972* (Baton Rouge: Louisiana State University Press, 1997), chap. 2. See also Philip A. Klinkner and Rogers M. Smith, *The Unsteady March: The Rise and Decline of Racial Equality in America* (Chicago: University of Chicago Press, 1999), 144–145; Lichtenstein, *State of the Union*, 73.

97. *A. S. Beck Shoe Corporation v. Johnson*, 274 N.Y. Supp. 946 (Sup. Ct. 1934); *Green v. Samuelson*, 178 A. 109 (Court of Appeals of Maryland 1935). These early harbinger cases predate the Supreme Court's Norris-LaGuardia decisions, though they postdate the passage of the Norris-LaGuardia Act itself (1932).

98. *Beck*, 274 N.Y. Supp. at 946. Keith Whittington has suggested to me that a dispute of the sort at the center of the *A. S. Beck* case—which involved employment and who would get it—has more in common with the quintessential "labor disputes" in picketing cases than when, say, Earth First! pickets McDonald's over the use of Amazon River Basin coffee. This is certainly true. What I argue here is not that the conceptualization of the "don't buy where you can't work" pickets is either fanciful or a stretch, but rather that it expanded the labor dispute category or (in legal jargon) it "extended" the earlier precedent.

99. *Green*, 178 A. at 114.

100. Comment, *Harvard Law Review* 48 (1935): 691.

101. Comment, *University of Pennsylvania Law Review* 83 (1935): 383, 384.

102. Ibid., 383, 384.

103. *New Negro Alliance v. Sanitary Grocery Co.*, 303 U.S. 552 (1938).

104. Justice Brandeis had long argued that a "proximate relation" between employers and employees should not be a requirement for bringing a dispute under the statutory auspices of progressive legislation regulating labor disputes. *Duplex Printing v. Deering* (J. Brandeis, dissenting). Brandeis wrote these views into law in his opinions for the Court in its Norris-LaGuardia decisions. See Kersch, *Constructing Civil Liberties*, 169, 179–186.

105. *New Negro Alliance*, 303 U.S., at 561.

106. Orren and Skowronek, "Institutions and Intercurrence," 111–171. See also Skowronek, *Building a New American State*.

107. The process by which civil rights disputes involving labor unions came, at this same time, to be constructed by courts as "labor disputes," is chronicled in detail in Kersch, *Constructing Civil Liberties*, chap. 3.

108. *Graham v. Brotherhood of Locomotive Firemen and Enginemen*, 338 U.S. 232 (1949). On civil rights as the tracing out of the principles of the New Deal, see Bruce Ackerman, *We the People: Foundations* (Cambridge, Mass.: Harvard University Press, 1991). On civil rights as the tracing out of the principles of liberal justice, see John Rawls, *A Theory of Justice* (Cambridge: Harvard University Press, 1971); and Ronald Dworkin, *A Matter of Principle* (Cambridge, Mass.: Harvard University Press, 1985). Not surprisingly, Ackerman's earlier, theoretical work is very much a part of the Rawls-Dworkin political/ideological projects. See Bruce Ackerman, *Social Justice in the Liberal State* (New Haven, Conn.: Yale University Press, 1980). For an extensive critique of Whiggish developmental narratives of twentieth-century American constitutionalism, see Kersch, *Constructing Civil Liberties*.

109. It is worth considering the departure marked by these rulings in light of the Court's contemporaneous collective bargaining decisions not involving race. The Taft-Hartley Amendments (1947) to the Wagner Act, Section 301, contained language that promised to sharply increase the power of federal courts to enforce collective bargaining agreements: "Suits for violation of contracts between an employer and a labor organization . . . may be brought in any district court of the United States having jurisdiction of the parties." In a series of cases premised on understandings of voluntarism and a vision of labor-management self-government and "industrial pluralism" culminating in the so-called Steelworker's Trilogy (1960), the Court held that arbitrators selected by the parties, and not the courts, were the proper resolvers of disputes involving collective bargaining agreements. *United Steelworkers v. American Manufacturing Co.*, 363 U.S. 564 (1960); *United Steelworkers v. Warrior & Gulf Navigation Co.*, 363 U.S. 574 (1960); *United Steelworkers v. Enterprise Wheel and Car Corp.*, 363 U.S. 593 (1960). The Court reaffirmed that the courts had sharply limited injunctive powers in collective bargaining contract cases right through the 1960s. See *Sinclair Refining Co. v. Atkinson*,

370 U.S. 195 (1962). It beat a full-scale retreat from this commitment and (as key commentators have characterized it) from the Norris-LaGuardia Act itself only in 1970. *Boy's Market, Inc. v. Retail Clerks Local 770*, 398 U.S. 235 (1970). Stone, "Post-War Paradigm," 1525–1544; Klare, "Labor Law and the Liberal Imagination." This history renders the Court's assertion of its injunctive powers in race cases all the more striking.

110. *Graham*, 338 U.S., at 237. On the ideological uses of differing conceptions of "labor" in American politics, see Gerring, *Party Ideologies in America*, 57–64.

111. The use of the word *notwithstanding*, however, seems to have been a departure—perhaps inadvertent—from the ideological script set out more affirmatively in *Graham*. *Brotherhood of Railroad Trainmen v. Howard*, 343 U.S. 768, 774 (1952).

112. Interestingly enough, Fred Vinson, the author of the *Shelley v. Kraemer*, 344 U.S. 1 (1948), concurred in this view. See also *Hurd v. Hodge*, 344 U.S. 24 (1948). Minton was not yet on the Court in 1948, and Reed did not participate in that decision. For an appeal to *Shelley* in seeking to invalidate race discrimination internal to labor unions, see *Syres v. Oil Workers Union*, 223 F.2d 739, 745–746 (5th Cir. 1955) (J. Rives, dissenting). The Fifth Circuit's decision in *Syres* was reversed by the Supreme Court, without opinion, 350 U.S. 892 (1955). The NLRA originally did not provide for court enforcement of collective bargaining arrangements: those remedies were provided in due course by the Taft-Hartley Act (1947). Hill, *Black Labor*, 100.

113. *Oliphant v. Brotherhood of Locomotive Firemen and Engineers*, 262 F.2d 359, 360 (1958), cert. denied, 359 U.S. 935 (1959).

114. *Oliphant*, 262 F.2d at 361, 362.

115. Ibid. at 363. After these decisions, beginning in the late 1950s and early 1960s, judicial assertiveness toward labor unions had begun to take hold in other doctrinal areas as well. See Schiller, "From Group Rights to Individual Liberties," 57–73.

116. In attaching dates to this sequence, I follow Lowi, *End of Liberalism*. See also Lichtenstein, *State of the Union*, 191–193 (dating "shift in liberal consciousness" to 1963). I depart from Lichtenstein in treating civil rights not as a matter of individual rights but as a matter of rival class, or group rights.

117. *Shelley v. Kraemer*, 334 U.S. 1 (1948); *Burton v. Wilmington Parking Authority*, 365 U.S. 715 (1961); *Heart of Atlanta Motel v. United States*, 379 U.S. 241 (1964).

118. Schiller, "From Group Rights to Individual Liberties," 48–73. Schiller's thoughtful and useful account of these developments deals with race and civil rights only in passing. This leads him to overstate the completeness of a movement from group to individual rights rubrics at about this time. Although, as he demonstrates, the courts become increasingly critical of the group rights claims of labor at this time, they were manifestly enthusiastic about approaching race through the prism of a group rights rubric. See Kersch, *Constructing Civil Liberties*, 188–233.

119. 42 U.S.C. Sec. 2000e-c,(1964). See also *Alexander v. Gardner-Denver Co.*, 415 U.S. 36 (1974).

120. *Hughes Tool Co.*, 147 NLRB 1573 (1964); *Independent Metal Works, Local 1 and 2*, 147 NLRB 1573 (1964); *Local 1367 International Longshoreman's Association*, 148

NLRB 897 (1964); *Local 2, United Rubberworkers*, 368 F.2d 12 (5th Cir. 1966). See Hill, *Black Labor*. In moving against union corruption, the Labor-Management Reporting and Disclosure Act (1959) (the Landrum-Griffith Act) had also moved to regulate the internal affairs of unions. 73 Stat. 519 (1959). These included a "Bill of Rights of Members of Labor Unions," guaranteeing due process rights and rights to equal privileges and speech and assembly, a requirement that dues be imposed only by majority rule, and a ban on restrictions of a union member's right to sue either the employer or the union itself. Schiller, "From Group Rights to Individual Liberties," 58–60.

121. *Brown v. Board of Education (II)*, 349 U.S. 294 (1955); Feeley and Rubin, *Judicial Policymaking and the Modern State*; Chayes, "Role of the Judge."

122. *Boys Market, Inc. v. Retail Clerks Union*, 398 U.S. 235 (1970); Klare, "Public/Private Distinction," 1389.

123. See, e.g., Jeffery Segal and Harold Spaeth, *The Supreme Court and the Attitudinal Model Revisited* (New York: Cambridge University Press, 2002).

Part III

Constructing Authoritative Constitutional Meaning

Chapter 6

(Re)Construction of Constitutional Authority and Meaning: The Fourteenth Amendment and Slaughter-House Cases

Wayne D. Moore

Authority and meaning are central concepts within theories and practices of constitutionalism. Accordingly, a good way to study important problems of constitutional development is through analysis of the construction and reconstruction of constitutional authority and meaning. I do so in this chapter through reconsideration of the U.S. Supreme Court's decision in *Slaughter-House Cases* (1873).[1] There are several reasons why this case provides excellent points of departure for examining the development of constitutional authority and meaning. Chronologically, the majority and dissenting opinions in *Slaughter-House* constitute the U.S. Supreme Court's initial treatment of the authority, meaning, and significance of the Fourteenth Amendment to the U.S. Constitution. Within political time, and taking into account institutional norms and constraints, the justices had unique opportunities to influence the shape of the Fourteenth Amendment's integration, across a number of dimensions, into the constitutional landscape.

No other formal amendment to the U.S. Constitution has had more problematic original authority than this one; and none has had greater legal or political significance. Accordingly, the justices' treating this text as a valid amendment was itself momentous. *Slaughter-House* warrants careful study if for no other reason than for the insights it provides into how text has gained authority within the American constitutional order. In other words, this case illuminates first-order problems of normative continuity and change, involving the identity of the Constitution itself (as distinct from its interpretation).

The ways the justices treated the meaning of the Fourteenth Amendment were also constitutionally significant. *Slaughter-House* was decided just seven years after this amendment was added to the Constitution, during the early stages of the Reconstruction after the American Civil War. Accordingly, all of the justices had witnessed those politically, economically, socially, and legally transformative events. Not surprisingly, the majority and dissenting opinions made competing claims about the amendment's original meaning. Equally significantly, they relied on a range of additional interpretive approaches. The judges did not claim that they were simply preserving the Fourteenth Amendment's original meaning. Nor did they presume or imply that such an approach was theoretically or practically viable or defensible. On the contrary, the justices acknowledged that they were "constructing" the Fourteenth Amendment's meaning, they pointed toward earlier "construction" of the amendment by other political actors, and they allowed room for its subsequent (re)construction.[2] Even in its early stages, then, this amendment's meaning was treated as multivocal, potentially dynamic, and (re)formed through pluralistic political processes involving multiple institutions—rather than univocal, static, or simply a function of judicial fiat.

The majority and dissenting opinions in *Slaughter-House* also provide valuable perspectives toward relationships between the authority of text and its meaning. In one sense, claims about meaning have been a subset of claims of authority more generally. Following interpretive conventions, the majority in this case claimed that its construction of the Fourteenth Amendment was its authoritative meaning; and the dissenters made competing claims about what the amendment's authoritative meaning either was or should have been.[3] Across this dimension, accounting for the Fourteenth Amendment's historically constructed authoritative meaning (as a function of its origins and/or otherwise) parallels accounting for the construction of its authority as such (based on the standards of Article V and/or other criteria). The opinions in *Slaughter-House* participated in important ways in both processes.

Equally significantly, the opinions in *Slaughter-House* suggest that controversies over the Fourteenth Amendment's authoritative meaning have been linked in several ways to controversies involving its authority as such. One way is that the amendment's initial meaning was constructed in part through debates surrounding its proposal and ratification. In other words, positions on the Fourteenth Amendment's meaning were critical components of processes of constitutional amending. Thus the outcome of those processes was not simply the authorization of text, but the authorization of text having meaning.

The opinions in *Slaughter-House* indicate that similar processes involving the construction of integrated meaning and authority continued following the Fourteenth Amendment's addition to the U.S. Constitution. One of my primary aims in this essay is to explain how this is so. Doing so requires paying close attention to the justices' reliance on multiple criteria of constitutional authority and complementary perspectives toward meaning. As I explain below, the majority and dissenting opinions indicate that considerations of meaning were pertinent to analysis, across several dimensions, of the authority of the Fourteenth Amendment itself—and vice versa.

Background: From Constitutional Amending to Constitutional (Re)Construction

Before turning to *Slaughter-House* itself, it is instructive to review earlier controversies involving the Fourteenth Amendment's authority and meaning. One reason is that the justices treated constitutional history as normatively and practically significant and constraining. Thus some familiarity with the Fourteenth Amendment's political history is necessary to grasp the issues at stake, comprehend the justices' analyses of them, and assess the case's significance. In addition, many of the factors that had earlier led individuals to propose or oppose constitutional amending between 1866 and 1868 had remained, in some form, in play around the time of the Court's decision in 1873. Much within the constitutional order characteristically had persisted, or at least was presumed to have persisted, even as the terms of constitutional contestation had shifted significantly within a relatively brief span of years.

Two sets of issues in particular had received a great deal of attention during debates surrounding the Fourteenth Amendment's proposal and ratification. First was its procedural validity. The focus of these debates was primarily, but not exclusively, on whether political practices were satisfying or had satisfied the criteria for constitutional amendment set forth in Article V of the U.S. Constitution. Second, the Fourteenth Amendment's proponents and opponents took competing positions on the amendment's substantive validity. In doing so, they explicitly and implicitly relied on several sets of evaluative criteria.

Criticism of the Fourteenth Amendment as procedurally invalid emphasized irregularities at both the proposing and ratifying stages. Briefly, the 39th Congress that proposed this amendment in the aftermath of the American Civil War did not include representatives of the eleven formerly rebellious states. Those states were, however, treated as within the Union for some purposes—including ratification, allegedly in pursuance of Article V, of the proposed Fourteenth Amendment. But after legislatures purporting to represent the Southern states unanimously rejected this proposal, the Republican-controlled Congress enacted military reconstruction and made ratification of the amendment by reconstructed state legislatures a condition precedent to those states' regaining representation within Congress. Critics of this addition to the text of the U.S. Constitution did not concede that the congressionally reconstructed legislatures were valid; and in any event their approval was dismissed as obtained through force and coercion rather than deliberation and voluntary consent.[4]

Critics of this "so-called amendment" also argued that it was substantively invalid. Most of these arguments focused on the scope of the changes purportedly brought about by the text, particularly across the dimension of federalism. These changes were too sweeping, argued some of the Fourteenth Amendment's critics, for a mere "amendment." Others argued that the new text was inconsistent with principles of constitutionalism presumed by the Constitution and on which it depended for its authority.[5]

The Fourteenth Amendment's supporters, not surprisingly, met these criticisms with counterarguments. For example, prominent Republicans defended the exclusion from the 39th Congress of purported representatives of the Southern states as legitimate in the war's wake. They, as with the Johnsonian state legislatures that rejected the proposed Fourteenth Amendment, were characterized as not sufficiently "republican." The primary reason given was that they excluded black men from the franchise. Building on this critique, leaders of Congress argued that the congressionally reconstructed state legislatures had superior rather than inferior credentials compared with the Johnsonian governments. Thus approvals of the proposed amendment by the former, as with those by legislatures representing the Northern and border states, were constitutionally effective. In any event, the amendment was proposed by two-thirds of the members of both houses of Congress and was ratified by legislatures representing three-fourths of the states. Thus it was possible to defend the Fourteenth Amendment as valid based on Article V, interpreted formally.[6]

The amendment's proponents also defended the Fourteenth Amendment as substantively legitimate. According to some of its defenders, for example, the Fourteenth Amendment's primary functions included reinforcing the Thirteenth Amendment and the Civil Rights Act of 1866 by defining criteria for citizenship and by making explicit limits on the states that already had been implicit within the constitutional order. While some viewed the Fourteenth Amendment as "radical" and defended it as such, others denied that it was so fundamentally transformative. Notwithstanding these differences, leading Republicans joined one another in claiming that the changes brought about by the Fourteenth Amendment were valid on the basis of their congruence with the U.S. Constitution's deepest commitments and aspirations, principles of constitutionalism, and standards of political morality.[7]

Controversy over the Fourteenth Amendment's original validity persisted well after Congress and Secretary of State William Seward formally (and equivocally, in the latter's case) declared it part of the U.S. Constitution in July of 1868.[8] Democrats made the validity of congressional reconstruction, including the South's military occupation and the Fourteenth Amendment's coerced ratification, a major issue in the 1868 presidential elections.[9] Although Republicans retained control of national institutions as a result of those elections, criticism of Reconstruction policies persisted in the North and West as well as the South, among both Republicans and Democrats.

Revealing was a comment by Oliver P. Morton, Republican Senator from Indiana, in the course of congressional debates over ratification of the Fifteenth Amendment. He complained on February 15, 1871,

> that the adoption of the [fourteenth] amendment was strongly opposed by the Democratic party in Congress and out; that the Democratic party everywhere denied the power of Congress to require the late rebel States to ratify the amendment as a condition to their restoration; that no Democratic convention, Legislature, or leading statesman, so far as I know, has accepted or admitted the validity of the amendment.[10]

This claim that "no Democrat" had yet "accepted the validity" of the Fourteenth Amendment as late as February of 1871 is remarkable. Although Morton's comment doubtless contained elements of overstatement, it seems accurate as a gauge of Democrats' continued opposition to military reconstruction and its legacies.[11] Morton's claim is not indicative, however, of the predominant rhetorical structure of Democratic positions on the Fourteenth Amendment as expressed in congressional debates beginning at least in 1871. In the course of debates over the 1871 Enforcement Acts, controversy centered on the authoritative meaning and implications of the Fourteenth Amendment's provisions rather than on the validity of the text as such. It is not surprising that most members of the Republican majority (especially moderates and radicals) took this position, because their party had been the amendment's primary supporters. More remarkable, notwithstanding comments like Morton's, was the willingness of most Democrats (along with conservative Republicans) to focus on the Fourteenth Amendment's meaning rather than its authority. There is little evidence that those who had initially opposed the Fourteenth Amendment as invalid persisted in pressing this position in the context of debates over passage of the 1871 Enforcement Acts (or afterward).[12]

Although we cannot be certain of all the reasons for this shift, one factor, in addition to considerations of who held power, was doubtless the relative malleability of the Fourteenth Amendment's primary prohibitions on the states. At least in the context of congressional debates over passage of the 1871 Enforcement Acts, it was unlikely that a majority of the members of either house of Congress would refuse to accept the amendment as valid. Following the readmission in 1868 of most Southern states to representation within Congress, however, it was less difficult to imagine a coalition forming around interpretive positions that conservatives along with moderates would be willing to endorse. In other words, there was no certainty, and perhaps not even a likelihood, that a radical gloss on the amendment would prevail in the short, medium, or longer terms.[13]

For the purposes of this essay, there is no need to document the dynamics of this shift more fully, in advance of the Supreme Court's decision in *Slaughter-House*, away from critics of the Fourteenth Amendment challenging its validity and toward their contesting its meaning. It is sufficient to have made the following introductory points. First, the amendment's opponents advanced serious arguments criticizing it as invalid. They were met by equally serious arguments defending it as valid. Awareness of these controversies, which had both procedural and substantive dimensions, is critical to understanding what was at stake in *Slaughter-House* and other early interpretive precedents involving the new text. Second, congressional debates (as summarized above) indicate that the course of constitutional debates within Congress had shifted at least by 1871. Although there is evidence that Democrats (and perhaps conservative Republicans) continued to regard the Fourteenth Amendment as invalid, they did not explicitly press that position in the course of debates over passage of the 1871 Enforcement Acts. Third, the malleability of the Fourteenth Amendment's terms allowed it to accommodate relatively readily this shift in the terms of political contestation. Stated differently, the amendment itself could accommodate a range of interpretive agendas, including those of its Democratic critics along with its Republican sponsors, many of whose views also shifted during the later stages of Reconstruction. Fourth, controversies surrounding formal processes of constitutional amending, along with the text's subsequent interpretation by members of Congress, frame questions about relationships between controversies involving the Fourteenth Amendment's authority and positions on its authoritative meaning.

Multidimensional Constitutional Authority

The Fourteenth Amendment's judicialization, as with its authoritative (re)construction more generally, had commenced well before the Court's decision in *Slaughter-House*. State and lower federal court judges, along with legislative and executive officials as indicated above, had already begun to interpret and apply the amendment.[14] These processes would also continue, of course, both outside the courts and through judicial decisions, after the Court's decision in *Slaughter-House*.

The justices understood, nevertheless, the importance of this case, particularly as a vehicle for taking positions on the Fourteenth Amendment's authority and meaning. Justice Samuel F. Miller indicated in his majority opinion that the butchers' lawsuit was moved forward on the docket on account of its importance. After initial arguments and early indications of divisions among the justices, *Slaughter-House* was reargued in February 1872. Other cases were apparently delayed so that the judges could offer their initial (re)construction of the Fourteenth Amendment in this context.[15] Justice Miller characterized their duty to do so as a "great responsibility." In his view, no other case, during the justices' official tenure, had raised "questions so far-reaching and pervading in their consequences, so profoundly interesting to the people of this country, and so important in their bearing upon the relations of the United States, and of the several States to each other and to the citizens of the States and of the United States."[16]

The case presented numerous ironies, and they were compounded by the justices' opinions. John A. Campbell, Democrat and former justice of the U.S. Supreme Court from Alabama, served as counsel for the butchers. Acting in that capacity, he turned Southern Democratic opposition to the Fourteenth Amendment on its head by invoking that amendment as a source of nationally enforceable rights of U.S. citizenship. In contrast, Louisiana's carpetbag legislature, which was heavily dependent on congressional policies of military reconstruction, defended the state's granting of an exclusive monopoly to a slaughterhouse company as within the state's police powers and as beyond the reach of federal judicial interference. Justice Miller's opinion for a majority of the Court maintained that the Fourteenth Amendment's primary purpose was to guard against state-supported discrimination based on race. But the case in which the justices chose to announce that position did not involve such discrimination. The majority's (re)construction of the Fourteenth Amendment's terms, moreover, could and would cut against an expansive view of that amendment's limitations and of federal authority to enforce them—including in cases involving discrimination against black persons. Meanwhile, the dissenters drew on interpretive precedents involving classifications based on race to support claims of economic rights. The approach they advocated would take hold later in the nineteenth century even as commitment to protecting rights of black persons waned. In important respects, then, extensions of aspects of the Fourteenth Amendment's (re)construction by justices in the majority and in dissent would ironically converge with one another.

Equally if not more significantly, there were deep resonances in the ways the justices handled matters of constitutional authority and meaning. Among other things, all of the justices in *Slaughter-House* united in assuming that the primary object of interpretation, identified as "the Constitution of the United States," had changed as a result of political developments between 1866 and 1868—or, also taking into account the Thirteenth and Fifteenth Amendments, between 1865 and 1870. More specifically, the justices presumed without exception that the U.S. Constitution had new text, including the provisions identified as "the Fourteenth Amendment." This shared position reflected the centrality of Article V of the U.S. Constitution, interpreted in conjunction with principles of popular sovereignty, as part of the "rule of recognition" (to use H. L. A. Hart's terminology) for identifying applicable constitutional norms within the United States.[17]

Although the justices' handling of formal processes and outcomes of constitutional amending tied to Article V framed their respective treatments of the issues in *Slaughter-House*, their opinions in that case would have been much different if they had been confined by an assumption that Article V was the exclusive—or even the most important or most relevant—criterion for analyzing problems of constitutional authority and meaning. Much of the text in the majority and dissenting opinions makes little sense except as proceeding from an assumption that additional criteria of constitutional authority and meaning—going beyond those formalized by Article V—were pertinent to deciding the lawsuit or at least to rationalizing positions taken in this context. In other words, the justices appear to have assumed that there were multiple rules of recognition for identifying constitutional norms and analyzing their implications. Stated differently, the opinions reflect a premise that in the United States there was a more complex and inclusive rule of recognition that embraced a variety of subsidiary components, rather than a single one based on Article V. The justices' analysis of that article pointed beyond its criteria and otherwise relied on a broader analytic and interpretive framework.

Accordingly, it is fitting to develop and draw on a model of pluralistic or multidimensional authority to address problems of constitutionalism raised by the opinions in *Slaughter-House*. This chapter does so by identifying and exploring the analytic contributions of six such sets of criteria. These criteria may be conceived, among other things, as representing or corresponding to discrete dimensions of constitutional authority.[18]

The six sets of criteria are as follows. The first, already introduced, are the standards of constitutional validity set forth in Article V of the U.S. Constitution. Second are procedural criteria of constitutional authorization based on principles of popular sovereignty conceived as extending beyond those set forth in Article V. Third are standards of internal constitutional coherence. Fourth are principles of constitutionalism. Fifth is the amendment's authority as measured by additional standards of political morality. And sixth is constructive authority, which involves attributing positions to "the people" beyond those expressed through conventionally recognized channels of constitutional authorization.[19]

As explained below, the opinions in *Slaughter-House* explicitly and implicitly invoke versions of all six criteria. Accordingly, the opinions in that case support a multidimensional model of constitutional authority and exemplify reliance on such a model to guide political decision making. The justices' strategy also invites analysis, drawing on these six sets of criteria, of the authority of their respective interpretive positions as with that of the Fourteenth Amendment itself.

The first and second sets of criteria are similarly oriented toward matters of process: those recognized by Article V and those rooted more directly in principles of popular sovereignty. These criteria converge in supporting analysis of whether political practices involving the Fourteenth Amendment satisfied applicable procedural standards of constitutional validity, thereby linking matters of substance and process to one another. Relying on those criteria, moreover, one may assess the extent to which—and how—presumptions of the sovereignty of "the people" have been realized—or not—through processes involving the Fourteenth Amendment's addition to the U.S. Constitution or through its subsequent interpretation.[20]

In contrast, the third, fourth, and fifth criteria—standards of internal constitutional coherence, principles of constitutionalism, and standards of political morality—are joined by a shared focus on matters of substantive congruence. Thus each depends on interpretation of the relevant norms: those purportedly brought about by the Fourteenth Amendment, the imperatives of other parts of the U.S. Constitution, other constitutional norms, principles of constitutionalism, and standards of political morality. Each frames in a different way relationships among constitutional meaning and authority, as with relationships among each and surrounding norms and practices.

The sixth criterion, constructive constitutional authority, bridges distinctively matters of process and substance. This criterion, as conceived for purposes of this essay, allows for the construction of constitutional authority not only through actual political practices, but also through imaginary or hypothetical processes. According to one version of this criterion, as explained more fully below, substantive outcomes may be considered authoritative as representations of the constitutional identities and commitments of "the people" on account of their constructive rather than actual procedural pedigree—for example, as norms that "the people" might approve (or might have approved) if given the opportunity to do so. Other versions of the sixth criterion focus more directly on substantive constitutional commitments not registered by conventional processes of constitutional representation, with the aim being to identify norms congruent with the constitutional identities and commitments of the whole people or a relevant portion thereof. The issues of substantive congruence raised by this inquiry thus parallel those implicated by the third, fourth, and fifth criteria.

Separately and together, through their complementary and competing implications, these six criteria provide frameworks for analyzing the construction and reconstruction of the Fourteenth Amendment's authority and meaning in the aftermath of its addition to the U.S. Constitution. There is no better case for reexamining these issues than *Slaughter-House*. The justices' opinions in that case demonstrate the contributions of plural criteria of constitutional authority and meaning; they support a conclusion that the Fourteenth Amendment's authority remained partial across at least some dimensions even after this decision; they highlight linkages among positions on authority and meaning; they underscore the centrality of these concepts, along with principles of popular sovereignty, within theories and practices of American constitutionalism; and they point toward relationships between constitutional adjudication and surrounding political developments.

The following six sections examine the justices' reliance on these six sets of criteria. Then a concluding section explores the combined contributions of those criteria to analyzing the authority of the Fourteenth Amendment and of the justices' initial reconstruction of it in *Slaughter-House*, along with intersections among those criteria. What emerges is the outlines of a distinctive framework for addressing a variety of problems of constitutional history, law, theory, and practice.

The "Voice of the People," as Recognized by Article V

Early in his opinion, Justice Miller referred to the Fourteenth Amendment, along with the Thirteenth and Fifteenth, as having been added to the U.S. Constitution "by the voice of the people." In this context, he referred to the "history of the times" as revealing "the occasion and the necessity for recurring again to the great source of power in this country, the people of the States, for additional guarantees of human rights." He described those events as "familiar to us all."[21]

Rather than avoiding problems of constitutional authorization, Justice Miller confronted them directly. He presumed that as a result of the Civil War, "slavery, as a legalized social relation, perished." In his view, then, President Abraham Lincoln's Emancipation Proclamation (1863) "expressed an accomplished fact." But those who had achieved military victory were not content to rest the abolition of slavery only on "the actual results of the contest or the proclamation of the Executive, both of which might have been questioned in after times." Accordingly, those who had succeeded in reestablishing the authority of the federal government "determined to place this main and most valuable result in the Constitution of the restored Union as one of its fundamental articles." Thus Justice Miller explicitly contrasted the authority of the Thirteenth Amendment, as a "fundamental article" of the Constitution, with results and proclamations having more tenuous authority.[22]

His treatment of the Fourteenth Amendment's authority and meaning were extensions of this line of argument. Notwithstanding the formal abolition of slavery through the Thirteenth Amendment, "the condition of the slave race would, without further protection of the Federal government, be almost as bad as it was before." As a result, "the statesmen who had conducted the Federal government in safety through the crisis of the rebellion" became convinced that "something more was necessary in the way of constitutional protection." These persons had "declined to treat as restored to their full participation in the government of the Union the States which had been in insurrection, until they ratified [the proposed Fourteenth Amendment] by a formal vote of their legislative bodies."[23]

These passages, along with others that reinforced them, relied on principles of popular sovereignty, including their institutionalization through processes of constitutional amending based on Article V of the U.S. Constitution. In addition to invoking the authority of "the people," Justice Miller's opinion also emphasized the roles of "the Congress which proposed these amendments" and of "the legislatures of the States which ratified them." In his view, Congress and especially state legislatures had acted on behalf of "the people," with the latter identified more specifically at one point as "the people of the States." Justice Miller's apparent premise was that "the people of the States," as represented by state legislatures for purposes of ratifying proposed constitutional amendments, had foundational political authority within the regime.

According to Bruce Ackerman, Justice Miller's reference to military reconstruction, including Congress's exclusion of the Southern states from readmission to national representation until they ratified the proposed Fourteenth Amendment, "cr[ies] out for a modicum of legalist hand-wringing over Article Five." In Ackerman's view, however, "the Court acted consistently with common law norms by ignoring the deep questions that everybody knew lurked just beneath the surface." His explanation of why they did so: "neither side of the *Slaughterhouse* controversy was interested in raising the question of validity."[24]

I agree with Ackerman that peculiar configurations of parties and issues in *Slaughter-House* made it relatively easy for the justices to finesse concerns about the Fourteenth Amendment's validity. But unlike Ackerman, I interpret the comments summarized above, along with those of the dissenters that are summarized below, as indicating that the justices deliberately meant to affirm the amendment as valid on the basis of the formal criteria of Article V.[25] Going further, I seek to account for ways that the majority and dissenting opinions explicitly and implicitly relied on additional criteria of constitutional validity, including those oriented primarily toward matters of substance, in an effort to reinforce, consolidate, and extend the Fourteenth Amendment's authority. The justices had various reasons of their own for doing so that went beyond those of the litigants.

These reasons paralleled and reinforced one another. Attorneys for the butchers could not invoke the Fourteenth Amendment's limitations without presuming their validity. For different reasons, including their broader political commitments, those defending the monopoly were also poorly positioned to claim that this amendment was completely unauthoritative. The willingness of those on both sides of the controversy to treat this text as part of the

U.S. Constitution was presumably informed, in addition, by an expectation that its provisions afforded substantial interpretive latitude. Rather than contesting the Fourteenth Amendment's validity, the litigants advanced interpretations of its provisions that supported their respective adversarial postures.

The Supreme Court justices were doubtless aware of arguments that this amendment was both procedurally and substantively invalid. Some of the justices may have been sympathetic with those arguments and were not dependent on the attorneys to bring them to their attention. The adversarial posture of the litigants would not have prevented the justices (whether a majority or in dissent) from declaring the Fourteenth Amendment invalid if they had wished to do so. At the same time, the willingness of both parties to treat the Fourteenth Amendment as valid made *Slaughter-House* a good case for the justices to take—and move forward on the docket—if they were interested in treating the Fourteenth Amendment as valid rather than invalid.

Like the litigants, the justices apparently had different reasons (indicated more fully below) for treating the Fourteenth Amendment as valid—or, more modestly, for presuming its validity at least for purposes of deciding this case. Because this issue had been largely settled through extrajudicial political practices by the time of the Court's decision, it would have required upsetting substantial reliance interests to declare the amendment invalid. As during prior stages of the Fourteenth Amendment's constitutionalization, the potential malleability of the amendment's terms may have been a factor in supporting the justices' implicit legalization of these constitutional developments. As an added variable, the justices also might have anticipated benefitting institutionally from ways that the amendment legitimated shifts in power from state to national institutions.[26] For whatever reasons, all of the justices in *Slaughter-House* reinforced rather than reversed the shift that had already taken place within other political arenas. The majority and dissenters alike supported moving away from debating the validity of the Fourteenth Amendment as such and toward contesting its authoritative meaning.

It is noteworthy in this connection that justices did not divide neatly across partisan or geographic lines, either in their treatment of the Fourteenth Amendment's validity or in taking positions on its authoritative meaning. There were four Republicans and one Democrat in the majority, and three Republicans and one Democrat in dissent. All came from the North or West. Democratic President James Buchanan had appointed Justice Nathan Clifford; two each of the remaining justices in the majority had been appointed by Republicans Abraham Lincoln and Ulysses Grant; three of the dissenters had been appointed by Lincoln and one by Grant.[27]

The justices' respective positions on the meaning of the Fourteenth Amendment would unfold on a case-by-case basis through what was doubtless an evolutionary process mediated by political and institutional factors. Linkages between issues of process and substance were especially transparent in the dissenters' brief references to Article V and principles of popular sovereignty. Justice Stephen J. Field claimed that the Fourteenth Amendment, if it referred only to preexisting rights of U.S. citizenship as claimed by the majority, was "a vain and idle enactment, which accomplished nothing, and most unnecessarily excited Congress and the people on its passage." He argued instead that "the Congress which framed and states which adopted" this amendment had intended it to "protect the citizens of the United States against the deprivation of their common rights by State legislation."[28] Justice Joseph P. Bradley similarly urged that "it was the intention of the people of this country in adopting that amendment to provide National security against violations by the States of fundamental rights of the citizen."[29] Justice Noah H. Swayne also criticized the majority's "construction" (his term) of the Fourteenth Amendment as "too narrow." It defeated "by a limitation not anticipated, the intent of those by whom the instrument was framed and of those by whom it was adopted." "Nowhere, than in this court," he continued, "ought the will of the nation, as thus expressed, be more liberally construed or more cordially executed."[30]

Significantly, then, the dissenters joined the majority in attributing the Fourteenth Amendment to "the people." Those in dissent, as with Justice Miller for the majority, explicitly and implicitly invoked Article V and structures of governmental representation. All of the opinions treated the Fourteenth Amendment's meaning as a function at least in part of its original pedigree. More specifically, the opinions in *Slaughter-House* reflect a shared premise that the new text's authoritative meaning was rooted in the expectations of those responsible for its addition to the Constitution. This is one way that the justices linked the Fourteenth Amendment's meaning to its presumably authoritative origins.

The "Voice of the People," as Expressed Outside Article V Processes

According to Bruce Ackerman, Justice Miller relied on the authority of "the people" not to affirm the Fourteenth Amendment's authority based on Article V, but to support a position that it was valid as a "non–Article V amendment." Remarkably, Ackerman has endorsed eighteenth-century Democratic arguments critical of this "so-called amendment" as invalid based on Article V. But unlike Reconstruction-era Democrats, Ackerman has argued that the amendment was fully valid originally on the basis of other procedural criteria of constitutional legitimacy rooted in principles of popular sovereignty. In Ackerman's view, "the People" approved the Fourteenth Amendment through structures and processes of national representation in ways that validated the amendment independently of Article V.[31]

Early versions of Ackerman's analysis appeared to rely heavily on claims of direct action by the people at large, such as the elections of 1866, as sources of constitutional authority.[32] More recently, however, he has denied that he regards "the People" as having approved the Fourteenth Amendment at any particular "decisive moment." Instead, he has described his conception of how "the People" have acted authoritatively in terms of structures and processes of national representation. More specifically, in We The People: Transformations, Ackerman defines "the People" as "the name of an extended process of interaction between political elites and ordinary citizens." Through "structured dialogue" during moments of "higher lawmaking," a "constitutional solution is hammered out" through which "the prevailing elites and the majority of citizens will share common concerns and basic aims to a much higher degree than usual." The "process ends as the general citizenry retreats from its extraordinary levels of engagement, leaving political elites to engage in normal electoral competition in a way that is broadly consistent with the terms worked out."[33]

Ackerman has not been entirely clear or consistent on when he has considered this process to have been completed with respect to the Fourteenth Amendment. In his 1989 article, "Constitutional Politics/Constitutional Law," and in his 1991 book, We the People: Foundations, he treated a fourth stage, an alleged "switch in time," as decisive.[34] Elaborating, he claimed in 1989 that as a result of President Andrew Johnson's switch in 1868 from opposing the Fourteenth Amendment to allowing its ratification to proceed,

> a new institutional situation emerged in the months after the impeachment trial. Instead of escalating the constitutional conflict yet further, all the previously dissenting parts of the government—the Presidency, the Court, the Southern States— now accepted (however reluctantly) the higher lawmaking pretensions of the Reconstruction Congress and allowed the ratification of the Amendment to proceed. This new *unanimity among the branches* gained its formal expression in . . . Secretary of State Seward's two July Proclamations concerning the Fourteenth Amendment.[35]

Here Ackerman ran together treatment of validity based on Article V with that based on supposed concurrence among the legislative and executive branches of the U.S. government. He also suggested that Secretary of State Seward's formal announcement was a significant consolidating event.

By comparison, in *We The People: Transformations* (1998), Ackerman explicitly adds a fifth stage, a "consolidating election," identified in chapter 1 as the 1868 presidential elections in the case of the Fourteenth Amendment. Chapter 8 elaborates on how Ulysses S. Grant's election in 1868 "marked a watershed" by "solidif[ying] the constitutional baseline established provisionally by the second proclamation issued by Secretary of State Seward on the Fourteenth Amendment." Here Ackerman suggests that "Reconstruction had reached a point of no return," as "the People" had "fully dedicated itself" to the principles of Section 1 of the Fourteenth Amendment and thereby "anchored their legal contribution into the very bedrock of our constitutional order."[36]

Curiously, however, chapter 1 of *Transformations* continues with a section on "Consolidation and the Court." After reviewing several cases in which the justices might have threatened aspects of congressional reconstruction if given the opportunity to do so, Ackerman cites *Slaughter-House* as a case in which the justices, in a "single sentence place[d] the country on notice that its period of anxiety was at an end." The important sentence, according to Ackerman: the one in which Justice Miller wrote in his opinion for the Court that the Thirteenth, Fourteenth, and Fifteenth Amendments had "been added by the voice of the people." Also significant, according to Ackerman, is that the justices allegedly voted "9-to-0" and announced a "unanimous decision" to uphold the validity of the Fourteenth Amendment. (Ackerman does not explain how they could "decide" this issue even though neither party in the litigation "was interested in raising the question of validity"—or how such a decision could establish a "decisive precedent" if the justices "ignor[ed] the deep questions [of constitutional validity] that everybody knew lurked just below the surface.") In any event, he concludes that "with *Slaughterhouse*, the bandwagon had come to rest at its final destination." The apparent presumption or implication of this passage, despite his earlier claims about the decisiveness of the 1868 elections, is that the Fourteenth Amendment's validity had not been finally settled before this decision.[37]

What, in Ackerman's view, was established as "bedrock"? His position on this issue has also been complex. As indicated, he has emphasized Section 1. More specifically, he has claimed that "the People" dedicated itself to "the proposition that '[a]ll persons born or naturalized' in America were entitled to 'the privileges [and] immunities of citizens of the United States' that were beyond the power of any state or locality to abridge.'"[38] How was this commitment consolidated by the justices in *Slaughter-House?* According to Ackerman, "The Justices speak with a unanimous voice. While they later divide sharply over the *meaning* of the amendments, all nine unconditionally accept their *validity*."[39] As if the justices did not disagree about meaning in this case!

My position both overlaps and departs from Ackerman's in important ways. I agree with Ackerman that there were problems with the Fourteenth Amendment's original pedigree based on Article V. But I disagree with him that this amendment completely lacked original validity based on Article V (or that the justices in *Slaughter-House* treated it as such). My position overlaps Ackerman's in allowing for constitutional authorization outside the mechanisms of Article V, including through government officials' acting on behalf of "the people." I go further in also allowing for the direct construction and reconstruction of constitutional norms by "the people" at large—and not only through representative structures. On the basis of a wider range of considerations (and thus for different reasons), I agree with Ackerman's implicit premise that the Fourteenth Amendment had only partial authority before the U.S. Supreme Court decided *Slaughter-House*. My position also overlaps Ackerman's in viewing the Court's decision in that case as constitutionally transformative, although I do not think it fully "consolidated" the amendment's authority—either descriptively or normatively, based on Article V or otherwise. Nor do I regard the justices' handling of issues of authority and meaning as dichotomous in the ways Ackerman suggested. On the contrary, I view these issues as integrally related to one another. Unlike Ackerman, moreover, I do not view the Fourteenth Amendment's subsequent authority (or its authoritative meaning) as entirely a function of its original pedigree (procedural or otherwise).

This is not the place for a thorough critique of Ackerman's arguments or a fuller elaboration of my positions on all of the matters just staked out. Here the focus is how the justices in *Slaughter-House* handled issues of constitutional authority and meaning involving the Fourteenth Amendment. These issues are not neatly severable from the broader problems of constitutional authority and meaning as indicated above. But looking at those problems through the lenses of the justices' opinions in that case does provide some means of focusing the analysis and thus limiting the scope of inquiry.

Justice Miller's initial reference to "the voice of the people," as indicated above, is followed closely by what appears to be an overlapping reference to "the great source of power in this country, the people of the States."[40] The surrounding comments linked those references, as with similar ones by Justices Bradley and Swayne, to processes and outcomes of constitutional amending based on Article V. Thus it is not obvious that Justice Miller or the other justices meant to refer, or would have been understood at the time as referring, to constitutional transformations taking place *outside* the mechanisms of Article V. Most of the references in the majority and dissenting opinions to "the people" may be understood more simply as denoting their representation through the mechanisms of Article V.

It was nevertheless significant that the justices referred to "the people" as a source of the recent amendments' authority. These references located Article V within a broader theoretical context that could serve at least seven distinct analytic functions. First, linking Article V to principles of popular sovereignty supported interpreting the former in ways that were consistent rather than inconsistent with regarding it as a vehicle for authoritative actions by "the people" or on their behalf and in their name. Which views of Article V satisfied this criterion depended on positions involving several intersecting issues including who was included in "the people," how they were politically configured (as members of a nation and/or as members of a state and/or otherwise), how they could act (such as directly and/or through representatives), and what levels of representation (of the whole and/or parts) and/or approval (majoritarian and/or supermajoritarian) were necessary to attribute actions to "the people" as such. Justice Miller focused on the identities of "the people" as members of "the states" and their roles in ratifying the proposed amendments through the respective state legislatures; and he also referred to Congress's role in proposing the amendment. Justices Field and Bradley's references to "the people" were more equivocal. In any event they, as with Justices Miller and Swayne, apparently viewed Article V as consistent with principles of popular sovereignty and as capable of supporting attributions of constitutional text to "the people."

The justices' apparent presumption that the Fourteenth Amendment was valid based on Article V depended not only on interpretation of the latter's provisions, but also on an implicit position that those requirements had been satisfied in practice. Principles of popular sovereignty could also inform treatment of this second issue. More specifically, those principles pointed toward questions, independent of those involving how to interpret Article V, about whether the actions of government officials in approving the Fourteenth Amendment adequately represented "the people." Many of the issues raised by this inquiry would parallel versions of several raised by the first. None of the justices in *Slaughter-House* expressed concerns about the adequacy of representative processes—although, as indicated above, Justice Miller did refer to Congress's exclusion of Southern states from national representation until they approved the proposed amendment.

Third, the justices' invocations of the authority of "the people" supported an inquiry into whether Article V processes produced a substantively valid result, considering that it had been designed to enable constitutional amending by the people or on their behalf and in their name. This inquiry shifts the focus beyond issues of procedure (including the propriety of processes set forth in Article V and representative processes more generally) to whether the Fourteenth Amendment adequately represented substantive constitutional commitments of "the people." This inquiry also depends on conceptualization of the identity or identities of "the people," understood substantively and not just formally. Claims by each of the justices about the importance of the Fourteenth Amendment's substantive aims were pertinent across this dimension, as was Justice Field's grouping together Congress and "the people" as having both been "excited" on the Fourteenth Amendment's passage. The dissenter's claim that the views of Congress and "the people" had been aligned in this respect supports a position that the former had properly represented the latter.

While the preceding three inquiries focus on the requirements of Article V and whether they were satisfied in the case at hand, a fourth and fifth center on political activities outside Article V but linked to it. The fourth is also suggested by Justice Field's comment that "the people" had been excited over the Fourteenth Amendment's enactment. Although he might have been referring to "the people" as represented by state legislatures, the passage may also be read as indicating involvement by "the people" *at large* in processes of constitutional amending. Justice Field does not seem to have been suggesting that ordinary citizens, acting as such, directly authorized constitutional amending (although such a position would have been both coherent and theoretically defensible). Instead, I read this passage as an expression of Justice Field's view that "the people" at large had participated in constitutional amending in ways not treated as authoritative by Article V but nevertheless relevant to evaluating the meaning and significance of representative actions that were recognized as authoritative by Article V. For example, citizens had debated the merits of the proposed amendment through speech, the press, and the like. Constitutional positions expressed through such channels, in addition to possibly influencing the course of the Fourteenth Amendment's proposal and ratification, also would have been relevant across the first three dimensions. Among other things, how the public viewed the amendment was relevant to analysis of the adequacy of processes and outcomes of governmental representation (issue 2) and whether the Fourteenth Amendment represented constitutional aims sought by "the people" (issue 3) and hence whether it was appropriate to treat it as valid (issue 1).

A fifth inquiry focuses on analogous governmental acts: those taken outside the channels of Article V but linked to them in some manner. Justice Miller's references to the Reconstruction acts were significant across this dimension. Even if those laws and policies and their enforcement were not themselves constitutionally transformative, they affected the course of constitutional amending through the channels of Article V. Justice Miller's treatment of the ends sought by the Reconstruction acts, moreover, informed analysis of the aims of the Fourteenth Amendment itself. His handling of this issue was also pertinent across the first three dimensions, as his emphasis on constitutional ends provided criteria for interpreting Article V and the Fourteenth Amendment as means to those ends. Those ends similarly provided criteria with which to evaluate the adequacy of representative structures, the Reconstruction policies at issue, and other actions taken by government officials on behalf of the people.

Sixth is constitutional change outside the mechanisms of Article V. Justice Miller, for example, presumed that "slavery, as a legalized social relation, perished . . . as a necessity of the bitterness and force" of the Civil War. Accordingly, "the proclamation of President Lincoln expressed an accomplished fact."[41] I read these passages, along with Justice Miller's comments on the advantages of formal amendments, as presuming that constitutional change had occurred in three stages: first, on the basis of the results of the war; second, through executive action; and third, through the mechanisms of Article V. Although Justice Miller treated the last as having the most secure authority, he implied that the first two—which persons might "question" in "after times"—had at least some forms of constitutional authority. Justice Miller's opinion in *Slaughter-House* thus exemplifies a theoretical framework that allows both for multiple sources of authority and for gradations of authority across at least some of them.

Seventh is authoritative constitutional (re)construction of text, following its addition to the U.S. Constitution. Justice Field, for example, referred to Congress's "construction of the thirteenth amendment" through passage of the Civil Rights Act of 1866. He also emphasized that one of the main reasons for adoption of the Fourteenth Amendment was to "obviate objections" to the validity of that law; and he noted that Congress in 1870 had given effect to this understanding by reenacting the Civil Rights Act of 1866. Thus Justice Field implied that Congress had already begun to "construct" the Fourteenth Amendment's meaning through passage of the Enforcement Act of 1870 (as it had constructed the Thirteenth's meaning through passage of the 1866 law). He viewed the authority of Congress's "construction" of the Fourteenth Amendment as reinforced, moreover, by original understandings of its meaning and implications.[42]

Justice Miller in his majority opinion similarly referred to the Court's decision in *Slaughter-House* as itself amounting to a "construction" of the three recent amendments.[43] The majority, as with the dissenters, presumed that this "construction" was legally authoritative. By linking the authority of the Fourteenth Amendment to that of "the people," the justices also invited evaluation of their respective opinions based on the extent to which they were consistent with principles of popular sovereignty. They presumed, in other words, that they were "constructing" the Fourteenth Amendment's authority and meaning on behalf of "the people."[44]

It is apparent that the justices considered their opinions, as with constitutional constructions by Congress and others, as authoritative not only according to procedural criteria, but also on the basis of substantive ones. Processes mattered: how the justices had been chosen, adversarial postures, majoritarian rules of decision, and the like. At the same time, the justices were offering substantive readings of constitutional guarantees. They invited evaluation of their opinions, as with the provisions being interpreted, based on substantive standards. Accepting that invitation, we may now explore the significance of the justices' reliance in *Slaughter-House* on substantive criteria of constitutional authority.

Standards of Internal Constitutional Coherence

All of the justices placed a premium in *Slaughter-House* on the U.S. Constitution's internal coherence. Thus all sought to reconcile the Fourteenth Amendment with other parts of the Constitution to which it was added and with other features of the constitutional order more generally. But the justices did so differently, on the bases of competing interpretations of the amendment and of other norms of American constitutionalism.

Justice Miller's opinion for the majority proceeded from an assumption that Louisiana had "ample" authority to pass the challenged law unless it was restrained by one of the recent amendments. In support of this position, the justice argued that with the exception of "very few express limitations," the "entire domain of the privileges and immunities of citizens of the States . . . lay within the constitutional and legislative power of the States and without that of the Federal government." He questioned, then, whether the purpose of the Fourteenth Amendment's privileges or immunities clause was to "transfer the security and protection" of all these "civil rights . . . from the States to the Federal government." Justice Miller suggested that such a result would "bring within the power of Congress the entire domain of civil rights heretofore belonging exclusively to the States" and would "constitute this court a perpetual censor upon all the legislation of the States, on the civil rights of their own citizens." He denied that those who had proposed and ratified the Fourteenth Amendment had intended consequences "so serious, so far-reaching and pervading, so great a departure from the structure and spirit of our institutions." The argument against such a "radical" construction of the Fourteenth Amendment was "irresistible, in the absence of language which expresses such a purpose too clearly to admit of doubt." Justice Miller likewise did not "see" in the other parts of the Fourteenth Amendment, or in the Thirteenth or Fifteenth Amendments, "any purpose to destroy the main features of the general system." Even under pressure of "the excited feeling growing out of the war," the "statesmen" responsible for these amendments "still believed that the existence of the States with powers for domestic and local government . . . was essential to the perfect working of our complex form of government." Thus the justices would "continue" to hold "with a steady and even hand the balance between State and Federal power." For Justice Miller, in short, the Fourteenth Amendment had not brought about fundamental change. Its provisions could be construed as consistent with the main features of the antebellum Constitution.[45]

As Walter F. Murphy has recognized, these arguments went to the Fourteenth Amendment's authority, not just its meaning. According to Murphy, Justice Miller's opinion in *Slaughter-House* may be viewed as an attempt to avoid interpreting the Fourteenth Amendment as having brought about fundamental changes to the constitutional order too sweeping for a mere constitutional "amendment." Part of the impetus for such a saving (re)construction of the amendment may have resulted from criticism of the Fourteenth Amendment, along with the Thirteenth and Fifteenth, as substantively invalid independently of the procedures through which these "so-called amendments" were added to the U.S. Constitution. Murphy's analysis of this issue, as with contemporaneous treatment of it during the Reconstruction era, has relied (among other things) on a distinction between constitutional "amending" (including as permitted by Article V) and more fundamental constitutional "re-formation." The central idea here is that a constitution cannot itself authorize movement to a fundamentally different political order. To be legitimate, such a movement must find its justification elsewhere.[46]

Principles of internal constitutional coherence, when linked to Miller's reading of the antebellum Constitution, thus support his reading of the Fourteenth Amendment.[47] Most immediately, his (re)construction of the amendment was a way of avoiding the problems of constitutional incoherence that he suggested would have plagued more "radical" interpretations of the amendment's meaning or of its effects on the constitutional order. More affirmatively, the majority's position may be viewed as an effort to reconcile the Fourteenth Amendment with other norms of U.S. constitutionalism. Holding other interpretive positions constant, it was relatively easy to achieve a substantial measure of internal constitutional coherence—with little disruption of established precedents and other existing institutions— by treating the new text as having brought about modest rather than sweeping changes to the constitutional order. Accordingly, a commitment to treating the Fourteenth Amendment as authoritative across this dimension appears to have exerted an influence, analytically, toward emphasizing constitutional continuities based on connections between the Fourteenth Amendment and antecedent norms.

The dissenting opinions indicate, however, that Justice Miller's approach was not the only available means of negotiating the imperatives of internal constitutional coherence. Justices Field, Bradley, and Swayne adopted versions of the general structure of Justice Miller's opinion by emphasizing ways that the Fourteenth Amendment was fundamentally conservative in character. They, like Justice Miller, argued that this amendment reinforced and extended antecedent norms in ways that promoted rather than undercut internal constitutional coherence. In handling this issue, however, the dissenters drew on perspectives toward the antebellum Constitution and toward the Fourteenth Amendment that were substantially different from Justice Miller's. By comparing their positions to the majority's, we can see that the implications of criteria of internal constitutional coherence were variable (or cross cutting) rather than constant (or unidirectional).

Justice Field maintained that the terms of the Fourteenth Amendment "inhibit any legislation which confers special and exclusive privileges like these under consideration." It "place[d] the common rights of American citizens under the protection of the National government." In his view, "The amendment does not attempt to confer any new privileges or immunities upon citizens, or to enumerate those already existing. It assumes that there are such privileges and immunities . . . and ordains that they shall not be abridged by State legislation." Relying on precedents interpreting the privileges and immunities clause of Article IV, Section 2 of the Constitution, Justice Field maintained that "what the clause in question did for the protection of the citizens of one State against hostile and discriminating legislation of other States, the Fourteenth Amendment does for the protection of every citizen of the United States against hostile and discriminating legislation against him in favor of others, whether they reside in the same or in different States." Justice Field similarly relied on a wide range of precedents that he regarded as affirming the equal right of citizens to pursue "the ordinary avocations of life" and as declaring that "all grants of exclusive privileges, in contravention of this equality, [were] against common right, and void." Although he claimed that the Fourteenth Amendment had significantly altered constitutional norms, he treated those alterations as extensions of deeply established norms. His analysis thus supported a conclusion that this amendment's addition to the U.S. Constitution promoted rather than undercut its internal coherence.[48]

Justice Bradley in his dissent also emphasized connections between the Fourteenth Amendment and antecedent constitutional norms. He referred to the "authoritative declaration of some of the most important privileges and immunities of citizens of the United States . . . in the Constitution itself." Other rights were no less inviolable on account of their not being enumerated in the constitutional text: "It was not necessary to say in words that the citizens of the United States should have and exercise all the privileges of citizens; . . . their very citizenship conferred these privileges, if they did not possess them before." The law in question went against those rights, and it was one of the primary purposes of the Fourteenth Amendment to make them enforceable by federal courts against the states. Justice Bradley emphasized, moreover, that the amendment's prohibitions were self-executing, and thus "very little, if any, legislation on the part of Congress would be required to carry the amendment into effect." Any increase in judicial workload could be handled by Congress's increasing the number of federal courts. Thus in his view the Fourteenth Amendment would not require reconceiving rights of citizenship, transforming governmental structures, or other fundamental change within the constitutional order.[49]

Justice Swayne made the strongest case for viewing the Fourteenth Amendment as radically transformative. He characterized it as "a new departure" that "mark[ed] an important epoch in the constitutional history of the country." He also described the amendment, along with the Thirteenth and Fifteenth, as "ris[ing] to the dignity of a new Magna Charta." He conceded the majority's premise that before the Fourteenth Amendment's adoption, the subject at hand "was wholly within the jurisdiction of the States." Before the war, "ample protection was given against oppression by the Union, but little was given against wrong and oppression by the States." In his view, the Fourteenth Amendment remedied "that want." But even he characterized the terms of this amendment as "eminently conservative in their character." And he pointed out that federal judges had ample experience interpreting the rights at issue and exercising "authority of the same amplitude."[50]

Some texts have been difficult to reconcile with the major features of an existing constitutional order without substantial disruption, and vice versa. The Fourteenth Amendment, because of its potentially vast reach, may readily be conceived as designed to have such an effect. In short, it may be viewed as widely and deeply transformative in its direct effects and indirect implications.

But its central prohibitions on the states—those contained in Section 1—have also afforded substantial interpretive latitude. The same has been true of many of the parts of the U.S. Constitution with which the Fourteenth Amendment's provisions most transparently have intersected: delegations of power to Congress in Article I, including the necessary and proper clause; the privileges and immunities clause of Article IV; the supremacy clause in Article VI; the Fifth Amendment's due process clause; the Ninth Amendment's reference to unspecified rights retained by the people; the Tenth Amendment's implication of limited delegations of power to national institutions along with its reservation of powers to the states and to the people; and the Thirteenth Amendment's abolition of slavery and involuntary servitude. There have been corresponding issues involving relationships between the Fourteenth Amendment and provisions in state constitutions; and unwritten or informal norms (at various levels of constitutional governance) have presented additional complications.

Standards of internal coherence have not themselves dictated how to interpret the relevant norms. These standards have, however, exerted gravitational pull in the direction of interpreting the applicable norms, to the extent reasonably practical, as largely consistent with one another. Thus it has been necessary for interpreters in the past to consult additional criteria that have further constrained choices among interpretive positions (involving the Fourteenth Amendment and other norms of U.S. constitutionalism) that have satisfied the criterion of internal constitutional coherence. We may now turn to the fourth and fifth criteria for their separate and combined contributions on this score.

Principles of Constitutionalism

One way to conceive of principles of constitutionalism is to think of them as constitutional norms extending beyond those established or authorized by any particular constitution. For example, John E. Finn has treated relationships between a given constitution and these broader principles of constitutionalism as analogous to those between a particular contract and general laws of contracting. Each instance of the former presupposes and draws authority from the latter. The same is true of constitutions as a generic category, of which the U.S. Constitution is an example. It may be understood as resting on and incorporating principles of constitutionalism that have grounded or reinforced its authority as a constitution. These broader principles thus have provided standards for evaluating the authority of the U.S. Constitution and for choosing among conceivable interpretations of it and its features.[51]

From perspectives within any particular constitutional order, understandings of principles of constitutionalism, as with other standards of political morality, have been highly contested. From more detached analytic perspectives, understandings of these principles appear to have evolved over time. From both perspectives, they have been pluralistic rather than unitary in their meaning and implications. Stated differently, political actors historically have treated principles of constitutionalism as plural rather than singular; and this feature becomes compounded within an interpretive posture, like the one I take in this essay, which embraces a multiplicity of subsidiary interpretive perspectives.

Consistently with this more general pattern, each of the opinions in *Slaughter-House* invoked some version of what we may regard as principles of constitutionalism. Those opinions support a conclusion that principles of popular sovereignty and self-governance, structures of governmental representation and limited governmental power, aspirations for internal constitutional coherence, and commitment to providing security for fundamental rights of persons, have each been conceived as aspects of constitutional governance with moral authority independently of their affirmation or establishment by the U.S. Constitution. The opinions thus offer useful analytic perspectives toward principles of constitutionalism as a subset of criteria of political morality more generally.

It is noteworthy in this connection that Justice Miller in his majority opinion relied heavily on principles of limited government, especially those associated with structures of federalism. For example, he treated as authoritative "the structure and spirit of our institutions." More specifically, he invoked "the whole theory of the relations of the State and Federal governments to each other and of both these governments to the people." Justice Miller also took a position that the Court had a responsibility to maintain "the perfect working of our complex form of government" by preserving "the balance between State and Federal power." Thus he urged interpreting the Fourteenth Amendment consistently with continued maintenance of such a balance. This is another way his opinion treated issues of authority and meaning as integrally linked with one another.[52]

Justice Field, in contrast, emphasized guarantees of rights that, in his view, "belong to citizens of all free governments." He also claimed that "our government [would] be a republic only in name" if it did not respect "the equality of rights." Going further, he urged that grants of exclusive privilege were "opposed to the whole theory of free government" and violated "the right of free labor." He continued: "That only is a free government, in the American sense of the term, under which the inalienable right of every citizen to pursue his happiness is unrestrained, except by just, equal, and impartial laws." Bringing together issues of meaning and authority, he took a position that the Fourteenth Amendment incorporated these fundamental tenets of constitutional governance as standards for measuring "the validity of the legislation of every State." Thus he treated meaning and authority as aligned across three levels: principles of constitutionalism, the positive law of the U.S. Constitution, and state legislation.[53]

Justice Bradley also referred to rights held by "citizens of any free government." Not only did he base them on the U.S. Constitution, as indicated above, but he also claimed that "the people of this country brought with them to its shores the rights of Englishmen; the rights which had been wrested from English sovereigns at various periods of the nation's history."[54] These passages, along with Justice Swayne's invocation of the Magna Charta, drew on traditions of constitutionalism deeper and broader than the positive law of the U.S. Constitution. Interpreting the Fourteenth Amendment as resonating with those principles and as advancing them were ways of reinforcing its authority across this dimension.

Other Standards of Political Morality

The justices also relied on other standards of political morality that they apparently conceived as not falling within any of the preceding categories and thus as extending beyond them. In the process, the justices both indicated that they conceived of (what I am referring to as) principles of constitutionalism as a subset of moral standards and they relied on such standards more generally. For example, Justice Miller suggested that the abolition of slavery and guarantees protecting basic rights of the former slaves were driven at least in part by moral considerations. He also suggested that fundamental rights of state citizenship were held by individuals even prior to the formation of governmental institutions.[55] Justice Field similarly invoked the idea of "just rights," and he maintained that the Fourteenth Amendment gave national institutions authority to secure their exercise. He clearly invoked moral standards when he claimed that Louisiana's establishment of a slaughterhouse monopoly deprived individuals of "common rights" and went against considerations of "abstract justice." In his view, a "free government" may not interfere with "the inalienable right of every citizen to pursue his happiness . . . except by just, equal, and impartial laws."[56] Justice Bradley described the monopoly as "onerous, unreasonable, arbitrary, and unjust."[57] Justice Swayne described the Fourteenth Amendment as "necessary to enable the government of the nation to secure to every one within its jurisdiction the rights and privileges enumerated, which, according to the plainest considerations of reason and justice and the fundamental principles of the social compact, all are entitled to enjoy."[58]

Underlying the majority and dissenting justices' respective invocations of moral standards to evaluate conceivable interpretations of the Fourteenth Amendment were two important premises and an implicit invitation. First, the justices united in taking a position, explicitly or implicitly, that the Fourteenth Amendment incorporated moral standards. Thus they considered those standards relevant to interpreting the amendment's terms. Second, and relatedly, the majority and dissenting opinions each reflect and proceed from a premise that it was appropriate for the justices to attempt to maintain or advance rather than weaken or diminish the Fourteenth Amendment's moral authority. By linking the first premise to the second while joining issues of meaning and authority, the justices presumed that they would advance the authority of both the Fourteenth Amendment and their interpretations of its terms by taking positions that were consistent rather than inconsistent with the applicable moral standards. Those standards, as indicated above, included what Justices Field and Bradley characterized as principles of "free government," other conceptions of what I have described as norms of constitutionalism, and additional criteria of political morality.

In addition, by invoking moral standards to defend their interpretive positions and to criticize opposing ones, the justices invited the readers of their opinions to draw on those standards to evaluate the precedents being set. Among the issues raised by such an inquiry would be: What moral authority did the justices attribute to the Fourteenth Amendment? More generally, in what ways were their (re)constructions of the amendment congruent with moral imperatives and aspirations? Conversely, in what ways did the opinions fall short of those ideals? Accordingly, to what extent would the majority and the dissenters' positions advance principles of constitutionalism, and in what ways would these positions go against those principles? Stated differently, what was the moral authority of the justices' opinions?

These types of inquiries, as with those raised by the first four criteria (and the sixth, considered below) were amenable to graded analysis and continue to call for corresponding conceptions of constitutional authority and meaning, not simply line drawing. They also lead to further questions about the characteristics and sources of the moral principles at issue. Were they independent of political practices or formed through them? Did the justices have comparative institutional advantages interpreting them and analyzing their implications? To what extent, if any, did the moral authority of the judges' efforts to reconstruct the Fourteenth Amendment's authority and meaning depend on their positions' resonating with broader political and social understandings of the matters of constitutional history, politics, law, and theory at stake?

There are numerous ways to engage these queries. One is to investigate the conceptions of morality on which the justices relied. Another is to situate the justices' positions within broader historical and theoretical contexts. A third is to rely on independent (external) evaluative standards, including those provided by contemporary perspectives. Although in this essay I provide the beginnings of each of these forms of analysis, space limitations preclude fuller treatment of them here except as follows. The following section, on constructive constitutional authority, offers distinctive evaluative perspectives toward several of the matters of political morality at stake in *Slaughter-House* and indicates some of the ways the justices in that case negotiated them. In addition, below, I explore relationships among the six criteria being considered here. These comments relate back to the queries being raised here by suggesting how the first, second, third, fourth, and sixth criteria may inform further analysis of the issues of moral authority raised by the fifth criterion—and vice versa.

Constructive Constitutional Authority

What distinguishes the sixth criterion is that it looks to hypothetical or constructive approval by the people or those acting on their behalf. Its underlying premise, like that of at least the first two criteria, is that the U.S. Constitution's authority has rested on that of "the people" whom it has purported to represent. The first two criteria are oriented toward actual political practices treated as constitutionally authoritative. The sixth allows for the possibility of attitudes, commitments, deliberations, and conceivable actions having been constitutionally authoritative in ways that have extended beyond what has been regarded as such by the first two as conventionally understood.[59]

Among other things, this sixth criterion potentially provides a partial remedy for deficiencies or limitations associated with the first two while intersecting distinctively with perspectives offered by the third, fourth, and fifth. Of particular relevance on this score have been barriers to political participation by "the people" themselves and related inadequacies in purportedly representative structures and processes of constitutional governance. As examples, exclusions of women and black men from the franchise have effectively disqualified them from participating fully (both directly and indirectly, on their own and through representatives) in important processes of constitutional (self-)governance. During the antebellum period, many women (although not enslaved black women) were widely presumed to be "citizens." There were good reasons to regard them, by extension, as among "the people." Despite the Supreme Court's decision in *Dred Scott*, there was also strong support for viewing many free black men and women as "citizens" and members of "the people"—both of the United States and of the states of their residence.[60] The Thirteenth Amendment, of course, formally abolished slavery; the Fourteenth Amendment set forth expansive criteria for "citizenship"; and one of the aims of the Reconstruction acts of 1867 and 1868, along with the Fifteenth Amendment, was to extend voting rights to many black men. But none of these developments ensured that women could vote, and exclusions from the franchise on the basis of race and sex persisted throughout the era of Reconstruction. These exclusions tainted the processes culminating in the addition of the Fourteenth Amendment to the Constitution as with its subsequent interpretation by governmental officials. This is another way that these processes could at best generate norms having partial authority, if measured by inclusive standards of rights of political participation.

Other issues of political inclusion and exclusion were also pertinent in the case of the Fourteenth Amendment. As indicated above, the formerly rebellious Southern states were excluded from the Congress that proposed the Fourteenth Amendment. In addition, former Confederate leaders were disqualified from participating in processes tied to ratification of the proposed amendment. There is evidence that many persons eligible to participate in those processes voluntarily abstained from doing so on the basis of principled opposition to the policies of military reconstruction of which those processes were parts.[61] Even if the resulting outcomes formally satisfied the requirements of Article V, their authority was diminished by these exclusions, as with those identified above.

The Southern states were eventually readmitted to representation in Congress. Disqualifications of former Confederates were eventually lifted. Many black men were able to vote and otherwise exercised rights of active citizenship (although many remained excluded, in various ways and for various reasons). Problems of authorization that originally plagued the Fourteenth Amendment may have been remedied to some extent (but not fully) through more inclusive representative processes at subsequent stages, including those involving the amendment's authoritative interpretation (such as by the justices in *Slaughter-House*).

But women, more than half the population, remained excluded from direct participation in many of these processes. What percentage of them approved the amendment—or would have voted for persons who, in turn, voted to approve it? Can we imagine how the text might have been different—or might have been interpreted differently—if women had been allowed to participate more fully at these stages (and beforehand) in structures and processes of constitutional governance? Is it likely that *Bradwell v. Illinois* (1873) and *Minor v. Happersett* (1875) would have followed immediately on the heels of *Slaughter-House*? Or, stated differently, was the authority of *Slaughter-House* (as with *Bradwell* and *Minor*) impaired on account of these exclusions? On this dimension as well, does it make sense to regard the justices' opinions as having had partial authority—here as measured by standards of constructive constitutional authorization taking into account the potential or imaginary contributions of a wider range of participants in processes of constitutional creation, amending, interpretation, and the like? The sixth criterion points toward questions like these and helps us to see (or appreciate more fully) the importance of investigating them.[62]

We have explored thus far how the idea of imaginary or constructive constitutional authorization may allow interpreters to look beyond actual decisions in the past or present by treating as authoritative alternative outcomes that might have flowed—or might flow—from perspectives going beyond those registered by actual processes and outcomes of constitutional decision making. Accounting for these broader perspectives allows a closer approximation (even if only imaginarily) of full representation of the entire/whole people upon whom the U.S. Constitution has rested for its authority and in whose name it has purported to speak. In this respect, a model of constructive constitutional authority accords more fully than conventional models with inclusive constitutional aspirations.

The sixth criterion also allows for expansion of temporal horizons. The text of the U.S. Constitution not only has had a historical pedigree and has depended for its continuing authority on its ongoing reaffirmation, it also has referred to "our posterity." Thus it has looked toward the future, along with the past and present; and it has depended on its interpreters to do likewise. The idea of hypothetical approval is one way of dealing with this issue. As the text has aspired to represent future generations of "the people," interpretive positions have had authority across the sixth dimension to the extent they have been likely to gain the assent of future citizens (whether expansively or narrowly conceived).

This perspective helps to illuminate important features of the majority and dissenting opinions in *Slaughter-House*. As with most judicial opinions, they looked toward the future as well as the past and present.[63] For example, Justice Miller suggested that if the justices had endorsed the butchers' position, two consequences would have followed. First, the Court's decision would have implied that Congress had authority not only to pass laws to remedy past wrongdoing by the states, but also to enact advance legislation "restricting the exercise of legislative power by the States, in their most ordinary and usual functions." Second, such a decision would have "constitute[d] this court a perpetual censor upon all legislation of the States, on the civil rights of their own citizens." In addition to denying that the Fourteenth Amendment's framers had intended such results, Justice Miller emphasized their far-reaching consequences. He also offered a relatively narrow view of the Fourteenth Amendment's equal protection clause—one that had transparent implications with respect to the issues in cases such as *Bradwell v. Illinois*. We may infer from passages such as these that the majority was concerned not only with whether their decision resonated with prior precedents, but also with whether it was capable of extension to other foreseeable controversies. The majority was attentive, in other words, to whether their (re)construction of the Fourteenth Amendment would be reaffirmed on the one hand or reversed on the other.[64]

The dissents were also forward-looking in orientation. All three dissenters articulated positions capable of extension in other cases. Justice Field, for example, emphasized the centrality of "free labor" principles within American constitutionalism. One aspect of those principles, he claimed, was "the inalienable right of every citizen to pursue his happiness ... unrestrained, except by just, equal, and impartial laws."[65] Justice Bradley made a complementary argument that the "right to choose one's calling, profession, or trade" was "an essential part of that liberty which it is the object of government to protect"—subject, however, to reasonable regulations.[66] Justice Swayne expressed hope that "the consequences to follow" from the majority's holding would be "less serious and far-reaching than the minority fear they will be."[67] All three opinions transparently reflect a strategy of planting doctrinal seeds capable of development in ways at odds with the majority's (re)construction of the Fourteenth Amendment's provisions.

It is noteworthy in this connection that *Slaughter-House* involved claims of economic rights where issues of race and gender were not directly implicated. The butchers' initiating the lawsuit, the respective attorneys' arguments challenging and defending the monopoly, the justices' moving the case forward on the docket, their emphasizing the importance of the issues at stake, and the ways they dealt with them, all reflect a shared assumption that constitutionalism in America was centrally concerned with economic rights. *Slaughter-House* alone did not end controversy over the character or scope of these rights—including what protection, if any, the Fourteenth Amendment provided them. But the opinions in that case—those in dissent as well as Justice Miller's majority opinion—were important as initial efforts to elaborate jurisprudential positions on relationships among governmental powers and commercial rights. The authority of these positions was partly a function of the support they were capable of receiving among relevant constituencies—including actual and conceivable constitutional decision makers in the wake of the Court's decision.

The attention given to the issues in this case also reflects a widespread assumption that maintaining and reinforcing the Fourteenth Amendment's authority following its addition to the U.S. Constitution depended (and was widely presumed to depend) in large measure on dealing effectively with its implications with respect to federal and state regulations of commercial rights (as well as issues of health more peculiar to this case). Democrats along with Republicans, those in the South as with those in the North and West, black and white persons, women along with men, might join in affirming the centrality of commercial rights within the constitutional order. To be sure, *Slaughter-House* signaled important differences in the conceptualization of those rights and which institutions were primarily responsible for their security. But it was at least imaginable that some measure of consensus might emerge capable of supporting a constitutional jurisprudence involving the Fourteenth Amendment that centered on commercial rights.

The story of judicial protection of commercial rights following *Slaughter-House*, as with that pertaining to constitutional developments more generally in the aftermath of this case, is long and complex. To identify one pertinent feature of it: Commercial rights did emerge as the centerpiece of constitutional jurisprudence from the late nineteenth century through the early twentieth, and the Fourteenth Amendment was at the core of that jurisprudence.[68] One need not view this result as preordained or predestined by *Slaughter-House* to regard as nonaccidental the justices' choice of that case to announce their initial (re)construction of the Fourteenth Amendment. In retrospect, it is remarkable the extent to which later doctrine built on central features of both the majority and dissenting opinions. If the justices could have neither completely controlled nor fully predicted what followed, at least they may have anticipated aspects of its broad outlines.

Conclusion

We may now move beyond consideration of ways that the six sets of criteria being investigated here (including their respective subsidiary components) contribute separately to analyzing the U.S. Supreme Court's (re)construction of the Fourteenth Amendment's authority and meaning in *Slaughter-House*. This essay concludes by exploring the combined contributions of those criteria, along with intersections among them. What emerges is the outlines of an overarching, multidimensional model of constitutional authority and a corresponding model of pluralistic meaning.

While each criterion on its own enables consideration of at least one dimension of constitutional authority and corresponding conceptions of meaning, together, these six sets of criteria facilitate analysis of problems of constitutional authority and meaning across several dimensions. Stated differently, one may combine the six sets of primary criteria into an overarching macrocriterion. That broader evaluative perspective, as with the more particular ones, may contribute to analyzing constitutional developments involving the Fourteenth Amendment and other parts of the U.S. Constitution—or problems of constitutionalism more generally.

One way to integrate the combined contributions of the relevant primary criteria is to treat constitutional authority from a macro perspective as greatest with respect to issues and positions finding support from multiple subsidiary criteria. In those cases, by extension, constitutional meanings have been relatively determinate and cohesive. On the other hand, one may view constitutional authority as weakest for issues and positions finding more slender support, or where the implications of the various microcriteria have been at odds with one another—thus yielding relatively indeterminate or pluralistic meanings. Intermediate positions may be located across these poles.

In this connection it again warrants emphasis that the various opinions in *Slaughter-House* support all six criteria, and vice versa. Neither the majority opinion nor any of the dissents in that case treat any one of the six primary criteria being considered here as exclusively relevant to deciding the case or defending interpretive positions in that context. Parts of each opinion, on the contrary, address issues pertinent across all six of these dimensions.

In addition, the analysis in each opinion addresses issues relevant across these six criteria in ways that treat them as mutually reinforcing. Stated differently, the opinions treat constitutional authority and meaning as functions of the combined implications of what I am referring to here as the six primary criteria. Accordingly, although the justices did not explicitly invoke the idea of a single macrocriterion, the opinions implicitly depend on some version of such a model for their overall intelligibility. The justices presented the components of their analysis as parts of integrated, coherent opinions—not as disparate or disjointed claims or arguments.

It is also significant that the opinions in *Slaughter-House* support treating principles of popular sovereignty as a common thread running through various components of their analysis. Although parts of each opinion are consistent with conceiving of versions of several of the six criteria as not dependent on principles of popular sovereignty, important passages in the majority and dissenting opinions explicitly invoke those principles. Of particular relevance on this score is Justice Miller's attributing the text of the Fourteenth Amendment to "the people," along with Justice Field and Justice Bradley's respective references to popular involvement in formal processes of constitutional amending. Those passages support conceiving of the first two criteria as resting on a premise that constitutional norms have depended for their authority and meaning on political activities by "the people" and on their behalf. They also support conceiving of the other four criteria as rooted in principles of popular sovereignty.

Turning those criteria around, what are their combined contributions to analyzing the opinions in *Slaughter-House?* They support a position that the justices' opinions, as with the Fourteenth Amendment and other pertinent parts of the U.S. Constitution, have depended for their authority at least in part on that of "the people of the United States." Going further, the subsidiary criteria invoked by the justices provide standards for assessing the extent to which that text, and the opinions seeking to (re)construct its authoritative meaning(s), have found support as authoritative representations of the constitutional activities and commitments of those people.

Relatedly, most of those criteria, still engaged at a relatively high level of generality, presume or imply that the authority and meaning of the Fourteenth Amendment—along with the justices' positions on its authority, meaning, and implications—have been linked in important ways to broader activities and commitments of constitutional politics. First, Article V has treated as authoritative processes of constitutional amending involving state legislators and members of Congress. As the justices recognized in *Slaughter-House*, moreover, the people at large participated various ways in those processes and influenced their outcomes. Across the second criterion, principles of popular sovereignty also supported the justices' treating additional representative actions as authoritative, including "constructions" of the Fourteenth Amendment by Congress, along with the Court's decision in *Slaughter-House*. Third, and for similar reasons, those principles supported the justices' efforts to achieve at least two forms of constitutional coherence: among the Fourteenth Amendment and other parts of the U.S. Constitution, from the "internal" perspective of constitutional precedent; and between these "internal" (judicial) and "external" (extrajudicial) perspectives.[69] The authority of the opinions themselves was thus a function of the extent to which they promoted one or both of these forms of coherence in ways that were reasonably attributable to "the people" whom the justices (as with the text they were interpreting) purported to represent. Fourth, the authority of the justices' positions on the elements and implications of principles of constitutionalism was likewise a function, at least in part, of their being congruent with (re)constructions of these norms by "the people" at large and those acting on their behalf. Fifth, the moral authority of the opinions was likewise a function of their resonance with social constructions of norms of political morality. Sixth, the idea of constructive constitutional authority supports treating as authoritative the justices' representation of voices among "the people" that were not otherwise represented within formal channels of constitutional amending, official interpretive practices, or predominant social constructions of principles of constitutionalism and standards of political morality more generally. The justices had distinctive institutional opportunities and responsibilities to represent these out of favor and/or anticipatory perspectives.

It is apparent that much of the majority and dissenting opinions was, not surprisingly, consistent with mainstream understandings of structures of constitutional amending, principles of popular sovereignty, relevant constitutional norms, principles of constitutionalism, and standards of political morality more generally. While there were important disagreements between the majority and dissenting justices and among the latter, those on both sides of this case treated the Fourteenth Amendment as valid, presumed that federal judges had authority to enforce its prohibitions, invoked principles of popular sovereignty, interpreted the Fourteenth Amendment as consistent with structures of American federalism and principles of limited government, took positions that the states had important commercial powers and that federal judges had authority to enforce fundamental rights as limits on them, and defended their positions on moral grounds.

It is particularly important that the justices united in treating commercial rights and their regulation as central concerns of American constitutionalism. While they disagreed about the validity and fairness of the slaughterhouse monopoly at issue in this case, neither the majority opinion nor any of the dissents appears to have been outside the bounds of major currents within political thinking at the time. Those on both sides found substantial support from constitutional precedents and subsequently received endorsements from influential constituencies.[70]

These considerations do not, however, support a conclusion that any of the opinions in *Slaughter-House* was fully authoritative across all six dimensions or treated the Fourteenth Amendment itself as such. On the contrary, the majority and dissenting opinions both actually and constructively underrepresented important constituencies and interests. Black men, along with women of all races and colors, had reasons to be ambivalent at best toward the justices' opinions. Although Justice Miller indicated that the overarching aim of the Fourteenth along with the Thirteenth and Fifteenth Amendments was to provide for "the freedom of the slave race, the security and firm establishment of that freedom, and the protection of the newly-made freeman and citizen from the oppressions of those who had formerly exercised unlimited dominion over him," other parts of his opinion implied that national institutions had limited authority to guarantee those rights.[71] The dissenters offered more expansive readings of federal power, but their positions on the scope of the Fourteenth Amendment's guarantees were also relatively confined—especially as compared with the "radical" commitments of at least some of the amendment's proponents.[72]

Accordingly, this chapter supports a tentative conclusion that the justices' opinions in *Slaughter-House*, as with the Fourteenth Amendment, which they (re)constructed in this case, had partial rather than complete authority across the six criteria examined above, both separately and as aspects of a more inclusive multidimensional macrocriterion. In addition, the justices in that case, far from settling the Fourteenth Amendment's authoritative meaning, contributed to processes involving the (re)construction of text having pluralistic rather than unitary meaning. There remains a need for further analysis, beyond the bounds of this essay, to refine, reinforce, extend, and perhaps qualify these conclusions—including through reconsideration of ways that a variety of political actors contributed to the Fourteenth Amendment's subsequent constitutional development. Of particular importance is accounting more fully for ways that constitutional developments have simultaneously enhanced the Fourteenth Amendment's authority across some dimensions while diminishing it across others.

Notes

1. *Slaughter-House Cases*, 83 U.S. 36 (1873).

2. The justices in *Slaughter-House* referred explicitly at least seventeen times to constitutional "construction." At least ten of these references were to actual or conceivable "constructions" of the Fourteenth Amendment by the justices in that case; at least one emphasized "construction" of constitutional provisions by Congress; and the other references were to problems of constitutional construction more generally or that involving other cases. See ibid. at 67, 69, 72, 75, 78, 81, 82, 89, 91, 97, 123, 124, 126, 129. See also note 42 below, and the accompanying text (Justice Field implied that Congress had begun "constructing" the Fourteenth Amendment through passage of the Enforcement

Act of 1870). Consistent with these passages and others like them, this chapter conceives of constitutional "construction" and/or "reconstruction" as including at least the creation, maintenance, revision, and destruction of constitutional norms, through interpretation and otherwise. The more equivocal designation, "(re)construction," is used where appropriate to hold open which characterization is more appropriate.

3. Whether the justices were making claims about what the Fourteenth Amendment's authoritative meaning was or should have been depends on their respective positions on the potential independence of constitutional meaning from authoritative judicial interpretation of the norms at issue.

4. For criticism of the Fourteenth Amendment as procedurally invalid, see, e.g., Joseph James, "Is the Fourteenth Amendment Valid?," *Social Science* 50 (1975): 3–9; Forrest McDonald, "Was the Fourteenth Amendment Constitutionally Adopted?," *Georgia Journal of Southern Legal History* 1 (1991): 1–20; Walter J. Suthon Jr., "The Dubious Origin of the Fourteenth Amendment," *Tulane Law Review* 28 (1953): 22–44. See also Bruce Ackerman, *We the People 2: Transformations* (Cambridge, Mass.: Harvard University Press, 1998); Wayne D. Moore, "The Fourteenth Amendment's Initial Authority: Problems of Constitutional Coherence," *Temple Political and Civil Rights Law Review* 13 (2004): 515–545.

5. See, e.g., the sources cited by Walter Murphy, "*Slaughter-House*, Civil Rights, and Limits on Constitutional Change," *American Journal of Jurisprudence* 12 (1987): 1–22, at 9n29. See also Moore, "Fourteenth Amendment's Initial Authority."

6. See, e.g., Ferdinand F. Fernandez, "The Constitutionality of the Fourteenth Amendment," *Southern California Law Review* 39 (1966): 378–407; John Harrison, "The Lawfulness of the Reconstruction Amendments," *University of Chicago Law Review* 68 (2001): 375–462.

7. Republican positions on several of these issues are developed in the *Report of the Joint Committee on Reconstruction*, First Session, Thirty-ninth Congress (Washington, D.C.: Government Printing Office, 1866). See also Fernandez, "Constitutionality of the Fourteenth Amendment"; Murphy, "*Slaughter-House*, Civil Rights."

8. See *United States Statutes at Large* 15 (1869): 706–711.

9. See, e.g., Frank P. Blair, Letter to Col. James O. Broadhead, 30 June 1868, reprinted in *Democratic Speaker's Handbook*, ed. Matthew Carey Jr. (pseud., supposedly Augustus R. Cazauran) (Cincinnati: Miami Printing, 1868), at 355; Eric Foner, *Reconstruction: America's Unfinished Revolution, 1863–1877* (New York: Harper & Row, 1988), 337–345; Arthur M. Schlesinger Jr., ed., *History of American Presidential Elections, 1789–1968* (New York: McGraw-Hill, 1971), 11:1247–1299.

10. *Congressional Globe*, 41st Congress, 3rd sess., part 2, 1252 (15 February 1871).

11. See ibid., part 3, app. 114 (15 February 1871). Francis Blair Jr., at that time a senator from Missouri, reminded his colleagues that "the Democratic party in the [1868] convention at New York [had] made this issue broadly and unmistakably: that the reconstruction acts of Congress were unconstitutional and void." He apparently thought this criticism, which implicated the Fourteenth Amendment itself, remained viable, at least

as of February 1871. See also Foner, *Reconstruction*, esp. 455 ("Democrats never accepted the legitimacy of the Enforcement Acts") and 590 (quoting a Southern newspaper for declaring in 1875 that the Fourteenth and Fifteenth Amendments "may stand forever; but we intend . . . to make them dead letters upon the statute-book").

12. For a reprint of debates surrounding passage of the Second and Third Enforcement Acts of 1871 (the latter known as the Ku Klux Klan Act), as excerpted from the *Congressional Globe*, see Alfred Avins, ed., *The Reconstruction Amendments' Debates: The Legislative History and Contemporary Debates in Congress on the 13th, 14th, and 15th Amendments* (Richmond: Virginia Commission on Constitutional Government, 1967), 480–574. Further confirming this shift in the terms of constitutional contestation, the 1872 Democratic platform conceded the Fourteenth Amendment's validity as such. See Donald Bruce Johnson, ed., *National Party Platforms* (Urbana: University of Chicago Press, 1978), 1:41–42. See also Bryan H. Wildenthal, "The Lost Compromise: Reassessing the Early Understanding in Court and Congress on Incorporation of the Bill of Rights in the Fourteenth Amendment," *Ohio State Law Journal* 61 (2000): 1051–1173, which emphasized that some leading Southern Democrats, as early as 1873–1874, supported a position that the Fourteenth Amendment made the Bill of Rights enforceable against the states, thus helping to account for the reasons at least some Democrats might have treated the Fourteenth Amendment as valid. But as I indicated in the previous note, even the settlements summarized herein were not complete. Some Democrats continued to contest the Fourteenth Amendment's validity and sought to gut its provisions of practical significance through restrictive interpretive practices. In addition, prominent critics of the Supreme Court's desegregation decisions in the middle of the twentieth century revitalized arguments that the Fourteenth Amendment itself was invalid. See, e.g., State Sovereignty Commission of Louisiana, "Unconstitutional Creation of the Fourteenth Amendment," *Georgia Bar Journal* 23 (1960): 147–239. More generally, much of the scholarly analysis of the Fourteenth Amendment's origins seems to have been precipitated by the Court's decisions in *Brown v. Board of Education*, 437 U.S.483 (1954), 349 U.S. 294 (1954), and related controversies.

13. The willingness of the Fourteenth Amendment's opponents to accept its validity is comparable in a number of respects to the willingness of the Anti-Federalists' to accept the validity of the original Constitution. For selected Anti-Federalist writings after ratification, see, e.g., David Siemers, *The Antifederalists: Men of Great Faith and Forbearance* (Lanham, Md.: Rowman & Littlefield, 2003), chap. 7. See also Mark A. Graber, "Settling the West: The Annexation of Texas, the Louisiana Purchase, and *Bush v. Gore*," in *The Louisiana Purchase and American Expansionism, 1803–1898*, ed. Sanford Levinson and Bartholomew Sparrow (Lanham, Md.: Rowman & Littlefield, 2005), for a complementary analysis of the dynamics of constitutional settlement involving Texas statehood.

14. See generally Robert J. Kaczorowski, *The Politics of Judicial Interpretation: The Federal Courts, the Department of Justice and Civil Rights, 1866–1876* (New York: Oceana, 1985); William E. Nelson, *The Fourteenth Amendment: From Political Principle to Judicial*

Doctrine (Cambridge: Harvard University Press, 1988), 151–155. On earlier stages of litigation in *Slaughter-House*, see Ronald M. Labbé and Jonathan Lurie, *The Slaughter-house Cases: Regulation, Reconstruction, and the Fourteenth Amendment* (Lawrence: University Press of Kansas, 2003).

15. The sequencing was significant across a number of fronts. First, it was easier to defend interpretive positions in this case, which had even more controversial implications in other cases, than it would have been to defend such positions in the first instance in such other (more controversial) cases. In addition, after the justices treated the Fourteenth Amendment as valid, it became more difficult, both theoretically and practically, to then deny its validity. Even when judicial doctrine has not been totally confining, it has not let left the normative terrain unaffected.

16. *Slaughter-House Cases*, 83 U.S., at 67. On the significance of the issues of public health raised by the case, see Wendy E. Parmet, "From *Slaughter-House* to *Lochner*: The Rise and Fall of the Constitutionalization of Public Health," *American Journal of Legal History* 40 (1996): 476–505; Michael A. Ross, "Justice Miller's Reconstruction: The Slaughter-House Cases, Health Codes, and Civil Rights in New Orleans, 1861 1873," *Journal of Southern History* 64 (1998): 649–676.

17. See I I. L. A. Hart, *The Concept of Law* (Oxford: Oxford University Press, 1961).

18. Although this essay is distinctive insofar as it explicitly develops a multidimensional model of constitutional authority and a corresponding model of pluralistic meaning and links them to principles of popular sovereignty, it has affinities to a number of works across several dimensions. For example, Robert G. McCloskey has explicitly relied on multiple criteria of constitutional authority to assess particular interpretive precedents. McCloskey, "Principles, Power, and Values," in *The Modern Supreme Court* (Cambridge: Harvard University Press, 1972), 290–321. The approach developed here also has affinities to that developed by Mark E. Brandon, "The 'Original' Thirteenth Amendment and the Limits to Formal Constitutional Change," in *Responding to Imperfection: The Theory and Practice of Constitutional Amendment*, ed. Sanford Levinson (Princeton, N.J.: Princeton University Press, 1999), chap. 10 (describes constitutional authority as operating across two axes, or dimensions—"horizontal" and "vertical"). In addition, Philip Bobbitt and William F. Harris II, by identifying various modes of constitutional argument, have implied that these forms of argument are authoritative. Bobbitt, *Constitutional Fate: Theory of the Constitution* (New York: Oxford University Press, 1982); Harris, *The Interpretable Constitution* (Baltimore, Md.: Johns Hopkins University Press, 1993). Similarly, Robert Post, "Theories of Constitutional Interpretation," in *Law and the Order of Culture*, ed. Robert Post (Berkeley: University of California Press, 1991), 13–41, describes three models of constitutional authority that have supported competing theories of constitutional interpretation. This chapter, as with several of the works cited in this note, emphasizes ways that problems of constitutional authority have been significant in ways that have extended beyond their relevance to defending particular interpretive positions.

19. To avoid possible misunderstanding, it bears emphasis here that this essay does not treat constructive authority as the sole mode of constitutional construction, or even

as a privileged mode. A variety of models of constitutional authority, including but not limited to that described here as a form of constructive authority, can support constitutional (re)construction.

20. Among recent works examining historical understandings of principles of popular sovereignty and exploring their normative and practical implications, especially in relation to constitutional amending, are: Bruce Ackerman, *We the People 1: Foundations* (Cambridge, Mass.: Harvard University Press, 1991), and *We the People 2: Transformations* (Cambridge, Mass.: Harvard University Press, 1998); Akhil Reed Amar, "The Consent of the Governed: Constitutional Amendment Outside Article V," *Columbia Law Review* 94 (1994): 457–508; Christopher L. Eisgruber, *Constitutional Self-Government* (Cambridge: Harvard University Press, 2001); Harris, *Interpretable Constitution*; Larry Kramer, *The People Themselves: Popular Constitutionalism and Judicial Review* (New York: Oxford University Press, 2004); Frank I. Michelman, "Law's Republic," *Yale Law Journal* 97 (1988): 1493–1537; Wayne D. Moore, *Constitutional Rights and Powers of the People* (Princeton, N.J.: Princeton University Press, 1996); Lawrence Gene Sager, *Justice in Plain Clothes: A Theory of American Constitutional Practice* (New Haven, Conn.: Yale University Press, 2004); Keith E. Whittington, *Constitutional Construction: Divided Powers and Constitutional Meaning* (Cambridge: Harvard University Press, 1998); Keith E. Whittington, *Constitutional Interpretation: Textual Meaning, Original Intent and Judicial Review* (Lawrence: University Press of Kansas, 1999).

21. *Slaughter-House*, 83 U.S., at 67, 71.

22. Ibid., at 68.

23. Ibid., at 70–71.

24. Ackerman, *We the People 2: Transformations*, 246. Ackerman has claimed, moreover, that Justice Miller was "hostile" to establishing the Fourteenth Amendment's legal pedigree on the basis of Article V and that his opinion is "unconcern[ed] with formalities" more generally (245). But the passages cited in the text of this chapter indicate that the majority opinion, on the contrary, was very much concerned about the Fourteenth Amendment's authority and issues of formality.

25. Stated differently: Justice Miller acknowledged some of the factual predicates to such criticism of the Fourteenth Amendment as procedurally invalid while treating them as insufficient to defeat claims of validity based on formal satisfaction of the criteria of Article V.

26. See generally Howard Gillman, "How Political Parties Can Use the Courts to Advance Their Agendas: Federal Courts in the United States, 1875–1891," *American Political Science Review* 96 (2002): 511–524; Mark A. Graber, "The Non-Majoritarian Difficulty: Legislative Deference to the Judiciary," *Studies in American Political Development* 7 (1993): 35–73; Ran Hirschl, *Towards Juristocracy: The Origins and Consequences of the New Constitutionalism* (Cambridge: Harvard University Press, 2004). The amendment's effects on configurations of political power has been complicated, of course, by the fact that Section 5 of the amendment has delegated primary enforcement to Congress, not the Court, as well as by controversy over the character and scope of the Four-

teenth Amendment's limitations on the states. On the former issue, see, e.g., Robert C. Post and Reva Siegel, "Protecting the Constitution from the People: Juriscentric Restrictions on Section Five Power," *Indiana Law Journal* 78 (2003): 1–45; Rebecca E. Zietlow, "Juriscentrism and the Original Meaning of Section Five," *Temple Political and Civil Rights Law Review* 13 (2004): 485–513.

27. The Republicans in the majority were Justices Davis, Hunt, Miller, and Strong; joined by the Democrat Clifford. The dissenting Republicans were Chief Justice Chase and Justices Bradley and Swayne, joined by the Democrat Field. Lincoln had nominated Chase, Davis, Field, Miller, and Swayne; Grant had nominated Bradley, Hunt, and Strong. For general information on these justices, see Richard L. Aynes, "Constricting the Law of Freedom: Justice Miller, the Fourteenth Amendment, and the Slaughter-House Cases," *Chicago-Kent Law Review* 70 (1994): 627–688; Labbé and Lurie, *Slaughterhouse Cases*, chap. 7.

28. *Slaughter-House*, 83 U.S., at 89, 96 (Field, J., dissenting). Chief Justice Salmon Chase joined Justice Field's dissent, as did Justices Joseph P. Bradley and Noah H. Swayne. The latter, but not the chief justice, also wrote separate dissents.

29. Ibid., at 122 (Bradley, J., dissenting).

30. Ibid., at 129 (Swayne, J., dissenting).

31. See Ackerman, *We the People 2: Transformations*.

32. See Bruce A. Ackerman, "The Storrs Lectures: Discovering the Constitution," *Yale Law Journal* 93 (1984): 1013–1072, esp. 1068–1069, 1056; Ackerman, "Constitutional Politics/Constitutional Law," *Yale Law Journal* 99 (1989): 453–547, esp. 504–507.

33. Ackerman, *We the People 2: Transformations*, 187–188.

34. See Ackerman, "Constitutional Politics/Constitutional Law," 506–509; Ackerman (1991), esp. 44–49.

35. Ackerman, "Constitutional Politics/Constitutional Law," 507 (emphasis in original).

36. Ackerman, *We the People 2: Transformations*, 20, 211, 234–238.

37. See ibid., 238–249.

38. Ibid., 237 (brackets in original).

39. Ibid., 245 (emphasis in original).

40. These references are on the same page of the *U.S. Reports:* 83 U.S., at 67.

41. See *Slaughter-House*, 83 U.S., at 68.

42. See esp. 83 U.S., at 92, 93, 97 (Field, J., dissenting). See also Whittington, *Constitutional Construction*, for analysis of the significance of (a distinctive model of) constitutional "construction" by legislative and executive officials. More generally, on the significance of constitutional interpretation and/or construction by nonjudicial actors (including the people at large along with legislative and executive officials, at the national and state levels), see, e.g., Louis Fisher, *Constitutional Dialogues: Interpretation as Political Process* (Princeton, N.J.: Princeton University Press, 1988); James E. Fleming, "The Constitution Outside the Courts," *Cornell Law Review* 86 (2000): 215; Barry Friedman, "Dialogue and Judicial Review," *Michigan Law Review* 91 (1993): 577;

Stephen M. Griffin, *American Constitutionalism: From Theory to Politics* (Princeton, N.J.: Princeton University Press, 1996); Ken I. Kersch, *Constructing Civil Liberties: Discontinuities in Development of American Constitutional Law* (Cambridge: Cambridge University Press, 2004); Kramer, *People Themselves*; Sanford Levinson, *Constitutional Faith* (Princeton, N.J.: Princeton University Press, 1988); Moore, *Constitutional Rights and Powers*; Walter F. Murphy, "Who Shall Interpret the Constitution?," *Review of Politics* 48 (1986): 401–423; Sager, *Justice in Plain Clothes*; Cass R. Sunstein, *The Partial Constitution* (Cambridge: Harvard University Press, 1993); Mark V. Tushnet, *Taking the Constitution Away from the Courts* (Princeton, N.J.: Princeton University Press, 1999).

43. See 83 U.S., at 67.

44. Justice Miller's *Slaughter-House* opinion, along with the dissenting opinions, thus call into question Keith Whittington's distinction between constitutional "interpretation" (a proper activity for judges) and "construction" of constitutional norms by other governmental officials. See Whittington, *Constitutional Construction* and *Constitutional Interpretation*. Among other things, the opinions in *Slaughter-House* support a view that judges, not only legislative and executive officials, have engaged in versions of what Whittington has defined as both constitutional "interpretation" and "construction," and that these activities have run together in practice rather than being mutually exclusive. Stated differently, it makes sense to regard constitutional "interpretation" as a form of constitutional "construction," and perhaps vice versa.

45. *Slaughter-House*, 83 U.S., at 66, 77–78, 82.

46. See Murphy, "*Slaughter-House*, Civil Rights."

47. But Murphy has criticized rather than endorsed the majority's opinion on this score. In his view, there was no need for the justices effectively to gut the meaning of the Fourteenth Amendment's central guarantees (as he claims they did) to avoid treating it as substantively valid. Thus Murphy has defended a more expansive conception of rights of national citizenship, along with corresponding shifts in power from institutions of state to national governance, as still within the scope of legitimate constitutional "amending." Accordingly, he endorsed the dissenters' positions, summarized in the text below, on the Fourteenth Amendment's meaning and significance. Ibid.

48. See *Slaughter-House*, 83 U.S., at 93, 96, 109 (Field, J., dissenting).

49. Ibid., at 118–119, 122–124 (Bradley, J., dissenting).

50. Ibid., at 125–126, 128–129 (Swayne, J., dissenting).

51. See John E. Finn, *Constitutions in Crisis: Political Violence and the Rule of Law* (New York: Oxford University Press, 1991), esp. 21–35.

52. See *Slaughter-House*, 83 U.S., at 78, 82.

53. See ibid., at 109–111 (Field, J., dissenting). See generally Alpheus T. Mason, *Free Government in the Making: Readings in American Political Thought* (New York: Oxford University Press, 1965).

54. 83 U.S., at 114 (Bradley, J., dissenting).

55. See 83 U.S., at 68–72, 76.

56. Ibid., at 86, 111 (Field, J., dissenting).

57. Ibid., at 119 (Bradley, J., dissenting).

58. Ibid., at 129 (Swayne, J., dissenting).

59. Some versions of the theory of constructive constitutional authority as outlined here draw on and have affinities to the notion of pure procedural justice as developed by John Rawls in A *Theory of Justice* (Cambridge: Harvard University Press, 1971). But other versions (also including some explored here) are rooted more firmly in actual political practices and proceed more directly from substantive understandings of principles of justice and assumptions of popular sovereignty.

60. Such a position might find support based on analysis of meaning and authority across the six dimensions being discussed here. For a preliminary treatment of this issue, without explicit reliance on those six criteria, see Moore, *Constitutional Rights and Powers*, chap. 2.

61. See Michael Perman, *Reunion without Compromise: The South and Reconstruction, 1865–1868* (Cambridge: Cambridge University Press, 1973), esp. 304–347.

62. For analysis of the history and significance of (non)voting and other forms of (non)participation by women, particularly in the nineteenth century, see, e.g., Reva B. Siegel, "She the People: The Nineteenth Amendment, Sex Equality, Federalism, and the Family," *Harvard Law Review* 115 (2002): 947–1046; Sandra F. VanBurkleo, *"Belonging to the World": Women's Rights and American Constitutional Culture* (New York: Oxford University Press, 2001); VanBurkleo, " 'Words as Hard as Cannon-Balls': Women's Rights Agitation and Liberty of Speech in Nineteenth Century America," in *Constitutionalism and American Culture: Writing the New Constitutional History*, ed. Sandra F. VanBurkleo, Kermit L. Hall, and Robert J. Kaczorowski (Lawrence: University Press of Kansas, 2002). Complicating analysis of the constructive authority of the Fourteenth Amendment and of the authority of interpretations of that amendment, it is apparent that efforts to enhance such authority across one dimension competed with efforts to maintain or enhance it across others. For example, it would have been difficult to secure the approvals required by Article V if the Fourteenth Amendment had explicitly guaranteed sexual equality. More generally, the weakening or destruction of some constitutional meanings typically accompanies the construction or reinforcement of others. See generally Robert M. Cover, "Forward: *Nomos* and Narrative," *Harvard Law Review* 97 (1983): 4–68.

63. On the idea of judges' "predicting progress," see generally Alexander M. Bickel, *The Least Dangerous Branch: The Supreme Court at the Bar of Politics*, 2nd ed. (New Haven, Conn.: Yale University Press, 1996).

64. See *Slaughter-House*, 83 U.S., at 78, 81. Eventually, in cases such as *Craig v. Boren*, 429 U.S. 190 (1976) and *United States v. Virginia*, 518 U.S. 515 (1996), the Court would also depart from the justices' dismissive treatment of classifications based on sex. The lessons from cases like these bridge issues of inclusion as considered above with those involving expansion of temporal horizons as considered here.

65. *Slaughter-House*, 83 U.S., at 111 (Field, J., dissenting).

66. Ibid., at 112, 116, 119 (Bradley, J., dissenting).

67. Ibid., at 130–131 (Swayne, J., dissenting).

68. See Howard Gillman, *The Constitution Besieged: The Rise and Demise of Lochner Era Police Powers Jurisprudence* (Durham: Duke University Press, 1993).

69. For a complementary treatment of issues of "vertical" and "horizontal" coherence, see Brandon, " 'Original' Thirteenth Amendment."

70. For overviews of reactions to the Court's decision in *Slaughter-House*, along with references to relevant primary sources, see Aynes, "Constricting the Law," 678–686; Charles Warren, *The Supreme Court in United States History* (Boston: Little, Brown, 1926), vol. 2, esp. chap. 32.

71. The quoted passage is from *Slaughter-House*, 83 U.S., at 71. See the text above, especially that accompanying notes 45–47, for quotations and summaries of other passages from Justice Miller's majority opinion suggesting either a narrow reading of the Fourteenth Amendment's guarantees and/or limited federal authority to enforce them.

72. See generally Foner, *Reconstruction*, and Nelson, *Fourteenth Amendment* (documenting support for the proposed Fourteenth Amendment among "radicals"). See also Michael Les Benedict, *A Compromise of Principle: Congressional Republicans and Reconstruction, 1863–1869* (New York: W. W. Norton, 1974) (emphasized the Fourteenth Amendment's "conservative" character while also documenting dissatisfaction with the amendment among leading "radicals").

Chapter 7

The Civil Rights Cases *and the* Lost Language *of* State Neglect

Pamela Brandwein

Consider a deceptively simple question: Why did the Supreme Court strike down the public accommodation provisions of the Civil Rights Act of 1875 in the *Civil Rights Cases?*[1] The conventional answer is that the Court invalidated these provisions because they regulated private action, and private action was beyond the reach of the Fourteenth Amendment. This answer is so long-standing and routine among academics that we may call it orthodox.[2] Just as familiar are the standard accounts of constitutional history[3] and political development[4] during the 1870s and 1880s. These accounts portray Court decisions invalidating Reconstruction legislation as a reflection of the Republicans' political retreat from Reconstruction and their turn to big business. We have, then, familiar accounts of the legal significance of the *Civil Rights Cases* as well its relationship to politics and history.

The goal of this chapter is to embark on a legal and historical rethinking of the *Civil Rights Cases.* I argue that the Court's reasons for striking down the public accommodation provisions have been misunderstood, and that the decision permits broader federal protections for civil rights than has been recognized. Twentieth-century legal actors have understood this canonical decision anachronistically, reading Justice Joseph P. Bradley's majority opinion through the lens of a rights paradigm established in the late 1930s. As a result, they have missed an old nineteenth-century legal language I call "state neglect," which was used by the Waite Court.

In order to get at the proper historical meaning of Bradley's pivotal opinion, we must recover this old institutional language. This legal idiom was associated with nineteenth-century conceptions of rights and rights protections. It was also associated with the idea that states had an affirmative duty to administer laws protecting physical security and property (but not access to public accommodations) equally on the basis of race. This duty, notably, created correlative rights. If a state punished physical violence against whites but was derelict in its duty to punish physical violence against blacks, the state failed in its duty to equally administer the law. The state's failure was a rights violation ("state action") within the meaning of the Fourteenth Amendment and Congress had the power to provide a remedy under Section 5 of that Amendment:[5] the federal prosecution of individuals who remained unpunished. This made the rights denial "innocuous."

The recovery of the language of state neglect means we must rewrite the story of constitutional development during the Waite era (1874–1888). Waite Court justices were not racial villains who had lost interest in Reconstruction, as conventional accounts of constitutional development suggest. Neither, however, did they endorse the vision of the more radical Republicans. This is clear in Justice Bradley's refusal to rate access to public accommodations as a fundamental right. State neglect concepts protected only those rights that a Republican consensus regarded as fundamental. These included rights to property, contract, and physical security, which enacted the "free labor" vision of the party. State neglect concepts, then, protected only the core body of rights that a Republican consensus deemed essential for blacks to become "free laborers" on terms equal with whites. This means that Waite Court justices are properly understood as racial moderates who negotiated a middle course—a politically centrist view of congressional power under Section 5—even as the population lost interest in the struggles of Southern blacks.

The Centrism of State Neglect

State neglect principles were politically centrist in that they rejected the preferences of both Democrats and the more radical Republicans. The Democrats rejected federal regulation of all private action under all circumstances. The radicals, for their part, sought federal regulation of a broad range of rights, including access to public accommodations, and they approved federal regulation regardless of whether states neglected their duty. In the *Civil Rights Cases* and other decisions, Waite Court justices charted a middle path, designing new legal rules they likely hoped would be politically acceptable and stabilizing. Indeed, institutional structure and stability could not be taken for granted.

This middle path, as I have suggested, permitted federal regulations of private individuals under Section 5, but only under certain conditions. First, only private wrongs against "civil rights" could be reached. (This is obviously a crucial category and it must be understood with a nineteenth-century concept, a "hierarchy of rights." I will return to this point shortly.) Second, these private wrongs had to be motivated "on account of" the race of the victim. Third, state failure to redress these wrongs had to be a "predicate" for federal intervention. All three conditions had to be met in order for federal prosecution of private individuals to be valid under Section 5. (My use of quotations around "civil rights," "on account of," and "predicate" indicates that these were the Court's words.)

A key point here is that state neglect concepts remained consistent with the *Slaughter-House Cases*,[6] and with state-centered federalism, which remained dominant after the war.[7] Today, we imagine there was only one version of state-centered federalism—that is, the Democrats' version. We think that if the Court rejected a nation-centered federalism (which it did in the *Slaughter-House Cases*), the Court endorsed the Democratic understanding of state-centered federalism.

There were, however, multiple versions of state-centered federalism, and state neglect concepts were associated with a moderate version. According to this moderate version, states retained primary control of local crime. Congress could not pass "municipal codes" (again, the Court's words), which took original control of wrongdoing. If, however, states defaulted in their duty to redress wrongs against "civil rights" equally on the basis of race, the federal government had the power to step in, perform that duty, and render that rights violation "innocuous."

A "Lost" Language

The language of state neglect is lost to the legal community. What does this mean? After all, state neglect concepts remain in the plain sight of anybody reading the *Civil Rights Cases*. There is also no recently discovered text that somehow unlocks the meaning of Bradley's opinion. State neglect concepts are "lost," then, in the sense that they are unrecognizable. This is because the old legal paradigm of the 1870s and 1880s has disappeared. We have lost the language of state neglect, in other words, because we have lost this old legal paradigm. The early decades of the twentieth century saw the establishment of a new rights paradigm: a new way of thinking about rights and rights protections. Today, we think and work within this paradigm. This paradigm— an institutional product—has mediated readings of the *Civil Rights Cases*. This mediation, however, has gone unnoticed. In order to see that the Waite Court permitted some Section 5 regulations of private individuals, we must recover the legal idiom of Waite Court justices.

In order to do this, we need methods developed by historians of political discourse, such as Quentin Skinner and J. G. A. Pocock.[8] Skinner and Pocock have developed techniques for studying language in institutional settings.[9] Languages, as they explain, are neither ideologies nor arguments. Rather, they are vocabularies, ideas, and concepts. These vocabularies develop over time, and they are shaped by institutionally defined interpretive communities. Institutional idioms, historically constructed and reconstructed over time, thus help define the institutional environment. The language of state neglect is an institutional language in the sense described by Skinner and Pocock.

The methodology they lay out requires us to trace the use of language. This methodological emphasis flows from the basic recognition that texts belonging to the history of political discourse were public acts of communication and argumentation. Usage had to be conventional for communication to take place. The challenge for historians of political discourse is the same challenge here: "to learn to read and recognize the diverse idioms of political discourse as they were available in the culture and at the time" being studied.[10] The historian must be able to identify what institutional actors can do with language,[11] for the historical job is not to enter the heads of long-dead thinkers. The goal "is simply to use the ordinary techniques of historical enquiry to grasp their concepts, to follow their distinctions, to appreciate their beliefs and, so far as possible, see things their way."[12] Historical understanding, as Skinner explains, "is a product of learning to follow . . . different styles of reasoning."[13]

Historical investigations of institutional languages are essential for the study of constitutional development. An understanding of legal idioms is a prerequisite not only for understanding Court doctrines within a particular historical period, but also for tracking long-term processes of doctrinal and legal change. Thus, it is surprising that New Historical Institutionalism scholars have not widely seized upon the methods of Skinner and Pocock.

The Current Stakes

High constitutional stakes attach to the recovery of state neglect concepts because in recent years, the Rehnquist Court has returned the *Civil Rights Cases* to legal prominence. In striking down a variety of civil rights laws as beyond Congress's power under Section 5 of the Fourteenth Amendment, the Rehnquist majority relied on this canonical case as a central source of authority.[14] That Court also treated the idea of "state sovereign immunity" with robustness,[15] trading silently on the historical view that Waite Court endorsed a conservative (as opposed to moderate) state-centered federalism.

The recovery of a proper historical reading of the *Civil Rights Cases* severely compromises the Rehnquist Court's decision to rely on the *Civil Rights Cases* to justify their Section 5 rulings. With the recovery of state neglect principles, a powerful precedent-based critique of these federalism and separation-of-powers cases becomes available.

The recovery of state neglect concepts, it should be noted, leaves a number of crucial questions unanswered. Indeed, a critique of these Rehnquist Court cases would require confrontation with these questions. How was state neglect to be established? How were actions "on account of race" to be established? Must "animus" be proven? Further, were conceptions of state "duty" evolving, and how might new duties become established? Perhaps most fundamentally, if the language of state neglect was associated with a nineteenth-century legal framework that has disappeared, can we simply pick it up again? The recovery of state neglect concepts might be interesting as a matter of history, but their applicability to contemporary contexts cannot be assumed. These are all open questions, which a historically proper reading of the *Civil Rights Cases* cannot answer.

Organization of the Chapter

This chapter is divided into three sections. First, I focus on the text of the *Civil Rights Cases*. I pay particular attention to a long-neglected portion: Justice Bradley's express approval for the Civil Rights Act of 1866. It is in this portion of the opinion that Bradley uses the language of state neglect. I then show that state neglect concepts were historically located. I trace the vocabulary of state neglect in the Reconstruction Congresses, the federal circuit courts between 1867 and 1871, and counsel briefs on behalf of William Cruikshank. I also take a detailed look at the text of *United States v. Cruikshank*, an early state-action decision, conventionally understood as hostile to Reconstruction. I challenge this conventional understanding of *Cruikshank*, revealing its moderate character. I next raise the problem of periodizing constitutional development in the late nineteenth century, arguing that the conventional account of constitutional development during this time flattens significant differences between the Waite and the Fuller eras. As a result, our understanding of Waite Court doctrine is obstructed.

Throughout the chapter, my goal is to contrast what we think we know about Waite Court decisions with what is actually there. The additional goal of examining the institutional developments that gave rise to distorted read-ings of the *Civil Rights Cases* must await another day. This chapter is long enough, and telling this part of the story would at least double its length.

Justice Bradley and the Civil Rights Act of 1866

The *Civil Rights Cases* is a canonical decision in American constitutional law for establishing the doctrine of "state action." According to this doc-trine, the Fourteenth Amendment protects individuals against govern-mental action but not against the action of private persons, no matter how injurious or wrongful.[16] A corollary, presumed to follow logically, is that Congress may not regulate private individuals under its Section 5 power to enforce the Fourteenth Amendment. The purpose of barring Congress from reaching private persons is dual: to preserve a conception of federal-ism, whereby states retain police power, and to preserve a realm of private freedom.[17]

A close historical reading of Justice Bradley's approval of the Civil Rights Act of 1866[18] gives us insight on the Waite Court's conception of state action. It also drives a wedge between state action doctrine and its presumed corollary. In other words, a close historical reading of the Court's approval for the Act of 1866 shows that the Court in fact approved certain Section 5 regulation of private individuals. The conceptions of state action and Section 5 power that appear in conventional scholarship on Recon-struction are narrower than the historical conceptions that appear in the *Civil Rights Cases*. To highlight this difference, an example might be help-ful. According to historical conceptions, if a state punishes physical vio-lence against whites but fails to punish private Klan violence against blacks, this failure is state action within the meaning of the Fourteenth Amend-ment and Congress has the power to provide a remedy: prosecution of Klansmen who escaped justice. In contrast, according to conventional scholarly conceptions of state action and Section 5 power, state failure to punish Klan lynching is not state action and Congress cannot authorize prosecution of Klansmen under Section 5. State neglect concepts thus posit a broader definition of state action and broader federal power to protect civil rights.

Let us now move to Justice Bradley's text in order to see his use of state neglect concepts. Bradley used his approval of the Civil Rights Act of 1866 to draw a distinction between valid ("corrective") and invalid ("general") legislation under Section 5. Congress, he explained, could provide corrective legislation that supplied "modes of relief . . . and redress" against "state action of every kind"[19] that violated the Fourteenth Amendment. Congress had the power "to adopt appropriate legislation for correcting the effects of . . . prohibited State laws and State acts, and thus to render them effectually null, void, and innocuous." Congress was not, however, authorized to pass a "code of municipal law for the regulation of private rights."[20] This was general legislation, prohibited under Section 5.

According to the traditional interpretation of the general/corrective distinction, all federal regulations of private persons fall immediately into the category of general legislation/municipal law. There is no possibility that some federal regulations are invalid codes of municipal law while others are valid modes of redress that correct the effects of state action, rendering that state action innocuous.

Such a possibility, in fact, is supported by Bradley's endorsement of the Civil Rights Act of 1866. Bradley called the act "clearly corrective in its character."[21] It was corrective because its regulations of private individuals were limited. Only those individuals, whose wrongs against "civil rights" had the "color of law . . . or custom" came within federal reach. "Under color of law . . . or custom" is an important legal phrase, which remains on the books in civil rights statutes that survived Reconstruction.[22] The concept "under color of law . . . or custom" was part of the language of state neglect, and its historical meaning has been lost as well.

The Civil Rights Act of 1866, it should be noted, was originally passed to enforce the Thirteenth Amendment.[23] It was also reenacted in the Enforcement Act of 1870, which was passed under the Fourteenth and Fifteenth Amendments.[24] In the *Civil Rights Cases*, the Court treated the Act of 1866 as valid under the Fourteenth Amendment. This is centrally important, because it means that the Court's approval of the Act of 1866 was part of its Section 5 jurisprudence.

What, then, made the Act of 1866 "clearly corrective" in nature? What did it mean when individual wrongs had the "color of law . . . or custom"? We must have answers to these questions in order to understand the Waite Court's distinction between corrective and general legislation. Once we have a working sense of why the Court viewed the Act of 1866 as constitutional, we can begin to get a fix on why the Court might have struck down the public accommodation provisions of the Act of 1875.

Bradley began his discussion of the Act of 1866 by emphasizing that it was corrective because it was "intended to counteract and furnish redress against State laws and proceedings, and customs having the force of law, which sanction the wrongful acts specified."[25] The penalty applied "only to those who should subject parties to a deprivation of their rights under color of any statute, ordinance, custom, etc., of any State or Territory."[26] Bradley then cited with approval sections 1977, 1978, 1979, and 5510 of the Revised Statutes, which derived from sections 1 and 2 of the Civil Rights Act of 1866. Explaining his approval, he stated,

> In this connection it is proper to state that civil rights, such as are guaranteed by the Constitution against State aggression, cannot be impaired by the wrongful acts of individuals, unsupported by State authority in the shape of laws, customs, or judicial or executive proceedings. The wrongful act of an individual, unsupported by any such authority, is simply a private wrong, or a crime of that individual; an invasion of the rights of the injured party, it is true, whether they affect his person, his property, or his reputation; but if not sanctioned in some way by the State, or not done under State authority, [the] rights [of the injured party] remain in full force, and may presumably be vindicated by resort to the laws of the State for redress. An individual cannot deprive a man of his right to vote, to hold property, to buy and sell, to sue in the courts, or to be a witness or a juror; he may, by force or fraud, interfere with the enjoyment of the right in a particular case; he may commit an assault against the person, or commit murder, or use ruffian violence at the polls, or slander the good name of a fellow citizen; but, unless protected in these wrongful acts by some shield of State law or State authority, he cannot destroy or injure the right; he will only render himself amenable to satisfaction or punishment; and amenable therefore to the laws of the State where the wrongful acts are committed.[27]

How should we understand this?[28] First, we must identify which individual wrongs Bradley identified as subject to federal regulation: assault, murder, and interferences in property, contract, and jury service.[29] These were "civil rights." This term is certainly familiar today, and it has an all-encompassing coverage. The old meaning of this term, however, was far narrower.

A nineteenth-century concept—a hierarchy of rights—is crucial to an understanding of this old meaning. The hierarchy-of-rights concept was part of an old rights regime, and it can be imagined as a pyramid.[30] At the base of this pyramid were "civil rights." There was consensus among Republicans that a core body of rights made up this category: the right to property, contract, sue, testify in court, be subject to the same criminal penalties as others, and protection from physical violence. These were the rights that moderate Republicans deemed necessary for blacks to compete as "free laborers" on an equal basis with whites.[31] These rights were listed in the Civil Rights Act of 1866; and as Eric Foner has explained, the Act of 1866 was a natural extension of "free labor" ideology of the Republican party.

Significantly, there was disagreement among Republicans about the status of public accommodation rights. Whereas radical Republicans such as Charles Sumner regarded public accommodation rights as civil rights, other Republicans regarded them as "social rights." Social rights were at the tip of the pyramid and considered nonbasic. The central point here is that access to public accommodations was not part of the group of rights that Republicans, by consensus, regarded as fundamental.

Note, then, that Bradley explicitly mentioned only those rights that enjoyed consensus as civil rights. In doing this, he was communicating to his audience a federal commitment to those rights. By leaving out those rights associated with the "social rights" category, namely public accommodation rights, marriage rights, and education rights, Bradley was communicating a lower commitment to these rights. Leaving off the list those rights that many deemed "social" was as important as including those that enjoyed consensus as fundamental. We must know the hierarchy of rights vocabulary, in short, in order to understand what Bradley was doing in this passage.

Now, we must also identify the circumstances under which federal regulation of individual wrongs became permissible. Some form of state "support" or "sanction"[32] had to be given to these wrongs. State authorities had to "protect" these wrongs "by some shield." The wrong had to "rest upon" some state authority "for its excuse and perpetration."[33] In what ways might state authorities shield, protect, or sanction, say, assault or murder on account of race? The practice of refusing to punish would certainly protect or shield such wrongs. Indeed, recall Bradley's statement: "unless protected in these wrongful acts by some shield of State law or State authority, [an individual] cannot destroy or injure the right; he will only render himself amenable to satisfaction or punishment." Here, Bradley indicates that individuals cannot deprive other individuals of rights. Only a state can deny rights, and states can do this by protecting, shielding, or excusing wrongful acts from due punishment.[34] This is the core of the state neglect concept. The active participation of officials in wrongdoing might also support or protect such wrongdoing. However, Bradley's language does not require the active participation of state agents in wrongdoing in order for that wrongdoing to have the "color of law . . . or custom."

Bradley's use of the term *individual* is critical here. Bradley's use of this word means there is no rule requiring the participation of state agents in order for wrongs to have the "color of law . . . or custom." Hundreds of federal court opinions before and after the *Civil Rights Cases* used a distinction between "individuals" and "officers,"[35] and there is overwhelming intertextual agreement on usage. Although "officials" might sometimes fall into the category of "individuals," the category of "individuals" cannot be limited to "officials." According to modern case law, the wrongs of private individuals can only qualify as action "under color of . . . law or custom" if state officials jointly participate.[36] There must be some "positive" action by state agents, in relation to this wrongdoing. This rule, however, cannot be squared with the excerpts above, for it requires that Bradley's category of "individuals" refer only to state agents. It is untenable however to interpret the word *individuals* in this way.

Three years before the *Civil Rights Cases*, another case, *Neal v. Delaware* (1880), explicitly used a conception of state action that included a state's failure to redress a race-based wrong against a civil right. In this little-studied but revealing jury case, the Court stated, "The refusal of the State court to redress the wrong by them [the jury officers] committed was a denial of a right secured to the prisoner by the Constitution. Speaking by Mr. Justice Strong, in *Ex parte Virginia*, we said, and now repeat, that 'a State acts by its legislative, its executive, or its judicial authorities.'"[37] To refuse to redress was to act. This conception of state action was consistent with Bradley's statement in the *Civil Rights Cases* that rights remained in "full force" until state authorities shielded or excused the crime in some way.

As Bradley explained, too, in approving the Act of 1866, Congress had the power to provide remedy for this form of rights denial. Section 5 legislation, however, had to be "predicated" on that rights denial:

> Hence, in all those cases where the Constitution seeks to protect the rights of the citizen against discriminative and unjust laws of the State by prohibiting such laws,[38] it is not individual offences, but abrogation and denial of rights, which [the Constitution] denounces, and for which it clothes the Congress with power to provide a remedy. This abrogation and denial of rights, for which the States alone were or could be responsible, was the great seminal and fundamental wrong which was intended to be remedied. And *the remedy to be provided must necessarily be predicated upon that wrong*. It must assume that in the cases provided for, the evil or wrong actually committed rests upon some State law *or State authority for its excuse and perpetration*.[39]

The absence of such a predicate was the problem with Section 5519 of the Ku Klux Klan Act of 1871, which the Court struck down the same year in *United States v. Harris*. This case involved private Klan violence unrelated to voting.[40] As Justice William B. Woods explained, the law under consideration was directed exclusively against the action of private persons, without reference to the laws of the State or their administration by her officers . . . When the State has been guilty of no violation of its provisions, when, on the contrary, the laws of the State, as enacted by its legislative, and construed by its judicial, *and administered by its executive departments*, recognize and protect the rights of all persons, the amendment imposes no duty and confers no power upon Congress.[41]

This rule was the same as that identified by Bradley in approving the Civil Rights Act of 1866, which was corrective in character because it limited federal penalties to individuals, whose race-based crimes against civil rights were shielded or protected from punishment in some way by state authorities. The act of shielding was a denial of equal rights because it made redress to the victim unequally unavailable; the victim was deprived of the equal benefit of the law. The federal government could provide a remedy by punishing the wrongdoer, but this punishment had to be predicated on state neglect. In sum, the Act of 1866 certainly invalidated the Black Codes, but it was not just discriminatory state laws or what we would call "positive" actions that triggered federal regulatory power.

To be sure, Bradley's approval of the Act of 1866 as model corrective legislation does not tell us anything directly about why the Civil Rights Act of 1875 was unconstitutional. Recall that access to public accommodations did not enjoy consensus as a fundamental "civil right" at the time. Bradley's opinion hinted that access to public accommodations was a social right, not a civil right, but he did not explicitly state this.[42] He implied it, however, in stating that blocked access to public accommodations was not a "badge of slavery"[43] and in making a hostile and gratuitous remark about the public accommodation claims of the plaintiffs.[44]

Bradley's ridicule for the public accommodation claim and his support for the Act of 1866 must both be placed in their proper historical context. The nineteenth-century hierarchy of rights concept helps delineate this context. Modern readers have failed to perceive hierarchy of rights language in Bradley's opinion, and this has led them to treat Bradley's ridicule as expressing an all-out hostility to enforcement legislation.[45] An anachronistic reading of Bradley's ridicule, then, impedes an understanding of the *Civil Rights Cases*. My point here is that Bradley could express disdain for public accommodation rights while remaining committed to "core" civil rights.

A handful of law professors have forwarded a state neglect interpretation of the *Civil Rights Cases*,[46] but they miss Bradley's hierarchy of rights language in another way. This makes their state neglect interpretation different from mine in a crucial respect. In overlooking the distinction between "civil rights" and "social rights" that was present in Bradley's opinion, they overstate the coverage of state neglect doctrine. They argue, in brief, that the *Civil Rights Cases* struck down the public accommodation provisions of the Civil Rights Act of 1875 because these regulations were not made contingent upon state failure to protect the right of access to public accommodations. Although this interpretation captures the general structure of state neglect doctrine (no federal regulation of private individuals until states fail in their duty to provide redress), it oversteps in counting public accommodation rights as clearly within the coverage of the doctrine.[47]

What is clear from the *Civil Rights Cases* is that the Court's definition of corrective legislation permitted federal regulations of at least *some* private individuals. There was no across-the-board rule that Section 5 regulations of private individuals were automatically invalid. The public accommodation provisions could not have been struck down, then, for this reason. There must have been some other reason.[48]

We may return, at this point, to classic quotes from the *Civil Rights Cases*:

> The first section of the Fourteenth Amendment . . . is prohibitory in its character, and prohibitory upon the States. . . . That Amendment erects no shield against merely private conduct, however discriminatory or wrongful.[49]
>
> It is State action of a particular character that is prohibited. Individual invasion of individual rights is not the subject-matter of the amendment.[50]
>
> [The Fourteenth Amendment] does not authorize Congress to create a code of municipal law for the regulation of private rights; but to provide modes of redress against the operation of State laws, and the action of State officers, executive or judicial, when these are subversive of the fundamental rights specified in the amendment.[51]

These quotes are fully consistent with state neglect concepts, which may now be elaborated as follows:

States have the duty to provide equal benefit and protection of the laws.

Private interferences in core civil rights that have been motivated by the race of the victim are "merely private" crimes, *unless* state officers systematically fail, refuse, or neglect to punish that crime.

It is a Fourteenth Amendment violation for states to systematically fail or neglect to punish such interferences. Thus, if a person is subjected to private interference in core civil rights on account of their race, which the state neglects to redress, the constitutional wrong under the Fourteenth Amendment is not the private act of the individual. Rather, the rights violation is the state's failure to equally administer the law.

The Fourteenth Amendment gives Congress authority to insure that state
failure to fulfill its duty to provide equal protection shall not result in
the injury or destruction of core civil rights. Thus, when states neglect
this duty, Congress may step in and provide redress by prosecuting the
offenders. This is a mode of redress that renders the constitutional violation innocuous.

Congress may provide in advance for possible state default in providing equal
protection of core civil rights. But if it does so, such regulations of private
action must be made conditional on the state's failure or default. This
condition insures that Congress does not take over municipal functions.

Our inquiry does not end here, however. Were concepts of state neglect
established or widely recognized? That is, was it part of a legal discourse?
In order to answer this question, we must go outside the text of the *Civil
Rights Cases*. We cannot know from Bradley's opinion alone if concepts of
state neglect had a characteristic or unusual place in the intellectual and
legal climate, or what conventions may have governed their treatment.[52]
Confidence that state neglect concepts existed, furthermore, will increase
the more it can be shown that a large and diverse group of legal actors used
these concepts for a diversity of purposes.[53]

Prevailing Conventions of Usage

The state neglect concepts used by Justice Bradley in the *Civil Rights Cases*
were not idiosyncratic but historically located. This can be seen by tracing,
intertextually, the use of these concepts. In this section, I look briefly at the
development of the state neglect concept by moderate Republicans in the
Reconstruction Congresses. I then examine federal circuit court decisions
between 1867 and 1873. Finally, I focus on *United States v. Cruikshank*
(1876). My overall objective is to flesh out the language of state neglect
and show that Bradley's discussion of the Act of 1866 did not introduce any
inconsistency into Waite Court jurisprudence on Section 5.

State Neglect in the Reconstruction Congresses

We look first to the Reconstruction Congresses, where moderate Republicans developed state neglect concepts and generated critical commentaries
that regulated it. In this section, we can see how "external" politics informs
the study of Bradley's language, for a sequence of events led Republicans to

develop the idea that state neglect was a constitutional violation that needed correction.

Our point of departure is the Reconstruction Act of 1867, which put Republicans in charge of Southern legislatures. This forced ex-Confederates to adapt the form of their resistance to Reconstruction. No longer able to make laws, Southerners retained executive power to enforce the law. A new Southern pattern took shape: the rise of Klan violence that targeted not only blacks but also white Republicans[54] and the local and systematic nonenforcement of laws.[55]

For Republicans, the nonenforcement of laws against Klansmen conflicted with their idea of republican government. They consistently cited this nonenforcement as a violation of republicanism and as a constitutional problem.[56] Consider the statement of moderate Republican James A. Garfield (Ohio congressman and future president), made during debate over the Ku Klux Klan Act of 1871. Garfield used the idea of state neglect and developed a specific limitation of it:

> But the chief complaint is not that the laws of the State are unequal, but that even where the laws are just and equal on their face, yet, by a *systematic maladministration of them, or a neglect or refusal to enforce their provisions*, a portion of the people are denied equal protection under them. Whenever such a state of facts is clearly made out, I believe the last clause of the first section [of the Fourteenth Amendment] empowers Congress to step in and provide for doing justice to those persons who are thus denied equal protection. Now if the . . . pending bill can be so amended that it . . . shall employ no terms which assert the power of Congress to take jurisdiction of the subject *until such denial be clearly made*, and shall not in any way assume the original jurisdiction of the rights of private persons and of property within the state— with these conditions clearly expressed . . . I shall give it my hearty support.[57]

For Garfield and the Republicans, a state denied equal protection when it neglected and refused to enforce the law equally.[58] But Garfield also specified limits to this concept of state neglect. Congress could not take jurisdiction of private crime until state failure to remedy that crime was clearly established. This criticism is what Pocock calls a "second-order language," which commented on and regulated the use of the state neglect concept. Garfield put forward this criticism to distinguish himself from both the more radical Republicans, who argued that Congress could take original jurisdiction of private crime regardless of state behavior, and from the Democrats, who argued that Congress could never regulate private crime. This middle view provided the basic structure for the Waite Court's concept of state neglect.

Significantly, opponents of the Klan Act, such as Rep. Francis Blair of Missouri, used the vocabulary of state failure and neglect. This shows that the concept was commonly understood:

> The new principle asserted in the bill is that the Government may interfere to put down insurrection in a State without the application of the State authorities, when the State being unable to do so shall fail, neglect or refuse to apply for aid . . . It is alleged that great disorders exist in a section of our country, and that numerous crimes are committed with impunity by a secret organization which pervades that community.[59]

Blair, then, used the vocabulary of state neglect but rejected it as a constitutional concept. Congress could do nothing even if states failed or refused to apply for aid. And like all Democrats, Blair denied or downplayed the reality of Klan violence.[60] He used the vocabulary of state neglect ("crimes committed with impunity") to challenge Republican claims that this state of affairs existed. Blair, therefore, used the language of neglect for purposes very different than Garfield. This increases our confidence that the concept was indeed an established one.

Republicans who enacted the Enforcement Act of 1870 and the Ku Klux Klan Act of 1871 held firm control of Congress and sought to highlight Southern abuses. The Reconstruction Congresses had become a battleground for constructing the meaning of the Civil War[61] and the definition of slavery's destruction.[62] Republicans used the language of state neglect to express their vision of what republican government required. Northern Democrats were the immediate target of the Republicans' state neglect discourse. (The Democrats, as Joel Silbey has shown, remained real competitors in Northern elections.[63]) But Republicans were speaking broadly to the Northern voting population. As we will see, some aspects of this discourse but not others were brought into the federal courts.

State Neglect in the Federal Circuit Courts, 1867–1873

The legal language of state neglect appeared in the federal circuit courts as challenges were brought to Reconstruction legislation. Between the passage of the Thirteenth Amendment[64] and the *Slaughter-House Cases*,[65] for example, there were thirty circuit court references to the Reconstruction Amendments and enforcement legislation. These thirty references appeared in twenty cases, written by nine justices and judges.[66] There were two references to the Thirteenth Amendment,[67] five references to the Civil Rights

Act of 1866,[68] seven references to the Fourteenth Amendment,[69] five references to the Fifteenth Amendment,[70] five references to the Enforcement Act of May 31, 1870,[71] and six references to the Ku Klux Klan Act of April 20, 1871.[72] Justice Bradley authored three of these circuit court opinions.[73]

In these cases, which discussed Reconstruction legislation at varying lengths, federal circuit courts often used the idea of state neglect when assessing the coverage of the Civil Rights Act of 1866, the Fourteenth Amendment, and Fifteenth Amendment. In the Act of 1866 and Fourteenth Amendment cases, the concept of state neglect permitted federal prosecutions of private individuals who committed physical violence "on account of race, color or previous condition of servitude" when state authorities neglected to redress those crimes. In the Fifteenth Amendment cases, the idea of state neglect permitted federal punishment of municipal officers who neglected their duty "on account of race, color, or previous condition of servitude." Circuit judges thus used state neglect concepts to permit federal prosecution of individuals under the Fifteenth Amendment, as well as the Fourteenth Amendment.

Circuit judges also developed their own "second-order languages" that limited federal enforcement power. In *United States v. Given*, Justice Strong emphasized that a municipal officer's refusal to collect taxes had to be on account of race in order to render him susceptible to federal prosecution. In *United States v. Crosby*, Judge Bond, who was deeply sympathetic to federal prosecution of Klansmen, quashed nine of eleven counts of an indictment because they were not correctly drawn. The identification of a racial motive was a significant device that limited federal prosecution. Without it, the federal government was regulating "ordinary" crime, off limits under both Amendments.

In none of these thirty circuit court references was the existence of state neglect disputed. Nonperformance of duty, courts agreed, was one way that states could deny equal protection and the right to vote. A dual conception of "denying rights" was apparent in the handful of decisions that discussed the issue at length; a denial of rights could take one of two forms: first, a positive invasion of rights, or second, omission to protect rights—that is, refusal to perform duties or give requisite relief:

> Congress has the power, by appropriate legislation, to protect the fundamental rights of citizens of the United States against unfriendly or *insufficient* state legislation, for the fourteenth amendment not only prohibits the making or enforcing of laws which shall abridge the privileges of the citizens, but prohibits the states from deny-

ing to all persons within its jurisdiction the equal protection of the laws. *Denying includes inaction as well as action, and denying the equal protection of the laws includes the omission to protect, as well as the omission to pass laws for protection.*[74]

Suppose, as is largely the case in Delaware, the state passes no unfriendly act, but *neglects to impose penalties* upon its election officers for making discriminations on account of race or color, and provides *no remedy* for such wrongs, of what value is the constitutional provision unless it means that congress may interfere? . . . When state laws have imposed duties upon persons, whether officers or not, the *performance or non-performance* of which affects rights under the federal government . . . I have no doubt that congress may make the non-performance of those duties an offence against the United States . . . Undoubtedly, *an act, or an omission to act,* may be an offence both against the state law and the laws of the United States.[75]

In these circuit decisions, it became clear that the concept of state neglect was designated by a host of words. No single keyword referenced this concept. The terms *duty* and *protect* were always present and constellations of terms consistently appeared with them. One constellation of words referred to the fact of neglect: "omission to protect, omission to pass laws for protection,"[76] "insufficient legislation,"[77] "prejudices affecting the administration of justice,"[78] "hostile . . . administ[ration of] justice,"[79] "no punishment could be awarded [for mischief],"[80] "state . . . neglects to impose penalties,"[81] "no remedy [provided by states for] discriminations on account of race."[82]

A second constellation referred to the consequences of that neglect: "crimes of the deepest dye . . . committed by white men with impunity,"[83] physical retaliation as the only available remedy,[84] the "mischief the act is intended to remedy would flourish,"[85] a condition of barbarism would result,[86] and constitutional rights would be inadequately protected.[87]

A third group of words referred to ideas about the proper nature and organization of the state. Government, for example, had an obligation to protect its citizens. Civilization should be maintained. These ideas served to explain why state neglect amounted to a constitutional violation and why federal intervention was necessary.

A more fleshed-out example would be helpful to illustrate the use of the state neglect concept in the circuit courts. The following passage comes from *United States v. Rhodes,* which upheld the Civil Rights Act of 1866.[88] The importance of *Rhodes* lies in Justice Swayne's identification of the constitutional problem the Civil Rights Act of 1866 remedied:

The difficulty was that where a white man was sued by a colored man, or was prosecuted for a crime against a colored man, colored witnesses were excluded. This in many cases involved a denial of justice. *Crimes of the deepest dye were committed by white men with impunity. Courts and juries were frequently hostile to the colored man, and administered justice, both civil and criminal, in a corresponding spirit.* Congress met these evils by giving to the colored man everywhere the same right to testify "as is enjoyed by white citizens," abolishing the distinction between white and colored witnesses, and by giving to the courts of the United States jurisdiction of all causes, civil and criminal, which concern him, wherever the right to testify as if he were white is denied to him or cannot be enforced in the local tribunals of the state.[89]

The idea that white men could commit crimes with impunity—that is, free or exempt from punishment or penalty, is central in *Rhodes*. If courts and juries "administered justice" in a "hostile" spirit, so that white men could commit crimes against blacks with impunity, this tells us something about the nature of this new kind of constitutional violation. Swayne's identification of a constitutional violation thus stemmed from the consequences of state neglect—white men committing crimes against blacks with impunity. It is significant that in 1873, Justice Miller made a similar comment in the *Slaughter-House Cases*, noting that black lives "were at the mercy of bad men, either because the laws for their protection were *insufficient* or were *not enforced.*"[90]

The circuit courts' Fifteenth Amendment cases also used the language of state neglect. As previously mentioned, some of these cases involved federal prosecutions of municipal election officials who had neglected their duty on account of the race of the prospective voter. These cases were prosecuted under the Enforcement Act of 1870. *United States v. Given*, for example, involved the federal prosecution of a local election official. The decision was written by Justice William Strong (on circuit), who emphasized that dereliction of duty had to be on account of race in order to incur federal penalty.[91] Again, the word *duty* was present (that is, the duty to permit all voters equally to pay the prerequisite tax for voting, to equally accept votes from qualified voters), appearing many times in the decision. The words *refusal, omit,* and *omission* referred to the nonperformance of this duty. Justice Strong also identified the consequences of this race-based neglect, a devaluation of constitutional rights, which acted at the same time as a justification for federal prosecution of these officials.

The second important Fifteenth Amendment case was *United States v. Crosby*,[92] one of the famous Klan trials in South Carolina. *Crosby*, written by Judge Hugh Bond, involved federal prosecution of private, racially motivated voter intimidation under the Fifteenth Amendment.[93] Referencing state failure to prosecute such action, Bond emphasized that without federal authority to prosecute Klan intimidation and violence, the "mischief the [Act of 1870] is intended to remedy would flourish."[94]

Thus, no single keyword referenced the concept of state neglect elaborated in these circuit cases. This is not surprising, because possessing a concept, as Quentin Skinner explains, is not the equivalent of knowing the meaning of a single word.[95] Rather, concepts are associated with groups of words. "The surest sign that a group or society has entered into the self-conscious possession of a new concept is that a corresponding vocabulary will be developed, a vocabulary which can then be used to pick out and discuss the concept with consistency."[96] These, then, were "the normal possibilities"[97] of state neglect language. With these possibilities identified, it is easier to see the presence of this language in Supreme Court decisions that followed. The Waite Court used the language of state neglect, but it did so in more minimalist fashion. (I explore the reasons for this minimalist approach below.)

State Neglect in United States v. Cruikshank (1876)

United States v. Cruikshank was an early state-action case, which stemmed from horrific racially and politically motivated election violence (a race for governor) in Louisiana.[98] Three men, William J. Cruikshank, John P. Hadnot, and William B. Irwin, were found guilty of conspiracy under Section 6 of the Enforcement Act of 1870.[99] Chief Justice Waite, writing for the Court, threw out all counts of the indictment, leaving no one legally accountable for the massacre. This is among the reasons scholars have viewed the decision as hostile to Reconstruction. Indeed, a view of *Cruikshank* as a judicial abandonment of blacks to Southern mobs has been conventional among liberal scholars since the *Brown* era.[100]

Cruikshank is significant here for a number of reasons. First, the case was a doctrinal precursor to the *Civil Rights Cases*, but not in the sense that scholars typically think. Recovering the Supreme Court's early uses of the state neglect/action concept is part of the job of examining the *Civil Rights Cases* intertextually. Second, the text of the Waite's opinion in *Cruikshank* does not support the historical "abandonment" reading. Third, Justice Bradley's circuit court opinion in *Cruikshank* demarcates a theory of rights and rights protections, rooted in both natural law and positive law, which he connects to state neglect concepts. This theory resembles nothing in use today, and recovering it helps us to understand the intellectual universe of Waite Court justices. Finally, the briefs filed by Cruikshank's lawyers are a rich source of documentary evidence on the conventional status of state neglect concepts. These briefs, moreover, help establish the moderate nature of *Cruikshank*'s reasoning.

When considering *Cruikshank*, the key thing to keep in mind is that the indictments could be thrown out under either a conservative or moderate theory of congressional power. Much hinged on which theory the Court used. The conventional view is that the Court threw out the equal protection and Fifteenth Amendment counts for conservative reasons— that is, because private individuals were beyond the reach of congressional enforcement power under the Fourteenth and Fifteenth Amendments. This reasoning, of course, closed the door to future indictments. The text of *Cruikshank*, however, shows that the Court rejected these counts for moderate reasons—that is, because the counts did not explicitly identify the crimes as motivated on account of race. This reasoning left intact federal power to pursue private Klansmen, if the power was used correctly.

We begin, then, with a brief look at Justice Bradley's circuit court opinion in *Cruikshank*.[101] Bradley (like the Supreme Court) threw out the indictments. His theory of congressional enforcement power, however, was moderate in nature. The problem with the indictment was that it was incorrectly drawn: "An indictment under the enforcement act [of 1870] or civil rights bill [of 1866] for violating civil rights, *should state that the offense charged was committed against the person injured by reason of his race, color, or previous condition of servitude*."[102] The specification of a racial motive was a key device limiting federal power. It was a move of enormous significance to expand federal oversight over race-based crimes, and this limiting device kept federal power within clear boundaries. (Recall that Judge Bond used this limiting device in *Crosby*.) Related to this, Bradley identified a distinction between "ordinary crime," which was under the exclusive jurisdiction of the states, and "federally cognizable crime," which included lawless combinations inflicted on account of race. Bradley clearly recognized federal power to prosecute private, racially motivated lawless conspiracies under the Civil Rights Act of 1866, which

> was intended to give to the colored race the rights of citizenship, and to protect them, as a race, or class, from unfriendly state legislation and from lawless combinations. An injury to a colored person, therefore, is not cognizable by the United States courts under that act, unless inflicted by reason of his race, color, or previous condition of servitude. An ordinary crime against a colored person, without having that characteristic, is cognizable only in the state courts.[103]

As did Rep. Garfield, Bradley rejected two extreme positions, each, in his view, with unacceptable consequences. One extreme position, urged by Democrats (including Cruikshank's lawyers), was that the sole condition under which Congress could pass enforcement legislation was the existence of objectionable state laws that violated the Constitution. At the other extreme, as already noted, were more radical Republicans who had argued that the federal government could take direct control of private individuals regardless of state behavior.

Bradley's distinction between ordinary crime (which remained within the exclusive jurisdiction of the states) and federally cognizable crime "on account of race," helped define his middle path. "Unless this distinction be made, we are driven to one of two extremes—either that congress can never interfere where the state laws are unobjectionable, *however remiss the state authorities may be in executing them, and however much a proscribed race may be oppressed;* or that congress may pass an entire body of municipal law for the protection of person and property within the states."[104]

Here, Bradley expressed an explicit concern for state failure and state dereliction of duty in executing laws, thus rejecting the Democrats' position. But Bradley worried, too, that Congress could be given authority to pass an "entire body of municipal law." By giving Congress power only over crimes on account of race, and by permitting "the duty and power of enforcement [to] take their inception from the moment that the *state fails to comply with the duty enjoined,* or violates the prohibition imposed,"[105] Bradley met both concerns. He carved out a middle view of congressional enforcement authority under the Fourteenth Amendment, rejecting the all-or-nothing options presented by radicals and Democrats.

In the *Civil Rights Cases,* Bradley stated again that Section 5 did not authorize Congress to pass a "code of municipal law for the regulation of private rights."[106] The canonical interpretation of this language is that the federal government may never regulate private individuals under Section 5. Bradley's *Cruikshank* opinion, however, used the no code of municipal law language—not to reject Congressional regulation of private individuals in all instances, but to reject the radical Republican position that would permit congressional enforcement regardless of state behavior. Bradley used the no-code language to carve out the middle path of state neglect, and his discussion in the *Civil Rights Cases* was consistent with this.

Bradley's theory of enforcement legislation under the Fifteenth Amendment is also significant here. The counts drawn under the Fifteenth Amend-

ment were invalid because they, too, were not limited to race-based conspiracies.

> The fifteenth amendment does not confer upon congress the power to regulate the
> right to vote generally; but only to provide against discrimination on account of
> race, color, or previous condition of servitude. Congress, therefore, cannot legislate
> in reference to any interference with the right to vote, *which does not proceed from
> that cause*, unless in elections of senators or representatives. A conspiracy to pre-
> vent a colored person from voting is no more a United States offense than a con-
> spiracy to prevent a white person from voting, *unless entered into by reason of the
> voter's race, color, or previous condition of servitude*.[107]

Although this view of congressional power under the Fifteenth Amendment sounds similar to Bradley's view of congressional power under the
Fourteenth Amendment, there was a significant difference: there was no
state neglect predicate for federal prosecutions of private, race-based interferences in voting rights under the Fifteenth Amendment.[108] This seems
jarring to contemporary readers. After all, the amendments share the "no
state" language. Bradley's opinion, however, articulated a theory of rights
that justified the different views of congressional power under each amendment. This theory of rights helps us to understand the intellectual context
in which state neglect concepts were developed. (Bradley's more nationalist view of the Fifteenth Amendment, by the way, would be endorsed by
C. J. Waite himself in a centrally significant but little-known circuit case
in 1877, *United States v. Butler*.[109])

Justice Bradley's theory of congressional enforcement power under the
Fourteenth and Fifteenth Amendment sat comfortably within the natural
law tradition. Legal thinkers within this tradition distinguished between
two types of rights: rights that preexisted the Constitution and constitutionally created rights. The idea that natural rights preexisted the Constitution is foreign to modern day legal positivists. But for legal thinkers in
the natural-law tradition, the Constitution could "declare" the existence
of rights[110] or "create" rights. Bradley, "one of the most systematic analysts
ever to serve as an associate justice"[111] and an accomplished mathemati-
cian, tried to build from this distinction a coherent approach to congressional enforcement of the different Reconstruction Amendments.

The nature of the right protected by the amendment, Bradley began,
determined the manner by which Congress could protect it. Rights in the
first category (rights that preexisted the Constitution) were "from that body
of natural rights which were recognized and regarded as sacred in all free

governments,"[112] or were part of the "political inheritance derived from the mother country" that belonged to every citizen "as his birthright."[113] In the tradition of natural law inherited in America, equality of basic rights was part of natural-law thinking.[114] (This is important to recognize, because it is easy for modern readers to regard federally guaranteed equal protection as a newly created Constitutional right.) The Fourteenth Amendment, as Bradley presented it, protected this first type of right.[115]

The second category of rights "derived from the grants of the constitution."[116] These grants "confer[red] a positive right which did not exist before."[117] Congressional authority to enforce these constitutionally conferred rights arose either "from the correlative duty of government to protect," or from "the general power 'to make all laws necessary and proper for carrying into execution the foregoing powers.'"[118] The Waite Court later embraced this concept of a federally or constitutionally created right, permitting the federal government to directly prosecute both private individuals[119] and state officials[170] who infringed upon these rights.

According to Bradley, Congress could not directly protect the category of preexisting rights. "This would be to clothe congress with power to pass laws for the general preservation of social order in every state." Rather, congressional protection of these preexisting rights had to be contingent upon the state's failure of duty or some other form of state violation. "The duty and power of [congressional] enforcement take their inception from the moment that the state fails to comply with the duty enjoined, or violates the prohibition imposed."[121] State neglect doctrine, then, attached to this first, preexisting category of rights.

Congress could, however, directly protect those rights in the second category: rights "created" by the Constitution. (Direct protection meant independent of state behavior—that is, federal protection was not contingent on state failure.) Congress, furthermore, could directly protect these rights against both private individuals and state officials. The Fifteenth Amendment (like the fugitive slave clause) created a new right, and so no state neglect predicate was required for federal intervention. The Fourteenth and Fifteenth Amendments, then, protected different types of rights, and this determined the different manners by which Congress could protect these rights.

The *Slaughter-House Cases* is conventionally regarded as an across-the-board rejection of the natural law tradition.[122] But although *Slaughter-House* did indeed reject certain elements of that tradition, the justices nevertheless endorsed the element of equality of basic rights. As we will see, Chief

Justice Waite stated for the Court in *Cruikshank*, "The equality of the rights of citizens is a principle of republicanism. Every republican government is in duty bound to protect all its citizens in the enjoyment of this principle."[123]

Contemporary eyes will "read over" these references to republicanism because they are not part of the modern vocabulary of rights. In 1874, however, the language of republicanism and duty was intelligible within the natural-law tradition. As Knud Haakonssen has explained, there was a harmony between republicanism and natural rights in the natural-law tradition.[124] In this tradition, rights and (republican) duties were correlative. Rights specified relationships among the offices, or role obligations, imposed upon individuals by natural law, and adherence to proper relationships led to the highest collective good. There were also reciprocal duties of citizen allegiance and government protection. Again, Waite explicitly acknowledged these reciprocal duties in his opinion for the Court in *Cruikshank*.[125]

Bradley's circuit opinion is important, then, because it offered a moderate theory of congressional power that resulted in the invalidation of counts drawn under the Fourteenth and Fifteenth Amendments. The fact that the counts were invalidated, then, is not automatic evidence that the doctrine in *Cruikshank* is conservative.

With Bradley's circuit opinion written, lawyers for William Cruikshank now set upon a specific task: assaulting Bradley's moderate theory of enforcement legislation.[126] David Dudley Field, who argued the case before the Supreme Court, was keenly aware of the moderate nature of Bradley's theory. Field understood that while Bradley threw out the indictment as incorrectly drawn and found Section 6 unsupported by the Constitution, Bradley handed to Congress and federal prosecutors a blueprint for writing future laws and indictments. Bradley's opinion, in other words, recognized federal power to pursue the Klan, if exercised correctly. Field sought to slam the door on the possibility of future federal prosecutions of Klansmen, devoting his presentation to a conservative theory of enforcement legislation. A chasm separated his theory from Bradley's.

Field urged that Section 6 was unconstitutional because it reached beyond state laws to regulate private action.[127] Indeed, Field used an extremely narrow definition of state action to limit the reach of the Fourteenth Amendment. For Field and others,[128] the sole condition on which Congress could act under the Fourteenth or Fifteenth Amendments was the existence of state laws that violated federally guaranteed rights. If a state "makes no law" abridging equality of rights, "the condition on which alone Congress can act has not arrived."[129] This extraordinarily narrow definition of state action was at odds with Justice Miller's opinion in *Slaughter-House*, which had explicitly stated that the validity of state laws was not the only concern of the Fourteenth Amendment.[130]

Field, not surprisingly, rejected the language of state neglect developed in the circuit courts.

> Will it be said . . . that the equal protection of the laws presupposes the existence and enforcement of laws, and that if the States do not make the laws, or, being made, *do not enforce them*, then Congress may interfere? . . . Let the question be put in this form: Suppose a State *not to provide adequate remedies* for the protection of life, liberty and property, what may Congress do? . . . The answer must be, Congress may do nothing whatever, beyond providing judicial remedies in Federal Courts for parties aggrieved by deprivation of their rights. Beyond this there is no alternative between doing nothing or doing everything.[131]

Recall, however, that Bradley's circuit opinion clearly identified a middle ground between "doing nothing" and "doing everything." Field ignored this, boiling down his main point: "*State inaction . . . is no cause for Federal action.* There must be affirmative action by a state tending to deprive a citizen of his rights before Congress can interfere . . . *Failure* to provide a remedy for a wrong is not the same thing as depriving of a right."[132]

An interesting dimension of the briefs for Cruikshank is their use of now-famous language by Justice Miller in *Slaughter-House*. Adopting Miller's language, they urged the Court to rule Section 6 unconstitutional[133] in order to preserve the "whole theory of the relations of the State and Federal governments to each other, and of both these governments to the people." If the Court were to let Section 6 stand, Field argued, this would "completely revolutionize" government and destroy the states[134]:

> All the serious, far reaching and pervading consequences, so forcibly depicted in the Slaughter House Cases, will be realized; and we shall have taken a fatal departure from the structure and spirit of our institutions. The State governments will be fettered and degraded, by subjecting them to the control of Congress in the exercise of powers, heretofore universally conceded to them, of the most ordinary and fundamental character.[135]

Against the urging of Field, the Court treated Section 6 as constitutional, although the Court never clearly explained why.[136] The Court's approval of Section 6 has scarcely been noticed by scholars who view the Court as hostile to Reconstruction. The Court's approval, however, tells us that the Court and these Democrats held different versions of state-centered federalism. The Court certainly rejected the view that the Fourteenth Amendment incorporated the Bill of Rights, refusing the vision of nation-centered federalism embodied in the incorporation thesis. There were, however, multiple versions of state-centered federalism, and moderate versions were consistent with new federal power over race-based wrongs against "civil rights."

Waite's opinion for the Court in *Cruikshank* is a skeletal version of Bradley's circuit opinion. In minimal fashion, Waite uses the moderate theory of congressional enforcement authority articulated by Bradley in his circuit opinion. Waite repeated Bradley's diagnosis of the flaw in the equal protection counts:

> The fourth and twelfth counts charge the intent to have been to prevent and hinder the citizens named, who were of African descent and persons of color, in "the free exercise and enjoyment of their several rights and privilege to the full and equal benefit of all laws and proceedings." . . . *There is no allegation that this was done because of the race or color of the persons conspired against.*[137]

The conventional reading of *Cruikshank* as hostile to Reconstruction ignores this last sentence, which should stop readers in their tracks. Why would it be relevant that there was no allegation of a racial motivation if the equal protection clause could never reach private individuals, as the conventional reading holds? If Waite was setting out a rule that private individuals were outside the reach of the equal protection clause, his attention to the missing allegation of racial motive is incomprehensible: the counts would have been bad even with the allegation of a racial motive. Why then would Waite have identified the absence? Clearly, it mattered to Waite that this allegation was absent. The only way it could have mattered is if there was constitutional authority to prosecute Cruikshank under the equal protection clause, but the absence of this allegation rendered the counts insufficient.

On the very next page, Waite made the same point with regard to the Civil Rights Act of 1866. The problem was not a lack of federal authority to prosecute Cruikshank under this act. The problem was an insufficient indictment:

> No question arises under the Civil Rights Act of April 9, 1866, which is intended for the protection of citizens of the United States in the enjoyment of certain rights, without discrimination on account of race, color, or previous condition of servitude, because, as has already been stated, *it is nowhere alleged in these counts that the wrong contemplated against the right of these citizens was on account of their race or color.*[138]

Again, the conventional reading of *Cruikshank* cannot make sense of this passage. Waite is clear here that a question under the Civil Rights Act would arise if federal prosecutors had alleged that Cruikshank's violence was "on account of race." There was no lack of power to prosecute Cruikshank under the Fourteenth Amendment; these counts failed on a technicality.[139]

Note, by the way, that this limitation on federal power (the indictment had to indicate that the offense was on account of "the race or color of the *persons conspired against*") excluded from the coverage of the enforcement acts Klan violence against white Republicans, which could also be conceived as "on account of race." Waite, like Bradley before him, placed violence on account of politics outside the scope of congressional enforcement,[140] even though moderate Republicans had sought to include these racial-political crimes within the coverage of the acts. The Court then reined in the congressional Republicans' concept of state neglect, refusing to count unpunished political violence against white Republicans as a violation under the Fourteenth Amendment.

What of the oft-quoted statement from *Cruikshank:* "the fourteenth amendment . . . adds nothing to the rights of one citizen as against another. It simply furnishes an additional guaranty against any encroachment by the States."[141] The conventional interpretation of this classic statement is that the Fourteenth Amendment flatly precludes federal regulation of private individuals. This interpretation, however, is difficult to square with the above excerpts, which identify the missing allegation of a racial motive as the flaw in the indictments. This difficulty should mitigate against the conventional interpretation of this quote (that is, no federal regulation of private individuals under Section 5 under any circumstances). This classic quote, moreover, is consistent with state neglect concepts. State neglect concepts arguably help us understand what Waite was doing in offering this statement. Given his identification of the flaw in the indictment (a missing charge of racial motive), and given Bradley's identification of state failure as a predicate for federal intervention under the Fourteenth Amendment, this statement can be read to indirectly flag the existence of this predicate.

Interestingly, there are "old" readings of *Cruikshank,* by both the Court (in 1892)[142] and by political scientists (in 1909),[143] which are consistent with this state-neglect reading. The existence of these old readings is highly significant, for it suggests that past interpretive communities saw *Cruikshank* in the way I suggest here.

It should be noted, finally, that Waite molded his opinion without the help of government lawyers, relying principally, it seems, on Bradley. The government brief was anemic and did not use state neglect concepts. Indeed, the government took no advantage of avenues of argument opened to it by

Bradley's circuit opinion.[144] The solicitor general, in fact, appeared less interested than the Court in maintaining federal authority to indict Klansmen, as long as indictments were properly drawn. The political context gave Republican government plenty of reasons for retreating from civil rights enforcement at this time, and the government brief must be understood within this political context. Indeed, the institutional relationship between the Court and Republican elites helps explain Waite's minimalism.

The Minimalist Expression of State Neglect

Waite's minimalist expression of state neglect principles, unlike Bradley's more robust presentation, invites questions about whether Waite sought to support state neglect principles with minimal antagonism to the South.[145] Indeed, there is a notable characteristic among the Waite Court cases associated with state action concepts.[146] In none of these cases does the Court repeat a statement made by Judge William B. Woods in *United States v. Hall* that "denying [rights] includes inaction as well as action [and] the omission to protect, as well as the omission to pass laws for protection."[147] In addition, the Court never directly rebuts David Dudley Field, who argued in his brief for William Cruikshank that "state inaction . . . is no cause for federal action."[148] It would have been easy, it seems, to either repeat Woods or directly repudiate Field.[149] The absence of such statements looks like evidence against the Court's use of state neglect concepts.

But would it really have been easy? The answer is no. Rogers M. Smith, in a founding essay on new historical institutionalism, has explained that the deliberate behavior of Court justices becomes understandable only in the context of institutionally constituted purposes and perspectives.[150] What institutionally constituted purposes and perspectives of Waite Court justices might have led them to use state neglect principles in minimal fashion? What institutional relationships tied the Republican justices of the Waite Court to Republican political elites? And how might these relationships have made a repetition of Woods or a direct repudiation of Field counterproductive?

The answers to these questions begin with an awareness that Republican support for black civil and political rights did not cease with the textbook end of Reconstruction in 1877.[151] Federal prosecutions of Klansmen did not cease,[152] and Republican congressmen, for their part, brought contested election cases in the House of Representatives. As Richard Bensel has explained, "Through the power of the House to rule on the qualifications of its members in these cases, the party of the Northern core attempted to impose standards of election conduct that the party was unwilling or unable to enforce through a resort to arms."[153] President Grant expressed genuine frustration with the media for making the military seem "despotic"[154] and with Southern justice systems for their failure to enforce the law.[155] President Hayes, for his part, vetoed seven times (in 1879–1880) Democratic efforts to rescind voting protections. Hayes pursued sectional reconciliation, but "he did not abandon southern blacks."[156] There are even indications that President Garfield retained a commitment to Reconstruction.[157]

A key point is that after the contested election of 1876, national elections remained tightly fought throughout the 1880s.[158] These razor-thin national contests insured that Republicans would be highly sensitive to a Northern electorate that now cared little for Reconstruction. What is clear is that the three Republican presidents in office during the Waite era faced a delicate political situation. A scaled-back civil rights strategy had become politically necessary.

Consider, then, the impact of repeating Woods or directly repudiating Field in this political environment. It would have put any of these Republican presidents in an awkward and very difficult political fix. To repeat Woods or directly repudiate Field would have put pressure on Republican political elites to act strongly and bring more prosecutions, which were expensive in both dollars and political capital. To repeat Woods or directly repudiate Field would have pointed a large finger at the South, casting Southern rights violations in high relief. It would have been a public slap at the Democrats and at the South, which Republican elites now felt it necessary to avoid.

There were also unique institutional concerns for the justices that had to do with preserving the prestige and influence of the Court itself, and repeating Woods or directly repudiating Field would have made the Court look weak because the executive branch could not and would not have undertaken broad prosecutorial efforts to remedy the inaction the Court had highlighted.[159] In short, there were good reasons to lay out state neglect principles in a minimalist way. A deliberate decision to avoid a direct repudiation of Field becomes understandable only in the context of institutionally constituted purposes and perspectives.

The "Abandonment Narrative" and Constitutional Development

What, then, of the conventional account of late nineteenth-century constitutional development, which casts Waite Court decisions as a retreat from

Reconstruction and which treats the last three decades of the nineteenth century as a single period? The recovery of state neglect concepts means we must reconsider this account.

Events during the Second Reconstruction played a major role in establishing this account, as it was during these years that liberal scholars built what I call the "abandonment narrative." According to this narrative, the Supreme Court abandoned blacks to their former masters between 1873 and 1896, leaving blacks largely under the control of the states, which were not disposed toward protecting their rights. These developments, the story goes, reflected the Court's retreat from Reconstruction—a reflection of the political retreat embodied in the Compromise of 1877. The Compromise of 1877 plays a key role in this narrative, linking Court decisions both immediately before (*Cruikshank*) and afterward (the *Civil Rights Cases*) in a story of swift downward progression of civil rights enforcement. Justice Bradley's association with this compromise, through his participation on the electoral commission that resolved the disputed election of 1876, is also invoked in the narrative, helping to "explain" the *Civil Rights Cases* and state action doctrine. State action doctrine (narrowly understood) thus appears to follow retreatist politics. The conventional narrative ends with *Plessy v. Ferguson*[160] and the Court's approval of Jim Crow segregation, which appears as a short and inevitable step from the *Civil Rights Cases*.

The early parts of this conventional story, which focus on the *Slaughter-House Cases,* have recently come under critical scrutiny.[161] For our purposes, the point is that this story erases significant political discontinuities between the 1870–80s and 1890s, obstructing our understanding of the *Civil Rights Cases.* The abandonment narrative containing historical anachronisms projects the politics, policies, and categories of thought of the 1890s backward onto the late 1870s and early 1880s. These anachronisms have impeded a proper reading of Waite Court decisions, because they make it difficult to imagine that the Court would take a moderate stance.

Public law scholars who seek to understand the Waite Court and American political development need a fresh look at political events after the Compromise of 1877. Once anachronistic understandings of the late 1870s and early 1880s are cleared away, it becomes easier to see that the political context of the Waite era would not have precluded the use of state neglect concepts.

The work of one historian, J. Morgan Kousser, is particularly relevant here. Kousser has sought to establish the disfranchisement movement, which begins in the late 1880s, as a historical divide.[162] Arguing that the late nineteenth-century must be divided into pre- and postdisfranchisment years, J. Morgan Kousser has identified anachronisms in the historical literature that have obscured recognition of this divide:

> By reading the characteristics of the twentieth-century Southern political structure back into the pre-disfranchisement era, historians holding this view dismiss too easily the national Republican party's post-1877 commitment to protecting the political rights of its Southern followers, under-estimate the residual power of the Southern GOP in the late nineteenth century, and disregard the transformation of Southern politics that took place about the turn of the century.[163]

Contributors to the legal literature on Reconstruction have naturally relied on the historical literature to inform their readings of cases, and this has inadvertently perpetuated the historians' anachronisms.

In order to develop a new account of the Waite Court and American political development, we need to confront the myth that the "Solid South" formed immediately after the Compromise of 1877, freezing blacks out of the political process.[164] What followed in the South, rather, "was a period of transition, uncertainty, and fluctuation."[165] Blacks continued to vote in significant, although reduced, numbers,[166] despite violence and fraud. Democratic victories were not easy during these years, except in Georgia. In short, blacks remained important players in Southern politics until the disenfranchisement campaigns that started in the late 1880s.

In the late 1870s and into the 1880s, then, there was no settled institutional environment. While the population turned away from Reconstruction, Republican elites were not always quick to follow. As mentioned earlier, Republicans continued to cite fraud and violence in Southern elections, helping to unify a party still *divided* over economic and fiscal issues. A recognition of this division disrupts anachronisms in Bensel's work on the Republican party. By projecting the big business image of the Republican Party of the 1890s backward onto the Republicans of the 1870s, Bensel obscures the political flux of this earlier period. If tariff protection for industry was the "unshakable pillar of party identify for the Republicans"[167] then these were not the Republicans of the 41st or 42nd Congresses, which passed the Enforcement Acts of 1870 and 1871.[168]

Eric Foner, too, has noted that "the coming of 'home rule' did not suddenly arrest the process of change . . . A new social order did not come into being immediately, nor could the achievements of Reconstruction be entirely undone."[169] Foner's discussion of Redemption does not emphasize a distinction between the pre- and postdisfranchisement periods, but his discussion lends weight to such a division. In highlighting the ways that the political context of Redemption differed from that of Reconstruction, Foner notes that Redeemers were "constrained only by the increasingly remote possibility of federal intervention, the survival of enclaves of Republican political power, and fear of provoking divisions with the now dominant Democracy."[170] Although these constraints were obviously weaker in comparison to earlier years, they were still significant in comparison with the postdisfranchisement era of the 1890s.

It was after the election of 1874, which returned the House to Democratic control, and through the predisenfranchisement period—a period of transition, fluctuation, and uncertainty—that the Waite Court used state neglect concepts in minimalist fashion, leaving intact federal power to reach private individuals under limited circumstances. The Waite Court's use of state neglect concepts is less surprising, in short, when we realize that Republicans did not completely abandon blacks until the 1890s.

Political developments in the 1890s would certainly make the judicial use of state neglect concepts implausible at this time. After 1890, there were "changes in the GOP."[171] In the 1890 and 1892 elections, the Republicans who remained from the Reconstruction Congresses lost their seats.[172] A reconstituted Republican party sacrificed the Lodge Election bill in 1892, the last attempt to Reconstruct the South,[173] "in exchange for legislative action on economic issues deemed to be of greater urgency—namely, the tariff and the currency."[174] In early 1894, furthermore, Democrats finally succeeded in repealing federal voting rights laws. Later that year, in the first congressional election that followed the depression of 1893, Republicans won one of the largest victories in congressional history.[175] In 1896, Republicans won the largest presidential victory in a quarter century, only to beat that margin in the 1900 election. In 1896, *The Nation* observed a "striking" shift from just four years earlier in "the entire absence of any allusion" to "black political rights in Republican Party state conventions."[176] These political changes took place in a context shaped by the rise of social Darwinism, which enormously strengthened the intellectual prestige of racist doctrines,[177] and in the age of empire.

A new account of constitutional development during the last three decades of the nineteenth century must pay more attention to the late 1880s as a significant historical divide. This will assist in reformulating the relationship between law and politics during the Waite era, a transitional era in which Republican support for civil rights was present, though muted.

Conclusion

The standard account of constitutional development during the late nineteenth century gets right the idea that the judicial abandonment of blacks follows political abandonment. However, this account gets wrong the timing of political and judicial abandonment and the case law that was the vehicle for judicial abandonment. It is the Fuller Court (1888–1910), beginning with *Plessy*,[178] that is mainly responsible for the judicial abandonment of blacks. This abandonment, not surprisingly, occurred during the worst period of black subordination since slavery. An elaboration of this argument would support the recovery of state neglect concepts. Indeed, a detailed look at Fuller Court cases on Reconstruction legislation would provide the foundation for a new look at constitutional developments during the Progressive Era. The conventional storyline of legal developments during the Progressive Era focuses on matters of political economy and *Lochner v. New York* (1905).[179] If the Fuller Court, however, departed from Waite Court principles in key cases in 1903 and 1906, then *Lochner* is not the only main development of this time.

In closing, we should ask what happens today when "state action" is conceived as excluding state derelictions of duty. The *DeShaney* case,[180] which involved the dereliction of duty by welfare state authorities, offers but one example of the impact of a narrow conception of state action in a modern context. The more recent case, *Gonzales v. City of Castle Rock*,[181] which involved the failure of police officers to enforce a restraining order against a man who ultimately killed his three children, offers another example. Regarding Rehnquist Court federalism cases, *United States v. Morrison* is the leading example. In *Morrison*, the Court ruled that Section 5 could not authorize §13981 of the Violence against Women Act of 1994. This law provided a civil remedy for victims of gender-based violence, on the view that state authorities were failing to provide remedies for violence against women while providing remedies for violence in other contexts. This law did not target state officials, stated Rehnquist, and this weighed against its Section 5 validity.[182]

The recovery of state neglect concepts in the *Civil Rights Cases* opens new avenues of argumentation for the plaintiffs in all these cases. This recovery would not guarantee victory for the plaintiffs, for courts would still have to accept the extension of state neglect principles to matters of domestic and sexual violence. But for the first time, precedent could support the legitimacy of the plaintiff's claims.

Notes

1. 109 U.S. 3 (1883). The public accommodation provisions granted "full and equal enjoyment" of inns, public conveyances, theaters, and places of public amusement. 18 Stat. 335 (1875).

2. See, e.g., Eugene Gressman, "The Unhappy History of Civil Rights Legislation," *Michigan Law Review* 50 (1952): 1323, 1336–1337; Robert J. Cottrol, "Civil Rights Cases," in *The Oxford Companion to the Supreme Court*, ed. Kermit Hall (New York: Oxford University Press, 1992), 149; Leonard W. Levy, "The Civil Rights Cases," in *Encyclopedia of the American Constitution*, ed. Leonard W. Levy and Kenneth L. Karst (New York: Macmillan, 2000), 408–410; William Wiecek, *Liberty under Law: The Supreme Court in American Life* (Baltimore, Md.: Johns Hopkins University Press, 1988), 100.

3. See, e.g., C. Vann Woodward, *The Strange Career of Jim Crow* (New York: Oxford University Press, 1955), 71; Robert J. Harris, *The Quest for Equality* (Baton Rouge: Louisiana State University Press, 1960), 82–91; Peter Magrath, *Morrison R. Waite* (New York: Macmillan, 1963), 130–149; William Gillette, *Retreat from Reconstruction, 1869–79* (Baton Rouge: Louisiana State University Press, 1979), 295; Robert J. Kaczorowski, *The Politics of Judicial Interpretation: The Federal Courts, the Department of Justice and Civil Rights, 1866–1876* (New York: Oceana, 1985), 217; Eric Foner, *Reconstruction: America's Unfinished Revolution, 1863–1877* (New York: Harper & Row, 1988).

4. See, e.g., Richard F. Bensel, *The Political Economy of American Industrialization, 1877–1900* (Cambridge: Cambridge University Press, 2000) and Bensel, *Sectionalism and American Political Development, 1880–1980* (Madison: University of Wisconsin Press, 1984).

5. U.S. Constitution, Fourteenth Amendment, section 5: "The Congress shall have power to enforce, by appropriate legislation, the provisions of this article."

6. 83 U.S. (16 Wall.) (1873).

7. On the dominance of state-centered federalism at the time, see Michael Les Benedict, "Preserving Federalism: Reconstruction and the Waite Court," *Supreme Court Review* 39 (1978): 41–53.

8. See, e.g., Quentin Skinner, *Visions of Politics*, vol. 1, *Regarding Method* (Cambridge: Cambridge University Press, 2002); J. G. A. Pocock, *Virtue, Commerce, and History: Essays on Political Thought and History* (Cambridge: Cambridge University Press, 1985); Pocock, "Texts as Events: Reflections on the History of Political Thought," in *The Politics of Discourse: The Literature and History of 17th Century England*, ed. Kevin Sharpe and Steven N. Zwicker (Berkeley: University of California Press, 1987). See

also Terence Ball and J. G. A. Pocock, *Conceptual Change and the Constitution* (Lawrence: University Press of Kansas, 1988); Terence Ball, James Farr, and Russell L. Hanson, eds., *Political Innovation and Conceptual Change* (Cambridge: Cambridge University Press, 1988).

9. Pocock, *Virtue, Commerce, and History*, 7–8.

10. Ibid., 9.

11. J. L. Austin explained that we must understand the intended point of a statement, i.e., what a given agent *is doing* in making a particular statement, in order to fully understand the statement. The social context cannot yield an answer to this question because it can reveal multiple possibilities. We must look at the relationship between text and context to get at an answer.

12. Skinner, *Regarding Method*, 3. I have argued elsewhere that lack of familiarity with the idioms of Republican congressmen prevented Charles Fairman from realizing that these congressmen intended to incorporate the Bill of Rights. See Pamela Brandwein, "Dueling Histories: Charles Fairman and William Crosskey Reconstruct 'Original Understanding,'" *Law and Society Review* 30 (1996): 289–334.

13. Skinner, *Regarding Method*, 47.

14. *City of Boerne v. Flores*, 521 U.S. 507 (1997) (invalidating the Religious Freedom Restoration Act of 1993); *Kimel v. Florida Board of Regents*, 528 U.S. 62 (2000) (invalidating the Age Discrimination in Employment Act of 1967), *United States v. Morrison*, 529 U.S. 598 (2000) (invalidating §13981 of the Violence against Women Act of 1994); *Board of Trustees of the Univ. of Ala. v. Garrett*, 531 U.S. 356 (2001) (invalidating Title II of the Americans with Disabilities Act of 1990).

15. See, e.g., *Seminole Tribe of Florida v. Florida*, 517 U.S. 44 (1996).

16. *Shelley v. Kraemer*, 334 U.S. 1, 13 (1948): "Since the decision of this Court in the *Civil Rights Cases*, the principle has become firmly embedded in our constitutional law that the action inhibited by the first section of the Fourteenth Amendment is only such action as may fairly be said to be that of the States. That Amendment erects no shield against merely private conduct, however discriminatory or wrongful."

17. See, e.g., *Lugar v. Edmondson Oil Co.*, 457 U.S. 922, 936 (1982): "Careful adherence to the 'state action' requirement preserves an area of individual freedom by limiting the reach of federal law and federal judicial power."

18. Act of 9 April 1866. 14 Stat. 27. Section 1 gave all persons the right "to make and enforce contracts, to sue, be parties and give evidence, to inherit, purchase, lease, sell, hold and convey real and personal property" as enjoyed by white citizens. It also provided for "the full and equal benefit of all laws and proceedings for the security of person and property, as is enjoyed by white citizens." Section 2 provided criminal penalties for "any person who under color of any law, statute, ordinance, regulation or custom" deprived anyone of rights secured or protected by Section 1 on account of color or race.

19. 109 U.S., at 11. Congress could "provide modes of redress against the operation of State laws, and the action of State officers executive or judicial, when these are subversive of the fundamental rights specified in the amendment."

20. Ibid.

21. 109 U.S., at 16. The Civil Rights Bill of 1866 was "different" from the public accommodations provisions of the act of 1875.

22. The "under color of" phrase appears today in §242 of the Criminal Code and its civil counterpart, 42 U.S.C. 1983. Both sections derive from Section 2 of the Civil Rights Act of 1866. For Court constructions of §242, see *Hague v. CIO*, 307 U.S. 496 (1939), *United States v. Classic* 313 U.S. 299 (1941), *Screws v. United States*, 325 U.S. 91 (1945), *Williams v. United States*, 341 U.S. 97 (1951), *United States v. Price*, 383 U.S. 787 (1966). For Court constructions of 1983, see *Monroe v. Pape*, 365 U.S. 167 (1961); *Adickes v. S. H. Kress & Co.*, 398 U.S. 144 (1970). In *United States v. Price*, the Court stated that "under color" of law means the same thing in §242 that it does in the civil counterpart of §242, 42 U.S.C. 1983, even though the word *wilfull* appears in §242 but not in 1983. 383 U.S., at 794–795. See also *Collins v. Hardyman*, 341 U.S. 651, 661 (1951), where the Court read a state-action requirement into 8 U.S.C. 47 (3), which provided a civil action in federal court for private conspiracies to deprive persons of the equal protection of the laws. "Private discrimination is not inequality before the law unless there is some manipulation of the law or its agencies to give sanction or sanctuary for doing so." Section 47 (3) was originally the civil counterpart to Rev. Stat. 5519, the criminal statute covering private conspiracies to deprive persons of the equal protection of the laws, which was ruled unconstitutional in *United States v. Harris*, 106 U.S. 629 (1883).

23. After the passage of the Civil Rights Act of 1866, some Republicans harbored doubts about its constitutionality. Further, all Republicans wanted to protect the act from repeal by later, hostile congressional majorities. In order to accomplish both ends, and for other purposes—e.g., giving constitutional status to the rights of citizenship and personhood—Republicans passed the Fourteenth Amendment. In the *Civil Rights Cases*, Bradley recognized the constitutional support the Act gained from the Fourteenth Amendment, while remaining uncommitted about the extent to which the act was authorized under the Thirteenth Amendment: "Whether [the Civil Rights Act of 1866] was fully authorized by the Thirteenth Amendment alone, without the support which it afterward received from the Fourteenth Amendment, after the adoption of which it was re-enacted with some additions, it is not necessary to inquire." 109 U.S., at 22.

24. The Civil Rights Bill of 1866 was reenacted in Section 18 of the Enforcement Act of 1870 (31 May 1870), 16 Stat. 140. Sections 16 and 17 of the Enforcement Act were also modifications of the Civil Rights Bill. For example, Section 2 of the Civil Rights Act of 1866 was reenacted in Section 17 of the Enforcement Act of 1870 with "aliens" added as a protected category. The word *citizens* also replaced "white persons." It was not unusual for Bradley to have noted the reenactment of the Act of 1866 in the Enforcement Act of 1870. A number of circuit court opinions noted the reenactment of the Civil Rights Act of 1866 with some modifications, in sections 16, 17, and 18. See, e.g., *Live-Stock Dealers' & Butchers' Assn. v. Crescent City Live-Stock Landing &*

Slaughter-House Co. 15 F. Cas. 649 (Case No. 8,408) (C.C.D. La) (1870); *In re Hobbs,* 12 F. Cas. 262 (Case No. 6,550) (C. C. N.D. GA) (1871).

25. *Civil Rights Cases,* 109 U.S. 16 (1883). (42 U.S.C. 1981 derives from §1977; 42 U.S.C. 1982 derives from §1978; 42 U.S.C. 1983 derives from §1979; 18 U.S.C. 242 derives from §5510.) For doctrine on these sections, see *Giles v. Harris,* 189 U.S. 475 (1903) (on §1979); *Runyon v. McCrary,* 427 U.S. 160 (1976) (on §1978); *Monroe v. Pape,* 365 U.S. 167 (1961) (on §1983); *United States v. Classic* 313 U.S. 299 (1941); and *Screws v. United States,* 325 U.S. 91 (1945) (on §242, which derived from §5510).

26. 109 U.S., at 16–17. This was not the first time Bradley had stressed the "under color of" requirement. In 1878, Bradley stated that the Civil Rights Bill "vindicated" the right to "the equal benefit of the laws" "against individual aggression; but only when committed under color of some 'law, statute, ordinance, regulation, or custom.'" *Ex parte Wells,* 29 F. Cas. 633 (C.C.D. La) (No. 17, 386).

27. 109 U.S., at 16, 17.

28. Several modern cases quote pieces of this discussion. See *Monroe v. Pape,* 365 U.S. 167, 216 (1961) (Frankfurter, J., dissenting); *Jones v. Alfred H. Mayer Co.,* 392 U.S. 409, 451, 453 (1968) (Harlan, J., dissenting); *Adickes v. S.H. Kress & Co.,* 398 U.S. 144, 162 (1970) (Harlan, writing for the majority); *Runyon v. McCrary,* 427 U.S. 160, 202–203 (1976) (White, J., dissenting); *Bell v. Maryland,* 378 U.S. 226, 307 (1964) (Goldberg, J., concurring). All of these discussions miss the historical meaning of Bradley's language.

29. The inclusion of the right to vote in this list was most likely due to the reenactment of the Act of 1866 in the Enforcement Act of 1870, which mainly protected voting.

30. Harold Melvin Hyman and William M. Wiecek present the hierarchy of rights as a pyramid in *Equal Justice under Law: Constitutional Development, 1835–1875* (New York: HarperCollins, 1982), 395–396. The best introduction to the "hierarchy of rights" concept is Mark Tushnet, "The Politics of Equality in Constitutional Law: The Equal Protection Clause, Dr. Du Bois, and Charles Hamilton Houston," *Journal of American History* 74 (1987): 884–890. See also Michael W. McConnell, "Originalism and the Desegregation Decisions," *Virginia Law Review* 81 (1995): 94, 1016 (noting that this concept of a hierarchy of rights has been forgotten today).

31. Foner, *Reconstruction,* 244.

32. 109 U.S., at 16.

33. 109 U.S., at 18.

34. Bradley's concept of "state injury of rights" is still consistent with the element of modern state action doctrine that holds that only the state can deprive individuals of rights.

35. A Lexis-Nexis search for Supreme Court cases between 1874 and 1888 using both the words *individuals* and *officers* produced 525 hits. I was unable to locate a case among these in which *individual* did not mean either human being or natural person.

36. In *United States v. Price*, 383 U.S. 787 (1966), the Court ruled that the private individuals who acted jointly with Deputy Sheriff Price in murdering Michael Schwerner, James Chaney, and Andrew Goodman acted "under color of law." Legal scholars, too, view the phrase narrowly. See, e.g., Theodore Eisenberg, "Color of Law," in *Encyclopedia of the American Constitution*, ed. Leonard W. Levy and Kenneth L. Karst (New York: Macmillan, 2000), 444–445: "the expansive extreme view of color of law arises not in interpreting the phrase itself but in interpreting it in conjunction with a series of nouns that accompany it" (e.g., "custom" or "usage"). Note that Eisenberg treats "under color of law" as "the phrase itself," which privileges the word *law* over *custom*. There is no textual or historical warrant for such treatment.

37. 103 U.S. 370, 397 (1880). As we will see, jury rights were regarded, by consensus, as "civil rights."

38. Bradley switched back and forth between references to state laws, and to references to state law or state authority. Compare this reference to state laws only with the reference to state law or state authority that concludes this paragraph.

39. 109 U.S., at 17–18, emphasis added.

40. 106 U.S. 629 (1883).

41. 106 U.S., at 639–640, emphasis added.

42. In the Civil Rights Bill of 1866, Congress understood to secure "those fundamental rights which are the essence of civil freedom . . . Congress did not assume . . . to adjust what may be called the social rights of men and races in the community." 109 U.S., at 22.

43. "Can the act of a mere individual, the owner of the inn, the public conveyance or place of amusement, refusing the accommodation, be justly regarded as imposing any badge of slavery or servitude?" 109 U.S., at 24. "It would be running the slavery argument into the ground to make it apply to every act of discrimination which a person may see fit to make as to the guests he will entertain, or as to the people he will take into his coach or cab or car, or admit to his concert or theater, or deal with in other matters of intercourse or business." 109 U.S., at 24–25.

44. "When a man has emerged from slavery, and by the aid of beneficent legislation has shaken off the inseparable concomitants of that state, there must be some stage in the progress of his elevation when he takes the rank of a mere citizen, and ceases to be the special favorite of the laws, and when his rights as a citizen, or as a man, are to be protected in the ordinary modes by which other men's rights are protected." 109 U.S., at 25.

45. To modern ears, Justice Harlan's dissenting argument that racially motivated exclusions of blacks from public accommodations were a badge of slavery rings true, as does his view that equal access to public accommodations was a civil right. But the urge to treat Harlan's more radical Republican perspective as "correct" has led modern readers to miss the historical reality that moderate Republicans could ridicule the right to public accommodation while remaining committed to core civil rights specified in the Civil Rights Act of 1866.

46. See, e.g., Laurent B. Frantz, "Congressional Power to Enforce the Fourteenth Amendment against Private Acts," *Yale Law Journal* 73 (1964): 1353; McConnell, "Originalism and the Desegregation Decisions," 1090; Geoffrey Stone, Louis Seidman, Cass Sunstein, and Mark Tushnet, *Constitutional Law* (Boston: Little, Brown, 1996), 1598; Paul Brest and Sanford Levinson, *Processes of Constitutional Decisionmaking* (Boston: Little, Brown, 1992), 1303; Robert C. Post and Reva Siegel, "Equal Protection of the Law: Federal Antidiscrimination Legislation after Morrison and Kimel," *Yale Law Journal* 110 (2000): 441, 475–476.

47. The law professors' interpretation also has a difficult time accounting for Bradley's ridicule for the public accommodation claim.

48. Bradley was carefully indirect about what was wrong with the public accommodations provisions. This indirect language and the purposes it might have served have never been the focus of scholarly inquiry, and unfortunately, it is beyond the scope of this essay to examine his indirection.

49. 109 U.S., at 9. Three years earlier, the Court had stated, "The provisions of the Fourteenth Amendment . . . all have exclusive reference to state action exclusively, and not to any action of private individuals." *Virginia v. Rives*, 100 U.S. 313, 318 (1880).

50. 109 U.S., at 11.

51. Ibid.

52. Skinner, *Regarding Method*, 84.

53. Confidence that an idiom existed for actors in history increases to the extent "(a) that diverse authors employed the same idiom and performed diverse and even contrary utterances in it, (b) that the idiom recurs in texts and contexts varying from those in which it was at first detected, and (c) that authors expressed in words their consciousness that they were employing such an idiom and developed critical and second-order languages to comment on and regulate their employment of it." Pocock, *Virtue, Commerce, and History*, 10.

54. See generally Allen W. Trelease, *White Terror: The Ku Klux Klan Conspiracy and Southern Reconstruction* (Westport, Conn.: Greenwood Press, 1971).

55. *Report of the Joint Select Committee to Inquire into the Condition of Affairs in the Late Insurrectionary States*, 13 vols. (Washington, D.C., 1872), *House Reports*, 42nd Cong., 2nd sess., No. 22 (serial 1529-41).

56. See, e.g., Hyman and Wiecek, *Equal Justice under Law*, 416, 419, 422, 425. See also Michael P. Zuckert, "Congressional Power under the Fourteenth Amendment: The Original Understanding of Section 5," *Constitutional Commentary* 3 (1986): 123.

57. *Congressional Globe*, 42nd Cong., 1st sess. 153 (Appendix) (1871), emphasis added.

58. See, e.g., the remarks of Rep. Horatio C. Burchard of Illinois: "If secret combinations of men are allowed by the Executive to band together to deprive one class of citizens of their legal rights without a proper effort to discover, detect, and punish the violations of law and order, the State has not afforded to all its citizens the equal

protection of the laws." 42nd Cong., 1st sess., App. 315. See, too, 42nd Cong., 1st sess. App. 315 (Rep. Hoar); ibid. at 182 (Rep. Mercur); 41st Cong., 2nd sess. 3611 (Sen. Pool); 42nd Cong., 1st sess. App. 251 (Morton); 42nd Cong., 1st sess. 375 (Lowe); ibid. at 514 (Poland); ibid. at 459 (Colburn).

59. 42nd Cong., 1st sess. App. 72, 117.

60. See, e.g., David Blight's discussion of the Democrats' minority report from the Klan hearings of 1871, which "fashioned an elaborate version of the victimized and oppressed South, and argued vehemently that most of the alleged Klan violence simply had not occurred." *Race and Reunion: The Civil War in American Memory* (Cambridge, Mass.: Harvard University Press, 2001), 121.

61. See Pamela Brandwein, *Reconstructing Reconstruction: The Supreme Court and the Production of Historical Truth* (Durham, N.C.: Duke University Press, 1999), 23–60; Blight, *Race and Reunion*, 31–63.

62. See Pamela Brandwein, "Slavery as an Interpretive Issue in the Reconstruction Debates," *Law and Society Review* 34 (2000): 315–366.

63. See Joel H. Silbey, *A Respectable Minority: The Democratic Party in the Civil War Era* (New York: W. W. Norton, 1977). In the 1874 elections, Democrats took control of the House of Representatives for the first time since the war. They turned a 198–88 Republican majority into a 169–109 Democratic majority.

64. The Thirteenth Amendment was added to the U.S. Constitution on 18 December 1865.

65. In the *Slaughterhouse Cases*, the Supreme Court gave its first elaborated discussion of the Reconstruction Amendments, and so I use this decision as a divide.

66. Supreme Court justices were Chase, Swayne, Bradley, and Strong. The circuit judges were Woods and Bonds. The district judges were Busteed, Erskine, and Drummond.

67. *In re Turner*, 24 F. Cas. 337 (Case No. 14, 247) (C.C.D. Md.) (1867); *United States v. Rhodes*, 27 F. Cas. 785 (Case No. 16,151) (C.C.D. KY) (1867).

68. *United States v. Rhodes*, 27 F. Cas. 785 (Case No. 16,151) (C.C.D. KY) (1867). *Live-Stock Dealers' & Butchers' Assn. v. Crescent City Live-Stock Landing & Slaughter-House Co.* 15 F. Cas. 649 (Case No. 8,408) (C.C.D. La) (1870); *In re Hobbs*, 12 F. Cas. 262 (Case No. 6,550) (C. C. N.D. GA) (1871); *Harrison v. Hadley*, 11 F. Cas. 649 (D.D.E.D. AR) (1873); *Gaughan v. Northwestern Fertilizing Co.*, 10 F. Cas. 91 (Case No. 5,272) (C. C. N. D. IL) (1873).

69. *Griffin's Case*, 11 F. Cas. 7 (Case No. 5,815) (C.C.D. VA) (1869); *Live-Stock Dealers' & Butchers' Assn. v. Crescent City Live-Stock Landing & Slaughter-House Co.* 15 F. Cas. 649 (Case No. 8,408) (C.C.D. La) (1870); *Ins. Co. v. New Orleans*, 13 F. Cas. 67 (Case No. 7,052) C.C.D. LA) (1870); *Marsh v. Burroughs*, 16 F. Cas. 800 (Case No. 9,112) (C.C.S.D. Ga) (1871); *United States v. Hall*, 26 F. Cas. 79 (Case No. 15,282) (C.C.S.D. AL) (1871); *In re Hobbs*, 12 F. Cas. 262 (Case No. 6,550) (C. C. N.D. GA) (1871); *Northwestern Fertilizing Co. v. Hyde Park*, 18 F. Cas. 393 (Case No. 10,336) (C. C. N.D. IL) (1873).

70. *Live-Stock Dealers' & Butchers' Assn. v. Crescent City Live-Stock Landing & Slaughter-House Co.* 15 F. Cas. 649 (Case No. 8,408) (C.C.D. La) (1870); *In re Hobbs*, 12 F. Cas. 262 (Case No. 6,550) (C. C. N.D. GA) (1871); *Kellogg v. Warmouth*, 14 F. 257 (Case No. 7,667) (C.C.D. LA) (1872); *Harrison v. Hadley*, 11 F. Cas. 649 (D.D.E.D. AR) (1873); *United States v. Collins*, 25 F. Cas. 545 (Case No. 14,837) (C.C.S.D. Ga) (1873).

71. *United States v. Crosby*, 25 F. Cas. 701 (No. 14,893) (C.C.S.C. 1871); *Belding v. Turner*, 3 F. Cas. 84 (Case No. 1,243) (C.C.D. CN) (1871); *Gaughan v. Northwestern Fertilizing Co.*, 10 F. Cas. 91 (Case No. 5,272) (C. C. N. D. IL) (1873); *Northwestern Fertilizing Co. v. Hyde Park*, 18 F. Cas. 393 (Case No. 10,336) (C. C. N.D. IL) (1873). *United States v. Given*, 25 Fed. Cas. 1324 (No. 15,210) (C.C.D. Del. 1873).

72. *In re Lindauer*, 15 F. Cas. 550 (C.C.S.D. NY) (1870); *Ex parte McIllwee*, 16 F. Cas. 147 (C.C.D. VA) (1870); *United States v. Canter*, 25 F. Cas. 281 (C.C.S.D. OH) (1870); *United States v. Hall*, 26 F. Cas. 79 (Case No. 15,282) (C.C.S.D. AL) (1871); *United States v. Clayton*, 25 F. Cas. 458 (C.C.E.D. AR) (1871); *Harrison v. Hadley*, 11 F. Cas. 649 (D.D.E.D. AR) (1873).

73. *Live-Stock Dealers' & Butchers' Assn. v. Crescent City Live-Stock Landing & Slaughter-House Co.* 15 F. Cas. 649 (Case No. 8,408) (C.C.D. La) (1870); *Marsh v. Burroughs*, 16 F. Cas. 800 (Case No. 9,112) (C.C.S.D. Ga) (1871); *United States v. Collins*, 25 F. Cas. 545 (Case No. 14, 837) (C.C.S.D. Ga) (1873).

74. *United States v. Hall*, 26 F. Cas. 79, 81 (No. 15,282) (C.C.S.D. Ala. 1871), emphasis added.

75. *United States v. Given*, 25 F. Cas, at 1327–1328, emphasis added. The decision was written by Supreme Court Justice William Strong, who would later write the Jury Decisions of 1880. Strong, like Bradley, would also sit on the electoral commission that appointed Hayes president in 1876.

76. *United States v. Hall*, 26 F. Cas. at 81–82.

77. Ibid.

78. Ibid.

79. *United States v. Rhodes*, 27 F. Cas. at 787.

80. *United States v. Crosby*, 25 F. Cas. 701. The word *mischief* denotes Klan voter intimidation.

81. *United States v. Given*, 25 F. Cas. at 1327.

82. Ibid.

83. *United States v. Rhodes*, 27 F. Cas. at 787.

84. Ibid. at 787–788.

85. *United States v. Crosby*, 25 F. Cas. at 704.

86. *United States v. Rhodes*, 27 F. Cas. at 787–788.

87. *United States v. Hall*, 26 Fed. Cas. at 81–82: "As [Congress] cannot compel the activity of state officials, the only appropriate legislation it can make is that which will operate directly on offenders and offenses, and protect the rights which the amendment secures." *United States v. Given*, 25 F. Cas. at 1328. "Any other doctrine would

place the national government entirely within the power of the states, and would leave constitutional rights guarded only by the protection which each state might choose to extend them."

88. *Rhodes* (decided before the passage of the Fourteenth Amendment) identified nonperformance of the duty to protect as a violation of the Thirteenth Amendment. All decisions afterward identified nonperformance as a violation of the Fourteenth Amendment and Fifteenth Amendment.

89. 27 F. Cas. at 787, emphasis added.

90. In *Slaughter-House*, Justice Miller explained that even after the passage of the Thirteenth Amendment, Southern states were not yet in their proper relationship to the Union. This was because the lives of black men "were at the mercy of bad men, either because the laws for their protection were *insufficient* or were *not enforced*" (83 U.S., at 70, emphasis added). Miller made clear that the validity of state laws was not the only concern of Reconstruction, "as it is a State that is to be dealt with, *and not alone the validity of its laws*" (83 U.S., at 81, emphasis added).

91. The Supreme Court opinion *United States v. Reese* endorsed the reasoning in *Given*. *Reese* is conventionally understood as supporting state action orthodoxy, in which dereliction of duty is excluded from the meaning of "state action." The explanation probably lies partly in the fact that the decision struck down two sections of the Act of 1870 (which looks like an across-the-board rejection of congressional power) and partly in guilt by association. *Reese* was the companion case to *United States v. Cruikshank*, and *Cruikshank* is conventionally understood as a state-action case.

92. 25 F. Cas. 701 (No. 14, 893) (C.C.S.C. 1871).

93. 25 F. Cas. at 704. "The constitution has declared that the states shall make no distinction on the grounds [of race &c]. And, by this legislation, congress has endeavored, in a way which congress thought appropriate, to enforce it. It is this act of appropriate legislation [the Act of 1870] and the first section of it, which the defendants are charged with violating, and we think it makes no difference at what election, whether it be state or federal, he is intimidated or hindered from voting because of his race, color, or previous condition of servitude. Congress may have found it difficult to devise a method by which to punish a state which, by law, made such distinction, and may have thought that legislation most likely to secure the end in view which punished the individual citizen who acted by virtue of a state law or upon his individual responsibility. If the act be within the scope of the amendment, and in the line of its purpose, congress is the sole judge of its appropriateness." 25 F. Cas. at 704.

94. 25 F. Cas. at 704.

95. "Language and Political Change," in Ball et al., *Political Innovation and Conceptual Change*, 7–8.

96. Ibid., 8.

97. The historian of political discourse must identify the "normal possibilities of the language" under investigation, "so that should we encounter the anomalies and inno-

vations that accompany paradigmatic change, we will be able to recognize them, reiterate them, and begin to see how they came to be performed." Pocock, *Virtue, Commerce, and History*, 30.

98. Ninety-seven individuals were originally indicted under sections 6 and 7 of the Enforcement Act of 1870. The first sixteen counts of the indictment, under the section 6, were for conspiracy. The next sixteen counts, under section 7, were for murder. Three of the men—William J. Cruikshank, John P. Hadnot, and William B. Irwin—were found guilty on the first sixteen counts, and so only section 6 was relevant for the Court. For reasons I do not know, U.S. attorneys identified only two men, Levi Nelson and Alexander Tillman, as victims, although it is estimated that about 300 people were killed.

99. Section 6 made it a felony for two or more persons to "band or conspire together, or go in disguise upon the public highway, or upon the premises of another, with intent to violate" any of the provisions of the Act of 1870, "or to injure, oppress, threaten, or intimidate any citizen with intent to prevent or hinder his free exercise and enjoyment of any right or privilege granted or secured to him by the constitution or laws of the United States, or because of his having exercised the same."

100. See, e.g., Leonard W. Levy, "*United States v. Cruikshank*," in *Encyclopedia of the American Constitution*, ed. Leonard W. Levy and Kenneth L. Karst (New York: Macmillan, 2000), 733: "*Cruikshank* paralyzed the federal government's attempt to protect black citizens by punishing violators of their civil rights and, in effect, shaped the Constitution to the advantage of the Ku Klux Klan." See also Kermit L. Hall, ed., *The Oxford Companion to the Supreme Court* (New York: Oxford University Press, 1992), 209.

101. 25 F. Cas. 707 (April 1874).

102. 25 F. Cas. at 707, emphasis added. This language is from headnote 1. For language in the opinion, see 25 F. Cas. at 715: "The [fourth] count manifestly refers to the rights secured by the civil rights bill . . . But the count does not contain any allegation that the defendants committed the acts complained of with a design to deprive the injured persons of their rights on account of their race, color or previous condition of servitude. This . . . is an essential ingredient in the crime to bring it within the cognizance of the United States authorities."

103. 25 F. Cas. at 708, emphasis added. This language is from headnote 5. For language in the opinion on the distinction between "ordinary" crimes and federally cognizable crime, see 25 F. Cas. at 711–712: "All ordinary murders, robberies, assaults, thefts, and offenses whatsoever are cognizable only in the state courts . . . To constitute an offense . . . of which congress and the courts of the United States have a right to take cognizance . . . there must be a design to injure a person, or deprive him of his equal right of enjoying the protection of the laws, by reason of his race, color or previous condition of servitude."

104. 25 F. Cas. at 714, emphasis added.

105. Ibid. at 715, emphasis added.

106. 109 U.S., at 11.

107. 25 F. Cas. at 708, emphasis added. This language is from headnote 6. For language in the opinion, see note 105. See also 25 F. Cas at 713–714. "Congress, so far as the fifteenth amendment is concerned, is limited to the one subject of discrimination—on account of race, color or previous condition of servitude. It can regulate as to nothing else. No interference with a person's right to vote, unless made on account of his race, color or previous condition of servitude, is subject to congressional animadversion. There may be a conspiracy to prevent persons from voting having no reference to this discrimination. It may include whites as well as blacks, or may be confined altogether to the latter. It may have reference to the particular politics of the parties. All such conspiracies are amenable to the state laws alone. To bring them within the scope of the amendment and of the power of congress, they must have for motive the race, color or previous condition of servitude of the party whose right is assailed."

108. "I am inclined to the opinion that Congress has the power to secure [the Fifteenth Amendment right] not only against the unfriendly operation of state laws but against outrage, violence, and combinations on the part of individuals, irrespective of state laws." 25 F. Cas. at 713.

109. *United States v. Butler*, 25 Fed. Cas. 213 (No. 14,700) (C.C.D.S.C. 1877). In *Butler*, it becomes clear that there is no state neglect predicate for federal regulations of private, race-based interferences in voting rights under the Fifteenth Amendment. On the Waite Court's nationalist Fifteenth Amendment jurisprudence, see Benedict, "Preserving Federalism."

110. See Akhil Reed Amar, *The Bill of Rights: Creation and Reconstruction* (New Haven, Conn.: Yale University Press, 1998), 148; Howard Jay Graham, "Our 'Declaratory' Constitution," *Stanford Law Review* 7 (1954): 3, 3–4; Jacobus tenBroek, *Equal under Law* (1961; reprint, New York: Collier, 1965), 90–91.

111. Hyman and Wiecek, *Equal Justice under Law*, 414.

112. 25 F. Cas. at 714.

113. 25 F. Cas. at 710.

114. Knud Haakonssen, "From Natural Law to the Rights of Man: A European Perspective on American Debates," in *A Culture of Rights: The Bill of Rights in Philosophy, Politics, and Law*, ed. Michael J. Lacey and Knud Haakonssen (Cambridge: Cambridge University Press, 1991), 51.

115. The idea of basic, natural rights—distinct from positive rights granted by the sovereign—had been used to justify the American Revolution: "If certain basic rights were to be the moral touchstone by means of which the conduct of all instituted authority was to be checked, such rights must exist on a basis that made them transcend all institutions of authority. They must somehow be inherent to the human species . . . Furthermore, the institutions of civil society must be seen primarily as safeguards for such rights." Haakonssen, "From Natural Law to the Rights of Man," 47–48. Thus inalienable rights—never conceived with exactitude—were a basic minimum. "The contract supporting civil government was between individuals who retained an identifiable core

of rights, for the sake of whose protection other [natural] rights were alienated to create government. At the same time, by limiting the natural rights proper to the well-known three, it underlined the alienable and adventitious character of the rest and so allowed wide scope for the assimilation of the historically contingent." Ibid., 50. Note that this framework allows for hierarchy of rights thinking. It also permits Bradley to limit "civil rights" to a core minimum, on which there was consensus.

116. 25 F. Cas. at 714.

117. 25 F. Cas. at 712. The fugitive slave clause in the U.S. Constitution, for example, created a new right.

118. Bradley cited *Prigg v. Pennsylvania* as the source of this doctrine. 25 F. Cas. at 709.

119. *Ex parte Yarbrough*, 110 U.S. 651 (1884); *United States v. Waddell*, 112 U.S. 76 (1884); *In re Neagle*, 135 U.S. 1 (1890).

120. *Ex parte Siebold*, 100 U.S. 371 (1880).

121. 25 F. Cas. at 710.

122. The majority rejected the robust conception of national citizenship that Republicans had developed within their natural rights framework. The majority also rejected Justice Bradley's argument that the butchers had a natural right to practice their trade.

123. 92 U.S., at 555.

124. Although the origins of Republican constitutionalism in natural-law theory have been well examined (see tenBroek, *Equal under Law*; Howard Jay Graham, "Our 'Declaratory' Fourteenth Amendment," *Stanford Law Review* 7 [1954]: 3; and William Wiecek, *The Origins of Antislavery Constitutionalism in America, 1760–1848* [Ithaca, N.Y.: Cornell University Press, 1977]), the harmony of natural rights thinking with republicanism has not usually been identified. Graham, for example, reduces the natural-law tradition of the Republicans to Locke's Second *Treatise* (at 3, 7)—a mistake, according to Haakonssen. On the correlative nature of rights and (republican) duties in the natural-law tradition inherited by the founders, see Haakonssen, "From Natural Law to the Rights of Man."

125. 92 U.S., at 549: "We have in our political system a government of the United States and a government of each of the several States. Each one of these governments is distinct from the others, and each has citizens who owe it allegiance, and whose rights, within its jurisdiction, it must protect."

126. *Landmark Briefs and Arguments of the Supreme Court of the United States: Constitutional Law*, ed. Philip B. Kurland and Gerhard Casper (Arlington, Va.: University Publications of America, 1975), 7:285–417. Filed by David Bryon (hereinafter the "Bryon Brief"), R. H. Marr (hereinafter the "Marr Brief"), John A. Campbell (hereinafter the "Campbell Brief"), and David Dudley Field (hereinafter the "Field Brief"). Field was the brother of Associate Justice Stephen J. Field.

127. See also Bryon Brief at 20, 26.

128. Bryon Brief at 20, 25 (a state acts "solely through its legally constituted legislature, or its people in general convention, legally assembled"); Campbell Brief at 24–26

(14th provided only for "an appeal by the citizens against an exorbitant law of the State") at 26; Field Brief at 4–5; Field Oral Presentation, at 20, 33.

129. Field Oral Presentation at 20. See also 30 ("Congress cannot act until the States have legislated in violation of the prohibition, and then only by way of nullifying their action through the Courts"). At one point, Field included the acts of corporate officers, although he argued that the *abuse* of official position was not "state action." This was simple trespass and hence not within reach of the amendments. The state can act only by its corporate officers, and then only in pursuance of state legislation. If a state governor despoils a citizen, he is a simple trespasser, unless there be a state law to justify him. Field Oral Presentation at 24.

130. "But as it is a State that is to be dealt with, and not alone the validity of its laws, we may safely leave that matter until Congress shall have exercised its power, or some case of State oppression, by denial of equal justice in the courts, shall have claimed a decision at our hands. We find no such case in the one before us." 83 U.S., at 81. (The brief of R. H. Marr quotes this sentence but leaves out the crucial fragment "and not alone the validity of its laws" without including an ellipsis. Marr Brief at 17.)

131. Field Oral Presentation at 22, emphasis added.

132. Field Oral Presentation at 18, emphasis added. See also Field Brief at 4–5. Marr's Brief also acknowledged that "faithless" state officials or a "corrupt" judiciary might impair rights. Laws might be maladministered, leading to the deprivation of rights. But according to Marr, Congress could not provide remedies for such wrongs. "The enforcement [of rights] devolves upon the officers of the State charged with the administration and execution of the laws; and it is difficult to perceive how individuals could hinder or prevent the free exercise and enjoyment, by any citizen, of the equal benefit of all the laws of the State or of the United States. *It might be done by an incompetent or corrupt Judiciary, possibly by other faithless officials*; but the redress of any such wrong is not within the legislative power of Congress. It would depend, in last resort, on this Court." Marr Brief at 28, emphasis added.

133. Bryon Brief at 27–28; Campbell Brief at 12, 13, 20; Field Oral Presentation at 1, 15.

134. Bryon Brief at 23, 24, 26, 30; Marr Brief at 13, 15–17, 30–31; Campbell Brief at 12, 13, 26, 28; Field Oral Presentation at 10, 26–32.

135. Marr Brief at 31. See also Campbell Brief at 28. Field's Oral Presentation suggested that if Section 6 were left standing, the government would become "consolidated" (at 26) and the Court would be turned into a "perpetual censor" (at 30).

136. Michael Les Benedict has noted that Waite's opinion was "unclear on the grounds on which the Justices upheld the constitutionality of the Enforcement Act provisions before them." "Preserving Federalism," 74. Waite stated several times, for example, that the counts of the indictment "do not present a case within the sixth section of the Enforcement Act." 92 U.S., at 543, 544. He also stated, "To bring this case under the operation of the statute . . . it must appear that the right . . . was one granted or secured by the constitution." 92 U.S., at 549.

137. 92 U.S., at 554, emphasis added.

138. Ibid. at 555, emphasis added.

139. The counts drawn under the Fifteenth Amendment (counts 6 and 14) failed on the same technicality. Stated Waite, "Inasmuch, therefore, as it does not appear in these counts that the intent of the defendants was to prevent these parties from exercising their right to vote on account of their race, &c., it does not appear that it was their intent to interfere with any right granted or secured by the constitution or laws of the United States. We may suspect that race was the cause of the hostility, but it is not so averred. This is material to a description of the substance of the offence, and it cannot be supplied by implication. Every thing essential must be charged positively, and not inferentially. The defect here is not in form, but in substance."

140. 25 F. Cas. at 713.

141. 92 U.S., at 542, 543.

142. See, e.g., *Logan v. United States*, 144 U.S. 263, 288, emphasis added, citing *Cruikshank* at 556. "[*Cruikshank*] held, in accordance with *Reese*, that counts for conspiracy to prevent and hinder citizens of the African race in the free exercise and enjoyment of the right to vote at state elections, or to injure and oppress them for having voted at such elections, *not alleging that this was on account of their race, or color, or previous condition of servitude, could not be maintained.*" *Logan* is an especially revealing case, for in addition to giving this "old" reading of *Cruikshank*, the decision quoted language from the *Civil Rights Cases* that has become the canonical expression of state action. The *Logan* Court treated this language as consistent with its reading of *Cruikshank* and as supporting the federal prosecution of Logan, a private individual, under §5508, which derived directly from Section 6. If the Court held a modern state-action reading of the *Civil Rights Cases*, its language could not have been used to support the prosecution of Logan. *Logan* was written by Justice Horace Gray, a justice with an ordinary, non-distinguished career. The fact that these readings of *Cruikshank* and the *Civil Rights Cases* came from Gray (and not from a justice with a high-profile, distinctive approach to constitutional interpretations) adds weight to the conclusion that they were conventional readings for the time.

143. See the 1909 reading of *Cruikshank* by John Mathews Mabry in *The Legislative and Judicial History of the Fifteenth Amendment* (Baltimore, 1909), 118: "The lack of proof that race was the cause of the discrimination was the ground upon which the decision directly turned." Mabry's study not only provided evidence that Republican congressmen understood state "denial" of voting rights to include dereliction of duty and "failure to make arrests, to put on trial, to convict or punish offenders" against the Fifteenth Amendment (at 94). Mabry argued that the circuit court decision *United States v. Crosby*, Bradley's circuit decision in *Cruikshank*, and Waite's opinion for the Court together established the principle that Congress had the power under the Fifteenth Amendment to punish private individuals who infringed on the right secured by the amendment (at 90, 104).

144. The Government Brief, for example, might have made use of Bradley's statement that a racial motive was necessary for the indictment to be good. The solicitor

general could have argued that racial motive was obvious given the facts, even though it was not explicitly charged, and agreed with Bradley that this element was necessary.

145. For example, Waite dropped elements from Bradley's circuit opinion that would likely have antagonized white Southerners, such as Bradley's use of *Prigg v. Pennsylvania*, 41 U.S. (16 Pet.) 539, a proslavery decision, as source of constitutional authority for congressional power to pass the Enforcement Act of 1870.

146. *United States v. Cruikshank, Civil Rights Cases, United States v. Harris*.

147. 26 Fed. Cas. at 81.

148. *Landmark Briefs* (supra note 126), at 7:437.

149. Benedict, "Preserving Federalism," 67, argues that it would have been easy to repeat Woods or repudiate Field.

150. Smith argues that legal institutions are independent influences in Court decision making, creating distinctively "legal" values, perspectives, and rhetorics of justification. "Political Jurisprudence, the 'New Institutionalism,' and the Future of Public Law," *American Political Science Review* 82 (1988). For a conceptualization of legal institutions as "constitutive" in nature, and for an overview of New Historical Institutionalism (NHI) that situates it relative to behavioral and strategic-rational choice approaches to the study of constitutional law, see Kahn and Kersch's Introduction to this volume.

151. See, e.g., Robert M. Goldman, *A Free Ballot and a Fair Count: The Department of Justice and the Enforcement of Voting Rights in the South, 1873–1893* (New York: Fordham University Press, 2001).

152. See *Ex parte Yarbrough*, 110 U.S. 303 (1884).

153. Bensel, *Sectionalism and American Political Development*, 87.

154. Grant to Edward Pierrepont, 13 September 1875, in Brooks D. Simpson, *The Reconstruction Presidents* (Lawrence: University Press of Kansas, 1998), 186.

155. Message to the Senate on 13 January 1875; and Sixth Annual Message, Simpson, *Reconstruction Presidents*, 179, 175.

156. Michael J. Klarman, *From Jim Crow to Civil Rights: The Supreme Court and the Struggle for Racial Equality* (New York: Oxford University Press, 2004), 14; Michael J. Klarman, "The Plessy Era," *Supreme Court Review* (1998): 317. Republican administrations continued to bring prosecutions under these statutes through the 1880s. The Republican commitment to black suffrage did not end until the 1890s, and Democrats finally succeeded in repealing these statutes in 1894.

157. A. G. Riddle reports that at the convention nominating Garfield for president, Garfield expressed support for the Wade-Davis bill (1864), a radical Republican alternative to Lincoln's 10 Percent Plan, and the Wade-Davis Manifesto, which contained harsh criticism of Lincoln for his pocket veto of the Wade-Davis bill. A. G. Riddle, *The Life of Benjamin F. Wade* (Cleveland, Ohio: W. W. Williams, 1886).

158. See Joel H. Silbey, *The American Political Nation, 1838–1893* (Stanford, Calif.: Stanford University Press, 1991).

159. Justices on the Warren Court worried that a decision striking down school segregation would go unenforced by the executive branch. Of course, the justices went

ahead in *Brown*. There were important differences, however, between the context of *Brown* and the context of Waite cases. *Brown* had a section of the country behind it. There were also large-scale developments (cold war politics) that made Jim Crow morally untenable as well as an albatross around the neck of the United States in its effort to condemn Soviet violations of human rights. See Mary Dudziak, *Cold War Civil Rights* (Princeton: Princeton University Press, 2000). In contrast, no large-scale currents supported state neglect principles after 1874, and the Court would have recognized this.

160. 163 U.S. 537 (1896).

161. See Michael A. Ross, *Justice of Shattered Dreams: Samuel Freeman Miller and the Supreme Court during the Civil War Era* (Baton Rouge: Louisiana State University Press, 2003).

162. The disfranchisement movement, in which such things as literacy tests and cumulative poll taxes were enacted, came in two waves, the years 1888 to 1893 and 1898 to 1902. "The former coincided with the threat of a Republican resurgence associated with the proposed Lodge Fair Elections Bill; the latter, with the ebbing of the Populist-Republican activities of the 1890s." Kousser, *The Shaping of Southern Politics: Suffrage Restriction and the Establishment of the One-Party South, 1880–1910* (New Haven, Conn.: Yale University Press, 1974), 239–240.

163. Ibid., 3.

164. "The notion that disfranchisement was simultaneous with the textbook end of Reconstruction in 1877 and that the South became 'solid' immediately after that date are myths." J. Morgan Kousser, *Colorblind Injustice: Minority Voting Rights and the Undoing of the Second Reconstruction* (Chapel Hill: University of North Carolina Press, 1999), 20.

165. Kousser, *Shaping of Southern Politics*, 11.

166. In the mid-1870s and 1880s, despite campaigns of violence in Louisiana, Alabama, Mississippi, and South Carolina, blacks still voted in substantial numbers. Blacks were elected to Southern state legislatures in significant numbers through the 1880s. Black office holding also persisted well past the compromise of 1877, in some states not peaking until the 1880s. Blacks continued to serve on Southern juries, at least through the 1880s and sometimes into the 1890s. Klarman, "*Plessy* Era," 307–308, 374. See also Foner, *Reconstruction*, 590.

167. Bensel, *Political Economy*, 107.

168. Ibid., 17.

169. Eric Foner, *Reconstruction*, 587.

170. Ibid. Kousser would likely contest Foner's description of a "now dominant Democracy" and cite numbers showing that the Solid South did not materialize until after the disfranchisement movement.

171. Kousser, *Shaping of Southern Politics*, 31.

172. "James G. Blaine, John Sherman, Benjamin Harrison, John J. Ingalls, Henry W. Blair, George F. Edmunds, William E. Chandler, Thomas B. Reed, and many others either died or left elective office during the nineties. In their places rose younger men to whom abolition and Reconstruction seemed irrelevant, merely picturesque, or even

evil. To the new generation of Republican leaders, domestic politics consisted almost entirely of the promotion and/or regulation of business." Kousser, *Shaping of Southern Politics*, 31. Giant corporations, made possible by completion of national railroad and telegraph lines, established full control of the Republican Party.

173. The 1890 elections bill proposed by Henry Cabot Lodge would have permitted federal supervisors to observe the registration of voters and guard against fraud at the polls. The Lodge bill would have had no effect in Mississippi, which had recently restricted suffrage through law (stuffing the ballot box was no longer necessary). Republican Congressman Hamilton G. Ewart predicted that passage of the Lodge bill would lead Democrats to use the law to pass disfranchisement measures. Cong. Record, 51st Cong., 1st sess., 6690. "The threat alone proved sufficient," notes Kousser in *Shaping of Southern Politics* (33).

174. Klarman, "*Plessy* Era," 318.

175. In the 1890s, the era of national political "stalemate" ended. Foner, *Reconstruction*, 523. See also Silbey, *American Political Nation*. Silbey argues that the period between the 1830s and early 1890s was characterized by a partisan political culture. Silbey uses electoral patterns to show that 1865 and 1877 were not turning points. The postwar pattern continued the prewar pattern of deep partisan division, and presidential elections from 1876 to 1888 were all decided by razor-thin margins. It was not until the elections of 1892 and 1896 that this pattern changed. In the election of 1900, Republicans increased their margin of victory even further.

176. Quoted in Klarman, "*Plessy* Era," 319.

177. See Rogers M. Smith, "Beyond Toqueville, Myrdal, and Hartz: The Multiple Traditions in America," *American Political Science Review* 87 (1993): 559.

178. See, e.g., *Williams v. Mississippi*, 170 U.S. 213 (1898), *Giles v. Harris*, 189 U.S. 475 (1903), and *Hodges v. United States*, 203 U.S. 1 (1906).

179. 198 U.S. 45 (1905).

180. *DeShaney v. Winnebago County Dept. of Social Services*, 489 U.S. 189 (1989). In *DeShaney*, the Court ruled that the failure of the Department of Social Services (DSS) to render protective services to a boy who was in danger from his father did not violate the due process clause of the Fourteenth Amendment. Although the DSS had knowledge of the danger from the father, there was no duty to protect the boy from dangers the state did not create. According to the Court, the DSS did not render the boy more vulnerable to dangers from the father. This was private violence, and state and local governments had no duty to protect its citizens from private violence.

181. *Gonzales v. City of Castle Rock*, 366 F. 3d 1093 (10th Cir. 2004). This case required the court to decide whether a court-issued domestic restraining order, whose enforcement was mandated by a state law, created a property interest protected by the due process clause of the Fourteenth Amendment. "At issue here is whether Ms. Gonzales' [procedural] due process rights, pursuant to the Fourteenth Amendment, were violated when the officers failed to enforce her restraining order against her husband." 366 F. 3d at 1098. Although the circuit court ruled, en banc, that such a procedural right

existed, the court affirmed the earlier dismissal of a substantive due process claim under the rule in *DeShaney* that the state does not have an affirmative duty to protect individuals from private third-party violence.

182. 529 U.S., at 626–627: "Sect. 13981 visits no consequence whatever on any Virginia public official involved in investigating or prosecuting Brzonkala's assault. The section is, therefore, unlike any of the §5 remedies that we have previously upheld." Citing *Katzenbach v. Morgan*, 384 U.S. 641, *South Carolina v. Katzenbach*, 383 U.S. 301, and *Ex parte Virginia*, 100 U.S. 339.

Part IV

Insiders and Outsiders: Development and the
Construction of Constitutional Inclusion

Chapter 8

Pace v. Alabama: *Interracial Love, the Marriage Contract, and Postbellum Foundations of the Family*

Julie Novkov

Constitutional development is a key piece of political development, and scholars of U.S. political development generally agree that the period after the Civil War was crucial in working out new political and institutional arrangements to address the collapse of slavery and Southern resistance to a national order. Although these arrangements had to be worked out on the ground, the prior issue was the construction of a constitutional order under which they would develop. Congress initiated the process, first legislatively in passing sweeping new regulations of civil rights, then constitutionally by proposing amendments to the Constitution that were sure to pass in the charged postwar political atmosphere.

The courts, however, and in particular the U.S. Supreme Court, would be major players in this process. The courts, charged with interpreting and applying the new legislation and amendments, were in a crucial position to influence development. Their critical role raises questions for scholars of political development. Scholars disagree about the specifics but mostly agree that the Supreme Court's rulings in the years between 1873 (the year when the Supreme Court ruled in the *Slaughter-House Cases*) and 1896 (the year of the decision in *Plessy v. Ferguson*) reflected the justices' interest in reining in the radical potential of the changes passed by Congress and approved by the people in the immediate postwar years. The doctrinal path the Court trod, however, did not emerge independently or solely through engagement with legal principles. Nor was the path fixed ahead of time, determined by doctrinal or constitutional imperatives. Significant institutional constraints inherent in the judicial process affected not only the outcomes in the key cases, but also how they were reached. As Moore and Brandwein suggest in this volume, the struggles in the judiciary did not simply establish the scope of the Fourteenth Amendment. Rather, early interpretations of the amendment helped to carve out the parameters of its legitimacy as a tool for the restructuring of the federal order in the wake of the Civil War's end.

In this chapter, I illuminate this process by addressing two puzzles in the context of an overlooked but crucial moment. First, what background cultural and political interests informed the debate over the new constitutional order, and how were these interests integrated into the debate? This question looks to the interplay between institutional structure and operation on the one hand and culture on the other. Second, was the Court's embrace of the constitutional principles that enabled the rise of Jim Crow in the South inevitable? This question implicates theories of path dependence. The story is not a simple one of cause and effect. Rather, it suggests that the negotiation over the creation of a postwar state was both contingent and bounded. To understand how this process worked and how it implicated the courts' capacity to interact with external factors, we can look to a specific moment of contingency that influenced later moments.

Law school textbooks and many other narratives of the early history of the Fourteenth Amendment consistently interpret the Supreme Court's first discussions of race in the postbellum era. In the beginning (1873) was *Slaughter-House*, which limited the Fourteenth Amendment by effectively gutting the privileges or immunities clause and circumscribing the application of the guarantees of equal protection and due process.[1] *Strauder v. Virginia* provided a glimmer of hope for African Americans in 1880 by declaring racially exclusionary juries to be unconstitutional, but the ruling in the *Civil Rights Cases* of 1883 clarified the Court's unwillingness to support broadbased statutory reform of the racial hierarchy being reestablished in the South.[2] The Court's final word on the postbellum subordination of blacks was issued in *Plessy v. Ferguson* in 1896, which legally legitimized the practice of Jim Crow throughout the South.[3] To the extent that there ever was a moment of contingency, it existed only for a few years after the ratification of the Fourteenth Amendment, and the Court quickly settled on an interpretation of the amendment that distinguished between political and social equality while defining political equality as narrowly as possible.

This narrative, however, can be challenged. Looking to the outcomes and reasoning in the leading cases lends an air of inevitability to the doctrinal path, but what if we do not assume at the outset that the path was fixed? Brandwein's chapter in this volume engages the same question, considering whether the rigid and familiar conception of the state action doctrine in the *Civil Rights Cases* was either as inevitable or as clear as later interpreters have understood it to be. Likewise, Moore suggests that significant questions of legitimacy were swirling around the Fourteenth Amendment that only reached settlement as it was interpreted in the federal courts. The cultural and political imperatives referred to above are often read as pushing the Court toward the path it took, but these imperatives, based principally on questions of race, are not often analyzed in their concrete relation to actual cases. In order to understand the interplay, we must look at the cases themselves, but not just at their presentation in the U.S. Supreme Court.

In studying the Supreme Court, we often forget that the rules the Court makes arise from specific cases that have both factual and legal backgrounds. Understanding a case's history before its review by the Court helps to untangle what was at stake from the point of view of the litigants and gives a better picture of the elements of uncertainty that required resolution. If we simply want to know the legal rules the Court established, a reading of the Court's opinion will often suffice, but in order to sort out the interplay between cultural and political forces on one hand and legal norms on the other, we must look beyond the opinion to the immediate history of the case. This dynamic interpretation sometimes brings to the fore questions of subnational development that are usually understood as mere background unless they themselves are the key points of legal contention.

Questions about constitutional legitimacy are likewise multidimensional and the process of creating legitimacy flows in different and conflicting directions. A familiar problem is whether the Court's rulings will be accepted by the public or the legal community as legitimate, but this framing assumes the prior and independent legitimacy of grounding documents like statutes and the Constitution itself. Dynamism in interpretation with more focus on state-level battles can show how the initial interpretive struggles over the Fourteenth Amendment laid out a framework for understanding the amendment itself as a legitimate and acceptable change in federal structure. The state court struggles primed the national inquiry into how far the Fourteenth Amendment's guarantees could extend and how much of state law the new federal order could rework.

In this chapter, I look at the often noted but rarely discussed case of *Pace v. Alabama*.[4] Because the U.S. Supreme Court's analysis in the case was quite brief and the outcome unsurprising to modern observers, few have considered it carefully. Looking at the history of the case, however, reveals the development of an underlying logic of local control over racial issues that the Court would consider and ultimately endorse fully in later rulings.

At first blush, the case is not remarkable. It involved Tony Pace's appeal of his conviction for violating Alabama's criminal prohibition of miscegenation. He and his partner Mary Ann Cox were convicted in 1881 of engaging in adultery or fornication, a felony because she was white and he was (in the statute's language) a Negro or a descendant of a Negro. The appeal to the U.S. Supreme Court raised the question of the Fourteenth Amendment's effect on Alabama's statutory efforts to suppress interracial marriage; Pace was appealing the Alabama Supreme Court's validation of the law in light of a challenge under the Fourteenth Amendment.

As in *Plessy v. Ferguson*, the Court upheld the law. Unlike *Plessy*, *Pace* was forgotten rather than being forever linked with the case that overturned antimiscegenation laws, *Loving v. Virginia*, which the Court decided in 1967.[5] Although *Pace* framed laws barring miscegenation as appropriate under equal protection because the penalties were the same for both whites and blacks, the landmark case of *Loving v. Virginia* explored the ideological message of racial hostility grounding criminal bans on interracial marriage. Studying the dynamics of *Pace v. Alabama* from its roots in Alabama's struggle over race in the postbellum era reveals the careful recrafting of the white family as a quasi-public entity at the state's center in response to the radical implications of Reconstruction. Alabama's discussion was the most extensive on the state level, but a few other states also grappled with the problem of squaring prohibitions against miscegenation with the Fourteenth Amendment's command of equality.

The transformation of private patriarchal control over both African Americans and families into a network of state intervention had significant implications both for the law of race and for the resurgence of state power in response to federal challenges. It also marked a significant step in the path that would ultimately lead to *Plessy* and the Court's full embrace of a distinction between legal and social equality. I tell the story of the state-level struggle with the law of race and the thirteen-year path in state court that led to the initial justifications for Jim Crow on both the state and federal levels. Looking specifically at Alabama, the narrative will also demonstrate why the legality of regulating miscegenation was such a pivotal question for the South and for the nation.

Reconstituting the State

Studies of Southern history have shown that the legal regulation of African Americans and their interactions with whites were not static over time. For complex reasons, coherent commitments to white domination in law and public policy increased in the antebellum era, and restrictions of black autonomy correspondingly grew for both slaves and free blacks. As Martha Hodes has shown, although miscegenation was socially disapproved even when practiced by white men with unwilling black women, in the early antebellum years, it was sometimes tolerated even when the participants were black men and white women.[6] In the late antebellum era, Alabama criminalized miscegenation but did not class it as a felony; Northern and Western states also passed criminal prohibitions against interracial marriage in the 1840s and 1850s.[7] As one might predict, relationships between white men and black women received far less scrutiny and condemnation than relationships between black men and white women, although in the early part of the nineteenth century, even the latter relationship occasionally existed without exciting violence.[8]

As the sectional crisis intensified, free blacks found it increasingly difficult to stay in the deep South. A network of legal regulations throughout the South made it harder for free blacks to work and live without harassment. In Alabama by the time of the Civil War, most free blacks, who had formerly composed a fairly significant body of the state's population, had left for more hospitable regions.[9] Some thinkers have speculated that the legal pressures on free blacks made it easier for deep Southern states to maintain a low level of regulation directed at slaves. Once almost all of the blacks in a state were slaves, there was no longer a need for explicitly race-based regulation to maintain the subordinate status of blacks.[10]

After the Civil War, the former slave states' laws regarding race were left in disarray. Under a moderate governor appointed by President Johnson, Alabama, like its neighbors, sought to reenter the nation without changing the status of blacks more than was absolutely necessary.[11] The constitutional convention that the new governor and legislature convened included many of the men who had been prominent citizens and politicians before the war. After the war had ended but before the radical Republicans in the U.S. Congress had pushed through the Fourteenth and Fifteenth Amendments, the reconstituted Alabama legislature met and passed a number of laws restricting blacks, among which was a new antimiscegenation measure.[12]

This measure differed substantially from its predecessor. The law, which persisted in the same basic form until 1970,[13] made miscegenation a felony. The law was framed neutrally with respect to gender and provided for a lengthy prison term on conviction:

> If any white person and any Negro, or the descendant of any Negro, to the third generation inclusive, though one ancestor of each generation was a white person,

intermarry or live in adultery or fornication with each other, each of them must on conviction be imprisoned in the penitentiary, or sentenced to hard labor for the county for not less than two nor more than seven years.[14]

The subsequent section provided that anyone attempting to officiate at such a marriage could be fined between one hundred and one thousand dollars and could be imprisoned or sentenced to hard labor for up to six months. Alabama's restriction was unusually harsh both in the length of the mandated prison term and in that it extended to relationships of adultery and fornication, but many states in the South and North defined miscegenation as a significant crime by the end of the 1860s.[15]

Radical Reconstruction began in 1867, leading to another constitutional convention in Alabama in which blacks were permitted to vote. A white delegate proposed a constitutional prohibition of miscegenation. Black delegates opposed the clause because they believed that such laws would be used to control the black population. Ultimately the new constitution had no provision regarding intermarriage but also said nothing about the laws passed during early Reconstruction.[16] The 1867 convention reflected the delegates' desire to steer a middle course among the fighting factions, but the new constitution failed to achieve popular approval as vast numbers of white voters boycotted the polls.[17]

The radical Republicans in Congress solved this problem by mandating that a new constitution need only receive a majority of the votes cast for ratification, and the Alabama government was up and running again in mid-1868.[18] For the first time, black men were elected to the Alabama legislature, but the arrival of a new political player on the scene limited substantive improvements in blacks' political fortunes: by 1870, the Ku Klux Klan was operating effectively enough for Alabama to elect a Democratic governor and legislature.[19] The congressional radical Republicans responded by legislating against the Klan and sending federal observers to Alabama for the 1872 elections, but this resulted only in confusion as two legislatures—one Democratic and one Republican—claimed to have won the elections. President Grant's attorney general worked out a compromise through which the Republicans held the legislature for the remainder of the term, but by 1874 the North had lost the will to impose its vision of the postwar order on the South. In 1874, the Democrats again took control of the state government.[20]

For the Alabama courts, these wild swings in political fortunes meant that the personnel and guiding philosophies of the judiciary were in constant flux. The initial composition of the high court after the war was upper middle-class, well educated, white men who were sympathetic to the old regime.[21] The Constitution of 1868, when finally approved, mandated the election of three state supreme court judges for six-year terms. The effective electorate at this point included a significant percentage of black voters. This electorate selected three white Republicans for the high court bench; after the Democrats had retaken control, the 1874 election resulted in an entirely Democratic bench.[22]

Once the legal prohibition against miscegenation had been reestablished, the obvious question for lawyers was how the ban would fit with the new national statutory and constitutional guarantees of the Reconstruction era. The Thirteenth Amendment had eliminated slavery in 1865, the Fourteenth Amendment had granted citizenship to blacks in 1868, and the Fifteenth Amendment had guaranteed black male suffrage in 1869. This question masked the deeper question about what remained of the rigid hierarchy of race in the wake of war and emancipation. Miscegenation quickly became a key point to address this question, as it struck at the heart of both the master frame of racial hierarchy in its disruptive and intimate impact.

The constitutional stakes were as high as the civic stakes, and Alabama would be one of the first states to address this issue in a criminal context, although Indiana's high court would also be a key player. The intensity of litigation over this issue suggests both that the stakes were high and that the outcome was in doubt. Would the new state judiciaries in the South interpret the guarantees of civil rights as a fundamental restructuring of the position and status of African Americans? If so, would they initiate such a reconsideration at the explosive site of miscegenation? And how would this struggle implicate the institution of the judiciary with its doctrinal practices? The high courts of the states were at critical cultural junctures, mediating social attitudes toward miscegenation through legal filters. Their agendas differed from the federal courts' concerns, however. Moore and Brandwein demonstrate the Supreme Court's crucial role not only in interpreting the Fourteenth Amendment, but also in crafting a Fourteenth Amendment that would work. The state courts had less institutional stake in legitimating the amendment itself and far more in advancing interpretations of it that would speak to their own processes of postwar reconstruction. Nonetheless, these state-centered struggles established the parameters of the federal and constitutional questions that the Supreme Court would ultimately face.

Ellis v. State and the Initiation of the Struggle

Thornton Ellis was classified as black by the state of Alabama, and Susan Bishop was understood to be white. In the spring of 1868, the couple was arrested for violating Alabama's prohibition against miscegenation. Ellis was charged with adultery or fornication, and Bishop with adultery. Both pleaded not guilty to the charge of adultery or fornication but were convicted. The judge sentenced both to pay fines of $100 for their offense; neither was sentenced to a jail or prison term. Both appealed their convictions.[23]

Their case was the first reported challenge to a criminal prohibition against miscegenation. Others would come soon, as white women in many states had to cope with the enormous loss of white men's lives during the Civil War.[24] As noted above, by the time the Fourteenth Amendment became law, many states had passed criminal statutes barring miscegenation. In the South, most of these provisions became law very shortly after the Civil War's end, and no state legislature would abrogate its law in the postbellum era until Illinois did so in 1874. Although four more states would follow Illinois' lead in the 1880s (Rhode Island, Maine, Michigan, and Ohio), not until Oregon's legislature acted in 1951 would another state eliminate its ban by vote of the legislature or people.[25]

The appeals of Ellis and Bishop were based on the legal turmoil in Alabama during the immediate postbellum years. They claimed that the court had erred by convicting them for violating a statute that "was not in force at the time of the cause."[26] The argument, although not spelled out in the record, was apparently that Congress's passage of antidiscrimination legislation superseded Alabama's earlier prohibition against miscegenation.

The Alabama Supreme Court considered the appeal in the summer of 1868 to address the validity of the statute. Arguing for the state was attorney general John William Augustine Sanford Jr., who served in that capacity from 1865 through 1868 and again from 1870 through 1878. A staunch advocate of states' rights, Sanford would defend Alabama's criminal prohibition of miscegenation before the high court five times within eleven years.[27] He was thus the main crafter of Alabama's strategy to maintain the implementation of a policy of racial separation with regard to families.

The Court opened its opinion by noting that two Alabama statutes addressed adultery or fornication. The first, Section 3598, declared adultery and fornication to be misdemeanors punishable by a $100 fine and/or a term in jail or at hard labor for not more than six months. Upon conviction for a third offense, the penalty increased to a term in the penitentiary or at hard labor for two years.[28] This statute did not address race as a component of the offense. Section 3602 addressed miscegenation and prescribed a two- to seven-year term in the penitentiary or at hard labor. Ellis and

Bishop, although accused and convicted of miscegenation, had been sentenced under the statute addressing only adultery or fornication.

The Court explained the sentence as the circuit court's effort to account for the congressional civil rights act of 1866, reasoning that Bishop and Ellis had been sentenced only for their violation of Section 3598. The problem for the Court was that the circuit court had erred in believing that Section 3602 did not comport with Congress's mandate.[29] The Civil Rights Act of 1866 mandated equal treatment and prohibited discrimination in "the imposition of punishment" but did not prohibit the state from "making . . . race and color a constituent of an offense, provided it does not lead to a discrimination in punishment."[30] The Court emphasized that all parties were punished equally under Section 3602: "The white man who lives in adultery with a black woman is punished in precisely the same manner, and to the same extent with the black woman. So also the white woman is punishable in precisely the same manner with the black man."[31] The Court read race as a status akin to one's status as a minor in other contexts; distinctions in status governed the capacity to form a legal marriage.

Ellis and Bishop won reversals of their fines, but the case was remanded to the circuit court to correct the error by resentencing them in accordance with the harsher prohibition of miscegenation. They thus ended up worse off than they would have been had they not appealed.[32] The Court explicitly avoided considering Section 3602's compliance with the new Fourteenth Amendment, explaining that the question was not before them and that their ruling should not be taken as an affirmation of the law's validity.[33] The end result was thus ambiguous; although the Court mandated strict application of the statute in the case at hand, its ultimate validity remained under a cloud.

The case established the initial framing of the questions at issue. The struggle over the meanings of Congress's actions during Reconstruction and the new amendments was to be fought in part around the difficult issue of miscegenation. Such an inquiry would focus on the core question of the constitutionality of antimiscegenation laws, shaping both policies on interracial romance and procreation and the scope of the constitutional change wrought by Reconstruction. But at least as significant was the question of how this issue was to be considered, and this question had implications beyond policies barring interracial marriage. Should the inquiry address the extent of the equality promised by civil rights laws and the Fourteenth Amendment? Was it about the federal government's power to impose national standards in areas traditionally under state, local, or private paternal control? Was it about the nature of contracts and families and their relationship to the state? Or was it about miscegenation itself and the precise nature of the threat whites perceived it as posing to the state? These alternative framings would require different types of argumentation from the parties in the cases and the judges ruling on them. They would be worked out first on the state level, and the successful frames would only later be transported to the highly public arena of federal constitutional litigation. Even by the time the Supreme Court considered the *Slaughter-House Cases* in the 1872 term, the state courts, in hearing *Ellis* and cases like it, had begun to establish the broad parameters within which the struggle for legitimacy that Wayne Moore describes would take place.[34]

Ellis v. State centered on the meaning of the equality in the Civil Rights Act of 1866, reading this equality as a superficial guarantee. Had they wished to do so, the judges in the case could have cited the congressional debates over the laws: at least some of the supporters argued that state regulations against miscegenation were acceptable as long as the penalties for whites and blacks were symmetrical.[35] The other significant development in the case was the Court's assertion that race was a status. At this stage, the Court did not publicly assert that blackness was an inferior status and whiteness was superior, although regulation of miscegenation rested on this assumption. Rather, the identification of race with status highlighted the problematic nature of interracial marriage. If an individual attempted to contract a marriage rendered illegal by his or her status, the marriage was not merely voidable by the state's intervention, but rather was void at the outset. The conception of race as status enabled the Court to focus on the differences between intra- and interracial sexual relationships, whether these relationships were legitimated through marriage or not. This distinction, as well as the status-like nature of race, would be significant in later debates over the issue and ultimately would shape the way the U.S. Supreme Court reached the question of miscegenation.

Burns v. State and the Interpretive Challenge

Ellis initiated the struggle, but other state high courts began to participate shortly afterward. In 1869, North Carolina's high court considered and upheld the convictions of a black man and white woman for fornication or adultery on the basis of facts that established a marriage between them.[36] Georgia likewise affirmed the convictions of a white man and black woman for fornication, refusing to require the admission of evidence that they had undergone a marriage ceremony.[37] The most important state court ruling outside of Alabama, however, came from the North in 1871, when the state of Indiana analyzed the question of miscegenation comprehensively in *State v. Gibson*.

Like most of the appeals of this era, the case involved the convictions of a white woman and a man "then and there having one-eighth part or more of negro blood."[38] The Indiana court took the opportunity to engage in an extensive analysis of the Fourteenth Amendment, basing its reasoning on the initial assumption that the amendment "did not enlarge the powers of the federal government, nor diminish those of the states."[39] The effect of the Fourteenth Amendment was thus only to extend citizenship to blacks, but the high court read citizenship narrowly and claimed that its content had traditionally been defined by the states and remained so defined under the new regime.[40]

The *Gibson* Court then turned to the question of contract as the basis for the claim that Reconstruction legislation and constitutional change abrogated the regime of antimiscegenation. Marriage, claimed the court, was more than a simple civil contract, and the states' stable social relations depended on their capacity to regulate it. Citing a recent Pennsylvania case allowing segregation on a railroad, the opinion found that racial separation was natural and reasonable and that states' decisions to maintain separate social spheres among the races did not send any impermissible message of inferiority to blacks.[41] The court engaged in no significant analysis of the federal mandate of equality or its extent.

The next case concerning miscegenation to reach the Alabama Supreme Court did so one year after Indiana's ruling. As noted above, by this time, Alabama's judiciary had changed dramatically. In place of the Democratic judges who had ruled in *Ellis* were Republicans elected under the constitution of 1868. This case presented the constitutional question squarely, and the Court invalidated Alabama's criminal prohibition of miscegenation, becoming the only state high court to overturn a conviction in the nineteenth century. One constant remained from *Ellis*: again John Sanford argued the state's position to the high court.

Little information is available regarding the background of the case. The Alabama Supreme Court's opinion notes that no briefs reached the court reporter. The case involved an appeal by a justice of the peace Burns, who was tried and convicted in Mobile's city court of violating Sections 3602 and 3603 of Alabama's code.[42] Burns had solemnized the rites of matrimony between an interracial couple. He appealed his sentence (which most likely was the $100 to $1,000 fine prescribed by the statute) on the grounds that the congressional Civil Rights Act of 1866 invalidated the statute and that it was furthermore rendered unconstitutional by the state and federal constitutions.[43] Although the question of the Civil Rights Act's applicability had been answered with respect to Section 3602 in *Ellis*, it was worth asking again, given the change in personnel on the bench.

The Court began with a discussion of the Civil Rights Act. Responding to the *Gibson* Court's analysis, the *Burns* Court described marriage as "a civil contract, and in that character alone is dealt with by the municipal law."[44] This description was not, however, the prelude to a discussion of the traditional scope of state authority over the family. Instead, the Court emphasized marriage's contractual nature and the Civil Rights Act's command of equality in contractual relations. Like the right to sue and be sued, denied in *Dred Scott* and explicitly granted in the postbellum era, Congress had specifically authorized blacks "to make and enforce contracts, amongst which is . . . marriage with any citizen capable of entering into that relation." In the Court's reading, contractual freedom was one of the hallmarks of citizenship, and marriage was merely a subspecies of contract.[45]

After summarily dismissing the objection that some citizens (women and children) were not permitted to exercise the types of rights characterized as cornerstones of citizenship, the Court turned to an analysis of the Fourteenth Amendment. The amendment served two purposes for the justices. First, it enabled them to dissipate any clouds over the constitutionality of the Civil Rights Act of 1866, and second, it provided them with an alternative and independent reason for invalidating the statute.

In 1872 Congress was still in the midst of crafting regulations within the framework of Reconstruction. Few, if any, federal courts had addressed the interplay between the Fourteenth Amendment and the legislation that preceded it. Alabama and other state courts thus had the first opportunity to interpret the amendment and its impact. The Alabama Supreme Court knew that it was blazing a jurisprudential trail that might guide other courts and shape the way that the federal courts ultimately addressed these issues.

Considering the relationship between the Civil Rights Act and the Fourteenth Amendment, the Court saw the main issue as a potential objection that the act itself had exceeded Congress' power under the Constitution. The Court rejected this claim on the ground that "the cardinal principle [of the act] is now declared by the 14th amendment to the Federal constitution."[46] Arguments concerning the permissible scope of federal influence over questions of marriage were percolating in the early 1870s, but they were not yet pervasive or definitive enough for the Alabama court to have to grapple seriously with this concern.[47] Further, the constitutional cloud on the act's legitimacy, explained the Court, arose from the U.S. Supreme Court's discredited ruling in *Dred Scott*.

The Court, rejecting the narrow framing of citizenship articulated in Indiana, sketched a vision of the core meaning of the Fourteenth Amendment as a broad and substantive guarantee of rights:

> The spirit and express declaration of this section are, that no person shall be disfranchised, in any respect whatever, without fault on his part . . . and that persons who acquire citizenship under it shall not be distinguished from the former citizens for any of the causes, or on any of the grounds, which previously characterized their want of citizenship.[48]

This sweeping interpretation did not emphasize any part of Section 1; rather it read the section as an organic whole designed to change the nature of citizenship for African Americans.

Legal scholars have argued at length about the original meaning and purpose of the Fourteenth Amendment without reaching a solid consensus. Members of Congress certainly intended the Fourteenth Amendment to bolster the legitimacy of the Civil Rights Act of 1866, but its additional uses were controversial. Scholars arguing that Congress did not envision radical change point out that language mandating comprehensive colorblindness in U.S. law were considered and rejected.[49] Advocates of expansive interpretations point out that the supporters of the amendment objected to criminal suppression of miscegenation in other contexts and that color blindness was a significant constitutional norm even before the passage of the Fourteenth Amendment.[50] Michael McConnell has even shown that the question of school desegregation, formerly thought to be unquestionably legitimate, was a live issue for Congress during Reconstruction.[51] Although some scholars like Bank and Marcosson have mentioned the role that state courts played in considering antimiscegenation laws, few have looked in depth at the opinions and their relationship to the framing of the questions on the federal level.

Burns v. State helps us to understand a few things about what contemporaneous observers thought the Fourteenth Amendment would accomplish. Certainly the idea that it might invalidate all racially charged legislation, regardless of whether the laws addressed so-called social or political equality, was under consideration. Otherwise, attorneys would not have attempted to fight convictions on the basis of the Fourteenth Amendment, and no court would have found in favor of such attorneys. The fact that similar challenges were being brought in other states and that Congress seriously debated wholesale racial reform suggests that others saw the early 1870s as a critical moment at which a radical agenda of racial equalization was possible. Although one should not minimize the fact that the Alabama judges who ruled against the state in *Burns* were Republicans, they were elected rather than imposed from above, and elected in a period when Alabama elections were more democratic than they would be for years to come.

Ultimately, *Burns* did three important things: first, it invalidated Alabama's antimiscegenation statute, thereby demonstrating that such an outcome was possible and sparking a concerted effort to reestablish the law. Second, it established a framework for interpretation based on the meaning of citizenship as an organic whole. And finally, the outcome and reasoning gave attorneys for others convicted of violating the antimiscegenation statute hope that they might be able to extend the ruling to apply to their circumstances. Both sides thus had strong incentives to continue litigating the question in Alabama and elsewhere.

Ford, Green, and *Hoover:* Chipping Away at *Burns*

The next cases to reach Alabama's high court took place in the mid- to late 1870s. By this time, Alabama's politics had transformed significantly, and the Democrats were once again in control of the Supreme Court. Other Southern states interpreting their laws barring interracial relationships were reaching mixed results. Tennessee refused to acknowledge interracial marriages contracted in Mississippi during the brief period when Mississippi was without a criminal prohibition.[52] North Carolina, faced with a similar question in 1877, invalidated the convictions of a couple who had married legally in South Carolina, although the majority strongly recommended that all states should adopt prohibitions on interracial marriage.[53] Texas and Louisiana initially allowed inheritance rights for interracial families, but by the mid-1870s, Texas had reversed course by upholding its criminal prohibition against interracial marriage on constitutional grounds.[54]

The Alabama cases of the late 1870s, all heard by the same Court and all of which upheld the constitutionality of Alabama's antimiscegenation laws, demonstrated both the growing acceptance of a distinction between social and political equality for African Americans and the seriousness with which the Alabama court took the challenge of the broad vision of racial equality articulated in *Burns*. Actors within the legal system took pains to work through the issues carefully, motivated in part by the structure of the adversarial system but also by the problem of defining the racial terrain precisely. The criminal prohibition maintained some significant support despite the ruling in *Burns*, as state actors continued to enforce it. Confused and angered litigants appealed their convictions; some apparently even knew of the ruling in *Burns* and had relied on it in marrying across the racial boundary.

For a contemporary observer, it is unsurprising that Alabama's high court ultimately supported antimiscegenation legislation. What is surprising is that the Court did not simply overrule *Burns* at the first opportunity. Instead, the Court struggled to harmonize its rulings of the later 1870s with *Burns*, first narrowing it, and even when overruling it, encouraging pardons for the defendants. Especially in light of the U.S. Supreme Court's early indication in the *Slaughter-House Cases* that the Fourteenth Amendment would not be read as a broad command to expand federal influence over the states, Alabama's wandering jurisprudential path is interesting. After tracing the contours of the path, we shall consider the reasons for the Alabama court's extended inquiry into the subject of miscegenation.

Before further litigation took place in Alabama, however, the states' legal systems had to consider the construction of the Fourteenth Amendment in the *Slaughter-House Cases*. The U.S. Supreme Court was not looking at a case implicating race directly, but the majority opinion clearly linked the Fourteenth Amendment to race in declaring that the amendment provided no refuge for litigants seeking to overturn a state-granted monopoly. The well known discussion of citizenship in the majority's ruling clearly differentiated between state and national citizenship, reading the new guarantee of national citizenship as a fairly thin right of free travel and trade along with the catalogue of rights in the 1825 case of *Corfield v. Coryell*.[55]

Less well known, however, is the Court's critical commentary on the postbellum activities of Southern legislatures, which immediately "imposed upon the colored race onerous disabilities and burdens and curtailed their rights . . . to such an extent that their freedom was of little value." These aggressive actions, explained the Court, drove the Congress to enact positive legislation and ultimately the Fourteenth Amendment to generate meaningful security for the persons and property of the former slaves and free blacks.[56] The Court did not mention antimiscegenation policies in its discussion. *Slaughter-House* thus gave no unambiguous signals to either side.

In Alabama, the first case to reach the state's high court after *Burns* and *Slaughter-House* was the case of *Ford et al. v. State* in 1875. Both Ford, a white man, and his unnamed lover, a black woman, were convicted of violating Section 3602, which rendered interracial adultery or fornication felonious and its perpetrators subject to a two-to-seven-year term in the state penitentiary. The existing record is sketchy, but their attorney John Foster argued on their behalf that *Burns v. State* governed the outcome by rendering Section 3602 unconstitutional. They claimed that Section 3602's failing was to make "an act which when committed by persons of the same race . . . only a misdemeanor, a felony when committed by persons of different races."[57] Their argument ignored the Civil Rights Act of 1866, resting instead on the federal and Alabama constitutions.

In response, attorney general John Sanford cited the recently decided *Slaughter-House Cases* for the proposition that "every State has the right to regulate its domestic affairs, and to adopt a domestic policy most conducive to the interests and welfare of its people."[58] His reasoning rested on the distinction the Supreme Court had drawn between state and national citizenship but did not mention the Court's recognition of the need for affirmative legislative protection for blacks' rights. Rooting his argument in the state's autonomy, he argued directly that *Burns* should be overturned, citing *Ellis* and Indiana's ruling in *Gibson*.

The court issued a short per curiam ruling that did not engage these arguments substantially. Rather, the justices explained that *Ellis* had covered the issue adequately and that the specific issue in this case departed from *Burns*. *Burns*, they claimed, dealt with the question of prohibiting marriage between blacks and whites. This case addressed adultery. They reasoned, "Marriage may be a natural and civil right, pertaining to all persons. Living in adultery is offensive to all laws human and divine, and human laws must impose punishments adequate to the enormity of the offence and its insult to public decency."[59] This reasoning differentiated between the legitimate act of marriage, presumed to be the subject of *Burns*, and the illegitimate acts of adultery and fornication. *Burns* was thus cut back to address only marriage or attempted marriage, defined as (possibly) a natural right governed by the Fourteenth Amendment.

The Court did not directly defend the statutory differentiation between intraracial and interracial adultery or fornication against the charge that it violated the Fourteenth Amendment. The Court's reasoning seemed to be that because both were illegitimate in a moral sense, the state was justified in punishing each to the extent that it insulted the (or most of the white) community's mores. No further analysis addressed the legitimacy of maintaining a racial classification in the statute, in part probably because the attorneys in the case framed their debate around the question of the applicability of *Burns*. Nonetheless, the ruling's specifics may have surprised both sides— *Burns* did not govern the result, but still remained a viable precedent.

Green v. State reached the high court next. This case, decided in early 1878, was the most extensive statement that the Alabama Supreme Court would ever make on the question of the constitutionality of antimiscegenation laws. In it, the Court established a dual frame for analysis that rested on the nature of marriage and the scope of the Fourteenth Amendment's guarantee of equality. This case was destined to become a national bellwether, cited broadly along with *Gibson* by state supreme courts justifying the validation of their own criminal prohibitions of miscegenation.

Julia Green, a white woman, and Aaron Green, a black man, had lived together for several years. At their trial, the prosecutor produced a marriage license dated 11 July 1876; the license had been issued by a probate judge in Butler County.[60] Under the probate judge's signature on the marriage license was a notation that Elder Robert Pounds had married the couple on 13 July. They had lived together and held themselves out as husband and wife before their arrest. Both were arrested and charged with violating the antimiscegenation law in 1877. At the trial level, the case had to be continued briefly because Aaron Green escaped and fled the court's jurisdiction; upon his recapture, the court tried both and found both guilty.[61] They had offered no defense at trial but did ask the judge to instruct the jury that "If the jury believe, from the evidence, that the defendants . . . represented themselves as man and wife, and openly and notoriously lived together and cohabited as man and wife, this would be evidence of marriage between the defendants."[62] The court refused to give the charge, and the record indicates that they were sentenced to three years' hard labor,[63] although Julia Green's sentence was apparently later changed to a two-year term in the state penitentiary.[64]

Julia Green's attorney appealed her conviction on the ground that it fell squarely within *Burns*'s ambit. Because the case involved a marriage, the question of *Burns*'s validity could not be avoided. The intrepid John Sanford (who had been reelected in 1876) again argued that *Burns* was ripe for reconsideration, repeating his appeal to the Court to consider Indiana's exhaustive consideration of antimiscegenation legislation's constitutionality in *Gibson v. State*. This time, the Court accepted his challenge to explore the issue comprehensively.

The Court's opinion began by explaining previous Alabama precedents, setting up *Ellis* and *Ford* against *Burns*. The justices then systematically attacked *Burns*, characterizing its approach as "narrow and . . . illogical" for several reasons.[65] The first objection to *Burns* was that the antimiscegenation statute did not criminalize marriage itself (still understood to be a civil right) but rather marriage "*between* a white person and a Negro."[66] They then introduced the principle of symmetry—the claim that no violation of equality or discrimination on the basis of race had ensued because both blacks and whites convicted under the statute faced the same legal penalty.[67]

The Court also challenged *Burns's* interpretation of the history of the Civil Rights Act of 1866 and the Fourteenth Amendment. The *Green* Court pointed out that many Northern states prohibited miscegenation at the time of the passage of both the Civil Rights Act and the Fourteenth Amendment, and that neither the act nor the Fourteenth Amendment referred to miscegenation specifically. Thus, reasoned the Court, the extent of black rights should be limited to their furthest expanse in the North during Reconstruction, because the political authorities in Congress presumably reflected these sentiments.[68] This reasoning ignored the *Burns* Court's broad reading of the Fourteenth Amendment as a new understanding of the scope of citizenship, perhaps because the Court now believed that *Slaughter-House* and *Bradwell v. Illinois* had definitively disposed of this vision.[69]

The heart of the Court's analysis, however, was its reconceptualization of marriage. *Burns* had read marriage as a contract covered by the language in the Civil Rights Act guaranteeing freedom of contract. The *Green* Court challenged this reading directly. The first principle the Court articulated was that marriage contracts differed substantially from other types of contracts. For instance, they could be formed by individuals (women) "not capable of forming any other lawful contract." Marriages, unlike other civil contracts, could be violated and annulled by law. The rights and obligations of marriage were legally determined rather than being subject to the rational will of the contracting parties.[70] This conceptualization of marriage, which the Court underlined by citing Story's well respected treatise on conflicts, presented marriage not primarily as a private agreement between individuals but rather as a relationship of public significance under the state's control. Citing a Kentucky case, the Court described marriage as "the most elementary and useful of . . . [all social relations], . . . regulated and controlled by the sovereign power of the State."[71] This interpretation of the state's intimate involvement with marriage had two purposes: it counteracted the claim that marriage was like any other private contract and thus was subject to the mandate of civil equality, and it placed the primary responsibility for regulating marriage squarely in the hands of the state, not the federal government.

Why, though, was marriage so connected to the state? The Court did not simply rely on history here—instead it posited a forward-looking conception of marriage as the fundamental relationship for social functioning and the family as the basic unit of the state. The justices reasoned:

> It is through the marriage relation that the *homes* of a people are created—those homes in which, ordinarily, all the members of all the families of the land are . . . assembled together; where the elders of the household seek repose . . . ; and where . . . the young become imbued with the principles, and animated by the spirit and ideas, which . . . give shape to their characters and determine the manner of their future lives. These homes, in which the virtues are most cultivated and happiness most abounds, are the true *officinae gentium*—the nurseries of States.[72]

The Court read public significance into the marriage relationship; the family's importance to the state served as ample justification for careful regulation of the process through which families were created.

The nature of the state's capacity to control and regulate marriage was nonetheless closely bounded. The purpose of prohibiting miscegenation was to prevent "the evil of introducing into their most intimate relations, elements so heterogeneous that they must naturally cause discord, shame, disruption of family circles, and estrangement."[73] The Court explicitly noted that the state had no authority to meddle with the "interior administration" of the family, reserving its power for "guard[ing] them against disturbances from without."[74] The Court's logic was circular—the state had a duty to protect white families against the introduction of blackness because blackness was by definition incompatible with family life, regardless of how an interracial family came into existence. The opinion sought to mask the inequality inherent in its reasoning by explaining that the protection was as necessary for blacks as for whites. Nonetheless, the need for separation rested on a simultaneous assertion that blacks and whites were too different to form successful nurseries of states and that the "more humble and helpless" families particularly needed the strong hand of the law to prevent them from allying with each other and finding commonalities.[75] This disingenuous reasoning also supported marriage's noncontractual nature; although marriage was not a contract in the context of miscegenation, Justice Manning, author of the ruling in *Green*, had, in a bigamy case appealed only a year earlier, ruled that a marriage between two whites was a contract.[76]

The opinion affirmed the judgment of the circuit court, but the Court recognized that the defendants had likely believed that their actions were legal. In light of the overruled precedent of *Burns*, the Court encouraged the governor to pardon Julia Green.[77] The record is silent on whether the executive took up the Court's invitation.[78]

Green reveals the extent to which miscegenation was intertwined with concerns about the family and the composition of the state. The Alabama Supreme Court's need to back away from *Burns* and to validate antimiscegenation laws pushed it toward an analysis that reserved enormous power for the states to regulate racial relations in the public's interest. Likewise, the location of the struggle around the issue of miscegenation shaped the Court's framing of the dichotomy between social and political equality. The battles over miscegenation fought at the national level during the ratification of the Civil Rights Acts of 1866 and 1875 and the Fourteenth Amendment raised the specter of an African American having a right to sue a white family for not allowing (usually) him access on an intimate basis.[79] The Alabama high court reframed the threat as coming from the established interracial family itself; in their interpretation, the threat was not to individual whites, but rather to the state itself. This reading of the threat of miscegenation posed a stronger justification for state intervention and began to outline the contours of a white state threatened by contamination from blackness. Later decades would see the full articulation of a theory and practice of the white state, but the first manifestations of its modern form emerged in *Green* as a response to the triple threat of federal control of race relations, earlier state sanctioning of black equality, and the establishment of legitimate black-white families.

The *Hoover* case, adjudicated in 1878, also involved an attempt by a black man and a white woman to live together in matrimony. Robert Hoover and Betsey Litsey were arrested and charged with living together in a state of adultery or fornication in violation of the antimiscegenation statute.[80] As in *Green*, a marriage license was introduced at the trial. Only Robert Hoover was tried for the crime of miscegenation; Betsey Litsey (who went by the surname Hoover), according to the record, was too close to delivering their child to appear in court.[81] Hoover sought to call the probate judge to the stand to testify that Hoover "had asked him if it was lawful for him (Hoover) to marry a white woman, and that he was informed that it was."[82] The state objected and the court did not allow the evidence to be introduced. Hoover was found guilty and sentenced to a two-year term in the state penitentiary.[83]

Hoover's attorney relied on *Burns* in challenging his client's conviction, but he also argued that the antimiscegenation statute had never been properly passed in accordance with Alabama law. He also claimed (somewhat confusingly) that "there never was a statute of Alabama forbidding marriage between whites and Negroes, and declaring it to be void *ab initio;* but only a statute . . . declaring that if any white person and any Negro intermarry each of them must, on conviction, be imprisoned in the penitentiary."[84] The thrust of this argument was apparently a simultaneous plea for jury nullification and a claim that interracial marriage could not be taken as a crime of strict liability. Rather, implied Hoover's attorney, the defendant had to intend to violate the law. In response, John Sanford cited *Green* and the authorities on which the ruling in *Green* had relied.

The Court opened with a reference to *Green*, declining to engage in sustained analysis. It also quickly dismissed the procedural challenge, ruling that the somewhat irregular passage of the original acts had been validated by the later adoption of the entire Alabama Code in 1867 and 1876. The opinion emphasized that the marriage of Robert and Betsey Hoover was not merely voidable but rather was "absolutely void." In technical terms, any long-term interracial sexual relationship could only be adultery or fornication, not marriage. Thus Hoover was guilty under the law prohibiting interracial adultery or fornication, and his attempt to prove marriage, rather than exonerating him, merely strengthened the case against him.[85]

The Court went even further in identifying miscegenation as an offense of strict liability. The justices were unpersuaded by Hoover's efforts to introduce evidence that he believed his actions were permissible under the then-current state of the law, ruling that ignorance of the law could provide no defense, even when this "ignorance" rested on a prior opinion of the Alabama high court itself. Again, the evidence of the marriage worked in precisely the opposite direction as Hoover hoped—it demonstrated that their act of cohabitation was intentional, and Hoover's question only revealed that he had known of the existence of the antimiscegenation statute. The Court's one concession to Hoover's unhappy plight was a recommendation that the case be considered for executive clemency, "on condition there be given satisfactory assurance of a discontinuance of this very gross offence against morals and decorum. Should this crime be repeated or continued, the law should lay a heavy restraining hand on the offenders."[86]

Hoover added to *Green's* comprehensive analysis the Court's insistence that interracial marriage itself was a legal contradiction of terms. This reasoning underlined the *Green* Court's emphasis on the centrality of marriage to the state's purpose and functioning and the interconnectedness of "pure" families with the state's mission. *Hoover* likewise undercut *Burns* even more by effectively eliminating the category of interracial marriage as a possibility. When read in tandem with *Ford*, an ongoing interracial sexual liaison could fall into but one of two categories: felonious adultery or felonious fornication. The only remnant of interracial marriage logically left in the Alabama code was an attempt to form a marriage that would be legally void and criminally sanctioned from the outset.

The cases of the 1870s thus saw a rapid retreat from *Burns* and a systematic and thorough dismantling of the adverse precedent. *Ford* initially limited *Burns* to cases involving interracial marriage, and *Green* and *Hoover* demolished *Burns's* remaining governance over interracial marriage. Read together, these cases declared such marriages to be inherently against the state's values and interests and to be logically impossible, given the nature of marriage and the state's intimate relationship with marriage as an institution. The careful trajectory that the state of Alabama plotted in its attack on *Burns*, both through the efforts of attorney general John Sanford and through the Democratic high court's rulings, shows the seriousness with which the white institutions of Alabama took *Burns's* challenge to a reestablishment of a status quo of subordination for African Americans.

These cases would resonate outside of Alabama as well. By setting up the constitutional questions within a framework of questioning the nature of marriage and its relationship to state power, the Alabama high court established the core inquiry into the Fourteenth Amendment's meaning as one of the extent of the federal government's power to intervene. With the scope of equality rendered an afterthought, establishing the principle of superficial symmetry as an acceptable measure would be easier in the years and cases to come.

Pace & Cox v. State and *Pace v. Alabama:* Constituting the State

Pace & Cox v. State would be the Alabama Supreme Court's last word on the constitutionality of its antimiscegenation legislation until the 1950s, and the U.S. Supreme Court's ruling in *Pace v. Alabama* in 1883 would stand until being undercut by *McLaughlin* in 1964 and definitively repudiated in *Loving v. Virginia* in 1967. For rulings of such monumental longevity, the background of the case was fairly unremarkable in the context of its companions at the state level.

As in *Ellis, Ford, Green,* and *Hoover,* the defendants were a black man and white woman who were charged with engaging in an interracial sexual relationship. Little is known about Tony (or Toney) Pace and Mary Ann (or perhaps it was really Mary Jane) Cox. They met and in 1881 were arrested for violating Section 4184.[87] At the time of their arrest, they were living in Clarke County, in the south-central region of Alabama, where many former slaves had remained after emancipation.[88] They were both charged with adultery or fornication rather than intermarriage or attempted intermarriage.[89] Both were convicted and sentenced to two-year terms in the state penitentiary.[90]

Both Pace and Cox appealed; each appeal had procedural elements that were quickly dismissed. They also claimed that the statute violated the U.S. Constitution. The Court spent some time addressing the constitutional challenge; the opinion could simply have cited *Green* and moved on, but apparently the justices felt that further elucidation would be helpful. The Court emphasized the Fourteenth Amendment's equal protection clause and addressed equality directly. The opinion explained that the difference between the punishment for intraracial and interracial adultery did not give rise to an equal protection problem because it did not constitute discrimination for or against either race.[91] This reasoning justified the targeting of differential punishments on the basis of the offense rather than the individuals who committed it. It was the offense of interracial adultery or fornication that differed from intraracial adultery or fornication, not the races of the individuals arrested for engaging in the prohibited activity.

Once this logical distinction was on the ground (however tenuously), the Court was off and running. "The evil tendency of the crime . . . is greater when . . . committed between persons of the two races. . . . Its result may be the amalgamation of the two races, producing a mongrel population and a degraded civilization, the prevention of which is dictated by a sound public policy affecting the highest interests of society and government."[92] This reasoning picked up on and extended the reasoning in *Green* concerning the central place of the family in state structure. *Green* and *Pace*, when read together, present a picture of sharply dichotomous families: the legitimate, intraracial, white cornerstone of the state, and the illegitimate, threatening, destructive interracial not-family. This reasoning rendered racial differentiation not merely permissible, but actually necessary for the future survival of the state. Although the Court had started with an analysis of equality, any substantive engagement with equality left the table quickly as the comparison between inter- and intraracial relationships and their place in the state became the crux of the constitutional question.

Tony Pace's attorney, John Tompkins, appealed the ruling against his client to the U.S. Supreme Court, and the justices placed the case on their docket. The U.S. Supreme Court had little guidance other than the litigation in Alabama; lower federal courts had considered statutes concerning miscegenation only twice, in 1871 and 1879, and had declined to invalidate them either on statutory or constitutional grounds.[93] Tompkins argued nonetheless that Alabama's antimiscegenation statute violated the Fourteenth Amendment's equal protection clause. In his brief to the U.S. Supreme Court, Tompkins attempted to reframe the question of equality around racial discrimination. He cited *Slaughter-House* in support of the proposition that the Fourteenth Amendment's specific purpose was to ameliorate black inequality and provide full citizenship for African Americans.[94] Citing several recent federal precedents acknowledging the unconstitutionality of racial differentiation, he based his analysis on a comparison between the establishment of intraracial adultery or fornication as a misdemeanor and interracial adultery or fornication as a felony.[95]

Tompkins sidestepped Alabama's prohibition of interracial marriage, focusing instead on the narrower issue of the differential penalty for interracial adultery or fornication. *Green*, he claimed, had answered the question of interracial marriage's illegitimacy definitively. Marriage, he conceded, was a social institution fully under control of the state and its particulars were not subject to federal intervention. Inverting the reasoning used in *Ford* to distinguish *Burns*, he claimed that because adultery and fornication were social evils rather than social blessings, "legislative power may not say how crimes . . . may be discriminately punished (where all are equal before the law) according to the caste of the individual who invades them."[96] This move sought to take miscegenation outside of the questions about social equality and render interracial sex a crime parasitic on the simple prohibition of sexual activity between individuals not married to each other.

Henry Tompkins, attorney general for the state of Alabama, filed a response defending the statute in broad terms.[97] Although the law had two purposes—the prevention of intermarriage and the prevention of illicit sexual intercourse between blacks and whites—the ultimate end of the statute was the same: to prevent "the amalgamation of the two different races."[98] The defense of the statute was thus not only a claim that punishing interracial adultery or fornication as a felony was legitimate, but also that the criminal suppression of miscegenation was constitutionally acceptable.

Pace's argument that the differential punishment of adultery constituted inequality failed on two grounds for the state. First, the state announced the principle of symmetry: because both parties were punished alike, regardless of race or gender, the statute did not create any inequality. Second, the crime of interracial adultery was in fact a greater crime than intraracial adultery and warranted greater punishment.[99] In making this claim, the state first noted that adultery between those whose status barred intermarriage often received greater punishment. This simple point introduced the need to examine the relationship between adultery and intermarriage, ultimately implicating the state's authority to regulate marriage.

The state argued that it had traditionally had extensive power to regulate marriage. Marriage was, as *Green* had noted, more than a private contractual relationship because of its implications for the state's future.[100] The antimiscegenation statute was akin in its purpose to the rules against consanguinity: "the prevention of the evil results which are supposed to be developed in their progeny."[101] Because of this particular threat to the state's interests, the state had additional criminal leverage against the couples who purveyed it. Having established the state's traditional powers over these questions, Henry Tompkins now turned to an analysis of the Fourteenth Amendment.

Tompkins articulated a limited vision of national power over state functions and placed the regulation of marriage and family firmly within the ambit of state authority. The primary question for equal protection was not whether the statute created any substantive inequality in its operation, but rather whether the states had the authority to forbid intermarriage. If this power existed, then the constitutionality of antimiscegenation measures was assured "so long as there is no discrimination in the punishment imposed upon the white and that imposed upon the Negro violator of the particular statute." To the response that such a measure stigmatized blacks (and possibly to defend against any latent claims under the Thirteenth Amendment, Tompkins argued that such regulations "[do] not place upon either [race] the badge of inferiority; they are based upon the idea of dissimilarity, which does not necessarily mean legal or civil inequality."[102] This analysis led inevitably to the principle of symmetry, but by framing the question as being primarily about the state's power rather than the scope and meaning of the Fourteenth Amendment, Tompkins pushed the Court toward a superficial review of the nature of the equality underlying the Fourteenth Amendment.

The High Court heard the case during its October 1882 term and issued its ruling on 29 January 1883. The ruling in the more famous *Civil Rights Cases*, argued the same term, would not be issued until October. The Court's consideration of the issue was superficial but picked up on the themes emerging from Alabama and other states, ultimately endorsing a thin conception of symmetry as the appropriate departure point for analysis under equal protection. Initially, the Court claimed that Pace was correct to identify the equal protection clause's purpose as that of "prevent[ing] hostile and discriminating State legislation against any person or class of persons."[103] Equality required accessibility to the legal process on the same terms for all as well as equality in legal outcomes, particularly punishments. In framing the principle this way, the Court relied on the Civil Rights Act of 1870, which included a clause concerning contracts and a requirement of equal legal consequences.[104]

The Court read the equality in punishment, however, as mandating equal sentences for black and white miscegenators, not equal treatment for the purveyors of intra- and interracial adultery or fornication. The code sections, claimed the Court, were entirely consistent: "The one prescribes . . . a punishment for an offence committed between persons of different sexes; the other describes a punishment for an offence which can only be committed where the two sexes are of different races."[105] The discrimination in question was not between blacks and whites but rather between two different offenses. The Court did not explicitly grant the state's rightful power to judge rationally the nature and appropriate punishments for the offenses, but this was the implication of the ruling.

On the state's side, the interplay between the Alabama and U.S. Supreme Courts demonstrated the state's need to justify both its specific policy on interracial sex and its assumption of the authority to regulate daily life in the wake of Reconstruction. On the U.S. Supreme Court's side, the Court's response signaled a tacit acceptance of a dividing line between state and federal authority as well as the federal government's willingness to read the Fourteenth Amendment's guarantees in superficial terms. Much has been made of the legal distinction between social and political equality, and this distinction did do significant analytical work enabling the rise of Jim Crow. Nonetheless, the fundamental distinction in Pace's appeals was between interracial sex's purported threat to the state and the lesser dangers posed by illicit intraracial sex. This reasoning began the process of closing the doctrinal path of reading substantive guarantees of citizenship rights through the Fourteenth Amendment, a path that would not reopen on racial grounds until the twentieth century.

While closing this door, the U.S. Supreme Court opened another. The reasoning in Pace v. Alabama suggested to the states that their articulations of the dangers posed by black equality and their need to develop legal means of articulating and entrenching white supremacy would largely be allowed to stand without serious review. In the South particularly, the states were not slow to see and accept the invitation.

Taking It to the Top: *Pace v. Alabama*, History, and the U.S. Supreme Court

The U.S. Supreme Court is a powerful and visible institution. We study it for that reason, and we look to understand the relationship between law and politics by trying to understand why it addresses cases in the ways that it does. Because of the hierarchic nature of courts and the Supreme Court's national influence, studying the Supreme Court provides a useful window on the development of legal and national norms over time.

We must, however, bound our study of the Court by looking to the ways that it does not necessarily shape its own agenda. Although a leading Supreme Court case may provide the first widely publicized look at a particular issue, most issues percolate through the legal system for years before reaching the U.S. Supreme Court. We need to understand how legal frames developed earlier and how litigation in the lower courts set up frameworks that shape the ways that cases reach the High Court. In doing so, we may need to pay more attention to subnational questions of development that have unintended effects and consequences on the framing and articulation of national questions.

The simple way to explain *Pace* is to say that the U.S. Supreme Court heard a case involving a challenge to state antimiscegenation statutes in the early 1880s; it ruled in favor of such laws by relying on a thin conception of equality based on the observation that blacks and whites were subject to the same punishment under Alabama's law. The case, coming before lengthier and more substantive analyses like the *Civil Rights Cases* and *Plessy v. Ferguson*, was unremarkable except insofar as it hinted at what was to come.

This interpretation, however, overlooks the back history of the case and thus misses its significance. *Pace v. Alabama* marked the first steps on a path that would lead to a comprehensive national acceptance of the systematic legal entrenchment of white supremacy in the South. *Pace* in fact marked the end of an era in a certain sense: after the ruling by the U.S. Supreme Court, no defendant in Alabama challenged a conviction for miscegenation on constitutional grounds again until 1954. Even outside of Alabama, no state court would seriously consider invalidating its antimiscegenation regime on constitutional grounds until the California high court ruled 4–3 that its statute was unconstitutional in *Perez v. Sharp* in 1948. The pattern of the late nineteenth and early twentieth centuries was rather for state supreme courts to address the question of constitutionality summarily by looking not only to the U.S. Supreme Court's ruling in *Pace*, but also to the Alabama high court's ruling in *Pace & Cox v. State* and even more so to *Green v. State*.

The period between 1868 and 1882 was a time of negotiation and contingency on the state level. The state courts genuinely struggled with the issue of interracial marriage, with the most fully developed and contested line of cases emerging in Alabama. As the debate progressed, the state courts winnowed through various arguments, and a gradual consensus on framing the issue emerged around a thin conception of equality as symmetry. The shape that the debates took influenced the way that the U.S. Supreme Court would ultimately address the issue, making it appear to be more of a foregone conclusion than it actually was, and the Supreme Court ultimately did not deal with the state courts' concerns about marriage's public significance. The Court's opinion thus left marriage simultaneously as a public institution but as wholly within the states' control.

By 1883, the U.S. Supreme Court's ruling was fairly predictable, but this settled expectation did not emerge without struggle. The trajectory of the case law in Alabama and elsewhere reveals this struggle and the need for a well articulated theory concerning the need for and legitimacy of anti-miscegenation laws. When read alongside the history of the unsettled nature of race relations in the South immediately after the Civil War, this trajectory suggests openness to change and a sense of historical contingency in the early 1870s. As Michael McConnell argues, segregation in education was debated fiercely and opposed by many Republicans during Reconstruction.[106] Barbara Welke, Grace Elizabeth Hale, and Martha Hodes have all shown that race and gender relations were left in a state of upheaval in the immediate postbellum era.[107] The full meaning and legitimacy of the Fourteenth Amendment were not set by its language and passage through Congress and the states, but rather depended on its early uses and interpretations.[108]

Former slaves immediately began exercising their rights after the war and the consumption patterns of a rising black middle class raised the specter of blacks' being able to purchase their way into equality, as other groups had begun to do.[109] Many whites' response was to work assiduously to prevent meaningful black equality. Although blacks could not be summarily dismissed from the political arena, their ability to exercise all of the privileges and benefits formerly reserved for whites was contingent on at least two things: the state's not stepping in to prevent them from exercising these privileges and benefits, and the state's active thwarting of those who would block African Americans from meaningful equality.[110] Whatever else can be said about Congress's actions and intentions during the late 1860s and early 1870s, the laws it passed addressed both of these themes.

This dynamic was complicated by the fact that the state itself, both on the federal and the local level, was under intense negotiation (as was the scope of federal governance). Of course individual state governments were reconstituted in the wake of secession, war, and the reestablishment of the union, but additional structural changes were afoot. Peter Bardaglio has suggested that the postbellum Southern states also faced the challenge of stepping into the role of the ultimate guarantor of patriarchal power, a position held privately by individual white men in the antebellum era.[111] The example of miscegenation illustrates Bardaglio's argument well: in the antebellum years, interracial sex was almost exclusively controlled and sanctioned by individual white men, but after the war's end, the state took on the regulatory role through the vehicle of criminal laws like Section 4184. Ultimately the patchwork of white supremacy established piecemeal in the years between 1866 (antimiscegenation laws) and the elimination of the black vote in the 1890s would be rationalized and institutionalized in a wave of new state constitutions debated and passed in the early twentieth century. The process of legitimizing legislation against miscegenation thus comprised a process of incorporating the enforcement of social norms into the state's structure and operation.

The cases in Alabama show this process in a microcosm. Although the legislature acted quickly to criminalize interracial sexual relationships, these statutes were initially in question. The questions of constitutionality and conflict with federal policies reached Alabama's highest court six times within thirteen years, and the decisions issued by the court ranged from a finding that the entire policy against miscegenation violated federal law and the constitution to a finding that all legal modes of suppressing miscegenation were permissible. The struggle over miscegenation enabled the rearticulation of the relationship between race and nationhood in the postbellum era. As such, it had high stakes both for the state of Alabama and for the nation as a whole. Pace v. Alabama may not have featured extensive constitutional analysis, but the ruling spoke volumes about what had been settled and what could be built on this settled ground.

The uncertainty of the 1870s generated a moment in which the Alabama high court had to work through in detail the meanings of marriage, family, and miscegenation to the state. The *Burns* Court, countering *Ellis*, read marriage as a simple contract, but later cases read the marriage contract not as a private agreement between individuals but rather as a unique instance of state control. The reasoning in *Ford*, *Hoover*, and *Green* illustrates Alabama's growing commitment to a conception of marriage as a quasi-public relationship, at least in terms of the state's ability to determine what constituted family and legitimacy. This reasoning allowed significant state control over marriage as an institution with a minimal control over the internal workings of marriage.[112] The post-*Burns* cases emphasized the threat that miscegenation posed to the state: the forming of mixed-race family units. Intraracial family units were crucial to the state's workings, because only among such units could the white families be acknowledged and nurtured as the backbone of state development.

Roughly the same developmental path would mark the emergence and validation of the whole panoply of Jim Crow laws. In both Alabama and Virginia, laws regarding miscegenation had been settled as constitutional and the basic form established by the early 1880s; the only changes until the 1960s were acts in the 1920s to make the laws more restrictive.[113] With the question of miscegenation definitively settled and the distinction between social and political equality off the ground, the path was clear for the development of other racially based restrictions framed in symmetrical terms. The U.S. Supreme Court's ruling in *Pace* put the South on notice that equality would not be deeply interrogated, and that state control over "fundamentally local" questions like marriage, transportation, public accommodations, and schooling would be sustained.

In the national arena, *Pace* was also a significant bellwether. The U.S. Supreme Court's lack of interest in deep analysis of equality embedded a conception of the Fourteenth Amendment that would support the outcomes and reasoning in the *Civil Rights Cases* and *Plessy*. This trajectory did not mean that the Fourteenth Amendment would remain dormant; already the state courts were deciding the precursors to *Lochner* and using the amendment to invalidate protective labor measures.[114] When viewed along with other cases decided between 1873 and the turn of the century, *Pace* provides the cornerstone for a narrative of a Court that sought to facilitate national rebuilding by allowing the South to exercise significant control over race relations while the judiciary aggressively enabled large-scale industrial development. This narrative, however, must necessarily depend on the state-level development of doctrinal justifications for federal abstention on questions of racial justice.

This narrative encourages rethinking of broad theories of political development to tailor them more closely to legal contexts. Structural analysis of institutions and their development, linked to path dependence, can help in providing a grand narrative of development. Focusing on the law, however, suggests that the process is more complex, contingent, and porous than such grand narratives would acknowledge. As Amy Bridges has cautioned, investigating a deeper context suggests that midlevel theories are more appropriate to account for complex phenomena.[115] Her insight applies particularly to the courts, passive institutions that by design must directly grapple with outside social and political phenomena without the capacity to exercise significant control in shaping their own broad agendas.

Looking to nodes of conflict—the moments of disruption and fissure in which actors in the legal system struggle over meaning—can help to unravel this process.[116] The battle over interracial marriage differed from the late nineteenth- and early twentieth-century litigation over the legitimacy of protective labor legislation. Unlike the struggles over limits on employers' relations with employees, there was very little elite support for or interest in invalidating bans on cross-racial intimacy. Nonetheless, lawyers representing convicted defendants appealing their draconian sentences had sufficient incentives to challenge the prohibitory regime on any grounds that could conceivably succeed. The threat of constitutional challenge under the Fourteenth Amendment raised whites' anxieties about the capacity of the state to reestablish and maintain racial hierarchy, and fears of miscegenation provided a sharp focus for unsettled broader issues with racial meaning, the new balance of power between the states and the national government, and the significance of families within the states' structure.

Reading *Pace* back into the early history of the Fourteenth Amendment sensitizes us to what was settled and what was open. On the national level, the case was a bellwether for future development, marking a course that later courts would adopt and refine in endorsing both a thin conception of equality and a strict separation between political and social equality. For the U.S. Supreme Court, *Pace*, not *Plessy*, initiated the line of cases permitting explicitly racial classifications under equal protection. *Plessy's* role was to harden this doctrinal commitment, and later analysts could reconceive this history as establishing a barrier that would require years of planned litigation to dismantle piece by piece.

Pace teaches two other lessons, however. First, the history of the case before its consideration by the U.S. Supreme Court suggests that the meaning of equal protection was anything but fixed during Reconstruction and the immediate post-Reconstruction era. Seeing the emergence of Jim Crow as a path-dependent result of institutional accommodations made in federal law during the years after the passage of the Fourteenth Amendment would miss the significant renegotiation of the relationship between race and the state that took place first on the state level and only later on the federal level. Although this renegotiation was not exclusively legal, looking to the law and particularly to the struggle over regulating interracial intimacy provides a sense of the range of alternatives available to policy makers in these years. The legal battles also highlight the extent to which private intimacy had public significance for many white elites. Establishing the constitutional capacity to bar interracial marriage was a high priority not only because of simple racism, but also to underline the states' continued authority over the day-to-day lives of citizens.

Pace also suggests that a narrow focus on doctrine at the federal level misses the extent to which both cultural conflicts and their mediation on the state level framed cases as they were presented at the federal level. If state-level debates had framed the questions differently, or if the regulation of miscegenation had not been contested at the state level, the federal courts' consideration of these issues and their ultimate path could have been different. This is not to suggest that the federal courts were constrained absolutely by what occurred at the state level. Rather, the process in the state courts refined the arguments made to the U.S. Supreme Court and provided available templates for analysis that the U.S. Supreme Court could accept or reject.

Both Pace and Plessy are dead, swept away by the Warren Court, but ghosts remain. In both cases, the Supreme Court refused to look beneath the surface of equality to consider the intentions driving the policies in question. A formal commitment to sameness in treatment was sufficient to justify these policies; some would argue that current equal protection doctrine features the same principle. The history of Pace, however, emphasizes that the meaning of equal protection is never fixed and that the U.S. Supreme Court's internal and external workings do not operate independently to produce doctrinal outcomes. Rather, moments of openness and contingency occur, and actors in all parts of the legal system seek to exploit them.

Notes

A version of this chapter was presented at the annual meeting of the American Political Science Association in 2002. I thank the American Philosophical Society, which generously funded my research with a Henry M. Phillips Jurisprudence grant; the National Endowment for the Humanities for a summer stipend; and the University of Oregon for a Bray Award. I also thank research assistants Jason Tanenbaum and Michelle Diggles as well as Ron Kahn, Peggy Pascoe, and Lane West-Newman for their helpful feedback.

1. *Slaughter-House Cases*, 83 U.S. 36 (1873).

2. *Strauder v. West Virginia*, 100 U.S. 303 (1880); *Civil Rights Cases*, 109 U.S. 3 (1883).

3. *Plessy v. Ferguson*, 163 U.S. 537 (1896); see, e.g., Walter Murphy, James Fleming, and Sotirios Barber, *American Constitutional Interpretation*, 2nd ed. (Westbury, N.Y.: Foundation Press, 1995), 896–908.

4. 106 U.S. 583 (1883).

5. *Loving v. Virginia*, 388 U.S. 1 (1967). Technically, an earlier case, the Court's ruling in *McLaughlin v. Florida* in 1964, invalidated the specific criminalization of interracial cohabitation, thus striking down the principle endorsed by *Pace*. Nonetheless, *McLaughlin* raised much less popular and jurisprudential interest than *Loving*. Peter Wallenstein, *Tell the Court I Love My Wife: Race, Marriage, and the Law—An American History* (New York: Palgrave Macmillan, 2002), 208–211.

6. Martha Hodes, *White Women, Black Men: Illicit Sex in the Nineteenth-Century South, 1890–1940* (New Haven, Conn.: Yale University Press, 1997).

7. Wallenstein, *Tell the Court I Love My Wife*, 74–75, 78.

8. Hodes, *White Women, Black Men*.

9. Peter Kolchin, *First Freedom: The Responses of Alabama's Blacks to Emancipation and Reconstruction* (Westport, Conn.: Greenwood Press, 1972).

10. Charles Robinson II, *Dangerous Liaisons: Sex and Love in the Segregated South* (Fayetteville: University of Arkansas Press, 2003), 8–20.

11. William Rogers, David Ward, Leah Atkins, and Wayne Flynt, *Alabama: The History of a Deep South State* (Tuscaloosa: University of Alabama Press, 1994), 230–232.

12. Ibid., 236–241.

13. As noted above, *Loving v. Virginia* invalidated Virginia's antimiscegenation law in 1967. Some states, including Alabama, maintained that *Loving* only applied in Virginia. An irritated federal district court judge struck down Alabama's statute in 1970 in *U.S. v. Brittain*, 319 F. Supp. 1058 (N.D. Ala. 1970). An initiative passed in November 2000 finally reversed Alabama's constitutional prohibition against miscegenation established in 1901.

14. Ala. Stat. 1866: Art. 1, sec. 61.

15. Wallenstein, *Tell the Court I Love My Wife*; Robinson, *Dangerous Liaisons*.

16. Robinson, *Dangerous Liaisons*, 28–29.

17. Rogers et al., *Alabama*, 247.

18. Ibid., 248–249.

19. Ibid., 251. The Alabama Klan of the late 1860s and early 1870s should not be confused with its later incarnation in the early twentieth century. Although the Klan of the late 1800s engaged in violent suppression of black political activity, it was neither as well entrenched nor as politically connected as the Progressive Era Klan. Glenn Feldman, *Politics, Society, and the Klan in Alabama* (Tuscaloosa: University of Alabama Press, 1999).

20. Rogers et al., *Alabama*, 254–264.

21. Mary Frances Berry, "Judging Morality: Sexual Behavior and Legal Consequences in the Late Nineteenth Century South," *Journal of American History* 78 (1991): 836.

22. Wallenstein, *Tell the Court I Love My Wife*, 377, 383.

23. *Ellis v. State*, 42 Ala. 525 (1868), Trial Record. Alabama Department of History and Archives, Montgomery, Ala., 1, 3.

24. Wallenstein, *Tell the Court I Love My Wife*, 61–62.

25. Ibid., 254.

26. Trial record, *Ellis v. State*, 4.

27. Wallenstein, *Tell the Court I Love My Wife*, n. 44.

28. *Ellis v. State*, 42 Ala. 525, 525 (1868).

29. Ibid. at 526.

30. Ibid.

31. Ibid.

32. Wallenstein, *Tell the Court I Love My Wife*, 378.

33. *Ellis v. State*, 526.

34. Wayne D. Moore, "(Re)Construction of Constitutional Authority and Meaning: The Fourteenth Amendment and *Slaughter-House Cases*," this volume.

35. Steven Bank, "Anti-Miscegenation Laws and the Dilemma of Symmetry: The Understanding of Equality in the Civil Rights Act of 1865," *University of Chicago Law School Roundtable* 2 (1995): 303.

36. *State v. Hairston and Williams*, 63 N.C. 439 (1869).

37. *Scott v. State*, 39 Ga. 321 (1869).

38. *State v. Gibson*, 36 Ind. 389 (1871).

39. Ibid., 393.

40. Ibid., 395–397.

41. Ibid., 404–405.

42. *Burns v. State*, 48 Ala. 195, 196 (1872).

43. Ibid.

44. Ibid., 197.

45. Ibid., 198.

46. Ibid., 198.

47. Reva Siegel, "Why Equal Protection No Longer Protects: The Evolving Forms of Status-Enforcing State Action," *Stanford Law Review* 49 (1997): 1123–1124.

48. *Burns v. State*, 198.

49. See, e.g., Samuel Marcossen, "Colorizing the Constitution of Originalism: Clarence Thomas at the Rubicon," *Law and Inequality* 16 (1998); Raoul Berger, "Robert Bork's Contribution to Original Intention," *Northwestern University Law Review* 84 (1990).

50. Bank, "Anti-Miscegenation Laws"; Andrew Kull, *The Color-Blind Constitution* (Cambridge, Mass.: Harvard University Press, 1992).

51. Michael McConnell, "Originalism and the Desegregation Decisions," *Virginia Law Review* 81 (1995).

52. *State v. Bell*, 66 Tenn. 9 (1872).

53. *State v. Ross*, 76 N.C. 225 (1877).

54. Wallenstein, *Tell the Court I Love My Wife*, 88–91.

55. *Slaughter-House Cases*, 83 U.S. 26, 72–73 (1873).

56. Ibid., 70.

57. *Ford v. State*, 53 Ala. 150, 151.

58. Ibid.

59. Ibid. *Green et al. v. State*, 59 Ala. 69 (1878).

60. *Green et al. v. State*, 59 Ala. 69 (1878).

61. *Green v. State*, 58 Ala. 190 (1877), Trial Record. Alabama Department of History and Archives, Montgomery, AL, 3, 6.

62. *Green et al. v. State*, 59 Ala. 68, 69 (1878).

63. *Green v. State*, trial record, 6.

64. *Green v. State*, 58 Ala. 190 (1878)

65. Ibid. at 92.

66. Ibid., emphasis in original.

67. Ibid.; see also Bank, "Anti-Miscegenation Laws."

68. *Green v. State*, 58 Ala. 190 (1878), at 192–193.

69. In *Bradwell v. Illinois*, decided the day after *Slaughter-House*, the U.S. Supreme Court denied Myra Bradwell's challenge to Illinois' refusal to grant her a license to practice law. The Court's majority simply relied on *Slaughter-House* to determine that the Fourteenth Amendment's scope was insufficiently broad to justify interpreting a license to practice law as a privilege or immunity protected by the U.S. Constitution. *Bradwell v. Illinois*, 83 U.S. 130 (1873).

70. *Green v. State* at 193, citing *Townsend v. Griffin*.

71. Ibid., citing *Maguire v. Maguire*.

72. Ibid., 194.

73. Ibid.

74. Ibid. This reservation of power enabled individual men to retain patriarchal authority in their families without undue fear of state intervention. See Siegel, "Why Equal Protection No Longer Protects."

75. Ibid.

76. Berry, "Judging Morality," 840.

77. *Green v. State*, 197.

78. The Greens, however, were not finished. A second case, under the management of a different attorney, reached the Alabama Supreme Court in 1878. The second appeal was based on procedural rather than constitutional grounds and was also rebuffed by the Court. The Greens argued that the trial court had refused to give a requested jury instruction that might have convinced the jury to view their relationship as a legitimate marriage rather than a long-term sexual liaison based on adultery or fornication. The Court noted that cohabitation was the key element of the offense of miscegenation, and the defendants' own production of their marriage certificate merely bolstered the case against them. *Green et al. v. State*, 59 Ala. 69, 70–71 (1878).

79. Bank, "Anti-Miscegenation Laws"; McConnell, "Originalism."

80. *Hoover v. State*, 59 Ala. 58 (1878).

81. *Hoover v. State*, 59 Ala. 58 (1878), Trial Record. Alabama Department of History and Archives, Montgomery, AL, 6.

82. *Hoover v. State*, 58.

83. Trial Record at 6.

84. *Hoover v. State*, 59.

85. Ibid. at 60.

86. Ibid.

87. *Pace & Cox v. State*, 69 Ala. 231 (1881), Trial Record, Alabama Department of History and Archives, Montgomery, Ala., 3.

88. Harvey Jackson, "The Middle-Class Democracy Victorious: The Mitcham War of Clarke County, Alabama, 1893," *Journal of Southern History* 57 (1991).

89. *Pace & Cox v. State*, 69 Ala. 231 (1882).

90. Trial Record, 3.

91. *Pace & Cox v. State*, 69 Ala. 231, 233 (1882).

92. Ibid.

93. Wallenstein, *Tell the Court I Love My Wife*, 108–110.

94. John Tompkins, *Brief for the Plaintiff in Error*. Filed in the U.S. Supreme Court (1882), 2.

95. Ibid., 3–4.

96. Ibid., 5.

97. John Sanford, who had defended against the previous challenges, was now the clerk of the Alabama Supreme Court and had overseen the preparation of the trial record for the U.S. Supreme Court's consideration. *Pace v. Alabama*, trial record, 10.

98. Henry Tompkins, *Brief and Argument for Appellee*, filed in the U.S. Supreme Court (1882), 2–3.

99. Ibid., 3.

100. Ibid., 4–5.

101. Ibid., 5–6.

102. Ibid., 13–14.

103. *Pace v. Alabama*, 106 U.S. 583, 584 (1883).

104. Ibid., 584–585.

105. Ibid., 585.

106. McConnell, "Originalism."

107. Barbara Welke, *Recasting American Liberty: Gender, Race, Law, and the Railroad Revolution, 1865–1920* (Cambridge: Cambridge University Press, 2001); Grace Elizabeth Hale, *Making Whiteness: The Culture of Segregation in the South, 1890–1940* (New York: Pantheon Books, 1998); Hodes, *White Women, Black Men.*

108. Moore, "(Re)Construction of Constitutional Authority and Meaning," this volume; Pamela Brandwein, "The *Civil Rights Cases* and the Lost Language of State Neglect," this volume.

109. Noel Ignatiev, *How the Irish Became White* (New York: Routledge, 1995); Hale, *Making Whiteness.*

110. See Brandwein, *"Civil Rights Cases,"* this volume.

111. Peter Bardaglio, *Reconstructing the Household: Families, Sex, and the Law in the Nineteenth-Century South* (Chapel Hill: University of North Carolina Press, 1995).

112. Siegal, "Why Equal Protection No Longer Protects."

113. Peter Wallenstein, "Race, Marriage, and the Law of Freedom: Alabama and Virginia, 1860s–1960s," *Chicago-Kent Law Review* 70 (1994): 406.

114. Julie Novkov, *Constituting Workers, Protecting Women: Gender, Law, and Labor in the Progressive Era and New Deal Years* (Ann Arbor: University of Michigan Press, 2001).

115. Amy Bridges, "Path Dependence, Sequence, History, Theory," *Studies in American Political Development* 14 (2000).

116. Novkov, *Constituting Workers, Protecting Women.*

Chapter 9

Constitutionalizing Terms of Inclusion: Friends of the Indian and Citizenship for Native Americans, 1880s–1930s

Carol Nackenoff

The Supreme Court is one important actor, but not necessarily the final arbiter, in struggles over the meaning of constitutional principles and rights. In this chapter, I consider how best to think about the relationship between activists and the Court in the context of the highly contested meaning of citizenship from approximately 1880 to the early 1930s, with special attention to forging the relationship between Native Americans and citizenship in the constitutional order. The period begins with the galvanization of reform efforts by the Ponca removal controversy and the publication of Helen Hunt Jackson's *A Century of Dishonor* (1881), a work highly critical of U.S. government policy toward Native Americans.[1] The defining feature of the period is the Dawes (General Allotment) Act of 1887, providing for the allotment of Native American lands to individuals—land in severalty—and granting citizenship to Indians who took up these allotments.[2] Supporters of allotment policy reasoned that if communal tribal property were broken up and distributed to Indian heads of household and single individuals—with remaining lands designated surplus available for sale—Indians would more quickly learn to become industrious and self-sufficient, earn bread by the sweat of their brow, and become prepared to join civilized society. The "Dawes Act era" refers to the period during which the allotment policy remained in effect, from 1887 until 1934, when the Indian Reorganization Act prohibited further allotment and instituted other significant reforms in federal government policy. Toward the end of this era, the Indian Citizenship Act of 1924 granted citizenship to all Native Americans within the territorial boundaries of the United States who had not yet been so designated, and political forces arose that pressed for acknowledgment that allotment policy had been a failure.

366

This was a period of intense negotiation about citizenship. Not only policy changes and constitutional constructions, but also the reach and structure of the federal court system were at issue. Several generations of mobilized activists and interest groups incorporated and drew upon lawyers, legal scholars, former members of the state and federal bench, social scientists, legislators and other political figures, journalists and editors with the capacity to reach a wide audience, and funders with networks of contacts as they played a key role in framing—and then in reframing—the nature of the "Indian problem." The Dawes Act era bore witness to two important and successive framings that would bear on understandings of what Native American citizenship entailed or required of various institutions and actors.

The first framing gave rise to the Dawes Act and successive statutes designed to implement allotment and promote the assimilation of the Indian into the wider society. Citizenship was tied to acceptance of property relations and understandings of independent agency and manhood prevalent in "civilized" society. Reforms were sometimes advanced in the name of breaking the dependence of Native Americans on government rations and handouts—a welfare reform measure, as it were, that would divest the federal government of financial responsibility for Indians as they presumably learned to take responsibility for themselves. But if government income supports were to be withdrawn, federal government legal authority over the Indian would tend to expand. These reformers tended to see citizens as those who were equally subject to, and who had equal recourse to, the rule of law. If Indians were treated by law rather than caprice, they would be tutored in citizenship. The reformers' desire to guide the Indian toward citizenship required increased federal intervention and suggested at least a short-term agenda of protection. The goal of civilizing the American Indian made many such reformers proponents of national state building during a state-building era.

The second framing arose chiefly after World War I and denounced federal government policy as harmful to Native Americans and in violation of important rights, including religious freedom. This new generation of activists, who mobilized vigorously and effectively to bring an end to the Dawes Act era, wished to preserve and celebrate Native American cultures and diversity, finding in them an alternative to some of the worst features of the industrial era. Tending to emphasize local knowledge and participatory governance, this subsequent generation of reformers pursued an agenda that had both nationalizing and decentralizing features. Their project involved returning jurisdiction over some matters to Native Americans and limiting the control of the administrative state in these areas. At the same time, they wished to break the power of state and local governmental institutions over land claims so they would no longer be resolved to the detriment of tribal Indians. This required a national solution.

Periods in which Native American issues were nationalized tended to be periods in which conflicts between state and federal government, between branches of the national government, and between organized groups with various kinds of material, political, and ideological stakes in the outcome of these conflicts intensified. When contestants in these struggles were able to successfully articulate the conflict in constitutional terms, the pace of institutional change often intensified. This dynamic had the capacity to draw the Supreme Court into significant periods of doctrinal activity and development involving Native Americans. At one point in the early twentieth century, the Court, having tried several different formulations of the citizenship issue that failed to reduce conflict, deferred to Congress, removing itself from further engagement in determining the relationship between wards and citizens. And in the final period of this study, policy change met some of the rights-based grievances occasioned by government action, removing some of the mounting pressure for Court engagement.

The Court and the Broader Interpretive Community

The Court is sometimes accused of making grandiose claims about its power to establish constitutional meanings and of preempting democracy through juristocratic interventions in political processes. In response, some current legal scholars urge a more populist or democratic deliberation about the meaning of the Constitution.[3] To reinvigorate democracy, the Court's own posture must be different.[4] Doctrines and rules of constitutional construction do not absolve the Court from the obligation of constitutional dialogue. However, other recent legal scholars have had a great deal to say about why and how courts fail to monopolize the Constitution's meaning. A jurisprudential model that focuses so exclusively on the Court's articulations incorrectly neglects the ways in which constitutional meanings are actually and actively constructed by other actors in the political process. There is a great deal of "elaboration of constitutional meaning outside the courts," and this is a central means of resolving textual indeterminacies.[5] According to Keith Whittington, "the jurisprudential model needs to be supplemented with a more explicitly political one that describes a distinct effort to understand and rework the meaning of a received constitutional text."[6] Judicial attempts to foreclose constitutional questions tend to leave unresolved many issues at stake in political disputes; "in both historical and modern contexts, public debate over constitutional meaning has been a significant component of developing the constructions."[7] The exploration below demonstrates that the Court does not monopolize the Constitution's meaning and offers corroboration of Whittington's insight. As Ronald Kahn argues, the world outside the Court factors into judicial decision making beyond taking cognizance of events and facts.[8] And as Ken I. Kersch demonstrates in his contribution to this volume, justices "had always brought the outside world into the sinews of the decisions issuing from the internal world of the Court"; this was no artifact of the purported revolution of 1937.[9]

The Supreme Court and lower federal court agendas were affected by funded, mobilized, and highly motivated organized interests that pressed Native American issues on the Court. The story of how pioneer feminist Belva Lockwood used her legal skills and hard-won access to the Supreme Court, aided by other women trained in law, to successfully litigate the largest monetary settlement of a land claim on behalf of Native Americans in 1906, is illustrative.[10] This is but one example of the impact on the Court's agenda that a dogged feminist lawyer who took an interest in a particular case was able to make after nearly fifteen years of work. Likewise, in the early 1920s, a group of wealthy California women facilitated the highly visible legal and political battles waged in the name of Native Americans by Stella Atwood, head of the General Federation of Women's Clubs' (GFWC) Committee on Indian Welfare, by then researcher John Collier, and by GFWC Indian Welfare Committee attorney Francis Wilson. These activists paid salaries for the researcher and attorney and expenses for Atwood.[11] Only those mobilized and equipped to use the federal courts to wage their battles are likely to turn to this arena. The availability of resources for litigation determines the sustained attention particular issue areas may receive. Because the Court is generally reluctant to take on issues that have been insufficiently litigated in lower courts, surmounting barriers to entry depends on the "availability of resources for legal mobilization."[12] Constitutional litigation requires institutional mechanisms that overcome cost barriers to the individual plaintiffs—support structures, financial resources, and, increasingly in the era of my investigation, law firms.[13]

Court decisions themselves can play a role in mobilizing groups to more political activity, including legal contestation.[14] And when decisions are undertheorized, organized groups may keep their focus trained on the Court, seeing there an opportunity for participation in shaping doctrinal developments. Whether wittingly or not, it appears the Court may have engaged in some cases of either democracy-promoting or democracy-permitting outcomes in fleshing out the relationship between protection and citizenship for Native Americans. These would seem to be moments particularly well described by Cass Sunstein's judicial minimalism, and reminiscent of Charles E. Lindblom's "science of muddling through," used to describe congressional policy making.[15] In a period of vigorous dialogue, the Court tended to feel its way toward the position it established in *United States v. Nice* (1916) that citizenship was "not incompatible with tribal existence or continued guardianship, and so may be conferred without completely emancipating the Indians or placing them beyond the reach of congressional regulations adopted for their protection."[16] This seems to have cleared the way for the Citizenship Act of 1924. Throughout the period leading up to *Nice*, policy makers in Congress, members of the executive branch, state governments, federal and state courts, and activists continued to respond and to reshape what they meant to say about the preconditions, parameters, and terms of citizenship. The Court did not quell democratic debate even when it attempted to settle the issue, and seemed sometimes to invite additional opportunities for response and reconsideration.

In periods of contestation such as occurred between *Matter of Heff* (1905) and *U.S. v. Nice* (1916), development of a national position on citizenship proceeded in a manner that could be characterized as iterative. Groups that were unhappy with a Court decision and were armed with particular understandings and expectations about citizenship pressed statutory reforms on Congress, and Congress responded in some measure. Congressional action affected the kinds of cases that came to the Court. The Court then engaged in statutory and constitutional construction that led to criticism by activist reformers and policy makers, including members of the legal community, followed by a new round of proposals and responses, with constitutional construction paying heed to new statutorily enshrined and administratively embellished political sentiment. The Court was not necessarily the leader and initiator in the process of conceptual change that impacted legal decision making.[17] The constitutional history of struggles over the meaning and scope of Native American citizenship involve "feedback loops." As Thomas J. Keck points out in this volume, "the 'legal' ideas that influence the justices . . . are derived in large part from ongoing debates in the broader political system, and the 'political' interests that pressure the Court are often constituted by legal categories created by the justices themselves."[18] Conceptions of citizenship and standing in the political order that energized activists influenced the Court, and doctrinal developments on the Court reshaped the efforts, strategies, and language of activists.

If it sometimes appears to settle constitutional matters for a time, the Court also frequently *unsettles* formulas. Some moments are more promising than are others for contesting particular constitutional meanings. Opportunities may come and go like "policy windows" that policy entrepreneurs attempt to exploit when a problem is recognized, a solution is developed in the policy community, and the opportunity for policy change is present. For John Kingdon, such windows "present themselves and stay open for only short periods," and it is then that items can move onto a decision agenda.[19] Organized activists who have managed to establish a claim to be heard can, at that point, function like policy entrepreneurs. Entrepreneurs willing to invest time, energy, reputation, money, and other resources to promote a position are found in multiple formal and informal locations in the political system.[20]

Allocation of attention to issues and problems on the Court may frequently be more episodic than incremental. Frameworks through which issues are analyzed in the Supreme Court may, somewhat like Congress, alternate between periods of relative stability and rapid change. Baumgartner and Jones find that "the American political system lurches from one point of apparent equilibrium to another."[21] This accords with Whittington's analysis of the "punctuated character of much of constitutional development," when political pressures and the preexisting institutions, norms, and settlements that hitherto contained them reach an untenable point.[22]

Investigations into the changing status of Native Americans in the polity have prompted some to claim that rules, doctrines, and precedents merely mask the extent to which Court decisions are rooted in politics. Political struggles over Reconstruction and the Civil War Amendments, the press of westward migration, and economic expansion form an inescapable backdrop to decisions that seem to have rather contingent constitutional rooting. More than one scholar has found a lack of principled decision making in the arena of Native American jurisprudence: "the Court is not wedded to constitutional, treaty, or legal principles so much as it is to ad hoc decision-making based on issues, players, and political circumstances."[23] If this is the case, then we might well go off to join the rational choice school.

However, doctrine and precedent matter. The Court viewed Native American citizenship issues in the Dawes Act era through channels of doctrinal development that included federalism, the Fourteenth Amendment, the commerce power, protective legislation, contracts, property, and treaty law. Some of these doctrinal areas were more closely and carefully developed than were others. Although many specific outcomes were left indeterminate, these framings shaped the terms and context within which members of the interpretive community fought out their battles and the outcomes that were thinkable and likely.

Precedents and stories about case law trajectories establish the terrain on which contestants will frame their complaints, but these precedents and stories are constantly reworked. As Austin Sarat contends, "the hegemony of liberal legality is measured in the extent to which it can induce its most disadvantaged citizens to fight their battles on the terrain of liberal legality itself."[24] But litigants bring their own understandings of and to law when they come to court, and this "contact" plays a vital role in keeping law in touch with the social order in which it is embedded.[25] Litigants play a role in the Court's reworking of these precedents and stories, but so, too, do the historical narratives, analogies, and metaphors the justices bring to their task.[26] We will have reason to see, in the struggle over the meaning and scope of Native American citizenship, both that legal elites influence public opinion and political movements and that legal ideas help shape political ideas and channel struggles for power.[27]

Although I have borrowed from models of congressional development, it is important to remember that the Court has its own norms, dynamics, and institutional history and is not an institution that simply resembles or mirrors others. Historical institutionalists Karen Orren and Stephen Skowronek posit the relative independence of different institutional formations, born of different historical origins and tending to different patterns of development.[28] They find "a political universe organized and activated by intercurrence—engagements throughout the polity of the different norms embedded in institutions, the terms of control contested, more or less intensely, in the ongoing push and pull among them."[29] Instead of an integrated political system, "at any moment in time several different sets of rules and norms are likely to be operating simultaneously"; "relations among political institutions are (at least) as likely to be in tension as in fit and the tension generated is an important source of political conflict and change."[30] Political actors may exploit tensions and contradictions that exist because of these institutional mismatches; in this context, one sees the potential for creativity by actors of all sorts. An "inherently open, dynamic, and contested" political universe means that "existing norms and collective projects, of varying degrees of permanence, are buffeted against one another as a normal condition."[31] As the Court encountered and interacted with other institutions during the Dawes Act era, there was indeed room for political actors to work creatively.

Interested actors may be viewed as constituting an interpretive community. Kahn sees the interpretive community engaged in a dialogic relationship with the Court; I prefer to envision the Court as constituting a part of that interpretive community.[32] Julie Novkov's imagery of "nodes of conflict" involving activist organizations, legal scholars, policy makers, and legal institutions is also quite helpful in thinking about this period of negotiation of the status and terms of incorporation of Native Americans. Recognizing that judges do not monopolize control over doctrine, Novkov enhances our ability to envision the dynamic production of meaning. Nodes of conflict are contested narrative spaces or "moments in the development of doctrine during which the various groups of actors who have access to the legal community struggle among themselves and with each other to establish their interpretations of a particular legal concept or phrase as the dominant norm."[33] During periods of contestation, decisions leave ambiguities, lacunae in doctrine that are taken up and used by other actors in the process of interpretation. Such nodes require "the creation and acceptance by the legal community of an ambiguity in the law, a contested social issue, and the development of a connection between the ambiguity and the social issue."[34] In the Dawes Act era, it appears that some moments may even give rise to multiple nodes. Different groups of actors may be involved in each issue, but there are conceptual linkages across contested issue areas. Overlap occurs because political and cultural discourse develops in ways that pattern thinking about social and economic problems, and because expectations about the role of the state in their resolution are likewise patterned. Overlap between issue areas also occurs because doctrinal developments help frame the ways in which members of the interpretive community link law and the Constitution to particular struggles.

I will examine some ways in which constitutional controversies helped frame the arguments about Native American citizenship and consider how frames dealt in and shaped the participation of other members of the interpretive community. I will look at ways in which initiatives undertaken by activists impacted constitutional frames and doctrines. Friends of the Indian often focused simultaneously on contesting rules, procedures, and values in both legislative and judicial arenas; it was not a sign of weakness when activists focused attention on the Court. These activists testified in Congress and pressed administrative agencies. They fought battles on several fronts that included bringing their arguments to the court of public opinion and to the federal court system. Let me now turn to some central ways in which the establishment and interpretation of precedent helped establish the terrain on which Native American citizenship was conceptualized and contested in the Dawes Act era.

Patterning and Nationalizing Conflict over Native American Citizenship: From the Marshall Court to the Dawes Act Era

Marshall Court cases such as *Cherokee Nation v. Georgia* (1831) and *Worcester v. Georgia* (1832) established a framework within which Native Americans were conceptualized as participating in a ward-guardian relationship with the national government.[35] These early decisions constructed the terrain on which many subsequent battles were fought. The Marshall Court asserted that the federal government alone had power to make treaties with the Indians and denied state power to abrogate or alter those formed between Indians and the federal government. State incapacity to legislate on Indian affairs was never successfully challenged in the Supreme Court following *Worcester*.[36] Marshall's image of Indians as wards was designed to authorize federal government claims to protect Indians from states and foreign nations.[37] The ward-guardian imagery, the denial of state authority to legislate on Indian matters, and the insistence that an Indian nation was not exactly akin to a foreign nation but rather a domestic dependent nation, would all have a very great impact on later controversies. Past decisions and precedents could be reworked, but they provided signals about what to contest and how.

President Jackson rebuffed the Court and the State of Georgia denied claims for exclusive federal jurisdiction, revealing that the Court surely did not have the final say in determining the status of treaties and of the relationship of the Indian nations to the law during antebellum removal controversies. As Shattuck and Norgren have argued, "the removal of the Cherokee after the *Worcester* decision demonstrated the limits of the judiciary's ability to reconcile basic conflict. In the 1830s the legal victories of *Worcester* could not be translated into political guarantees,"[38] underscoring Whittington's point that many issues at stake in political disputes remain unresolved by judicial attempts to foreclose constitutional questions and that public debate is a significant component of developing constitutional construction. Although Jackson's response to the Court may have made for high drama, the role of other institutional actors and of public debate in constitutional construction will be apparent in less dramatic situations.

Another point warrants notice here. Dialogue, negotiation, and contestation involving the Court and other members of the interpretive community tend to intensify when an issue is becoming *nationalized*. When land claims, rooted within the boundaries of what many citizens increasingly perceived to be the recognizable outlines of a state (in this case, Georgia), are taken out of the orbit of state courts and legislatures, interested parties and activists with visions of state sovereignty that differ from the vision articulated by the Supreme Court are likely to claim the Constitution in different terms. The State of Georgia refused, as it had in *Chisholm v. Georgia* in 1793, to appear before the Supreme Court in *Worcester* and *Cherokee Nation v. Georgia*. The state had executed a Cherokee in 1830, directly defying John Marshall's personally signed habeas corpus writ.[39] The people of Georgia had already been rebuffed by the Supreme Court's nationalizing decision in *Fletcher v. Peck* some twenty years earlier, when Marshall held contracts sacrosanct and argued that even the near-wholesale bribery of the Georgia legislature in the great Yazoo land fraud could not justify legislative reversal of the massive land grants following popular ouster of the legislature at the next election.[40] By taking land claim issues out of the hands of Georgia legislators and politicians and nationalizing the issue by raising it to an issue of constitutional law, the Court is likely to spur actively interested parties to mobilize at the level of national politics (if some do not choose to simply defy the Court, as was the case here). We will find another important moment of nationalization in the era between *Ex Parte Crow Dog* (1883) and *U.S. v. Kagama* (1886).

When we turn to another key formative period, we see that gender and the status of Native Americans figured alongside race in framing and interpreting the Civil War Amendments. What was the relative authority of states and the federal government over privileges and immunities of citizenship, and what were these privileges and immunities? Despite some aspirations that the Fourteenth Amendment would undo *Barron v. Baltimore* (1833), extending rights and provisions of the Bill of Rights to the states,[41] there was considerable effort in Congress to control the scope of the Fourteenth Amendment. Congressional authors of the Civil War Amendments drafted the texts to avoid enfranchising women; the record speaks repeatedly of women's representation through male heads of household.[42] Did the Fourteenth Amendment make Indians citizens? Congress was aware of the question of whether there was some analogy between the situation of Native Americans and former slaves, but seemed to think not. The Constitution declared that Indians not taxed would not be counted as "free persons" in determining a state's representation in Congress (Article I, Section 2). The Fourteenth Amendment's second section retained the exclusion of Indians not taxed, as did the Civil Rights Act of 1866 in its declaration of federal citizenship. The relationship of citizenship in the state wherein one resided (or was born) and citizenship in the United States would become especially interesting in the case of nonreservation Indians.

Activists mobilized around new constitutional language to press their understandings on the Court, and the Court crafted readings that, in rebuffing the claims of women and limiting the scope of remedy for newly freed blacks, also affected understandings of Native American citizenship. *Slaughter-House* looms over the debates on the relation of Native Americans and the state, and decisions involving women's claims were also germane. Even before *Minor v. Happersett* (1875) settled the issue of whether voting was a privilege of citizenship, the issue of women's claim to the privileges or immunities of citizenship loomed in thinking about the construction of the Fourteenth Amendment in the *Slaughter-House Cases* (1873), and *Bradwell v. Illinois* (1873) followed the announcement of the *Slaughter-House* decision by one day.[43]

Because dominant constructions in the era failed to make the right to vote a central component of democratic citizenship, federal citizenship and nonvoting status for Native Americans were often assumed to be compatible. Determination of who could vote was increasingly left to states under the Court's construction of the Civil War Amendments. Following passage of the Fifteenth Amendment and the Civil Rights Act of 1870, a United States District Court for Oregon held that "an Indian . . . who is a citizen of the United States . . . cannot be excluded from this privilege [of voting] on the ground of being an Indian, as that would be to exclude him on account of race."[44] But relatively few Indians had been granted citizenship in the United States by statute or treaty at this point. If an Indian merely left the reservation and adopted civilized ways, was that Indian eligible to vote? There was no such guarantee prior to the Dawes Act, and because Indian allottees who became citizens under the Dawes Act were subject to state law, as voting and citizenship were further pulled asunder during the rise of Jim Crow, no federal right to vote would be forthcoming.

The 1884 case of *Elk v. Wilkins* was instructive, and served as a catalyst to reformers pressing for the General Allotment Act of 1887. John Elk, leaving the reservation for Omaha as a young man and later severing his ties to his tribe, presented himself to vote in Omaha. Denied on the grounds that he was not a citizen of the United States, Elk appealed to the Supreme Court on Fourteenth and Fifteenth Amendment grounds with the aid of two attorneys experienced in Native American litigation. The Court rejected the argument that Elk had surrendered himself to the jurisdiction of the United States and was entitled to the rights and privileges of citizens. Justice Gray, writing for the Court, insisted that "the alien and dependent condition of the members of the Indian tribes could not be put off at their own will, without the action or assent of the United States. They were never deemed citizens of the United States, except under explicit provisions of treaty or statute to that effect."[45] The Fourteenth Amendment contemplates two and only two sources of citizenship: birth and naturalization; Indians born within the territorial limits of the United States may be geographically born within the United States but are not thereby citizens by birth, and can become citizens only by naturalization or by treaty or statute. "No one can become a citizen of a nation without its consent."[46] Further, despite the fact that national legislation was increasingly tending toward fitting the Indians for citizenship, "the question whether any Indian tribes, or any members thereof, have become so far advanced in civilization, that they should be let out of a state of pupilage, and admitted to the privileges and responsibilities of citizenship, is a question to be decided by the nation whose wards they are."[47] Congress would have to make a declaration authorizing such a change in their status. Reformers who crafted and lobbied for the General Allotment Act believed this 1887 measure settled the question of citizenship in the affirmative; however, some states continued to deny Native Americans the right to vote to the mid-twentieth century on grounds that they were "Indians not taxed" or, in one 1928 ruling, that Indians living on reservations were "persons under guardianship."[48] If states lacked responsibility for noncitizen Indians, the Dawes Act failed to make clear the relationship between federal tutelage and the advent of citizenship.

Friends of the Indian who had experience in the field were often engaged during the 1880s and beyond as mediators in decisions about when an Indian was fit for citizenship. Educators, missionaries, superintendents, and other reform-minded whites living among the Indians could serve as gatekeepers to courts, encouraging or discouraging individual Indians from seeking a decision from a federal district court on fitness for citizenship. Evidence presented to a court tended to include sufficient intelligence and prudence to control one's own affairs, having adopted the habits of civilized life, and proof that the Indian had supported himself and his family for the previous five years.[49]

Law and Lawlessness: Activists and the Assimilationist Agenda for Native American Citizenship in the Time after Treaties

The volume of activism on behalf of what was widely termed the "Indian problem" was quite impressive beginning around 1880, and the visions of activists would be important in shaping the policy debates until the early years of the new century.[50] I will focus first on the proponents, shapers, and supporters of the Dawes Act, with its massive effort to make Indians citizens by extending the promise of individual property holdings and a tutelage period during which children would become men. There is a great deal of communication from organized groups to policy makers and the Court—and vice versa.

The Lake Mohonk Conference of Friends of the Indian was a remarkable organization, and surely the most influential of the various organizations pressing for Native American reform during the 1880s and 1890s. The group constituted a sort of Bohemian Grove, bringing together policy makers and activists, legal authorities, journalists, clergy, and "experts" who had been out in the field, some of them newly professionalizing social scientists. Senator Henry Dawes, considered the author of the General Allotment Act of 1887, was an active participant in the early years. Alice Fletcher, an ethnologist who had experience allotting land in the early 1880s among the Omahas, was an active and highly regarded authority there, whether in attendance or writing from her allotment assignments as A Special Agent with the Department of Indian Affairs. Former Supreme Court Justice William Strong and former President Rutherford B. Hayes (who had appointed the Mohonk conference organizer Albert Smiley to the Board of Indian Commissioners in 1879) attended once each, as did Theodore Roosevelt and John D. Rockefeller. Organizations such as the Indian Rights Association, under the leadership of Herbert Welsh, and the Women's National Indian Association, led by Mary Bonney, Sara Thompson Kinney, and Amelia Stone Quinton, were very well represented.

The advocates who gathered there annually beginning in 1883 deliberated bills before Congress, passed resolutions, drafted legislative proposals, lobbied Congress, paid visits to the president, and certainly had a major impact on shaping the Dawes Act (General Allotment Act of 1887). Senator Dawes emphasized the importance of Smiley's Lake Mohonk conferences for government Indian policy: "The remedy is *here*. Public sentiment for the Indian has had its inspiration *here*."[51] And Dawes remarked that "The new Indian policy of the government . . . was born of and nursed by the women of this Association."[52] The conferees of Lake Mohonk supported allotment of tribal lands and, more broadly, efforts to assimilate Native Americans into Victorian America as soon as was practicable. If not always of one mind, they were generally prepared to intervene in Native American community and family life, educate and Christianize Indians, and advance their "civilization." Citizenship was linked to strides taken toward civilization.

Lake Mohonk activists frequently deliberated when Indians should have access to the ballot *in light of* their reading of the lessons learned from experience in the aftermath of passage of the Fourteenth and Fifteenth Amendments. Legal scholar and Harvard Law School professor James Bradley Thayer worked with the Lake Mohonk Conference for some years, served on its Committee on Laws, and was among the legal activists who were constructing "social facts" and attempting to forge some consensus about what experience with black voting taught with regard to Native Americans. He wrote articles in wide-circulation magazines on the legal status of Indians, in the process criticizing certain Supreme Court decisions, pointing out the need to move beyond the Dawes Act, and advocating and attempting to influence policy and the legal climate.[53] Thayer's reading of experience, coupled with evaluations of participants who had been among the tribes, shaped recommendations made at Mohonk.

The perception that the sudden thrust of unprepared voters into the electorate, and the harmful and disruptive effect this had on Southern state governments, was read in the aftermath of Reconstruction as a mistake not to be repeated with Native Americans. As Thayer explained to *Atlantic Monthly* readers midway between the *Civil Rights Cases* (1883) and *Plessy* (1896):

> The great body of the tribal Indians are totally unfit for the ballot, and it would be inexcusable to force such a body of voters suddenly upon the States where they live. It was bad enough, although politically necessary, to do this sort of thing at the end of the war, in communities which had revolted, staked all upon war, and lost. It would be inexcusable to do it in the midst of a loyal population, who are entitled to have their wishes consulted by the government. And above all, it would be an abandonment by the government of its highest present duty to the red men, that of governing and sheltering them. In view of what has happened at the South with the negroes, and of the well-known local hostility to the Indians at the West, it cannot be doubted that they would suffer much.[54]

Gradual tutelage and preparation of Indians for citizenship were seen as the lessons learned from "social facts" of the experience of race and Reconstruction. This construction of the errors of Reconstruction helped create a climate within which state restrictions on black suffrage would be viewed in light of the need to be prepared to vote. By using the Constitution as a vehicle of social memory, reformers established a narrative about the proper relation of Native Americans to the constitutional order. Reva Siegel argues that

> when lawyers interpret the Constitution, they engage the task as carriers of social memory, equipped with certain belief structures that will shape the way in which they understand law. But it also seems clear that when lawyers interpret the Constitution they are contributing to the stock of narratives that, passed from generation to generation, constitute our civic identity, norms, and purposes. Judicial decisions are thus products of social memory; at the same time, they are one of the many social institutions that produce social memory.[55]

Or, as Kersch argues, one can see in this era the formulation of constitutive stories recalling lessons learned.[56] The reworking of the history and lessons of the Fourteenth and Fifteenth Amendments in law reviews, essays, exchanges at Mohonk, in congressional debates and elsewhere both responded to, and in turn reshaped, official narratives told by the Court.

Former Supreme Court Associate Justice William Strong, who retired in 1880, spoke forcibly at Mohonk in 1885 for cleaving citizenship from suffrage: "The immediate admission of the Indians to all the rights of citizenship, including suffrage, I cannot agree to that. I am in favor of their being admitted to citizenship as rapidly as there is any degree of fitness for it. I believe, all those Indians, who have lands in severalty, ought to be admitted to citizenship; but whether to admit them to the suffrage, is another question. I am greatly in favor of education. Suffrage is not an indispensable requisite to citizenship."[57] Brandwein argues in this volume that major shifts in racial politics occurred in the late 1880s and early 1890s; here, we see that even among liberal reformers, suffrage was not consistently seen as a necessary requisite of citizenship in the mid to late 1880s. Thayer's remarks above, coming in 1891—the same year the Republicans failed to pass the Lodge Bill and were widely perceived by white Southerners as having invited them to enact formal disenfranchisement laws[58]— might conceivably be read as an apologia for Republican politics. However, Strong and many of the like-minded at Lake Mohonk reveal that the nexus was never irrevocably established. Perhaps, too, the uncoupling became more palatable to reformers as the influx of Southern and Eastern European immigrants fueled criticism of urban machine politics.

Lake Mohonk reformers were also deeply concerned with extending the reach of federal law into "Indian country." There was a perception of lawlessness that became a central focus for many self-styled friends of the Indian. If activists were divided over the question of how immediately citizenship should follow upon allotment under the Dawes Act, the most influential among those at Lake Mohonk were generally supportive of Theodore Roosevelt's posture, articulated in 1889, that "we undoubtedly ought to break up the great Indian reservations, disregard the tribal governments, allot the land in severalty (with, however, only a limited power of alienation), and treat the Indians as we do other citizens, with certain exceptions, for their sakes as well as ours."[59] Because the federal government, and not the states, was the locus of any United States authority over tribal Indians under John Marshall's construction, reformers seeking to extend the rule of law sought to broaden the reach of federal law; circumstances made them allies of the forces of nationalization. Although they claimed to want agreements negotiated with the Indians honored, they also wanted to bring Native Americans under federal law like other citizens, a goal that stood in some tension with the desire to respect treaties since general provisions of law could differ from special arrangements embodied in treaties. These reformers "linked adherence to principles of legal rationality and morality with the pragmatic needs of manifest destiny."[60]

The Court had already done some important work to facilitate changes that would make the activists' law-extending agenda conceivable. Amid postwar pressures for economic development and expansion, the federal government rethought the treaty relationship. There followed both new statutory language and new constructions placed on the reach of federal law into Indian tribes covered by prior treaty arrangements. The Commissioner of Indian Affairs, himself a Seneca Indian, supported closing the treaty-making process in his 1869 *Annual Report*.[61] In 1872, an amendment to the Interior Department appropriation bill terminated the treaty-making process. Even though existing treaties were to retain their force, "hereafter no Indian nation or tribe within the territory of the United States shall be acknowledged or recognized as an independent nation, tribe, or power, with whom the United States may contract by treaty."[62] Agreements negotiated subsequently would not have the same force of law; Congress could simply deal with Native Americans by statutory law, without tribal consent.

Following the treaty termination amendment, the Supreme Court tended to read that enactment to mean that congressional acts applied to tribes unless Congress specifically excluded them. Despite extant treaties, tribes did not have to explicitly consent to inclusion in congressional enactments. This trend in interpretation began even before treaty cessation. In the *Cherokee Tobacco Case* (1870), also known as *Two Hundred and Seven Half-Pound Papers of Smoking Tobacco, etc., v. United States*, Justice Swayne wrote for a divided Court that an 1868 general revenue law posting taxes on alcohol and tobacco also applied to the territory of the Cherokee nation, despite a pre-existing 1866 treaty.[63] Congress acquired even greater powers to ignore or override the wishes of Indian tribes, and Justice Harlan could argue that because railroads are public highways, "established primarily for the convenience of the people, and to subserve public ends," they are subject to governmental control and regulation. Therefore, Congress could appropriate "private property" for a railroad right of way so long as there was just compensation, regardless of treaties with the Cherokee Nation.[64]

When Alice Fletcher, a pioneer advocate of the government's allotment policy, argued at Lake Mohonk a little more than a decade after treaty making ceased that one could not expect to get two-thirds of a tribe to vote in support of allotting lands in severalty (which would generate set-sized private plots and release surplus tribal lands for sale), she averred, "Indians are, like the rest of mankind, unwilling to vote for present trouble in order to secure an unknown and uncertain benefit. The work must be done for them, whether they approve or not."[65] She reflected prevalent views that Indians, like children, could not necessarily see what was in their best interest. Moreover, Native Americans were being held back by a surplus of land that keeps contact with civilization at bay; all this land "isolates him [the Indian] from the industries that teem throughout the length and breadth of our land."[66] For Reverend Dr. Lyman Abbott, another Lake Mohonk activist, the interest in gaining access to land was even more pronounced: "A people do not occupy a country simply because they roam over it. Three hundred thousand people have no right to hold a continent and keep at bay a race able to people it and provide the happy homes of civilization."[67] We were, he argued, beyond the era of treaties.

As a means of making the Indian more self-reliant and "manly," predominant reform voices of the 1880s wanted to undercut tribal government and the authority of tribal councils so that the Indian could better mature and integrate into white society. Alice Fletcher spoke and wrote influentially on this question of dissolving the power of tribal governance. She vigorously pressed Dawes to hasten the breakup of tribal relations because they were obstacles to progress, surely endorsing the view that "all political progress has its foundation in the individual." Dawes rewrote the bill in light of some of her ideas.[68] Fletcher spoke of the Indians as her children and her babies; she was hardly alone among female activists in speaking of "[our] children, the Indians."[69] The image had important policy consequences. In Fletcher's view, for Indians to attain the "manly rights," they must have responsibility and property, and must no longer be governed *en masse* by agents or by tribal governments. She and her allies likened life on the reservation to a prison, an environment "from which every elevating and inspiring element has been eliminated."[70] In the words of another highly influential Lake Mohonk participant, isolation from American civilization (to which the reservation system contributed) denied Native Americans opportunities of a man and a citizen.[71]

As these reformers managed any measure of success on the dimension of tribal governance, however, the problems of lawlessness became exacerbated. Weakened tribal councils had little capacity to resist incursions on territory and self-determination. For mainstream reformers in the Lake Mohonk constellation, the only proper measure of self-government was that shared by all other Americans. Reformers had mobilized for extension of federal law over tribal Indians even before the Dawes Act. In a report to the president in 1881, a commission to investigate matters relating to the Poncas reported:

> All Indians should have an opportunity of appealing to the courts for the protection and vindication of the rights of person and property. Indians cannot be expected to understand the duties of men living under the forms of civilization until they know, by being subject to it, the authority of stable law as administered by the courts, and are relieved from the uncertainties and oppression frequently attending subjection to arbitrary personal authority.[72]

Another important node of conflict—this time, around the reach of courts in criminal convictions involving crimes between Indians on the reservation—produced more scope for the exercise of federal authority. There was wide sentiment among liberal reformers that Congress should address defects in another recent Supreme Court ruling. The unpopular holding of *Ex Parte Crow Dog* (1883) established the general rule that "as long as the Indian maintained his tribal relationship, he was in effect a citizen of that tribe. His individual rights and privileges were determined therefore not by the Constitution or laws of the United States, but by his tribal customs and rules."[73] Crow Dog, a Sioux, had been sentenced to death by a federal circuit court for the murder of the chief of his own tribe, a murder that occurred on the reservation. Justice Stanley Matthews wrote for the Supreme Court that, under existing treaties, statutes, and practices, this was a matter for tribal jurisdiction. Matthews reasoned that when the United States contracted with these Indians as a distinct political body, promising to secure to them "an orderly government, by appropriate legislation thereafter to be framed and enacted," that among the arts of civilized life meant to be encouraged among them, self-government was the highest, "the regulation by themselves of their own domestic affairs, the maintenance of order and peace among their own members by the administration of their own laws and customs."[74] The opinion's author suggested that if Congress passed specific subsequent legislation for or concerning the Indians, it could alter the situation.

Public protest over the Court's decision led to an alteration of law. The 1885 Indian Appropriations Act gave federal and territorial courts jurisdiction over persons on the reservation in the case of certain crimes, including murder and manslaughter, assault with intent to kill, rape, arson, burglary and larceny.[75] Although the constitutionality of this law was challenged in *United States v. Kagama* (1886), the 1885 Major Crimes Act was upheld by the Court, which also reasserted that only the federal government—not the states—had jurisdiction over reservation Indians. The clear responsibility for the "Indian problem" rested, then, with Congress.[76]

Limits of the Activists' Ability to Deliver on Law and Courts

Reform voices continued and even stepped up efforts to extend the rule of law to Native Americans; Dawes had, in their view, not gone far enough. In their analysis, law offered Native Americans support, protection, and tutelage; absence of law meant that Native Americans were subject to arbitrary individual authority.

In 1890, the American Bar Association unanimously resolved "that the United States should provide, at the earliest possible moment, courts and a system of law for the Indian reservations."[77] The Lake Mohonk Conference of the Friends of the Indians, the Philadelphia-based Indian Rights Association led by Herbert Welsh (Secretary), and the Boston Indian Citizenship Committee had all either drafted legislation or pressed Congress throughout much of the 1880s for "the immediate extension of the ordinary laws of the land over the Indian reservations."[78] This influential group of activists heavily dominated by the Indian Rights Association claimed that their draft legislation had the support of some of the best lawyers in the country. Despite their efforts to fix "upon the Indian the same personal, legal, and political status which is common to all other inhabitants," Dawes was not supportive, questioning the constitutionality of Thayer's measure, and Congress was largely uninterested.[79] Many considered the General Allotment Act, the product of their recent attention, sufficient; lack of interest also stemmed from the desire to retain flexible federal power to access tribal lands based in concern for development and expansionist interests.

The Dawes Act era witnessed the alienation of approximately two-thirds of all tribal lands held at the outset of the General Allotment Act. About half the lands lost resulted from sale of what government deemed surplus land. Legal informality permitted Congress to breach treaty agreements when it thought necessary, and legal informality facilitated the alienation of vast tracts of Native American lands not allotted to individuals. Nearing the outset of an era that would later be characterized by "legal formalism," the Lake Mohonk reformers frequently decried the absence of established law that would protect Native Americans just as it protected other Americans. But the ward-guardian legacy did not map readily onto developing industrial-era legal doctrine that treated able-bodied (especially male) workers and employers as equally entitled by law to make contracts according to their own best judgment. Reformers also wanted to operate upon dependents, to have authority to break up their traditional governments and customs in the name of Christianity, civilization, progress, and maturation. They wanted to be able to expunge tribal rituals and inculcate Christianity. Moreover, reformers wanted to be able to protect Native American landholders from those who would engage them in disadvantageous, unscrupulous exchanges that would leave individual allottees impoverished. Allotment would only work if Indians kept their lands and were able to produce their sustenance. And because liquor often figured in disadvantageous contracts, reformers wanted to keep liquor away from the Indian. How could these reformers bar the very exchanges in which ordinary citizens were free to engage? Some further elaboration of a legal doctrine of protection was necessary.

If Congress had greater powers to reach into reservations with general enactments, then the reach of law over the Indians could, at least in some ways, be extended. However, this power did not necessarily extend to protection, and the question of special legislation remained open. Just what Marshall's "state of pupilage" would mean remained for the reformers around the turn of the century to flesh out.

The Court often deferred to congressional designs on tribal lands. In an important reading in 1903, the *Lone Wolf* Court announced that Indians were an "ignorant and dependent race," "dependent largely for their daily food. Dependent for their political rights."[80] In a decision that has been called the Indians' *Dred Scott*,[81] Justice White upheld against a Fifth Amendment challenge congressional action transferring 2.5 million "excess" acreage from Apache, Kiowa, and Comanche Indians to the federal government without having obtained consent from the tribes. (The land was sold to white settlers.) The Court essentially announced that the matter was an unreviewable political question, deferring to the political will expressed by the legislature. In a statement remarkable for reconstructing history to meld the Treaty Cessation Act of 1872 with a reading of the status of preexisting treaties, Justice White announced that "plenary authority over the tribal relations of the Indians has been exercised by Congress from the beginning, and the power has always been deemed a political one, not subject to the control of the judicial department of the government."[82] The Court reasoned that the Indians' right of self-government could be contravened when Congress found it necessary to do so. Interest in the case was great; the Senate deliberated whether 500 or 1,000 copies should be printed.[83]

This type of reading of constitutional history—however it may have blatantly disregarded treaties and traditions of self-government—more clearly dealt in the reformers and Friends of the Indian to implement the plans that they were convinced were in the interests of these children. Individuals could be made capable of governing themselves, and then they would be citizens subject to the laws of the United States and of the states wherein they resided; there would—and could—be no such thing as a self-governing tribe. Native Americans who sought to preserve separate and self-governing tribal entities had little remaining voice.

Competence, Guardianship, and Citizenship in the Era of Protective Legislation

There was a process of negotiation through which special legislation and provision became constitutionally permissible *alongside* citizenship. Activists and organizations involved at Lake Mohonk generally believed the achievement of the ballot and full citizenship to mean the abandonment of Native Americans to the states: "Remember that with the giving of full citizenship there would take place a loss of all power in the federal government to legislate specially for them."[84] This was contrary, they argued, to what Native Americans required, namely "for a good while, the very careful and exceptional protection of the nation."[85] Henry Dawes thought that the end of the twenty-five-year period of grace and tutelage embedded in the General Allotment Act also meant the loss of federal government power to legislate specifically for the Indian. The question of the capacity for Indians to be "citizens and pupils of the United States at the same time" was one that continued to be debated, and the *Congressional Record* of 1897 reveals continuing confusion over the political status of Native American recipients of land allotments under the Dawes Act. One representative from a western state said this matter "ought to be passed upon and determined by the courts."[86]

Evidence of the effects of allotment since the General Allotment Act was not so rosy.[87] Assimilation proved more difficult and protracted than reformers envisioned, and the Dawes Act produced many destructive consequences for Native American life. Reformers had begun with optimistic expectations that the Indian could mature at least as quickly as a child made the journey from infancy to adulthood; a generation or so would bring an end to the "Indian problem." Although Alice Fletcher had argued with Dawes at Mohonk that ten years was a sufficient period during which to insist on the inalienability of allotted lands, Dawes had persisted with his twenty-five-year interregnum in the final bill.[88] This grace period during which the federal government could maintain its oversight and protection of Native American properties allotted in severalty was surely enough time, reformers believed, to make Indians individual men and self-sufficient citizens. If children and wards were not to be abandoned, how could citizenship and protection be made compatible in the case of Native Americans? There would have to be legal and juridical underpinning for continued coercive intervention and protection. Necessity became the mother of invention.

Settling the matter of the compatibility of guardianship and citizenship, and the status of federal legislation singling out Native Americans for benevolence or different treatment took place in the context of a classic protective legislation issue of the Progressive Era: alcohol. Prohibition of the sale of alcohol hinged on the Court's reading of congressional authority to regulate commerce with the Indian tribes. Since the Jefferson administration, the federal government had contended that regulation of liquor traffic with the Indians was designed both to benefit Indians and protect whites, because abuse of liquor was considered linked to wars and violence between Indians and whites. By 1865, the Supreme Court had opined that "commerce with the Indian tribes, means commerce with the individuals composing those tribes." This power can be exercised within the limits of a state, for "the locality of the traffic can have nothing to do with the power."[89] It could be exercised over adjoining or buffer zones, and it appeared—from the governing statute of 23 July 1892—that it could be exercised over a ward of the United States (including a Dawes Act allottee whose land remained in trust) when that ward was outside of Indian territory.[90] Several Supreme Court cases and dozens of district and circuit court cases were heard concerning the sale or possession of alcohol between the 1892 statute and the decisive case of U.S. v. Nice in 1916.

The Heff matter was precipitated by the sale of liquor to Native Americans by whites off the reservation in the aftermath of the federal government ban on such sales. The issue reached the Federal Circuit Court in 1901, in the case of Farrell v. United States. The decision reasoned that federal citizenship for an Indian was not incompatible with the federal government's treatment of the Indian as a ward in need of protection from the evils of alcohol.[91] The Court argued that "the deprivation of these Indians of the right to buy intoxicating liquors is not the taking away from them of any privilege or immunity of citizenship, but it is an attempt to confer upon them an additional immunity which some citizens do not possess, an immunity from drunkenness and its pernicious consequences."[92]

However, four years later, in Matter of Heff (1905), the Supreme Court determined that Indians accepting allotments immediately became American citizens. In a formalistic and nonprotectionist argument that failed to subdue political opponents, Justice Brewer reasoned: "Can it be that because one has Indian, and only Indian blood in his veins, he is to be forever one of a special class over whom the General Government may in its discretion assume the rights of guardianship which it had once abandoned, and this whether the State or the individual himself consents? We think the reach to which this argument goes demonstrates that it is unsound."[93] Citizens are those whose consent cannot be sidestepped. In one reading, Heff accords Native Americans a dignity and political status at law that does not warrant any breach of consent.

However, the suggestive connection between the language of Heff and Justice Bradley's majority opinion in the Civil Rights Cases (1883) serves as a reminder of the limits and narrowness of the guarantees that citizenship under the Fourteenth Amendment provided, and the absence of affirmative obligations placed on the federal government in light of the Amendment's promise during this era:

When a man has emerged from slavery, and by the aid of beneficent legislation has shaken off the inseparable concomitants of that state, there must be some stage in the progress of his elevation when he takes the rank of a mere citizen, and ceases to be the special favorite of the laws, and when his rights as a citizen, or a man, are to be protected in the ordinary modes by which other men's rights are protected.[94]

There is a connection between how the relationship between protective legislation and the commerce power was forged with regard to Native Americans and with regard to other citizens. One might even make the case that reasoning about protection and the boundaries of the federal commerce power in relations with Indian tribes paved the way, despite the unpopular *Heff* decision, for broader readings of the commerce power in regulating relations among the several states. The Court heard oral arguments six weeks before hearing *Lochner*, and decided *Heff* one week prior to *Lochner*;[95] the issue seems clearly related to reasoning about protective legislation and federal police powers under the commerce clause more broadly.

Heff and *Lochner* stood at odds with certain other cases expressing a broader federal power to regulate harm through the commerce power, and in the next decade, there would be significant opportunities to rethink the impact of protection on citizenship. In *Champion v. Ames* (1903), Justice Harlan, writing for a 5–4 Court, supplied the rationale that "the suppression of nuisances injurious to public health or morality is among the most important duties of Government."[96] In *Hipolite Egg Co. v. United States* (1911), Justice McKenna wrote for a unanimous Court that articles that are outlaws of commerce may be seized wherever they are found. In *Hoke v. United States* (1913), the unanimous Court followed McKenna's reasoning that congressional power over transportation "among the several States" extends not only to means necessary but also convenient, "and the means may have the quality of police regulations."[97] In *Heff*, Justice Brewer construed the Dawes Act and its amendments to mean that "when the United States grants the privileges of citizenship to an Indian, gives to him the benefit and requires him to be subject to the laws, both civil and criminal, of the State, it places him outside the reach of police regulations on the part of Congress."[98]

The Court may have spoken, but other members of the interpretive community also constructed *Heff*. A month after the decision, the acting attorney general issued an opinion that although the decision was conclusive Congress lacked police jurisdiction over Native American allottees off the reservation, the most that can be claimed for the *Heff* decision is that it holds that, by making Indian allottees citizens and subject to the laws of the State, Congress has divested itself of this purely personal jurisdiction over them. But the jurisdiction which Congress exercises over them upon the reservations is authorized by the fact that they are inmates, so to speak, of Federal institutions; and while subject generally to State jurisdiction, that jurisdiction can not be exercised so as to interfere with the conduct of these institutions or to defeat the treaty stipulations which the United States may have made with the Indians.[99]

President Roosevelt rejected the idea that Indians were no longer subject to federal control; he asserted that *Heff* had "struck away the main prop on which has hitherto rested the Government's benevolent effort to protect [the Indian] against the evils of intemperance."[100] Commissioner of Indian Affairs Francis Leupp contended that *Heff* "simply places the ignorant, incapable, and helpless Indian citizens at the mercy of one class of evil doers."[101] Many federal policy makers and activists were surprised and disturbed by *Heff*; citizenship and a twenty-five-year period of continued tutelage were thought compatible. *Heff* was unpalatable to reformers and self-styled "Friends of the Indian." Congress responded with alacrity, passing the 1906 Burke Act.

The Burke Act, passed as a response to *Heff*, provided an opportunity to withhold citizenship from Indians accepting allotments until the twenty-five-year trust period had expired and allottees held a fee patent to their land. This established, however, a dual system in which Natives who had accepted allotments prior to the Burke Act could not be protected, whereas those who accepted land in severalty after 1906 could. And Congress permitted the Secretary of the Interior to grant citizenship and fee-simple title to any Indians who he determined were "competent" in the management of their own affairs.

Who would be considered "competent" to alienate lands under this arrangement? Were Native American tribal governments that still owned communal land capable of selling such lands to whites, or were these sales subject to repudiation by the federal government? Economic expansion would again bear on determinations of capacity, agency, and ability to contract. The elaborate quasi-judicial competency hearings occasioned after the 1906 Burke Act, with their rituals and ceremonies renouncing Indian arrows and ways—held with or without the permission of the Native American involved—were clearly about property and not just about citizenship. An adjudged competent Native could buy and (more usually) sell property in the marketplace like any other citizen, regardless of potential susceptibility to the wiles of the unscrupulous. Competency proved to be another vehicle for surrender of land and economic resources, with many incentives to find Indians competent. And alternatively, a finding of incompetence by an Indian Agent could place a Native American's home and land in the hands of said agent to make determinations in the Native's supposed best interest.

The post-*Heff* period was one of considerable intensity, reiteration, and reinterpretation as the relationship between Indian citizens and the federal government was revisited. A variety of cases involving such issues as the reach of federal criminal sanctions and the capacity of Indians to alienate their lands narrowed the reach of *Heff* prior to *Nice*. In *United States v. Celestine* (1909), the Court constructed recent events to suggest that "Congress in granting full rights of citizenship to Indians, believed that it had been hasty."[102] In *United States v. Pelican* (1914), the Court constructed the purpose of the Burke Act "distinctly to postpone to the expiration of the trust period the subjection of allottees under that act to state laws."[103]

The important case of *U.S. v. Sandoval* (1913) was again triggered by liquor sales to Indians, this time by a Spanish American introducing liquor into Santa Clara and San Juan Pueblos. At issue was the status of a provision of the 1910 Enabling Act requiring New Mexico, upon admission to the union as a state, to surrender jurisdiction over the lands of any Indians who derived their title from the United States or a prior sovereignty. The Supreme Court upheld federal government jurisdiction, reaffirming that the United States maintained responsibility for the Pueblos because they were wards of the government. The implications involved title to property. The holding meant that since 1848, Pueblo Indians had not been competent to alienate individual or communal landholdings, leaving 3,000 land claims indeterminate.[104]

The key Supreme Court decision in this dispute would come with *U.S. v. Nice* (1916), with the majority opinion written by Justice Van Devanter. Overturning *Matter of Heff* (1905) in short order, this decision removed the chief objections to extension of citizenship to those Native Americans not yet granted citizenship. Van Devanter reasoned: "Citizenship is not incompatible with tribal existence or continued guardianship, and so may be conferred without completely emancipating the Indians or placing them beyond the reach of congressional regulations adopted for their protection."[105] Coming during the period when the Court was negotiating its posture on protective legislation involving women, children, and the occasional group of able-bodied but endangered male workers (*Holden v. Hardy*), Van Devanter argued that it had been the intent of Congress to maintain certain protections for

Native Americans—for example, oversight and management of funds from land sales. If Congress intended to maintain these oversight provisions, then such protection or special consideration was not inconsistent with citizenship. This decision became a kind of settling that paved the way for the Indian Citizenship Act of 1924, the act signed by Coolidge that granted citizenship to remaining noncitizen Indians living within the boundaries of the United States and not previously made citizens through statute or treaty.[106]

Cultural Pluralism and the Administrative State: The Rise of a New Generation of Activists and the Struggle for Native American Reform

The very naming of the "Indian problem" in the late nineteenth century supported a vision congruent with the rise of the administrative state. With the professionalization of the social sciences and medicine came a growing emphasis on scientific management of "problems" to be solved. In the Progressive Era, many social problems were redefined as problems of proper administration. Knowledge and information, properly applied, yielded solutions to such problems. Dawes Act–era reformers had faith that by staying the course, the envisioned results would be forthcoming. The Indian was a "problem" that late nineteenth century reformers thought could be "solved" within a generation: disease, nutrition, sanitation, education, and ultimately civilization were all problems that would yield to intervention and the persistent implementation of proper methods. Each of these arenas dealt in reformers, many of them women. Maternalists and progressive activists believed in the power of expertise, even if they often differed significantly about the role to be played by local knowledge and by the understandings and wishes of those who were the objects of social policy.[107]

There were outcries about corruption of Indian agents, who ruled autocratically and personified the government to Native Americans (who were therefore given very poor lessons in government). Government agents who helped deprive their charges of their lands after the Dawes Act helped fuel the muckraking era's battle against corruption and the progressive impetus for civil service reform. The Progressive Era good-government movement fueled the engine of activists who pressed for reform of the Bureau of Indian Affairs (BIA) and cessation of the system of Indian Agents. Corruption mobilized groups outside the Court to press not only for BIA reform, but also for substitution of a system of law and courts for human corruption and lawlessness.

Proper administration and good governance were rallying cries that also dealt in maternalist reformers of the early twentieth century. Writer and activist Mary Austin, who spent time in New Mexico near the Pueblo Indians, contended that women were administrators of the goods of the material realm, that women had the intellectual gift of administration and a genius for organization. Administration required a capacity for fluidity and incremental adjustment to change, attention to the environment, to movement and to progress.[108] Jane Addams's vision of administration also rejected mere efficiency: administrators needed to recognize the power of experience. Detachment and objectivity were poor administrative strategies; dealing with substantive problems and making room for the democratic voice were proper ones.[109] These women also thought in terms of the importance of groups rather than of individuals.

Such arguments were helpful to the later generation of friends of the Indian, who mobilized around 1920 to help bring an end to the Dawes Act era. It was clear to them that the "Indian problem" was not being solved. Alienation of allotted land, forced sale of better communal landholdings, and loss of resources such as water rights left widespread poverty. Disease, decimation of Native populations, alcoholism, and forced removal of children for education off the reservation all took a major toll on Native Americans as well. With ample evidence of the suffering and impoverishment visited upon many groups of Native Americans following implementation of Dawes Act–era policies, this later generation of reformers tended to repudiate the assimilationist policies of the Lake Mohonk period. In an era when maternalists such as Addams delivered critiques of individualism, competitive capitalism, and militarism—all of which detracted from the development of a sense of interdependence and a social ethic—some reformers began to argue for preservation of indigenous traditions.[110] As historian Frederick Jackson Turner declared the frontier closed and activists mobilized to preserve wilderness and oppose such projects as the Hetch Hetchy dam, a romantic effort to preserve what was seen as the natural blossomed. Nature was the refuge from industrial ills,[111] and Indians were seen as retaining a close relationship with it. Some key figures and organizations among this new generation of activists included John Collier and the American Indian Defense Association, and Stella Atwood and the two-million-strong General Federation of Women's Clubs, a formidable force in the 1920s.

John Collier, an increasingly important player and leader of the American Indian Defense Association, spoke for appreciation and preservation of the uniqueness, history, and culture of Native Americans. Drawing from his experience with the Pueblos around 1920, Collier and his allies among artists and intellectuals in the Santa Fe–Taos area valued Native American communal traditions. These Native Americans lived a critique of materialism, industrialism, consumer culture, and individualism.[112] Artists and intellectuals mobilized in opposition to the Bursum Bill in 1922–1923, which would have resolved many Pueblo land and important water rights claim conflicts in favor of white settlers. They feared it would threaten the culture they loved. They went public, signing a "Proclamation to the American Public" protesting the impending destruction of Pueblo land rights; setting aside their other artistic projects, they wrote essays and articles attacking Secretary of the Interior Fall and the proposed legislation.[113] One of Collier's pieces in *Sunset Magazine* presaged doom in its banner headline: "The Pueblos' Last Stand: If the Arizona and New Mexico Tribes Lose Their Land, Their Ancient Civilization Dies," and the article extolled the Pueblos' self-governing democratic institutions and spiritually conscious civilization, their system of moral education that "puts Americans to shame," and their "cooperative arts of song, dance, and drama."[114] Collier and his allies helped mobilize Pueblos against the threat of the government's proposed measures and assisted them in sending several delegations to Washington to speak on their own behalf.[115]

Many of these same artists and writers struggled to prevent prohibitions on Native American rites and dances. Collier considered native dances the closest American equivalent of the "mighty dramas of the Greeks."[116] An earlier generation of Americanizers had attempted to Christianize the Indians and purge them of their pagan gods. The struggle over culture and its preservation became more pronounced in the fifteen to twenty years before reorganization of the BIA in 1934 and the abandonment of allotment policies. This pronounced interest came somewhat later than pioneering interest among social workers at Hull House in preserving immigrant cultures and arts. By the early 1920s, as the meaning and scope of the First Amendment was beginning to get closer attention in the federal courts, these activists began to speak of the struggle to preserve rites and dances in terms of freedom of religion.

Although relatively little legislation concerning Native Americans passed in the 1920s, pressures for reforms mounted. Some inaction resulted from the successes of reformers in politicizing and defeating administration-supported measures in Congress. These activists did a great deal to politicize the problem of land alienation and loss, and to defend Pueblos against such losses and against loss of mineral rights. They confronted Department of the Interior policies in the press, mobilized Pueblos, supported court battles, offered legislative testimony, and raised funds for their battles. Much of the legislative attention to Native Americans in the 1920s and an occasional court case during this period focused on the Pueblos, the very Indians who had captured the attention of reformers. They were elaborating constitutional meaning at a time when the Court was relatively quiescent on Native American issues but heavily engaged in commerce, contracts, protective legislation, takings, and increasingly, incorporation of the First Amendment against the states. Invoking constitutional values and terminology, activists were offering alternatives to dominant constitutional constructions that would eventually reshape prevailing policy.

The General Federation of Women's Clubs, an organization that could never unite on the federal suffrage amendment until it became enshrined in the Constitution, formed a Committee on Indian Welfare in 1921, with statewide committees and chairs following suit. Californian Stella Atwood pressed for the formation of this committee and became its first chair. Collier found that Atwood "was fighting almost alone for the Indians' cause" at that time.[117] Under Atwood's leadership, the Committee on Indian Welfare of the GFWC was concerned with more than the common health, education, and family issues. Atwood vocally urged court challenges and constitutionalized rights issues. Atwood and committee members were active in getting unworthy Indian agents investigated and sometimes dismissed, interfacing with the Indian Office and the Department of the Interior. The committee mounted a large congressional effort, and the General Federation *News* announced in August of 1921 that Indian welfare would be "pushed through appeals to state senators and representatives in Congress." Atwood instructed members that "the legislative program, of course, is the crux of the whole matter. All the legislation affecting the Indian emanates from Congress. The legislative committees of the various states . . . have under consideration the bills affecting their states and such committees communicate with their congressmen where they feel that is necessary."[118]

Stella Atwood was a highly visible advocate. She sent telegrams around the nation on 22 December 1922, protesting Interior Secretary Fall's threatened eviction order, and sent one to the White House warning President Harding of the "grave political consequences" that would follow Fall's scheme.[119] The next month, during the uproar over the Bursum Bill, Fall announced he was shortly leaving office; no tears were shed by reformers.[120] Atwood also testified before the Senate Committee on Public Lands and

Surveys in January 1923, both as a spokesperson for the Pueblos and also expressing the opposition of the General Federation of Women's Clubs to the manner in which the Department of the Interior handled Pueblo land claims. She reminded legislators she spoke for 2 million women voters.[121] She made clear that both the GFWC and the Indian Defense Association were "going to give all necessary publicity and more publicity to the Indian question"—a question which involved the "whole subject of the conservation and utilization of natural resources," and which required "defending the rights, as my organization sees them, of the Indians."[122] She worked tirelessly to defeat the Bursum and Lenroot Bills, both of which the GFWC judged unfavorable to Pueblo land claims; she helped press for passage of the Pueblo Lands Act of 1924, which contained a provision that in land claim disputes, Indians had the right to hire attorneys and "assert and maintain unaffected by the provision of this act their title and right to any land" in court.[123] The 1920s GFWC was seen as a formidable force in legislative battles.

Some GFWC detractors were unhappy with Atwood's heavily legal and political focus; if the Indians were encouraged and helped to develop proper homes, the "Indian problem" would, in their view, be solved. Atwood was removed from her chairmanship of the GFWC committee amid controversy in 1924.[124] However, she continued her work with Collier and the American Indian Defense Association and remained an active spokesperson and leader within the General Federation of Women's Clubs, writing repeatedly and eloquently in the mass-circulation newsletter about Native American rights and calling members to action.

From this position of high visibility, Atwood helped constitutionalize the struggle over the terms of Native American citizenship in the 1920s, perhaps even more vocally after passage of the Indian Citizenship Act of 1924.[125] The 1924 Act had been accomplished with the aid of progressives on the Senate Committee on Indian Affairs, who were committed to the reformers' agenda of curbing the authority of the BIA and the Interior Department.[126] With the financial assistance of California supporters, she and John Collier hired legal counsel and filed legal briefs. Judge Richard H. Hanna, formerly of the New Mexico Supreme Court, was enlisted on behalf of the Pueblos. Collier reported that the American Indian Defense Association "financed the legal representation of all the New Mexico Pueblos before the Pueblo Lands Board and before the courts. This legal representation, although not much more than its office costs were met, consumed one-half of the Association's income through all the years [after 1924 and into 1933]."[127]

Atwood demanded redress in increasingly constitutional language. In 1925, she wrote in the General Federation *News*: "The Indian should have the right as has every other citizen, to petition the government for a redress of his grievances." She demanded the right to peaceful assembly, and the right not to be arrested or to have one's household searched without a warrant. In this wide-circulation GFWC membership publication, she called for the "establishment through test cases of the Indian's right to civil and religious liberty and the protection of the courts," reacting to the ban on certain secret and allegedly immoral ritual dancing, and to the Indian Bureau's attempts to stop Pueblo boys from receiving a period of tribal religious training.[128] She would continue to point to federal government abuses in constitutional terminology:

> The American Indians constitute a body of citizens which we segregate and deny the due processes of law as guaranteed to them under our constitution.
>
> This involves the denial of court review of the acts of their guardian. They are the only wards who cannot demand an accounting of their estate from their guardian. They are denied the right to have a court pass on their competency.[129]

Three years after the Indian Citizenship Act of 1924, Atwood found that Indians had no power to make contracts or form themselves into corporations without the consent of the Indian Bureau. "The time has come for our great organization to arise and demand that these first Americans should no longer be aliens."[130]

For Atwood, Collier, and a large contingent of 1920s Native American activists, rights under the Constitution became a means of mobilization. They argued in a grammar that was both legally and politically attuned during an era of rising rights consciousness. Although these reformers did not completely reject a theory of guardianship, they embraced a concept of citizenship that included Native American capacity to use law and courts for their own protection against an encroaching state. Many of the rights of which Atwood spoke were individualized rights, but it also appears that reformers wished tribes as corporate bodies to be able to protect themselves against wrongs and encroachments. Despite the Indian Bureau's attempt to brand the American Indian Defense Association as a Russian Communist tool "financed by Soviet Moscow," the activists and their allies in Congress (including Senators LaFollette and Wheeler and Representatives Frear and Howard) were transforming public perceptions of the "Indian problem."[131] The proponents of assimilation were losing their capacity to define Native American policy.

The Indian Reorganization Act of 1934, also known as the Wheeler-Howard Act, was realized in considerable measure due to the battles waged by Native Americans and their organized, mobilized allies in the 1920s. John Collier, now serving as Indian Commissioner, worked to unite the American Indian Defense Association, the National Association on Indian Affairs (formerly the Eastern Association on Indian Affairs), and the Indian Rights Association behind legislation to reverse allotment policy and replace the Dawes Act. The General Federation of Women's Clubs, the American Civil Liberties Union, and the National Council of American Indians also attended a meeting Collier called, as did Lewis Meriam, author of a highly regarded report on Indian administration.[132] Interior Department Solicitor Nathan R. Margold and his legal staff, including prominent authority on Indian law Felix S. Cohen, worked with the Indian Bureau to draft the Indian Reorganization Act.[133] Provisions of the bill met significant resistance in Congress, with resistance and concern among various Native Americans as well; some of the latter resistance centered on new communal claims upon lands previously held as private property (the Umatilla of Oregon wrote Collier, calling it a plan for "Socialization and Communism"). Some more assimilated Indians rejected attempts to recreate tribal entities.[134]

Commissioner Collier decided to convene a number of Indian congresses throughout the country to attempt to build support for the bill; he personally attended most of the ten congresses held and ultimately offered amendments to the Wheeler-Howard bill on the basis of what he heard. Congress made other significant changes, eliminating the Title I provision allowing tribal communities to receive, upon application and ratification of a certain percentage of tribal members, charters of incorporation and establishment of municipal home rule, with power to borrow money from a special credit fund. Title IV, providing for a federal court of Indian affairs, with jurisdiction over all matters concerning Native American chartered communities, was scuttled in Congress with the blessing of Senator Wheeler. Collier had wanted this provision to increase Native American access to the federal courts and because it extended the jurisdiction of federal courts beyond the few legal problems they had previously been authorized to address. A further weakened and altered bill passed only with the president's intervention. The final version of the Indian Reorganization Act prohibited any further allotment of Native American lands, restricted further alienation of land, and restored some surplus lands to tribes. The act provided for limited tribal self-government.[135]

The Wheeler-Howard Act did not accomplish everything reformers wanted and did not have the support of some Native Americans consulted. Nevertheless, it marked the end of the Dawes era and established a new framework through which legislators, lawyers, courts, and activists would carry on their discourse.

Conclusion

The Dawes Act era was witness to a great deal of conflict over the meaning of Native American citizenship and to frequent interaction between courts and other members of the interpretive community. Some of the key conflicts revolved around property and its alienation, the pace of movement toward citizenship, the reach and impartial application of federal law to all citizens, federal jurisdiction over criminal convictions and liquor sales, the status of tribal governing bodies and tribal existence itself, and tribal dances and religious freedoms. During these periods of conflict, the Court did not monopolize the Constitution's meaning. Several judicial attempts to resolve conflict occasioned rather quick response by activists and their allies in Congress and demonstrated the limited ability of the judiciary to reconcile basic conflict. Sometimes, judicial deference to Congress permitted political solutions to develop, removing the Court from a sustained controversy (as in *Nice*). Sometimes, the effect of such deference to political branches (as in *Lone Wolf*) appeared as a renunciation of any notion that Native Americans had claims the Court was bound to acknowledge, and did not long insulate the Court from politics. Legal formalism (as in *Heff*) met with stiff opposition and revisionist activism. Not only was public debate an important component of developing constitutional construction, but members of the interpretive community participated in constructing decisions the Court made.

Members of the legal community, social scientists, writers, artists, journalists, and politicians participated in the work of interest and advocacy groups. As these groups framed arguments about the "Indian problem" and pressed for policy change, analyzed and criticized Court decisions, and endorsed or fought specific legislative proposals, they played a vital role in reshaping the political and policy environment in which Native American issues were considered. Many Friends of the Indian were highly mobilized and blessed with time and economic resources. They drafted and deliberated policy and were influential in the halls of Congress, in the legal community, and in shaping public opinion. While pressure and activity levels varied in this period, activists were vital in keeping Native American citizenship issues on the national agenda and before the Court from the 1880s to the 1930s.

Protestant reformers had a vision of the path from childhood to maturation the Indians should take. The government's wrongs against the Indian that Helen Hunt Jackson had identified were linked to the land; acquisition and government recognition of individual holdings of property figured quite importantly in Lake Mohonk activists' diagnosis and treatment. With allies such as Henry Dawes, they were able to implement a policy of assimilation and allotment that would have far-ranging implications both for Native Americans and for opening up vast tracts of land for white settlement. But pressures for economic development also had an important bearing on how property rights would be construed, and on congressional willingness to extend the rule of law to Indians. The Lake Mohonk agenda was also consonant with—and could be seen as supporting—the growth and expansion of the American state. The progressive movement's emphasis on cleaning up corruption, good government, civil service reform, and the science of administration helped frame the kinds of national interventions in the life of reservation Indians that would—and would not—be seen as appropriate.

Although there were and are unique features to the relationship between Native Americans and the state, debates about citizenship and the status of Native Americans were intertwined with debates over African Americans, immigrants, women, and workers in the late nineteenth and early twentieth centuries. All entailed some expectations about what qualities citizens needed to possess. Property, independence, agency, manhood, earning one's bread by the sweat of one's brow, the role of civic knowledge and political awareness in voting, temperance, the protection of children, the construction of ward-guardian relations, and ideas about what made some people fit to make contracts and alienate labor or property, all figured importantly. The contests and intellectual framings in these various arenas interacted, informing the "social facts" surrounding the development of legal doctrine concerning the "Indian problem." Thus, protective legislation debates figured not only in gender and labor law, but also in law concerning Native Americans. Negotiations about the impact of the Civil War Amendments on jurisdictional boundaries between state and nation on matters of citizenship for recently freed blacks impacted law for women and for Native Americans. Debates about federalism and the reach of the commerce power (especially but not exclusively in light of congressional power to regulate commerce with the Indian tribes) had implications for the status of Native Americans at law.

These doctrinal connections helped frame the ways in which members of the interpretive community would link law and Constitution to particular Native American causes for which they struggled. Past decisions and precedents provided signals to the interpretive community about what to contest and how. Decisions—and sometimes developing precedent as in the arena of First Amendment jurisdiction—provided activists with new constitutional language to use and construct, and around which to mobilize. Policies and judicial decisions alike could be woven into constitutive stories about lessons learned from failures and missteps, designed to reorient federal Indian policy.

When issues surrounding the status of Native Americans in the polity were nationalized, conflict tended to expand and intensify, involving different branches of the national government and often pitting conceptions of the relationship between state and federal governments against each other. When activists and interested parties played a role in constitutionalizing conflict as well, the pace of change seemed to accelerate. Nationalization and constitutionalization of Native American citizenship issues took place on several dimensions. The jurisdictional issue, establishing the federal government's authority over the Indian, mapped onto conflicts over federal-state relations, both in the antebellum era and subsequent to the Civil War Amendments. The attendant issue of nationalization of authority over Native Americans occasioned constructions of the status of treaties with and statutes over them. Increasingly in the Progressive Era—despite exceptions such as *Heff*—the reach of the federal government's authority over tribal Indians expanded. Reformers in the late nineteenth century and early years of the twentieth century required federal authority for many of their projects and became advocates for the extension of the reach of federal law to Native Americans. Struggles to extend the reach of national law and federal authority drew in activists, legislators, and courts. Reformers of the 1920s determined that government policies were tending to harm, rather than protect, Native Americans, based in part on their own critique of atomistic individualism and capitalism characterizing the society Native Americans were supposed to join. These new activists celebrated communities and their social ethic, and pointed to what other cultures could teach. They increasingly turned to the emerging language of rights, although they wished to protect groups and not merely individuals from harm at the hands of the federal government. This later generation of reformers turned to the national state, including the Court, for authoritative solutions, even to grant some decision-making power to tribal authorities. John Collier noted with satisfaction that, by 1925 in the House and 1928 in the Senate, "Indian questions are no longer, in Congress, 'local' questions."[136]

Negotiation and dialogue among members of the interpretive community became intense in the final years of the Dawes Act era, even though the Court was only indirectly a central player. The Court was providing cues and language to activists that they would employ in the public arena. Growing rights consciousness and attendant developments in federal case law added an important dimension to arguments and assaults on assimilation and prevailing federal policies. During the second wave of Native American reform efforts, activists who engaged the language of rights, freedom of religion, the ability to make contracts, presence or absence of legal recourse, and equality under the law consciously constitutionalized conflict. The absence of key markers of civil liberty—such as security against arbitrary violence promised by civil law, capacity to plead and sue in court with an impartial judge, and guaranteed access to law—indicated denial of citizenship rights.[137] Framing wrongs against Native Americans in this manner became an important vehicle for mobilizing popular opinion and pressure against current government initiatives. Such constitutionalized conflict rather quickly resulted in major policy innovation. Although the language and concepts with which courts deal had been engaged, the period following *U.S. v. Nice* was somewhat more subdued in terms of court battles, since the 1916 decision seemed to settle the issue of the compatibility of the status of citizen and ward. The constitutional ferment of the 1920s did not follow one or a set of "minimalist" decisions, but rather followed a decision in which the Court finally deferred to Congress to determine the time and manner of ending its guardianship over tribal Indians.

What should also not be forgotten about the Dawes Act era is that inclusion and incorporation of Native Americans under "protection" of federal law was an agenda that took very little account of the wishes of the Native American tribes that had previously thought themselves entitled to internal self-government under treaties and statutes negotiated with the federal government. During most of the era when allotments were distributed, citizenship meant renunciation of tribal membership. Citizenship did not confer voting rights, unless a state wished to recognize such rights. And citizenship, even if granted to entire tribes, did not protect many tribal landholdings because Native Americans were also wards. Native Americans experienced their membership in the polity differently depending on their location. In these constructions of citizenship, courts, other political institutions, and other members of the interpretive community had sometimes differing approaches, investments, and interests, but all were engaged in interactions that made constitutional law.

Notes

I thank Michael Pasahow, who provided invaluable research assistance for this project. I also owe thanks to Joshua Hudner, Noah Metheny, Will Ortman, and Phil Spector for additional research assistance. I am grateful to the General Federation of Women's Clubs for access to their archives.

1. Helen Hunt Jackson, *A Century of Dishonor* (1881; reprint, Boston: Roberts Brothers, 1886). The book was called "the *Uncle Tom's Cabin* of the Indian race" by Ray Allen Billington on the back cover of the original edition. Jackson, known for poetry and prose, was galvanized by an Indian rights lecture concerning the Ponca removal controversy, which she heard in Boston on a return visit from her then home in Colorado in 1879. She viewed Secretary of the Interior Carl Schurz as a major obstacle to Indian policy reform; some of the letters exchanged between Jackson and Schurz concerning the forced relocation of the Poncas were published in the *New York Tribune* and the *Boston Daily Advertiser* in 1879 and 1880. Her book was designed to demonstrate and expose the wrongs the government had inflicted upon Native Americans; to insist upon the natives' right of occupancy to the soil (which she found upheld in U.S. Supreme Court decisions); and to condemn the theft of land and the violation of treaties and rules of international law, along with the 1871 congressional determination to cease treaty making with Indians altogether. Chapters explored governmental wrongs against different tribes. Jackson called for citizenship for Indians as soon as they were fit, and protection until that time; she appealed for protection of the law for Indian's rights of property, life, liberty, and the pursuit of happiness (341–342). She had no known direct contact with any tribes but conducted her research in the Astor Library. She produced a work whose intent was to "appeal to the heart and the conscience of the American people. What the people demand, Congress will do" (30). A copy was sent to each member of Congress.

2. The Dawes Act also permitted the government to sell off "excess" land after the allotments were made. The act made provision for 160-acre allotments to heads of households and 80-acre allotments to each single person over eighteen (with additional provisions for orphaned minors).

3. See Mark Tushnet, *Taking the Constitution Away from the Courts* (Princeton, N.J.: Princeton University Press, 1999). Tushnet, "*Marbury v. Madison* and the Theory of Judicial Supremacy," in *Great Cases in Constitutional Law*, ed. Robert P. George (Princeton, N.J.: Princeton University Press, 2000), 21–22. Cass R. Sunstein, *One Case at a Time: Judicial Minimalism on the Supreme Court* (Cambridge, Mass.: Harvard University

Press, 1999), makes a case for judicial minimalism to the extent it promotes democratic deliberation as well as accountability and reflection.

4. Bruce Ackerman's First Amendment argument for permitting the California recall election to proceed as scheduled can be read as one particular vision of democracy-enhancing jurisprudence ("Worse yet, the decision disrupts the First Amendment interests of the millions of Californians who have participated in the recall effort"). Ackerman, "The Vote Must Go On," *New York Times*, September 17, 2003, A27. However, Laurence H. Tribe argues that "California's denial of equality will be unmistakably systematic. It will predictably discriminate against urban minorities . . . In short, this case is about enforcing the bedrock guarantee of equality in the right to vote." Which is the democracy-enhancing posture? Tribe, "The Ninth Circuit Got It Right," *Wall Street Journal*, September 18, 2003, A16.

5. Keith E. Whittington, *Constitutional Construction: Divided Powers and Constitutional Meaning* (Cambridge, Mass.: Harvard University Press, 1999), 207, 9.

6. Ibid., 5.

7. Ibid., 226.

8. See Ronald Kahn, "Institutional Norms and the Historical Development of Supreme Court Politics: Changing 'Social Facts' and Doctrinal Development," in *The Supreme Court in American Politics: New Institutionalist Interpretations*, ed. Howard Gillman and Cornell W. Clayton (Lawrence: University Press of Kansas, 1999), 43–59. Kahn uses the term *social facts* to talk about the conditions under which new circumstances put pressure on existing beliefs, leading the Court to change its beliefs about social reality. I am suggesting that activists contest visions of social facts and sometimes succeed in impressing this new vision on the Court. See also H. N. Hirsch, *A Theory of Liberty: The Constitution and Minorities* (New York: Routledge, 1992). Hirsch points out the inevitable embeddedness of constitutional doctrine in social and political reality, including societal consensus or lack thereof about a given moral issue.

9. Ken I. Kersch, "The New Deal Triumph as the End of History?: The Judicial Negotiation of Labor Rights and Civil Rights," this volume.

10. The case would become *Eastern and Emigrant Cherokees v. United States*, and in the U.S. Supreme Court, bundled with three other cases, it would be referred to as *The United States v. Cherokee Nation* 202 U.S. 101 (1906). See generally Jill Norgren, "Before it Was Merely Difficult: Belva Lockwood's Life in Law and Politics," *Journal of Supreme Court History* 23 (1999): 16–42.

11. Kenneth R. Philip, *John Collier's Crusade for Indian Reform, 1920–1954* (Tucson: University of Arizona Press, 1977), 43.

12. Charles R. Epp, "External Pressure and the Supreme Court's Agenda," in *Supreme Court Decision Making: New Institutionalist Approaches*, ed. Cornell W. Clayton and Howard Gillman (Chicago: University of Chicago Press, 1999), 255–279; quote 259–260.

13. Ibid., 261 and passim.

14. See Michael McCann, "How the Supreme Court Matters in American Politics," in *The Supreme Court in American Politics: New Institutionalist Interpretations*, ed. Howard Gillman and Cornell Clayton, 71–72 (Lawrence: University Press of Kansas, 1999).

15. Sunstein, *One Case at a Time*; Charles E. Lindblom, "The Science of Muddling Through," *Public Administration Review* 19 (1959): 79–88. Keith Bybee has also noticed the connection between Sunstein's minimalism and Lindblom's muddling through in "Book Review Essay: The Jurisprudence of Uncertainty: Cass R. Sunstein, *One Case at a Time*," *Law and Society Review* 35 (2001): 943.

16. *United States v. Nice*, 241 U.S. 591 (1916). Act of 2 June 1924, 43 Stat. 253, 8 U.S.C. 3. See Felix S. Cohen, *Handbook of Federal Indian Law*, United States Department of the Interior, Office of the Solicitor (Washington, D.C.: U.S. Government Printing Office, 1942), 156–157.

17. Pamela Brandwein, "The *Civil Rights Cases* and the Lost Language of State Neglect," this volume.

18. Thomas M. Keck, "From *Bakke* to *Grutter*: The Rise of Rights-Based Conservatism," this volume.

19. John W. Kingdon, *Agendas, Alternatives, and Public Policies* (Boston: Little, Brown, 1984), esp. 173–218; quote 174.

20. Ibid., 188.

21. Frank R. Baumgartner and Bryan D. Jones, *Agendas and Instability in American Politics* (Chicago: University of Chicago Press, 1993), 12.

22. Whittington, *Constitutional Construction*, 216.

23. David E. Wilkins, *American Indian Sovereignty and the U.S. Supreme Court* (Austin: University of Texas Press, 1997), 86.

24. Austin Sarat, "Going to Court: Access, Autonomy, and the Contradictions of Liberal Legality," in *The Politics of Law: A Progressive Critique*, ed. David Kairys, 3rd ed. (New York: Basic Books, 1998), 110.

25. Ibid., 111.

26. On the latter point, see Cornell W. Clayton, "The Supreme Court and Political Jurisprudence: New and Old Institutionalisms," in *Supreme Court Decision-Making: New Institutionalist Approaches*, ed. Cornell W. Clayton and Howard Gillman (Chicago: University of Chicago Press, 1999), 32. Clayton is somewhat critical of this historical-interpretive institutionalist approach, referring to Howard Gillman, Karen Orren, Stephen Skowronek, and Rogers Smith.

27. Robert A. Kagan, Bryant Garth, and Austin Sarat, "Facilitating and Domesticating Change: Democracy, Capitalism, and Law's Double Role in the Twentieth Century," in *Looking Back at Law's Century*, ed. Austin Sarat, Bryant Garth, and Robert A. Kagan (Ithaca, N.Y.: Cornell University Press, 2002), 7.

28. Karen Orren and Stephen Skowronek, "Institutions and Intercurrence: Theory Building in the Fullness of Time," in *Political Order*, ed. Ian Shapiro and Russell Hardin (*Nomos* 38) (New York: New York University Press, 1996), 140.

29. Ibid., 112.

30. Ibid., 111. Karen Orren and Stephen Skowronek, "In Search of Political Development," in *The Liberal Tradition in American Politics*, ed. David F. Ericson and Louisa Bertch Green (New York: Routledge, 1999), 39.

31. Orren and Skowronek, "In Search of Political Development," 39; Orren and Skowronek, "Institutions and Intercurrence," 140, 139.

32. Ronald Kahn, *The Supreme Court and Constitutional Theory, 1953–1993* (Lawrence: University Press of Kansas, 1994). I am somewhat reticent to speak in terms of dialogue because I believe that sometimes the participants are speaking in different languages. The question is when these discourses engage. Not always are the issues framed and constitutionalized in a way that is likely to engage the Court. Barry Friedman seems to have a looser notion of dialogue in "Dialogue and Judicial Review," *Michigan Law Review* 91 (1993): 577.

33. Julie Novkov, *Constituting Workers, Protecting Women* (Ann Arbor: University of Michigan Press, 2001), 16.

34. Ibid., 21.

35. *Cherokee Nation v. Georgia*, 5 Peters 1 (1831) and *Worcester v. Georgia*, 6 Peters 515 (1832).

36. Cohen, *Handbook of Federal Indian Law*, 116.

37. See Wilkins, *American Indian Sovereignty*, 116.

38. Petra T. Shattuck and Jill Norgren, *Partial Justice: Federal Indian Law in a Liberal Constitutional System* (New York: Berg, 1991), 50. It is also noteworthy, for our purposes, that the Cherokee Nation chose to contest decisions in the Court, hiring attorneys and pressing their claims in constitutional terms. See Jill Norgren, *The Cherokee Cases: The Confrontation of Law and Politics* (New York: McGraw-Hill, 1996). Their sustained litigation kept Cherokee issues before the courts. Shattuck and Norgren also demonstrate that the antebellum Court was not completely consistent in following the vision of *Worcester*.

39. R. Kent Newmyer, *John Marshall and the Heroic Age of the Supreme Court* (Baton Rouge: Louisiana State University Press, 2001).

40. *Fletcher v. Peck*, 6 Cranch 87 (1810).

41. See, e.g., Akhil Reed Amar's discussion of Congressman John Bingham in *The Bill of Rights: Creation and Reconstruction* (New Haven, Conn.: Yale University Press, 1998), 147, 164–165. For a wonderful treatment of the Fairman-Crosskey debate in light of investments in the Frankfurter-Black debate over incorporation, as well as more recent incarnations, see Pamela Brandwein, *Reconstructing Reconstruction: The Supreme Court and the Production of Historical Truth* (Durham, N.C.: Duke University Press, 1999).

42. Reva B. Siegel, "Collective Memory and the Nineteenth Amendment: Reasoning about 'the Woman Question' in the Discourse of Sex Discrimination," in *History, Memory, and the Law*, ed. Austin Sarat and Thomas R. Kearns (Ann Arbor: University of Michigan Press, 1999), 147–148, citing evidence in the *Congressional Globe* for the 38th–40th Congresses. See also Siegel, "She the People: The Nineteenth

Amendment, Sex Equality, Federalism, and the Family," *Harvard Law Review* 115 (2002): 947.

43. Although *Bradwell v. Illinois* was heard two weeks before the *Slaughter-House Cases*, the decisions were made a day apart, with *Slaughter-House* (5–4) splitting the Court and *Bradwell* (8–1) giving the justices little difficulty.

44. *McKay v. Campbell*, 16 Fed. Cas. No. 8840 (D.C. Ore. 1871), quoted in Cohen, *Handbook of Federal Indian Law*, 158.

45. *Elk v. Wilkins*, 112 U.S. 94, 100 (1884). See Shattuck and Norgren, *Partial Justice*, 95 for background on the case. See also Wilkins, *American Indian Sovereignty*, 119–120.

46. *Elk v. Wilkins*, 112 U.S. 94, 103 (1884).

47. Ibid., at 106.

48. Cohen, *Handbook of Federal Indian Law*, 157–159. The latter was the case in Arizona. South Dakota, Colorado, Utah, Idaho, New Mexico, and Washington were also among states continuing to maintain some restriction on Native American suffrage following the Indian Citizenship Act of 1924. See Wilkins, *American Indian Sovereignty*, 119–120, for the connection between the *Elk* decision and the General Allotment Act. See also *Proceedings of the Lake Mohonk Conference*.

49. These were criteria that had been in use in certain treaties and statutes since 1870. See Cohen, *Handbook of Federal Indian Law*, 153.

50. Lake Mohonk activists began to turn their attention to the Philippines, to Porto Rico [sic] and other places touched by imperial ventures in the early years of the new century; this change of focus also seems to occur because of the failure of early optimism that the Dawes Act would lead to assimilation and civilization of the Indians in short order.

51. Senator H. L. Dawes, *Proceedings of the Eighth Lake Mohonk Conference* (1890), 84, quoted in Larry E. Burgess, "We'll Discuss It at Mohonk," *Quaker History* 60 (Spring 1971): 20.

52. Robert Winston Mardock, *The Reformers and the American Indian* (Columbia: University of Missouri Press, 1971), 199.

53. He addresses the Lake Mohonk Conference at some length in 1887; Thayer's appointment to the Committee on Laws can be found in the *Proceedings of the Lake Mohonk Conference*. See James Bradley Thayer, "The Dawes Bill and the Indians," *Atlantic Monthly* 61 (March 1888): 315–322; and "A People without Law," *Atlantic Monthly* 68 (October 1891): 540–551, and 68 (November 1891): 676–687. He makes reference to *Harvard Law Review* 1 (1887–1888): 149–152, where "The Law School/In the Moot Court" section contains a report of a case he gave his students to argue: "Tribal Indians, while off their reservation and within a State, are protected by the 14th amendment of the Constitution of the United States, as being persons entitled to the equal protection of the laws. Where a statute giving an action against towns for injuries suffered by reason of a defect in the highway excepts such Indians from the benefits of it, the excepting clause is unconstitutional and void." Thayer, writing the opinion of the Court, found that the exclusion was unconstitutional.

54. Thayer, "People without Law," 682–683.

55. Siegel, "Collective Memory and the Nineteenth Amendment," 134–135.

56. Kersch, "The New Deal Triumph as the End of History?," this volume.

57. Justice William Strong, *Proceedings of the Lake Mohonk Conference*, 1885, 33–34.

58. See Brandwein, *"Civil Rights Cases,"* this volume.

59. Theodore Roosevelt, *The Winning of the West*, vol. 10 in *Theodore Roosevelt*, ed. Hermann Hagedorn (New York: Charles Scribner's Sons, 1926), 80.

60. Shattuck and Norgren, *Partial Justice*, 79.

61. Wilkins, *American Indian Sovereignty*, 52–53.

62. U.S. Commissioner of Indian Affairs, *Annual Report* (1871), 1154 quoted in Wilkins, *American Indian Sovereignty*, 53.

63. Wilkins, *American Indian Sovereignty*, 54–55.

64. *Cherokee Nation v. Southern Kansas Railway*, 135 U.S. 641, 657–658 (1890).

65. Alice Fletcher, *Proceedings of the Lake Mohonk Conference*, 1884, 5. Fletcher personally and forcefully carried out some of these allotments both before and after the Dawes Act, beginning with the Omahas in 1883, when she was appointed Special Agent to the Office of Indian Affairs. She was treated as the authority on the Indians at Lake Mohonk.

66. Joan Mark, *A Stranger in Her Native Land: Alice Fletcher and the American Indians* (Lincoln: University of Nebraska Press, 1988), 118, quoting Alice Fletcher, "Between the Lines," in *Lend a Hand* (July 1886), the paper of the Hampton Institute.

67. Lyman Abbott, Remarks, *Proceedings of the Lake Mohonk Conference*, 1885, 51.

68. Mark, *A Stranger in Her Native Land*, 106, 117. The quote is from Mr. John H. Oberly, Superintendent of Indian Schools, Department of the Interior, *Proceedings of the Lake Mohonk Conference*, 1885, 55.

69. The phrase "the sorry case of your children the Indians" appears in correspondence between Mrs. H. A. (Stella) Atwood, California representative, Division of Industrial and Social Conditions, Department of Public Welfare, General Federation of Women's Clubs, and Belle Sherwin, newly elected president of the League of Women Voters, 31 May 1924 (Atwood to Sherwin) and 3 June 1924 (Sherwin to Atwood). Sherwin uses the phrase, apparently from the Atwood letter, which is missing from the file. Papers of the League of Women Voters, Library of Congress.

70. Miss Alice C. Fletcher, "The Indian and the Prisoner," *Southern Workman* 17 (1888): 45. Originally published in the *International Record of Charities and Correction*.

71. This is the language of Professor C. C. Painter, *Proceedings of the Lake Mohonk Conference*, 1885, 29.

72. General Crook, General Miles, and others quoted in Thayer, "People without Law," 685.

73. Michael T. Smith, "The History of Indian Citizenship," *Great Plains Journal* 10 (Fall 1970): 26–29. Smith points out that in fact, some whole tribes were granted citizenship, which made this position hard to sustain. In these cases, it appeared that such an Indian had to be a member of a tribe to become a citizen.

74. *Ex Parte Crow Dog*, 109 U.S. 556, 558 (1883).

75. Smith, "History of Indian Citizenship," 28.

76. Ibid.

77. Quoted in Thayer, "People without Law," 686n1.

78. Ibid., 685–686.

79. See Shattuck and Norgren, *Partial Justice*, 99–100.

80. *Lone Wolf v. Hitchcock*, 187 U.S. 553, 565, 567 (1903).

81. Senator Matthew Quey, Republican of Pennsylvania, called *Lone Wolf* a very remarkable decision. "It is the *Dred Scott* decision No. 2, except that in this case the victim is red instead of black. It practically inculcates the doctrine that the red man has no rights which the white man is bound to respect, and, that no treaty or contract made with him is binding. Is that not about it?" *U.S. Congressional Record* (1903), 2028 quoted in Wilkins, *American Indian Sovereignty*, 116.

82. *Lone Wolf v. Hitchcock*, 187 U.S. 553, 555 (1903). See also Shattuck and Norgren, *Partial Justice*, 76–77; Wilkins, *American Indian Sovereignty*, 114–115.

83. Wilkins, *American Indian Sovereignty*, 116.

84. Thayer, "People without Law," 683.

85. Ibid., 683.

86. Representative Robert Gamble (R., South Dakota), quoted in Wilkins, *American Indian Sovereignty*, 120. The impossibility of being both a citizen and a pupil of the United States is quoted from an immediately preceding remark by Representative Bailey in the 1897 *Congressional Record*.

87. Although not readily recognized by reformers, some allotments were inadequate for grazing; some lands were of poor quality; not all Native Americans were from farming traditions; and as some Indians were made eligible to alienate their lands, they became landless, without the rations and other government supports that had predated the Dawes Act.

88. For example, Fletcher, *Proceedings of the Lake Mohonk Conference*, 1884, 26.

89. On the liquor traffic, see Cohen, *Handbook of Federal Indian Law*, 352. *U.S. v. Holliday*, 3 Wall 407, 418 (1865), citing Marshall in *Gibbons v. Ogden* (1824); quoted in Cohen, *Handbook of Federal Indian Law*, 90n20. This would seem to follow Marshall's jurisdictional reasoning in the lottery ticket case of *Cohens v. Virginia* (1821).

90. Cohen, *Handbook of Federal Indian Law*, 354–355. The 1892 statute in question is 27 Stat. 260.

91. Wilkins, *American Indian Sovereignty*, 121, citing 110 Fed. 942, 947–948 (1901). This was a South Dakota case.

92. *Farrell v. United States* 110 Fed. 942, 948 (1901) quoted in Wilkins, *American Indian Sovereignty*, 122. Cohen, *Handbook of Federal Indian Law*, 354: "the privilege of buying liquor is not one of the privileges of citizenship"; see also *Mulligan v. United States*, 120 Fed. 98 (1903).

93. *Matter of Heff*, 197 U.S. 488, 508 (1905).

94. *Civil Rights Cases*, 109 U.S. 3 (1883), Justice Bradley writing for the Court.

95. *Matter of Heff* was argued 9 and 10 January 1905 and decided 10 April 1905. *Lochner v. New York* was argued 23 and 24 February 1905 and decided 17 April 1905.

96. *Champion v. Ames*, 188 U.S. 321 (1903). Justice Brewer, who would write the unpopular *Heff* decision, dissented in *Champion*, arguing both that lottery tickets were not in themselves injurious and that the Congress lacked general police powers; such power was reserved to the states by the Tenth Amendment.

97. *Hipolite Egg Co. v. United States*, 220 U.S. 45 (1911); *Hoke v. United States*, 227 U.S. 308 (1913).

98. *Matter of Heff*, 197 U.S. 488, 509 (1905).

99. U.S. Commissioner of Indian Affairs, *Annual Report* (1905). Quoted in Wilkins, *American Indian Sovereignty*, 124–125.

100. President Theodore Roosevelt, Fifth Annual Message, 5 December 1905, quoted in Wilkins, *American Indian Sovereignty*, 124.

101. U.S. Commissioner of Indian Affairs, *Annual Report* (1906), quoted in Wilkins, *American Indian Sovereignty*, 123.

102. *United States v. Celestine*, 215 U.S. 278, 291 (1909).

103. *United States v. Pelican*, 232 U.S. 442, 450 (1914).

104. Philip, *John Collier's Crusade*, 28–30. This issue would remain contested well into the 1920s and deal in another generation of Native American activists and white reformers. See below on the Bursum and Lenroot bills, both of which reformers saw defeated.

105. *United States v. Nice*, 241 U.S. 591, 598 (1916).

106. 43 Stat. 253, 8 U.S.C. 3 (2 June 1924). Note that some migratory Indians whose lands crossed the Canadian border did not fall within the description of those who now became citizens.

107. Jane Addams, for example, clearly believed that those to be served were partners in defining what they required. Direct involvement and engagement with the poor taught activists. Camilla Stivers, "A Civic Machinery for Democratic Expression: Jane Addams on Public Administration," paper presented at Exploring Jane Addams, Twenty-ninth Annual Richard R. Baker Philosophy Colloquium, University of Dayton, 8–9 November 2002. See also Camilla Stivers, *Bureau Men, Settlement Women: Constructing Public Administration in the Progressive Era* (Lawrence: University Press of Kansas, 2000); Wendy Sarvasy, "Social Citizenship from a Feminist Perspective," *Hypatia* 12 (1997): 54–73.

108. Mary Austin, *The Young Woman Citizen* (New York: Women's Press, 1918). I am indebted to Teena Gabrielson for pointing out Austin's understanding of administration in "Avenues to Virtue: Gender, Nature, and Citizenship at the Turn of the Century," paper presented at the American Political Science Association Meeting, 27–31 August 2003.

109. Stivers, "Civic Machinery," citing Jane Addams, "The Problems of Municipal Administration," *American Journal of Sociology* 10 (January 1905): 425–444. When John Collier became Indian Commissioner in the Roosevelt administration, he prided himself on the extensive and organized field consultation with tribal Indians that preceded

formulation of what he liked to call the Indian New Deal (the Indian Reorganization Act). John C. Collier, *From Every Zenith* (Denver: Sage Books, 1963), 174–175.

110. On Addams's critique, see Carol Nackenoff, "Gendered Citizenship: Alternative Narratives of Political Incorporation in the United States, 1875–1925," in *The Liberal Tradition in American Politics*, ed. David Ericson and Louisa Bertch Green (New York: Routledge, 1999), 137–169.

111. William Cronon, "The Trouble with Wilderness, or Getting Back to the Wrong Nature," in *Uncommon Ground: Toward Reinventing Nature*, ed. William Cronon (New York: W. W. Norton, 1995), 69–90. Raymond Williams, "Ideas of Nature," in *Problems in Materialism and Culture: Selected Essays* (London: New Left Books, 1980), 67–85.

112. Philip, *John Collier's Crusade*, 2–4, 33–34. John Collier began his career as a social worker, joining the People's Institute in New York and working toward its goal of "giving the immigrant masses a sense of brotherhood in their local neighborhoods" and of advancing social democracy. Collier helped organize a Pageant and Festival of Nations in 1914; he was convinced that industrialism had led to dehumanization and sundering of collective units, including families and neighborhoods. He sought to preserve various national cultures, not unlike Addams. He met Mary Austin through the Training School for Community Workers he established, loosely connected with the People's Institute. Philip, *John Collier's Crusade*, 9–21, 10 (quote); Collier, *From Every Zenith*, 155.

113. The proclamation was signed by Vachel Lindsay, Edgar Lee Masters, Carl Sandburg, and William Allen White, among others. See Philip, *John Collier's Crusade*, 34. Mabel Dodge, an instigator of a great deal of artistic interest in the area, persuaded D. H. Lawrence to move to the area and write about Native American life.

114. John Collier, "The Pueblos' Last Stand," *Sunset Magazine* (February 1923): 20–22.

115. Philip, *John Collier's Crusade*, chap. 2.

116. Collier, *From Every Zenith*, 137.

117. Ibid., 131. Atwood shared credit for founding the Committee on Indian Welfare with South Dakota Yankton Sioux Zitkala-Sa, also known as Mrs. Gertrude Bonnin, a proponent of Indian self-determination, tribal identity, and cultural pluralism.

118. Report of the Committee on Indian Welfare, Sixteenth Biennial Convention of the General Federation of Women's Clubs, Chatauqua, New York, 28 June 1922, 508. General Federation of Women's Clubs Convention Records, 1896–1930. Record Group 3, Series 1.

119. Philip, *John Collier's Crusade*, 37–38. Fall apparently felt that by threatening to evict white settlers if the Bursum Bill or similar measure did not pass, backlash and even violence would turn public sentiment against the Pueblos and their allies.

120. Fall's departure was precipitated by the Teapot Dome scandal. See also Philip, *John Collier's Crusade*, 38. Unflattering references to Fall appear in the records of the General Federation of Women's Clubs; in 1927, Stella Atwood refers to Fall as the "late unlamented Secretary of the Interior" (General Federation of Women's Clubs, Twelfth Biennial Council, 1927, Report of the Division of Indian Welfare), 46. An editor of the

New York Sun, Lemuel Parton, told members of Congress that John Collier made Albert Fall "bark like a coyote at the mention of his name" (quoted in Philip, *John Collier's Crusade*, 116).

121. *Pueblo Indian Lands*. Hearings before a Subcommittee of the Committee on Public Lands and Surveys, United States Senate, Sixty-seventh Congress, Fourth Session, on S. 3865 and S. 4223 (Washington, D.C.: Government Printing Office, 1923), 114–120. Alice Robertson from Oklahoma, who had been present at one or more of the Lake Mohonk Conference sessions in later years, was serving in the U.S. House of Representatives when Atwood testified there. Robertson attacked Atwood's disinterestedness and questioned whether she acted with approval of the federation's board of directors in collecting funds for Pueblo defense. John Collier came to Atwood's defense. See Philip, *John Collier's Crusade*, 43–44.

122. Atwood testifying before the Subcommittee of the Committee on Public Lands and Surveys, United States Senate, 16 January 1923, 116.

123. Philip, *John Collier's Crusade*, 53.

124. Ibid., 62, citing Collier, *From Every Zenith*. Controversy in the General Federation of Women's Clubs was rarely apparent in reports from conventions, and Stella Atwood is listed as chairman of the Division of Indian Welfare in the Twelfth Biennial Council Report (see notes 129 and 130 below). The personal attacks on Atwood by members of the House Committee on Indian Affairs are described in Philip, *John Collier's Crusade*, 43–44; Collier charges the Indian Bureau with the attack that drove Atwood out of her chairmanship of Indian Affairs in the GFWC (*From Every Zenith*, 141).

125. When Native Americans became citizens, they became subject to the laws of the states wherein they resided; it is interesting to note that pressing Native American rights as a matter for constitutional protection occurred alongside increasing attention to developing jurisprudential rationale for which provisions of the Bill of Rights applied to the states.

126. Gary C. Stern, "The Indian Citizenship Act of 1924," *New Mexico Historical Review* 47 (July 1972): 266.

127. Collier, *From Every Zenith*, 141, 153, 157. Collier also recounts the spring 1923 dismissal of earlier and more costly counsel, Francis C. Wilson of Santa Fe. Wilson had spoken out of turn in Washington by endorsing, on behalf of the General Federation of Women's Clubs, the Indian Defense Association, and the Pueblos, a bill that practically duplicated the Bursum Bill minus the religious persecution clauses (153).

128. Stella Atwood, *General Federation News* (April 1925). Some of the pleas for religious freedom during the period came from a different direction: some friends of the Indian and some Pueblos themselves sought freedom to practice Christianity without encumbrance from tribal religious leaders. Collier felt that the Bureau of Indian Affairs orchestrated these voices in an attempt to derail reformers' charges.

129. General Federation of Women's Clubs, Twelfth Biennial Council 1927 (Grand Rapids, Mich., Report of the Division of Indian Welfare; chairman, Mrs. Stella Atwood).

130. Ibid.

131. Collier, *From Every Zenith*, 134, 157 (quote).

132. Philip, *John Collier's Crusade*, 135. The Meriam Report, *The Problem of Indian Administration*, represented the findings of an investigation of Indian affairs conducted by the private-sector Institute for Government Research. Dean of Harvard Law School Felix Frankfurter was consulted on Collier's appointment. On Collier's belief that Felix Frankfurter had offered his unsolicited support for the nomination, see Collier, *From Every Zenith*, 171–172; Philip believes Frankfurter's first choice nominee was fellow attorney Nathan Margold, who had also served as legal adviser for the Pueblos (Philip, *John Collier's Crusade*, 114–115). Collier considered ACLU founder and director Roger N. Baldwin an important helper in bringing about reform (*From Every Zenith*, 159). The ACLU, founded in 1920, litigated cases of World War I dissidents and took up the cause of First Amendment freedoms.

133. Collier, *From Every Zenith*, 173.

134. See Philip, *John Collier's Crusade*, 143–159, for a discussion of objections to various provisions of the bill.

135. Ibid., 141–143, 156–159. Collier was proud of this process of consultation: "Perhaps never in American history has any legislation been written and enacted so completely in a goldfish bowl—been by governmental intent so exhaustively a subject for popular consideration prior to its enactment. . . . In fact, it can be said that the renaissance of the Indians as self-governing, self-respecting men came to fruition in and through their thorough discussion of the Reorganization Act" (Collier, *From Every Zenith*, 175). On the final version, see 48 Stat. 984, 25 U.S.C. 461. See Cohen, *Handbook of Federal Indian Law*, 84.

136. Collier, *From Every Zenith*, 163, quoting his own remarks in his 1922–1933 periodical, *American Indian Life*.

137. See Margaret R. Somers, "Rights, Relationality, and Membership: Rethinking the Making and Meaning of Citizenship," *Law and Social Inquiry* 19 (Winter 1994): 106.

Chapter 10

From Bakke to Grutter:
The Rise of Rights-Based Conservatism

Thomas M. Keck

Supreme Court decisions are shaped by forces both external and internal to the institution itself. These factors have conventionally been characterized as "political" and "legal," respectively, but those terms imply a greater degree of independence from each other than actually exists. The "legal" ideas that influence the justices, after all, are derived in large part from ongoing debates in the broader political system, and the "political" interests that pressure the Court are often constituted by legal categories created by the justices themselves. In this chapter, I explore the interaction of such legal and political factors in the context of a failed assault on a landmark precedent, the Court's 1978 decision in *Regents of the University of California v. Bakke* (1978).

In the *Bakke* case, Justice Powell sought to settle the affirmative action issue with a judicial compromise, striking down the strict racial quota used for medical school admissions at the University of California–Davis (UC-Davis), but indicating that some more flexible race-conscious policies would survive constitutional scrutiny. In the wake of this effort, however, a variety of conservative legal activists waged a sustained campaign to persuade the Court to abandon Powell's compromise and to invalidate all race-conscious admissions policies nationwide. Led by the Center for Individual Rights (CIR), this campaign had much going in its favor and might well have succeeded, but twenty-five years later, it produced another landmark decision reaffirming *Bakke*. Justice O'Connor, casting the deciding vote and writing for the Court in *Grutter v. Bollinger* (2003), upheld the University of Michigan Law School's admissions policy, and in doing so, entrenched Powell's vulnerable compromise into constitutional law for decades to come. Despite legal arguments that appeared compelling to many—and despite substantial political support from policy elites and ordinary citizens alike—CIR failed to persuade the Court to outlaw race-conscious affirmative action policies.

CIR's defeat was not total, however, as it did succeed in imposing significant limits on such policies at the margins. During the quarter century between *Bakke* and *Grutter*, CIR's lawyers successfully persuaded a number of federal courts to invalidate race-conscious policies, and its lawsuits contributed to a number of parallel efforts outlawing such policies by means of statewide initiative.[1] On the same day as *Grutter*, moreover, the Court also decided *Gratz v. Bollinger* (2003), invalidating the University of Michigan's undergraduate admissions policy as an impermissible quota under *Bakke*, thereby forcing several large public universities to reshape their admissions procedures.[2] Despite the significant defeat in *Grutter*, then, organized interest group litigation has had a substantial influence on the constitutional law of affirmative action.

To understand the relative influence of such external pressures on the Court, however, we must attend to their interaction with a variety of internal influences on judicial decision making. In particular, CIR's success in advancing its color-blind vision of the equal protection clause was limited by the continued commitment of key members of the Rehnquist Court to a particular vision of the judicial role. Justice O'Connor had been quite critical of affirmative action on a number of occasions, but she was also determined to move cautiously in imposing constitutional limits on a policy supported by large numbers of university, corporate, and military elites. So long as she continued to follow Powell in exercising significant deference to university officials on matters of educational policy—and so long as she held the Court's deciding vote—CIR was unable to achieve the sweeping declaration of color-blind law that it has sought.

In an important sense, moreover, it is misleading to characterize CIR's litigation campaign as an "external" pressure on the Court because that campaign has in fact been shaped by the Court itself to a significant degree. In other words, the rise of such litigation has been a consequence as well as a cause of the Court's decisions. As I will argue below, Powell's *Bakke* opinion played a significant, although unintended, role in sparking the rights-based legal campaign on behalf of white "victims" of affirmative action. As with other government policies, Supreme Court decisions sometimes reshape the terrain of politics, calling forth political identities and interests that return to influence the Court in subsequent cases. As Michael McCann has noted, the High Court often serves as a catalyst, shaping the legal agendas, opportunities, and resources of political movements with its key decisions: "When the Court acts on a particular disputed issue, it can at once elevate the salience of that issue in the public agenda, privilege some parties who have perceived interests in the issue, create new opportunities for such parties to mobilize around causes, and provide symbolic resources for those mobilization efforts in various venues." Rather than settling political conflicts, Supreme Court rulings more "often serve to encourage or generate further litigation on public issues."[3] This sort of feedback process is an important feature of political development more generally, and although Court scholars have not often addressed it, this dynamic has been receiving substantial attention elsewhere in the discipline.

Building on a seventy-year-old remark of E. E. Schattschneider's—that "new policies create a new politics"—contemporary students of American political development have been pointing out that "policies function as institutions, imposing particular norms and rules on recipients, and thus, in turn, reshaping politics itself." Because such "policies convey to citizens their rights and privileges as well as their duties and obligations as members of the community," they sometimes produce political demands that would not otherwise have emerged.[4] As Karen Orren and Stephen Skowronek have observed, "anyone who cares to look back far enough in time will likely find that government has a strong hand in creating the interests it appears to be mediating later on." Thus, "the effects of government policy . . . are of interest . . . not only because they determine who gets what in the here and now but also because they classify the groups, impart the identities, forge the divisions, and strike the alliances that channel future political action."[5] In Paul Pierson's words, "major policies frame the choices of political actors both by creating resources and incentives and by influencing the efforts of individuals to interpret the social world."[6]

In this light, our investigations of Supreme Court decision making and constitutional development must attend to the role of the Court's own decisions in calling forth particular constitutional demands from the public. Like other announcements of public policy, the language of Supreme Court opinions shapes the context in which "individual citizens acquire perceptions of their role in the community, their status in relation to other citizens and government, and the extent to which a policy has affected their lives."[7] As Pierson notes, policies send "signals [that] may influence individuals' perceptions about what their interests are, whether their representatives are protecting those interests, who their allies might be, and what political strategies are promising."[8] In short, whereas Charles Epp and a variety of other judicial scholars have emphasized that support structures in civil society are a significant independent variable shaping judicial action, the reverse also appears to be true.[9] Rights-based litigation encourages the courts to exercise rights-based activism, but such activism in turn encourages the development of rights-based litigation organizations. Thus, students of law and courts have rightly identified organized interest group litigation as a key influence on the Court, but we cannot fully understand either the origins or the relative influence of this "external" factor without reference to internal dynamics on the Court itself.

Powell's Judicial Compromise

Justice Powell's opinion announcing the Court's judgment in *Bakke* is widely regarded as an example of pragmatic judicial compromise.[10] On the one hand, Powell held that UC-Davis's racial quota was unconstitutional, and he appeared to endorse a color-blind reading of the Fourteenth Amendment in doing so. He emphasized that "the guarantees of the Fourteenth Amendment extend to all persons," and he insisted that the principle "of equal protection cannot mean one thing when applied to one individual and something else when applied to a person of another color. If both are not accorded the same protection, then it is not equal." Observing that we live in "a Nation of minorities," in which "the white 'majority' itself is composed of various minority groups, most of which can lay claim to a history of prior discrimination at the hands of the State and private individuals," he insisted that "it is far too late to argue that the guarantee of equal protection to all persons permits the recognition of special wards entitled to a degree of protection greater than that accorded others."[11] Critics of affirmative action, both liberal and conservative, had been advancing such a color-blind reading of the Fourteenth Amendment for several years, and Powell's opinion appeared to give it the Court's imprimatur.[12]

On the other hand, Powell balanced this commitment to color-blindness against a competing concern for judicial restraint, as he was determined to avoid the active judicial supervision of university admissions procedures that the color-blind principle might be thought to require. He had advocated judicial deference in the equal protection context before, and he had recently insisted that such deference was particularly appropriate toward the academic decisions of a public university.[13] Powell was thus faced with competing constitutional commitments, which he sought to balance in the course of case-by-case decision making. As his biographer has noted, "faced with two intellectually coherent, morally defensible, and diametrically opposed positions, Powell chose neither."[14] On the specific question of university admissions, he held that the medical school could no longer set aside sixteen spots in its entering class solely for racial minorities, but he indicated that he would have upheld the policy used by Harvard College, which had been detailed in an amicus brief submitted on behalf of several prestigious private universities. Under the Harvard plan, as Powell described it, "race or ethnic background may be deemed a 'plus' in a particular applicant's file, yet it does not insulate the individual from comparison with all other candidates for the available seats."[15]

Given his color-blind reading of the Fourteenth Amendment, Powell insisted that all race-conscious affirmative action policies should be subjected to strict judicial scrutiny, but he thought that policies modeled on the Harvard plan would sometimes be able to meet this high burden. Although strict quotas would never be "precisely tailored to serve a compelling governmental interest" because they sweep too broadly, policies of individualized consideration might be permissible (even though race-conscious), provided that they did indeed serve some "compelling" purpose.[16] UC-Davis had advanced four justifications for its admissions policy, but Powell rejected three of them as constitutionally insufficient. It was unacceptable, in his view, for a public university to discriminate against white applicants for the purpose of "(i) reducing the historic deficit of traditionally disfavored minorities in medical schools and in the medical profession; (ii) countering the effects of societal discrimination; [or] (iii) increasing the number of physicians who will practice in communities currently underserved." Such discrimination might be constitutionally permissible, however, when it was precisely tailored to "obtaining the educational benefits that flow from an ethnically diverse student body."[17]

This aspect of Powell's holding shaped the admissions policies at public and private universities for a generation. As Louis Menand has noted, *Bakke* "changed the language of college admissions by decreeing that if admissions committees wanted to stay on the safe side of the Constitution, they had to stop talking about quotas and to begin talking about diversity instead."[18] Before the *Bakke* decision, as Daniel Lipson notes, "compensation [for past discrimination] stood out as the primary justification for affirmative action among its proponents." Subsequently, however, "the Supreme Court's resistance to a broad interpretation of the compensation rationale led universities and other institutions to abandon [it] and instead elevate the diversity rationale as the primary justification for race-based affirmative action."[19] The shift did not happen overnight, but Powell put university officials on notice that compensatory justifications were virtually out of bounds, and over time, higher education leaders (and admissions office staffs) adopted the mission of "educational diversity" wholeheartedly.

Even if university administrators initially made this decision simply to comply with a legal rule, the shift had wide-ranging political effects over time, leading to the emergence of what Lipson has called the "diversity consensus" among university and corporate elites. In both the higher education context and in corporate America, a new breed of diversity management specialists was charged with the task of implementing affirmative action policy. These organizational actors were so successful in entrenching themselves in the institutional culture of higher education that support for affirmative action became a litmus test for employment in university admissions offices—and often in other administrative posts as well.[20] When the issue returned to the Court in *Gratz* and *Grutter*, scores of colleges and universities joined a variety of amicus briefs noting that they had relied heavily on Powell's opinion in designing their post-*Bakke* admissions policies.[21] By this point, the diversity consensus had become almost as entrenched in the corporate world, which explains why scores of large corporations signed a similar amicus brief in *Gratz* and *Grutter* as well.[22] In short, Powell's opinion significantly shaped the stated goals of affirmative action policies at colleges and universities nationwide, and it shaped the operational details of those policies as well.[23]

In the pages that follow, however, I am primarily interested in a different set of the *Bakke* decision's effects. It was either the great genius or the great failing of Powell's opinion that it shaped the arguments, tactics, and even identities of actors on both sides of the affirmative action debate, and here I focus on its impact on the conservative opposition. In particular, Powell's opinion contributed to the rise of anti–affirmative action litigation groups like CIR. In addition, as amplified by the Court's subsequent holdings and CIR's own litigation efforts, Powell's opinion fostered the widespread self-perception of white individuals as aggrieved rights-bearers, treated unfairly by powerful liberal institutions and ready to seek their day in court.

The Rise of Rights-Based Conservatism

Powell's balancing act in *Bakke* was typical for him, and over the next several years, he continued to lead the Court in straddling the fence on the question of affirmative action's constitutionality.[24] His approach remained influential even after his retirement in 1987, as O'Connor took his place as the swing vote on affirmative action, explicitly following the path that he had marked out. Once the Court's conservative majority was consolidated, however, it became clear that *Bakke* would be the first in a line of decisions striking down race-conscious affirmative action policies. In *Richmond v. Croson* (1989), O'Connor relied heavily on Powell's *Bakke* opinion in holding that the city of Richmond, Virginia, could not constitutionally set aside a fixed percentage of public contracting dollars for minority-owned firms. Six years later, in *Adarand Constructors, Inc. v. Pena* (1995), O'Connor again wrote for the Court and again relied heavily on Powell, this time subjecting a similar minority business set aside at the federal level to similarly strict constitutional scrutiny. With these decisions, the Rehnquist Court made clear that race-conscious affirmative action policies would face a heavy presumption of unconstitutionality. In each case, however, O'Connor pointedly insisted that although the specific policy before the Court went too far, some race-conscious policies might be constitutionally legitimate.

Because the end result in each of these cases was to strike down a race-conscious policy, conservative legal activists supported the Court's decisions, but they were not content to leave matters to the justices themselves. In particular, they urged the Court to overcome O'Connor's hesitation and to actively enforce the principle of color-blind law in all circumstances. CIR has been the most influential of an increasingly prominent group of public interest law firms that have advanced this argument, hoping to prod and support the conservative justices in their efforts.[25] Founded in 1989, the same year as the Court's *Croson* decision, CIR has dedicated itself to "re-impos[ing] constitutional limits on a meddlesome, interest-group-infested government," and its leaders have viewed the anti–affirmative action campaign as an important front in this battle.[26]

Thus, CIR's anti–affirmative action campaign has been part of a more general rise of rights-based conservatism. Following the model used by so many liberal and progressive organizations—most notably, the NAACP's Legal Defense and Education Fund—these conservative groups use strategically planned constitutional litigation to promote their political ends. The language of individual liberty, equal treatment, and even judicial activism is as much a part of contemporary conservatism as it is of modern liberalism. Besides the very name of the organization, CIR's Web site and publications repeatedly refer to the affirmative action lawsuits as "civil rights" cases and describe the organization's goal as "the defense of individual liberties." The group's mission statement notes that "CIR provides free legal representation to deserving clients who cannot otherwise afford or obtain legal counsel and whose individual rights are threatened,"[27] and its legal arguments have built on landmark rights-protecting precedents that conservatives once criticized. In the Michigan law school case, for example, CIR's lawyers began the substantive portion of their Supreme Court brief by quoting Robert Carter's oral arguments for the NAACP in *Brown v. Board of Education* (1954).[28]

In 1998, CIR's then senior counsel (and later CEO) Terence Pell made the organization's strategy particularly plain in a solicitation of conservative foundation money in *Philanthropy*. Calling for conservatives to "make copious use of the courts in their efforts to rein in an increasingly out of control bureaucratic state," Pell noted that although "once the Ford and Rockefeller Foundations used the courts to push through broad programs of social reform, now it is conservative activists who are mounting high-profile cases to further policy objectives that could not be secured readily through more representative branches of government."[29] This sort of rights-based legal strategy has played an increasingly prominent role in contemporary conservative movements, despite the significant tension between these strategies and conservatives' own long-standing critique of judicial activism.

The rise of such rights-based litigation in pursuit of conservative ends cannot be explained without reference to the constitutional decisions of the Burger and Rehnquist Courts. If the conservative justices, having taken over the Court during the 1980s and 90s, had adopted a posture of Holmesian self-restraint, conservative litigators would have had little incentive to begin appealing to the Court to defend conservative visions of constitutional rights. In actual fact, however, the Rehnquist Court has sent a very different signal. Rather than abandoning Warren Court–style activism in favor of judicial restraint, the Court has retained much of that liberal activism and supplemented it with a distinctive style of conservative activism.[30] As a result, the later Rehnquist Court had a solid majority of five justices who were willing to actively exercise their power to defend constitutional principles of color-blindness and limited government, and thanks to groups like CIR, these justices had a steady stream of opportunities to do so. Where some of these justices were troubled by a countervailing commitment to judicial restraint, moreover, CIR's legal activists encouraged them to ignore such considerations.[31]

In the affirmative action context in particular, the Court's *Bakke* decision promoted the rise of this conservative rights campaign. By handing affirmative action opponents a victory, but only a partial one, the decision contributed to the emergence and development of organized interests seeking to render that victory more complete. From one angle, after all, Powell's opinion was a call to arms for white "victims" of affirmative action. Holding that the liberal educators and bureaucrats who ran the University of California had violated Allan Bakke's constitutional rights, Powell encouraged other rejected white university applicants to seek similar redress in the federal courts. The *Bakke* decision also encouraged conservative legal activists to provide free legal representation to such applicants, and even to solicit such applicants when they were not readily presenting themselves. Since its founding, CIR has repeatedly broadcasted its support for Powell's holding that "the guarantee of equal protection cannot mean one thing when applied to one individual and something else when applied to a person of another color. If both are not accorded the same protection, then it is not equal."[32]

The interest group litigators who emerged in *Bakke*'s wake have also appealed to Powell's opinion in seeking to mobilize mass support for their efforts. In pursuit of both individual plaintiffs and broader public support, CIR has encouraged whites to identify as victims of affirmative action policies. After all, the perception of a white university applicant that she has faced illegal discrimination requires not just the existence of a race-conscious admissions policy but also an awareness of the principle of constitutional equality, a willingness to adopt a racialized identity, and a belief that it was her race that made the difference in her adverse admissions decision. As Murray Edelman has noted, "perception of deprivation, . . . like all perception, is a function of social cues regarding what is to be expected and what exists; it does not correlate directly or simply with objective conditions or with any particular measure of them."[33] For a white applicant to take the additional step of suing the university that rejected her, moreover, she must perceive the university's admissions policy as not only "unjust" but also "subject to change"—two perceptual conditions identified by Doug McAdam as necessary elements for the emergence of oppositional political activity.[34]

In the affirmative action context, neither the Supreme Court nor CIR created these perceptions in the public at large, but they certainly fostered and encouraged them. Before initiating the Michigan undergraduate suit, for example, CIR and four conservative state legislators held a press conference in the summer of 1997, asking anyone who felt unjustly rejected from UM to contact them. They also placed a number of newspaper advertisements looking for whites who had faced discrimination, and they distributed a brochure that asked, "Do you know a victim of affirmative action or racial quotas?" Republican State Senator Dave Jay later explained these actions by noting that "affirmative action is 'the No. 1 economic and social issue' in the working class Detroit suburbs he represents, where, he says, nearly everyone knows someone 'who has suffered a loss due to minority preferences.'"[35] In this way, Senator Jay encouraged his white constituents to identify themselves as victims of discrimination, and many of them came to do just that.[36] This effort was also successful in its short-term goal of identifying potential plaintiffs. Senator Jay and his colleagues forwarded more than fifty names to CIR's offices in Washington, after which about a dozen of the potential plaintiffs were interviewed in person. As lead plaintiff in the undergraduate suit, CIR's lawyers selected Jennifer Gratz, a blond, telegenic, articulate, high school cheerleader with good grades, who had nonetheless been rejected by UM.

In January 1999, CIR expanded this effort nationwide, publishing an affirmative action "handbook" that urged college students to investigate their school's admissions policies and promoting the handbook in advertisements placed in college newspapers. Other organizations opposed to affirmative action assisted CIR in spreading the message that our nation's universities were illegally discriminating against white applicants. Linda Chavez's Center for Equal Opportunity (CEO), for example, issued a steady stream of reports and press releases to that effect, and used its interactive Web site to bring the point home as well.[37]

In light of this process, some supporters of affirmative action have accused CIR of duping rejected white applicants into serving as the smiling public face of its anti–affirmative action agenda. Both CIR's lawyers and the plaintiffs themselves, however, deny this charge, insisting that the plaintiffs' perceptions of their own victimization are sincere. Pell insisted, for example, that the lawsuits "were built around the experiences of real individuals. Cheryl Hopwood, Katuria Smith, Jennifer Gratz, and Patrick Hamacher were not token plaintiffs recruited to support a right-wing ideological agenda. They were individuals who independently had concluded they had been discriminated against by university admissions officials."[38] Gratz and her fellow plaintiffs have told the same story. In a 1998 magazine interview, Gratz described the day three years earlier when she received her rejection letter from UM. If her own version of the story is accurate, she opened the envelope, read the letter, and then immediately turned to her father and asked if they could sue the university. Noting that she knew minority students with lower grades than hers who had been admitted, she recalled her immediate suspicion that "I was discriminated against because of my race." In the same interview, Gratz's father expressed a similar sense of rights consciousness and white victimization: "We tell our kids to work hard and the right things will come to you. . . . But I've been in the work-force; I've been around. . . . The system is set up so no longer is it about be-ing the most qualified. It's a numbers game. That's the way we've allowed the government to do it."[39]

Given the highly organized and strategic process by which CIR re-cruited Gratz as a plaintiff, these observations should be taken with a grain of salt. Nonetheless, it is certainly true that many white Americans per-ceive themselves as victims of affirmative action, and there is no reason not to believe that Gratz and her father experienced that common reaction when she was rejected by UM. Judging by their own public statements, Gratz and her fellow plaintiffs think of themselves as aggrieved rights-bearers who are seeking their day in court. Gratz has repeatedly insisted that the affirmative action policies "are wrong. I believe I was racially dis-criminated against. It's probably happening to a lot of other people who are applying to colleges and it shouldn't keep going on."[40] She has also won-dered publicly, "What would I be saying to my children if I didn't challenge something so clearly wrong?"[41] In a television interview, Barbara Grutter, the lead plaintiff in the UM law school case, said that what made her most angry was "the fact that someone has the arrogance to think that they have the right to treat me differently, to take away my rights."[42] Similarly, the *Seattle Post-Intelligencer* reported in 1998 that Katuria Smith, the lead plain-tiff in one of CIR's other cases, "says filing the lawsuit was a matter of prin-ciple. It's wrong, she says, to treat people differently based on race."[43]

Thus, CIR's strategic campaign against *Bakke* fostered the development of rights consciousness among whites who already suspected—or were at least susceptible to the suspicion—that they had been victims of discrimi-nation. Significantly, these perceptions have required such applicants to adopt a racialized identity, even though they repeatedly insist that race is an irrelevant characteristic. For instance, their own claims of discrimina-tion are rooted in a narrative of white racial victimization at the hands of elite liberal institutions such as the University of Michigan. CIR's plain-tiffs were recruited and coached by legal activists seeking to abolish affirma-tive action, but their rights consciousness appears to have preceded their involvement with CIR. In other words, Gratz and her fellow plaintiffs have not simply been deploying the rhetoric of constitutional rights in an effort to promote a political agenda; they have been articulating a right that they believe themselves to possess. Here as elsewhere, rights discourses play both a strategic and a constitutive role in political change. On the one hand, activists recognize that rights are valuable strategic resources that carry substantial weight in American law and culture, and they understandably try to use these resources to promote their own political ends. On the other hand, rights also constitute the very identities and interests of these same activists to a significant degree.[44] After all, it is because so many of us actually believe in rights that their mobilization is so often successful. And it is clear that many of the supporters of the anti–affirmative action campaign led by the Center for Individual Rights sincerely believe that they are, in fact, fighting to defend their individual rights.

They have come to this belief, moreover, at least in part because the Supreme Court has been endorsing such rights claims since 1978. Although public knowledge of the Supreme Court is generally quite limited, it is nonetheless the case that the language of particular disputes is often traceable to appellate doctrine of which the proponents are not even aware.[45] In short, both the individual and the organizational face of the anti–affirmative action movement were shaped by the Court's color-blind rhetoric. In a recent survey of the "policy feedback" literature, Suzanne Mettler and Joe Soss noted that one potential impact of public policy is to "foster group divisions within the polity . . . play[ing] an active role in constructing and positioning [social] groups, defining their boundaries, and infusing them with political meaning." In addition to the group divisions themselves, "policies can [also] affect citizens' ideas about which groups are deserving or undeserving, with major implications for the content of subsequent policy making."[46] In this sense, the Court's decisions fostered both a white racial consciousness among ordinary citizens and a set of organized groups committed to representing those citizens, and these ideas and interests influenced the Court's subsequent decisions in turn.

CIR in Court

Because Powell's endorsement of educational diversity and the "Harvard plan" was the legal ground on which colleges and universities stood in continuing their race-conscious policies, CIR was forced to launch a full-scale effort to overturn this ground. Thus, even though they had borrowed much of their color-blind rhetoric from Powell's opinion, CIR's lawyers began to target that opinion as ripe for ridicule, and in a carefully planned series of lawsuits, they urged the federal courts to abandon Powell's compromise.

CIR's first significant victory came in the widely noted *Hopwood* case in 1996, when the Fifth Circuit Court of Appeals declared that Powell's

Bakke opinion was no longer good law and held that the University of Texas Law School (UT) was unconstitutionally discriminating against white applicants. The year after *Hopwood v. Texas*, CIR successfully defended California's Proposition 209, which had amended the state Constitution to prohibit all affirmative action in the areas of education, employment, and government contracting.[47] CIR then filed suit against the Universities of Washington (UW) and Michigan (UM) in the hopes of persuading the Supreme Court to eliminate affirmative action in public university admissions nationwide. The Washington suit was largely derailed in 1998 when the state's voters adopted an initiative modeled on Prop. 209.[48] The adoption of I-200 rendered much of CIR's lawsuit moot, but the organization continued to pursue damages for the four white plaintiffs who had allegedly been harmed by the old policy. In December 2000, the Ninth Circuit upheld UW's no-longer-existing affirmative action policy, thus creating a conflict among the federal circuits and thereby increasing the chances for Supreme Court review.[49]

Because UW's affirmative action policy was no longer operating, however, the case was not a good vehicle for the High Court, and so all eyes turned to the Michigan litigation. In two separate lawsuits filed in 1997, CIR had challenged UM's affirmative action policies in both law school and undergraduate admissions. The organization had mixed success in the lower courts, but in December 2002, the Supreme Court agreed to hear both cases. In the space of less than a decade, CIR had persuaded the Court to revisit *Bakke*.

In all of these cases, CIR's lawyers advanced two distinct legal claims. They hoped at the very least to convince the federal courts that existing university admissions practices were not in compliance with *Bakke*. In advancing this claim, they acknowledged Powell's holding that educational diversity was a compelling government interest, and hence that race-conscious policies may be used to further that interest, but argued that Powell imposed two important limitations on such policies. First, he held that public universities can only consider the race of applicants if they do so in a flexible, individualized manner that does not amount to a quota. On CIR's reading, this holding proscribed not just fixed and rigid quotas, but all "dual" or "two-track" race-based systems. Although UM did not set aside a specific number of slots for minority applicants, CIR insisted that both its undergraduate and law school policies were more rigid and race-conscious than the flexible "Harvard plan" that Powell had endorsed.[50] Second, CIR's lawyers read *Bakke* to hold that race-conscious policies could only be justified as part of a broader effort to procure the educational benefits of a diverse student body, and not merely as an attempt to increase the proportion of minority students at the school. This line may appear a distinction without a difference, but CIR contended that Powell only endorsed policies that pursued diversity in a variety of forms, including race, and not those that exclusively pursued racial diversity, at the expense of other forms of diversity carrying an equally significant educational value.[51]

Although they tried to amplify a particular reading of *Bakke* that was conducive to their cause, CIR's lawyers also advanced the broader argument that Powell's opinion was no longer good law, and indeed may never have been. In their view, Powell spoke only for himself, and not for the Court, when he held that educational diversity represented a compelling government interest that could justify affirmative action policies even under strict scrutiny.[52] Even if Powell did speak for the Court on this point, moreover, they insisted that subsequent decisions had rejected this holding. Relying on the Rehnquist Court's decisions in *Croson, Adarand,* and a series of racial gerrymandering cases, CIR argued that race-conscious admissions policies could never be justified except as remedies for specific instances of past racial discrimination.[53]

In this sense, CIR's lawyers were engaged in an ongoing dialogue with the justices of the Rehnquist Court, with CIR's legal arguments and political rhetoric significantly shaped by the Court's own color-blind reading of the Fourteenth Amendment. When O'Connor took over for Powell in trying to mark out a judicial compromise on the issue, Scalia and later Thomas began writing separately to express their impatience with her approach. Concurring in the judgment in *Croson,* for example, Scalia objected to O'Connor's apparent belief that, "despite the Fourteenth Amendment, state and local governments may in some circumstances discriminate on the basis of race in order (in a broad sense) 'to ameliorate the effects of past discrimination.'" In Scalia's view, "only a social emergency arising to the level of imminent danger to life and limb—for example, a prison race riot, requiring temporary segregation of inmates—can justify an exception to the principle embodied in the Fourteenth Amendment that our Constitution is colorblind." This color-blind principle was so important to Scalia because he saw its opposite—that is, "the tendency . . . to classify and judge men and women on the basis of . . . the color of their skin"—as the source of all racial inequality.[54]

Writing separately again in *Adarand,* Scalia reiterated that "government can never have a 'compelling interest' in discriminating on the basis of race in order to 'make up' for past racial discrimination in the opposite direction." In his view, there should be "no such thing as either a creditor or a debtor race" because "that concept is alien to the Constitution's focus upon the individual, and its rejection of dispositions based on race." As he had argued six years earlier in *Croson*, he insisted that "to pursue the concept of racial entitlement—even for the most admirable and benign of purposes—is to reinforce and preserve for future mischief the way of thinking that produced race slavery, race privilege and race hatred. In the eyes of government, we are just one race here. It is American."[55] Thomas also wrote separately in *Adarand*, insisting that "as far as the Constitution is concerned, it is irrelevant whether a government's racial classifications are drawn by those who wish to oppress a race or by those who have a sincere desire to help those thought to be disadvantaged." Indeed, he went so far as to insist "that there is a moral [and] constitutional equivalence between laws designed to subjugate a race and those that distribute benefits on the basis of race in order to foster some current notion of equality."[56]

Scalia and Thomas have pressed this point most persistently, but Kennedy has not been far behind. Kennedy first made his color-blind views known in an apocalyptic dissenting opinion in *Metro Broadcasting v. FCC* (1990), invoking Jim Crow segregation, South African apartheid, and Nazi citizenship law to express his sense of the affirmative action program at issue.[57] Writing for the Court five years later in *Miller v. Johnson* (1995), he cited *Bakke*, *Croson*, and *Adarand* for the proposition that the "central mandate" of the equal protection clause is "racial neutrality in governmental decisionmaking," and he insisted that "this rule obtains with equal force regardless of the race of those burdened or benefited by a particular classification." Holding that "the Government must treat citizens as individuals, not as simply components of a racial, religious, sexual, or national class," he invalidated a race-conscious districting scheme from Georgia.[58] Rehnquist did not often write opinions of his own in the affirmative action cases, but he consistently signed on to the color-blind arguments of his colleagues, meaning that throughout the 1990s—or at least since Thomas's 1991 appointment—CIR's lawyers and a solid four-justice wing of the Court were advancing mutually reinforcing arguments regarding the unconstitutionality of affirmative action.

Alone among her conservative colleagues, O'Connor regularly expressed some concern with the Court's sweeping interventions in this context. She cast a number of deciding votes to strike down affirmative action policies, but she often limited the reach of the Court's holdings by suggesting other circumstances under which such policies might survive constitutional scrutiny. Writing for the Court in *Adarand*, she extended *Croson* by holding that strict scrutiny should apply to race-conscious policies at the federal as well as state levels, but she pointedly insisted that such scrutiny would not always be fatal and that some race-conscious plans might still be upheld. Exercising the "passive virtues," she would not even let the Court issue a final decision on the particular dispute, which she reversed and remanded without an explicit declaration of unconstitutionality.

Similarly, in a series of "racial gerrymandering" decisions beginning with *Shaw v. Reno* (1993), O'Connor joined her conservative colleagues to hold that government should generally not consider race when drawing electoral districts, but stopped short of their insistence that such race-conscious districting was always invalid. In O'Connor's decisive view, race could not be the predominant factor in districting decisions, but it could be considered in an effort to achieve some particularly important state interests. As in the government contracting cases, she frequently wrote for the Court in the districting cases, relegating Scalia and Thomas's views to concurring opinions. In *Bush v. Vera* (1996), she took the unusual step of writing both the Court's plurality opinion and a separate concurring opinion in the same case, with the concurring opinion an effort to clarify the limited reach of the main opinion. And in *Easley v. Cromartie* (2001), when North Carolina's Twelfth Congressional District came back to the Court for the fourth time, O'Connor voted with her four liberal colleagues to uphold it, despite what Thomas characterized as a persistent pattern of race-conscious districting.[59] Her deciding vote had led the Court into this "political thicket" eight years earlier, and it was now her deciding vote that marked the limits of this field of conservative activism.

In the university admissions context, then, the task for CIR's lawyers was clear. They had to persuade O'Connor to continue enforcing her color-blind reading of the Fourteenth Amendment and to ignore any countervailing concern for judicial restraint. In the Michigan cases, they failed.

The Internal and the External in *Bakke*, *Gratz*, and *Grutter*

In *Gratz* and *Grutter*, O'Connor thwarted the conservative litigators (and her conservative colleagues) by adhering to Powell's compromise from *Bakke*. She voted with the four conservatives (and Justice Breyer) to strike down Michigan's undergraduate admissions policy, which weighed applicants on a numerical scale and automatically awarded a twenty-point bonus to all underrepresented minorities, but she voted with the four liberals to uphold Michigan's law school admissions policy, which gave a more flexible boost to such minorities in the course of individualized consideration of every applicant. In doing so, she garnered a judicial majority for Powell's long-contested endorsement of race-conscious measures to promote educational diversity, thus entrenching his analysis into constitutional law for the foreseeable future.

Writing for the Court in *Grutter,* O'Connor began the substantive portion of her opinion by reviewing Powell's analysis from *Bakke.* She endorsed his insistence that "the guarantee of equal protection cannot mean one thing when applied to one individual and something else when applied to a person of another color," but she also endorsed his holding that "student body diversity is a compelling state interest that can justify the use of race in university admissions." Most importantly, she followed Powell in balancing the principle of color-blind equality with a healthy dose of deference to university officials.[60]

Powell had emphasized the importance of such deference on more than one occasion. Just a few months before the *Bakke* decision, concurring in *Board of Curators of the University of Missouri v. Horowitz* (1978), he had noted that "university faculties must have the widest range of discretion in making judgments as to the academic performance of students and their entitlement to promotion or graduation."[61] Several years later, in *Regents of the University of Michigan v. Ewing* (1985), he had again emphasized "the respect and deference that courts should accord academic decisions made by the appropriate university authorities. . . . Judicial review of academic decisions, including those with respect to the admission or dismissal of students, is rarely appropriate, particularly where orderly administrative procedures are followed."[62] O'Connor picked up on these arguments in *Grutter,* citing *Horowitz* and *Ewing* as well as *Bakke* in noting that her holding was "in keeping with [the Court's] tradition of giving a degree of deference to a university's academic decisions, within constitutionally prescribed limits." Remarkably, given the Rehnquist Court's willingness to enforce its vision of color-blind law in earlier cases, she held that "the Law School's educational judgment that [student body] diversity is essential to its educational mission is one to which we defer."[63]

O'Connor's deference to university officials was apparently buttressed by the fact that those officials were supported by an overwhelming elite consensus in defending the importance of racial diversity. The University of Michigan called this consensus to the Court's attention by mobilizing a remarkable list of individuals and organizations to file amicus curiae briefs on its behalf. These supporters included many traditional civil rights groups and liberal elected officials, and a distinguished list of higher education leaders, institutions, and associations.[64] More surprisingly, twenty-two state governments and two large cities signed such briefs, with only the state of Florida filing a brief on the other side. More remarkable still were the briefs filed by General Motors and sixty-five other "leading American businesses" on Michigan's side, and most remarkable of all was the brief filed by twenty-nine "former high-ranking officers and civilian leaders of the Army, Navy, Air Force, and Marine Corps, including former military-academy superintendents, Secretaries of Defense, and present and former members of the U.S. Senate."[65]

The military officers' brief was a key focus of the justices' questions during oral arguments, and O'Connor quoted extensively from it in her opinion in *Grutter*. Quoting from several of the other briefs as well, she noted that

> the Law School's claim of a compelling interest is further bolstered by its *amici*, who point to the educational benefits that flow from student body diversity. In addition to the expert studies and reports entered into evidence at trial, numerous studies show that student body diversity promotes learning outcomes, and "better prepares students for an increasingly diverse workforce and society, and better prepares them as professionals." These benefits are not theoretical but real . . . as major American businesses have made clear that the skills needed in today's increasingly global marketplace can only be developed through exposure to widely diverse people, cultures, ideas, and viewpoints. What is more, high-ranking retired officers and civilian leaders of the United States military assert that, "[b]ased on [their] decades of experience," a "highly qualified, racially diverse officer corps . . . is essential to the military's ability to fulfill its principal mission to provide national security."[66]

In light of these arguments, it is no surprise that many informed observers pointed to the military brief in particular—and the elite consensus more generally—as a key factor influencing O'Connor's decisive vote.[67]

O'Connor's deference was not without limits, and she undertook an independent review of the university's evidence for the educational benefits of diversity. That review, however, was much more deferential than the one that CIR was urging. Quoting Powell, she insisted that "'good faith' on the part of a university [should be] 'presumed' absent 'a showing to the contrary.'" This deference was justified for O'Connor because, like Powell, she was convinced that "not every decision influenced by race is equally objectionable" and that federal judges should generally avoid imposing sweeping constitutional limits on other agencies of government.[68] In other words, the elite consensus in support of diversity was relevant for O'Connor because her understanding of the judicial role deemed it relevant in this context. In contrast, it was irrelevant for her four conservative colleagues, who had long insisted "that there is a moral [and] constitutional equivalence between laws designed to subjugate a race and those that distribute benefits on the basis of race in order to foster some current notion of equality."[69] Although O'Connor was willing to presume good faith on the part of university admissions officials, her fellow conservatives expressed a great deal of mistrust toward them.[70] Because Scalia's vision of the judicial role called for actively policing the liberal cultural elites who were so often out of touch with the principles and preferences of the American people, for example, the consensus of those elites played no role in his constitutional judgment.

This conservative mistrust of liberal educators is rooted in a long-standing critique of multicultural egalitarianism and liberal social engineering. Rehnquist, Scalia, Thomas, and Kennedy's reading of the equal protection clause as a per se prohibition of affirmative action policies simply cannot be understood without reference to the conservative political backlash that emerged as soon as the first such policies had been adopted. The key mechanisms by which such external influences have been brought to bear on the Court are the presidential power of judicial appointment, on the one hand, and the constitutional litigation of the executive branch and organized interest groups, on the other. If Republican Presidents Nixon, Reagan, and Bush had not had the chance to fill the Court with conservative appointees, there would have been no one to act on CIR's arguments. But if CIR and its allies had not waged a concerted rights-based litigation campaign on behalf of white "victims" of affirmative action, there would have been no arguments on which the conservative justices could act.

Although the rise of the constitutional critique of affirmative action cannot be understood without reference to interest group litigation, the Court's partial rejection of that critique cannot be explained by such external factors alone. O'Connor's commitment to a particular vision of the judicial role prevented her, and hence the Court, from invalidating race-conscious admissions policies nationwide. This vision of the Court's role is a form of judicial restraint, a value to which constitutional conservatives have long expressed devotion, but O'Connor has operationalized this value somewhat differently than her colleagues. Most constitutional conservatives—and, for that matter, most constitutional liberals—have marked off a discrete set of contexts in which the Court should defer to the decisions of the elected branches. In the affirmative action cases, for instance, Scalia and Thomas are fully willing to exercise their power to strike down democratically enacted policies (because they read the Fourteenth Amendment as prohibiting such policies), but in abortion or gay rights cases, they insist on deferring to the democratic will (because they read the Constitution as silent on such matters).

O'Connor's conception of judicial restraint works differently. Unlike most of her colleagues, she recognizes no "political thickets"—no political or policy contexts in which judicial intervention is inappropriate. Instead, she is willing to actively enforce a wide variety of constitutional rights guarantees, in both liberal and conservative directions, but whenever she does so, she seeks to temper the reach of such guarantees at the margins. Thus, she will vote with her conservative colleagues to strike down affirmative action policies, and with her liberal colleagues to strike down antiabortion laws, but in both contexts, she will limit the reach of the Court's decision.[71]

Scalia and Thomas often support their judgments with sweeping categorical principles—insisting that "only a social emergency arising to the level of imminent danger to life and limb . . . can justify an exception to the principle embodied in the Fourteenth Amendment that our Constitution is colorblind" or that "a State's use of racial discrimination in higher education admissions is categorically prohibited by the equal protection clause."[72] In contrast, O'Connor regularly seeks to confine her own judgments with narrow, fact-specific discussions of the particular case. Even when exercising her own power quite actively—as in *Croson, Adarand, Gratz,* and *Grutter*—O'Connor generally proceeds cautiously or, in Cass Sunstein's words, "one case at a time." In the first three of these decisions, she endorsed the conservative rights argument, handing legal victories to white "victims" of affirmative action, but pointedly insisting that that rights guarantee might have a limited reach. In *Grutter,* she finally drew the line, making clear that the right to color-blind law would sometimes be outweighed by other constitutional considerations. When the deciding vote was hers, she was unwilling to invalidate the admissions policies used at, and defended by, scores of colleges and universities nationwide. Absent O'Connor's commitment to this sort of "judicial minimalism," CIR would have won a sweeping legal victory.[73]

Policy Feedback and Constitutional Development

CIR's anti–affirmative action campaign represented an organized and sustained assault on a landmark Supreme Court precedent. To explain the Court's decisions in *Gratz* and *Grutter*—and to understand the relationship between internal and external factors in shaping Supreme Court decision making more broadly—we need to view these decisions as part of an ongoing historical process. As Theda Skocpol has noted, social scientists "too often . . . forget that policies, once enacted, restructure subsequent political processes. Analysts typically look only for synchronic determinants of policies—for example, in current social interests or in existing political alliances. In addition, however, we must examine patterns unfolding over time."[74] Given the interaction of multiple, relatively autonomous factors, we must attend to matters of timing and sequence to explain the Court's decision whether or not to overturn a landmark precedent.

A number of external factors presented the Rehnquist Court with both the demand for overturning *Bakke* and the opportunity to do so. In particular, the New Right critique of liberal egalitarianism that emerged during the late 1970s rendered precarious the political support for race-conscious affirmative action policies. And the rise of rights-based conservatism in general, and conservative public interest litigation organizations in particular, called on the conservative justices of the Rehnquist Court to actively enforce conservative constitutional commitments, such as the right to color-blind treatment by the government. Other external factors may have been significant as well, but as I have tried to show, these influences are not, in fact, fully external to the Court itself. In particular, it is misleading to characterize interest group litigators as independent forces acting on a dependent Court because the justices shape the litigators' actions at least as much as the reverse.

If this claim is correct, then the scholarly literatures on constitutional development and legal mobilization have much to teach each other. These two bodies of work have been more or less distinct from one another, largely because the former has been relatively Supreme Court–centered (and Constitution-centered), whereas the latter has focused on a much broader range of legal disputes. Because organized litigation activities do sometimes promote constitutional change, however—and because constitutional changes spur more such litigation in turn—there are some clear interconnections between these literatures that should be drawn out. In their current guise, the principal theme of the constitutional development literature is the political foundations of judicial power, whereas the principal theme of the legal mobilization literature is the legal foundations of political power.[75] My goal is to look more explicitly at the loop that links these processes to one another, and the policy feedback rubric strikes me as a promising avenue toward that end.

I do not mean to suggest that Court scholars have never noticed the sort of effects that I am highlighting here. In an influential 1976 article on "The Supreme Court and National Policy Making," for example, Jonathan Casper called attention to a variety of ways in which the Court's decisions reshape politics. Toward the end of the article, Casper gave several examples in which Supreme Court decisions had shaped "both the nature of subsequent policies—their breadth, their statutory and administrative form—and the constellation of political forces in the society." The increasingly libertarian character of the Court's post-1957 obscenity decisions, for example, had been such that even if those decisions were overturned, "experience with the availability of pornography . . . would probably produce policies permitting substantially greater availability than existed in the pre-1957 period. Moreover, the political and economic interests with an investment in protecting the freedom to distribute and profit from such materials have greatly increased in recent years and would also operate to dampen . . . the ability of the 'anti-obscenity' interests to impose restrictive policies." In addition, because access to federal court can sometimes be gained with fewer, or at least different, resources than are required to lobby Congress or the federal executive, Court decisions may be particularly significant in "placing issues on the agenda of other political institutions and in [the] development of interest groups." After all, "the legitimacy conferred by victory in court may be useful in attracting members and resources and mobilizing others."[76]

Although others have identified this sort of political effect of Supreme Court decisions, these effects have not often been the subject of explicit examination, in part because they have cut against the grain of a dominant argument in the field. Casper's 1976 article represented a sustained critique of an earlier article by Robert Dahl which had characterized the Court as relatively powerless, and because more scholars have followed Dahl than Casper, there is a well-entrenched paradigm of research contending that the Court's decisions do not have much impact on politics or policy.[77] To examine the feedback effects that I have highlighted here will require moving beyond this Dahlian framework.

In sum, we cannot understand either the origins or the relative influence of CIR's litigation without reference to certain internal dynamics on the Court. The Court's willingness to actively scrutinize race-conscious affirmative action policies in *Bakke* and subsequent cases—and its willingness to exercise judicial power in pursuit of other conservative ends as well—was a crucial step in the emergence of the rights-based conservative movement that in turn tried to shape and direct the Court's decisions. The conservative litigators of CIR have seen themselves as mobilizing against Powell's opinion, but even so, their arguments and strategies have been shaped by his account of color-blind equality.

Only by attending to the interaction of such internal and external factors can we explain why conservative political movements began adopting rights-based arguments in the late twentieth century, and why and to what degree those movements have succeeded in persuading the Court. Powell's opinion contributed to the development of organized interest groups devoted to litigating against affirmative action and to the emergence of individual citizens willing to lend their names to such lawsuits. The opponents of affirmative action have exhibited a rights consciousness more often associated with left-liberal political movements, and the judicial conservatism of the Rehnquist Court was a rights-based conservatism. These developments, moreover, reinforced one another. Sparked by the Court's decisions, CIR's attorneys mobilized rejected white applicants like Jennifer Gratz, encouraging them to magnify their perceptions of their own victimization. In this way, the Court's decisions created new constituencies, fostering the development of organized interests committed to pushing the Court even further.

These "external" pressures, however, have only influenced constitutional doctrine to the extent that the conservative justices have been willing to abandon, or at least cabin, their commitment to judicial restraint. O'Connor developed her own distinctive version of such restraint, and this internal factor continued to influence her constitutional decisions. It is for this reason that the Rehnquist Court refused to dismantle Powell's affirmative action compromise despite substantial conservative pressure to do so. On this issue as on many others, it is O'Connor who had the deciding vote, and she had self-consciously modeled her approach on Powell's, enforcing a color-blind constitutional vision on the American polity but tempering that vision with a continuing commitment to judicial minimalism.

Notes

For helpful comments on earlier versions of this article, I thank Ron Kahn, Ken Kersch, Julie Novkov, Amanda Winkler, Steve Wasby, Kevin den Dulk, Keith Bybee, Erika Wilkens, Suzanne Mettler, Dan Lipson, and my fellow participants at the 2003 Annual Meeting of the Western Political Science Association, the 2003 Annual Meeting of the American Political Science Association, and the Sawyer Law and Politics Program Research Workshop at Syracuse University's Maxwell School.

1. CIR's first significant victory in the affirmative action context came in *Hopwood v. Texas*, 78 F.3d 932 (5th Cir. 1996), in which the Fifth Circuit struck down the admissions policy at the University of Texas law school and the Supreme Court refused to review the decision. Over the next several years, CIR's lawsuits played a supporting role in successful anti–affirmative action initiative campaigns in California and Washington. See *Coalition for Economic Equity v. Wilson*, 122 F.3d 692 (9th Cir. 1997), and *Smith v. University of Washington Law School*, 233 F.3d 1188 (9th Cir. 2000).

2. Peter Schmidt, "Affirmative Action Remains a Minefield, Mostly Unmapped," *Chronicle of Higher Education*, 24 October 2003, A22–A25.

3. Michael McCann, "How the Supreme Court Matters in American Politics: New Institutionalist Perspectives," in *The Supreme Court in American Politics: New Institutionalist Interpretations*, ed. Howard Gillman and Cornell Clayton (Lawrence: University Press of Kansas, 1999), 71.

4. Suzanne Mettler, "Bringing the State Back in to Civic Engagement: Policy Feedback Effects of the GI Bill for World War II Veterans," *American Political Science Review* 96 (June 2002): 352. See also E. E. Schattschneider, *Politics, Pressures, and the Tariff: A Study of Free Private Enterprise in Pressure Politics, as Shown in the 1929–1930 Revision of the Tariff* (New York: Prentice-Hall, 1935).

5. Karen Orren and Stephen Skowronek, "The Study of American Political Development," in *Political Science: State of the Discipline*, ed. Ira Katznelson and Helen V. Milner (New York: W. W. Norton, 2002), 741–742.

6. Paul Pierson, "When Effect Becomes Cause: Policy Feedback and Political Change," *World Politics* 45 (July 1993): 628.

7. Mettler, "Bringing the State Back," 352.

8. Pierson, "When Effect Becomes Cause," 621.

9. Charles Epp, *The Rights Revolution: Lawyers, Activists, and Supreme Courts in Comparative Perspective* (Chicago: University of Chicago Press, 1998).

10. See, e.g., Keith Bybee, "The Political Significance of Legal Ambiguity: The Case of Affirmative Action," *Law and Society Review* 34 (2000): 263–290.

11. 438 U.S. 265, 289–296 (1978).

12. See, e.g., Alexander Bickel and Philip Kurland's amicus curiae brief on behalf of the Anti-Defamation League of B'nai B'rith in *DeFunis v. Odegaard* 416 U.S. 312 (1974), and Kurland's reprise of the same argument in a similar brief for the ADL in *Bakke*. As Andrew Kull, *The Color-Blind Constitution* (Cambridge, Mass.: Harvard University Press, 1992), has noted, moreover, this color-blind vision of legal equality had deep roots in American constitutional history.

13. For Powell's deference to public universities, see *Board of Curators of the University of Missouri v. Horowitz* 435 U.S. 78 (1978), and for his deference in the equal protection context more generally, see his opinions in *Frontiero v. Richardson* 411 U.S.

677 (1973), *Keyes v. School District No. 1, Denver, Colorado* 396 U.S. 1214 (1973), and *San Antonio Independent School Dist. v. Rodriguez* 411 U.S. 1 (1973).

14. John C. Jeffries Jr., *Justice Lewis F. Powell Jr.* (New York: Charles Scribner's Sons, 1994), 469.

15. 438 U.S. 265, 317 (1978).

16. Ibid., at 299.

17. Ibid., at 306.

18. Louis Menand, "College: The End of the Golden Age," *New York Review of Books*, 18 October 2001, 46.

19. Daniel Lipson, "The New Politics of Affirmative Action: How an Endangered, Liberal, Civil Rights Policy Has Transformed into an Entrenched, Conservative, Diversity Management Policy," paper presented at the annual meeting of the Canadian Political Science Association, Winnipeg, Manitoba, 3–5 June 2004, 8.

20. Ibid., 21–26. See also Daniel Lipson, "As American as Apple Pie: The Rise of the Diversity Consensus in Undergraduate Admissions at UC-Berkeley, UT-Austin, and UW-Madison," paper presented at the annual meeting of the Midwest Political Science Association, Chicago, Ill., 3–6 April 2003.

21. *Grutter v. Bollinger*, 123 S.Ct. 2325, 2336 (2003), citing the briefs for Judith Areen et al. (a group of ten law school deans) and Amherst College et al. (a group of twenty-eight selective, private liberal arts colleges). Note also the amicus curiae brief filed by Harvard University and seven other selective private universities.

22. Lipson, "As American as Apple Pie," 26–29.

23. A close examination of the operational details of the policy implementation is beyond the scope of this article, but to take just one example, eliminating the compensatory rationale removed any justification for limiting the policy's pool of beneficiaries to African Americans. If the policy is intended to promote educational diversity rather than to provide reparations for slavery and segregation, then it makes sense to extend it to all underrepresented racial minorities, and perhaps to other groups as well.

24. See, e.g., *Fullilove v. Klutznick* 448 U.S. 448 (1980) and *Wygant v. Jackson Board of Education* 476 U.S. 267 (1986).

25. The *Adarand* case was litigated by another such group, the Mountain States Legal Foundation.

26. This statement is from a 24 November 1998 letter from Michael S. Greve to CIR supporters, in which he noted that "CIR has pursued this goal in the nation's courts with single-minded devotion for almost ten years." CIR's official publications regularly describe the organization's goal as seeking "the re-invigoration of meaningful constitutional constraints on government" (CIR, 1997–1998 Annual Report).

27. See "The Mission of CIR," at http://www.cir-usa.org/mission_new.html.

28. The brief quoted Carter's opening statement that "we have one fundamental contention which we will seek to develop in the course of this argument, and that contention is that no state has any authority under the equal protection clause of the Four-

teenth Amendment to use race as a factor in affording educational opportunities among its citizens." Brief for the Petitioner, *Grutter v. Bollinger*, 18.

29. Terrence Pell, "Conservatives and the Courts: Judicial Activism on the Right?," *Philanthropy* (May/June 1998): 28.

30. Thomas M. Keck, *The Most Activist Supreme Court in History: The Road to Modern Judicial Conservatism* (Chicago: University of Chicago Press, 2004).

31. Michael S. Greve, "The Demise of Race-Based Admissions Policies," *Chronicle of Higher Education*, 19 March 1999, B6–B7.

32. For example, this language appears as a pull quote in a CIR document entitled "A Commitment to Protecting Civil Rights," available at http://www.cir-usa.org/civil_rights_theme.html.

33. Murray Edelman, *Politics as Symbolic Action: Mass Arousal and Quiescence* (Chicago: Markham, 1971), 107. See also Stuart A. Scheingold, *The Politics of Rights: Lawyers, Public Policy, and Political Change* (New Haven: Yale University Press, 1974), 133–134.

34. Doug McAdam, *Political Process and the Development of Black Insurgency, 1930–1970*, 2nd ed. (Chicago: University of Chicago Press, 1999), 34.

35. Peter Schmidt, "U. of Michigan Prepares to Defend Admissions Policy in Court," *Chronicle of Higher Education*, 30 October 1998, A34.

36. Other conservative litigation organizations have undertaken similar efforts in different legal contexts. In 2003, for example, the Alliance Defense Fund published a series of advertisements in student newspapers under the headline, "Are You Experiencing Anti-Christian Bigotry on Campus?" The ads went on to note that "in the name of 'diversity' and 'tolerance,' schools are systematically violating the rights of students who follow Jesus." Quoted in Burton Bollag, "Choosing Their Flock," *Chronicle of Higher Education*, 28 January 2005, A33.

37. For a long list of CEO reports documenting allegedly illegal discrimination at colleges and universities, see "Preferences in Higher Education," available at http://www.ceousa.org/html/edprefs.html. Note also the group's "University of Michigan at Ann Arbor Admissions Predictor," which provides an interactive form prompting students to enter their SAT scores, high school GPA, and race, and then informing them of their probability of being admitted to the university in 1995. See http://www.ceousa.org/html/umich5.html.

38. Pell, "Conservatives and the Courts," 29.

39. Lisa Belkin, "She Says She Was Rejected by a College for Being White: Is She Paranoid, Racist, or Right?" *Glamour*, November 1998. See also Anne Hull, "A Dream Denied Leads Woman to Center of Suit," *Washington Post*, 23 February 2003, A1.

40. Rene Sanchez, "Final Exam for Campus Affirmative Action?," *Washington Post*, 5 December 1997, A1. See also Jacques Steinberg, "3 Look to College Suit to Show Their Merits," *New York Times*, 23 February 2003, 32.

41. Quoted in CIR Docket Report, vol. 11, no. 1 (Fall 2000).

42. Transcript, *60 Minutes* (CBS News Broadcast, 29 October 2000), available at http://www.cir-usa.org/articles/michigan_60minutes.html.

43. *Seattle Post-Intelligencer*, 15 October 1998.

44. Michael McCann, *Rights at Work: Pay Equity Reform and the Politics of Legal Mobilization* (Chicago: University of Chicago Press, 1994).

45. Ibid. Michael Paris and Kevin J. McMahon, "The Politics of Rights Revisited: Rosenberg, McCann, and the New Institutionalism," in *Leveraging the Law: Using the Courts to Achieve Social Change*, ed. David A. Schultz (New York: Peter Lang, 1998), 63–134.

46. Suzanne Mettler and Joe Soss, "The Consequences of Public Policy for Democratic Citizenship: Bridging Policy Studies and Mass Politics," *Perspectives on Politics* 2 (March 2004): 61.

47. Prop. 209 provided that "the state shall not discriminate against, or grant preferential treatment to, any individual or group on the basis of race, sex, color, ethnicity, or national origin in the operation of public employment, public education, or public contracting." *Coalition for Economic Equity v. Wilson*, 122 F.3d 692 (9th Cir. 1997).

48. Washington's I-200 provided that "the state shall not discriminate against, or grant preferential treatment to, any individual or group on the basis of race, sex, color, ethnicity, or national origin in the operation of public employment, public education, or public contracting."

49. *Smith v. University of Washington Law School*, 233 F.3d 1188 (9th Cir. 2000).

50. Plaintiffs' Memorandum in Opposition to Defendants' Motion for Summary Judgment and Reply Memorandum in Support of Plaintiffs' Motion for Partial Summary Judgment, *Gratz v. Bollinger*, 30 May 1999.

51. Memorandum of Law in Opposition to Defendants' Partial Summary Judgment Motion, *Smith v. UW*, 20 January 1998, 8; Complaint filed in the U.S. District Court for the Eastern District of Michigan, *Gratz v. Bollinger*, 14 October 1997. See also Greve, "Demise of Race-Based Admissions Policies."

52. CIR's lawyers have advanced this argument by rhetorically denigrating "Justice Powell's lonely opinion" throughout their legal briefs and public comments. They have remarked upon Powell's "alleged endorsement of a 'Harvard' plan (whatever that is)" and have insisted that Powell's opinion never "command[ed] the allegiance of anyone on the Court but him." See Brief for the Petitioner, *Grutter v. Bollinger*, at 22; Memorandum in Opposition to Defendants' Partial Summary Judgment Motion, *Smith v. UW*, 17 June 1998, at 7–9; Plaintiffs' Memorandum of Law in Support of Motion for Partial Summary Judgment, *Gratz v. Bollinger*, 8 April 1999; Greve, "Demise of Race-Based Admissions Policies," B6.

53. See, e.g., Memorandum in Opposition to Defendants' Partial Summary Judgment Motion, *Smith v. UW*, 17 June 1998; Plaintiffs' Memorandum of Law in Support of Motion for Partial Summary Judgment, *Gratz v. Bollinger*, 8 April 1999; Plaintiffs' Memorandum in Opposition to Defendants' Motion for Summary Judgment and Reply Memorandum in Support of Plaintiffs' Motion for Partial Summary Judgment, *Gratz v. Bollinger*, 30 May 1999.

54. 488 U.S. 469, 520–521 (1989).

55. 515 U.S. 200, 239 (1995).

56. Ibid., at 240.

57. 497 U.S. 547, 631–638 (1990).

58. 515 U.S. 900, 904, 911–912 (1995). Note also Kennedy's opinion for the Court in *Rice v. Cayetano* 528 U.S. 495 (2000).

59. Although Breyer, rather than O'Connor, wrote for Court in this case, he peppered his opinion with quotations from her opinions in *Shaw v. Reno, Miller v. Johnson,* and *Bush v. Vera.*

60. *Grutter v. Bollinger,* 123 S.Ct. 2325, 2336–2337 (2003).

61. 435 U.S. 78, 96, n. 6 (1978).

62. 474 U.S. 214, 230 (1985).

63. *Grutter,* 123 S.Ct. 2325, 2339 (2003).

64. The civil rights organizations included the ACLU, the Lawyers' Committee for Civil Rights under Law, the Leadership Conference on Civil Rights, the NOW Legal Defense and Education Fund, the National Urban League, the National Rainbow/PUSH Coalition, and both the NAACP and the NAACP Legal Defense and Educational Fund. The elected officials included well over 100 members of the U.S. Congress, 30 members of the New York City Council, 36 past and present members of the Pennsylvania legislature, the governor of Michigan, and the mayor of Detroit. From the field of higher education, Michigan's supporters included the Association of American Law Schools; the American Law Deans Association; 10 leading law school deans, acting as individuals; the Society of American Law Teachers; the American Council on Education, the Association of American Medical Colleges, and more than 60 other higher education organizations and associations; the National Academy of Sciences; Harvard, Yale, Princeton, and Stanford Universities, along with over 60 other private colleges and universities; and a number of professional associations from the social sciences, including the American Psychological Association, the American Sociological Association, and the Law and Society Association.

65. Brief for Amici Curiae 65 Leading American Businesses in Support of Respondents, *Grutter v. Bollinger,* 18 February 2003; Consolidated Brief of Lt. Gen. Julius W. Becton Jr. et al. as Amici Curiae in Support of Respondents, *Grutter v. Bollinger,* 19 February 2003.

66. 123 S. Ct. 2325, 2340 (2003).

67. Linda Greenhouse, "Context and the Court," *New York Times,* 25 June 2003, A5; Michael S. Greve, personal interview, 2004.

68. 123 S.Ct. 2325, 2338–2339 (2003).

69. The quote is from Thomas's concurring opinion in *Adarand Constructors, Inc. v. Pena,* 515 U.S. 200, 240 (1995).

70. See, e.g., Rehnquist's opinion for the Court in *Gratz* and dissenting opinion in *Grutter;* Kennedy's dissenting opinion in *Grutter;* and Scalia's opinion concurring in part and dissenting in part in *Grutter.*

71. I have told this story at some length elsewhere. See Keck, *Most Activist Supreme Court.*

72. The quotes are from Scalia's opinion concurring in the judgment in *Richmond v. Croson*, 488 U.S. 469, 520–521 (1989), and Thomas's concurring opinion in *Gratz*, 123 S.Ct. 2411, 2433 (2003).

73. The term *judicial minimalism* is Sunstein's as well. See Sunstein, *One Case at a Time: Judicial Minimalism on the Supreme Court* (Cambridge, Mass.: Harvard University Press, 1999).

74. Theda Skocpol, *Protecting Soldiers and Mothers: The Political Origins of Social Policy in the United States* (Cambridge, Mass.: Harvard University Press, 1992), 58.

75. Mark A. Graber, "Constructing Judicial Review," *Annual Review of Political Science* 8 (2005): 425–451; McCann, *Rights at Work*.

76. Jonathan D. Casper, "The Supreme Court and National Policy Making," *American Political Science Review* 70 (March 1976): 50–63.

77. For the leading example of this Dahlian paradigm, see Gerald N. Rosenberg, *The Hollow Hope: Can Courts Bring About Social Change?* (Chicago: University of Chicago Press, 1991). For the original argument, see Robert A. Dahl, "Decision-making in a Democracy: The Supreme Court as a National Policy-Maker," *Journal of Public Law* 6 (1957): 279–295.

Conclusion

Supreme Court Decision Making and American Political Development

Ronald Kahn and Ken I. Kersch

How can we explain the emergence of new constitutional doctrine on the U.S. Supreme Court? How can we explain the persistence of settled doctrine? How might we explain the unique mixture of the new and old that, when viewed over the long term, comprises the landscape of American constitutional development? How do the features of that landscape, and the forces that shape them, relate to those behind the more expansive landscape of American political—as opposed to constitutional—development? What can our understanding of American political development teach us about the nature of American constitutional development, and vice versa? How distinctive is the Court as an institution that institutes, absorbs, and negotiates constitutional and political change?

This book is offered as a call for more searching and subtle inquiries into these and related questions. By way of illustration, it has suggested an array of ways that law and courts scholars can begin to ask more interesting questions, and to find more sophisticated answers to them. The contributors to this volume share an animating belief that fresh and more sophisticated inquiry in the study of law and courts will be driven by efforts to illuminate simultaneously the way in which internal and external influences interact to shape Supreme Court decision making and the way in which the long-term processes of political and constitutional change affect that dynamic. In this, our contributors have insisted on moving beyond an increasingly stale and ideologically rigid research agenda that has insisted that the most relevant questions in the field involve debates over the respective influence of "law" versus "politics," or internal or external factors in explaining judicial "votes." Our contributors, by contrast, favor approaches that are open to the possibility that new questions are in order, that different, more complex and more interesting dynamics are at work, and that new empirical evidence is needed to formulate those questions and move toward arriving at answers.

In contrast to behavioralist scholars of various sorts, and to "big bang" historians (who focus on the impact of single, large-scale events on constitutional change), our contributors embrace complexity, and the possibility that the process of American constitutional development is multifaceted. However much aspiring "scientists" may wish it were otherwise, constitutional law—and, perhaps, politics more generally—as understood across time, because of its very nature, must be approached simultaneously as a normative, interpretative, and descriptive (or empirical) enterprise. This is essential even though ordinary, everyday politics constructs the world through dichotomous categories—law versus politics, the state versus the individual, liberty versus equality, liberal versus conservative, one right versus another. But as politics moves through time, categories arise, alter, shift, and die. Constitutional law and politics are, in significant part, about the developmental life of categories. This book takes that developmental life seriously. Moreover, it raises questions about whether the developmental life of courts—the active adherence to (or rejection of) precedent, the application of principles to facts in perpetually altering contexts—is operationally and empirically distinctive in this regard. As we see it, when considered together, the contributions to this book, although far from arriving at universal agreement on all points, have taken an important step toward a preliminary mapping of the dynamic, mutually constitutive relationship between politics and law in shaping the fate of constitutional categories over time within the developmental life of courts. Within that mapping, some significant themes have clearly emerged.

Supreme Court Decision Making Is Unique

In writing about the Court, many political scientists have a tendency to borrow understandings derived from the study of other institutions—like Congress or the executive branch—and apply them mechanically to the Court, as if there were nothing politically distinctive about jurisprudence, and as if constitutional decisions were not distinctive from legislative ones. We believe that our contributors have shown that such accounts have flattened the unique properties and processes at work in courts. Courts, our contributors have shown, are not parties, not legislatures, not bureaucracies, and not the presidency (although they may share attributes of each of these). Judges cannot be accurately understood as simply providing additional data sets believed to speak to hypotheses fashioned with other political institutions in mind. They must be understood for who they are, where they sit, and what they do.

The Internal-External Dynamic Is at the Core of Supreme Court Decision Making

Although all of our contributors share an appreciation for the virtues of complexity and the necessity of understanding Supreme Court decision making across time, they disagree on the way in which internal and external forces interact to shape the path of American constitutional development.

Mark A. Graber opens the volume with the assertion that the disentanglement of the internal and external in Supreme Court decision making is well-nigh impossible because each set of influences is constitutive of the other. Graber does not deny what many mainstream students of judicial politics assert—that attitudes, strategies, and policy preferences are important to Supreme Court decision making. But unlike those students, he also takes internal legal factors unique to courts seriously and explains just how it is that they come into relation with attitudes, politics, and strategies. Ostensibly "legal" precedent is often shaped by the strategic and political calculations of an earlier time, and thus the categorical distinctions that analysts traditionally rely on collapse. In this regard, viewed over the long term, law is politics and politics is law. Judges who follow the law are, by the very nature of legal development, also taking into account political imperatives. Similarly, political argument is also often an argument about the normative requirements of law. The only way that one can see this is to be open to taking both the law and politics seriously, and making the effort to consider both, not at a single snapshot point in time, but in history. The implication of Graber's argument is that developmental approaches are the approaches most likely to transcend the law versus politics debate to yield persuasive understandings of Supreme Court decision making.

Ronald Kahn's essay also collapses the distinction between politics and law emphasizing the degree to which, in its "internal" legal reasoning in particular cases, the Court, as part of the process by which it maintains its legitimacy as a legal institution, is forced to apprehend and construct the social, economic, and political world outside its chambers, even in the politically charged areas of gay rights and the right of abortion choice. Moreover, there is a feedback loop between this process and external politics, one in which Court autonomy prevails even in periods of contested politics in which the place of the Court in the American political system is being questioned. For this reason, arguments about the requirements of law are arguments about politics, and vice versa.

In her study of postbellum family law, Julie Novkov finds similar processes at work in the courts. She demonstrates that as the Alabama state court system struggled with the issues of interracial marriage, its judges were constant consumers of cultural ideas, and they used those ideas in their efforts to construct the legal conceptions of marriage and the family. Over time, the Alabama Supreme Court altered its understanding of marriage as an ordinary contract and moved toward an understanding of it as a contract with special status with unique importance for the health of the state—a recategorization that, in time, would have significant effects. Eventually, these constructions, which originated in the state courts, worked their way into the jurisprudence of the U.S. Supreme Court. In this way, once again, the sharp distinction between the internal and external in Supreme Court decision making is collapsed. The courts, Novkov insists, were significantly influenced by legal principles: they worked hard to fit their conceptions of marriage and interracial relations into the ideas of equality from the Fourteenth Amendment. Although these legal influences predominated at first, the Alabama Supreme Court gradually backed away from this strong equality conception, ending up with a weak equality principle. A legal explanation alone, though, is insufficient. Both culture and ordinary politics were involved as well: the switch from a Republican to a Democratic court was plainly significant in this regard. To understand these developments in judicial decision making, one needs to map the complex interplay of these elements across time.

The Relationship between Constitutional Development and Political Regimes Is Multidimensional, Dynamic, and Complex

Several of our contributors begin with an animating interest in the relationship between the Court and the broader political regime—that is, with a classically externalist model. Mark Tushnet explores the role the Court plays as a component part of a broader national governing order. He finds that in acting against parts of that order in what is often taken to be an unambiguously countermajoritarian fashion, a "collaborative Court" allies itself with other parts of that order, thus contributing to the affirmative process of "build[ing] a stable political order by helping some parts of the system destabilize other parts as a preliminary to the construction of a new system." But for Tushnet, this is more interesting than the familiar story about the Court simply ratifying majoritarian political preferences, because courts are unique institutions and do politics in a distinctly legal way. Legal legitimacy counts for Tushnet too. Were the Court to act as a mere echo chamber for majoritarian politics, he argues, it would vitiate its claim to engaging in a "constitutional" project, which is essential to the maintenance of its institutional power and authority. The Court thus acts distinctively and creatively, not as a rubber stamp for majoritarian preferences, but as a court. It does not ratify everything that emerges from the national political system. It proceeds in a way that allows it to meld its charge to decide cases legally with its charge to act, in key respects, as a voice of the people. Tushnet writes, "The very fact of collaboration connects the courts' constitutional law to the people. Judicial lawmaking when collaboration is impossible eliminates this form of connection, weakening the overall connection between constitutional law and the people. Such lawmaking is not only peculiarly unstable; it also rests on a weaker normative foundation as well."

Howard Gillman, perhaps the most purely externalist contributor to this collection, shares Tushnet's focus on the Court's ties to the ambient political regime, arguing that constitutional change sometimes reflects an effort at "political entrenchment," by which a governing coalition attempts to protect a political agenda by placing supporters of the agenda on the bench, where they will stay long after the coalition that appointed them is out of power. In his contribution, Gillman argues that such an effort at entrenchment goes a long way toward explaining the origins of the modern judicial liberalism of the Warren and post-Warren era. Gillman, however, complicates this seemingly straightforward picture by arguing from historical observation that the nature of particular political landscapes at particular times varies. There are, for example, fluctuations in the strength and scope of governing coalitions. Because of this, different coalitions will select differing approaches to enlisting the judiciary in service of their agendas. The judiciary may be enlisted, under different circumstances, to advance policy agendas, partisan agendas (that is, to shore up party support), or personal agendas. Gillman goes on to formulate, in preliminary form, a theory as to when efforts at entrenchment are likely to take place, when they are likely to succeed, and when they are likely to fail. He details, moreover, the ways in which, mindful of the character of the judiciary's orientation toward particular policies at particular times, each of the government's branches— including the courts themselves—work to either expand or contract the power of courts to decide cases in particular policy areas.

Even for Gillman, who links the justices closely to political parties, judges are best analogized not to legislators but to executive branch appointees to administrative agencies—that is, to people who are responsible for "a specialized subset of everyday policy making and/or particularized decision making." Even so, the "justices must reconcile their preferences with a web of 'internal' institutional constraints, perspectives, and responsibilities, including (perhaps) legal norms" in a way that purely policy-regarding administrators need not. The justices, in sum, may have a close connection to political regimes. But they build "jurisprudential regimes." Jurisprudential regimes and political regimes are not the same thing. His contribution suggests that further reflection on the relationship between the two is in order.

Wayne D. Moore also suggests that the nature of the collaboration between the Court and other institutions is far more complex than models of collaboration emphasizing external elements can account for. Moore argues that when the Court was considering internal legalist factors, such as reconciling the Fourteenth Amendment with other parts of the Constitution to secure constitutional coherence, the Court had to demonstrate it was collaborating in some respectful way with political branches and the states. Thus, for example, the Court had to evince a concern for states rights by not making too sweeping a change. For Moore, the issue of collaboration is recast into the somewhat different, and morally infused, issue of the systemic coherence of a governing order. The criteria of constitutional coherence is an important one, which requires the Court to look at both past legal decisions and the political and social world outside the Court. Interpretive stances, Moore explains, were established to meet rules of coherence. Like Tushnet, Gillman, Kahn, and Graber, Moore agrees that the Court has a certain amount of agency in the collaborative process. But for Moore, like Kahn, there is a strong, transformative, theoretical project that stands at the center of the Court's negotiation with other political institutions. This involves a search for authoritative constitutional interpretations that is, in notable part, a normative moral project. This project implicates the constitutional text, but, ultimately, is not derivable from it. For Moore, this means that the separation of the "oughts" and "ises," a categorical distinction commonly drawn by judges and scholars alike, is simply not possible as the Court makes constitutional choices. Thus, for scholars to facilely separate the two is to misdescribe what it is the Court does.

Ken I. Kersch's chapter resonates with Moore's on the issue of collaboration with a political regime. Kersch charts the Court's collaboration in the construction of a stable New Deal order by negotiating that regime's assimilation of the (at the time) antagonistic demands of two sequentially arrayed reformist imperatives, labor rights and civil rights. The collaboration versus conflict dichotomy is vexed for Kersch. As he sees it, the regime is not unified in theory, nor are particular viewpoints necessarily anchored in any single governmental branch like Congress or the presidency. The regime, for Kersch, is neither stable nor coherent as it moves through time. It is precisely the stream of change within a regime that the Court, through an active theoretical engagement involving the reimagining of the way in which principles apply to an altering external world, is working to negotiate.

As with Moore and Kersch, Pamela Brandwein sees the Court as engaging in a process of negotiation within a political regime. She describes the Court in the *Civil Rights Cases* as seeking to bridge antagonistic elements within the governing coalition to reach a politically palatable and ultimately stable solution through creative constitutional theorizing. This negotiation, as for Moore and Kersch, clearly has a moral dimension, which is part of the process of its becoming authoritative. Tushnet, Gillman, Kersch, and Brandwein thus all find a Court striving for some form of governmental stability.

The Construction of Constitutional Authority Is Central to the Process of Constitutional Development

Even the heavily "externalist" or "political" analysis undertaken by Gillman, which ties the trajectory of doctrinal development directly to partisan political regimes, takes account of the evident historical fact that legal doctrine sticks. If it did not, after all, entrenchment would be more difficult to come by as the personnel behind it died off and were replaced. How does that stickiness come to pass? For Kersch, who—like all of our contributors—takes the problem of legitimacy as central to understanding what it is that judges do, political ideology and constitutional memory are crucial. Stories of the trajectory of constitutional development in the United States, Kersch argues, serve as "constitutive stories" of the modern American nation. So far as twentieth-century constitutionalism is concerned, the story of the New Deal Constitutional Revolution of 1937 as a breakthrough triumph over legal formalism, misguided ideals of class neutrality in legislation, and aggressive assertions of judicial power, is key to sustaining as an active force the constitutional understandings forged in its aftermath. In his study of the trajectory of constitutional development of labor rights and civil rights, Kersch provides a case study in the construction of a modern constitutive story central to contemporary constitutional liberalism. That story involves the sequential, linear triumphs of labor rights and civil rights in the aftermath of the removal of the constitutional barriers set by in the *Lochner* era.

This was no simple task because the politics of this regime—liberal, Democratic Party politics—was complex and conflicted. At its core stood two antagonistic elements of a single coalition: blacks and organized labor. The Court was put in the position of having to negotiate an accommodation between them. It acted not only to entrench or consolidate the new regime (in the way emphasized by Gillman), but also to assimilate new reformist projects into the bosom of that regime. Kersch argues that the simultaneous process of consolidation and assimilation by the Court was, in significant respects, an ideological endeavor. Reconciling the diverse regime elements in the name of progress and reform was, of necessity, an exercise in forging new political theory.

Like Kahn, Kersch demonstrates how internal legalist doctrine must be revised to make a better fit with social facts. Internal doctrine was important to the justices, but over time it was revised in light of the world outside the Court. In this way, for Kersch, the Court is both tied to the new regime in some ways, and semiautonomous from it in others (a state of affairs described, in a somewhat different way, by Tushnet). Where Kersch differs from Tushnet and Gillman (but echoes the approach of some of our other contributors like Novkov, Brandwein, Nackenoff, and Keck) is in devoting sustained attention to the negotiation of legal doctrine in light not only of the regime, considered electorally, but also in light of the ideas (including the contested ideas and categories) that sustain, undermine, and trouble it.

For Kersch, the political triumph of the New Deal, and the set of ideologies and imperatives that sustain it, is not the end of the story, but the beginning. A central theme of many of the essays in this volume is that constitutional authority and constitutional settlements are not dictated or ratified by the adoption of constitutional text alone; rather, they are built. One cannot understand this building process without considering, as part of a single, fused process, developments inside and outside the Court. Wayne Moore methodically sets out the way this process worked in the construction of an authoritative meaning of the Fourteenth Amendment. This authority, Moore shows, was not entirely a function of the amendment's original pedigree, procedural or otherwise. Rather, it was the product of a complex relationship between text, principles, and politics outside the

Court. The mutual construction process engaged in by the Supreme Court plays a major role in defining what the Constitution means, but it is only a part of a broader process that must be considered as a whole. In a contribution that in some ways echoes Graber's, Moore shows in meticulous detail just how it is that law is about politics and politics is about law. This process Moore describes was fed by a series of debates taking place in various aspects of the polity over the proper meaning of the amendment's broadly worded provisions. These debates reflected a range of interpretive agendas, undertaken by a wide number of interpreters over time. Most of the meanings arrived at in those debates, Moore claims, could be fairly accommodated by the literal terms of the constitutional text.

Moore's six criteria through which authoritative constitutional interpretations are established as "rules of recognition" are simultaneously legal and political, internal and external, a conclusion that once again collapses the rigid but familiar "law" versus "politics" distinctions. Like Gillman, among others, Moore is concerned with the construction of a relatively stable regime of legal meaning. Like Kersch, Moore sees a process of legal, intellectual, and political negotiation on the Court as a prelude to constitutional consolidation and settlement. As with Graber, Kahn, Kersch, and other contributors, it is clear from Moore's contribution that separation of the "oughts" and "ises" in empirical and descriptive work on the choices justices make is simply not possible. "Oughts" are implicated in judicial assessments about what is (as Pamela Brandwein and Carol Nackenoff show in their accounts of the way in which the Court's readings of the perceived "lessons" of Reconstruction affected subsequent developments in Fourteenth Amendment doctrine), and perceptions of what is are affected by normative judgments about what ought to be. Brandwein's account of belated development of the state action doctrine under the Fourteenth Amendment, like many of our chapters, places the Court at the center of a process of negotiation among competing constitutional visions roiling political actors outside the Court. She demonstrates that in arriving at the "lost language" of state neglect as settlement—subsequently supplanted by the state action doctrine—the Court was driven by its effort to negotiate what it hoped would be a stable middle path between Democrats and Radical Republicans in the post–Civil War era.

Brandwein's chapter on the negotiation of a settlement in the service of a regime devotes sustained attention to a dynamic raised in a number of our other chapters: the role of what we call the "interpretive community" in framing constitutional negotiations and sustaining constitutional settlements. As Kersch in particular has emphasized, and as Moore anatomatized, regimes sustain themselves not through the exercise of coercive power alone but through the institutionalization of more or less accepted patterns of beliefs or ideologies, which have the salutary effect of obviating the need for coercion to win and sustain political obedience. Put otherwise, they sustain themselves by transforming politics, power, and history into law. Brandwein emphasizes the role that elite constitutional "experts" play in constructing the authority of legal doctrine or regime-sustaining constitutional settlements. These elites explain the legal meaning of the constitution to others. In the process, they influence not simply the general public, but also other participants in the legal system, such as lawyers, lower court judges, and politicians. That is, they help invent and sustain—and institutionalize as a form of orthodoxy—highly influential constitutional categories.

Brandwein shows this process at work by comparing our contemporary, widely accepted understandings of the meaning of the *Civil Rights Cases*, which treat the decision as having launched the state action doctrine, with a persuasive reconstruction of how that decision was understood—and made sense—at the time it was handed down. At the heart of the original understanding and meaning of those cases, Brandwein shows, was the language, not of state action, but of state neglect. That language—which does not exist as a category within contemporary constitutional law—allowed the federal government to bring a legal action when states neglected their responsibilities to adequately police the violation of private rights (so far as certain categories of rights were concerned). The language of state neglect, Brandwein shows, moreover, was the product of a carefully crafted constitutional settlement in which the justices in the *Civil Rights Cases* acted advisedly to take a middle path interpretation of the Fourteenth Amendment that would protect core civil rights against state neglect in instances of racially motivated transgressions while steering clear of the more radical injunction that the federal government act more aggressively to protect "social" rights as well. This meaning of the *Civil Rights Cases*, Brandwein explains, became "lost" only in the 1920s, when a retrospective reconstruction of the meaning of those decisions took place. The language of state neglect was lost because the categorical legal framework on which it rested— the concept of hierarchy of rights—fell out of favor in the interpretive community. New thinking about rights and rights protection rendered the vocabulary of state neglect unrecognizable. Ever since—crucially—students have been taught that the *Civil Rights Cases* created the state action doctrine. And for all intents and purposes, from that time forward, saying it made it so. An authoritative and seminal constitutional meaning had been constructed.

Negotiations of the sort that Brandwein identified Justice Bradley as having undertaken in the *Civil Rights Cases*, our other contributors make plain, are a common and important part of the story of American constitutional development and represent a unique contribution on the part of courts to American political life. In an era of Republican ascendancy on the Court, Thomas M. Keck found Justice Powell seeking a similar middle ground between color-blindness and judicial restraint in his affirmative action opinion in *Bakke*—a middle ground that gradually was written into the Court's majority opinion in the recent University of Michigan affirmative action case of *Grutter v. Bollinger*. Kersch finds the Court negotiating between the sequential imperatives of labor rights and civil rights. All of these accounts raise questions about the broader institutional conditions under which certain types of regime-sustaining—or regime-creating—doctrinal settlements are likely to be reached, and, for that matter (as Brandwein shows), deconstructed and, in time, lost to constitutional practice and memory.

The Relationship between External Advocacy Politics and Internal Legalisms is Bidirectional

The contributions of Novkov, Nackenoff, and Keck emphasize the significance of advocacy politics for Court decision making. Characteristically, however, the story they tell is not one of simple, unidirectional interest group influence that has become a staple of mainstream positivistic political science. These contributors show how, in constitutional development, internal principles and institutional norms interact with advocacy politics in a complex, bidirectional, and mutually constitutive way. Under certain conditions internal factors are important in influencing external politics by creating and collapsing new legal, intellectual, and political categories, in the process setting up frames and agendas for an ensuing politics. Under others, the Court is solicitous of external advocacy politics as it makes decisions in cases and lines of cases.

Julie Novkov finds that Supreme Court doctrine involving interracial marriage was strongly influenced by the conceptual framework developed by state courts in key interracial marriage cases. Novkov finds, moreover, that the conceptual apparatus arrived at by the state courts was itself structured by broad ranging and contentious debates in the wider state polity concerning the meaning of marriage, contract, and family. A thirteen-year legal, political, and cultural battle over interracial marriage produced a constitutional negotiation at the state court level that arrived at the understanding of the white family as a quasi-public definition.

Carol Nackenoff explains that advocacy groups are essential to understanding the path of constitutional development in the Supreme Court's late nineteenth and early twentieth-century American Indian cases. But this is no simple, unidirectional matter, involving the influence of "politics" on "law." Nackenoff's groups, like the Lake Mohonk Conference of the Friends of the Indian, were involved in theoretically rich normative, iterative, conceptually laden policy debates that ended up constructing the very contours of Supreme Court analysis. The dynamics here, however, were bidirectional, involving multiple feedback loops. Within these loops, the legal categories concerning citizenship created by the Court (and by legislation and administrative decisions) provided the framing through which these outside groups conceptualized the issue. To complicate matters further, both Court decisions and advocacy group politics in this area were also shaping legislative and administrative public policy regarding Indians. Nackenoff shows how the Court works alongside political institutions and the interpretive community as "one important actor, but not necessarily a final arbiter, in struggles over the meaning of constitutional principles and rights." Nackenoff's chapter demonstrates, as do many of our other chapters, that the constitutional language, norms, principles, and metaphors defined by courts are used in the politics outside the courts. That politics then comes back from the outside to influence subsequent Court rulings. In such a dynamic constitutional context, efforts to effect a hermetic separation between external and internal influences on Supreme Court decisions in constitutional cases is unwise, and, for that matter, impossible.

Thomas Keck's chapter, in looking at contemporary constitutional politics, in many respects, shows the same thing. Like many political scientists, Keck shares a belief that interest group litigation plays an important part in setting the Court's agenda and in shaping the development of constitutional doctrine. Keck argues, however, that focusing on the activities of such groups alone is inadequate. Keck contends that the purchase of arguments made by these groups about affirmative action can only be understood by appreciating the wider contemporaneous and New Right critique of liberal egalitarianism, a critique that is, in part, a normative argument about constitutional law provoked by Justice Powell's effort to reach a doctrinal compromise on the issue in *University of California Board of*

Regents v. Bakke. Keck usefully reminds us that the Court doesn't simply settle legal or political disputes: it creates them, and, in many respects, sets their categories and frames their terms. Moreover, it does so through a unique, courtlike process involving the incremental adjudication of highly concrete, but related, cases with slightly varying fact scenarios over time. Like Nackenoff, Keck also finds a dynamic policy feedback loop operating in the affirmative action cases, a loop in which law and politics, and internal and external influences are mutually stimulating and mutually constitutive. Keck, who may speak here for many of our other contributors, concludes in light of his study of affirmative action, that law and politics are too intertwined to really be called separate factors. "The 'legal' ideas that influence the justices, after all, are derived in large part from ongoing debates in the broader political system, and the 'political' interests that pressure the Court are often constituted by legal categories created by the justices themselves."

Constitutional Development in the Supreme Court Involves an Extended Engagement with the Interpretive Community

Constitutional decision making, analysis, and development, as it is practiced in the Supreme Court of the United States, is, in significant part, an exercise in applied political thought and political theory. Many of our contributors have found that the opinions of the legal interpretive community—law professors, social scientists, and legally oriented journalists and members of the informed public—play a crucial role in helping judges frame and resolve constitutional questions and problems. Indeed, discussions within the interpretive community may serve as the major arena in which internal and external influences on the Court are brought into relation with one another. Kersch argues that the interpretive community plays a subtle but important role in helping the judges think about and theorize the new constitutional problems. In spotlighting the relationship between political thought outside the Court concerning labor and civil rights and the development of Court doctrine, Kersch charts the process by which, under modern constitutional conditions, the Court becomes a functioning part of the interpretive community that surrounds it. In the process, the Court acted as the political theorist for the emergent regime, negotiating a modus vivendi between these sequentially arrayed but antagonistic developmental imperatives.

As Brandwein explains, Justice Bradley's opinion in the *Civil Rights Cases* was built on a foundation supplied by the interpretive community, which made categorical distinctions between different sorts of rights. In the early twentieth century, however, these understandings were subsequently transformed. In the aftermath of those transformations, Bradley's carefully structured opinion, and the language of state neglect that it had meticulously fashioned, suddenly made no sense. With its meaning lost, a retrospective meaning characterizing it as a state action doctrine decision was projected onto it. Developmentally speaking, the effects of the replacement of the lost language of state neglect by the state action doctrine proved profound.

Kahn argues that the nature of the polity and rights principles that are applied by individual justices through the social construction process is guided by different normative visions of what the interpretive process undertaken by the Court should be. Legalist scholars play a key role in elaborating and advocating such normative visions. Moreover, social science evidence and methods of inquiry inform the manner in which the Court's justices choose to engage in the social construction process. Kahn argues that the interpretive community is influential in persuading the justices whether, in a certain case or line of cases, they should engage in this process. Members of that community can also be highly influential in arguing just how wide-ranging that process should be, as evidenced by classic battles between originalists and nonoriginalists, and within the wider community, over the appropriateness of a robust social construction process and the Court's role as an actor within the American political system.

The interpretive community, defined broadly as including not just legalists, social scientists, journalists, and the informed public, but also legal and political advocacy groups, is, for Carol Nackenoff, very important to understanding Supreme Court decision making. Nackenoff shows the way the Court, as part of an iterative process, interacted with a wide range of advocacy groups, and other members of the interpretive community. When groups disagreed with Court decisions, they encouraged Congress to pass relevant new legislation. Influential parts of this legislation were then filtered back through the courts, in the process helping to shape the Court's agenda, and the terms of the ongoing constitutional debate. "Doctrinal connections," she writes, "helped frame the ways in which members of the interpretive community would link law and Constitution to particular Native American causes for which they struggled. Past decisions and precedents provided signals to the interpretive community about what to contest and how."

Interestingly, Nackenoff demonstrates that the particular view of history that was taken by the legal community in the period under study was an important external influence on the Court's decision making. Stories were formed that focused on learning lessons from the experience of African Americans under the Fourteenth and Fifteenth Amendments. "The reworking of the history and lessons of the Fourteenth and Fifteenth Amendments in law reviews, essays, exchanges at Mohonk, in congressional debates and elsewhere both responded to, and in turn reshaped, official narratives told by the Court."

Like Nackenoff, Wayne Moore takes a more expansive view of the relevant interpretive community. Moore's chapter charts how the Fourteenth Amendment's initial interpreters—including members of Congress, executive officials, attorneys, federal and state judges, and the people at large—reinforced the authority of the Fourteenth Amendment itself. By doing so, they directly and indirectly remedied vulnerabilities and weaknesses in the Amendment's original authority. The Court's decision in *Slaughter-House* was a significant step in this process.

Thomas Keck presents clear evidence that the interpretive community has been influential as an external influence on Court decision making in the area of affirmative action. For him, it is impossible to understand these decisions without taking account of the influence of the New Right critique of liberal egalitarianism that emerged during the late 1970s. This critique went a long way toward undermining political support for race-conscious affirmative action policies. He notes, in addition, that the rise of rights-based conservatism generally, and conservative public interest litigation organizations in particular, played a crucial part in calling on the conservative justices of the Rehnquist Court to actively enforce conservative constitutional commitments, such as the right to color-blind treatment by the government.

Constitutional Development Is About the Construction of Constitutional Narratives or Stories

One of the distinct and, in many respects, novel themes that emerges from many of the contributions to this volume is that constitutional development and narratives about the trajectory of constitutional development are not necessarily the same thing. Many of our contributors either implicitly or explicitly conclude that backward-looking, after-constructed "constitutive stories" of constitutional development are an important form of constitutional construction. These constructions can act in concrete ways to shape the contours of constitutional development. The interpretive community, of course, is an active participant in the process of constructing authoritative constitutional stories.

Significantly, Kersch, Nackenoff, Novkov, Brandwein, and Graber frame their contributions as revisionist challenges to some of the most influential of our conventional constitutional narratives. All explore how the stories told about constitutional change, on the Court and off, opened up, and at other times closed up, distinctive developmental trajectories, and thus are integral to the process of reaching and reworking constitutional settlements. These contributors show how the Court works through stories, analogies, and metaphors, and reworks them. They show how, in turn, these stories, analogies, and metaphors are taken into the interpretive and advocacy community, to be accepted, contested, or reworked. Many of these narratives are fashioned in light of the Court's unique needs as an institution. The complexity of the mutual construction process engaged in by the Court and the wide range of institutions and actors who are involved in that process, means that the effort to construct dominant developmental narratives is a complicated affair, with important political and distributional consequences. The project of crafting these narratives, whose characters are past cases (stare decisis), principles, doctrines, and (ostensible) constitutional turning points, are part of the process of forging a useable past, and creating new constitutional meanings.

We see the place of narratives or backward-looking memory in Brandwein's critique of the later conceptualizations of the *Civil Rights Cases* in light of her analysis of what the justices had actually said and done in that decision. At the core of Brandwein's contribution is a pairing of the text of the *Civil Rights Cases* themselves with the subsequent constitutional meaning attributed to those cases in constitutional law hornbooks and political science textbooks, which, she argues, changed radically over time. The after-constructed meaning of the *Civil Rights Cases* was reinforced, she finds, by the narrative of Reconstruction purveyed by influential historians subscribing to the liberal abandonment thesis. Those historians focused on the 1877 end of Reconstruction as a critical, sharp-break constitutional moment and, in turn, linked the *Civil Rights Cases* with decisions such as *Plessy v. Ferguson* as part of the story of a post-1877 linear, downward spiral in the path of civil rights.

Kersch's contribution takes on one of modern constitutionalism's defining narratives, that of the Whiggish unidimensional and linear path of progress narrative that dominates our understanding of the birth of the modern in constitutional law. That narrative has posited a break from a shopworn legal formalism, misguided ideals of class neutrality in legislation, and aggressive assertions of judicial power, to a new, "living constitutionalism" that took constitutional development in an altogether new, and more modern, direction. Kersch emphasizes that, ironically, a significant part of the Court's success in creating a sense of a fundamental break with the past stemmed from the Court's ability to create regime-reinforcing new formalisms, new claims for the ideal of class neutrality, and newly aggressive assertions of judicial power—the very commitments that had ostensibly been discarded in the earlier break. This successful progressive origins myth, in turn, informed and shaped many of the Court's most important subsequent opinions.

We see a similar process at work in Novkov's and Nackenoff's chapters. Novkov shows that influential and crucial nineteenth-century precedent concerning interracial marriage has been dropped from constitutional narratives recounting the developmental road leading to the Jim Crow case of *Plessy v. Ferguson.* To have taken account of that precedent—the genuine developmental path to *Plessy*—would have complicated a developmental narrative whose simplicities proved politically useful to the governing regime. Carol Nackenoff finds that narratives of the ostensible "lessons" of Reconstruction exerted a powerful influence over the debates over whether Native Americans should be accorded the vote. The meaning of those ostensible lessons greatly affected how the Court thought and what it did in its American Indian cases. Moreover, the politics of acceptance, rejection, and modification of stories concerning the path of key rights by advocates outside the Court, such as (among other things) religious liberty and the right to make contracts, proved central, in Nackenoff's account, to the development of public laws concerning Native American citizenship. These narratives affected the shape of legislation, administration, and constitutional doctrine. As she describes it in light of her evidence, "Litigants play a role in the Court's reworking of these precedents and stories, but so, too, do the historical narratives, analogies and metaphors the justices bring to their task." These narrative framings became an important vehicle for mobilizing popular opinion and pressure for and against key government initiatives.

The Supreme Court and American Political Development: Questions for the Future

The contributions to this volume suggest an array of questions involving the relationship between the Court and time that may guide scholarly inquiry in the future. One set of questions would pick up on the theme of the distinctiveness of the Court and consider it more explicitly as an institution operating in the stream of American political development. In what ways is the Court distinctive in the way it moves through time in comparison to the analogous movement by the legislature, the executive, and administrative agencies? Is the way the Court does law and politics simultaneously different from the way that these other institutions do? Many of our contributors have understood the Court to be engaged in the process of political and ideological negotiation across time. Does this process proceed in a court differently from the way it would proceed in the hands of a political party, a politician, or the mind of political strategist? Is constitutional compromise akin to political compromise?

We have argued that the mutual construction process, in which both internal legalist and external political and social factors play a key role, is one of the things that makes the Court unique as an institution. Might it be that this understanding, derived from a close empirical study of courts, can help us to better understand the nature of political decision making in other institutions? Why is it, after all, that scholars reflexively take insights distilled from the behavior of other institutions and apply them to courts, and not the other way around? Does a deep understanding of the judicial process really provide not a single insight that is applicable to our understanding of the nature of politics more generally? The construction of authority, Orren and Skowronek have argued, is at the core of the process of American political development. Courts construct and reconstruct authority on a daily basis. Is there nothing to be learned about the construction of authority more generally over time from this process? It is possible, of course, that courts define issues of authority and meaning in a way that is different from more directly politically accountable institutions. To date, however, no one has asked in a sustained and serious way whether or not this is true.

A better understanding of the processes of American constitutional development has the potential to contribute a great deal to the project of understanding legal and institutional development more generally, not only in the United States, but around the world. Developmental studies of American constitutionalism and court power can similarly speak to those scholars concerned with the development of the authority of international law and transnational courts. What does the American experience tell us about the conditions and prospects for these endeavors? How significant are transformative, revolutionary moments for the likely successes and failures in this regard? How much depends on incremental change in the after-math of such moments?

One of the contributions that American political development schol-ars make to the study of American politics more generally is that, like com-parativists, they are willing to chart political directions and the processes of political change across time by allowing that causal arrows may run in multiple directions simultaneously. They welcome not only what has been described as dialogue between key governing institutions, but also the pos-sibility of feedback loops—whether of ideas, consequences, or other polit-ical phenomenon. Many of our contributors place courts within larger models of institutional and political relations as they move through time. We believe that the studies offered here are insightful in this regard. They chart the way politics actually works, in practice, across time, dynamically. They also raise questions about the applicability of distinctive develop-mental dynamics identified by APD scholars with other institutions in mind—like path dependency, sequencing, layering, intercurrence, and mul-tiple orders—to the Supreme Court and the processes of constitutional development. The essays presented here are suggestive. But so far, this remains relatively uncharted territory.[1]

In recent work in APD theory, scholars have become engaged by the question of the unique role of time in the processes of American political development. How does that work speak to the empirical studies offered here, and vice versa? When considered together, the contributions to this book suggest that the concept of "political time," which Stephen Skowronek applies to what he read as the largely cyclical developmental pattern in the American presidency, may have less applicability to the sort of time that has shaped the development of constitutional doctrine in the U.S. Supreme Court. Can such a cyclical understanding explain the developmental pat-terns we see at work in the Court? If so, is it a simple matter of the Court's position as an agent, via the appointment process, of the presidency? If not, what exactly is the relationship between the legal, constitutional, or jurispru-dential time on the Court and political time in the presidency?

Skowronek, moreover, found that the "political time" of the presidency was limited by a process of institutional thickening, or settlement of norms, procedures, and practices, that occurred over secular (or normal) time. Does the Court move the same way through secular time with similar institutional effects? Or is it freer, and its path more contingent, in this regard? In light of the contributions to this volume, what is the best way to think about the special time in which the Supreme Court exists in American political life?

Scholars like David Mayhew have recently raised questions about the usefulness for the realignment model generally in explaining the patterns of American political development. Mayhew emphasized the importance of external events, like wars, economic depressions, and social movements, on the paths of political change. How do the contributions made here fit into this growing debate? It is quite possible that a study of the relationship between constitutional development and the question of periodization could go a long way toward informing scholars of other institutions on the forces driving long term political change.

Conclusion

When considered together, the chapters in this volume point the way toward a new theory-building project concerning the nature of American constitutional development. The questions raised by these essays about the linkages between conditions outside the Court and Court decision making suggest that the familiar models that pit "law" against "politics" and "internal" against "external" influences as alternative explanations for Supreme Court behavior are so far removed from actual developmental patterns viewed over the long term that they serve to impede rather than advance our understanding of the Supreme Court and its role in American constitutional development. New questions and a new openness to a variety of empirical observations are in order.

The chapters contained in this book suggest an array of avenues of future inquiry. Although we have highlighted what we believe are some of these, there are many others we might just as easily have treated. Although we hope that this conclusion has helped stimulate a deeper engagement with the work of our contributors and has prompted new questions about their findings and the interrelations among the chapters, there remains considerable room for readers to take things further, and in different directions. We very much hope that they will do so.

We believe that the most fruitful new direction for law and courts scholars will involve a willingness by those scholars to be engaged with the broader works and theoretical insights associated with the study of American political development. Law and courts scholars can learn much from APD. But we should be open to a possibility that, in our view, is too infrequently considered: that a close study of law and courts, rather than just taking ideas and insights from the study of other institutions and political processes, can yield insights into the nature of politics that prove useful to our understanding of politics taking place elsewhere, outside the courts. Put otherwise, we believe not only that law and courts scholars can learn from APD, but also that APD can learn from the study of law and courts. The ultimate test, though, should not be too cognizant of these methodological and subfield boundaries. It should be the reality test: does this describe and explain the nature of judicial decision making and the path of American constitutional development in fresh and interesting ways?

A robust engagement between those who study law and courts and APD, we would be remiss to omit, promises a special added benefit. It is much more capacious than the approaches to the study of law and courts—which have emphasized the prediction of judicial votes—that have predominated for the last half century. An APD orientation invites scholars and students alike to not only consider an array of foundational questions concerning order, authority, change, and time, but also to study the substantive areas of politics that they find most pressing and of the most interest. And it gives them a broad license to do so in diverse and creative ways, with the injunction to find out what it is substantively they most want to know. We believe that, as such, at the beginning of a new century, it is the best path to a worthwhile—and more relevant—political science.

Note

1. Paul Pierson, *Politics and Time: History Institutions and Social Analysis* (Princeton, N.J.: Princeton University Press, 2004); Karen Orren and Stephen Skowronek, *The Search for American Political Development* (New York: Cambridge University Press, 2004); Eric Schickler, *Disjointed Pluralism: Institutional Innovation and the Development of the U.S. Congress* (Princeton, N.J.: Princeton University Press, 2001).

CONTRIBUTORS

Pamela Brandwein is Associate Professor of Sociology and Government and Politics at the University of Texas at Dallas, where she teaches courses on civil rights and American constitutional development. Brandwein has published articles in the *Law and Society Review*, the *Ohio State Law Review*, and the *Michigan Journal of Law Reform*, and she is the author of the award-winning book, *Reconstructing Reconstruction: The Supreme Court and the Production of Historical Truth* (Duke University Press, 1999). She is currently working on a book entitled *The Supreme Court and the Lost Language of State Neglect*. Brandwein received her B.A. from Michigan and her Ph.D. from Northwestern.

Howard Gillman is Professor of Political Science, History, and Law, and Associate Vice Provost for Research Advancement at the University of Southern California, where he teaches courses on judicial politics and American constitutional development. Gillman is the author of articles published in the *American Political Science Review*, *Law and Social Inquiry*, the *Law and Society Review*, the *Political Research Quarterly*, *Studies in American Political Development*, and elsewhere, and many book chapters. He has published four books: *The Votes that Counted: How the Court Decided the 2000 Presidential Election* (University of Chicago Press, 2001), *Supreme Court Decision-making: New Institutionalist Approaches* (University of Chicago Press, 1999) (with Cornell Clayton), *The Supreme Court in American Politics: New Institutionalist Interpretations* (University Press of Kansas, 1999) (with Cornell Clayton), and *The Constitution Besieged: The Rise and Demise of Lochner Era Police Powers Jurisprudence* (Duke University Press, 1993), which was awarded the C. Herman Pritchett Award for the country's best book on law and courts and selected by *Choice* as an Outstanding Academic Book selection for 1993. Gillman received his B.A. and Ph.D. from the University of California–Los Angeles.

Mark A. Graber is Professor of Political Science and Law at the University of Maryland, College Park, and a Professor of Law at the University of Maryland School of Law. He teaches courses on constitutional law, American political thought and development, and political theory. He is the author of many articles in journals such as *Constitutional Commentary*, the *Journal of Supreme Court History*, the *Vanderbilt Law Review*, the *Review of Politics*, and *Studies in American Political Development*, as well as many book chapters. He has published four books: *Transforming Free Speech: The Ambiguous Legacy of Civil Libertarianism* (University of California Press, 1991), *Rethinking Abortion: Equal Choice,* *the Constitution, and Reproductive Politics* (Princeton University Press, 1996), *Marbury v. Madison: Documents and Commentary* (Congressional Quarterly Press, 2003), and *Dred Scott and the Problem of Constitutional Evil* (Cambridge University Press, forthcoming). Graber received his B.A. from Dartmouth, his J.D. from Columbia, and his Ph.D. from Yale.

Ronald Kahn is James Monroe Professor of Politics and Law and Director of the Law and Society Program at Oberlin College. He teaches courses on American constitutional law, American political development, the First Amendment, equal protection and implied fundamental rights, and contemporary constitutional theory. He was a Liberal Arts Fellow in Law and Political Science at Harvard Law School, 1979–1980. He is the author of many book chapters, as well as articles and reviews on constitutional law and theory, which have appeared in such venues as *Constitutional Commentary, Studies in American Political Development, Journal of Politics, Stanford Law Review, Case Western-Reserve Law Review, Journal of Legal Education, Polity, American Historical Review,* and the *American Political Science Review.* He is the author of *The Supreme Court and Constitutional Theory, 1953–1993* (University Press of Kansas, 1994) and is currently at work on a book entitled *The Outside World in Supreme Court Decision Making: Constructing the Rights of Subordinated Groups in Post-Pluralist America.* Kahn received his B.A. from Rutgers and his Ph.D. from the University of Chicago.

Thomas M. Keck is Assistant Professor of Political Science at the Maxwell School of Citizenship and Public Affairs at Syracuse University, where he teaches courses on the Supreme Court, law and society, American constitutional development, and American politics. He is the author of several book chapters and reviews. He is the author of *The Most Activist Supreme Court in History: The Road to Modern Judicial Conservatism* (University of Chicago Press, 2004). He is currently working on a book entitled *Race and Rights in a Conservative Era: The Legal Assault on Affirmative Action.* Keck received his B.A. from Oberlin and his Ph.D. from Rutgers.

Ken I. Kersch is Assistant Professor of Politics at Princeton University, where he teaches courses in American constitutional development, American political thought, and civil liberties. He has published articles in *Political Science Quarterly, Studies in American Political Development,* the *Journal of Supreme Court History,* the *University of Chicago Law Review,* the *University of Pennsylvania Journal of Constitutional Law, The Public Interest, Commentary, Critical Review,* and other journals. Kersch was the recipient of the Edward S. Corwin Award from the American Political Science Association in 2000. He was the Ann and Herbert W. Vaughan Scholar at Princeton's James Madison Program in American Ideals and Institutions (2001–2002) and a research scholar at the Social Philosophy and Policy Center in Bowling Green, Ohio (2005). Kersch is the author of *Freedom of Speech: Rights and Liberties Under the Law* (ABC-Clio, 2003) and *Constructing Civil Liberties: Discontinuities in the Development of American Constitutional Law* (Cambridge University Press, 2004). He is currently working on a book-length study of constitutional liberalism in the twentieth century, as viewed through the prism of the thought and jurisprudence of Justices Brandeis, Brennan, and Breyer. Kersch received his B.A. from Williams, his J.D. from Northwestern, and his Ph.D. from Cornell.

Wayne D. Moore is Associate Professor of Political Science at Virginia Polytechnic Institute and State University, where he teaches courses on constitutional law and politics, comparative constitutionalism, and political theory. He has served as a Fulbright Fellow teaching in the faculty of Law at Osaka University in Japan. Moore is the author of *Constitutional Rights and Powers of the People* (Princeton University Press, 1996), which won the 1997 C. Herman Pritchett Award for the country's best book by a political scientist on law and courts. Moore has also published a number of articles and book chapters and is currently working on several book projects involving matters of constitutional history, politics, law, and theory. He received his B.A. from the University of Virginia, his J.D. from the University of Virginia School of Law, and his Ph.D. in politics from Princeton University.

Carol Nackenoff is Professor of Political Science at Swarthmore College. She is the author of various articles and reviews and of *The Fictional Republic: Horatio Alger, Jr. and American Political Discourse* (Oxford University Press, 1994). She is currently at work on a new book, *Contested Citizenship*, which explores the meaning of citizenship in the United States in the late nineteenth and early twentieth centuries, with an emphasis on women's activism and their visions of citizenship and the state. Nackenoff received her B.A. from Smith and her Ph.D. from Chicago.

Julie Novkov is Associate Professor of Political Science and Director of the Women's and Gender Studies Program at the University of Oregon, where she teaches courses in constitutional law, civil rights, racial theory, civil liberties, and women and the law. She is the author of several articles in journals such as the *Law and History Review*, the *American Journal of Legal History*, and *Law and Social Inquiry*, and of a book, *Constituting Workers, Protecting Women: Gender, Law, and Labor in the Progressive and New Deal Years* (University of Michigan Press, 2001). She recently completed a book manuscript entitled *Racial Constructions: Regulating Interracial Sex and Building the White State in Alabama, 1865–1954*, and is currently at work on a book entitled *Making a Nation of Future Citizens: Political Development, Race, and the Regulation of Children's Work*. Novkov received her A.B. from Harvard/Radcliffe, her J.D. from New York University, and her Ph.D. from Michigan.

Mark Tushnet is the Carmack Waterhouse Professor of Constitutional Law at the Georgetown University Law Center, where he teaches courses on constitutional law and theory, and comparative constitutionalism. He is the coauthor of the nation's leading constitutional law casebook, as well as sixteen other books, including the definitive study of the life and work of Justice Thurgood Marshall (for whom Professor Tushnet served as a law clerk) and *Taking the Constitution away from the Courts* (Princeton University Press, 1999), *The New Constitutional Order* (Princeton University Press, 2003), and *A Court Divided: The Rehnquist Court and the Future of Constitutional Law* (W. W. Norton, 2004). He is also the author of many scholarly articles on constitutional law and constitutional history. He has been the recipient of Guggenheim, Rockefeller Foundation, and Woodrow Wilson Center fellowships. He received his B.A. from Harvard and his M.A. and J.D. degrees from Yale.

INDEX

Abbott, Lyman, 382

abortion rights cases, 74–75, 76, 83, 108n73. See also *Planned Parenthood of Southeastern Pennsylvania v. Casey; Roe v. Wade*

Ackerman, Bruce, 161n13, 240, 242, 243–45, 270n24

ACLU, 192, 214n29, 398, 413n132

activists

conservative, 414–17

for Native Americans, 367, 369, 373, 378–86, 387, 392–99, 400, 401, 403n1, 406n69, 411n113, 411-12n121, 412n124, 412n127, 412n128, 413n132, 413n135

Adarand Constructors, Inc. v. Pena (1995), 420, 427, 428, 429

Addams, Jane, 393, 410n107

Adkins v. Children's Hospital of District of Columbia (1923), 67, 69, 70, 73, 99

adultery and fornication laws, 332, 336–37, 338, 344, 348, 349–50, 351–54, 364n78

affirmative action

Center for Individual Rights (CIR), 414–15, 419, 420–27, 429, 431–32, 433, 435–36, 437n1, 438n26, 440n52

Fourteenth Amendment and, 417, 418, 427, 429, 433, 438–39n28

Rehnquist Court on, 414–15, 417–19, 420, 422, 427, 428, 420, 422, 424, 425–27, 428, 429–30, 431, 432–33, 436, 440n52, 453, 454

University of Texas Law School and, 426, 437n1

See also *Regents of the University of California v. Bakke*; University of Michigan affirmative action cases

AFL-affiliated unions, 182, 193

African Americans

discrimination and, 70–71, 74, 84, 105n17, 120, 121, 123, 292–93, 306, 312–13n45, 317n100, 317n102, 317n103, 318n107

interracial relationships and, 84, 105n17, 331–38, 339–60, 361n13, 364n78

judicial abandonment of, 304, 307

judicial and political appointments of, 148, 149

labor issues and, 171, 172, 173, 190–207, 209, 218n67, 219n70, 219–20n74, 221n81, 221n85, 221–22n87, 222n89, 222n90, 223n95, 224–25n109, 225n112, 225n116, 225n118, 225–26n120, 276

Republicans on civil rights of, 140, 276, 282–83, 288–89, 302, 303, 305–7, 310n23, 312n45, 322n156, 333, 334, 335, 339, 342, 356, 380

segregation and, 70–71, 74, 122, 129, 162n26, 163n45, 304, 322–23n159

voting rights of, 120–21, 232, 258–59, 292–93, 303, 304–5, 306, 311n29, 316n93, 318n107, 318n109,

CPSIA information can be obtained
at www.ICGtesting.com
Printed in the USA
LVHW041941020323
740756LV00001B/9